# *The* American Heritage®
# WORD FINDER

## Build Vocabulary Quickly and Easily

*by*
*Paul Hellweg*
*and*
*Phạm Đinh Thanh Nhàn*

Visit our website: hmhco.com

*Library of Congress Cataloging-in-Publication Data is available.*

Book design by Christopher Granniss

1 2 3 4 5 6 7 8 9 10 – DOC – 25 24 23 22 21 20 19

4500757507

Printed in the United States

*The* American Heritage®
# Word Finder

*This book is dedicated to*
*Michele Hellweg*
*and*
*Robert D. Hellweg, Jr.*

# Acknowledgments

*The American Heritage Word Finder* is based in part on *The American Heritage Children's Thesaurus.*

The authors would like to recognize these people involved with the *Children's Thesaurus:* **Susannah LeBaron** and **Joyce LeBaron** for their editorial contributions; **Robyn Battle** and **Marvin Vernon** for their work with an earlier database; and **Margery S. Berube, David Pritchard,** and **Beth Anderson** of Houghton Mifflin Harcourt for their roles in its development.

For *The American Heritage Word Finder,* the authors would like to recognize **Steve Kleinedler** and **Peter Chipman** at Houghton Mifflin Harcourt for their roles in its development.

The authors are indebted to all of the above.

# How to Use This Word Finder

## What Is *The American Heritage Word Finder?*

This book is a vocabulary study guide for beginning learners of the English language. It shows synonyms (words that share the same or nearly the same meaning), antonyms (words that are opposite in meaning), and word groups (closely related words). Not all words have synonyms, but many do. We have listed more than 4,000 of them as main entries in this book, with over 36,000 synonyms included in all.

*The American Heritage Word Finder* is based on the principle of *semantic connection*. That's a fancy term that means the best way to learn a new vocabulary word is to connect it to some-thing you already know. It's easier to identify, understand, and later recall words memorized with some type of connection in mind. To learn the color **green**, for example, you might want to learn it with the noun **grass**. Later on, you'll be more likely to remember both words because your brain naturally associates **green** with **grass**. Synonyms work the same way—use them to associate a word you want to learn with a word that you already know. Synonyms in *The American Heritage Word Finder* are listed in order of closeness of meaning to the main entry. This feature is intended to help nonnative speakers improve their vocabulary by making it easier to identify those words which are the closest in meaning.

## Why Use the Word Finder?

If you want to succeed in an English-speaking environment, you need a large vocabulary of English words. That's what *The American Heritage Word Finder* will help you acquire. Research has shown that a person's vocabulary level is the single best indicator of the likelihood of future success. Quite simply, the higher your vocabulary level, the greater your chances of success in *any* career. Learning new words requires no special skills or talents. Everybody can improve their vocabulary level, and you need to do that first because having a large vocabulary comes before career success, not after.

If you are a beginning learner, exposure to too much information can be overwhelming. That's why this book is for you. In more advanced ESL books, it's difficult to wade through the vocabulary lists, not knowing which words you need now, and which should be learned later as your proficiency improves. You won't have that problem here. Every entry in this book has been selected with the needs of beginning learners in mind. *The American Heritage Word Finder* is a vocabulary builder. Use it to learn the basic vocabulary that you will need to achieve your goal, whether that is entering an English-language university, doing well on an English proficiency test, finding a good job, or simply getting through everyday life in an English-speaking society.

## How Do You Use the Word Finder?

For vocabulary building, your best option is to simply open the book and browse through it. It's easier to learn a new word when you connect it with one you already know. That's why this book is so useful — listing words with their synonyms makes a convenient study tool. Open to any page. Scan the page. Select a main entry word you already know, then look at the words

that are similar in meaning. If you know all those synonyms, randomly pick another word for study. But if you don't know all the synonyms, pick one to commit to memory, keeping in mind the connection to the word you already know.

A different approach would be to look for a main entry that you don't know, and learn about it by learning its synonyms. For example, perhaps you don't know the word *browse*. You can look it up — you'll find it on page 20. Look at the synonyms and the sample sentence. The synonyms in order of relevance are: **look through, scan, skim, read,** and **survey**; the sample sentence is "Chaewon enjoys learning new words by *browsing* through a dictionary." If you know the meaning of one or more of these synonyms and understand the sample sentence, you'll have learned the word *browse*.

Most of the synonyms listed in *The American Heritage Word Finder* are also entry words. You can increase your understanding of any word you don't know by studying its synonyms. In the above example, *scan* is shown as a synonym for *browse*. Thus you can improve your comprehension of *browse* by looking up the entry for **scan**. Here it is:

Lookout

**scan** *verb* ✦ search, survey, examine, inspect, study ✧ explore, look The lookout used binoculars to *scan* the horizon.

Whatever your approach, you should randomly select words to learn. Traditionally, vocabulary has been taught and learned in groups. One day you study animals, another day you learn colors, and so on. There is a problem here: A large body of evidence indicates studying words in related groups inhibits vocabulary learning because it is easy to confuse and misremember closely related words. Let's say you memorized the words for many different animals yesterday. Today you remember all the words, but you could have trouble remembering which word corresponds to which animal. Overall, learning words in groups is more difficult because it takes more time to memorize them, and later on they are harder to recall. To improve your English vocabulary, you'll get your best results by studying miscellaneous

words, each of which is connected to a word you already know. *The American Heritage Word Finder* is ideal for such study.

## Using Synonyms

In *The American Heritage Word Finder,* synonyms are listed in order of closeness of meaning to the main entry. Here's an example that shows how synonyms are organized:

**mixture** *noun* ✦ blend, combination, compound, mix ✧ assortment My favorite drink is a *mixture* of iced tea and lemonade.

In the above entry, it would be acceptable to say "My favorite drink is a blend of iced tea and lemonade," or "My favorite drink is a combination of iced tea and lemonade," and so on for all the solid symbol (✦) synonyms. But the open symbol (✧) synonym won't work in this particular sentence. You wouldn't say "My favorite drink is an assortment of iced tea and lemonade." Open symbol (✧) synonyms will fit better in a different sentence, and you will be able to find examples throughout this book.

Most of the synonyms listed in this book are also entry words. So if you want to see one of the synonyms listed after the open symbol (✧) in a sample sentence, just look it up in the book. In the example given above, **assortment** is a main entry where you will find this sample sentence:

**assortment**: "Françoise gave her mother an *assortment* of Swiss chocolates."

Many synonyms can be substituted for one another just as they are, but others need to add a preposition or change the preposition that follows the entry word to make their use grammatically correct. In some cases we have placed a preposition in parentheses as a reminder that it will need to be used with that synonym.

Here's an example:

**suspension** *noun* ✦ interruption, pause (in), halt (in), stoppage ✧ break, discontinuity The cable company announced a brief *suspension* of service while they replaced their old equipment.

In this example, you would write or say, "The cable company announced a brief *interruption* of service while they replaced their old equipment," or "The cable company announced a brief *pause in* service while they replaced their old equipment," but not "The cable company announced a brief *pause* of service while they replaced their old equipment."

## Antonyms

In addition to synonyms, many English words also have *antonyms*—words that are opposite in meaning. We have included a varied selection of antonyms in feature boxes at the entry word to which they refer.

For example, here is the entry for **fresh** on page 75:

**fresh** *adjective* 1. ✦ unspoiled, unpreserved, new ✧ current, recent The local supermarket always has *fresh* fruits and vegetables. 2. ✦ another, new, additional, further ✧ different, more These dingy walls sure could use a fresh coat of paint. 3. ✦ clean, pure, invigorating, refreshing ✧ healthy I opened a window to let some fresh air into the room.

> **Antonyms** fresh
>
> *adjective* 1. musty, old, stale 3. dirty, impure, polluted, tainted

Note that numbered lists of antonyms correspond to the numbered items in the main entry and some numbers might not be included. Thus **musty, old,** and **stale** are antonyms for the first meaning in the main entry **fresh**, while

**dirty, impure, polluted,** and **tainted** are for the third meaning. Antonyms are not listed for the second item because there are no good ones for that meaning.

## Word Groups

*The American Heritage Word Finder* includes words that do not have actual synonyms but instead have a group of closely related words. For example, no words mean exactly the same thing as *knife*. Many words, however, refer to different types of knives, and we have put these related words in a Word Groups box.

Word Groups are entered alphabetically with the main entry words. For example, you will find the Word Groups box for *knife* on page 104 between the main entries for **kneel** and **knit:**

> **Word Groups**
>
> A **knife** is a sharp instrument used for cutting and piercing. **Knife** is a general term with no true synonyms. Here are some different kinds of knives to investigate in a dictionary: **cleaver, dagger, dirk, jackknife, machete, pocketknife, scalpel, stiletto, switchblade**

Use the Word Groups to explore the richness and variety of English. But when reviewing the Word Groups, don't try to memorize all the related terms—at least not all at once. Remember, the best way to acquire vocabulary is to do it randomly.

## Homographs

Words with the same spelling but different meanings are called *homographs*. These words are entered separately in the text, and each is followed by a small raised number, such as **present¹** and **present²** on page 143.

## Improving Your Writing

Most beginning learners will eventually need or want to start writing in English. Once you have learned sufficient vocabulary, you can use the synonyms in this book to improve your writing. To see how using synonyms works, imagine that you are writing an essay on the subject of winter where you live. You want to describe

what a really harsh winter can feel like, so you begin:

> *Of course, winter is normally a **cold** time of the year, but last January was unbelievably **cold**. I would go outside wearing boots and two pairs of socks, and my feet would still feel **cold**! I couldn't wait for spring to arrive so the **cold** weather would end.*

You read your paragraph and realize something seems wrong. Your words just don't communicate the idea you want to get across. How can you make the story sound more interesting? At the entry for **cold**, you find **chilly, cool, icy, frigid, frosty,** and **frozen** as choices to use here. It appears you will be able to improve your essay simply by changing a few words:

> *Of course, winter is normally a **cold** time of the year, but last January was unbelievably **frigid**. I would go outside wearing boots and two pairs of socks, and my feet would still feel **frozen**! I couldn't wait for spring to arrive so the **icy** weather would end.*

Now imagine that you're taking an English language proficiency test, and you have to write an essay on the same subject. The second version above would almost certainly receive a higher score because it shows knowledge of synonyms.

## Test Vocabulary

*The American Heritage Word Finder* is an excellent resource for anyone preparing for an English language proficiency test or an American college admissions test (SAT or ACT). The Word Finder's A–Z text includes thousands of basic words all test takers should know. But if you just want to focus on test vocabulary, see Appendix I—it contains a list of essential words to learn.

## American English vs. British English

*The American Heritage Word Finder* is based on American English. If you have been studying the English language somewhere other than in the United States, you may have been learning British English. The two versions of English are sufficiently similar to be mutually understandable. However, many words are spelled differently in British vs. American

English, and a few words are so different that they are likely to be unknown to someone unfamiliar with both styles of English. Please refer to Appendix II for a discussion of spelling rules and a list of the most common words likely to be confused.

## The Main Entry

Here's how a typical entry in this book works:

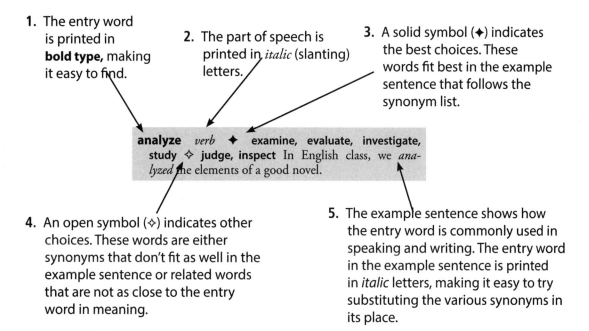

1. The entry word is printed in **bold type,** making it easy to find.

2. The part of speech is printed in *italic* (slanting) letters.

3. A solid symbol (✦) indicates the best choices. These words fit best in the example sentence that follows the synonym list.

> **analyze** *verb* ✦ examine, evaluate, investigate, study ✧ judge, inspect In English class, we *analyzed* the elements of a good novel.

4. An open symbol (✧) indicates other choices. These words are either synonyms that don't fit as well in the example sentence or related words that are not as close to the entry word in meaning.

5. The example sentence shows how the entry word is commonly used in speaking and writing. The entry word in the example sentence is printed in *italic* letters, making it easy to try substituting the various synonyms in its place.

All the entries in this Word Finder work in the same way, but some of them have more parts, like this one:

6. Sometimes an entry word can be used as more than one part of speech. Each part of speech is always presented separately within the main entry.

7. If the entry word has more than one meaning for a particular part of speech, each meaning is numbered.

> **cast** *verb* ✦ throw, toss ✧ fling, hurl, lob, pitch We need to *cast* the dice to see who goes first. —*noun* 1.✦ throw, toss ✧ fling, heave, lob, hurl The fisherman caught a big fish on the first *cast* of his lure. 2. ✦company, troupe ✧ actors, players, performers The director told the entire *cast* to attend tonight's rehearsal.

**A**

**abandon** *verb* 1. ✦ desert, forsake ✧ leave, reject, discard Brittany took home a puppy that someone had *abandoned*. 2. ✦ cease, discontinue, give up, quit, stop Rescuers had to *abandon* their search for the missing plane when night fell.

**abandoned** *adjective* ✦ deserted, empty, unoccupied, vacant ✧ forgotten, neglected The *abandoned* house had broken windows and an overgrown lawn.

**abbreviate** *verb* ✦ shorten, condense, contract ✧ compress, reduce, abridge "Doctor" is commonly *abbreviated* as "Dr."

**abdicate** *verb* ✦ resign, quit ✧ renounce, retire, yield When the king *abdicated*, his son became the new ruler.

**ability** *noun* ✦ capability, capacity, power ✧ aptitude, skill, talent My computer has the *ability* to run several programs at the same time.

**able** *adjective* ✦ competent, capable, proficient, skilled ✧ fit, qualified The company's new director has proven herself to be very *able*.

**abnormal** *adjective* ✦ strange, weird, eccentric, odd ✧ uncommon, unusual My friends think I'm *abnormal* because I like to wear socks that don't match.

**abolish** *verb* ✦ do away with, eliminate, disallow, end ✧ cancel Many people believe that the death penalty should be *abolished*.

**about** *preposition* 1. ✦ concerning, regarding, dealing with ✧ involving I am reading a book *about* international relations. 2. ✦ approximately, around, roughly ✧ almost, nearly The fireworks will start at *about* 7 p.m.

**above** *adverb* ✦ overhead ✧ over I'm friends with the people who live in the apartment *above*. —*preposition* ✦ beyond, over, past, exceeding, surpassing Children *above* the age of twelve must pay full price at our movie theater.

**abroad** *adverb* ✦ overseas ✧ away, elsewhere The college student spent her summer vacation *abroad*.

**abrupt** *adjective* 1. ✦ hasty, quick, rapid, sudden ✧ unexpected. The driver brought his car to an *abrupt* stop when a dog ran in front of it. 2. ✦ rude, uncivil, curt, impolite ✧ blunt, gruff The police officer warned the angry men not to be *abrupt* with him.

**absence** *noun* 1. ✦ nonattendance (at) ✧ absenteeism, truancy Fatima's *absence* from the choir was due to a cold. 2. ✦ lack, shortage, deficiency ✧ need, want The *absence* of fresh snow made our ski trip less enjoyable.

**absent** *adjective* ✦ missing, not present, away, gone ✧ truant Fatima was *absent* from choir practice today.

**absolute** *adjective* 1. ✦ complete, total, utter, downright ✧ perfect, pure I think that people who talk during movies are an *absolute* nuisance. 2. ✦ unlimited, unconditional, unrestricted, full ✧ unqualified Russian czars once ruled with *absolute* power.

**absorb** *verb* 1. ✦ soak up, take up ✧ hold, retain, swallow Jennifer used a kitchen towel to *absorb* the spilled milk. 2. ✦ take in, understand ✧ assimilate, learn I listened hard but I couldn't *absorb* what our professor was telling us.

**absorbing** *adjective* ✦ engrossing, captivating, fascinating, interesting, intriguing Samaira found the novel so *absorbing* that she recommended it to all her friends.

**abstain** *verb* ✦ refrain from, forgo, keep from, avoid ✧ pass, resist Hiro has to *abstain from* eating spicy foods now that he has stomach problems.

**abstract** *adjective* ✦ philosophical, theoretical ✧ obscure, vague, hypothetical Aristotle's writings are too *abstract* for me to understand.

**absurd** *adjective* ✦ ridiculous, preposterous, foolish, senseless, silly, stupid Before the airplane was invented, many people thought the idea of flying was *absurd*.

**abundance** *noun* ✦ lot, plenty, profusion, wealth ✧ excess, surplus The farmer was happy because his orchard produced an *abundance* of apples.

**abundant** *adjective* ✦ ample, plentiful, full, generous, rich ✧ **sufficient** The accountant has an *abundant* supply of pens and pencils.

---

**Antonyms** abundant

*adjective* **deficient, insufficient, meager, scant, scarce, sparse**

---

**abuse** *verb* ✦ **mistreat, misuse** ✧ **harm, hurt, take advantage of** In many countries it is illegal to *abuse* animals. —*noun* ✦ **mistreatment, misuse** ✧ **damage, harm, hurt** This old tennis racket looks like it has taken a lot of *abuse*.

**abyss** *noun* ✦ **chasm, crevasse, void** ✧ **gulf, hole, pit** Riko became dizzy when she looked over the edge of the *abyss*.

**accelerate** *verb* ✦ **go faster, speed up, quicken** ✧ **hasten, hurry, rush, speed** The sled suddenly *accelerated* when it hit a patch of ice.

**accent** *noun* ✦ **inflection, pronunciation** ✧ **emphasis, stress, tone** My friend Heidi speaks English with a German *accent*.

**accept** *verb* 1. ✦ **welcome, receive, take** ✧ **acquire, gain, get, obtain.** Yasir happily *accepted* my dinner invitation. 2. ✦ **acknowledge, agree, believe** ✧ **admit, affirm, claim** Is there anyone who does not *accept* that the world is round?

**acceptable** *adjective* ✦ **satisfactory, agreeable, fair, suitable, adequate** We bought the car because the price was *acceptable*.

**access** *noun* ✦ **admission, admittance, entrance, entry** ✧ **passage** You need a password to gain *access* to some webpages.

**accessory** *noun* 1. ✦ **extra, supplement** ✧ **addition, attachment** My new computer came with a mouse, cables, cleaning kit, and various other *accessories*. 2. ✦ **accomplice, partner** ✧ **assistant, associate, confederate** The cashier was convicted of being an *accessory* to the robbery.

**accident** *noun* 1. ✦ **chance, fluke, fortune, luck, coincidence** Sir Alexander Fleming discovered penicillin by *accident* when he found mold growing on an unwashed petri dish. 2. ✦ **mishap, crash** ✧ **disaster, misfortune, collision** My friend broke his leg in a skiing *accident*.

**accidental** *adjective* ✦ **chance, unexpected, unintentional, unplanned, lucky** The farmer's *accidental* discovery of oil made him very rich.

**acclaim** *verb* ✦ **praise, applaud, commend, hail** ✧ **approve, compliment** The movie was *acclaimed* by all the critics. —*noun* ✦ **praise, recognition** ✧ **approval, honor, applause** The author was pleased by the great *acclaim* that her novel received.

**accommodate** *verb* ✦ **hold, contain** ✧ **house, lodge, shelter** This classroom *accommodates* twenty students.

**accompany** *verb* ✦ **go with, attend, escort** ✧ **follow, guide** In the United States, Secret Service agents always *accompany* the president in public.

**accomplice** *noun* ✦ **partner, ally, associate, accessory, confederate, conspirator** ✧ **helper** Police investigators believe the bank robber had at least one *accomplice*.

**accomplish** *verb* ✦ **achieve, attain, complete, realize** ✧ **finish, reach** My girlfriend *accomplished* one of her major goals when she graduated from college last year.

**accomplishment** *noun* ✦ **achievement, feat, attainment** ✧ **success, triumph** Learning to play the saxophone is quite an *accomplishment*.

**accord** *verb* ✦ **agree with, coincide with, concur with, correspond to, match** The theory of evolution does not *accord with* the beliefs of some religions. —*noun* ✦ **agreement, concurrence** ✧ **harmony, rapport** The statements of the two witnesses were not in *accord* with each other.

**account** *noun* 1. ✦ **description, report, narrative** ✧ **explanation, story, tale, version** Ahmed gave his friends a detailed *account* of his trip abroad. 2. ✦ **importance, consideration, significance, value, worth** A job applicant's race, creed, or gender should be of no *account* to employers. —*verb* ✦ **explain** ✧ **clarify, justify, answer** The book's high price likely *accounts for* its poor sales.

**accumulate** *verb* ✦ **collect, assemble, gather, amass** ✧ **acquire, gain** Paul has *accumulated* an impressive collection of arrowheads.

**accuracy** *noun* ✦ **correctness, exactness, precision, rightness** Good accountants double-check their work for *accuracy*.

**accurate** *adjective* ✦ **correct, exact, precise, right, true** ✧ **perfect, truthful** A fact checker's job is to ensure all information is *accurate* before an article is published.

**accuse** *verb* ✦ **charge (with)** ✧ **allege, blame, de-**

**nounce** The diplomat was *accused* of spying for a foreign power.

**accustomed** *adjective* ✦ customary, habitual, normal, usual, traditional ◇ ordinary, routine In France, the *accustomed* greeting is a kiss on the cheek.

**ache** *verb* 1. ✦ hurt, throb ◇ pain, smart, suffer My legs *ache* from playing soccer all afternoon. 2. ✦ long, yearn, desire, want ◇ covet, crave Yaakov *aches* to be reunited with his family. —*noun* ✦ hurt, pain, soreness ◇ discomfort If that *ache* persists, you should see a doctor.

**achieve** *verb* ✦ accomplish, attain, fulfill, complete, reach, realize Seo-yeon recently *achieved* her dream of getting a black belt in tae kwon do.

**achievement** *noun* ✦ accomplishment, feat, triumph, attainment ◇ deed, exploit Zachary's proudest *achievement* is having won the regional chess tournament.

**acknowledge** *verb* 1. ✦ concede, admit, grant ◇ accept, allow Despite being 30 points behind, the basketball team refused to *acknowledge* defeat. 2. ✦ consider, deem, hold, recognize, regard Everyone *acknowledges* that Mitsuko is the best English speaker in our ESL class.

**acknowledgment** *noun* ✦ admission, concession, confession ◇ acceptance, recognition Ali's *acknowledgment* that he had been wrong helped us forget our anger at him.

**acquaintance** *noun* ✦ associate, colleague, companion, comrade I have many *acquaintances*, but only a few close friends.

**acquire** *verb* ✦ get, gain, obtain, procure, attain ◇ receive Robin recently *acquired* a beautiful kachina doll for her collection.

**acquit** *verb* ✦ absolve, clear, pardon ◇ discharge, excuse, forgive The jury *acquitted* the suspect when the evidence proved his innocence.

**act** *verb* ✦ function, operate, work, perform ◇ serve The lawyer *acted* on her client's behalf. —*noun* 1. ✦ deed, feat, action ◇ accomplishment, achievement, performance The legendary Hercules performed many heroic *acts*. 2. ✦ law, statute ◇ bill, decree In the United States, Abraham Lincoln's birthday was made a national holiday by an *act* of Congress.

**action** *noun* ✦ act, deed ◇ accomplishment, effort, performance Jamal's swift *action* saved the drowning boy's life.

**active** *adjective* 1. ✦ energetic, lively ◇ dynamic, industrious, busy My uncle is so *active* he walks at least five miles every day. 2. ✦ functioning, operating, working ◇ alive, running Italy's Mount Vesuvius is an *active* volcano.

**activity** *noun* 1. ✦ hobby, pastime, pursuit, project, interest ◇ endeavor Skiing and snowboarding are popular winter *activities*. 2. ✦ bustle, commotion, tumult ◇ action, movement There was a great deal of *activity* on the day of my friend's wedding.

**Antonyms** activity
*noun* 2. calm, lull, peace, quiet, serenity, tranquility

**actor** *noun* ✦ entertainer, performer, player ◇ star Pedro wants to be a movie *actor*.

**actual** *adjective* ✦ definite, real, true ◇ authentic, certain, genuine The *actual* size of the universe is still unknown.

**actually** *adverb* ✦ in fact, genuinely, really, truly ◇ indeed Much to Farrah's amazement, she *actually* enjoyed visiting her in-laws.

**acute** *adjective* 1. ✦ keen, powerful, sharp ◇ intense, strong, sensitive Eagles have *acute* vision. 2. ✦ serious, severe, critical, dire ◇ crucial, urgent California experienced an *acute* drought in the early 21st century.

**adapt** *verb* ✦ adjust, conform ◇ change, fit Ling *adapted* quickly to her new job.

**add** *verb* 1. ✦ sum up, total, calculate, compute ◇ figure, reckon Lloyd can *add* numbers so fast that we call him a human calculator. 2. ✦ include, insert ◇ attach, combine, join Our peanut butter cookie dough looked so rich that we decided not to *add* chocolate chips.

**addiction** *noun* ✦ dependence (on) ◇ fixation, obsession, preoccupation Do you think someone can have an *addiction* to sugar?

**addition** *noun* ✦ annex, extension ◇ attachment, expansion, increase, enlargement The new sunroom is a welcome *addition* to our house.

**additional** *adjective* ✦ extra, added, more ◇ supplementary, further The book's new edition includes *additional* information about the author's research.

**address** *noun* 1. ✦ residence, home ✧ abode, location, place Santiago's family moved to a new *address*. 2. ✦ speech, talk, oration ✧ lecture, sermon A popular senator gave the opening *address* at the convention. —*verb* ✦ speak to, talk to ✧ lecture, discuss The president will *address* the nation tomorrow.

**adequate** *adjective* ✦ enough, sufficient ✧ satisfactory, suitable, acceptable It is important to have *adequate* vitamins and minerals in your diet.

**adhere** *verb* 1. ✦ attach, cling, hold on, stick ✧ fasten There were many burs *adhering* to my socks after I took a shortcut through the empty lot. 2. ✦ follow, keep to, maintain, stick to ✧ heed, obey, observe Success comes to those who *adhere to* their goals.

**adjacent** *adjective* ✦ alongside, next to, touching ✧ close to, near I think it is funny that the diet center is *adjacent to* a donut shop.

**adjust** *verb* 1. ✦ change, modify, correct, regulate, set ✧ fix, repair Anna helped her little brother *adjust* the seat height on his bicycle. 2. ✦ adapt, conform ✧ reconcile, settle, fit Khalid had a hard time *adjusting* to life in a new country.

**adjustment** *noun* ✦ alteration, change, modification, adaptation, improvement A few *adjustments* to the satellite dish improved our television reception.

**administer** *verb* 1. ✦ direct, manage, run, supervise, lead ✧ control An experienced employee *administered* the summer arts program for the whole city. 2. ✦ dispense, give, provide, apply ✧ supply, furnish Paramedics *administered* first aid to the injured woman.

**admirable** *adjective* ✦ commendable, praiseworthy ✧ beneficial, excellent, good, superb Victoria makes *admirable* use of her spare time by volunteering at the local hospital.

**admiration** *noun* ✦ esteem, regard, respect, praise ✧ approval, reverence Ivanna earned her competitors' *admiration* when she won the race despite her asthma.

**admire** *verb* ✦ esteem, respect ✧ honor, revere, venerate, commend I *admire* Hasreet for being able to speak three foreign languages.

**admit** *verb* 1. ✦ acknowledge, concede, confess ✧ disclose, reveal Linda *admitted* that she had difficulty remembering the names of all fifty US states.

2. ✦ accept at, let in ✧ include, receive, take My friend Manoj was just *admitted to* Harvard University.

**adopt** *verb* ✦ embrace, endorse, accept, approve ✧ borrow, take on The chess club *adopted* a new set of tournament rules.

**adorable** *adjective* ✦ lovable, charming, delightful ✧ attractive, captivating, appealing Nicole is the only one who thinks that her pet iguana is *adorable*.

**adore** *verb* ✦ love, cherish, treasure ✧ revere, worship I *adore* my great-aunt because she is loving and wise.

**adorn** *verb* ✦ decorate, ornament, trim, deck, embellish Leah *adorned* her old hat with ribbons and flowers.

**adult** *noun* ✦ grown-up ✧ man, woman, elder Airlines typically require young children to be accompanied by an *adult*. —*adjective* ✦ mature, full-grown, grown ✧ aged, developed *Adult* blue whales are the world's largest living animals.

**advance** *verb* 1. ✦ move, proceed, progress ✧ hasten, speed, go The army *advanced* across the field. 2. ✦ further, improve, promote, boost ✧ assist, benefit Marie Curie's discoveries *advanced* our knowledge of radioactivity. 3. ✦ suggest, propose, introduce, offer, present The crackpot scientist *advanced* a theory that the Earth is square. —*noun* ✦ advancement, development, improvement, progress, gain ✧ headway *Advances* in technology have made computers faster and more powerful.

**Antonyms** advance

*verb* 1. recede, retreat, withdraw 2. hinder, impede, obstruct 3. repress, suppress, withhold
*noun* reversal, setback

**advantage** *noun* ✦ benefit, blessing ✧ asset, edge, favor, help Antonio helps those who have fewer *advantages* than he does by volunteering at a soup kitchen.

**advantageous** *adjective* ✦ beneficial, helpful, useful ✧ favorable, valuable Valentina finds it *advantageous* to live with a roommate rather than on her own.

**adventure** *noun* ✦ escapade, exploit, feat, venture ✧ experience, undertaking Going over the rapids in an inner tube was the greatest *adventure* of our trip.

**adventurous** *adjective* ✦ daring, intrepid, bold, brave, courageous The *adventurous* children explored a cemetery after dark.

**adversary** *noun* ✦ opponent, rival, competitor ✧ enemy, foe The two friends often are fierce *adversaries* on the tennis court.

**adverse** *adjective* ✦ bad, unfavorable ✧ unfortunate, unlucky, hostile *Adverse* weather forced us to postpone our baseball game.

**advertise** *verb* ✦ promote, publicize, pitch, announce ✧ feature Diya *advertises* her availability as a language tutor in the local paper and online.

**advice** *noun* ✦ counsel, guidance, recommendation, suggestion ✧ directions, help Sometimes it's difficult to follow all of your doctor's *advice*.

**advise** *verb* ✦ counsel, recommend, suggest ✧ caution, warn, encourage An accountant often *advises* clients on how to invest their money.

**affect** *verb* 1. ✦ alter, change, modify, influence ✧ disturb, transform The airline strike *affected* our vacation plans. 2. ✦ move, stir, touch ✧ impress, upset, reach The sad movie *affected* me deeply.

**affection** *noun* ✦ fondness, love, tenderness, warmth ✧ devotion Samar feels great *affection* for his little brother.

**affectionate** *adjective* ✦ loving, warm, tender, caring, fond The *affectionate* child likes to give people hugs.

**affirm** *verb* ✦ confirm ✧ assert, avow, claim, declare, insist, swear A witness *affirmed* that the defendant was telling the truth.

**afford** *verb* 1. ✦ pay for ✧ manage, support, sustain If I save a little each week, I'll soon be able to *afford* a new motorbike. 2. ✦ furnish, give, provide, supply ✧ produce, grant This window *affords* a fine view of the ocean.

**afraid** *adjective* 1. ✦ fearful, frightened, scared, terrified, intimidated The little boy was *afraid* of his neighbor's dog. 2. ✦ sorry, regretful ✧ reluctant, unhappy I'm *afraid* that I won't be able to attend your party.

**after** *preposition* ✦ behind, following, later than, past Dessert typically comes *after* the main course. —*conjunction* ✦ as soon as, once, when Employees can take a day off *after* the big job is finished. —*adverb* ✦ afterward, later, next, thereafter, then You go on ahead, and I'll come *after*.

**again** *adverb* ✦ once more, over ✧ anew, often Hiroshi liked the movie so much that he decided to see it *again*.

**against** *preposition* 1. ✦ into, opposite to, toward, facing ✧ across The flight was bumpy because the plane had to fly *against* a strong headwind. 2. ✦ on, upon, next to, alongside Hoang leaned his motorbike *against* a wall.

**age** *noun* ✦ epoch, era, period, time, phase Dmitry loves to read about the *age* of the dinosaurs. —*verb* ✦ ripen, develop, grow, mature ✧ season Letting tomatoes *age* on the vine ensures that they will have a better flavor.

**aged** *adjective* ✦ elderly, old ✧ advanced, ancient, mature, senior My grandfather is now *aged* and living in a nursing home.

**agency** *noun* ✦ bureau, business, office, firm, company ✧ department, organization Zahra works for a real estate *agency*.

**agent** *noun* 1. ✦ representative ✧ broker, delegate, negotiator Pedro's acting *agent* got him a job in a television commercial. 2. ✦ cause, force, instrument, medium ✧ means, mechanism, power Carbon dioxide is one of the *agents* that cause global climate change.

**aggravate** *verb* 1. ✦ intensify, worsen, magnify ✧ complicate, increase When I scratched my mosquito bites, I only *aggravated* the itching. 2. ✦ irritate, irk, annoy, bother, exasperate, provoke The woman's loud singing in the shower *aggravated* her roommates.

**agile** *adjective* ✦ nimble, limber, dexterous, spry ✧ deft, quick One needs to be very *agile* to excel in gymnastics.

**agitate** *verb* 1. ✦ churn, shake, stir, toss, jiggle A washing machine *agitates* clothes in soapy water to get the dirt out. 2. ✦ disturb, upset, shake up, unsettle ✧ arouse, excite, provoke The speaker's angry remarks *agitated* the audience.

**agony** *noun* ✦ anguish, distress, pain, torment ✧ suffering, misery I was in *agony* when I stubbed my toe a second time.

**agree** *verb* 1. ✦ consent, assent, allow, permit ✧ concur The judge *agreed* to let the defendant out on bail. 2. ✦ coincide with, concur with, correspond to, fit, match, accord My boyfriend's opinion of the movie didn't *agree* with mine.

**agreement** *noun* 1. ✦ accord, concurrence, harmony ✧ conformity My sister and I are usually in *agreement* about what to watch on TV. 2. ✦ deal, pact, bargain, compact ✧ treaty, understanding, arrangement Sarkis and his friend made an *agreement* to settle their argument by flipping a coin.

### Word Groups

Agriculture is the business of cultivating soil, producing crops, and raising livestock. **Agriculture** is a general term with no true synonyms. Here are some related words to investigate in a dictionary: **breeding, cultivating, farming, grazing, harvesting, ranching, reaping**

**ahead** *adverb* ✦ in front ✧ before, first, leading, onward Eli pulled *ahead* of the other cyclists just in time to win the race.

**aid** *verb* ✦ help, assist ✧ support, relieve A stranger stopped to *aid* the stranded motorist. —*noun* ✦ help, assistance, guidance ✧ service, support I could never have fixed my computer without my friend's *aid*.

**ailment** *noun* ✦ disease, illness, sickness, affliction, disorder Juan worried that he had a serious *ailment*, but he only had a bad cold.

**aim** *verb* ✦ point, sight ✧ direct, level, train Pete *aimed* at the bull's-eye, but he missed the target entirely. —*noun* ✦ goal, objective, intention ✧ plan, purpose, target Jeneane's *aim* in life is to become a senator.

**air** *noun* ✦ atmosphere, sky ✧ space The eagle spread its wings and soared through the *air*. —*verb* 1. ✦ ventilate, aerate ✧ freshen, refresh This stuffy room needs to be *aired*. 2. ✦ express, voice, communicate, state ✧ declare, display The manager plans to call a meeting for her employees to *air* their complaints.

**aisle** *noun* ✧ corridor, lane, passage, passageway, walkway, path A little boy got lost in the *aisles* of the grocery store.

**alarm** *noun* 1. ✦ apprehension, dismay, distress, fear, fright, worry, anxiety The doctor assured me that my stomachache was no cause for *alarm*. 2. ✦ alert, signal, warning ✧ bell, buzzer, horn, siren When the fire *alarm* went off, we all had to go outside. —*verb* ✦ frighten, scare, startle, shock ✧ dismay, upset Caroline likes to *alarm* her friends with her daredevil antics.

**alert** *adjective* ✦ attentive, vigilant, watchful ✧ observant, ready, aware The lifeguard at the pool is always *alert* for signs of distress. —*verb* ✦ advise, notify, warn, caution ✧ inform, signal We were *alerted* to prepare for more flooding. —*noun* ✦ alarm, signal, warning ✧ siren Everyone ran to their storm cellars when they heard the tornado *alert*.

### Word Groups

An **alibi** is a claim that a person was elsewhere when a crime took place. **Alibi** is a very specific term with no true synonyms. Here are some related words to investigate in a dictionary: **account, excuse, explanation, reason, report, statement, story, version**

**alike** *adjective* ✦ identical, like, similar, uniform ✧ matched No two snowflakes are *alike* in every detail. —*adverb* ✦ identically, similarly ✧ equally, uniformly, evenly The twin sisters usually dress *alike*.

**alive** *adjective* ✦ living, live ✧ breathing, existing, animate, active After the accident, the man was badly hurt but still *alive*.

**allegiance** *noun* ✦ loyalty, fidelity, ✧ devotion, obedience, faithfulness My dog gives his *allegiance* to whoever feeds him.

**alliance** *noun* ✦ pact, union, coalition ✧ agreement, treaty Australia, New Zealand, and the United States have formed a military *alliance* known as ANZUS.

**allied** *adjective* ✦ combined, joint, united ✧ associated, connected, aligned Several nations formed a pact, and their *allied* fleet contained more than 300 ships.

**allot** *verb* ✦ allocate, allow, assign, give ✧ distribute, share The professor *allotted* all students five minutes for their speeches.

**allow** *verb* ✦ let, permit ✧ approve, authorize, consent My young nephew is not *allowed* to stay out late.

**ally** *verb* ✦ join, unite, combine ✧ associate, unify The citizen groups *allied* with each other to lobby for a public park. —*noun* ✦ partner ✧ assistant, associate, colleague, confederate The United States was Britain's *ally* during World War II.

**almost** *adverb* ✦ nearly, practically ✧ about, mostly, virtually, approximately Binh *almost* flew off his motorbike when he hit the big pothole.

**alone** *adjective* ✦ unaccompanied, unattended, companionless ✧ isolated, secluded, solitary Hillary was *alone* all afternoon while her roommate was at work.

**aloud** *adverb* ✦ out loud ✧ audibly, loudly, openly My literature professor enjoys reading *aloud* to the class.

**also** *adverb* ✦ too, in addition, as well, besides ✧ additionally, furthermore Wherever I go, my dog wants to go *also*.

**alter** *verb* ✦ change, modify, transform, vary ✧ revise, adjust Chanay's new haircut completely *alters* her appearance.

**alternate** *verb* ✦ switch, shift, rotate, take turns ✧ vary My cat *alternates* between sleeping and eating. —*adjective* 1. ✦ alternating, every other ✧ recurring, successive Ray mows the yard on *alternate* Sundays. 2. ✦ substitute, another, different, replacement The bridge was closed, so we had to take an *alternate* route.

**alternative** *noun* ✦ choice, option, selection, possibility ✧ substitute There are so many *alternatives*, I can't decide which movie to see.

**altogether** *adverb* ✦ completely, entirely, totally, wholly, absolutely A librarian warned the children that they were being *altogether* too rowdy.

**always** *adverb* ✦ forever, eternally, everlastingly ✧ constantly, perpetually I will love you *always*.

**amateur** *noun* ✦ nonprofessional, dabbler ✧ beginner, novice The singing competition is open only to *amateurs* who have never been paid for a performance.

**amaze** *verb* ✦ astonish, astound, awe, surprise, impress ✧ shock Tiana *amazes* me with her ability to remember people's names.

**amazement** *noun* ✦ astonishment, awe, wonder, bewilderment, surprise, shock I watched in *amazement* as the tightrope walker ventured out on a wire stretched between two tall buildings.

**ambition** *noun* ✦ aim, goal, objective, aspiration ✧ desire, wish Diep's *ambition* is to become a veterinarian.

**ambitious** *adjective* 1. ✦ aspiring, determined ✧ eager, hopeful, purposeful The *ambitious* actor hopes to land a starring role someday. 2. ✦ bold, daring ✧ challenging, difficult, grandiose The

mayor unveiled her *ambitious* plan to build a new civic center.

**amble** *verb* ✦ ramble, saunter, stroll, walk, wander We *ambled* along the river, enjoying the sunny day.

**amend** *verb* ✦ revise, alter, change, modify, reform ✧ correct, improve The US Constitution has been periodically *amended*.

**amiable** *adjective* ✦ friendly, good-natured, pleasant ✧ congenial, sociable, agreeable Jayden likes his new job because his coworkers are *amiable*.

**Antonyms** amiable
*adjective* **mean, nasty, spiteful, unfriendly**

**among** *preposition* ✦ amongst, between ✧ amid, amidst, with The bank robbers divided the loot *among* themselves.

**amount** *noun* ✦ sum, total, quantity ✧ number, measure The *amount* you owe for dinner is five dollars. —*verb* ✦ total, equal ✧ match, reach, approach My expenditures for the weekend camping trip *amounted to* thirty-five dollars.

**ample** *adjective* ✦ abundant, plenty of, enough, sufficient, adequate ✧ plentiful, unlimited Even though Dave ate two hamburgers, he had *ample* room for dessert.

**amplify** *verb* ✦ intensify, magnify, strengthen, boost ✧ expand, increase A loudspeaker system *amplified* the band's music.

**amuse** *verb* ✦ entertain, divert, delight, please, charm ✧ interest Justine *amused* us with a song she made up.

**amusement** *noun* ✦ enjoyment, entertainment, diversion, fun ✧ mirth, pleasure The circus provides *amusement* for people of all ages.

**amusing** *adjective* ✦ entertaining, comical, funny, witty ✧ charming, delightful Pierre told us an *amusing* story about the time he got lost on the way to see his girlfriend.

**analyze** *verb* ✦ examine, evaluate, investigate, study ✧ judge, inspect In English class, we *analyzed* the elements of a good novel.

**ancestor** *noun* ✦ forebear ✧ forefather, foremother In Vietnam, many homes have an altar devoted to the family's *ancestors*.

**anchor** *verb* ✦ attach, fasten, fix, secure ✧ hold,

**moor** The climber looked for a safe place to *anchor* her rope.

**ancient** *adjective* ✦ age-old, archaic, old, olden ✧ aged, antique Angkor Wat is a complex of *ancient* temples in Cambodia.

**anger** *noun* ✦ fury, ire, rage, wrath, outrage ✧ annoyance, irritation My *anger* caused me to say things that I later regretted. —*verb* ✦ incense, infuriate, outrage, upset ✧ annoy, offend A customer's rude remarks *angered* the waitress.

**angry** *adjective* ✦ mad, furious, irate, incensed ✧ annoyed, upset My friend and I were *angry* when a stranger insulted us.

**anguish** *noun* ✦ distress, misery, grief, torment, agony ✧ pain, suffering We all felt great *anguish* when our beloved grandmother passed away.

**animal** *noun* ✦ beast ✧ being, creature, organism Our local zoo has *animals* from all over the world.

**animosity** *noun* ✦ hate, hatred, hostility, enmity ✧ bitterness, resentment There was *animosity* between the warring clans.

**annex** *verb* ✦ appropriate, seize, add, attach ✧ connect, join, unite After the war, the victorious country *annexed* some of the loser's territory. —*noun* ✦ addition, extension, wing ✧ branch The museum built an *annex* to house its new exhibit.

**announce** *verb* ✦ declare, proclaim ✧ disclose, report, tell The couple held a big party to *announce* their engagement.

**annoy** *verb* ✦ bother, disturb, trouble, irk, irritate, pester My roommate *annoys* me with his constant complaining.

**answer** *noun* 1. ✦ reply, response ✧ acknowledgment I emailed an *answer* to the birthday party invitation. 2. ✦ solution ✧ key, explanation, resolution, result Some people believe that learning to eat insects is the *answer* to world hunger. —*verb* ✦ reply, respond ✧ acknowledge, react Tricia *answered* with a nod.

**antic** *noun* ✦ caper, prank, stunt ✧ frolic, joke, trick Your childish *antics* are not as charming as you seem to think.

**anticipate** *verb* ✦ await, expect, hope for ✧ foresee, predict My dog eagerly *anticipates* our evening walks.

**anticipation** *noun* ✦ expectancy, expectation ✧ hope, prospect The delicious smells coming from the kitchen made my mouth water in *anticipation* of a great meal.

**antique** *noun* ✦ heirloom, antiquity ✧ artifact, relic, souvenir This doll is an *antique* that has been handed down from my great-grandmother.

**anxiety** *noun* ✦ apprehension, nervousness, uneasiness, concern, distress, worry Gabriela felt some *anxiety* about speaking before such a large group.

**anxious** *adjective* 1. ✦ apprehensive, worried, nervous, fearful, uneasy Mateo was *anxious* about his visit to the dentist. 2. ✦ eager, impatient ✧ desirous, expectant, keen Miranda is *anxious* to go away to college.

**apathy** *noun* ✦ indifference, disinterest ✧ unconcern The last election had a low turnout due to voter *apathy*.

**Antonyms** apathy
*noun* attention, care, concern, interest, regard

**appall** *verb* ✦ shock, dismay, horrify, alarm, stun Simon is *appalled* that so many people continue to deny the perils of global climate change.

**apparatus** *noun* ✦ equipment, gear, implements ✧ device, machinery Cayce enjoys using gym *apparatus*, especially the balance beam.

**apparel** *noun* ✦ attire, clothes, clothing, garments, garb The basketball player is looking for a store that sells *apparel* for tall men.

**apparent** *adjective* ✦ obvious, plain, clear, evident ✧ visible, noticeable It's *apparent* that you don't like these chocolate-covered grasshoppers.

**appeal** *noun* 1. ✦ bid, call, entreaty, plea, request The public television station is making an *appeal* for contributions. 2. ✦ attraction, allure, draw ✧ charm, fascination Sometimes TV commercials have more *appeal* than the show I'm watching. —*verb* 1. ✦ apply, ask, beg, plead to ✧ pray, request The earthquake victims *appealed to* the government for assistance. 2. ✦ interest, attract, fascinate, draw, tempt Windsurfing *appeals to* Kim.

**appear** *verb* 1. ✦ come out, emerge, show up ✧ materialize, issue The moon *appeared* from behind clouds. 2. ✦ look, seem ✧ act, feel, sound Jerome *appears* to be enjoying his book.

**appearance** *noun* 1. ✦ arrival, emergence ✧ coming, entrance We were thrilled by the sudden *ap-*

*pearance* of dolphins behind the boat. **2.** ✦ **look** ✧ **aspect, demeanor, image, bearing** Yusif always has a neat *appearance*.

**appease** *verb* ✦ **pacify, quiet, soothe, calm, placate** ✧ **satisfy** The mail carrier *appeased* the barking German shepherd with a dog biscuit.

**appendix** *noun* ✦ **addition, attachment, supplement** ✧ **index** My ESL book has an *appendix* that lists answers to the self-test questions.

**appetite** *noun* ✦ **desire, stomach, hunger, taste, craving** ✧ **demand, need** Holly had no *appetite* for the peanut butter and pickle sandwich.

**appetizing** *adjective* ✦ **appealing, delicious, inviting, pleasing, tempting** During the holidays, our kitchen is filled with *appetizing* aromas.

**applaud** *verb* ✦ **praise, commend, acclaim, laud, approve** ✧ **cheer** I *applaud* your courage to stand up for your beliefs.

**applause** *noun* ✦ **clapping, ovation** ✧ **acclaim, cheers, praise** The *applause* that followed Natalia's cello recital was very enthusiastic.

**appliance** *noun* ✦ **apparatus, equipment** ✧ **device, implement, machine** Kitchen *appliances* range from electric can openers to refrigerators.

**application** *noun* **1.** ✦ **function, purpose, use, employment** ✧ **operation, value** A pocketknife has many practical *applications*. **2.** ✧ **appeal, petition, request, requisition** I have sent *applications* to many different colleges.

**apply** *verb* **1.** ✦ **administer to, put on, spread on, place** ✧ **deposit, lay** Aloe vera gel can be safely *applied to* minor burns. **2.** ✦ **employ, exercise, use, utilize, engage** Skyler *applied* all of his strength to open the tightly sealed jar. **3.** ✦ **pertain, relate, fit** ✧ **concern, involve, refer** Honesty is an old-fashioned value that still *applies* today.

**appoint** *verb* ✦ **designate for, name to, select for** ✧ **assign, delegate, elect** A senator has been *appointed to* the president's cabinet.

**appointment** *noun* **1.** ✦ **selection (for), assignment, designation** ✧ **election, placement** Anastasia was pleased by her *appointment* to the research board. **2.** ✦ **date, engagement** ✧ **booking, meeting** I made an *appointment* to see the doctor.

**appreciate** *verb* **1.** ✦ **cherish, prize, treasure, value** ✧ **esteem, like** Beatriz *appreciates* the time she is able to spend with her family when she is home

from college. **2.** ✦ **comprehend, perceive, understand** ✧ **acknowledge, recognize, grasp** I *appreciate* your viewpoint, but you still haven't changed my mind.

**appreciation** *noun* **1.** ✦ **awareness, perception, understanding, regard** ✧ **enjoyment** Francesco developed a new *appreciation* of music after starting guitar lessons. **2.** ✦ **gratitude, gratefulness, thankfulness, thanks** Greta expressed her *appreciation* for the gift by writing a thank-you note.

**apprehensive** *adjective* ✦ **anxious, nervous, uneasy, afraid, fearful, frightened** ✧ **jittery** I'm usually *apprehensive* when I have to speak before a large group.

**approach** *verb* **1.** ✦ **near, reach, come to** ✧ **gain** The train slowed down as it *approached* the station. **2.** ✦ **begin, commence, initiate, start, undertake** Li Juan *approaches* each assignment with a positive attitude. —*noun* **1.** ✦ **method, way, procedure, system, technique** ✧ **attitude, style** When I have a big project, my *approach* is to do a little work every day. **2.** ✦ **avenue, passage, route** ✧ **entrance, entry** The soldiers guarded all *approaches* to their camp.

**appropriate** *adjective* ✦ **proper, correct, right, fitting, suitable, apt** Jocelyn wears *appropriate* shoes when she plays golf. —*verb* ✦ **allocate, allot, assign, authorize, designate** ✧ **devote** Construction will begin as soon as funds are *appropriated*.

**approval** *noun* **1.** ✦ **praise, respect, admiration, regard** ✧ **acceptance, favor** The crowd cheered with *approval* when the runner got back to her feet and finished the race. **2.** ✦ **consent, agreement, authorization, permission** The president will sign the bill into law if it meets with his *approval*.

**approve** *verb* **1.** ✦ **commend, praise, respect** ✧ **accept, appreciate, favor** Sakura's parents have always *approved of* her desire to study abroad. **2.** ✦ **authorize, permit, allow, endorse, confirm** The editor *approved* the reporter's suggestion for a news story.

**approximate** *adjective* ✦ **close, estimated, rough, loose** ✧ **relative** What is the *approximate* number of people at this party?

**approximately** *adverb* ✦ **about, nearly, roughly, around** ✧ **almost** My sister is *approximately* two years younger than I.

**aptitude** *noun* ✦ **gift, talent, ability, capability, skill**

✧ inclination, knack My friend Kim Ngan has a natural *aptitude* for writing.

**arctic** *adjective* ✦ freezing, frigid, icy, cold ✧ chill, chilly, cool The sudden blast of *arctic* air meant winter had arrived.

**area** *noun* 1. ✦ place, region, terrain, territory ✧ district, zone Mosses grow best in *areas* that receive a lot of rain. 2. ✦ room, space ✧ expanse, extent, scope My bed and desk take up most of the *area* in my bedroom.

**argue** *verb* 1. ✦ contend, plead ✧ assert, reason, state The defense attorney *argued* that his client was innocent. 2. ✦ quarrel, bicker, fight ✧ disagree, dispute, feud Muriel and her boyfriend rarely *argue* because they are so much alike.

**argument** *noun* 1. ✦ dispute, disagreement ✧ fight, quarrel, spat The two friends resolved their *argument* by flipping a coin. 2. ✦ reason, case, grounds, justification, defense The politician presented a compelling *argument* in favor of the new legislation.

**arid** *adjective* ✦ dry ✧ barren, parched, waterless My uncle moved to Arizona because its *arid* climate is very good for his arthritis.

**arise** *verb* ✦ appear, begin, start, emerge, originate, result, rise A disagreement *arose* when my friends and I tried to decide which movie to see.

**arm** *noun* ✦ firearm, gun, weapon, weaponry ✧ armament In the American Revolutionary War, Paul Revere warned the Massachusetts minutemen to ready their *arms*. —*verb* ✦ equip, outfit ✧ prepare, protect, provide The man *armed* himself with a baseball bat when he heard a strange noise outside.

**army** *noun* ✦ horde, swarm, host, mass ✧ force, troop, crowd I watched in fascination as an *army* of ants descended on the cookie crumbs.

**aroma** *noun* ✦ fragrance, smell, odor, scent, savor I love the *aroma* of freshly baked bread.

**around** *preposition* ✦ about, near, near to, close to I'll be home *around* dinnertime. —*adverb* ✦ about ✧ everywhere, all over Juana looked *around* until she found her missing comb.

**arouse** *verb* ✦ awaken, rouse, stir, excite, kindle, provoke, stimulate My friend's talk about her life abroad *aroused* my interest in traveling.

**arrange** *verb* 1. ✦ order, organize, sort ✧ place, position Bookstores *arrange* books alphabetically by author. 2. ✦ plan, prepare, schedule, manage A good travel agent will *arrange* all the airline and hotel reservations for you.

**arrangement** *noun* 1. ✦ layout, order ✧ distribution, formation, organization The bride and groom planned the seating *arrangement* for their wedding reception. 2. ✦ plan ✧ measure, preparation, provision, program My college advisor made *arrangements* for me to meet with representatives from several universities.

**arrest** *verb* ✦ apprehend, capture, catch, seize, detain Police officers *arrested* the robbery suspect. —*noun* ✦ apprehension, capture, seizure, detention The *arrest* was made by an undercover detective.

**arrival** *noun* ✦ appearance, coming ✧ approach, entrance My aunt's unexpected *arrival* was a wonderful surprise.

**arrive** *verb* ✦ come, get in, show up ✧ appear, approach, reach When does the next train *arrive*?

**arrogant** *adjective* ✦ conceited, egotistical, haughty, disdainful ✧ insolent, proud, vain The *arrogant* actress treated everyone disrespectfully.

**art** *noun* ✦ craft, skill, technique, methods Giorgia learned the *art* of calligraphy at school.

**article** *noun* 1. ✦ feature, piece, story ✧ essay, review, report This magazine is well known for its travel *articles*. 2. ✦ item, object, piece, thing ✧ commodity, entity A shirt is an *article* of clothing.

**artificial** *adjective* ✦ fake, imitation, phony, mock, simulated, synthetic Only an expert can tell *artificial* gems from real ones.

**Word Groups**

An **artist** is a person who creates works of art. **Artist** is a general term with no true synonyms. Here are some different kinds of artists to investigate in a dictionary: **artisan, composer, illustrator, musician, painter, sculptor, writer**

**ascend** *verb* ✦ climb, mount, move up ✧ rise, scale Geckos are lizards that can *ascend* smooth walls.

**ascent** *noun* ✦ climb ✧ ascension, scaling The first *ascent* of Mount Everest was made by Edmund Hillary and Tenzing Norgay.

**ashamed** *adjective* ✦ embarrassed, humiliated,

guilty ◇ sorry I feel so *ashamed* for having lied to you.

**ask** *verb* 1. ✦ request ◇ appeal, beg, plead, seek Wei *asked for* a new smartphone for his birthday. 2. ✦ inquire, query, question ◇ examine, interrogate My friend *asked* if she could borrow my laptop.

**asleep** *adjective* ✦ dozing, napping, sleeping, slumbering ◇ dormant My cat is *asleep* on the windowsill.

**aspect** *noun* ✦ appearance, look, air ◇ face, surface, shape Our yard took on a whole new *aspect* when we planted flowers around the edge.

**aspire** *verb* ✦ desire, strive, seek, want, wish, yearn ◇ crave The young soccer player *aspires* to become a champion.

**assassin** *noun* ✦ killer, murderer, slayer ◇ executioner In the United States, the Secret Service protects the president from would-be *assassins*.

**assassinate** *verb* ✦ kill, murder, slay ◇ execute, slaughter President Lincoln was *assassinated* five days after the American Civil War ended.

**assault** *noun* ✦ attack, strike, raid ◇ offensive, onslaught The soldiers made an *assault* on the enemy fort. —*verb* ✦ attack, raid ◇ bombard, charge, rush, storm Terrorists *assaulted* the local police station.

**assemble** *verb* 1. ✦ congregate, gather, rally, collect, group ◇ accumulate The football team *assembled* around the coach. 2. ✦ put together, construct, make, fabricate ◇ connect, join My friend helped me *assemble my* new bookshelves.

**assembly** *noun* 1. ✦ gathering, meeting ◇ convention, rally, conference In some schools, an *assembly* is held every morning to bring students and teachers together before classes start. 2. ✦ construction, fabricating ◇ connecting, fitting, joining The directions said that some *assembly* would be required.

**assert** *verb* ✦ affirm, claim, contend, announce, declare ◇ insist, swear The defendant *asserted* his innocence.

**asset** *noun* 1. ✦ advantage, aid, benefit, resource, boon, help, strength Having a large vocabulary is a great *asset* for taking college entrance exams. 2. ✦ possessions, property ◇ capital, wealth, resources My father's *assets* include two houses and a boat.

**assign** *verb* 1. ✦ appoint, designate, name, post ◇ charge, nominate The officer *assigned* two soldiers to stand guard. 2. ✦ give ◇ allocate, allot, dispense, distribute I hope the professor doesn't *assign* us any more book reports.

**assignment** *noun* ✦ task, duty, mission, job ◇ chore, responsibility The soldier's *assignment* was to stand guard.

**assist** *verb* ✦ aid, help ◇ serve, support, relieve Joo-won often *assists* his little sister with her homework.

**Antonyms** assist
*verb* hamper, hinder, impede, obstruct, restrict

**assistance** *noun* ✦ aid, help ◇ backing, service, support, hand The reporter asked his colleague for *assistance* writing the big story.

**assistant** *noun* ✦ aide, helper ◇ attendant, auxiliary, subordinate, deputy The scientist has several *assistants* to help with her research.

**associate** *verb* 1. ✦ identify with, connect to, link to, relate to Jack-o'-lanterns and haunted houses are *associated with* Halloween. 2. ✦ socialize, fraternize, mingle, mix, consort I don't like to *associate* with people who use illegal drugs. —*noun* ✦ colleague, partner, peer ◇ confederate, coworker The lawyer invited several business *associates* out to dinner.

**association** *noun* ✦ club, group, organization, society ◇ alliance, league Margaret Anne joined a national *association* of stamp collectors.

**assortment** *noun* ✦ selection, variety ◇ array, collection, mixture Françoise gave her mother an *assortment* of Swiss chocolates.

**assume** *verb* 1. ✦ presume, suppose, believe ◇ surmise, suspect, think Lee *assumes* that she will have a party on her birthday. 2. ✦ take on, incur, undertake ◇ acquire, adopt, embrace, take Keegan had to *assume* more responsibility around the house when his brother left for college.

**assure** *verb* ✦ promise, guarantee, reassure ◇ confirm, pledge The veterinarian *assured* me that my iguana would be fine.

**astonish** *verb* ✦ amaze, astound, stun, surprise ◇ startle, shock The acrobats *astonished* us with their daring feats.

**astonishment** *noun* ✦ amazement, surprise, awe

✧ **confusion, disbelief, wonder** I gaped in *astonishment* when a pigeon flew into our car.

**athletic** *adjective* ✦ **active, energetic, vigorous, robust** Kareem is an *athletic* man who loves to play hockey and other sports.

**atmosphere** *noun* 1. ✧ **air, sky, space** The space shuttle takes only a few minutes to exit the Earth's *atmosphere*. 2. ✦ **ambiance, feel, feeling, mood, spirit** ✧ **climate, environment** I love the cozy *atmosphere* at this café.

**atrocious** *adjective* ✦ **abominable, bad, dreadful, terrible, poor** ✧ **cruel, wicked** After World War II, some Nazi officers were accused of having committed *atrocious* war crimes.

**attach** *verb* ✦ **fasten, connect, secure, affix, join** Toshi *attached* a luggage rack to his motorbike.

**attachment** *noun* 1. ✦ **accessory** ✧ **addition, supplement, extra** Our new vacuum cleaner has an *attachment* for cleaning upholstery. 2. ✦ **bond, tie** ✧ **affection, devotion, love, fondness** Rebecca has a strong *attachment* to her best friend.

**attack** *verb* 1. ✦ **assault, charge, storm, raid** ✧ **assail, strike** Attila the Hun invaded Italy, but he did not *attack* Rome. 2. ✦ **criticize, denounce, fault** ✧ **censure, berate** During an election campaign, candidates commonly *attack* their opponent's beliefs. —*noun* ✦ **assault, charge, offensive, raid, strike, invasion** The enemy forces launched their *attack* at dawn.

**attain** *verb* ✦ **accomplish, achieve, reach, realize** ✧ **acquire, gain, win** Kwan *attained* her dream of becoming captain of the swim team.

**attempt** *verb* ✦ **try, endeavor** ✧ **seek, strive, struggle** I *attempted* to move the heavy desk by myself, but I had to ask for help. —*noun* ✦ **try, effort** ✧ **endeavor, venture, go, bid** Marcy cleared six feet on her first *attempt* at the high jump.

**attend** *verb* 1. ✦ **go to, appear at** ✧ **frequent, visit** Marcus *attends* hockey practice every afternoon. 2. ✦ **tend, care for, take care of, serve, assist** ✧ **accompany, escort** When the invalid came home from the hospital, she hired a nurse to *attend* her.

**attendant** *noun* ✦ **assistant, helper, aide** ✧ **servant, escort** A zoo *attendant* gave us directions to the koala enclosure.

**attention** *noun* ✦ **heed, regard, care** ✧ **concentration, notice** In my ESL class, I always pay close *attention* to the teacher.

**attentive** *adjective* ✦ **alert, heedful, observant, watchful** ✧ **considerate, thoughtful** An *attentive* waiter constantly refilled my water glass.

**attire** *noun* ✦ **apparel, clothing, clothes, garments, outfit** ✧ **costume, dress** Youssef wore comfortable *attire* for the plane ride.

**attitude** *noun* ✦ **outlook, perspective** ✧ **approach, disposition, mood** Mateo is easy to work with because he brings a good *attitude* to everything he does.

**attract** *verb* ✦ **draw, lure, pull, bring** ✧ **charm, entice** Don't leave the food uncovered or it will *attract* flies.

**attraction** *noun* ✦ **appeal, draw, pull** ✧ **allure, charm** The baby elephants are the main *attraction* at our zoo.

**attractive** *adjective* ✦ **appealing, pleasing, pretty, beautiful, becoming, lovely** That shirt is an *attractive* shade of green.

**audience** *noun* ✦ **crowd, onlookers, spectators** ✧ **following, gathering** The street juggler was so good that he soon attracted a large *audience*.

**authentic** *adjective* ✦ **genuine, real, actual, true** ✧ **valid** A good art dealer can usually tell if a painting is *authentic* or a forgery.

## Word Groups

The **author** of a written work is its original creator. **Author** is a general term with no true synonyms. Here are some different kinds of authors to investigate in a dictionary: **essayist, journalist, novelist, playwright, poet, scribe, scriptwriter**

**authority** *noun* 1. ✦ **authorization, control, power, right** ✧ **command, influence** The clerk told us that only the manager has the *authority* to change prices. 2. ✦ **expert, specialist** ✧ **master, professional** That professor is an acknowledged *authority* on Medieval art.

**authorize** *verb* ✦ **allow, enable, permit, approve, sanction** ✧ **warrant** Dinh has a visa that *authorizes* her to travel to the United States.

**autograph** *noun* ✦ **signature** ✧ **inscription, mark, sign** Michele asked the soccer star for his *autograph*. —*verb* ✦ **sign** ✧ **endorse, inscribe** The symphony conductor *autographed* my program.

**automatic** *adjective* ✦ automated, self-acting, self-operating, mechanical ✧ independent Our electric heater has an *automatic* shutoff as a safety feature.

**available** *adjective* ✦ free, open, obtainable ✧ accessible, ready, usable We asked the restaurant hostess if any booths were *available*.

**avenue** *noun* ✦ boulevard, road, street, thoroughfare ✧ route, lane We drove down a tree-lined *avenue* on our way to the park.

**average** *noun* ✦ mean, norm, par, standard, ordinary Maya's ability in English is above the *average*. —*adjective* 1. ✧ mean, middle, medium The *average* temperature of the Earth is 61 degrees Fahrenheit (16 C). 2. ✦ ordinary, typical, usual, normal, regular, standard The *average* candy bar has more than two hundred calories.

**avoid** *verb* ✦ elude, escape, evade ✧ dodge, shun, sidestep We went to the beach on Wednesday in order to *avoid* the weekend crowds.

**award** *verb* ✦ confer, bestow, give, grant, present ✧ assign Alice Munro was the first short-story writer to be *awarded* the Nobel Prize in Literature. —*noun* ✦ prize, trophy ✧ decoration, honor, medal, tribute The starlet was thrilled to receive the *award* for best actress.

**aware** *adjective* ✦ conscious, mindful ✧ informed, knowledgeable Caution signs are intended to make drivers *aware* of dangers ahead.

**awful** *adjective* ✦ bad, dreadful, hideous, horrible, terrible, abominable I didn't go to the movie because I heard it was *awful*.

**awfully** *adverb* ✦ extremely, immensely, terribly, very ✧ greatly I had an *awfully* hard time walking all three dogs at once.

**awkward** *adjective* 1. ✦ clumsy, uncoordinated, unskilled, graceless, inept Before I took tennis lessons, my serve was *awkward*. 2. ✦ cumbersome, difficult, unwieldy ✧ unmanageable The large suitcase was *awkward* to carry.

# B

**babble** *verb* ✦ chatter, blabber, jabber, talk ✧ gurgle, murmur My girlfriend *babbled* on and on about how excited she was to get the job she wanted. —*noun* ✦ babbling, burble, gurgle, murmur ✧ chatter, jabbering Listening to the brook's gentle *babble* is very relaxing.

**baby** *noun* ✦ infant, newborn, babe ✧ toddler, tot According to centuries-old German folklore, *babies* are delivered by a stork.

**back** *noun* ✦ rear, rear end ✧ end, reverse, stern, tail The driver asked us to please move to the *back* of the bus. —*adjective* ✦ rear, hind ✧ behind, end, tail Deliveries should be made to the *back* door. —*verb* ✦ sponsor, support, endorse, aid, help ✧ encourage The university is *backing* our debate team by paying our travel expenses.

**background** *noun* 1. ✦ distance, backdrop ✧ landscape, setting, surroundings My painting of a bighorn sheep has mountains in the *background*. 2. ✦ experience, training ✧ preparation, qualifications, history The interviewer had lots of questions about the job applicant's *background*.

**bad** *adjective* 1. ✦ awful, lousy, poor, terrible ✧ imperfect, inferior During the storm, our television reception was *bad*. 2. ✦ disagreeable, nasty, unpleasant, offensive, repulsive ✧ disturbing Rotten eggs have a *bad* odor. 3. ✦ disobedient, naughty ✧ unruly, wrong, mean Our dog was *bad* when he dug a big hole in the backyard. 4. ✦ damaging, harmful, hurtful, injurious Reading without enough light can be *bad* for your eyes. 5. ✦ regretful, remorseful, sorry, guilty ✧ upset The girl felt *bad* for yelling at her sister.

**baffle** *verb* ✦ bewilder, confuse, mystify, perplex, puzzle, stump I was *baffled* when my little sister refused the cookie I offered her.

**bag** *noun* ✦ sack, tote, tote bag ✧ pouch, bundle, container Jasmine brought her lunch to work in a paper *bag*.

**bait** *noun* ✦ lure ✧ attraction, magnet, temptation Many people use worms for *bait* when they fish. —*verb* ✦ taunt, goad, harass, provoke, tease ✧ torment As the player came up to bat, the other team *baited* him with jeers and insults.

**balance** *noun* 1. ✦ equilibrium, stability, steadiness ✧ poise The skier lost his *balance* and fell into a snowbank. 2. ✦ remainder, rest, leftover ✧ difference, residue, excess Karyn put half her income in savings then spent the *balance* on rent and food. —*verb* ✦ stabilize, steady ✧ poise, level When first learning to ride a bicycle, it takes a while to learn how to *balance* yourself.

**bald** *adjective* ✦ bare, smooth, barren, exposed ✧ hairless The tires on my motorbike are worn almost completely *bald*.

**balk** *verb* ✦ refuse, resist, stop ✧ hesitate The mule *balked* and would not carry the heavy load.

**ban** *verb* ✦ forbid, disallow, outlaw, prohibit, bar The city council has *banned* smoking in public places. —*noun* ✦ prohibition, restriction ✧ boycott, injunction During the 1920s, there was a nationwide *ban* on the production and sale of alcohol in the United States.

**band** *noun* 1. ✦ gang, crew, company, group, pack, party ✧ team The legendary Robin Hood had a *band* of merry men. 2. ✦ ensemble, group ✧ combo, orchestra My friend's *band* rehearses in his garage. —*verb* ✦ join, unite ✧ assemble, merge The citizens *banded* with the police to stop crime.

**bandit** *noun* ✦ outlaw, robber, thief ✧ criminal In America's Old West, *bandits* frequently robbed trains.

**bang** *verb* ✦ beat, hammer, pound, thump ✧ strike The little baby likes to *bang* on the table with his spoon.

**banish** *verb* ✦ exile, deport, eject, evict, expel Napoleon was *banished* to the island of Elba.

**banquet** *noun* ✦ dinner, feast, meal, fete Our company has an awards *banquet* twice a year.

**bar** *noun* 1. ✧ rod, shaft, rail, pole The lion gnawed on the iron *bars* of its cage. 2. ✦ impediment, obstacle, obstruction, barrier, hindrance ✧ block The applicant's lack of experience was a *bar* to getting the job she wanted. 3. ✦ pub, saloon, tavern

◇ canteen, lounge, nightclub Some *bars* sell only beer. —*verb* ✦ prevent, prohibit, restrict, forbid ◇ block, obstruct The criminal was deported and *barred* from ever entering the country again.

**bare** *adjective* ✦ bald, barren, uncovered, clear ◇ empty, naked, vacant There's a *bare* patch on the lawn where we can't get grass to grow. —*verb* ✦ expose, reveal, show, uncover, display Our new kitten *bared* its little claws when it saw our dog.

**barely** *adverb* ✦ just, scarcely, hardly ◇ only, almost The snow *barely* covered the ground.

**bargain** *noun* 1. ✦ agreement, arrangement, deal, pact, promise ◇ treaty The roommates made a *bargain* to determine who would do which chores. 2. ✦ buy, deal, good buy, value ◇ discount, steal We found some real *bargains* at the used clothing shop. —*verb* ✦ negotiate, deal, haggle ◇ barter, trade The prices at this shop are not fixed, so be sure to *bargain* before you buy anything.

**barren** *adjective* ✦ bare, empty, vacant ◇ infertile, unproductive Rin admired the open views as she hiked up the *barren* hillside.

**Antonyms barren**

*adjective* lush, fertile, fruitful, productive, profuse, rich

**barrier** *noun* ✦ obstacle, obstruction, impediment ◇ barricade, blockade The river was a *barrier* that the fire couldn't cross.

**barter** *verb* ✦ exchange, swap, trade ◇ bargain The farmer *bartered* his surplus rice for fish and meat.

**base** *noun* 1. ✦ bottom, foundation ◇ foot, seat The *base* of a pyramid is square, but the sides are triangular. 2. ◇ camp, installation, post, station, headquarters Fort Bragg in North Carolina is said to be the largest army *base* in the world. —*verb* ✦ ground, found, model ◇ build, construct, establish Even though the movie was *based* on a true story, I found it hard to believe.

**bashful** *adjective* ✦ shy, timid, reserved, reticent ◇ modest, uncertain Ara felt *bashful* on his first day at his new job.

**basic** *adjective* ✦ fundamental, primary, key, elementary ◇ core, essential, vital Flour is one of the *basic* ingredients in a cake.

**battle** *noun* ✦ combat, conflict, fight, war, struggle The soldiers were armed and ready for *battle*.

—*verb* ✦ combat, fight, struggle with ◇ duel, skirmish, contest The little yacht had to *battle* strong winds to get safely back to port.

**bawl** *verb* ✦ cry, howl, wail, sob ◇ shout, shriek, weep The toddler *bawled* when she couldn't find her teddy bear.

**bay** *noun* ✦ cove, harbor ◇ inlet, lagoon, gulf The crew anchored their ship in a secluded *bay*.

**beach** *noun* ✦ shore, seashore, seaside ◇ coast, seacoast Hiro looked for shells as he walked along the *beach*.

**beacon** *noun* ✦ signal, guide, light, beam ◇ landmark, pointer The lighthouse was a welcome *beacon* to the crew of the stormbound ship.

**beam** *noun* 1. ◇ brace, girder, rafter, stud, timber, trestle The cabin's ceiling has *beams* made of pine. 2. ✦ ray ◇ gleam, glow, shaft, streak The flashlight's *beam* became dim as the batteries faded. —*verb* ✦ shine, blaze, gleam, glimmer, radiate The sun *beamed* from behind the clouds.

**bear** *verb* 1. ✦ carry, tote, shoulder, support, hold ◇ sustain, take Mules can *bear* surprisingly heavy loads. 2. ✦ abide, endure, stand, tolerate ◇ suffer Many nonsmokers cannot *bear* to be seated next to someone with a lit cigarette. 3. ✦ produce, yield, develop, generate ◇ deliver, make Apple trees *bear* fruit in late summer and early fall.

**bearing** *noun* ✦ connection (to), relation (to) ◇ application, relevance, significance Our sense of smell has a strong *bearing* on our sense of taste.

**beast** *noun* ✦ animal ◇ creature, critter, mammal The lion has been said to be the king of *beasts*.

**beat** *verb* 1. ✦ drum, pound, strike, hit ◇ punch, whack, thump Hail was *beating on* the roof. 2. ✦ defeat, best, conquer, vanquish, whip, overcome My friend usually *beats* me at tennis. —*noun* ✦ pulse, rhythm, throb, tempo ◇ blow, sound, stroke Everybody danced to the *beat* of the music.

**beautiful** *adjective* ✦ lovely, pretty, gorgeous ◇ attractive, pleasing Your flower arrangement is very *beautiful*.

**beckon** *verb* ✦ gesture, motion, signal ◇ call, summon, wave Miguel *beckoned* for us to follow him.

**become** *verb* ✦ change into, convert to, grow into, turn into, develop into Caterpillars *become* either moths or butterflies.

**becoming** *adjective* ✦ attractive, flattering, pleasing, pretty ✧ **appropriate** Your dress is very *becoming.*

**before** *adverb* ✦ **already, previously** ✧ **earlier, formerly, beforehand** I've seen this episode of the show *before.* —*preposition* ✦ **prior to, preceding** ✧ **ahead of, in front of** I always wash my hands *before* dinner.

**beg** *verb* ✦ **beseech, implore, plead with, appeal to, ask** The homeless man *begged* us to help him.

**begin** *verb* ✦ **commence, start** ✧ **open, initiate, originate, undertake** The fireworks will *begin* as soon as it's dark.

---

**Antonyms** begin

*verb* cease, check, discontinue, finish, halt, quit, stop

---

**beginning** *noun* ✦ **start, opening, commencement** ✧ **outset, introduction** We found our seats before the *beginning* of the concert.

**behavior** *noun* ✦ **conduct, manners** ✧ **actions, attitude** Talking with one's mouth full is often considered to be rude *behavior.*

**behind** *preposition* ✦ **in back of** ✧ **after, following, beyond** My cat likes to hide *behind* the couch. —*adverb* ✧ **after, following, back, in back of** Mitsuko ran so fast that she left her friends *behind.*

**behold** *verb* ✦ **look at, gaze upon, observe, see, watch, witness** The sunset was beautiful to *behold.*

**belief** *noun* ✦ **conviction, feeling, opinion, position, theory, view** It is my *belief* that honesty is the best policy.

**believe** *verb* ✦ **accept, think** ✧ **hold, presume, suppose** Some people *believe* that ghosts are real.

**belly** *noun* ✦ **abdomen, stomach, tummy** ✧ **underside** The boy crawled through the grass on his *belly.*

**belong** *verb* ✦ **go, reside, stay, fit** ✧ **remain** The scissors *belong* in the top drawer.

**belongings** *noun* ✦ **possessions, property, things, goods** ✧ **gear, effects** When my family moved, we packed all our *belongings* into boxes.

**below** *adverb* ✧ **beneath, lower, under, underneath** From the hilltop, we could see the town *below.* —*preposition* ✦ **beneath, under, underneath** Sasha's dog is sitting *below* the table, begging for scraps.

**bend** *verb* ✦ **twist, flex, curve, turn, wind, coil** Wire sculpture is made by *bending* metal wire into artistic shapes. —*noun* ✦ **curve, turn, crook, twist, angle** Kim's house is just past the *bend* in the road.

**beneath** *preposition* ✦ **below, under, underneath** I found my other shoe *beneath* the bed.

**beneficial** *adjective* ✦ **helpful, useful, good, advantageous, productive, valuable** Proper nutrition is *beneficial* to your health.

**benefit** *noun* ✦ **advantage, asset, aid, help** ✧ **blessing, profit, use** A good education is a real *benefit* when you're looking for a job. —*verb* ✦ **help, aid, assist, serve** ✧ **support, sustain** Clean air *benefits* everyone.

**best** *adjective* ✦ **finest, greatest, principal** ✧ **foremost, top** Tetyana is my *best* friend. —*adverb* ✦ **most, most of all, above all** ✧ **extremely, fully, greatly** What flavor of ice cream do you like *best*?

**bet** *noun* ✦ **wager** ✧ **gamble, stake, venture, chance** Mark made a *bet* that he could win the race. —*verb* ✦ **wager** ✧ **chance, gamble, challenge, dare, risk** I *bet* my friend that I could beat him at badminton.

**betray** *verb* ✦ **deceive, double-cross** ✧ **abandon, desert, mislead, fail** I know that my friend won't *betray* me by telling my secret to anyone else.

**better** *verb* ✦ **improve, enhance, help, strengthen** ✧ **advance, beat** The runner hoped to *better* his race times by training harder. —*adjective* ✦ **finer, preferable (to), superior (to)** ✧ **greater** I think that homemade tomato sauce tastes *better* than store-bought ones. —*adverb* ✦ **more** ✧ **greater, finer, preferably** I like Thai food *better* than Italian.

**beware** *verb* ✦ **heed, mind, watch out for** ✧ **notice, regard** The swimming hole had a sign that warned people to *beware* of the deep water.

**bewilder** *verb* ✦ **baffle, confuse, mystify, perplex, puzzle** When my friend and I tried to assemble my new bicycle, the directions completely *bewildered* us.

**beyond** *preposition* ✦ **past, after, behind, farther than** ✧ **across** Our house is just *beyond* that grove of trees.

**bias** *noun* ✦ **leaning, preference, prejudice** ✧ **inclination, slant, tendency** A good referee has no *bias* toward either team. —*verb* ✦ **influence, prejudice, sway, slant, distort** Don't let my opinion *bias* your decision.

**bid** *verb* 1. ✦ command, order, direct, instruct, tell ✧ ask, require The queen *bid* her subjects to kneel in her presence. 2. ✦ offer ✧ propose, submit Kay *bid* twelve dollars for the old hat. —*noun* ✦ proposal, estimate ✧ offer, offering The contract will be awarded to the company with the lowest *bid*.

**big** *adjective* 1. ✦ large, enormous, gigantic, huge, immense, colossal Great Danes are *big* dogs. 2. ✦ important, consequential, major ✧ significant, vital, great Our soccer team practiced hard for the *big* game.

**bill** *noun* 1. ✦ check, tab, invoice, statement ✧ account After the meal was over, the waiter brought us our *bill*. 2. ✦ act ✧ draft, measure, program, proposal In the United States, a *bill* becomes law if passed by Congress and signed by the president.

**bind** *verb* ✦ fasten, connect, join, secure ✧ tie, wrap The pages of a book are commonly *bound* by sewing or gluing them together.

**birth** *noun* 1. ✦ delivery ✧ bearing, childbirth Baby elephants weigh about 250 pounds at *birth*. 2. ✦ beginning, dawn, start, origin ✧ creation, emergence The 200th anniversary of the *birth* of the United States was celebrated in 1976.

**bite** *verb* ✦ chomp, gnaw, nip, champ, chew ✧ nibble, munch I accidentally *bit* my tongue while chewing gum. —*noun* 1. ✦ sting ✧ prick, puncture, wound Try not to scratch those mosquito *bites*. 2. ✦ morsel, crumb, piece, scrap, mouthful ✧ nibble, taste I'm so full that I can't eat another *bite*.

**bitter** *adjective* 1. ✦ acrid, biting, pungent, sharp, tart ✧ harsh, stinging, unpleasant Coffee has a *bitter* taste. 2. ✦ resentful, sullen ✧ spiteful, angry, hostile, upset The politician was *bitter* when he lost the election to an inexperienced newcomer.

**blade** *noun* ✦ cutting edge, edge Chopping knives have sharp *blades*.

**blame** *verb* ✦ accuse, charge, criticize, fault, reproach Don't *blame* me for your problems. —*noun* ✦ responsibility ✧ accountability, fault, guilt The zookeeper took the *blame* for the penguins getting out of their enclosure.

**blank** *adjective* ✦ empty, unmarked, open ✧ bare, clear, unused, vacant The directions on the form said to leave the bottom half *blank*.

**blast** *noun* ✦ bang, boom, roar, burst ✧ eruption, explosion The hunters heard the distant *blast* of a shotgun. —*verb* ✦ dynamite, explode, detonate ✧ burst, demolish Miners *blasted* their way through the rock.

**blaze** *noun* ✦ fire, flames, inferno ✧ burning, glare, glow It took firefighters two hours to extinguish the *blaze*. —*verb* ✦ burn, flame ✧ flare, glow, shine The campfire *blazed* cheerfully.

**bleak** *adjective* ✦ depressing, dismal, dreary, cheerless, forbidding, gloomy, grim The constant rain made everything look *bleak*.

**blemish** *noun* ✦ defect, flaw, imperfection ✧ blotch, impurity, stain I got the ceramic pot at a discount because it has a slight *blemish*. —*verb* ✦ flaw, mar, spoil, tarnish, harm The gymnast's fall *blemished* an otherwise perfect performance.

**blend** *verb* ✦ combine, mix, stir ✧ scramble, unite, merge François *blended* the cake ingredients in a large bowl. —*noun* ✦ combination, mix, mixture ✧ compound, fusion, union This shirt is a *blend* of cotton and polyester.

**blight** *noun* ✦ affliction, plague, pest, disease, decay, sickness ✧ bane, curse Ireland's great famine of 1845-1849 was caused by a *blight* that destroyed the potato crop.

**blind** *adjective* 1. ✦ sightless ✧ unseeing, visionless My dog is *blind* in one eye. 2. ✦ ignorant of, unaware of ✧ naive, unknowing, unmindful We're usually *blind to* our own faults. 3. ✦ concealed, hidden, unseen ✧ obscure The mountain road had many *blind* curves.

**bliss** *noun* ✦ rapture, ecstasy, happiness, joy, delight Moira's idea of *bliss* is a day all to herself.

**blizzard** *noun* ✦ snowstorm, winter storm ✧ storm, flurry, tempest Yesterday's *blizzard* left huge snowdrifts behind.

**block** *noun* ✦ cube, chunk, piece ✧ brick, slab, wedge The ancient Egyptians used huge *blocks* of sandstone to build their pyramids. —*verb* ✦ halt, hinder, obstruct, stop ✧ interfere A herd of cattle *blocked* traffic.

### Word Groups

A **blockade** is the closing off of an area to stop people or supplies from getting through. **Blockade** is a very specific term with no true synonyms. Here are some related words to investigate in a dictionary: **attack, barricade, barrier, encirclement, obstacle, obstruction, siege**

**bloom** *noun* ✦ blossom, flower ✧ bud Cherry trees can have either pink or white *blooms*. —*verb* ✦ blossom, flower ✧ flourish, thrive, open, sprout The African violet is a flower that can *bloom* all year long.

**blow**[1] *verb* 1. ✦ fly, float, flutter ✧ move, sail Tumbleweeds *blew* across the road. 2. ✦ breathe, exhale, puff ✧ expel I *blew* on the campfire to get it going. 3. ✦ blast, dynamite, explode, burst ✧ detonate, erupt Work crews used dynamite to *blow* a tunnel through the mountain.

**blow**[2] *noun* ✦ hit, jab, punch, stroke, rap, swat The boxer raised his arms to block the *blows* of his opponent.

**bluff** *verb* ✦ deceive, fool, delude, mislead, trick My dog's growling often *bluffs* people into thinking that he's fierce. —*noun* ✦ deception, pretense, ruse ✧ fake, fraud, lie The detective hoped the suspects would believe his *bluff* that he knew more about the crime than he really did.

**blunder** *noun* ✦ error, mistake ✧ oversight, slip, lapse I made a *blunder* when I used salt instead of sugar in the cookie dough. —*verb* ✦ stumble, stagger ✧ bungle, flounder I *blundered* around in the dark trying to find the light switch.

**blunt** *adjective* 1. ✦ dull, unsharpened It's hard to cut tomatoes with a *blunt* knife. 2. ✦ candid, direct, abrupt, frank, tactless, straightforward My friend was a little too *blunt* when she said my new dress was hideous.

**blur** *verb* ✦ cloud, dim, obscure, shroud, veil ✧ darken, shadow Mist *blurred* our view of the mountaintop.

**board** *noun* 1. ✦ plank, slat, timber ✧ beam, panel, wood Ying made a bookshelf from bricks and *boards*. 2. ✦ committee, council, panel ✧ cabinet, commission The company is presided over by a *board* of directors.

**boast** *verb* ✦ brag, vaunt, gloat ✧ exaggerate, flaunt The young girl *boasted* about winning the dance competition.

**body** *noun* 1. ✦ physique, build, figure ✧ form, frame, person Exercise is good for both the *body* and the mind. 2. ✦ group, mass, unit ✧ assembly, party, society A few soldiers went on ahead, and the main *body* of troops followed behind.

**bold** *adjective* ✦ brave, courageous, daring, fearless, audacious, heroic A *bold* climber scaled the cliff without using a rope for protection.

**bolt** *noun* 1. ✦ pin, rod, fastener ✧ rivet, spike, screw I can adjust the height of my bicycle seat by loosening this *bolt*. 2. ✦ dart, dash, rush, run, sprint ✧ bound, spring The field mouse made a *bolt* for safety when it saw a hawk. —*verb* 1. ✦ fasten, latch, lock, secure ✧ bar Please *bolt* the door and turn off the porch light. 2. ✦ dash, dart, fly, race, run, rush, sprint When I opened the gate, all the horses *bolted* out.

**bond** *noun* ✦ attachment, connection, link, tie ✧ binding, union There is a strong *bond* between Pasha and his dog.

**bonus** *noun* ✦ addition, extra, reward ✧ benefit, gift, prize Some companies give their employees a *bonus* at the end of the year.

**boom** *noun* 1. ✦ clap, report, roar, rumble ✧ blast, bang, thunder A sonic *boom* shook our windows. 2. ✦ expansion, growth, upswing, advance, gain ✧ boost, prosperity The electronics industry experienced a *boom* when smartphones became popular. —*verb* 1. ✦ crash, roar, rumble ✧ blast, sound Thunder *boomed* in the distance. 2. ✦ increase, mushroom ✧ flourish, prosper, thrive, grow Alaska's population *boomed* when oil was discovered there.

**boost** *verb* 1. ✦ hoist, lift, raise, heft ✧ push, shove Shira *boosted* her little sister onto the pony. 2. ✦ increase, raise, build up, expand, improve ✧ amplify, hike Winning the first game of the season *boosted* our team's confidence. —*noun* ✦ lift ✧ heft, hoist, push, raise, shove Jayden gave his brother a *boost* over the wall.

**booty** *noun* ✦ loot, plunder, pillage, take, spoils The pirates buried their *booty* on a deserted island.

**border** *noun* 1. ✦ edge, margin, perimeter, rim ✧ fringe, limits Kenji planted bamboo around the *border* of his garden. 2. ✦ boundary, frontier ✧ line, threshold The Rio Grande River runs along the *border* between the United States and Mexico.

**bore** *verb* ✦ weary, tire, fatigue ✧ annoy, irritate The long and uninteresting speech *bored* me.

---

**Word Groups**

To **borrow** is to get something from someone else with the intention of returning it later. **Borrow** is a very specific term with no true synonyms. Here are some related words to investigate in a dictionary: **adopt, appropriate, assume, confiscate, grab, obtain, seize, take**

---

**boss** *noun* ✦ supervisor, manager, employer ◇ administrator, chief, leader My *boss* said that I was doing great work.

**bother** *verb* ✦ aggravate, annoy, disturb, irritate, pester The hum of the overhead lights really *bothers* me. —*noun* ✦ nuisance, annoyance, irritation, problem ◇ strain The mosquitoes in the backyard were such a *bother* that we had to move into the house.

**bottom** *noun* ✦ base, foot, lowest point ◇ foundation, ground, seat The tourists paused at the *bottom* of the monument before starting up the many stairs.

**bounce** *verb* ✦ bound, jump, leap, hop ◇ rebound, recoil, spring Children *bounced* up and down on the trampoline. —*noun* ✦ rebound, hop, jump, skip ◇ elasticity, spring The shortstop caught the baseball on its second *bounce*.

**bound**¹ *verb* ✦ hop, spring, jump, leap, skip ◇ bounce, vault The rabbit *bounded* away when it saw me. —*noun* ✦ hop, jump, leap ◇ spring, vault, skip The deer cleared the stream in a single *bound*.

**bound**² *noun* ✦ limit, boundary, border ◇ edge, perimeter Hunting is not allowed within the *bounds* of the nature reserve.

**bound**³ *adjective* 1. ✦ obligated, obliged, committed, required I am *bound* by my promise to help my daughter with her homework. 2. ✦ certain, sure ◇ destined, fated, likely I'm *bound* to get a high score on the proficiency test if I study hard.

**boundary** *noun* ✦ border, edge, limit, perimeter ◇ fringe, rim, frontier My family planted a bamboo hedge along the *boundary* of our property.

**bow** *verb* 1. ◇ curtsy, kneel, salute, stoop Everyone *bowed* to the king and queen. 2. ✦ submit, yield, succumb, surrender, concede ◇ bend We had to *bow* to the referee's decision even though we knew he was wrong. —*noun* ◇ curtsy, nod, salute, greeting The entire cast of the play came on stage for a final *bow*.

**box** *noun* ✦ carton ◇ case, container, crate, trunk, package Andrea's cat likes to play in cardboard *boxes*. —*verb* ✦ pack, package ◇ crate, wrap, load I *boxed* up my books to move them to my new apartment.

**brace** *noun* ✦ support, prop, reinforcement, strut ◇ buttress The *braces* of the bridge were made of steel. —*verb* ✦ reinforce, steady, support ◇ fortify, strengthen We used a board to *brace* the old fence.

**brag** *verb* ✦ boast, vaunt ◇ bluster, crow, gloat, exaggerate The mountaineer *bragged* about his daring exploits.

**brake** *verb* ✦ halt, stop ◇ decelerate, slow I *braked* suddenly when a dog ran in front of my motorbike.

**branch** *noun* 1. ✦ limb, bough ◇ stem, arm Our cat climbed to the top *branch* of the tree. 2. ✦ division, extension, department ◇ bureau, chapter The nationwide bank has at least one *branch* in every state. —*verb* ✦ divide, fork ◇ diverge, part, separate When the trail *branched*, I didn't know which way to go.

**brand** *noun* 1. ✦ kind, sort, type, variety, make What's your favorite *brand* of cereal? 2. ✦ mark, sign, symbol, stamp ◇ emblem, label The sheriff inspected the steer's *brand* to determine its rightful owner.

**brave** *adjective* ✦ courageous, fearless, heroic, valiant, valorous A *brave* girl rescued the small boy from the river. —*verb* ✦ endure, face, meet, bear ◇ challenge, defy, undergo In the United States, pioneers *braved* many dangers in their westward journey.

**break** *verb* 1. ✦ shatter, splinter, fracture ◇ crack, smash, burst The plate *broke* when I accidentally dropped it. 2. ✦ violate, breach, betray ◇ disregard, ignore, neglect My friend *broke* her promise to meet me after work. 3. ✦ end, halt, stop ◇ cease, interrupt, suspend Last week's rain *broke* the long drought. 4. ✦ beat, exceed, surpass, top, outdo Juan *broke* his college's record for the fifty-yard dash. —*noun* 1. ✦ rest, respite ◇ breather, intermission, pause, recess I took a *break* from my chores after washing the dishes. 2. ✦ opening, breach, gap, hole ◇ crack, split The sun shone through a *break* in the clouds.

**breed** *verb* 1. ✦ raise, rear, grow, nurture ◇ cultivate That farmer *breeds* and sells hogs. 2. ✦ generate, produce, cause, create, foster, promote Fear can often *breed* panic. —*noun* ✦ kind, sort, strain, type, variety, manner The border collie is my favorite *breed* of dog.

**brief** *adjective* 1. ✦ fleeting, momentary, quick, short, hasty ✧ temporary Our neighbor stopped by for a *brief* visit. 2. ✦ concise, short, succinct ✧ terse The newlyweds sent *brief* thank-you notes for all their wedding presents. —*verb* ✦ inform, instruct, advise ✧ explain, prepare Our coach *briefed* us on the other team's strengths and weaknesses.

**bright** *adjective* 1. ✦ brilliant, glowing, vivid ✧ shining, shiny, dazzling Tanya painted her apartment *bright* yellow. 2. ✦ intelligent, smart, brilliant, clever, quick The *bright* student finished the test before anyone else.

**brilliant** *adjective* 1. ✦ bright, gleaming, shining, sparkling ✧ intense, vivid I polished the silverware to a *brilliant* shine. 2. ✦ gifted, talented, magnificent, outstanding, remarkable, splendid, superb Beethoven was a *brilliant* composer.

**bring** *verb* 1. ✦ carry, take, tote ✧ bear, deliver, haul, transport I *bring* my lunch to work every day. 2. ✦ bring about, cause, create, generate, make, produce April showers *bring* May flowers.

**brink** *noun* ✦ verge, threshold, edge, point ✧ margin The Amur leopard is so endangered it's on the *brink* of extinction.

**brisk** *adjective* 1. ✦ energetic, vigorous, active, lively ✧ quick, swift My grandmother takes *brisk* walks to stay fit and healthy. 2. ✦ bracing, crisp, invigorating, stimulating, sharp, fresh The *brisk* wind made my ears numb.

**brittle** *adjective* ✦ crumbly, breakable, delicate, fragile, frail, weak, crisp I was gentle with the old book because its pages were *brittle*.

**Antonyms** **brittle**
*adjective* flexible, firm, mobile, pliable, solid, strong

**broad** *adjective* ✦ comprehensive, extensive, wide ✧ immense, large, spacious The man has gained a *broad* knowledge of birds since he took up bird watching as a hobby.

**broken** *adjective* 1. ✦ fractured, cracked, shattered ✧ injured The doctor put my *broken* arm in a plaster cast. 2. ✦ defective, faulty ✧ imperfect, out of order We had to recycle our *broken* fan because it could not be fixed.

**browse** *verb* 1. ✦ look through, scan, skim ✧ read,

survey Chaewon enjoys learning new words by *browsing* through a dictionary. 2. ✦ graze, eat, feed ✧ crop, nibble Deer *browsed* in the meadow.

**bruise** *noun* ✧ hurt, injure, wound, harm, damage The girl *bruised* her elbow when she fell off her mountain bike.

**brush¹** *verb* 1. ✦ curry, groom, smooth ✧ polish, sweep, clean Liana *brushes* her horse every day. 2. ✦ graze, skim, touch ✧ caress, kiss, tickle A butterfly *brushed* my arm as it flew past.

**brush²** *noun* ✦ thicket, underbrush, undergrowth ✧ bushes, shrubs, scrub Quails build nests in dense *brush*.

**brutal** *adjective* ✦ cruel, ruthless, merciless, harsh, vicious, barbaric The *brutal* dictator imprisoned and tortured his political opponents.

**buckle** *noun* ✧ catch, clasp, fastener, hook, clip My belt has a brass *buckle*. —*verb* 1. ✦ fasten, clasp, hook, secure, connect Be sure to *buckle* your seat belt snugly. 2. ✦ sag, warp, bend ✧ twist, collapse, crumble The boards on the porch have *buckled* with age.

**buddy** *noun* ✦ friend, mate, pal, chum ✧ comrade Last weekend Aaron played baseball with his *buddies*.

**budge** *verb* ✦ move, yield, shift ✧ dislodge, stir, push The stubborn mule refused to *budge*.

**budget** *noun* ✦ allotment, allocation ✧ allowance, funds, resources The university has a *budget* of ten million dollars to build a new library. —*verb* ✦ ration, plan, schedule ✧ allot, distribute Yusuf has to *budget* his salary so that it lasts all month.

**build** *verb* ✦ construct, erect, make, assemble ✧ fabricate, manufacture My family plans to *build* our new house on that vacant lot. —*noun* ✦ body, physique, frame ✧ figure, form, shape He has a good *build* for rock climbing.

**building** *noun* ✦ structure, construction, edifice ✧ erection The new apartment *building* is 30 stories high.

**bulletin** *noun* ✦ announcement, message, report, statement ✧ notice, notification A news *bulletin* interrupted my television show.

**bully** *verb* ✦ intimidate, menace, frighten, harass, threaten, domineer over Older children should not *bully* younger and smaller kids.

**bump** *verb* ✦ hit, knock, smack, bang ✧ collide,

strike I accidentally *bumped* against the corner of the table. —*noun* **1.** ✦ **jar, jolt, thump** ✧ **crash, knock, shock** We felt a slight *bump* as the airplane touched ground. **2.** ✦ **lump, swelling** ✧ **bulge, knob, knot, nodule** A *bump* formed on my leg where the bee stung me.

**bunch** *noun* ✦ **clump, cluster, bundle, batch** ✧ **crowd, group, quantity** The gorilla ate a *bunch* of bananas. —*verb* ✦ **huddle, crowd, cluster, flock, gather, herd** ✧ **collect** Antelope *bunch* together for safety when they see a lion.

**bundle** *noun* ✦ **bunch, collection, batch** ✧ **pack, package, stack** We took a *bundle* of old newspapers to the recycling center.

**burden** *noun* **1.** ✦ **load, weight, cargo, freight** ✧ **baggage, payload** Elephants can carry a heavier *burden* than many other animals. **2.** ✦ **difficulty, hardship, strain, trial, worry** I believe that friends help lighten the *burdens* of life. —*verb* ✦ **encumber, load, afflict, oppress, tax, weight** Our vacation *burdened* us with many expenses, but we were glad we went anyway.

**burglar** *noun* ✦ **robber, thief** ✧ **criminal, crook, prowler** The police caught the *burglar* as he came out of the house.

**burn** *verb* **1.** ✦ **fire, ignite, incinerate, kindle, torch** ✧ **blaze, combust** The spy *burned* his instructions after reading them. **2.** ✦ **char, scorch, sear, singe, blacken** I *burned* the toast.

**burst** *verb* ✦ **blow up, explode, pop** ✧ **rupture, split** If you don't punch holes in a potato, it will *burst* when you bake it. —*noun* ✦ **eruption, outbreak, gush, outpouring** ✧ **release** There was a *burst* of applause when the magician made the camel disappear.

**bury** *verb* **1.** ✦ **inter, lay to rest, entomb** Humans first started to *bury* their dead more than 100,000 years ago. **2.** ✦ **conceal, cover, hide** ✧ **secrete, veil** Squirrels *bury* nuts in order to save them for winter.

**business** *noun* **1.** ✦ **profession, trade, industry** ✧ **career, job, occupation, work** The servicing and repair of electronic equipment is a booming *business*. **2.** ✦ **selling, trade, transaction** ✧ **commerce, marketing** This department store does most of its *business* during the holidays. **3.** ✦ **company, firm, store, establishment** ✧ **enterprise, industry, office** Lin works part-time for a catering *business*. **4.** ✦ **affair, concern, interest, matter** ✧ **duty, responsibility** What actors do offscreen should be none of our *business*.

**busy** *adjective* ✦ **active, engaged, occupied** ✧ **absorbed, involved** Between work and soccer practice, Antonia is usually *busy*.

**but** *conjunction* ✦ **however, nevertheless, yet** ✧ **although, though** I thought that the roller coaster would scare me, *but* I enjoyed it. —*adverb* ✦ **only, merely, just** ✧ **solely, simply** I have *but* twenty dollars left to buy food for the rest of the week. —*preposition* ✦ **except, excepting, other than, save** Everybody has had the flu *but* me.

### Word Groups

A **button** is a disk used to fasten two pieces of material together. **Button** is a very specific term with no true synonyms. Here are some related words to investigate in a dictionary: **buckle, clasp, hook, link, snap, zipper**

**buy** *verb* ✦ **purchase, pay for** ✧ **acquire, get, obtain** Hiroko used her savings to *buy* a new smartphone.

**by** *preposition* ✦ **at, before, no later than** I have to be at work *by* eight o'clock in the morning.

**cab** *noun* ✦ taxi, taxicab ✧ hired car, limousine When my roommate's car broke down, she took a *cab* to work.

**cabin** *noun* 1. ✧ bungalow, cottage, hut, lodge, chalet Most of these lakeside *cabins* are used as vacation homes. 2. ✦ compartment, stateroom, berth, room Francesca and her best friend booked a private *cabin* for their cruise to the Greek Islands.

**cable** *noun* 1. ✦ guy, wire ✧ line, rope, strand, chain The telephone pole blew over when its anchoring *cables* broke. 2. ✦ cablegram, telegram, wire ✧ message The overseas reporter sent an urgent *cable* to her editor back in the United States.

**cafeteria** *noun* ✦ lunchroom ✧ café, dining room, restaurant, snack bar Everyone complains about the bland food that our company *cafeteria* serves.

**cage** *noun* ✧ coop, enclosure, pen, cell, prison I keep my parrot in a large wire *cage.* —*verb* ✦ confine, enclose, pen, fence in ✧ restrain There are numerous zoos worldwide where animals are allowed to roam free without being *caged.*

**calculate** *verb* ✦ add up, compute, determine, figure ✧ count, reckon I planned a budget by *calculating* all my expenses for the month.

**call** *verb* 1. ✦ cry, scream, shout, yell, holler ✧ hail Bjorn heard a lost hiker *calling* for help. 2. ✦ summon, bid ✧ command, order, ask My dog always comes to me whenever I *call* him. 3. ✦ address, name, designate ✧ label, title We *call* Manuel by the nickname "Einstein" because he's so smart. 4. ✦ telephone, phone, ring, dial I *called* the restaurant to see if I would need a reservation. —*noun* ✦ hail, summons ✧ cry, scream, shout, yell, signal I get frustrated when my cat ignores my *call.*

**calm** *adjective* ✦ composed, collected, cool, self-possessed ✧ peaceful, quiet, serene, still, tranquil Danielle was the only one who remained *calm* when the fire alarm went off. —*verb* ✦ pacify, quiet, relax, soothe ✧ tranquilize, settle Whenever my little sister gets agitated, I *calm* her with hugs.

**camouflage** *noun* ✦ concealment, cover ✧ cloak, disguise, mask, screen The soldiers changed the color of their *camouflage* when they moved from jungle to desert. —*verb* ✦ cloak, conceal, disguise, hide ✧ cover, mask Some species of chameleons can *camouflage* themselves by changing skin color to blend in with their surroundings.

**campaign** *noun* ✦ drive, crusade, movement ✧ effort, operation, project Simon helped start a *campaign* to raise awareness of global climate change. —*verb* ✦ run, stump ✧ crusade, push, contest Our mayor is *campaigning* for reelection.

**can** *noun* ✦ tin, canister ✧ container, jar, receptacle I had a *can* of soup for lunch today. —*verb* ✦ jar, bottle, tin, preserve ✧ keep My grandmother decided to *can* most of this year's tomato crop.

**cancel** *verb* ✦ drop, stop, call off ✧ repeal, revoke, void The airline *canceled* dozens of flights during the snowstorm

**candidate** *noun* ✦ contender, runner, nominee ✧ applicant, contestant There are three *candidates* for the open Senate seat.

**capable** *adjective* ✦ able, competent ✧ qualified, talented, skilled, apt *Capable* teachers are always in demand.

**capacity** *noun* ✦ volume ✧ content, room, size, space, limit The *capacity* of a typical oil barrel is fifty-five gallons.

**capital** *noun* ✦ assets, cash, funds, money, savings, wealth The film director was looking for an investor with sufficient *capital* to finance a movie.

**captain** *noun* ✦ head, leader ✧ chief, commander, master In American football, the team *captains* meet for a coin toss to see who gets the ball first. —*verb* ✦ command, head, lead ✧ direct, pilot, control My dream is to *captain* a cruise ship someday.

**capture** *verb* ✦ seize, take, grab ✧ apprehend, catch, hold Rebels tried to *capture* the government's headquarters. —*noun* ✦ apprehension, arrest, seizure The bank robber evaded *capture* for several days, but he was eventually arrested.

**car** *noun* ✦ auto, automobile, motor vehicle, motor-

**car** ◆ **vehicle** A coupe is a small *car* with only two doors.

**care** *noun* 1. ◆ **anxiety, concern, worry, trouble** ◇ **burden, fear** The resort claims that guests can leave all their *cares* behind. 2. ◆ **attention, caution** ◇ **effort, heed, wariness** Even though she was performing a routine operation, the surgeon worked with great *care*. 3. ◆ **charge, custody, keeping, protection, supervision** My friend left her purse in my *care* while she went swimming. —*verb* 1. ◆ **desire, like, want** ◇ **love, wish** Would you *care for* more ice cream? 2. ◆ **attend, look after, mind, protect, watch** The neighbors are going to *care for* our pets while we're on vacation.

**career** *noun* ◆ **job, occupation, vocation, work** ◇ **trade, profession** Felix hopes to have a *career* in law enforcement.

**careful** *adjective* ◆ **cautious, vigilant, wary, alert, watchful** I'm always *careful* when I cross a street.

**careless** *adjective* ◆ **negligent, mindless, thoughtless, unthinking, remiss** It was *careless* of the circus performer to leave the tiger's cage unlocked.

**carriage** *noun* ◆ **buggy, coach** ◇ **cart, wagon** My friends and I rented a horse-drawn *carriage* to go on a sightseeing tour.

**carry** *verb* 1. ◆ **bear, convey, transport, lug** ◇ **bring, move** The campers *carried* everything they needed in their backpacks. 2. ◆ **maintain, support, sustain, uphold** ◇ **continue, extend** My salary is supposed to *carry* me through the week, but somehow I always run short. 3. ◆ **have, stock, supply, furnish, provide** ◇ **offer** I'm looking for a market that *carries* organic produce.

**carve** *verb* ◆ **sculpt, whittle** ◇ **cut, form, shape, fashion** The retired man likes to *carve* little wooden animals to give as gifts.

**case¹** *noun* ◆ **instance, occurrence, episode, incident** ◇ **example** The police are investigating two separate *cases* of vandalism.

**case²** *noun* ◆ **box, carton** ◇ **container, crate, package, bin** Bottled water is usually cheaper if you buy it by the *case*.

**cash** *noun* ◆ **currency, money** ◇ **bills, change, coins** Our local market accepts only *cash* or personal checks.

**cast** *verb* ◆ **throw, toss** ◇ **fling, hurl, lob, pitch** We need to *cast* the dice to see who goes first. —*noun*

1. ◆ **throw, toss** ◇ **fling, heave, lob, hurl** The fisherman caught a big fish on the first *cast* of his lure. 2. ◆ **company, troupe** ◇ **actors, players, performers** The director told the entire *cast* to attend tonight's rehearsal.

### Word Groups

A **castle** is a large building with strong walls and other defenses against attack. **Castle** is a very specific term with no true synonyms. Here are some related words to investigate in a dictionary: **chateau, citadel, fort, fortress, palace, stronghold**

**casual** *adjective* ◆ **informal, relaxed, easygoing** ◇ **spontaneous, unplanned** Riya invited some friends over for a *casual* dinner.

**casualty** *noun* ◆ **victim** ◇ **dead, fatality, injured, wounded, missing** The papers reported that there were no *casualties* from yesterday's earthquake.

**catalog** *noun* ◆ **directory, index, list, register** ◇ **inventory, bulletin** Most universities publish *catalogs* that describe the courses they offer. —*verb* ◆ **list, record, register, categorize, classify** Aline *cataloged* all of the stamps in her collection.

**catastrophe** *noun* ◆ **calamity, disaster, tragedy** ◇ **accident, misfortune** The sinking of the *Titanic* was a great *catastrophe*.

**catch** *verb* 1. ◆ **capture, grab, grasp, seize, get** My cat *caught* a mouse yesterday. 2. ◆ **detect, discover, find, spot** ◇ **surprise** My roommate *caught* me wrapping her birthday present. 3. ◆ **contract, get, develop** ◇ **receive, take** I *caught* a cold while on vacation. —*noun* 1. ◆ **grab, snatch** ◇ **capture, grasp, seizure** Maya made a spectacular *catch* while playing softball with her friends. 2. ◆ **clasp, latch** ◇ **bolt, fastener, hook, clip** I put a *catch* on the cupboard door to keep it from swinging open.

**category** *noun* ◆ **class, group, classification, type** ◇ **division, section, order** Our local bookstore shelves novels by *category* such as "Westerns" and "Science Fiction."

**cause** *noun* 1. ◆ **reason (for), basis, origin** ◇ **source, root** Investigators are still trying to determine the *cause* of the accident. 2. ◆ **goal, principle** ◇ **crusade, purpose, ideal** My friends Jim and Mary contribute their time and money to support environmental *causes*. —*verb* ◆ **create, generate, produce** ◇ **begin, make** Yesterday's heavy rain *caused* some flooding.

**caution** *noun* ✦ alertness, attention, care, carefulness, vigilance Proceed with *caution* if you have to walk through a busy intersection. —*verb* ✦ advise, warn, forewarn ✧ alert, counsel In the United States, yellow road signs *caution* motorists of hazards ahead.

**cautious** *adjective* ✦ alert, attentive, careful, vigilant, wary, watchful The gymnast was *cautious* the first time she tried the balance beam.

**cavity** *noun* ✦ hole, hollow, opening, crater, pit ✧ space Erosion from running water has left many small *cavities* in the soft sandstone.

**cease** *verb* ✦ quit, stop, terminate, discontinue, halt ✧ end The officer ordered his soldiers to *cease* firing.

**celebrate** *verb* ✦ commemorate, honor, observe ✧ keep, remember Sharon prepared a special feast to *celebrate* Passover.

**celebrity** *noun* ✦ star, superstar ✧ dignitary, notable The tourists hoped to see some *celebrities* when they visited Hollywood.

**cell** *noun* ✦ room, chamber, compartment, cubicle ✧ cage, pen The sheriff's office has several small *cells* for holding prisoners.

**cement** *noun* ✧ adhesive, glue, mortar, concrete, paste Concrete is made by mixing *cement*, sand, water, and gravel together. —*verb* ✦ glue, stick, join, bond ✧ bind, fasten, fix I *cemented* the lamp's broken pieces back together.

**cemetery** *noun* ✦ burial ground, graveyard ✧ tomb, catacomb, churchyard We went to the *cemetery* to visit my grandfather's grave.

**center** *noun* ✦ inside, interior, middle, core ✧ nucleus, heart I prefer chocolate candies that have soft *centers*.

**central** *adjective* 1. ✦ middle, midway ✧ inside, interior, inner The *central* part of the United States is known as the Midwest. 2. ✦ chief, main, principal, head ✧ key, leading, prime The librarian at our local branch said that the *central* library has the book I want.

**ceremony** *noun* ✦ rite, ritual, service, celebration, observance ✧ custom The couple were married in a simple *ceremony* attended only by family and a few close friends.

**certain** *adjective* 1. ✦ sure, positive, confident ✧ satisfied, guaranteed I am absolutely *certain* that

I do not want anchovies on my pizza. 2. ✦ particular, precise, specific, definite, established Hunting is not allowed in *certain* areas of the National Forest.

**certainly** *adverb* ✦ definitely, positively, surely, undoubtedly, absolutely Juan said that he would *certainly* attend my birthday party.

**chain** *noun* ✦ sequence, series, cycle ✧ line, progression, set, string, train The unfortunate *chain* of events started when someone brought a dog to the cat show. —*verb* ✧ fasten, connect, bind, lock, secure, tie, hold Esmeralda *chained* her bicycle to a lamppost before she went into the store.

### Word Groups

A **chair** is a piece of furniture built for sitting on. **Chair** is a general term with no true synonyms. Here are some different kinds of chairs to investigate in a dictionary: **armchair, highchair, love seat, recliner, rocker, stool, throne**

**chairperson** *noun* ✦ chair, chairman, chairwoman ✧ director, leader, head The committee's *chairperson* welcomed everyone to the meeting.

**challenge** *noun* 1. ✦ dare ✧ bid, call, invitation, summons After Lauren beat Keegan at the video game, she accepted his *challenge* to a rematch. 2. ✦ trial, test, difficulty, struggle ✧ problem Running the full 26.2 miles of a marathon can be a real *challenge*. —*verb* ✦ dare ✧ bid, call, summon, invite My girlfriend *challenged* me to a game of Scrabble.

**champion** *noun* ✦ winner, victor ✧ conqueror, hero, master The world *champion* earned three gold medals at the Olympics.

**chance** *noun* 1. ✦ accident, luck, coincidence ✧ fate, fortune Wilhelm Roentgen discovered x-rays by *chance*. 2. ✦ likelihood, possibility, probability, prospect There's a good *chance* that the company picnic will be postponed if it rains. 3. ✦ opportunity, occasion, opening ✧ moment Please give me a call when you have a *chance*. 4. ✦ risk, gamble ✧ danger, peril, hazard The police chief warned his officers against taking unnecessary *chances*. —*verb* 1. ✦ happen, come ✧ fall, occur My birthday *chances* to fall on the same day as my father's. 2. ✦ attempt, hazard, risk, try, venture, dare Keiko wasn't sure if she could ski down the steep slope without falling, but she decided to *chance* it.

**change** *verb* 1. ✦ alter, modify, adjust ✧ adapt,

shift, vary When it started to rain, we *changed* our plans and decided to stay home. **2.** ✦ **exchange, replace, substitute, swap, trade** My roommate asked me to wait a few minutes while she *changed* her clothes. *—noun* ✦ **alteration, modification, switch, transition, variation** A sudden *change* in the weather forced us to postpone our ball game.

**channel** *noun* ✦ **course** ✧ **artery, passage, route, streambed** The main *channel* of the Amazon River is more than 4,300 miles long.

**chaos** *noun* ✦ **confusion, disorder, turmoil** ✧ **tumult, mess, uproar** The streets were in total *chaos* the day a power outage caused all the traffic lights to fail.

**chapter** *noun* **1.** ✧ **section, division, part, portion, topic** After reading the first *chapter*, I looked forward to the rest of the book. **2.** ✦ **branch** ✧ **group, unit, affiliate** A running club known as the Hash House Harriers has more than 2,000 *chapters* worldwide.

**character** *noun* **1.** ✦ **temperament, nature, personality** ✧ **attribute, feature, quality, trait** I thought that my dog was timid, but he showed his true *character* when he chased away a bear. **2.** ✦ **integrity, honor, morality** ✧ **fiber, honesty** I believe that a political leader should be a person of strong *character*.

**characteristic** *adjective* ✦ **normal, typical** ✧ **distinctive, particular, specific** Cold days are *characteristic* of winter weather in Canada. *—noun* ✦ **attribute, feature, quality, trait, property** I think that Ji-woo's kindness is her nicest *characteristic*.

**charge** *verb* **1.** ✦ **bill, ask, demand, require** ✧ **assess** Hanh *charges* ten dollars an hour as a Vietnamese language tutor. **2.** ✦ **rush, push, storm, thrust** ✧ **attack, assault, invade** Our quarterback *charged* through a hole in the other team's defensive line. **3.** ✦ **accuse (of), cite (for), indict (for)** ✧ **blame** The suspect was *charged with* one count of armed robbery. *—noun* **1.** ✦ **cost, expense, fee, price, payment** The salesman said that there was no additional *charge* to have our new refrigerator delivered. **2.** ✦ **care, custody** ✧ **guardianship, protection, responsibility** The nuns who run the orphanage have more than one hundred children in their *charge*. **3.** ✦ **accusation, allegation** ✧ **complaint, indictment** The suspect was arrested on a *charge* of shoplifting. **4.** ✦ **assault, attack, rush** ✧

invasion, raid, offensive A cavalry *charge* routed the enemy soldiers.

**charm** *noun* ✦ **appeal** ✧ **allure, attraction, attractiveness, beauty, magnetism** My uncle's log cabin is small, but it has a lot of *charm*. *—verb* ✦ **captivate, delight, enthrall, fascinate, thrill, bewitch** The clown's silly antics *charmed* everyone in the audience.

**charming** *adjective* ✦ **attractive, captivating, delightful, enchanting, engaging** My friend Oanh has a *charming* smile.

**chase** *verb* **1.** ✦ **pursue, run after** ✧ **follow, hunt, trail** My dog loves to *chase* rabbits. **2.** ✦ **drive away, drive, evict, oust, dispel** A security guard *chased* the trespassers from the scrapyard. *—noun* ✦ **pursuit** ✧ **race, hunt, search** Police officers caught the speeding car after a long, dangerous *chase*.

**chat** *verb* ✦ **converse, talk** ✧ **chatter, discuss, gossip** Phuong enjoys *chatting* with her friends over coffee. *—noun* ✦ **conversation, talk** ✧ **discussion, gossip, dialogue** I wondered what was up when my boss invited me into her office for a *chat*.

**cheap** *adjective* **1.** ✦ **inexpensive, low, bargain** ✧ **budget, reasonable, sale** This new restaurant has great meals at very *cheap* prices. **2.** ✦ **inferior, mediocre, poor, shabby, shoddy** ✧ **useless, worthless** This *cheap* pen keeps leaking ink.

**Antonyms** cheap
*adjective* **1.** costly, expensive, high-priced, precious, pricey **2.** excellent, high-quality, select, superior, well-made

**cheat** *verb* ✦ **swindle, defraud** ✧ **deceive, fool, mislead, trick** The dishonest art dealer *cheated* his customers by selling them forgeries.

**check** *verb* **1.** ✦ **curb, halt, restrain, stop, impede** ✧ **prevent** Workers built a sandbag dike to *check* the rising floodwater. **2.** ✦ **inspect, examine, survey** ✧ **review, compare, test** We *checked* the hotel room to make sure that we weren't forgetting anything. *—noun* **1.** ✦ **under control, restraint** ✧ **barrier, block, obstacle** I count to ten when I'm angry in order to keep my temper *in check*. **2.** ✦ **inspection, investigation, examination** ✧ **search, study, test** The security guard made routine *checks* of the building. **3.** ✦ **bill, tab** ✧ **invoice, receipt, ticket** After we had finished eating, the waiter brought our *check*.

**cheer** *verb* 1. ✦ hurrah, shout, yell, applaud ✧ praise The crowd *cheered* when our team scored a goal. 2. ✦ gladden, hearten ✧ comfort, console, encourage My friend tried to *cheer* me *up* when I was sick. —*noun* 1. ✦ cry, hurrah, shout, yell ✧ applause When the band began to play its hit song, the *cheers* of the fans grew deafening. 2. ✦ cheerfulness, delight, gladness, happiness, joy My grandmother's visits always fill me with *cheer*.

**cheerful** *adjective* ✦ glad, happy, joyful, merry ✧ pleasant All of the employees were in a *cheerful* mood on the last day of work before the holidays.

**cherish** *verb* ✦ prize, treasure, adore, love, revere, appreciate, value I *cherish* my family more than anything else.

**chest** *noun* ✦ trunk ✧ box, carton, container, crate The carpenter keeps his tools in a large wooden *chest*.

**chew** *verb* ✦ gnaw, munch, bite, chomp, nibble, champ Dogs like to *chew* on bones.

**chief** *noun* ✦ head, director, leader, supervisor, captain ✧ ruler The *chief* of our local fire department conducted a safety inspection of the new building. —*adjective* ✦ leading, first, main, primary, principal, major My *chief* concern is trying to find a good job.

**chiefly** *adverb* ✦ mainly, mostly, primarily ✧ especially, essentially Our house is made *chiefly* of wood.

**child** *noun* 1. ✦ kid, boy, girl, youth ✧ juvenile, toddler, baby We moved from our old house when I was just a young *child*. 2. ✦ offspring, descendant ✧ daughter, son, heir Michele is her parents' only *child*.

**chill** *noun* ✦ chilliness, coldness, coolness, cold ✧ nip There was a *chill* in the cabin until we got a fire going. —*adjective* ✦ chilly, cold, cool ✧ frigid, icy When autumn days turn *chill*, winter is close at hand. —*verb* ✦ cool, refrigerate ✧ freeze, ice Pudding should be *chilled* before serving.

**chilly** *adjective* ✦ chill, cold, cool ✧ icy, frigid, nippy Xiulan wore a wool sweater because the day was *chilly*.

**chip** *noun* ✦ fragment, piece, scrap ✧ bit, flake, shaving Sergei used some wood *chips* to start his campfire. —*verb* ✦ nick ✧ break, crack, splinter, damage I accidentally *chipped* the teacup when I dropped it.

**chisel** *verb* ✦ carve, sculpt, cut ✧ form, shape The names on these old tombstones were *chiseled* by hand.

**choice** *noun* ✦ pick, selection, preference, option, alternative ✧ decision You have your *choice* of apple or pumpkin pie for dessert. —*adjective* ✦ excellent, fine, select, special, superior We had *choice* seats for the concert.

**choke** *verb* 1. ✦ strangle ✧ smother, suffocate, throttle, stifle I had to loosen my tie because it was *choking* me. 2. ✦ block, clog, congest, obstruct, plug, close The freeway was *choked* by traffic.

**choose** *verb* ✦ pick, select ✧ decide, determine, elect We need to *choose* sides before we can start the game.

**chop** *verb* ✦ cut, hack ✧ sever, slice, split, hew I *chopped* onions for the spaghetti sauce. —*noun* ✦ blow, hit, punch, stroke, whack ✧ cut The karate master broke a board with a single *chop* of his hand.

**chore** *noun* ✦ task, duty, job ✧ work, assignment, responsibility My daily *chores* include doing the laundry and taking out the trash.

**chronic** *adjective* ✦ constant, continual, persistent, lingering ✧ habitual The asthmatic man had a *chronic* cough.

**chubby** *adjective* ✦ plump, fat ✧ heavy, stocky, stout Little babies often have *chubby* legs.

**chuckle** *verb* ✦ chortle, giggle, laugh ✧ snicker, smile Itsuko *chuckled* to herself as she read the humorous manga. —*noun* ✦ chortle, giggle, laugh ✧ snicker, smile My grandfather's corny jokes usually get a *chuckle* out of me.

**chum** *noun* ✦ buddy, friend, pal ✧ companion, mate My uncle said that he was looking forward to seeing his childhood *chums* again.

**church** *noun* ✦ house of worship ✧ cathedral, chapel, mosque, synagogue, temple Jimena attends a Bible study class at her *church*.

**circle** *noun* ✦ ring ✧ hoop, loop, disk We sat in a *circle* around the campfire. —*verb* ✦ encircle ✧ enclose, loop, ring, surround I *circled* the correct answers on my driver's license test.

**circulate** *verb* 1. ✦ move ✧ flow, swirl, turn, spin If it gets too hot, turn on a fan to *circulate* the air. 2. ✦ distribute, pass, spread, disperse, disseminate

Victoria *circulated* a petition to raise the minimum wage.

## Word Groups

A **citizen** is an official member of a country, state, or city. **Citizen** is a very specific term with no true synonyms. Here are some related words to investigate in a dictionary: **civilian, colonist, emigrant, immigrant, inhabitant, native, resident, settler, subject**

**city** *noun* ✦ metropolis, municipality ✧ town Tokyo is said to be the largest *city* in the world.

**civil** *adjective* 1. ✦ civic, communal, public ✧ civilian In the United States, *civil* liberties are protected by law. 2. ✦ cordial, courteous, polite ✧ kind, pleasant, decent Stuart gave a *civil* answer to the rude question.

**civilization** *noun* ✦ culture, society ✧ community, nation Most Native American *civilizations* had highly developed religious and social customs.

**claim** *noun* ✦ right, title ✧ call, demand, suit The two princes disagreed over who had legitimate *claim* to the throne. —*verb* 1. ✦ demand, occupy, require, take ✧ deserve My work *claims* so much of my time that I'm almost never home. 2. ✦ assert, declare, contend, maintain, profess ✧ believe My friend *claims* that one of her ancestors was an African king.

**clamor** *noun* ✦ commotion, din, noise, racket, uproar ✧ disturbance The *clamor* from our neighbor's party kept me awake until after midnight. —*verb* ✦ holler, howl, roar, shout, yell, bawl The audience *clamored* for the rap group to perform another song.

**clap** *verb* 1. ✦ applaud ✧ cheer, root Everyone *clapped* enthusiastically when the high diver completed his daring ninety-foot jump. 2. ✦ pat, slap, smack ✧ strike, whack, hit The whole team *clapped* Kyle on the back after he scored the winning goal. —*noun* ✦ peal, report ✧ boom, crack, bang We saw the bolt of lightning just seconds before we heard the thunder's loud *clap*.

**clarify** *verb* ✦ clear up, explain ✧ simplify, define When my boss saw my look of confusion, he *clarified* his directions.

**class** *noun* 1. ✦ category, classification, set, division, group, kind, sort My friend divides all movies into two *classes*—the good ones and the bad. 2. ✦ course, subject, session ✧ grade, lecture, section The university offers adult education *classes* in English as a Second Language. —*verb* ✦ classify, group, arrange, categorize, rank Whales and gorillas can be *classed* together because they are both mammals.

**classify** *verb* ✦ arrange, class, organize, rank, sort Diamonds are *classified* according to their quality.

**clean** *adjective* ✦ unsoiled, cleansed, spotless, washed ✧ fresh, neat, tidy I changed into *clean* clothes after painting my room. —*verb* ✦ cleanse, scrub, wash ✧ neaten, tidy, launder My roommate said that it was my turn to *clean* the bathroom.

**clear** *adjective* 1. ✦ bright, cloudless, sunny ✧ empty, open, vacant On a *clear* day, you can see the mountains from here. 2. ✦ see-through, translucent, transparent Jelly jars are usually made of *clear* glass. 3. ✦ apparent, obvious, plain, understandable, evident The interviewer said that I should make my answers to her questions as *clear* as possible. —*verb* 1. ✦ clean, tidy ✧ empty, open I will *clear* the table if you will do the dishes. 2. ✦ exonerate, absolve, acquit ✧ free, release New evidence *cleared* the couple who had originally been charged with the crime.

**clearly** *adverb* ✦ certainly, definitely, obviously, plainly ✧ really, surely The sick man *clearly* needs to see a doctor.

**clever** *adjective* ✦ bright, intelligent, quick, sharp, smart, alert The *clever* monkey quickly learned how to unlatch the door of the cage.

**client** *noun* ✦ customer, patron ✧ buyer, shopper, consumer A good accountant is likely to have many *clients*.

**cliff** *noun* ✦ bluff, precipice, rock face ✧ crag The mountaineer was easily able to climb the steep *cliff*.

**climate** *noun* ✦ clime, weather ✧ atmosphere, environment, nature, temperature Arizona is an American state that has a warm and dry *climate*.

**climax** *noun* ✦ high point, culmination, peak, zenith ✧ head, summit During the movie's *climax*, the mystery was solved and the murderer revealed.

**climb** *verb* 1. ✦ ascend, go up, mount, scale ✧ scramble Most expeditions to *climb* Mount Everest take several months. 2. ✦ ascend, lift, rise ✧ soar The airplane *climbed* steeply as it cleared the runway. —*noun* ✦ ascent ✧ grade, incline It looks like an easy *climb* to the top of that hill.

**cling** *verb* ✦ adhere, stick, clasp, fasten ✧ grasp, hang, hold Barnacles commonly *cling* to the hulls of ships.

**clip** *verb* ✦ cut, snip ✧ crop, trim, shear My roommate frequently *clips* discount coupons out of the Sunday newspaper.

**cloak** *noun* 1. ✦ cape, mantle ✧ robe, wrap, shawl In early movies, you could frequently identify the villain by the black *cloak* he wore. 2. ✦ veil, screen, cover ✧ mask, blanket A *cloak* of fog kept us from seeing the boat. —*verb* ✦ conceal, cover, hide, screen ✧ disguise, mask America's Stealth Bomber has features that *cloak* it from radar.

**close** *adjective* 1. ✦ at hand, imminent, near, nearby, approaching ✧ next When the sun began to set, I realized nightfall was *close*. 2. ✦ careful, firm, strict, tight, thorough, rigorous The lioness kept a *close* watch over her cubs. 3. ✦ equal, even ✧ alike, narrow, similar Everyone thought it would be a *close* game, but our team won easily. —*adverb* ✦ near, nearby ✧ almost, closely I don't like to sit *close* to a movie screen. —*verb* 1. ✦ shut ✧ fasten, lock, seal, secure Please *close* the gate when you leave. 2. ✦ complete, conclude, end, finish, stop, wrap up The politician *closed* his speech with a funny story. —*noun* ✦ conclusion, end, finish, stop, termination, closure Our conversation came to a *close* when my friend said that she had to be going.

**cloudy** *adjective* ✦ overcast, sunless, hazy ✧ dark, dim, muddy It was *cloudy* in the morning, but the sun came out in the afternoon.

**clown** *noun* ✧ comedian, comic, jester, joker, prankster They call him a *clown* because he's always doing something foolish. —*verb* ✦ fool, play ✧ jest, joke, kid My little brother likes to *clown* around by imitating a monkey.

**club** *noun* 1. ✦ cudgel ✧ bat, mallet, staff, stick In England, many police officers carry *clubs* instead of guns. 2. ✦ association, group, organization, society, league Tiep is a member of a *club* where people practice their English. 3. ✦ center, facility ✧ hall I'm taking swimming lessons at the local athletic *club*. —*verb* ✦ beat, hit, pound, strike ✧ batter, hammer My friend wanted to *club* the snake, but I persuaded him to leave it alone.

**clue** *noun* ✦ sign, trace, evidence, lead ✧ hint, suggestion Police said that the burglar left no *clues*.

**clumsy** *adjective* ✦ awkward, uncoordinated, inept, graceless My friend is so *clumsy* that he broke three plates while washing the dishes.

**cluster** *noun* ✦ batch, bunch, clump ✧ bundle, group, set I bought some grapes and ate the entire *cluster*. —*verb* ✦ bunch, collect, flock, gather, mass, assemble Whenever the farmer feeds his chickens, they *cluster* around him.

**coach** *noun* 1. ✦ carriage ✧ stage, stagecoach The queen's *coach* was drawn by a team of six gray horses. 2. ✦ trainer ✧ instructor, adviser, manager, teacher My soccer team has a new *coach*. —*verb* ✦ drill, instruct, teach, train, tutor The lawyer *coached* her client on what to say in court.

**coarse** *adjective* ✦ gritty, rough, grainy, sandy, scratchy Sandpaper has a *coarse* texture.

**coast** *noun* ✦ seacoast, seashore, seaside, shore, shoreline A lighthouse warns ships that the *coast* is near. —*verb* ✦ glide, slide ✧ drift, flow, roll, sail, slip Kari *coasted* down the steep hill on her bicycle.

**coat** *noun* 1. ✦ jacket ✧ overcoat, raincoat, windbreaker, wrap I always wear a warm *coat* when I walk in the snow. 2. ✦ coating, covering, layer ✧ surface, blanket When we fixed up our house, we put on a fresh *coat* of paint. —*verb* ✦ cover, blanket, layer ✧ smear, spread A thin layer of frost *coated* the trees.

**coax** *verb* ✦ persuade, urge, wheedle ✧ lure, influence My friends *coaxed* me to join their soccer team.

**code** *noun* ✦ regulations, rules, standards ✧ law, system According to the local fire *code*, we can't burn trash in the backyard.

**coil** *noun* ✦ reel, roll ✧ loop, ring, spiral The rancher bought a *coil* of barbed wire. —*verb* ✦ twist, wind, wrap, curl, roll, turn The python *coiled* itself around a tree branch.

**coin** *noun* ✦ coinage, change, cash, money Old-fashioned parking meters would only take *coins*. —*verb* ✦ create, invent, originate, make up, devise William Shakespeare is said to have *coined* over 1,700 new words.

**coincide** *verb* ✦ accord, agree, concur, correspond, match Sometimes the interests of government and the needs of the public do not *coincide*.

**coincidence** *noun* ✦ fluke, accident, chance ✧

**fate, luck** It is just a *coincidence* that my best friend and I have the same last name.

**cold** *adjective* 1. ✦ **chilly, cool, icy, frosty** ✧ **frigid, frozen** A glass of *cold* lemonade tastes wonderful on a hot summer day. 2. ✦ **unfriendly** ✧ **aloof, haughty, stony** The losing boxer gave the judges a *cold* stare. —*noun* 1. ✦ **chill, coldness, coolness, iciness** ✧ **freeze, frost** When I went outside without my jacket, I shivered in the *cold*. 2. ✧ **illness, fever, sickness, virus** I missed two days of work because I had a bad *cold*.

**collapse** *verb* ✦ **buckle, cave in, crumple, topple** ✧ **fall, fail** The cheap lawn chair *collapsed* when I sat on it. —*noun* ✦ **cave-in** ✧ **breakdown, disintegration, failure, crash** No one knew what caused the tunnel's sudden *collapse*.

**colleague** *noun* ✦ **associate, coworker, confederate, partner** ✧ **aide, comrade** What I enjoy most about my job is the friendliness of my *colleagues*.

**collect** *verb* 1. ✦ **accumulate, amass, gather** ✧ **assemble** These old books are just *collecting* dust. 2. ✦ **acquire, obtain, raise, secure, accrue** The government *collects* money through taxes.

**collection** *noun* ✦ **accumulation, hoard, mass, stockpile, assortment** My friend has a large *collection* of classical music.

**collide** *verb* ✦ **bump, crash, hit, slam, smash, strike** Two basketball players *collided* when they both ran toward the ball.

**collision** *noun* ✦ **accident, crash, impact, smashup, wreck** When the driver saw the oncoming car, she swerved away in order to avoid a *collision*.

**color** *noun* ✦ **hue, shade, tint, tinge, tone** My favorite *color* is purple. —*verb* ✦ **dye, stain, tint, tinge, paint** The tradition of *coloring* eggs at Easter time is believed to have been started by early Christians in Mesopotamia.

**colorful** *adjective* ✦ **bright, loud, vivid** ✧ **gaudy, flashy** My friend likes to wear *colorful* plaid shirts.

**combat** *verb* ✦ **battle, fight, struggle against** ✧ **oppose, resist, attack** Our mayor says that her top priority is to *combat* poverty. —*noun* ✦ **battle, war, action** ✧ **conflict, fight, struggle** The Air Force's newest jet fighter has not been tested in *combat*.

**combination** *noun* ✦ **blend, mix, mixture, com-**
pound ✧ **merger, union** This ice cream shop serves customers any *combination* of flavors they desire.

**combine** *verb* ✦ **blend, mix** ✧ **join, merge, unite** If you *combine* blue and yellow paint, you'll get green.

**Antonyms combine**
*verb* **detach, divide, segregate, separate, split, sunder**

**come** *verb* 1. ✦ **go (to), move (to), approach** ✧ **advance, near, proceed** Mohamed's family *came to* America last year. 2. ✦ **appear, arrive, show up** ✧ **reach** My commuter van *comes* at seven o'clock in the morning. 3. ✦ **fall, happen, occur, take place** ✧ **develop** Christmas *comes* only once a year. 4. ✦ **hail** ✧ **arise, issue, originate, spring** My friend Olaf *comes* from Norway.

**comfort** *verb* ✦ **console, soothe, hearten** ✧ **ease, pacify, relieve** Whenever I'm feeling bad, my friends try to *comfort* me. —*noun* 1. ✦ **solace, aid, help, relief, support** For many small children, it's a real *comfort* to hold a cherished blanket or stuffed animal. 2. ✦ **ease, well-being** ✧ **contentment, pleasure, satisfaction, luxury** It's possible to camp in *comfort* if you have the proper equipment.

**comfortable** *adjective* 1. ✦ **cozy, snug** ✧ **pleasant, pleasurable, satisfying** Cool autumn nights really make me appreciate my warm and *comfortable* bed. 2. ✦ **calm, at ease, easy, relaxed** ✧ **contented, serene** I didn't feel *comfortable* the first time I flew on a plane.

**comical** *adjective* ✦ **amusing, funny, humorous, laughable** ✧ **ridiculous** My puppy is *comical* when he chases his tail.

**command** *verb* 1. ✦ **order, direct, bid** ✧ **demand, require** Soldiers have to do what their officers *command*. 2. ✦ **lead, head** ✧ **control, govern, rule, supervise** A lieutenant *commands* a platoon of approximately forty soldiers. —*noun* 1. ✦ **order, direction, demand** ✧ **instruction, decree** I trained my dog to obey my *commands*. 2. **authority, control, leadership, charge** ✧ **power, mastery** A naval captain has *command* over both a ship and its crew.

**commemorate** *verb* ✦ **celebrate, honor, memorialize** ✧ **keep, observe, remember** The United States' Independence Day *commemorates* the adoption of the Declaration of Independence.

**commence** *verb* ✦ begin, open, start ✧ initiate, originate The graduation ceremony will *commence* at three o'clock.

**commend** *verb* ✦ compliment, praise, applaud, congratulate ✧ acclaim, honor My boss *commended* me for my excellent work.

**comment** *noun* ✦ observation, remark, statement ✧ note, opinion My friend's *comment* that I was an interesting person made me feel good. —*verb* ✦ mention, remark, say, state, express, reflect Everyone in the class *commented* on how difficult it was.

**commerce** *noun* ✦ business, trade, trading ✧ exchange, traffic Many jobs depend upon *commerce* with other countries.

**commit** *verb* 1. ✦ carry out, do, perform ✧ complete, execute, make, effect The police do not know who *committed* the crime. 2. ✦ assign, confine, institutionalize (in) ✧ imprison, deliver The emotionally disturbed man was *committed to* a mental hospital for treatment. 3. ✦ devote, pledge, resolve ✧ promise, vow I respect people who are *committed* to making the world a better place.

**common** *adjective* 1. ✦ general, universal, public ✧ joint, mutual, shared It is *common* knowledge that the dinosaurs are extinct. 2. ✦ ordinary, routine, typical, usual, average, normal ✧ simple Sprains and strains are the most *common* types of sports injuries.

**commonly** *adverb* ✦ ordinarily, regularly, usually, widely ✧ frequently, often Doctors *commonly* prescribe antibiotics for the treatment of infectious diseases.

**commotion** *noun* ✦ disturbance, uproar, turmoil, clamor, confusion There was a *commotion* in our house when a raccoon came in the pet door.

**communicate** *verb* ✦ convey, impart, inform ✧ declare, relate, report, state When my dog dropped his leash in my lap, I knew what he was trying to *communicate* to me.

**community** *noun* 1. ✦ city, town, neighborhood ✧ population, public Our mayor hopes to get the entire *community* involved in his anticrime campaign. 2. ✦ body, group, set, circle ✧ association, society The scientific *community* feels that more money should be devoted to research.

**compact¹** *adjective* 1. ✦ dense, firm, hard, solid, compressed ✧ thick An igloo is made from blocks of snow that are almost as *compact* as ice. 2. ✦ miniature, little, small, tiny ✧ cramped, limited, shrunken, undersized Recreational vehicles have *compact* kitchens. —*verb* ✦ compress, crush, cram, pack, squeeze Our kitchen has an appliance that *compacts* trash into small bundles.

**compact²** *noun* ✦ accord, pact, treaty, agreement ✧ deal, understanding The two nations signed a secret *compact* to help defend each other.

**companion** *noun* ✦ comrade, friend, partner, associate ✧ attendant, escort It's safer to go hiking if you have a *companion* along.

**company** *noun* 1. ✦ guests, visitors, callers I need to clean my apartment because I'm expecting *company*. 2. ✦ companionship, comradeship, fellowship ✧ friendship, society My grandfather says that he enjoys my *company* very much. 3. ✦ business, establishment, firm ✧ corporation, concern My friend works for a small *company* that makes gardening supplies. 4. ✦ troupe ✧ band, corps, group, party, troop A traveling ballet *company* will perform in our town next week.

**compare** *verb* 1. ✦ contrast, relate, consider ✧ analyze, examine Before I bought a new smartphone, I went to several stores to *compare* prices. 2. ✦ compete with, equal, match, correspond ✧ resemble Swimming in a pool is fun, but it can't *compare with* actually going to the beach.

**comparison** *noun* 1. ✦ assessment, evaluation, appraisal, ranking, rating ✧ judgment A *comparison* of the two stereos quickly revealed which one had the better sound. 2. ✦ similarity, resemblance, correspondence ✧ connection, relationship To me, there's no *comparison* between a frozen pizza and a fresh one from my favorite pizzeria.

**compassion** *noun* ✦ empathy, concern, sympathy, mercy ✧ love, tenderness Good doctors have *compassion* for their patients.

**compel** *verb* ✦ force, oblige, require, drive ✧ cause, make Bad weather *compelled* us to change our vacation plans.

**compete** *verb* ✦ contend, take part ✧ strive, vie, challenge, rival Natasha will *compete* in next Saturday's golf tournament.

**competent** *adjective* ✦ proficient, skilled, able, capable, good, qualified A *competent* accountant rarely makes mistakes.

**competition** *noun* 1. ✦ rivalry, competing ✧ contention, struggle, conflict The *competition* at the Olympics is intense. 2. ✦ contest, meet ✧ game, match, tournament, event Valentina was thrilled to win first place in the surfing *competition*.

**compile** *verb* ✦ put together, assemble, accumulate, collect, gather Astrid *compiled* a list of people she wanted to invite to her birthday party.

**complain** *verb* ✦ grumble, gripe, whine ✧ criticize, denounce, object, protest During last week's heat wave, many people *complained* about the temperature.

**complaint** *noun* ✦ criticism, objection, protest, gripe ✧ dissatisfaction Meiling loved the book; her only *complaint* was that it was too short.

**complete** *adjective* 1. ✦ intact, whole, entire, full ✧ total Whenever we play rummy, I count the cards to make sure the deck is *complete*. 2. ✦ absolute, perfect, thorough, utter ✧ sheer The camping trip was a *complete* disaster because of an unexpected snowstorm. —*verb* ✦ accomplish, conclude, end, finish, wrap up ✧ fulfill Our manager said we can have a day off as soon as we *complete* this job.

**Antonyms complete**
*adjective* 1. incomplete, partial, unfinished
*verb* begin, commence, inaugurate, initiate, launch, open, start, start up

**complex** *adjective* ✦ complicated, intricate, difficult, hard ✧ elaborate, involved A jigsaw puzzle with 5,000 pieces is too *complex* for my tastes.

**complicate** *verb* ✦ confuse, mix up, muddle ✧ handicap, involve Please don't *complicate* our game by adding all those new rules.

**complicated** *adjective* ✦ complex, intricate, difficult, hard ✧ involved, elaborate My new computer software is so *complicated* that I haven't been able to figure it out yet.

**compliment** *noun* ✦ commendation, praise ✧ admiration, approval, flattery, acclaim After the reading, the poet received many *compliments* on the beauty of her writing. —*verb* ✦ commend, praise, admire ✧ approve, flatter The chef was pleased when we *complimented* his cooking.

**comply** *verb* ✦ abide (by), carry (out), obey ✧ observe, respect, follow The emperor expected everyone to *comply with* his wishes.

**compose** *verb* 1. ✦ constitute, form, make, make up, fashion, build Hydrogen and oxygen are the elements that *compose* water. 2. ✦ write, author, create, make, produce ✧ devise, invent As part of the proficiency test, I have to *compose* a 500-word essay. 3. ✦ calm, quiet, relax, settle, soothe The actor took a few minutes to *compose* himself before the performance.

**compound** *noun* ✦ mixture ✧ blend, combination, union, composite Concrete is a *compound* of cement, sand, gravel, and water. —*verb* ✦ blend, combine, mix ✧ join, link Incense is made by *compounding* various scents with a combustible powder.

**comprehend** *verb* ✦ grasp, perceive, understand, know ✧ fathom I know how to use my computer, but I don't really *comprehend* how it works.

**comprehensive** *adjective* ✦ complete, full, thorough, exhaustive ✧ broad, large This history book has a *comprehensive* index that lists every subject covered.

**comprise** *verb* ✦ contain, include, incorporate, constitute ✧ embrace, involve Japan *comprises* more than 3,500 islands.

**compromise** *noun* ✦ agreement, settlement, arrangement, bargain, concession The agreed-upon price is a *compromise*—the buyer offered less, the seller wanted more. —*verb* ✦ meet halfway, settle ✧ agree, concede, give in, negotiate When my friend and I couldn't agree which restaurant to go to, we *compromised* by getting a pizza to eat in.

**compulsory** *adjective* ✦ mandatory, required, obligatory, necessary ✧ imperative On an airplane, wearing a seat belt is *compulsory* during takeoffs and landings.

**compute** *verb* ✦ calculate, determine, figure, reckon, ascertain ✧ estimate Can you *compute* the average of 106, 119, 125, and 130 without using a calculator?

**Word Groups**

A **computer** is a programmable electronic machine that processes information. **Computer** is a very specific term with no true synonyms. Here are some types of computers to investigate in a dictionary: **desktop, laptop, mainframe, notebook, smartphone, tablet**

**comrade** *noun* ✦ buddy, companion, friend, mate, pal, partner The ex-soldier has stayed in touch with many of his army *comrades*.

**conceal** *verb* ✦ hide, cover, mask, screen ✧ camouflage The top of the mountain was *concealed* by clouds.

**concede** *verb* 1. ✦ acknowledge, admit, accept, agree, confess, grant I *conceded* that I was lost and asked for directions. 2. ✦ give up, surrender, yield ✧ give in, resign The candidate *conceded* the election before the final votes were counted.

**conceited** *adjective* ✦ arrogant, haughty, vain, smug, self-centered The *conceited* artist claimed that he was the best painter around.

**conceive** *verb* ✦ envision, imagine, picture, think (of) ✧ form, develop Leonardo da Vinci *conceived* of many inventions that he was unable to construct.

**concentrate** *verb* 1. ✦ focus, pay attention ✧ apply, dedicate, devote, contemplate, think I was *concentrating* on piano practice and didn't hear the doorbell. 2. ✦ center, centralize, cluster, focus ✧ collect, gather The American motion picture industry is *concentrated* in Southern California.

**concept** *noun* ✦ idea, notion, conception, theory ✧ thought Jules Verne wrote about the *concept* of space flight nearly a century before it became a reality.

**concern** *verb* 1. ✦ affect, involve, pertain (to), interest Environmental issues *concern* all of us. 2. ✦ distress (by), disturb (by), trouble (by), worry ✧ bother We were *concerned about* my grandfather's health until the doctors said that he would be fine. —*noun* 1. ✦ affair, business, matter, consideration, issue ✧ interest Religious beliefs are a private *concern*. 2. ✦ apprehension, anxiety, worry ✧ care, trouble Amy took the stray cat home because she felt *concern* for its well-being.

**concert** *noun* ✦ performance ✧ program, recital, show I want to go to next week's *concert* because my friend is in the orchestra.

**concise** *adjective* ✦ brief, terse, short, succinct, condensed The interviewer said that my responses should be clear and *concise*.

**conclude** *verb* 1. ✦ close, complete, end, finish, terminate The celebration *concluded* with a display of fireworks. 2. ✦ determine, judge, decide, deduce, resolve, settle ✧ assume The doctor *concluded* that I was in excellent health.

**conclusion** *noun* 1. ✦ close, end, ending, finish, termination ✧ finale The start of the movie was boring, but the *conclusion* was very exciting. 2. ✦ deduction, determination, judgment, decision, verdict ✧ opinion The detective's *conclusion* was that the butler had committed the crime.

**concrete** *adjective* ✦ actual, definite, real, tangible ✧ firm, solid The judge ruled that the case could not be tried unless the police found some *concrete* evidence.

**concur** *verb* ✦ agree with, assent to ✧ consent, accord, approve The jurors were asked if they *concurred* with the verdict.

**condemn** *verb* 1. ✦ denounce, deplore, criticize, attack ✧ blame In last week's sermon, our minister *condemned* the use of illegal drugs. 2. ✦ doom, sentence, convict ✧ punish During the Roman Empire, prisoners were frequently *condemned* to serve as galley slaves.

**Antonyms** **condemn**

*verb* 1. admire, applaud, commend, esteem, extol, honor, praise 2. acquit, clear, excuse, forgive, pardon

**condense** *verb* ✦ abbreviate, abridge, crop, reduce, shorten ✧ curtail, thicken The editor *condensed* the author's book by cutting out five chapters.

**condition** *noun* 1. ✦ form, order, repair, shape, state, status I am looking for a used car that's in good *condition*. 2. ✦ ailment, disease, illness, malady, sickness ✧ affliction Anyone with a heart *condition* should be under a doctor's care. 3. ✦ qualification, provision, restriction, stipulation, requirement One *condition* of my tourist visa is that it must be used within a year of being issued. —*verb* ✦ prepare, ready, shape, train ✧ strengthen, adapt The coach began *conditioning* the team on the first day of practice.

**conduct** *verb* 1. ✦ escort, lead, direct, guide, steer ✧ usher, supervise A flight attendant *conducted* us to our seats. 2. ✦ behave, comport, acquit ✧ act, bear, carry The lawyer told her client that he *conducted* himself perfectly during his court appearance. —*noun* ✦ behavior, manner, actions, ways ✧ attitude The American military has a medal which is given for good *conduct*.

**confer** *verb* 1. ✦ consult, deliberate ✧ discuss, speak, talk, converse The jurors *conferred* for two days before reaching a verdict. 2. ✦ award (to), bestow, give (to), grant (to), present (to) A special award was *conferred on* the hometown hero by the mayor of the city.

**conference** *noun* ✦ consultation, discussion, meeting, talk, interview The manager scheduled a *conference* with all his employees to discuss the new regulations.

**confess** *verb* ✦ acknowledge, admit, concede, disclose, reveal After several hours of interrogation, the suspect *confessed* his guilt.

**confide** *verb* ✦ disclose, reveal, tell, whisper ✧ commit, entrust, turn over My best friend *confided* a secret to me because she knows that I'll never tell anyone.

**confidence** *noun* 1. ✦ self-confidence, self-reliance, assurance, aplomb ✧ poise After practicing at home, I was able to stand up in front of my ESL class and speak with *confidence*. 2. ✦ faith, reliance, trust ✧ belief, conviction We have complete *confidence* in our family dentist.

**confident** *adjective* ✦ certain, positive, sure, convinced ✧ assured Our baseball team is *confident* that we will win tomorrow's game.

**confidential** *adjective* ✦ classified, restricted, secret ✧ personal, private The lawyer keeps *confidential* files locked up whenever she is away from the office.

**confine** *verb* ✦ hold, limit, restrict, restrain ✧ detain, imprison We built a fence to *confine* our dog to the backyard.

**confirm** *verb* ✦ corroborate, support, uphold, verify ✧ approve, certify When I consulted a second doctor, she *confirmed* the original diagnosis.

**confiscate** *verb* ✦ appropriate, seize, take, take away, impound My toothpaste was *confiscated* by an airport security agent.

**conflict** *noun* 1. ✦ war, warfare ✧ battle, combat, fight The small border dispute quickly escalated into armed *conflict*. 2. ✦ clash, disagreement, argument, dispute ✧ feud, struggle The president tried to stay out of the *conflict* that arose among the advisors. —*verb* ✦ contradict, differ (from), disagree (with), vary (from) ✧ clash, diverge The second witness gave testimony that *conflicted with* what the first witness had said.

**conform** *verb* ✦ comply (with), correspond (to), agree (with), follow ✧ obey, observe People often feel pressured to *conform to* what family and friends expect of them.

**confront** *verb* ✦ challenge, defy, face ✧ encounter, meet When I *confronted* the growling dog, it turned tail and ran away.

**confuse** *verb* 1. ✦ baffle, bewilder, mystify, perplex, puzzle My friend's map *confused* me, and I ended up going in the wrong direction. 2. ✦ mistake, mix up ✧ jumble, misjudge, confound Ground squirrels look so much like chipmunks that people often *confuse* the two.

**confusion** *noun* ✦ chaos, disorder, turmoil ✧ bewilderment, perplexity There was much *confusion* when our plane landed in the wrong city.

**congratulate** *verb* ✦ applaud, cheer, hail, praise, compliment ✧ honor We all *congratulated* Mallory when she won the short-story contest.

**connect** *verb* 1. ✦ join, link ✧ attach, couple, fasten, unite The Channel Tunnel *connects* Great Britain with France. 2. ✦ associate, identify, relate, link, equate It was hard for me to *connect* names and faces during the first few days at my new job.

**connection** *noun* 1. ✦ coupling, attachment, junction ✧ bond, link, union My car wouldn't start because the battery *connection* was loose. 2. ✦ association, link, relation, relationship, relevance The police said that there was no apparent *connection* between the two bank robberies.

**conquer** *verb* ✦ defeat, overcome, vanquish, subdue ✧ beat, triumph Rome *conquered* England during the first century CE.

**conscious** *adjective* 1. ✦ aware, knowledgeable, mindful, heedful ✧ alert, awake The man gradually became *conscious* of the fact that he was not alone in the haunted house. 2. ✦ deliberate, intentional, planned, purposeful, willful Zhang Wei has been making a *conscious* effort to exercise more.

**consecutive** *adjective* ✦ successive, uninterrupted, continual, continuous, subsequent It rained for four *consecutive* days and nights last week.

**consent** *verb* ✦ assent, agree ✧ allow, approve, authorize, permit Both husband and wife *consented* to the divorce terms. —*noun* ✦ agreement, approval, assent, authorization, permission Surgery could not be performed without the patient's *consent*.

**consequence** *noun* ✦ result, aftermath ✧ effect,

end, outcome, product I missed the bus and as a *consequence* had to walk to work.

**conservative** *adjective* ✦ traditional, conventional, reasonable, standard, restrained The executive wore a *conservative* gray suit to the business meeting.

**conservation** *noun* ✦ preservation, protection, saving ✧ care, maintenance The *conservation* of natural resources is important to ensure future availability.

**conserve** *verb* ✦ preserve, save, spare ✧ keep, maintain, protect We were asked to *conserve* water during the long drought.

**Antonyms** conserve

*verb* consume, misuse, spend, squander, use up, waste

**consider** *verb* 1. ✦ contemplate, deliberate, ponder, reflect (on), think (about), examine Before I make a decision, I need to *consider* all options. 2. ✦ believe, judge, reckon, regard (as), view (as) This painting is *considered* to be one of the artist's best. 3. ✦ allow (for), heed, note, remember, count The veterinarian said that my cat was in excellent condition, if you *consider* his age.

**considerable** *adjective* ✦ extensive, great, significant, substantial ✧ big, large The famous earthquake that hit San Francisco in 1906 caused *considerable* damage.

**considerate** *adjective* ✦ thoughtful, kind, polite ✧ attentive, friendly, courteous It was very *considerate* of you to send me such a nice get-well card.

**consideration** *noun* 1. ✦ deliberation, reflection, study, thought, contemplation Agustín gave the job offer careful *consideration*. 2. ✦ concern, factor, issue, point ✧ circumstance When planning a camping trip, the weather is an important *consideration*. 3. ✦ regard, respect, concern ✧ courtesy, thoughtfulness, attention Alejandra always shows *consideration* for other people's feelings.

**consist** *verb* ✦ comprise, contain, include, incorporate, have This English proficiency test *consists* of four sections—listening, reading, writing, and speaking.

**consolidate** *verb* ✦ combine, join, link, merge, unite ✧ connect The business owner *consolidated* the company's debts by getting one bank loan that covered everything.

**conspicuous** *adjective* ✦ noticeable, obvious, prominent, recognizable ✧ clear, evident, plain, visible A giraffe's long neck is its most *conspicuous* feature.

**conspiracy** *noun* ✦ plot, scheme, plan ✧ intrigue Several generals were heavily involved in a *conspiracy* to overthrow their country's corrupt government.

**constant** *adjective* ✦ ceaseless, endless, continuous, perpetual, steady A newborn infant requires almost *constant* attention.

**constantly** *adverb* ✦ always, continually, continuously ✧ forever, often, regularly, nonstop Clouds *constantly* change size and shape on windy days.

**construct** *verb* ✦ build, fabricate, make, erect ✧ assemble, manufacture The university hired a contractor to *construct* the new library.

**consult** *verb* ✦ confer, deliberate, discuss ✧ speak, talk The defendant *consulted* with his lawyer before answering the question.

**consume** *verb* 1. ✦ devour, ingest, eat, swallow, down ✧ digest, feed The giant anteater of South America can *consume* over 30,000 ants in a day. 2. ✦ destroy, use up, waste, ravage ✧ exhaust, finish, devour The forest fire *consumed* more than five hundred acres of parkland.

**contact** *noun* ✦ communication ✧ connection, encounter, meeting, touch, union Some people believe that extraterrestrial beings are trying to make *contact* with humans. —*verb* ✦ communicate (with), call ✧ connect, reach, touch I tried all last week to *contact* you, but you didn't answer your phone.

**contain** *verb* 1. ✦ have, hold, include ✧ bear, carry That file box *contains* all my tax receipts from last year. 2. ✦ check, control, limit, restrain, stop, suppress Firefighters were able to *contain* the blaze before it destroyed the building.

**contaminate** *verb* ✦ foul, pollute, dirty, spoil, taint ✧ poison The oil spill *contaminated* several miles of shoreline.

**contemplate** *verb* ✦ consider, deliberate, ponder, reflect (on), think (about), study My best friend and I are *contemplating* renting an apartment together.

**contempt** *noun* ✦ disdain, disgust, disrespect,

**scorn** ✧ **hatred** The haughty billionaire felt *contempt* for people with less money.

**contend** *verb* **1.** ✦ **battle, combat, fight, struggle, duel, wrestle** We had to *contend with* a lot of mosquitoes on our last kayaking trip. **2.** ✦ **compete, vie, strive** ✧ **challenge, contest** The runners are *contending* for a chance to go to the state championship. **3.** ✦ **assert, claim, declare, affirm, allege, say, state, argue** My friend *contends* that he is a better swimmer than I am.

**content** *adjective* ✦ **contented, pleased, satisfied, happy** ✧ **gratified** If you aren't *content* with your score, you can take the proficiency test again. —*verb* ✦ **appease, gratify, satisfy** ✧ **delight, please** Because Akira couldn't go to the baseball game, he had to *content* himself with watching it on television.

**contented** *adjective* ✦ **content, gratified, pleased, satisfied, happy** The *contented* baby fell asleep in her mother's arms.

**contentment** *noun* ✦ **pleasure, satisfaction, happiness** ✧ **gratification** We all sighed with *content* after finishing the delicious meal.

**contest** *noun* ✦ **competition, rivalry** ✧ **meet, tournament, fight, struggle** Chloe was delighted to win the photo *contest* for best selfie. —*verb* ✦ **challenge, dispute, object (to)** ✧ **oppose, resist, struggle** The losing candidate *contested* the election results by calling for a recount.

**continual** *adjective* ✦ **constant, continuous, perpetual, persistent, steady** It's hard to concentrate with these *continual* interruptions.

**continue** *verb* **1.** ✦ **endure, go on, last, persist, remain, stay** The drought is expected to *continue* for the remainder of this year. **2.** ✦ **resume, carry on (with), pick up** ✧ **renew, restart** The speaker paused for a moment and then *continued* her lecture.

**continuous** *adjective* ✦ **constant, continual, endless, nonstop, perpetual, uninterrupted** The human brain needs a *continuous* supply of oxygen-rich blood.

**contract** *noun* ✦ **agreement, arrangement, compact** ✧ **bargain, deal, pact** When my friend bought a new car, he signed a *contract* that committed him to making monthly payments. —*verb* **1.** ✦ **shorten, tighten, compress** ✧ **decrease, reduce, shrink** Your muscles *contract* when you lift

a heavy object. **2.** ✦ **agree, pledge, promise, undertake** ✧ **vow** The disposal company *contracted* to pick up our trash once a week. **3.** ✦ **catch, develop, get** ✧ **acquire, obtain** My uncle *contracted* malaria while traveling in the tropics.

**contradict** *verb* ✦ **challenge, refute, deny, dispute** ✧ **disagree, oppose** Several new studies *contradict* the notion that sugar is harmless.

**contrary** *adjective* **1.** ✦ **contradictory, counter, opposed, opposite** ✧ **different** *Contrary* to popular belief, wolves do not howl at the moon. **2.** ✦ **headstrong, obstinate, stubborn, perverse** ✧ **disobedient** My *contrary* dog never comes when I call him.

**contrast** *verb* ✦ **compare, differentiate, oppose** ✧ **differ, distinguish, vary** I am reading an article that *contrasts* the lives of African Americans today to those of their ancestors. —*noun* ✦ **difference (from), divergence, variation** ✧ **comparison, counterpoint** The coolness of the air-conditioned room was a refreshing *contrast* to the heat outside.

**Antonyms** contrast

*noun* **agreement, harmony, likeness, resemblance, similarity, uniformity**

**contribute** *verb* **1.** ✦ **donate, give, grant, bestow, present** ✧ **furnish, supply** Bill and Melinda Gates have *contributed* more than thirty billion dollars to charitable causes. **2.** ✦ **add (to), influence, aid, help, support** ✧ **cause, make** The gold-medal gymnast said that her parents' support *contributed to* her success.

**contribution** *noun* ✦ **donation, gift, offering, present** ✧ **payment, handout** The American Red Cross is funded by voluntary *contributions*.

**contrive** *verb* ✦ **concoct, improvise, devise, create, design, invent** ✧ **plan, scheme** I *contrived* a no-kill mousetrap out of a board, spring, and tin can.

**control** *verb* **1.** ✦ **direct, govern, manage, supervise, administer, rule** Air traffic is *controlled* by specialists whose job is to keep the skies safe. **2.** ✦ **check, curb, restrain, subdue, suppress, repress** When the rude man insulted me, I had to struggle to *control* my temper. —*noun* **1.** ✦ **authority, command, direction, power, rule, management** The club's finances are under the treasurer's *control*. **2.** ✦ **check, curb, restraint, restriction, regulation** The mayor is trying to impose strict *controls* on public spending.

**controversy** *noun* ✦ contention, disagreement, dispute, argument, debate The president's plan to raise taxes was a source of much *controversy*.

**convene** *verb* ✦ assemble, congregate, meet, get together, gather ✧ rally America's first Continental Congress *convened* on September 5, 1774.

**convenience** *noun* ✦ advantage, benefit, comfort, ease ✧ aid, help, use, service The bank installed more ATMs for the *convenience* of its customers.

**convenient** *adjective* ✦ advantageous, beneficial, helpful, handy, useful ✧ suitable It is very *convenient* for me to live so close to my work.

**conventional** *adjective* ✦ traditional, customary, normal, regular, standard, usual The couple thought about getting married in a hot air balloon, but they settled on a *conventional* wedding in a church.

**conversation** *noun* ✦ chat, discussion, talk ✧ conference, speech I had a long *conversation* with my best friend when she got home from her trip abroad.

**converse** *verb* ✦ chat, speak, talk ✧ confer, discuss The two men spent the morning *conversing* about the weather and their grandchildren.

**convert** *verb* ✦ change, alter, turn, modify, transform ✧ switch The big mansion on the edge of town has been *converted* into a museum. —*noun* ✦ believer (in), follower (of), recruit ✧ disciple, devotee Marshall is a new *convert* to environmental causes such as recycling.

**convey** *verb* 1. ✦ bring, carry, transport, bear, move ✧ transmit The ancient Romans built an elaborate system of aqueducts to *convey* water to their cities. 2. ✦ communicate, express, relate, state ✧ disclose I searched for the right words to *convey* my thoughts.

**convict** *verb* ✦ condemn, sentence ✧ find guilty, judge The jury *convicted* the defendant on two counts of armed robbery. —*noun* ✦ inmate, prisoner ✧ captive, criminal, felon, outlaw Three *convicts* escaped from the state prison.

**convince** *verb* ✦ assure, persuade, satisfy ✧ impress, sway, influence Your story has *convinced* me that you are telling the truth.

**cook** *verb* ✦ make, prepare ✧ heat, bake, broil, fry, grill, microwave, roast My roommate said it was my turn to *cook* dinner tonight.

**cool** *adjective* 1. ✦ chill, chilly ✧ cold, icy, frigid It was warm on the beach, but the wind off the ocean was *cool*. 2. ✦ calm, collected, composed, serene, detached When the plane went into a spin, the pilot remained *cool* and quickly regained control. 3. ✦ aloof, distant, reserved, unfriendly ✧ haughty, remote My friend's *cool* stare turned into a warm smile when I apologized for having offended him. —*verb* ✦ chill ✧ freeze, frost, ice, refrigerate We *cooled* the soda by putting the bottle in a mountain stream.

**cooperate** *verb* ✦ collaborate, work together ✧ coordinate, join, participate, unite If we *cooperate*, we can get this job done in no time.

**cooperation** *noun* ✦ participation, teamwork, partnership ✧ aid, help, support Keeping the streets free of litter requires the *cooperation* of all citizens.

**coordinate** *verb* ✦ synchronize, adapt, conform, harmonize, integrate, unite Good swimmers *coordinate* their breathing with the rhythm of their strokes.

**cope** *verb* ✦ contend with, deal with, handle, manage ✧ control The babysitter had a tough time *coping with* five children at once.

**copy** *noun* ✦ duplicate, reproduction, double ✧ facsimile, imitation Medieval monks created beautiful hand-drawn *copies* of important manuscripts. —*verb* 1. ✦ write down, duplicate, reproduce, replicate Our ESL teacher asked us to *copy* the vocabulary words that she had written on the chalkboard. 2. ✦ imitate, mimic, follow ✧ fake, repeat, steal Many writers have *copied* the style of Ernest Hemingway.

**cord** *noun* ✦ string, twine ✧ line, rope, thread Soyeon used a length of *cord* to tie up the bundle of newspapers.

**cordial** *adjective* ✦ courteous, friendly, warm, pleasant, nice The hosts bid every guest a *cordial* welcome.

**core** *noun* 1. ✧ kernel, pit, nut, seed We put our apple *cores* in the compost pile. 2. ✦ center, middle, interior ✧ essence, heart, nucleus The Earth's *core* is believed to be a ball of solid iron and nickel.

**corner** *noun* 1. ✦ edge ✧ angle, bend, end Angelica folded the *corner* of a page to mark her place in the book. 2. ✦ intersection, junction, juncture,

**crossroads** Eric lives near the *corner* of First and Maple streets.

**corporation** *noun* ✦ business, company, firm, establishment ✧ enterprise My friend works for a *corporation* that develops computer software.

**correct** *verb* ✦ fix, remedy, repair ✧ adjust, amend, improve These eyeglasses will *correct* your vision. —*adjective* 1. ✦ accurate, exact, precise, right, true The *correct* spelling of most words can be found in a good dictionary. 2. ✦ right, decent, proper, respectable ✧ appropriate, fitting The *correct* thing to do is to return the lost wallet to its rightful owner.

**correction** *noun* ✦ revision ✧ adjustment, amendment, improvement, remedy The editor made a few minor *corrections* before approving the story for publication.

**correspond** *verb* 1. ✦ agree, concur, fit, match ✧ accord, harmonize The newspaper article does not *correspond* with what I saw on the television news. 2. ✦ communicate (with), exchange letters (with), write (to), contact Duyen regularly *corresponds with* her friend in Japan.

**corridor** *noun* ✦ hall, hallway ✧ aisle, passage, passageway The director's office is at the end of the main *corridor*.

**corrode** *verb* ✦ eat away, erode, wear away ✧ rust, destroy Acid rain *corrodes* railroad tracks, stone buildings, statues, and much more.

**corrupt** *adjective* ✦ dishonest, crooked, immoral ✧ bad, evil, wicked The *corrupt* boxer accepted a bribe to lose the big fight. —*verb* ✦ degrade, warp, subvert ✧ contaminate, pollute, taint Some people fear that too much violence on television can *corrupt* a person's values.

**cost** *noun* 1. ✦ charge, expense, price ✧ amount, payment If you buy these sunglasses, the case will be included at no extra *cost*. 2. ✦ loss, sacrifice, toll ✧ damage, injury, penalty The general believed that the enemy had to be defeated at any *cost*.

**costume** *noun* ✦ attire, dress, outfit, apparel, clothing ✧ disguise Leather pants known as "lederhosen" are part of Bavaria's traditional folk *costume*.

## Word Groups

A **council** is a group of persons who are called together to discuss or decide something. **Council** is a very specific term with no true synonyms. Here are some related words to investigate in a dictionary: **assembly,** board, bureau, cabinet, caucus, committee, congress, jury, panel

**counsel** *noun* ✦ guidance, advice, recommendation, opinion ✧ suggestion The couple sought a priest's *counsel* before making their marriage plans. —*verb* ✦ advise, guide ✧ direct, recommend, instruct, suggest My university has several psychologists available to *counsel* students who are having problems.

**count** *verb* 1. ✦ add up, tally, total ✧ calculate, compute, figure The chaperone *counted* heads to make sure that everyone was present. 2. ✦ have worth, matter, signify ✧ consider, regard, concern The last basket didn't *count* because the shot was made after the buzzer went off. 3. ✦ depend, rely, plan, trust (in) Yujin said that we could *count on* her to help with the party decorations. —*noun* ✦ tally, calculation, computation ✧ sum, total, result By my *count*, there were twenty-three people at the meeting.

**counter** *adjective* ✦ opposing, opposite, contrary, the reverse (of) ✧ contradictory, different The used car dealer made me a *counter* offer. —*verb* ✦ oppose ✧ answer, respond, return, retort My friend *countered* my suggestion that we get a pizza by proposing hamburgers instead.

**counterfeit** *verb* ✦ forge, fake ✧ copy, reproduce, imitate Federal agents arrested the criminal who had been *counterfeiting* twenty-dollar bills. —*adjective* ✦ fake, forged, imitation, phony, false, fraudulent These *counterfeit* bills don't look very much like the real thing. —*noun* ✦ forgery, fake, imitation ✧ facsimile, reproduction, copy This stock certificate looks real, but it is a *counterfeit*.

**country** *noun* 1. ✦ nation, state ✧ domain, kingdom, realm Mexico and Canada are the two *countries* that share borders with the United States. 2. ✦ land, terrain, territory ✧ district, region, area California's vast Central Valley is good farming *country*. 3. ✦ countryside, rural area ✧ farmland, provinces, backcountry My dream is to someday own a house in the *country*.

**couple** *noun* ✦ duo, pair, twosome ✧ team Fourteen *couples* entered the dance contest. —*verb* ✦ attach, connect, fasten ✧ join, link, unite I helped my friend *couple* the trailer to the pickup truck.

**courage** *noun* ✦ bravery, gallantry, fearlessness, heroism, valor, mettle The firefighter showed great *courage* when she entered the burning building to rescue people who were trapped.

**courageous** *adjective* ✦ brave, fearless, gallant, heroic, valiant, intrepid The *courageous* boy climbed a tree to rescue his neighbor's cat.

**course** *noun* 1. ✦ chain, series, procession, sequence, order, progression The *course* of events that led up to the American Revolutionary War started at least a dozen years earlier. 2. ✦ direction, heading, bearing, path, route, track, way The ocean liner changed *course* to avoid running into an iceberg. 3. ✦ class, subject, seminar ✧ lecture, lesson Jimena is taking an English Learner's *course* at the university. —*verb* ✦ flow, run, stream ✧ gush, surge, race Tears were *coursing* down the woman's cheeks while she chopped the onion.

**courteous** *adjective* ✦ polite, civil, considerate, respectful, well-mannered, mannerly A *courteous* driver let me pull into the lane.

**Antonyms** **courteous**

*adjective* discourteous, disrespectful, ill-mannered, impolite, impudent, rude

**cover** *verb* 1. ✦ blanket, coat ✧ cloak, hide, layer, screen After the volcano erupted, a thick layer of ash *covered* the ground for miles around. 2. ✦ comprise, contain, include, embrace, occupy This cattle ranch *covers* more than 5,000 acres. 3. ✦ journey, pass over, travel, cross The backpackers *covered* ten miles on their first day of hiking. —*noun* 1. ✦ shelter, refuge, protection ✧ asylum, haven, concealment, screen The rabbit took *cover* under a bush. 2. ✦ lid, top ✧ cap, covering, stopper, crown Please put the *cover* on the kettle so the water will boil faster.

**covet** *verb* ✦ crave, desire, want, wish (for), long (for) ✧ envy I think my dog *covets* my peanut butter sandwich.

**cozy** *adjective* ✦ comfortable, snug, warm, pleasant ✧ easy, safe, secure We felt *cozy* in front of the fireplace as we listened to the sound of the wind and rain outside.

**crack** *verb* 1. ✦ snap ✧ bang, beat, slap, pop, smack The horses reared when the cowboy *cracked* his whip. 2. ✦ break, fracture, splinter, split ✧ rupture A passing car kicked up a piece of gravel that *cracked* our windshield. —*noun* 1. ✦ bang, blast, report ✧ burst, clap, pop, snap The deer ran for

cover when it heard the loud *crack* of a rifle. 2. ✦ gap, split, break, chink, crevice ✧ cleft, fissure, opening The boy peeked through a *crack* in the fence.

**craft** *noun* 1. ✦ ability, art, expertise, skill, talent The embroidery on this scarf was done with great *craft*. 2. ✦ handicraft, trade, job, occupation, profession, work Violin-making is a difficult *craft* to learn. 3. ✦ boat, ship, vessel, watercraft ✧ aircraft, airplane, plane The Coast Guard warned all small *craft* to stay in port during the storm.

**cram** *verb* ✦ jam, squeeze, stuff, load, pack ✧ force, compress Zhang Li *crammed* all her travel clothing into one suitcase.

**cramp** *noun* ✦ contraction, spasm, convulsion ✧ kink, twitch I awoke in the middle of the night with a *cramp* in my leg. —*verb* ✦ contract, convulse ✧ tighten, stiffen Runners typically stretch before a race to keep their muscles from *cramping*.

**cranky** *adjective* ✦ cross, grouchy, grumpy, irritable, peevish, testy My little brother gets *cranky* if he doesn't take an afternoon nap.

**crash** *verb* ✦ smash (into), collide (with), hit, bump (against), strike The car *crashed into* a tree. —*noun* 1. ✦ bang, slam, smash ✧ clatter, racket, din I accidentally dropped a bowling ball, and it hit the floor with a loud *crash*. 2. ✦ smashup, wreck, accident, smash ✧ collision, impact The pilot parachuted to safety, but the plane was destroyed in the *crash*.

**crave** *verb* ✦ covet, desire, hunger (for), long (for), want, yearn (for) After eating freeze-dried foods for two weeks, the backpackers *craved* fresh fruits and vegetables.

**crawl** *verb* ✦ creep, inch ✧ drag, slither, wriggle, writhe I watched a snail *crawl* across the patio. —*noun* ✦ creep, snail's pace ✧ plod, walk, trudge Traffic slowed to a *crawl* during rush hour.

**crazy** *adjective* 1. ✦ absurd, dumb, foolish, silly, stupid Most people would say that believing the Earth is flat is a *crazy* notion. 2. ✦ enthusiastic, excited, passionate, wild, mad ✧ ardent I'm *crazy* about rap music.

**crease** *noun* ✦ fold, wrinkle, rumple ✧ line, pleat I ironed the *creases* out of my new shirt. —*verb* ✦ fold ✧ bend, crinkle, pleat, wrinkle It's easier to tear a piece of paper in half if you *crease* it first.

**create** *verb* ✦ generate, make, produce, start ✧ design, devise, invent The new factory is expected to *create* a lot of jobs.

**creation** *noun* 1. ✦ making, production, formation ✧ development, establishment, generation The *creation* of a seven-layer cake can take many hours from start to finish. 2. ✦ product, work, achievement ✧ invention, masterpiece The artist's latest *creation* is a marble sculpture of a bird in flight.

**creative** *adjective* ✦ ingenious, imaginative, inventive, innovative ✧ resourceful The fantasy novelist was known for her *creative* plots.

**creature** *noun* ✦ animal, beast, being ✧ organism, person Unicorns are mythical *creatures* revered for their beauty and grace.

**credit** *noun* ✦ acknowledgement, recognition, praise, acclaim ✧ honor The manager gave the staff all the *credit* for the work being done so well.

**creed** *noun* ✦ belief, faith ✧ doctrine, principle, teaching In the United States, employers cannot discriminate on the basis of race, color, or religious *creed*.

**creek** *noun* ✦ brook ✧ rill, stream, streamlet, spring The cattle get fresh water from a *creek* that runs through the ranch.

**creep** *verb* ✦ crawl, slink, slip, steal ✧ sneak, inch, slide The lion *crept* silently toward its prey.

**crest** *noun* ✦ summit, top, tip, peak, crown Lynn climbed to the *crest* of a hill to get a better view of the skyline.

**crew** *noun* ✦ group, gang, band, company, team ✧ staff My friends and I joined the *crew* that was cleaning up the lake shore.

**crime** *noun* 1. ✦ offense, violation ✧ felony, misdemeanor, infraction Shoplifting is a *crime*. 2. ✦ outrage, shame ✧ sin, wrong, wrongdoing, vice It would be a *crime* to throw away these old clothes when there are so many people who could use them.

**criminal** *noun* ✦ crook, felon, lawbreaker ✧ gangster, outlaw Police are searching for the *criminal* who robbed the local convenience store. —*adjective* ✦ illegal, unlawful, illicit, lawless ✧ dishonest, wrong Stealing a car is a *criminal* act.

**cringe** *verb* ✦ cower, flinch, recoil ✧ start, tremble, shy I *cringe* every time I hear the doctor say, "This won't hurt."

**cripple** *verb* ✦ disable, paralyze, immobilize, damage ✧ hurt, injure, weaken A heavy snowstorm *crippled* the city's transportation system.

**crisis** *noun* ✦ emergency ✧ predicament, problem, trouble, catastrophe There was a financial *crisis* when the county government ran out of money.

**critical** *adjective* 1. ✦ disapproving, condemning ✧ judgmental The librarian was *critical* of the plan to save money by ordering fewer books. 2. ✦ grave, serious, severe, dangerous, desperate, acute We experienced a *critical* shortage of water during last year's drought.

**criticize** *verb* ✦ evaluate, judge, review ✧ attack, condemn, denounce How can you *criticize* that movie when you haven't seen it?

**crook** *noun* ✦ cheat, swindler, criminal, thief ✧ scoundrel, villain That *crook* is trying to sell fake lottery tickets.

**crop** *noun* ✦ harvest, yield ✧ growth, produce, production Farmers are expecting a good *crop* of rice this year. —*verb* ✦ clip, cut, shear, trim ✧ mow, prune The barber *cropped* your hair pretty short.

**cross** *noun* ✦ crossbreed, hybrid ✧ blend, combination, mixture Alexandra's dog is a *cross* between a golden retriever and a Siberian husky. —*verb* 1. ✦ move across, transit, travel over, traverse ✧ pass An airplane can *cross* the United States in about five hours. 2. ✦ intersect, join, meet, converge ✧ connect, crisscross The intersection where the two busy streets *cross* would be a good place to build a gas station. —*adjective* ✦ angry, annoyed, mad ✧ grouchy, grumpy, irritable When the man was late to work several days in a row, his supervisor was *cross* with him.

**crouch** *verb* ✦ squat, stoop ✧ bend, hunch, kneel, huddle The tall man had to *crouch* to get under the railing.

**crowd** *noun* ✦ mob, flock, horde, multitude, swarm, throng A *crowd* of people gathered to watch the parade. —*verb* ✦ cluster around, flock around, gather around, mob, swarm, throng Fans *crowded around* the television star, trying to get his autograph.

**crude** *adjective* 1. ✦ makeshift, primitive, simple, rough, coarse ✧ unfinished When we first moved into our apartment, we used *crude* furniture made from old boards and packing crates. 2. ✦ impolite, rude, crass, tasteless, uncivilized My grandmother says that she will not tolerate *crude* behavior at her dinner table.

**cruel** *adjective* ✦ brutal, mean, ruthless, harsh, heartless, unkind I believe that people should never be *cruel* to animals.

---

**Antonyms** cruel

*adjective* compassionate, forgiving, gentle, kind, soft, softhearted, tender

---

**cruise** *verb* ✦ navigate, sail, voyage, boat, travel ✧ roam, wander We *cruised* out to Catalina Island in our neighbor's sailboat. —*noun* ✦ boat trip, sail, voyage ✧ jaunt, passage More people take *cruises* to the Caribbean than anywhere else in the world.

**crumble** *verb* ✦ break, pulverize, crunch, crush, mash ✧ grind I like to *crumble* my crackers before putting them in my soup.

**crumple** *verb* 1. ✦ wrinkle, rumple, crease, crinkle, crimp I *crumpled* my clothes when I packed my suitcase carelessly. 2. ✦ buckle, collapse, cave in, fall, topple, tumble Heavy snow made my tent *crumple*.

**crush** *verb* 1. ✦ squash, mash, compress, press, squeeze ✧ trample I always *crush* my soda cans before recycling them. 2. ✦ subdue, suppress, extinguish, quench ✧ defeat, destroy, overwhelm, vanquish The dictator tried to *crush* all opposition.

**cry** *verb* 1. ✦ shed tears, sob, weep ✧ wail, bawl If weddings are happy occasions, why do so many people *cry* at them? 2. ✦ call, shout, yell, bellow ✧ bawl, scream Sakura *cried* out a warning when she saw the car come around the corner too fast. —*noun* ✦ exclamation, call, scream, shout, yell The woman gave a *cry* of delight when she saw her long-lost brother.

**cuddle** *verb* ✦ snuggle, nuzzle, nestle ✧ embrace, hug, pet Olivia likes to *cuddle* with her cat.

**culprit** *noun* ✦ guilty party, offender, wrongdoer ✧ criminal, lawbreaker, outlaw, convict The police arrested several suspects, but the real *culprit* was never found.

**cultivate** *verb* 1. ✦ grow, raise ✧ farm, plant, till, breed The French are famous for *cultivating* fine grapes. 2. ✦ nourish, nurture, foster ✧ develop, improve, promote Reading can help to *cultivate* your mind.

**culture** *noun* ✦ civilization, society, customs ✧ lifestyle, cultivation, refinement The *culture* of ancient Greece evolved over hundreds of years.

**cunning** *adjective* ✦ clever, crafty, shrewd, sly, tricky The *cunning* spy avoided being captured.

**cure** *noun* ✦ remedy ✧ therapy, treatment, medicine, relief Medical researchers have yet to find a *cure* for the common cold. —*verb* ✦ heal, remedy, relieve ✧ help, improve These aspirin should *cure* your headache.

**curious** *adjective* 1. ✦ inquisitive, interested (in) ✧ inquiring, questioning My ESL class was *curious* about our new teacher. 2. ✦ peculiar, odd, remarkable, strange, unusual, weird The pack rat has the *curious* habit of stealing a shiny object and leaving a stone or twig in its place.

**currency** *noun* ✦ money, cash, legal tender ✧ bills, coins When we traveled to Mexico, we had to exchange our US dollars for Mexican *currency*.

**current** *adjective* ✦ latest, new, up-to-date, contemporary ✧ modern, present I went to a newsstand to get the *current* issue of my favorite magazine. —*noun* ✦ flow, draft ✧ course, stream, tide Many birds use air *currents* to glide across the sky.

**currently** *adverb* ✦ at present, now, presently ✧ today There are *currently* twenty-three students in my ESL class.

**curse** *noun* 1. ✦ hex, oath, spell ✧ jinx, charm A witch doctor tried to convince tourists that his amulet would ward off evil *curses*. 2. ✦ scourge, bane, affliction, evil, ill, woe Pollution and overcrowding are two *curses* of modern civilization. —*verb* 1. ✦ afflict, plague, torment, torture, trouble, burden The unfortunate man seems to be *cursed* with an incredible run of bad luck. 2. ✦ revile, condemn, denounce ✧ swear (at) The farmer *cursed* the tornado that destroyed his barn and ruined his crops.

**curve** *noun* ✦ bend, turn, twist, arc, crook, bow There are a lot of dangerous *curves* in the road ahead. —*verb* ✦ bend, swerve, turn, twist, wind The trail *curves* around the base of that hill.

**cushion** *noun* ✧ pillow, mat, pad, padding Our couch needs new *cushions*. —*verb* ✦ soften, dampen, deaden, lessen, suppress The thick carpet *cushioned* my fall from the chair.

**custody** *noun* ✦ guardianship, care, charge, keeping, supervision The court granted sole *custody* of the children to their mother.

**custom** *noun* ✦ rite, ritual, practice, rule, tradition ✧ habit, routine Many Jews observe the *custom* of not eating or drinking on the day of Yom Kippur.

**customary** *adjective* ✦ common, normal, routine, standard, traditional, usual In the United States, it is *customary* to leave a tip when dining in a restaurant.

**customer** *noun* ✦ buyer, consumer, shopper, patron ✧ client The department store was swamped with *customers* on the day of its big back-to-school sale.

**cut** *verb* 1. ✦ slice, carve ✧ incise, chop, pierce, sever, slit Please use this knife to *cut* the melon. 2. ✦ clip, snip, trim, crop ✧ mow, prune, shorten The barber *cuts* my hair with clippers. 3. ✦ halt, interrupt, stop ✧ end, quit, cease The driver *cut* the engine and allowed his car to coast to a stop. 4. ✦ decrease, lower, reduce, lessen, curtail ✧ remove The candidate promised to *cut* taxes. —*noun* 1. ✦ laceration ✧ gash, slash, wound The doctor said that my *cut* would not require stitches. 2. ✦ cutback, decrease, reduction, slash ✧ decline, fall Because of recent *cuts* in the state budget, no new highways will be built this year.

**cute** *adjective* ✦ adorable, attractive, charming, pretty ✧ beautiful The baby looks *cute* in her new Easter dress.

**cycle** *noun* ✦ chain, course, period, phase, sequence, series A caterpillar is just one stage in the life *cycle* of a butterfly or moth.

# D

**dab** *verb* ✦ daub, smear, wipe, swab, pat, slap Rafaela *dabbed* some grease on the bicycle chain. —*noun* ✦ bit, drop, touch ✧ speck, pat, daub Nikki put on a *dab* of perfume.

**dabble** *verb* ✦ putter, tinker, trifle ✧ play, toy Wyatt does not *dabble* in poetry; he takes it very seriously.

**dainty** *adjective* 1. ✦ delicate, fine ✧ exquisite, elegant, pretty Ballet slippers look *dainty*, but in fact they are very sturdy and strong. 2. ✦ choosy, picky, finicky, fussy, particular ✧ discriminating You're such a *dainty* eater that I never know what to cook for you.

**damage** *noun* ✦ destruction, harm, hurt, injury ✧ loss, wreckage A hailstorm did serious *damage* to the lilies in our garden. —*verb* ✦ harm, hurt, impair, injure ✧ ravage, wreck, ruin I had to return my new lamp because it was *damaged* in shipment.

**damp** *adjective* ✦ moist, wet ✧ clammy, dripping, soaked, soggy After soccer practice, my shirt was *damp* with perspiration.

**dance** *verb* ✦ frolic, gambol, prance, skip, cavort ✧ jiggle, shake, sway My dog *dances* with joy whenever I ask him if he wants to go for a walk. —*noun* ✧ ball, formal, party, prom, hop, social Are you going to the *dance* next Saturday?

**danger** *noun* ✦ in peril, at risk, in jeopardy ✧ hazard, threat The officer put her own life *in danger* when she rescued the driver from the burning car.

**dangerous** *adjective* ✦ hazardous, perilous, risky, unsafe ✧ chancy, precarious Riding a bicycle at night can be *dangerous*.

**dangle** *verb* ✦ hang, suspend, swing ✧ droop, sag, sling Jung *dangled* a toy mouse in front of her cat.

**dare** *verb* 1. ✦ challenge, defy, goad, provoke, taunt My friend *dared* me to ski down the steep hill. 2. ✦ venture, brave, risk ✧ attempt, face, gamble The explorer *dared* to journey into unknown and uncharted territory. —*noun* ✦ challenge, provocation, taunt ✧ bet I accepted my boyfriend's *dare* to jump from the highest diving board.

**daring** *adjective* ✦ bold, brave, courageous, gallant, fearless, intrepid The band of warriors made a *daring* attack against their enemy. — *noun* ✦ boldness, bravery, courage, nerve, valor, mettle The spy was told that the mission would require great skill and *daring*.

<hr>

**Antonyms** daring

*adjective* afraid, anxious, cowardly, fearful, nervous, scared, shy, timid
*noun* anxiety, cowardice, fear, nervousness, shyness, timidity

<hr>

**dark** *adjective* 1. ✦unlit, dim, murky ✧ black, gloomy, inky, sunless I could barely see my way along the *dark* hallway. 2. ✧ black, charcoal, brown, dusky, tan Some Arctic animals have *dark* coats in summer that turn white in the winter. —*noun* 1. ✦ darkness, blackness, dimness, murk ✧ gloom, gloominess When the lights went out, I groped around in the *dark* to find a flashlight. 2. ✦ dusk, evening, twilight, night, nightfall, nighttime I have to be home by *dark* because my motorbike's headlight is broken.

**darling** *noun* ✦ beloved, dear, precious, sweetheart, pet ✧ favorite After all these years, Grandmother still calls me her *darling*. —*adjective* 1. ✦ beloved, cherished, dear, dearest, loved, treasured ✧ favorite, precious This is Tinkerbelle, my *darling* cat. 2. ✦ adorable, cute, enchanting, charming, sweet You look *darling* in your new Easter dress.

**dart** *verb* ✦ bolt, dash, hurry, race, run, scurry, zip I caught a glimpse of a mouse as it *darted* under the sofa.

**dash** *verb* 1. ✦ bolt, race, run, rush, speed, sprint, dart, hurry Li Min *dashed* across the finish line to win the race. 2. ✦ fling, hurl, knock, slam, smash, throw, heave A large wave *dashed* a rowboat against the pier. —*noun* 1. ✦ bolt, run, rush, sprint, dart ✧ beeline The rabbit made a *dash* for safety when it saw a fox. 2. ✦ bit, pinch, touch, trace, hint ✧ drop The soup tasted bland, so I added a *dash* of pepper.

**data** *noun* ✦ information, facts, figures, statistics ✧

evidence, details The scientist collected a mass of *data* to prove the theory.

**date** *noun* 1. ✧ day, time, hour, month, year The *date* of the first crewed spaceflight was April 12, 1961. 2. ✦ appointment, engagement ✧ meeting, rendezvous, commitment Takumi made a *date* to see his counselor next Friday. 3. ✦ companion, partner, escort ✧ boyfriend, girlfriend My friend and her *date* went to dinner and a movie.

**dawn** *noun* 1. ✦ daybreak, sunrise, sunup, first light ✧ daylight, morning, twilight I have to get up before *dawn* to get to swimming practice on time. 2. ✦ arrival, beginning, birth, commencement, onset, origin, start The invention of the steam engine marked the *dawn* of the Industrial Age.

**day** *noun* 1. ✦ daytime ✧ daylight, sunlight, sunshine Most owls sleep during the *day* and hunt for food at night. 2. ✦ age, epoch, era, period, time ✧ generation In my great-grandfather's *day*, people did not have televisions.

**daze** *verb* ✦ stun, stupefy, disorient, bewilder, confuse ✧ numb, shock A blow on the head momentarily *dazed* the soccer player. —*noun* ✦ stupor, trance, haze, muddle ✧ confusion, astonishment, bewilderment I was in a *daze* after staying up all night working on my thesis.

**dead** *adjective* 1. ✦ deceased, expired, lifeless, perished ✧ departed, late There were *dead* bugs floating in the pond. 2. ✦ spent, finished, inoperative, worn out, exhausted, inactive ✧ useless My flashlight won't work because the batteries are *dead*. 3. ✦ absolute, complete, entire, total, utter There was *dead* silence in the room when our manager announced the company would be closing. —*adverb* 1. ✦ absolutely, completely, entirely, thoroughly, totally, altogether My neighbor is *dead* certain that she saw a ghost in her apartment. 2. ✦ directly, due, right, straight ✧ exactly, precisely The lookout gave a cry of warning when he saw another ship *dead* ahead.

**deadly** *adjective* ✦ fatal, lethal, mortal ✧ destructive, harmful, malignant In the fourteenth century, a *deadly* plague killed almost half the population of Europe.

**deal** *verb* 1. ✦ concern, have to do (with), involve, consider, treat Geology *deals with* the history of the earth. 2. ✦ buy and sell, sell, market, trade (in) ✧ traffic, peddle This store *deals in* both new and used books. 3. ✦ allot, give (out), hand (out), dis-

tribute, dispense ✧ administer, deliver The store manager *dealt out* the weekly work assignments. 4. ✦ cope (with), contend (with), handle, manage ✧ control I might need some help *dealing with* this problem. —*noun* ✦ agreement, arrangement, bargain, contract ✧ understanding I made a *deal* with my boss to get a day off if I could get my work done early.

**death** *noun* ✦ dying, passing, demise ✧ loss, departure, end, extinction We were saddened by the *death* of our grandfather.

**debate** *noun* ✦ discussion ✧ argument, disagreement, dispute, quarrel The candidates held a *debate* on television. —*verb* ✦ deliberate, discuss ✧ argue, dispute, quarrel The city council *debated* for several weeks before finally voting the new tax into law.

**debt** *noun* ✦ liability, obligation, debit ✧ bill, claim, dues I borrowed the money for my new motorbike, and I plan to pay off my *debt* as quickly as possible.

**decay** *noun* 1. ✦ decomposition, rot ✧ corrosion, spoilage The main cause of tooth *decay* is bacteria. 2. ✦ collapse, dilapidation, ruin ✧ decline, deterioration The old barn was in a state of *decay*. —*verb* ✦ break down, decompose, rot ✧ disintegrate, spoil, corrode The fallen leaves and twigs *decayed* into soil.

**deceive** *verb* ✦ fool, mislead, trick, bluff, dupe ✧ betray, cheat An opossum sometimes *deceives* predators by pretending to be dead.

**decent** *adjective* 1. ✦ appropriate, proper, right, seemly, suitable, fit ✧ respectable, virtuous The *decent* thing to do is to apologize to your friend for missing the party. 2. ✦ considerate, generous, kind, nice, thoughtful It was *decent* of Janine to offer to give you help with your work load. 3. ✦ adequate, fair, passable, reasonable, satisfactory ✧ mediocre, ordinary The meals at this restaurant aren't too good, but they make a *decent* dessert.

**decide** *verb* 1. ✦ conclude, determine, resolve ✧ establish, choose, select I *decided* that one ride on the giant roller coaster was enough for me. 2. ✦ rule, judge, settle ✧ decree The jury *decided* in favor of the defendant.

**decision** *noun* ✦ conclusion, judgment, selection, choice ✧ resolution, ruling, verdict The judges of the poetry contest are ready to announce their *decision*.

**decisive** *adjective* 1. ✦ conclusive, definite, significant ✧ deciding, convincing The winning candidate defeated his opponent by a *decisive* margin. 2. ✦ determined, firm, resolute ✧ assured, positive The *decisive* manager responded without hesitation to the emergency.

**declare** *verb* 1. ✦ affirm, assert, claim, say, state ✧ swear The witness *declared* that she was telling the truth. 2. ✦ announce, decree, proclaim, pronounce, rule The governor *declared* a state of emergency after the earthquake.

**decline** *verb* 1. ✦ refuse, reject, turn down ✧ deny, spurn, dismiss My friend *declined* my invitation to go to a movie. 2. ✦ decrease, diminish, wane, deteriorate, lessen, subside ✧ sink, weaken We're worried about my grandfather because his health continues to *decline*. —*noun* ✦ decrease, reduction, slump, downturn, drop, dip ✧ wane There has been a *decline* in the demand for watches since the introduction of smartphones.

**decorate** *verb* ✦ adorn, ornament, trim, dress ✧ beautify, fix up We *decorated* our Christmas tree with red and white lights.

**decrease** *verb* ✦ reduce, lower, lessen, diminish ✧ drop, dwindle My doctor advised me to *decrease* the amount of fat in my diet. —*noun* ✦ decline, drop, reduction, slump, cutback ✧ loss There has been a *decrease* in the sales of both white and wheat bread because people are becoming more health conscious.

**decree** *noun* ✦ mandate, proclamation, declaration, law, order, command ✧ decision The dictator issued a *decree* that made his birthday a national holiday. —*verb* ✦ mandate, proclaim, command, order, rule ✧ announce, decide In 1574, England's Queen Elizabeth *decreed* that only royalty could wear purple clothing.

**dedicate** *verb* ✦ devote, commit, give ✧ present, apply, pledge, surrender Mother Teresa *dedicated* her life to helping poor and needy people.

**deduct** *verb* ✦ remove, subtract, take, take off ✧ withdraw, eliminate My employer *deducts* taxes from my weekly paycheck.

**deed** *noun* ✦ act, action, exploit, feat ✧ accomplishment, achievement Sir Lancelot is a legendary knight known for his heroic *deeds*.

**deep** *adjective* 1. ✧ cavernous, low, yawning, bottomless The pirates buried their treasure in a *deep* hole. 2. ✦ great, intense, powerful, profound, strong, sincere Chelsea has a *deep* respect for people who volunteer their time to help others. 3. ✦ absorbed, engrossed, lost ✧ occupied, preoccupied Whenever I'm *deep* in thought, I don't hear what's going on around me. 4. ✦ profound, complex, difficult, obscure ✧ mysterious, subtle My intellectual friend likes to discuss *deep* subjects, such as philosophy and religion.

**defeat** *verb* ✦ beat, overcome, vanquish, conquer ✧ crush, rout, triumph The United States achieved independence by *defeating* England in the Revolutionary War. —*noun* ✦ loss, failure, beating ✧ downfall, rout, upset My favorite football team has suffered three *defeats* in the first five games of the season.

**Antonyms** **defeat**
*noun* conquest, success, supremacy, triumph, victory

**defect** *noun* ✦ fault, flaw, imperfection, blemish, shortcoming ✧ weakness This diamond didn't cost very much because it has a *defect*.

**defective** *adjective* ✦ faulty, flawed, imperfect ✧ broken, impaired, incomplete Our new TV was *defective*, so we returned it.

**defend** *verb* 1. ✦ guard, protect, safeguard, secure ✧ preserve, shield The commander called for reinforcements to help *defend* the fort. 2. ✦ support, sustain, uphold, maintain ✧ champion, endorse The scientist used facts and figures to *defend* the new theory.

**defense** *noun* ✦ protection, safeguard, guard, shield ✧ security, preservation The best *defense* against cavities is to brush your teeth after every meal.

**defer** *verb* ✦ delay, postpone, put off, stall, suspend ✧ wait I *deferred* making my decision about which college to attend until I knew where my friends were going.

**defiance** *noun* ✦ disobedience, resistance, rebellion ✧ opposition The antiwar protesters were arrested for their *defiance* of a police order to disperse.

**deficiency** *noun* ✦ lack, scarcity, shortage ✧ inadequacy, need, deficit If you drink a lot of milk, you are unlikely to have a calcium *deficiency*.

**define** *verb* ✦ characterize, describe, explain, interpret, name I believe that a person's essence is *defined* by what they do, not what they say.

**definite** *adjective* ✦ certain, positive, sure, unqualified, clear ✧ absolute, exact, precise Instead of saying "maybe," I wish you would give me a *definite* "yes" or "no."

**definition** *noun* ✦ meaning ✧ description, explanation, interpretation, sense If you don't know what a word means, you can look up its *definition* in a dictionary.

**deform** *verb* ✦ distort, contort, disfigure ✧ twist, mar, damage Is it true that you can *deform* your spine by slouching too much?

**defy** *verb* 1. ✦ challenge, dare ✧ summon, brave, confront, face The bull pawed the ground and snorted, *defying* the matador to move closer. 2. ✦ disobey, oppose, resist, disregard ✧ rebel, ignore, withstand. During the 1920s, many Americans *defied* the constitutional ban on the production and sale of alcoholic beverages.

**degrade** *verb* ✦ demean, disgrace, dishonor, shame, lower ✧ cheapen Nicole refused to *degrade* herself by cheating, even though she had a perfect opportunity.

**degree** *noun* 1. ✦ level, measure, order, grade ✧ class, phase, stage, step Maylin's gymnastic routine has a high *degree* of difficulty. 2. ✦ amount, extent, quantity ✧ range, scope There is a certain *degree* of truth in what he said, but it's not the whole story.

**dejected** *adjective* ✦ depressed, gloomy, sad, unhappy ✧ discouraged, down The *dejected* woman did her best to try to look cheerful.

**delay** *verb* 1. ✦ postpone, put off, defer ✧ interrupt, suspend, stay The movie's release was *delayed* due to production problems. 2. ✦ detain, hold up, impede, slow, hinder ✧ obstruct, retard The bus was *delayed* by heavy traffic. —*noun* ✦ postponement, holdup, wait, pause ✧ lag, stop The pilot announced that there would be a half-hour *delay* before takeoff.

**delegate** *noun* ✦ agent, representative, deputy, appointee ✧ ambassador, envoy Each local club sent a *delegate* to the national conference. —*verb* ✦ appoint, assign, designate, name ✧ commission, nominate The manager *delegated* the assistant to train the new employees.

**deliberate** *adjective* ✦ intentional, willful ✧ careful, planned, thoughtful The man pretended to be joking, but he was actually making a *deliberate* insult. —*verb* ✦ confer, consult, debate, discuss, consider ✧ reflect, study The jury *deliberated* for several days before reaching a verdict.

**deliberately** *adverb* ✦ consciously, intentionally, knowingly, purposely, on purpose, willfully The swindler *deliberately* misled his victims.

**delicate** *adjective* 1. ✦ dainty, exquisite, fine ✧ elegant, refined, nice The child in the painting has *delicate* features. 2. ✦ demanding, tricky, exacting, sensitive, touchy, difficult Repairing a watch is a *delicate* task. 3. ✦ breakable, fragile ✧ frail, weak, brittle, flimsy Eggs break easily because their shells are *delicate*.

**delicious** *adjective* ✦ delectable, appetizing, savory, tasty, tasteful ✧ good Those strawberries look *delicious*.

**delight** *noun* ✦ gladness, happiness, joy, pleasure, rapture, bliss ✧ enjoyment Francisco was filled with *delight* when he received a new smartphone. —*verb* ✦ gladden, cheer, please, thrill ✧ enchant, gratify, excite Nothing *delights* me more than going shopping with my friends.

**delightful** *adjective* ✦ enjoyable, happy, pleasant, pleasing, pleasurable, charming Rachel and her friends had a *delightful* day at the beach.

**deliver** *verb* 1. ✦ bring, carry, convey, ship, transport, bear ✧ provide, supply Your order will be *delivered* to your apartment. 2. ✦ administer, deal, give, inflict ✧ hurl, launch, throw The winning boxer *delivered* a knockout punch to his opponent. 3. ✦ give, present, proclaim ✧ communicate, say, speak The new president will *deliver* his inaugural address tomorrow. 4. ✦ save, free, liberate, release, rescue The hostages never lost hope of being *delivered* from their captors.

**demand** *verb* 1. ✦ insist on, appeal for ✧ claim, order, request, seek The workers *demanded* a raise in pay. 2. ✦ call for, need, require, compel ✧ necessitate, beg This problem is so serious that it *demands* our immediate attention. —*noun* 1. ✦ appeal, call ✧ command, order, request, bid The players tried their best to meet the coach's *demand* for better teamwork. 2. ✦ need, interest (in), market ✧ requirement, want, desire There isn't much *demand* for hot chocolate in the middle of summer.

**demolish** *verb* ✦ destroy, ruin, wreck, devastate,

level ✧ **smash, tear down** A tornado *demolished* the farmer's barn.

**demon** *noun* ✦ **evil spirit, devil, fiend** ✧ **beast, monster, ghoul** An exorcist is someone who supposedly can drive away *demons*.

**demonstrate** *verb* 1. ✦ **show, exhibit, display** ✧ **describe, explain, illustrate, teach** My personal trainer *demonstrated* the proper way to do a pull-up. 2. ✦ **march, protest, rally** ✧ **parade, picket, strike** Thousands of people *demonstrated* against the war.

**demonstration** *noun* 1. ✦ **presentation, show, display** ✧ **explanation, illustration, lesson** A salesperson gave us a *demonstration* of how the digital camera works. 2. ✦ **march, protest, rally** ✧ **meeting, sit-in, strike** Martin Luther King Jr. led numerous peaceful *demonstrations* in support of the American civil rights movement.

**den** *noun* ✦ **lair** ✧ **nest, retreat, shelter, cave, hideaway** A wolf's *den* is usually an underground burrow.

**denote** *verb* ✦ **designate, indicate, mean, signify, symbolize** ✧ **point out, show** A skull and crossbones on a sign usually *denotes* danger.

**denounce** *verb* ✦ **condemn, criticize, deplore, disapprove (of)** ✧ **assail, attack, curse** The preacher strongly *denounced* the use of illegal drugs.

**dense** *adjective* ✦ **thick, tight, compact, solid** ✧ **crowded, heavy, packed, close** The rabbit ran into a *dense* thicket just in time to escape from the hungry coyote.

**Antonyms** dense

*adjective* **meager, scanty, scattered, sparse, thin**

**deny** *verb* 1. ✦ **dispute, contradict, refute** ✧ **disagree, protest** The suspect *denied* that he had committed the crime. 2. ✦ **forbid, refuse, disallow, reject, veto** ✧ **withhold, oppose** US Immigration has the right to *deny* entry to anyone who is considered a threat to national security.

**depart** *verb* ✦ **go, leave, move out** ✧ **embark, exit, withdraw** My bus *departs* at three o'clock.

**department** *noun* ✦ **area, division, section** ✧ **branch, bureau, unit, quarter** The store was so large I had to ask a clerk for directions to the clothing *department*.

**departure** *noun* ✦ **going, leaving** ✧ **exit, start,** **withdrawal** Our *departure* will be delayed because the airport has been closed by fog.

**depend** *verb* 1. ✦ **hang, hinge, rest, be subject (to)** Whether or not I go to the movie *depends on* how much studying I get done. 2. ✦ **count (on), rely (on), trust** ✧ **believe (in)** Pets *depend on* their owners for food and shelter.

**dependable** *adjective* ✦ **faithful, reliable, responsible, trustworthy, trusty, steadfast** A *dependable* friend is someone who will always be there in time of need.

**depict** *verb* ✦ **picture, portray, show, tell, describe, relate** ✧ **represent** This film *depicts* the life of American President George Washington.

**deposit** *verb* ✦ **place, put, put down, set, leave, drop** ✧ **accumulate** The wind *deposited* a pile of leaves on our doorstep. —*noun* 1. ✦ **assets, cash, money** ✧ **savings** As part of my visa application, I had to show all the *deposits* in my bank account. 2. ✦ **down payment, installment** ✧ **pledge, security, retainer** I had to leave a *deposit* in order to rent the apartment. 3. ✦ **lode, vein** ✧ **accumulation, layer, sediment** The miner was excited when he found a large *deposit* of silver.

**depress** *verb* 1. ✦ **deject, discourage, dishearten, sadden, weary, oppress** Long spells of rainy weather always seem to *depress* me. 2. ✦ **press, push** ✧ **flatten, lower, thrust, drop** *Depress* the Escape key to take you back to the main menu.

**depression** *noun* 1. ✦ **dejection, despair, melancholy, sadness, gloom, despondency** The university has counselors to help students suffering with *depression*. 2. ✦ **cavity, hole, hollow, indentation, basin** ✧ **dent** When I turned the rock over, I found that the *depression* underneath was full of ants. 3. ✦ **recession, slump, economic decline** ✧ **crash, downturn** Many people lost their jobs during the worldwide *depression* of the 1930s.

**deprive** *verb* ✦ **rob, strip, divest** ✧ **deny, refuse, withhold** Don't let your worries *deprive* you of sleep.

**derelict** *adjective* ✦ **abandoned, deserted, neglected, dilapidated** ✧ **forgotten, forsaken, rundown** The *derelict* shipwreck has long been part of the local seascape.

**derive** *verb* ✦ **draw, gain, get, obtain, receive, take, secure** Haley *derives* a lot of satisfaction from helping other people.

**descend** *verb* 1. ✦ come down, drop, fall, sink ✧ dip, plunge The parachutist *descended* slowly to the ground. 2. ✦ come ✧ derive, issue, originate, spring My friend Sawa *is descended* from Miwok Indian ancestors.

### Word Groups

A **descendant** is a person who is related to a particular ancestor. **Descendant** is a very specific term with no true synonyms. Here are some related words to investigate in a dictionary: **child, grandchild, heir, kin, offspring, progeny**

**descent** *noun* 1. ✦ decline, drop ✧ dip, dive, fall We stood on our balcony and watched the sun's *descent* toward the horizon. 2. ✦ ancestry, heritage, lineage, origin, parentage, birth Afshin is of Iranian *descent*.

**describe** *verb* ✦ recount, relate, tell (about), narrate ✧ depict, recite, report Sofia *described* her trip to Hawaii in vivid detail.

**description** *noun* ✦ depiction, portrayal, representation ✧ account, report, statement I recognized the wombat at the zoo from its *description* in my book about Australia.

**desert** *verb* ✦ abandon, forsake, give up, leave, quit, vacate The birds *deserted* their nest when they flew south for the winter.

**deserve** *verb* ✦ earn, merit, rate, warrant, qualify ✧ gain, win Diego has been working so hard he feels like he *deserves* a raise.

**design** *noun* ✦ pattern, plan, diagram ✧ blueprint, drawing, sketch This *design* shows how to build your own kite at home. —*verb* ✦ devise, plan, conceive ✧ create, fashion, invent The family hired an architect to *design* their new home.

**designate** *verb* 1. ✦ indicate, mark, point out, show, specify, identify Brenda tied balloons to a telephone pole to *designate* where her party was being held. 2. ✦ appoint, name, select, choose, pick ✧ elect, nominate My boss *designated* me to represent our company at the conference.

**desirable** *adjective* ✦ agreeable, attractive, good, pleasing, nice ✧ beneficial, worthwhile Many people believe that small towns are *desirable* places to live.

**desire** *noun* ✦ wish, want, longing, yearning ✧ ambition, craving, goal, hunger My *desire* is for the world to live in peace. —*verb* ✦want, wish, covet, crave, long, yearn Many university students *desire* to study abroad.

**despair** *noun* ✦ dismay, desperation, hopelessness, discouragement, distress We looked at each other in *despair* as we realized that we were lost. —*verb* ✦ give up hope, lose hope ✧ resign, quit, surrender The shipwrecked sailors *despaired* of ever reaching shore safely.

**desperate** *adjective* 1. ✦ frantic, frenzied, mad, urgent ✧ drastic, intense I got up late and made a *desperate* attempt to get to work on time. 2. ✦ bold, daring, rash, reckless, risky ✧ hopeless, dangerous The convict hatched a *desperate* scheme to escape from prison.

**despise** *verb* ✦ detest, dislike, hate, loathe ✧ scorn, disdain I *despise* people who mistreat their pets.

**destination** *noun* ✦ stop, stopping place ✧ station, terminal, end, goal This plane will make two stops before it reaches its final *destination*.

**destroy** *verb* ✦ annihilate, demolish, devastate, ruin, wreck, level, raze In this movie, a giant lizard *destroys* much of downtown Tokyo.

**destruction** *noun* ✦ devastation, ruin, wreckage, havoc, damage ✧ loss The hurricane caused widespread *destruction*.

**detach** *verb* ✦ remove, take off, disconnect, unfasten ✧ disassemble, separate, free If you want to get your bike into the car's trunk, you'll have to *detach* its wheels.

**detail** *noun* ✦ element, feature, particular, item, part, specific Mick's model of a steam locomotive is authentic in every *detail*. —*verb* ✦ describe, itemize, recite, relate, recount, specify My friend's long email *detailed* everything that she had been doing abroad.

**detain** *verb* 1. ✦ delay, hinder, hold up, impede, slow ✧ stall, obstruct, retard We were *detained* by heavy traffic. 2. ✦ confine, hold, keep, restrain ✧ arrest Police officers *detained* the suspect for questioning.

**detect** *verb* ✦ discover, notice, find, spot ✧ expose, reveal, see An odor is added to natural gas to help people *detect* leaks.

**deter** *verb* ✦ discourage, hinder, dissuade, prevent, stop ✧ restrain Car alarms are supposed to *deter* thieves.

**determine** *verb* 1. ✦ decide, resolve, settle, establish ✧ **affect, choose, influence** This field goal attempt will *determine* which team wins the game. **2.** ✦ **detect, discover, find out, learn, ascertain** ✧ **conclude** Investigators are trying to *determine* what caused the fire.

**determined** *adjective* ✦ **intent, persevering, purposeful, steadfast, persistent** ✧ **firm, tough** Only the most *determined* players will be able to make it to the final competition.

**detest** *verb* ✦ **despise, dislike, hate, loathe, abhor** I *detest* people who make fun of someone with a disability.

**detour** *noun* ✦ **alternate route, diversion** ✧ **bypass, byway, substitute** We had to take a *detour* because the bridge was closed.

**devastate** *verb* ✦ **demolish, destroy, ruin, wreck, raze, level, ravage** The Italian city of Pompeii was *devastated* by the eruption of Mount Vesuvius in 79 CE.

**develop** *verb* **1.** ✦ **expand, improve, build up, broaden** ✧ **grow, increase, mature** Reading is a good way to *develop* your mind. **2.** ✦ **acquire, form, gain** ✧ **establish, generate** I *developed* an interest in international relations while studying abroad.

**development** *noun* ✦ **creation, production** ✧ **advancement, evolution, growth, progress** Medical researchers are always working on the *development* of newer and more effective medicines.

**device** *noun* **1.** ✦ **gadget, tool, apparatus** ✧ **appliance, instrument, utensil** Laptops, tablets, and smartphones are electronic *devices*. **2.** ✦ **ploy, gimmick, maneuver, trick** ✧ **plan, plot, scheme** A child's tantrum is often just a *device* for getting attention.

**devise** *verb* ✦ **concoct, contrive, create, fashion, invent, make, design** ✧ **plan** Scientists are trying to *devise* a robot with artificial intelligence.

**devote** *verb* ✦ **commit, dedicate, give, apply** ✧ **direct, focus** Dian Fossey *devoted* her life to studying and protecting the endangered mountain gorilla.

**devoted** *adjective* ✦ **committed, dedicated, faithful, loyal, true, staunch** The two girls are *devoted* friends.

**devotion** *noun* ✦ **affection, fondness, love, loyalty, commitment** ✧ **attachment, liking** The bride and groom exchanged rings as a token of their *devotion*.

**devour** *verb* ✦ **consume, eat, eat up, ingest, gobble** ✧ **swallow** I'm so hungry that I could *devour* an entire large pizza.

**devout** *adjective* ✦ **pious, religious, reverent** ✧ **earnest, sincere, devoted** *Devout* Muslims pray five times every day.

**diagram** *noun* ✦ **design, drawing, chart** ✧ **model, outline, pattern, plan, scheme** This *diagram* shows the parts of the human digestive system. —*verb* ✦ **draw, illustrate, picture, portray, sketch** ✧ **map, show, outline** The basketball coach used a chalkboard to *diagram* how the zone defense is supposed to work.

**dialogue** *noun* ✧ **speech, talk, conversation, discussion, script** I loved the movie's *dialogue* because the actors sounded exactly like my friends and me.

## Word Groups

A **diary** is a daily written account of one's thoughts and experiences. **Diary** is a very specific word with no true synonyms. Here are some related words to investigate in a dictionary: **chronicle, daybook, journal, log, notebook, record, yearbook**

**dictate** *verb* **1.** ✦ **read aloud** ✧ **pronounce, say, speak, utter, communicate** The lawyer *dictated* a letter to her secretary. **2.** ✦ **command, decree, direct, order, prescribe, impose** The tyrant had so much power that he was able to *dictate* how the government should be run.

**die** *verb* **1.** ✦ **expire, perish, pass away, decease** ✧ **depart, succumb** My African violet *died* because I forgot to water it. **2.** ✦ **diminish, dwindle, ebb, fade, subside, wane** The sound of the train's whistle gradually *died away* in the distance.

**differ** *verb* **1.** ✦ **vary, deviate** ✧ **alter, change, contrast** These two cars *differ* in price because one has air conditioning and the other doesn't. **2.** ✦ **clash, conflict, disagree, vary** ✧ **contradict, oppose, dissent** We all wanted to dine out, but our opinions *differed* when we tried to choose a restaurant.

**difference** *noun* **1.** ✦ **distinction, dissimilarity, variation, contrast, disparity** A big *difference* between whales and sharks is that whales are mammals and sharks are fish. **2.** ✧ **balance, remainder, rest, residue** The *difference* between 11 and 7 is 4. **3.** ✦ **disagreement, dissension, discord** ✧ **dispute,**

**quarrel** The two men settled their *differences* and became friends again.

**different** *adjective* 1. ✦ dissimilar, divergent, unlike, contrasting, varied My roommate and I have *different* opinions about who should do the cooking. 2. ✦ separate, distinct ✧ diverse, individual, unique, particular The two friends are both teachers, but they work at *different* schools.

**difficult** *adjective* 1. ✦ hard, rough, tough, demanding ✧ strenuous, tedious The scientist said that sending astronauts to Mars would be *difficult*, but not impossible. 2. ✦ obstinate, perverse, stubborn ✧ unmanageable, unruly, troublesome The *difficult* child constantly refused to do what his parents wanted.

**difficulty** *noun* ✦ hardship, obstacle, problem, trouble, adversity, trial The Pilgrims who founded Plymouth Colony overcame many *difficulties*, including food shortages and harsh weather.

**dig** *verb* 1. ✦ excavate ✧ burrow, scoop, shovel Workers *dug* a deep trench for the new building's foundation. 2. ✦search, delve, probe, sift ✧ investigate, look, research The reporter *dug* through several boxes of files to find the facts he needed for his article.

**digest** *verb* ✦ absorb, assimilate, take up ✧ consume, eat, ingest The Venus flytrap is an unusual plant that can trap and *digest* insects.

**dignified** *adjective* ✦ formal, noble, majestic, proper, stately, solemn ✧ elegant The queen spoke with an authoritative and *dignified* tone.

**dignity** *noun* ✦ formality, nobility, solemnity, seriousness ✧ honor, prestige Judges typically preside over their courts with *dignity*.

**diligent** *adjective* ✦ industrious, persevering, persistent ✧ careful, earnest, steadfast The best way to improve your English vocabulary is to be more *diligent* in your studying.

**dilute** *verb* ✦ cut, thin, water down ✧ mix, weaken A can of condensed soup should be *diluted* with water or milk before cooking.

**dim** *adjective* 1. ✦ low, faint, weak, soft ✧ dark, murky I strained my eyes when I tried to read in the *dim* light. 2. ✦ indistinct, blurry, vague, faint, hazy, unclear On misty days, Seattle residents can see only the *dim* outline of nearby Mt. Rainier. —*verb* ✦ turn down, lower, reduce, darken ✧

**blur, dull** In a movie theater, the lights are *dimmed* just before the film starts.

**dimension** *noun* ✦ measurements, proportions, size ✧ expanse, extent, length, width We need to know the window's *dimensions* so that we can buy curtains of the proper size.

**diminish** *verb* ✦ decrease, ebb, lessen, wane, abate ✧ lower, reduce With the loss of our star player, our chances for winning the tournament are *diminishing*.

**din** *noun* ✦ clamor, noise, racket, tumult, uproar, commotion The barking dogs made so much *din* that I couldn't sleep.

**dine** *verb* ✦ eat, have supper ✧ sup, consume, feast, feed Let's *dine* at that new restaurant tonight.

**dingy** *adjective* ✦ dirty, grimy, soiled ✧ dark, drab, gloomy, murky I couldn't see out of the *dingy* window on the subway.

**dip** *verb* 1. ✦ duck, dunk, immerse, submerge, submerse ✧ douse I *dipped* my hand in the bath water to see if it was the right temperature. 2. ✦ descend, drop, sink ✧ fall, lower, settle, slump The hawk *dipped* out of sight behind the ridge of the mountain. —*noun* 1. ✦ duck, dunk, plunge, swim ✧ immersion, soak Eduardo went for a *dip* in the swimming pool to cool off. 2. ✦ depression, pit, hollow ✧ drop, fall, slope The driver slowed down when he saw a big *dip* in the road.

### Word Groups

A **diplomat** is a person who represents a government in its relations with other countries. **Diplomat** is a general term with no true synonyms. Here are some related words to investigate in a dictionary: **agent, ambassador, consul, emissary, envoy, representative, statesman, stateswoman**

**direct** *verb* 1. ✦ aim, point, guide, lead, show, steer ✧ usher Could you *direct* me to the bathroom? 2. ✦ supervise, control, govern, manage, run, administer A store's manager *directs* the activities of the other employees. 3. ✦ instruct, order, tell, command ✧ bid A police officer *directed* everyone to stand back. —*adjective* ✦ straightforward, straight, shortest, short ✧ through, unswerving The *direct* route to the coast is about twenty miles shorter than the scenic road.

**direction** *noun* 1. ✦ control, leadership, management, supervision, guidance The corporation is under the *direction* of a new CEO. 2. ✦ guideline, instruction, directive ◇ **rule, command, order** To do well on a proficiency test, you must follow the *directions* carefully. **3.** ✦ **course, track** ◇ **path, route, way** The wind blew in a northerly *direction*.

**directly** *adverb* **1.** ✦ **right, straight, due, direct** ◇ **exactly, precisely** My friend's apartment is *directly* across the hallway from mine. **2.** ✦ **immediately, right, promptly, shortly, soon, just** I have a doctor's appointment *directly* after work.

**director** *noun* ✦ **leader, head, chief, manager, supervisor, boss** ◇ **executive** The museum's new *director* said her goal was to increase attendance.

**dirt** *noun* **1.** ✦ **earth, soil, loam** ◇ **ground** To safely put out a campfire, drown it with water then cover it with *dirt*. **2.** ✦ **filth, grime** ◇ **dust, mire, mud, soil** The mechanic always had a lot of *dirt* on his hands.

**dirty** *adjective* **1.** ✦ **filthy, grimy, soiled, unclean** ◇ **messy, polluted** My hands were *dirty* after I worked in the garden. **2.** ✦ **angry, disapproving, hostile, resentful, bitter** ◇ **low, mean** The server gave the customer a *dirty* look because he didn't leave a tip.

**disadvantage** *noun* ✦ **drawback, liability, problem, shortcoming, handicap, weakness** Flying is the fastest way to travel, but it has the *disadvantage* of being expensive.

**disagree** *verb* ✦ **differ, dissent, vary** ◇ **oppose, argue, quarrel** My friend and I always seem to *disagree* over which movie we want to see.

**disagreeable** *adjective* **1.** ✦ **bad, offensive, repulsive, repugnant, unpleasant, distasteful** Rotten eggs have a *disagreeable* odor. **2.** ✦ **bad-tempered, cross, grouchy, grumpy, irritable, quarrelsome, unfriendly** My friend is in a *disagreeable* mood because she didn't get much sleep last night.

**disagreement** *noun* **1.** ✦ **conflict, opposition** ◇ **difference, dissension, disparity** These two books are in *disagreement* over who really discovered America. **2.** ✦ **argument, dispute, fight, quarrel** ◇ **feud** The two friends had a big *disagreement*, but they finally worked it out.

**disappear** *verb* **1.** ✦ **vanish** ◇ **dissolve, evaporate, fade away** The day was warm until the sun *disappeared* behind clouds. **2.** ✦ **become extinct, die out, perish** ◇ **end, expire, cease, stop** The wooly mammoth *disappeared* about 10,000 years ago.

**disappoint** *verb* ✦ **let down** ◇ **displease, fail, frus-** trate, sadden You will *disappoint* your friend if you don't invite her to your dinner party.

**disappointment** *noun* **1.** ◇ **discontent, displeasure, dissatisfaction, frustration, regret, sadness** I tried to hide my *disappointment* when my friend canceled our dinner date. **2.** ✦ **letdown** ◇ **dud, flop, failure, disaster** The sequel to my favorite movie turned out to be a real *disappointment*.

**disapprove** *verb* ✦ **frown (on), object (to), condemn, denounce, dislike** ◇ **criticize** Michele *disapproves of* littering.

**disaster** *noun* ✦ **calamity, catastrophe, cataclysm, tragedy** ◇ **accident, misfortune, trouble** One of the biggest natural *disasters* ever was the eruption of the Krakatoa volcano in 1883.

**disbelief** *noun* ✦ **doubt, skepticism, unbelief** ◇ **distrust, rejection** The sailors' tales of giant sea serpents were met with *disbelief*.

**discard** *verb* ✦ **dispose (of), dump, eliminate, throw out, scrap** ◇ **abandon** We *discarded* a lot of old junk when we cleaned out the garage.

**discharge** *verb* **1.** ✦ **disembark, offload, let out, unload** ◇ **dump, empty** The flight from Houston will *discharge* its passengers at gate 17. **2.** ✦ **dismiss, release, let go** ◇ **excuse, free, expel, remove** The doctor *discharged* her patient from the hospital. **3.** ✦ **eject, emit, expel, gush, pour** ◇ **drain, leak** The broken fire hydrant *discharged* water all over the street. —*noun* ✦ **release, dismissal** ◇ **termination, liberation, expulsion, ejection** The soldier received an honorable *discharge*.

**disciple** *noun* ✦ **devotee, follower, adherent, believer** ◇ **pupil, student, supporter** The religious leader had many *disciples*.

**discipline** *noun* **1.** ✦ **self-control, diligence** ◇ **exercise, practice, preparation, training** It takes a lot of *discipline* to write a book. **2.** ✦ **correction, punishment** ◇ **control, penalty, reprimand** Cadets at the military academy were occasionally subjected to harsh *discipline*. —*verb* **1.** ✦ **drill, train, coach, instruct, teach, educate** The captain *disciplined* the crew to be expert sailors. **2.** ✦ **correct, punish, chasten** ◇ **penalize** The child is unruly because his parents never *discipline* him.

**disclose** *verb* ✦ **expose, reveal, tell** ◇ **relate, report, show, bare** The reporter refused to *disclose* the source of her information.

**discomfort** *noun* ✦ **pain, suffering** ◇ **annoyance,**

distress, irritation, misery Headaches can cause a lot of *discomfort.*

**discontinue** *verb* ✦ cease, end, halt, stop, terminate, suspend I *discontinued* my subscription to the magazine.

**discord** *noun* ✦ conflict, strife, dispute, dissent, disagreement, disharmony The meeting ended in *discord* with everybody shouting at each other.

**discount** *noun* ✦ deduction, reduction ✧ cut, decrease, markdown Senior citizens receive a *discount* at most movie theaters.

**discourage** *verb* 1. ✦ daunt, dishearten, intimidate, dispirit ✧ bother, depress The minor fall did not *discourage* the climber, and she continued on to the top of the cliff. 2. ✦ deter, dissuade, divert ✧ restrain, prevent, warn The city started an ad campaign to *discourage* young people from smoking.

**discover** *verb* ✦ find, locate, detect, spot ✧ identify, notice, recognize The Spanish explorer Ponce de León hoped to *discover* the legendary Fountain of Youth.

**discovery** *noun* ✦ detection, finding, identification ✧ location, recognition Madame Curie won a Nobel Prize in 1911 for her *discovery* of radium.

**discuss** *verb* ✦ confer about, talk about, consider ✧ debate, deliberate My friend and I have spent hours *discussing* our vacation plans.

**discussion** *noun* ✦ dialogue, talk, conversation ✧ conference, debate We need to have a *discussion* about whose turn it is to do the dishes.

**disease** *noun* ✦ illness, ailment, malady, sickness, affliction, disorder Modern medicine can cure many *diseases.*

**disgrace** *noun* 1. ✦ disrepute, dishonor, humiliation, shame, disfavor The politician resigned in *disgrace* when the public learned that she had accepted a bribe. 2. ✦ scandal, embarrassment, stigma ✧ blemish, stain I think it's a *disgrace* that there are so many homeless people in America. —*verb* ✦ dishonor, humiliate, shame ✧ embarrass, tarnish, stain The warrior's cowardice *disgraced* his entire tribe.

**disguise** *noun* ✦ costume, getup, outfit, concealment ✧ camouflage, cover, mask The actress wore a *disguise* to keep from being recognized. —*verb* ✦ costume, camouflage, dress ✧ conceal, cover,

mask The Greek god Zeus is said to have walked the Earth *disguised* as a human beggar.

**disgust** *noun* ✦ aversion, revulsion, nausea, queasiness ✧ annoyance, distaste I was filled with *disgust* when I saw rats in the restaurant's kitchen. —*verb* ✦ appall, nauseate, repel, revolt, sicken, offend The stench from the garbage dump *disgusts* everyone who lives nearby.

**dishonest** *adjective* ✦ deceitful, untruthful, false ✧ corrupt, crooked, fraudulent A person who tells lies is *dishonest.*

**disintegrate** *verb* ✦ break up, fall apart, crumble, fragment, shatter, splinter The spaceship *disintegrated* when it collided with an asteroid.

**dislike** *verb* ✦ despise, detest, hate, loathe ✧ scorn, resent I *dislike* people who are rude. —*noun* ✦ aversion (to), distaste (for), revulsion (toward) ✧ hatred, loathing My cat has an obvious *dislike* of dry food.

**dismal** *adjective* ✦ bleak, dreary, cheerless, dark, gloomy, depressing Rain clouds made the sky look *dismal.*

**dismay** *verb* ✦ alarm, distress, daunt ✧ appall, frighten, scare, shock The picnickers were *dismayed* to see the approaching storm. —*noun* ✦ anxiety, apprehension, distress, alarm ✧ dread, fright I was filled with *dismay* when I realized I'd locked myself out of the apartment.

**dismiss** *verb* 1. ✦ send away, excuse, let go, free, release The queen *dismissed* her servants when she wanted to be left alone. 2. ✦ discharge, fire, terminate, release, drop, lay off ✧ expel, oust Because sales were slow, the company had to *dismiss* several employees.

**disobedient** *adjective* ✦ defiant, rebellious, insubordinate ✧ naughty, stubborn, unruly The *disobedient* child refused to do what he was told.

**disobey** *verb* ✦ break, disregard, ignore, violate ✧ defy, rebel, resist The driver received a ticket for *disobeying* the speed limit.

**disorder** *noun* 1. ✦ disarray, chaos, commotion, confusion, turmoil ✧ jumble The soldiers retreated in *disorder* when the enemy attacked. 2. ✦ affliction, ailment, disease, illness, malady, sickness Asthma is a breathing *disorder.*

**disorderly** *adjective* 1. ✦ cluttered, jumbled, disorganized, messy, untidy Our hall closet is a *disor-*

*derly* jumble of hats, coats, boots, and umbrellas. 2. ✦ **disruptive, unruly, rowdy** ✧ **obstinate, improper, unlawful** A *disorderly* passenger was removed from the plane.

**dispel** *verb* ✦ **banish, drive away, put an end to, remove** ✧ **disperse, erase, scatter** The flight attendant helped to *dispel* my fear of flying.

**dispense** *verb* ✦ **distribute, give out, hand out, allot** ✧ **supply, administer, award** This clinic *dispenses* medicines free of charge to the needy.

**disperse** *verb* ✦ **dissipate, scatter, break up** ✧ **disband, dispel, separate** High winds caused the clouds to *disperse*.

**display** *verb* ✦ **demonstrate, exhibit, reveal, show, present** The firefighter *displayed* great courage by saving people from the burning building. —*noun* ✦ **show, spectacle** ✧ **demonstration, exhibit, exhibition, presentation, scene** Everyone enjoyed the New Year's fireworks *display*.

**dispose** *verb* ✦ **dispense with, discard, throw away** ✧ **dump, junk, scrap** We *dispose of* our old magazines and newspapers at the recycling center.

**dispute** *verb* 1. ✦ **argue, quarrel, squabble, clash, fight** ✧ **contend, debate** Art experts have *disputed* over the painting's authenticity. 2. ✦ **challenge, contest, question, doubt, oppose** ✧ **contradict** The customer *disputed* his bill because he thought he had been overcharged. —*noun* 1. ✦ **disagreement, contention, argument, quarrel** ✧ **conflict, controversy, fight, hostility** The two countries found a peaceful solution to their *dispute*.

**disregard** *verb* ✦ **ignore, overlook, pass over** ✧ **forget, neglect, slight** We *disregarded* the instructions for the board game and made up our own rules.

**disrupt** *verb* ✦ **disturb, interfere (with), interrupt, upset** ✧ **confuse, mess up** Some fans *disrupted* the rock concert when they rushed onto the stage.

**dissent** *verb* ✦ **be opposed, differ, disagree, vote no** ✧ **contradict, dispute, protest** Congress was unable to approve the controversial bill because so many senators *dissented*. —*noun* ✦ **disagreement, dissension, opposition, difference, discord** ✧ **protest** A verdict could not be reached because the jurors' *dissent* could not be resolved.

**dissolve** *verb* ✦ **liquefy** ✧ **break down, disintegrate, melt, mix, soften** The directions on the medicine bottle said to *dissolve* two tablets in a glass of water.

**distance** *noun* ✦ **length, space, interval** ✧ **gap, span, stretch, expanse** The shortest *distance* between two points is a straight line.

**distant** *adjective* ✦ **far, faraway, far-off, remote** ✧ **removed, separate** We could hear the *distant* thunder of the waterfall.

**distaste** *noun* ✦ **aversion (to), dislike (of)** ✧ **disgust, loathing, revulsion** My vegetarian friend makes her *distaste for* meat all too obvious.

**distinct** *adjective* 1. ✦ **obvious, unmistakable, clear, definite** ✧ **apparent** A *distinct* aroma of baking bread filled the house. 2. ✦ **different, dissimilar, individual, unlike, separate, singular** It's easy to tell the man apart from his twin brother because they have such *distinct* personalities.

**distinguish** *verb* 1. ✦ **differentiate, discern, discriminate, know, tell, determine** ✧ **divide, separate** It is important to be able to *distinguish* right from wrong. 2. ✦ **identify, make out, perceive, recognize, tell, detect** I could see someone approaching though the fog, but I couldn't *distinguish* who it was. 3. ✦ **honor** ✧ **exalt, dignify, glorify, elevate** Antonia *distinguished* herself by winning a short-story contest.

**distort** *verb* 1. ✦ **warp, contort, deform, twist, bend** ✧ **ruin, wreck** Don't leave DVDs in the sun because heat can *distort* them. 2. ✦ **alter, change, misrepresent, twist, falsify** ✧ **deceive, mislead** Supermarket tabloids are famous for *distorting* the truth.

**distract** *verb* ✦ **bother, disturb, interrupt** ✧ **divert, interfere** My roommate closed her door so the noise from the TV wouldn't *distract* her.

**distress** *noun* 1. ✦ **anxiety, concern, worry, care, anguish** ✧ **pain, sorrow, suffering** Not having enough money to get by is a constant source of *distress* for some people. 2. ✦ **danger, peril, trouble** ✧ **difficulty, need, misfortune** The ship in *distress* radioed an urgent appeal for assistance. —*verb* ✦ **trouble, upset, worry, bother, concern, disturb** I don't want to *distress* you, but I think you should know that they're towing your car.

**distribute** *verb* 1. ✦ **dispense, give out, hand out, issue, allot** ✧ **divide** Our local charity *distributes* food to needy families. 2. ✦ **disperse, spread** ✧ **scatter, diffuse** Please *distribute* the icing evenly over the entire cake.

**district** *noun* ✦ **area, quarter, section, zone, neigh-**

borhood, region, precinct New York's financial *district* is located on Wall Street.

**disturb** *verb* 1. ✦ disarrange, disorder, disorganize ✧ handle, move, shift, touch We were careful not to *disturb* any of the museum's exhibits. 2. ✦ agitate, distress, perturb, trouble, upset, worry The man's angry outbursts *disturbed* his friends and family. 3. ✦ annoy, bother, distract, interrupt, pester ✧ disrupt, interfere Please don't *disturb* the baby while she's sleeping.

**disturbance** *noun* 1. ✦ distraction, interference, interruption, disruption ✧ bother, annoyance The writer likes a quiet place where he can work without *disturbance*. 2. ✦ commotion, tumult, turmoil, uproar, ruckus ✧ riot The elephant created quite a *disturbance* when it escaped from the zoo.

**dive** *verb* ✦ plunge, leap, jump ✧ descend, drop, sink, submerge The swimmers *dove* into the pool at the start of the race. —*noun* ✦ descent, plunge, nosedive ✧ dip, drop, fall The test pilot wanted to see how the new jet would perform in a steep *dive*.

**diverse** *adjective* ✦ different, dissimilar, varied, various, assorted ✧ miscellaneous One of the strengths of the United States is the *diverse* backgrounds of its citizens.

**divert** *verb* 1. ✦ redirect, shift, turn aside, deflect ✧ sidetrack, swing, veer Bad weather caused our Chicago flight to be *diverted* to Indianapolis. 2. ✦ distract, absorb, amuse, entertain, occupy, engage ✧ delight Street musicians *diverted* us while we stood in line at the theater.

**divide** *noun* 1. ✦ cut, separate, split ✧ part, segment, break We *divided* the cake into six equal pieces. 2. ✦ distribute, deal out, split up, dispense, portion, share The bank robbers *divided* their loot among themselves.

**divine** *adjective* ✦ holy, religious, sacred, hallowed ✧ heavenly The *divine* scripture of the Islamic religion is known as the Koran.

**division** *noun* 1. ✦ partition, parting, segmentation, separation ✧ split The *division* of the year into twelve months began about 713 BCE. 2. ✦ department, section, branch ✧ component, part, segment Ji-yeon works in her company's sales and marketing *division*. 3. ✦ divider, partition, barrier, wall ✧ border, boundary, frontier The company installed vertical *divisions* to give each worker more privacy.

**divorce** *noun* ✦ breakup, separation, split, dissolution I was glad that my friend's parents decided not to get a *divorce*. —*verb* ✦ break up, part, separate, split, divide, sever The young couple *divorced* after only three months of marriage.

**do** *verb* 1. ✦ accomplish, execute, perform, carry out ✧ act, behave, conduct Soldiers are expected to *do* whatever they're told. 2. ✦ create, fashion, render, make, produce, compose ✧ design, form My artist friend is *doing* a portrait of me. 3. ✦ bring about, lead (to), result (in), effect ✧ cause, give, perform Complaining won't *do* any good. 4. ✦ figure out, solve, work out ✧ complete, resolve, finish My grandfather likes to *do* crossword puzzles. 5. ✦ suffice, serve, be fine ✧ answer, satisfy, suit Those tennis shoes will *do* for the hike, though boots would be better. 6. ✦ fare, make out, manage, get along ✧ continue How are you *doing* with your language lessons?

**docile** *adjective* ✦ gentle, manageable, tame, meek, obedient, submissive ✧ mild I'm not going to get on that horse unless he's very *docile*.

**doctor** *noun* ✦ physician, general practitioner, surgeon, medic ✧ healer, intern Lanh would like to be a *doctor* because she wants to help sick and injured people.

**doctrine** *noun* ✦ belief, creed, principle, teaching, tenet, dogma Abdullah is studying the *doctrines* of his religion.

### Word Groups

A **document** is an official paper containing information or proof. **Document** is a general term with no true synonyms. Here are some related words to investigate in a dictionary: **certificate, contract, deed, license, memo, petition, record, testament, will**

**dodge** *verb* ✦ duck, move aside, shift, sidestep, weave, swerve ✧ avoid, escape, evade The boxer *dodged* every time his opponent tried to punch him.

**domain** *noun* ✦ realm, dominion, territory ✧ property, region The king extended his *domain* by conquering two neighboring countries.

**domestic** *adjective* 1. ✦ family, familial, home, household ✧ residential The newlyweds rarely go out because they're enjoying the freshness of their *domestic* life together. 2. ✦ tame ✧ docile, obedient, trained Horses and cows are *domestic* animals.

**dominant** *adjective* ✦ controlling, ruling, commanding, leading, main, principal The young wolf did not dare challenge the *dominant* male of the pack.

**dominate** *verb* ✦ lead, rule, command, control ✧ direct, govern Among many animals, it is the strongest male that *dominates* the group.

**donate** *verb* ✦ contribute, give, present ✧ award, confer, grant Rodrigo *donated* clothing, shoes, and books to the local orphanage.

**donation** *noun* ✦ contribution, gift, offering ✧ present, grant, award The charity received *donations* from all over the world.

**donor** *noun* ✦ contributor, donator, giver, provider, supplier The Red Cross has issued an appeal for blood *donors*.

**doom** *noun* ✦ destruction, death, end, fate, ruin ✧ destiny Sirens were mythological beings whose beautiful voices lured sailors to their *doom*. —*verb* ✦ condemn, destine, fate ✧ finish, ruin The plan was *doomed* to fail because no one supported it.

**door** *noun* ✦ doorway, entrance, entry, gateway, threshold, portal A good education can be the *door* to success.

**dormant** *adjective* ✦ inactive, sleeping, asleep ✧ dead, idle, resting Geologists say the *dormant* volcano could erupt sometime soon.

**dosage** *noun* ✦ dose, amount, measure, portion, quantity When using any medicine, you should read the label to determine the proper *dosage*.

**doubt** *verb* ✦ disbelieve, distrust, question ✧ challenge, dispute, query I *doubt* that ghosts really exist. —*noun* ✦ misgiving, question, suspicion, uncertainty, reservation I have some *doubts* about whether he's telling the truth.

**doubtful** *adjective* ✦ dubious, questionable, unlikely, improbable ✧ uncertain, unclear It's *doubtful* that I'll be ready in time.

**down** *adverb* ✦ downward ✧ below, low, beneath, under I tripped and fell *down*. —*preposition* ✦ along ✧ into, through, by We walked *down* the block to the ice cream shop. —*verb* 1. ✦ bring down, shoot down ✧ fell, drop, hit, strike The fighter pilot *downed* two enemy aircraft. 2. ✦ drink, gulp, guzzle, swallow ✧ bolt, wolf, gobble Arike *downed* three glasses of water after the basketball game.

**doze** *verb* ✦ drowse, nap, sleep, slumber, snooze ✧ rest My cat likes to *doze* on the couch.

**drab** *adjective* ✦ colorless, dull, flat, dreary, somber ✧ uninteresting Zoe thought that her desk was too *drab*, so she painted it bright yellow.

**draft** *noun* 1. ✦ breeze ✧ air, current, wind, flow If the *draft* is bothering you, feel free to close the window. 2. ✦ version ✧ outline, plan, sketch, rough The author spent an entire year writing the first *draft* of her novel. —*verb* ✦ outline, plan, formulate ✧ diagram, draw, sketch The minister spent all week *drafting* the next sermon.

**drag** *verb* 1. ✦ draw, tow, tug, haul, pull ✧ lug It took two of us to *drag* the fallen tree branch off the road. 2. ✦ plod, trudge ✧ crawl, creep, straggle, poke, dawdle The weary hikers *dragged* into camp and collapsed in front of the fire.

**drain** *verb* 1. ✦ draw off, let out, empty ✧ discharge, release, flow, leak Every winter we have to *drain* all the water from the swimming pool so it won't freeze. 2. ✦ consume, deplete, exhaust, sap, use up ✧ remove, diminish The long swim *drained* all my strength.

**dramatic** *adjective* ✦ exciting, sensational, spectacular, thrilling, impressive The movie opened with a *dramatic* high-speed chase scene.

**drastic** *adjective* ✦ extreme, radical, rash, severe ✧ powerful, strong Starving yourself is a *drastic* and dangerous way to lose weight.

**draw** *verb* 1. ✦ pull, tow, drag, haul, tug Pioneers used horses, oxen, or mules to *draw* their covered wagons. 2. ✦ extract, remove, take, withdraw ✧ produce Let's pick teams by *drawing* names from a hat. 3. ✦ sketch, trace ✧ create, diagram, outline Many artists *draw* on a canvas with charcoal prior to painting. 4. ✦ attract, entice, lure, pull in, summon ✧ get, obtain, receive The department store's big sale *drew* hundreds of shoppers. —*noun* ✦ tie, deadlock, stalemate, standoff If the score is still tied after overtime in professional hockey, the game is declared a *draw*.

**drawback** *noun* ✦ disadvantage, problem (with), trouble (with) ✧ defect, difficulty, handicap There are *drawbacks* to both country and city living.

**Antonyms** drawback

*noun* advantage, benefit, blessing, convenience, favor, profit

**dread** *noun* ✦ apprehension, fear, fright, horror, terror, alarm Just thinking about rattlesnakes fills me with *dread*. —*verb* ✦ be afraid (of), fear ✧ worry (about), concern I used to *dread* flying, but I've learned how to overcome my fear.

**dreadful** *adjective* ✦ awful, horrible, terrible, frightful, dire ✧ bad, wicked The pilot regained control of the aircraft in time to prevent what could have been a *dreadful* accident.

**dream** *noun* ✦ ambition, aspiration, goal, hope ✧ vision, desire, wish Julieta's *dream* is to become an astronaut. —*verb* ✦ imagine, suppose, think, conceive ✧ fantasize, daydream I never *dreamed* that I'd be admitted to such a prestigious university.

**dreary** *adjective* ✦ bleak, cheerless, dismal, gloomy, somber, dull I think that *dreary* winter days are best spent at home by the fireplace.

**drench** *verb* ✦ douse, saturate, soak, wet, drown A sudden downpour *drenched* me as I biked home from work.

**dress** *noun* 1. ✦ frock ✧ gown, skirt Constanza bought a new *dress* to wear to her friend's party. 2. ✦ apparel, attire, clothes, clothing, garments The dinner invitation stated that formal *dress* was required. —*verb* ✦ attire, clothe, outfit ✧ adorn, trim, robe The golfer was *dressed* in shorts and a polo shirt.

**drift** *verb* 1. ✦ cruise, float, sail, coast, skim ✧ idle, meander, wander The hot-air balloon *drifted* over a hill. 2. ✦ accumulate, pile up, bank, collect, mass ✧ stack The wind caused snow to *drift* against our front door. —*noun* ✦ dune, bank, heap, mound, pile ✧ hill, mass These *drifts* were formed by big waves that carried sand onto the beach.

**drill** *noun* ✦ exercise, practice, rehearsal, training ✧ study Los Angeles schools hold regular earthquake *drills*. —*verb* 1. ✦ bore ✧ pierce, penetrate, puncture, ream The rancher *drilled* a well in order to get water for the cattle. 2. ✦ coach, rehearse, instruct ✧ teach, train, practice The teacher *drilled* her students by making them recite new vocabulary words over and over.

**drink** *verb* ✦ down, gulp, guzzle, sip, swallow, swig Kara *drinks* a glass of orange juice every morning. —*noun* 1. ✦ beverage ✧ fluid, liquid, refreshment My favorite *drink* is homemade lemonade. 2. ✦ sip, swallow, draft ✧ cup, glass, taste May I have a *drink* of water?

**drive** *verb* 1. ✦ operate, run, pilot, steer ✧ control You need a license in order to legally *drive* a car. 2. ✧ transport, convey, bus, chauffeur, taxi I *drove* my friend to her ESL class last night. 3. ✦ force, push, shove, compel, impel, press The climber tried to make it to the top of the mountain, but he was *driven* back by high winds. 4. ✦ hit, knock, hammer, propel ✧ pound, strike Mike Austin once *drove* a golf ball 515 yards, which is the current world record. —*noun* 1. ✦ excursion, ride, spin ✧ journey, tour, trip My family enjoys taking weekend *drives* in the country. 2. ✦ campaign, crusade, movement ✧ cause, effort My city is sponsoring a *drive* to collect canned foods for homeless families.

**droop** *verb* ✦ hang down, sag, slump, bend, drop, dangle ✧ wilt Heavy snow caused the tree branches to *droop*.

**drop** *noun* 1. ✦ bead, droplet, globule ✧ dribble, drip, trickle *Drops* of sweat formed on my forehead in the hot sun. 2. ✦ decline, decrease, dip, reduction, slump There's been a *drop* in the price of corn due to an abundant harvest. 3. ✦ descent, fall, plunge ✧ slope, pitch It's a long *drop* from the top of the cliff to the river below. —*verb* 1. ✦ fall, plunge, descend, sink, plummet ✧ lower, reduce The temperature *dropped* more than thirty degrees last night. 2. ✦ eliminate, leave out, remove, exclude, omit ✧ skip We'll have to *drop* one of these poems from the literary magazine because there isn't enough room for both. 3. ✦ give up, cease, discontinue, end, stop, terminate When my friend joined a softball league, she had to *drop* her piano lessons.

**drown** *verb* 1. ✦ drench, saturate, soak, douse ✧ flood, inundate, wet I like to *drown* my pancakes in maple syrup. 2. ✦ overpower, overwhelm, overcome ✧ smother, stifle, submerge The audience's applause *drowned out* the speaker's final words.

**drowsy** *adjective* ✦ sleepy, tired, dozy ✧ groggy, listless If you feel so *drowsy*, why don't you take a nap?

**drug** *noun* 1. ✦ medication, medicine, pharmaceutical ✧ pill, remedy Aspirin is one of the most commonly used *drugs* in America. 2. ✦ substance ✧ narcotic, opiate, depressant, stimulant People who sell illegal *drugs* run the risk of imprisonment.

**drunk** *adjective* ✦ drunken, intoxicated, inebriated

✧ **tipsy, groggy, impaired** *Drunk* drivers cause a lot of serious accidents.

**dry** *adjective* ✦ **waterless, arid, parched, rainless** ✧ **thirsty** Deserts can be hot or cold, but they're always *dry.*

**duck** *verb* 1. ✦ **crouch, stoop, dip, bend** ✧ **drop, lower** When the hiker saw a bear, he *ducked* behind a bush to avoid being seen. 2. ✦ **avoid, dodge, elude, escape, evade, sidestep** The politician *ducked* reporters by sneaking out the back door.

**due** *adjective* 1. ✦ **appropriate, fitting, proper, suitable, adequate** Use *due* care when handling a knife. 2. ✦ **anticipated, expected, scheduled, slated, booked** The flight from Tokyo is *due* at three o'clock. —*adverb* ✦ **directly, straight** ✧ **exactly, right, dead** We drove *due* east across the desert.

**dull** *adjective* 1. ✦ **blunt, unsharpened** ✧ **edgeless** It's hard to cut cleanly with a *dull* knife. 2. ✦ **boring, monotonous, tedious, tiresome, uninteresting, dreary** I fell asleep during the *dull* film. —*verb* ✦ **blunt, dim, diminish, lessen, reduce** ✧ **fade** Age has *dulled* our cat's eyesight.

**dumb** *adjective* ✦ **crazy, foolish, silly, stupid, unintelligent, thoughtless** I made a *dumb* mistake when I told you that George Washington was the mother of our country.

**dummy** *noun* 1. ✧ **puppet, mannequin, doll, figure, marionette, model** The ventriloquist's *dummy* has a funny-looking head. 2. ✦ **fake, imitation, simulation** ✧ **copy, counterfeit** There was a big scare, but the bomb turned out to be just a *dummy.*

**dump** *verb* ✦ **discard, drop, deposit, pour out, unload, empty, release** I get aggravated by people who *dump* trash in vacant lots. —*noun* ✦ **landfill** ✧ **junkyard, rubbish heap, trash pile** Because there is no trash collection in our town, we have to take our garbage to the *dump.*

**duplicate** *noun* ✦ **copy, reproduction, double** ✧ **image, replica** Because I worry about losing my house key, I have a *duplicate* hidden outside. —*verb* ✦ **replicate, repeat, reproduce, copy, imitate** ✧ **simulate** The scientist is *duplicating* her original experiment to see if she can get the same results.

**durable** *adjective* ✦ **enduring, lasting, long-lasting** ✧ **permanent, strong, sturdy, firm** These jeans are made of a *durable* fabric that can withstand hundreds of washings.

**duration** *noun* ✦ **length, course, period, extent** ✧ **span, term, time** Please keep your seatbelt fastened for the *duration* of the flight.

**dusk** *noun* ✦ **evening, nightfall, sundown, sunset, twilight, night** Rice farmers work in their paddies from dawn to *dusk.*

**duty** *noun* 1. ✦ **assignment, job, obligation, responsibility, task, business** A police officer's *duties* include enforcing the law and keeping the peace. 2. ✦ **tariff, tax** ✧ **fee, levy, assessment** The tourist had to pay a *duty* on the pearls that she brought back from Japan.

**dwell** *verb* ✦ **live, reside, abide, stay, lodge** ✧ **inhabit** People have *dwelled* in cities for thousands of years.

**dwindle** *verb* ✦ **decrease, diminish, shrink, thin out** ✧ **decline, ebb, lessen, reduce** The crowd began to *dwindle* before the game was over.

**Antonyms** **dwindle**
*verb* **build, expand, flourish, grow, increase, sprout, swell**

**dye** *noun* ✦ **coloring** ✧ **color, pigment, stain, tint** This red *dye* is guaranteed not to fade. —*verb* ✦ **color, tint** ✧ **shade, stain, tinge** People often *dye* their hair unusual colors as a form of self-expression.

**dynamic** *adjective* ✦ **energetic, forceful, lively, vigorous, active, strong** The *dynamic* performer had the whole audience singing along with her during the encore.

**eager** *adjective* ✦ **keen, avid, impatient, anxious, enthusiastic** Bianca is *eager* to start her new job.

**early** *adjective* ✦ **beginning** ✧ **initial, opening, first** My oldest brother is in his *early* thirties. —*adverb* ✦ **prematurely** ✧ **beforehand, before, ahead, in advance** Alexandra arrived *early* and helped us with the party decorations.

**earn** *verb* 1. ✦ **make, receive, get** ✧ **collect, gain** Juan Pablo *earns* more at his new job than he ever did before. 2. ✦ **gain, win, deserve, merit** Susannah *earned* our admiration when her essay was printed in a national magazine.

**earth** *noun* 1. ✦ **world, planet** ✧ **globe** Soviet astronaut Yuri Gagarin was the first person to orbit the *Earth*. 2. ✦ **soil, dirt, loam, ground, land** Most gardeners enjoy the smell and feel of rich, moist *earth*.

**ease** *noun* 1. ✦ **leisure, comfort, relaxation, rest, contentment** My cat lives a life of total *ease*. 2. ✦ **easiness, facility** ✧ **efficiency, dexterity** Isabella won the race with *ease*. —*verb* ✦ **lessen, lighten, relieve, soothe** ✧ **comfort** The doctor's cheerful words helped to *ease* my anxiety when she set my broken ankle.

**easy** *adjective* 1. ✦ **simple, uncomplicated** ✧ **effortless, light** Ji Won picked an *easy* pattern for her first sewing project. 2. ✦ **carefree, comfortable, cozy, pleasant** ✧ **prosperous** My grandparents have been enjoying an *easy* life since they retired. 3. ✦ **lenient, undemanding, soft** ✧ **casual, informal, tolerant** Our coach was *easy* on us for the first two or three practices of the season.

**Antonyms** **easy**
*adjective* 1. arduous, difficult, hard 2. shaky, troubled, uncomfortable 3. harsh, severe, strict

**eat** *verb* 1. ✦ **consume, devour, swallow** ✧ **dine, feast, feed** An adult elephant *eats* as much as one thousand pounds of food every day. 2. ✦ **wear away, corrode, erode** ✧ **destroy, waste** Sea water has been slowly *eating away* the boat's iron anchor.

**ebb** *verb* 1. ✦ **recede, retreat, flow back, withdraw, subside** When the tide *ebbed*, I went looking for seashells. 2. ✦ **decline, decrease, diminish, lessen** ✧ **reduce** The runner was only halfway through the race when his strength began to *ebb*.

**echo** *noun* ✦ **reverberation, reflection** ✧ **answer, response, repetition** The quiet *echo* of voices could be heard throughout the museum. —*verb* ✦ **reflect, resound, ring** ✧ **rebound, repeat** The crowd's cheers *echoed* loudly in the gymnasium.

**eclipse** *verb* 1. ✦ **block, obscure, conceal, hide, shadow** ✧ **darken, dim** When the moon passes between the sun and the Earth, the sun is *eclipsed*. 2. ✦ **overshadow, surpass, outdo, exceed** ✧ **excel** At the art contest, Miranda's drawing was so good that it totally *eclipsed* all the other entries.

**economical** *adjective* ✦ **frugal, thrifty, prudent** ✧ **careful, cheap, saving** Waiting until a store puts its merchandise on sale is an *economical* way of shopping.

**edge** *noun* 1. ✦ **border, margin, side, fringe** ✧ **rim** The lake has a beautiful sandy beach along its southern *edge*. 2. ✦ **advantage** ✧ **asset, benefit, head start** Madelyn's height gives her a definite *edge* when she plays basketball. —*verb* 1. ✦ **ease, creep, inch, slide** ✧ **budge, glide, move** I slowly *edged* away from the growling dog. 2. ✦ **trim, border, outline** ✧ **decorate** We decided to *edge* our gravel driveway with red bricks.

**edit** *verb* ✦ **revise, rewrite** ✧ **check, correct, proofread** A large newspaper typically has several people whose job is to *edit* articles before publication.

**educate** *verb* ✦ **instruct, teach** ✧ **coach, train, tutor** A teacher's main job is to *educate* his or her students.

**education** *noun* ✦ **knowledge, learning, schooling** ✧ **information, instruction** A good *education* can help you get a better job.

**eerie** *adjective* ✦ **frightening, scary, spooky, strange, uncanny, weird** We heard *eerie* noises coming from the old abandoned house.

**effect** *noun* 1. ✦ **consequence, end, outcome, result** ✧ **conclusion** Tooth decay is one of the bad *effects* of consuming too much sugar. 2. ✦ **impact, influ-**

ence ✧ **impression, significance** So far all my attempts to diet have had little *effect* on my weight. —*verb* ✦ **accomplish, achieve, bring about, cause, make** The development of electricity *effected* many changes in the way people live.

**effective** *adjective* 1. ✦ **efficient, practical, productive** ✧ **successful** Good students make *effective* use of their study time. 2. ✦ **operational, operative, in effect** ✧ **active, functioning, real** The new law will become *effective* in January.

**efficient** *adjective* ✦ **effective, practical, productive** ✧ **capable, competent, proficient** When microchips were developed, computers became much more *efficient*.

**effort** *noun* 1. ✦ **work, exertion, labor, toil** ✧ **strain, struggle** Writing a book takes much more *effort* than most people realize. 2. ✦ **attempt, endeavor** ✧ **try, bid** Huong is making an *effort* to improve her language skills.

**eject** *verb* ✦ **expel, spew, discharge, erupt, force out** ✧ **remove** The geyser *ejected* a spray of hot water and steam.

**elaborate** *adjective* ✦ **complex, complicated, detailed, intricate** ✧ **fancy, thorough** The couple made *elaborate* preparations for their wedding. —*verb* ✦ **expand, amplify, develop, enlarge (upon), explain** ✧ **add (to), improve** When Minju gave a brief answer, the interviewer asked her to *elaborate on* it.

**elastic** *adjective* ✦ **stretchable** ✧ **flexible, pliable, adaptable** These gym shorts have an *elastic* waistband.

**elder** *adjective* ✦ **older** ✧ **senior** My *elder* sister is a doctor. —*noun* ✦ **senior** ✧ **senior citizen, ancestor** In many Asian countries, *elders* are highly respected.

**elderly** *adjective* ✦ **aged, aging, old, senior** ✧ **mature** The *elderly* man has been retired for twenty years.

**elect** *verb* 1. ✦ **vote in, ballot** ✧ **appoint, designate, name, nominate** Workers *elected* a new president for their union. 2. ✦ **choose, decide, pick, select, opt** ✧ **prefer** Wang Li *elected* to major in anthropology instead of history.

**elegant** *adjective* ✦ **exquisite, fancy, fine, stylish** ✧ **graceful, grand** The actress wore an *elegant* gown to the awards ceremony.

**element** *noun* ✦ **component, feature, ingredient, part, factor** ✧ **item, piece** The basic *elements* of a successful movie include an interesting story and good acting.

**elementary** *adjective* ✦ **basic, beginning, introductory, fundamental** ✧ **simple** This class is for students who already have an *elementary* knowledge of English.

**elevate** *verb* ✦ **raise, lift, pick up** ✧ **boost, hoist** The nurse *elevated* the patient's legs to make him more comfortable.

**eligible** *adjective* ✦ **qualified, authorized** ✧ **acceptable, fit, suitable, worthy** You must be a citizen in order to be *eligible* to run for public office.

**eliminate** *verb* ✦ **remove, drop, omit, exclude, leave out** ✧ **discard** When the factory installed automated machinery, many jobs were *eliminated*.

**elude** *verb* ✦ **evade, avoid, dodge, duck, escape** ✧ **lose, shun** The cat *eluded* the dogs that were chasing him.

**embarrass** *verb* ✦ **disconcert, fluster, discomfort, upset** ✧ **humiliate, shame** The audience's heckles *embarrassed* the actors.

**embarrassment** *noun* ✦ **chagrin, discomfort, uneasiness** ✧ **awkwardness, shame, shyness** I blushed in *embarrassment* when I realized that my shirt was on inside-out.

**emblem** *noun* ✦ **symbol, insignia, sign, crest** ✧ **badge, token** Canada's official *emblem* is the maple leaf.

**embrace** *verb* 1. ✦ **hug, clasp** ✧ **cuddle, grip, hold, squeeze** The couple *embraced* each other at the end of their wedding ceremony. 2. ✦ **accept, adopt, endorse** ✧ **choose, welcome** By the fifth century CE, most of the Roman world had *embraced* Christianity. 3. ✦ **comprise, include, contain, embody, encompass** ✧ **cover, hold** The United Kingdom *embraces* four countries: England, Wales, Scotland, and Northern Ireland. —*noun* ✦ **hug, clasp** ✧ **caress, pat, squeeze** The young couple held each other tight in a loving *embrace*.

**emerge** *verb* ✦ **appear, come out, materialize** ✧ **arise, surface** After the storm, the sun *emerged* from behind a rain cloud.

**emergency** *noun* ✦ **crisis, extremity** ✧ **accident, difficulty, predicament, trouble** Many people store extra food and water for use in case of an *emergency.*

**emigrate** *verb* ✦ migrate, move, relocate ✧ immigrate Yoshiko has relatives in Japan who are planning to *emigrate* to the United States.

**eminent** *adjective* ✦ famous, celebrated, distinguished, outstanding, prominent, top Thomas Edison was an *eminent* American scientist and inventor.

**emit** *verb* ✦ give off, discharge, expel, release ✧ issue, vent That factory *emits* too much air pollution.

**emotion** *noun* ✦ feeling, sentiment ✧ affection, passion, ardor Some people are so shy they have difficulty expressing their *emotions.*

### Word Groups

An **emperor** is a man who is the ruler of an empire. **Emperor** is a very specific term with no true synonyms. Here are some related words to investigate in a dictionary: **czar, king, majesty, monarch, raja, ruler, sovereign, sultan**

**emphasis** *noun* ✦ attention, stress, importance, significance, weight My ESL teacher puts a lot of *emphasis* on learning basic vocabulary.

**emphasize** *verb* ✦ stress, highlight, feature, accentuate ✧ insist My new boss *emphasizes* the importance of never being late to work.

**employ** *verb* 1. ✦ hire, engage, take on ✧ enlist, recruit The new factory will *employ* three hundred workers. 2. ✦ use, utilize ✧ apply, exercise, operate Early computers were bulky because they *employed* vacuum tubes instead of transistors and microchips.

**employee** *noun* ✦ worker ✧ assistant, helper, laborer, staff I work at a small bakery that has just five *employees.*

**employer** *noun* ✦ boss, manager, supervisor, director ✧ business, company Delfina's *employer* gave her a promotion and a raise.

**employment** *noun* ✦ job, occupation, work ✧ profession, trade, vocation Ged is seeking *employment* as an architect.

### Word Groups

An **empress** is a woman who is the ruler of an empire. **Empress** is a very specific term with no true synonyms. Here are some related words to investigate in a dictionary: **czarina, maharani, majesty, monarch, queen, ruler, sovereign**

**empty** *adjective* 1. ✦ bare, unoccupied, vacant ✧ blank, clear, free Neighborhood children use this *empty* lot as a playground. 2. ✦ meaningless, unreal, hollow, idle ✧ insincere, useless My dog is quite harmless, and his growling is just an *empty* threat. —*verb* ✦ clean out, clear, clear out ✧ evacuate, vacate We had to *empty* the closet before we could paint it.

**enable** *verb* ✦ allow, let, permit ✧ authorize, empower Baby monitors *enable* parents to keep an eye on their sleeping infant without actually being in its room.

**enclose** *verb* 1. ✦ close in, envelop, surround ✧ fence, circle, cover, wall in The cabin's back porch is *enclosed* by screens. 2. ✦ include, insert, put in ✧ add If paying this bill by mail, be sure to *enclose* a check with your statement.

**encounter** *noun* ✦ meeting, contact ✧ brush, confrontation, rendezvous Fortunately the hiker's unexpected *encounter* with a bear was peaceful. —*verb* ✦ meet, come across, run into ✧ experience, face Kim loves to travel because she enjoys *encountering* people from different cultures.

**encourage** *verb* 1. ✦ inspire, motivate, persuade, urge, stimulate, prompt My friends *encouraged* me to apply for a scholarship to study abroad. 2. ✦ promote, advance, foster, further, support ✧ help Regular exercise *encourages* good health.

### Antonyms encourage

*verb* 1. deter, discourage 2. hinder, impede, inhibit, obstruct, retard

**end** *noun* 1. ✦ edge, extremity ✧ border, limit, margin This highway runs from one *end* of the continent to the other. 2. ✦ finish, conclusion, ending, closure ✧ close, finale I read the entire book from beginning to *end* in one afternoon. 3. ✦ aim, goal, objective, purpose ✧ intent The movie's villain would stop at nothing to achieve his *end.* —*verb* ✦ conclude, finish, cease, halt, stop ✧ close, complete The game will *end* at sunset, regardless of the score.

**endeavor** *verb* 1. ✦ strive, attempt, seek, try, undertake ✧ struggle I believe that everyone should *endeavor* to be as good a person as possible. —*noun* ✦ effort, venture, attempt, try ✧ exertion, pains, struggle, undertaking Duyen's latest *endeavor* is starting her own online clothing business.

**endorse** *verb* ✦ approve, agree (to), support, uphold, back ✧ allow The mayor *endorsed* the city council's plan for urban renewal.

**endure** *verb* 1. ✦ tolerate, bear, suffer, take, withstand When I broke my arm, I *endured* the pain without complaining. 2. ✦ last, continue, persist, remain, survive The Roman empire *endured* for hundreds of years before it was finally conquered.

**enemy** *noun* ✦ foe, adversary, antagonist, assailant, attacker, opponent ✧ competitor, rival In the American Civil War, the North and the South were *enemies*.

**energetic** *adjective* ✦ vigorous, active, dynamic, lively, spirited If you take an aerobics class, be prepared for *energetic* exercise.

**energy** *noun* ✦ vitality, vigor, pep, spirit ✧ force, power, strength Some people are so full of *energy* that they have a hard time sitting still.

**enforce** *verb* ✦ administer, implement, apply, impose ✧ accomplish, perform A lifeguard *enforces* the safety rules at my apartment's swimming pool.

**engage** *verb* 1. ✦ employ, hire, retain, enlist ✧ take on The firm *engaged* a consultant to help develop an advertising campaign. 2. ✦ engross, captivate, absorb, fascinate, interest, involve ✧ occupy I was so *engaged with* my new book that I lost all track of time.

**engagement** *noun* ✦ appointment, date, meeting ✧ commitment, booking My boyfriend and I have a dinner *engagement* planned for Saturday night.

**engrave** *verb* ✦ etch, carve, cut, inscribe ✧ chisel, stamp The jeweler *engraved* my name on my new silver bracelet.

**enhance** *verb* ✦ heighten, increase, intensify ✧ improve, strengthen I use herbs to *enhance* the flavor of my homemade spaghetti sauce.

**enjoy** *verb* 1. ✦ delight (in), like, love, relish ✧ appreciate, savor Chau *enjoys* listening to Vietnamese folk music. 2. ✦ have, possess ✧ command, hold, own Despite our cat's age, he still *enjoys* good health.

**enjoyment** *noun* ✦ pleasure, amusement, fun, delight, joy ✧ satisfaction Maria gets more *enjoyment* from going to a live concert than from watching a band on TV.

**enlarge** *verb* ✦ build up, expand, increase, extend ✧ amplify, augment The city is planning to *enlarge* the airport by building two new runways.

**enlighten** *verb* ✦ inform, educate, instruct, teach ✧ notify, tell The movie *enlightened* us about the traditional way of life of a group of indigenous people living in the rainforest.

**enlist** *verb* 1. ✦ enter, join, sign up ✧ enroll, volunteer My friend *enlisted* in the American army in order to get US citizenship. 2. ✦ recruit, engage, obtain, get, procure, secure The US Forest Service *enlists* the help of volunteers to maintain trails.

**enormous** *adjective* ✦ gigantic, huge, immense, giant, tremendous ✧ big, large, vast Tyrannosaurus was an *enormous* dinosaur.

**enough** *adjective* ✦ adequate, sufficient ✧ ample, satisfactory, plenty I'm saving a little of my income until I have *enough* money to buy a new smartphone.

**enrage** *verb* ✦ anger, incense, infuriate, madden ✧ provoke The man was *enraged* when he found that his car had been stolen.

**enrich** *verb* ✦ enhance, improve, better, develop, refine A good education will *enrich* your mind.

**enroll** *verb* ✦ register, enter, join, sign up ✧ enlist Ji-hye wants to *enroll in a*n advanced ESL class.

**ensure** *verb* ✦ assure, insure, make sure, check, confirm ✧ guarantee Please *ensure* that your seat belt is properly fastened.

**enter** *verb* 1. ✦ go in, come in ✧ arrive, penetrate In Japan, it's polite to take off your shoes before *entering* someone's house. 2. ✦ enroll (in), join, register (for), sign up (for), begin, start ✧ Luis will be *entering* college next fall. 3. ✦ record, write, list, post, note ✧ file, insert The professor *entered* our test scores in his grade book.

**enterprise** *noun* ✦ endeavor, project, undertaking, adventure, venture ✧ task Amundsen's journey to the South Pole by dogsled in 1911 was a daring *enterprise*.

**entertain** *verb* ✦ amuse, delight, divert ✧ interest, occupy When our TV was broken, we had to find some other way to *entertain* ourselves.

**entertainment** *noun* ✦ amusement, enjoyment, diversion, recreation, fun, pleasure My friend and I play video games for *entertainment*.

**enthusiasm** *noun* ✦ eagerness, excitement, zeal ✧

fire, passion, zest Nicole got the job because she showed so much *enthusiasm* at her interview.

**enthusiastic** *adjective* ✦ ardent, fervent, avid, eager, passionate ✧ earnest My dog always gives me an *enthusiastic* welcome when I get home.

**entire** *adjective* ✦ complete, whole ✧ full, total, intact I'm so hungry that I could eat an *entire* pizza.

**entitle** *verb* 1. ✦ title, call, name ✧ designate, dub, label The scientist wrote a research paper *entitled* "The Body Language of Fish." 2. ✦ permit, allow, authorize, qualify, empower In the United States, all adult citizens are *entitled* to vote.

**entrance** *noun* 1. ✦ entry, appearance ✧ admission, approach, arrival Everyone bowed when the queen made her *entrance*. 2. ✦ entry, entryway, gate ✧ door, doorway, passageway There was a long line at the *entrance* to the stadium.

**entry** *noun* 1. ✦ entrance, appearance ✧ admission, approach, arrival Loud applause greeted the orchestra's *entry* onto the stage. 2. ✦ entrance, door, doorway, entryway, passageway ✧ gate A security guard asked people to not block the *entry*. 3. ✦ posting, note, record ✧ statement At the end of each day, the ship's captain made an *entry* in the logbook.

**envelop** *verb* ✦ enclose, cover, wrap, cloak, shroud, surround ✧ hood The silky cocoon completely *enveloped* the caterpillar.

**Word Groups**

An **envelope** is a flat paper wrapper used mainly for mailing letters. **Envelope** is a very specific term with no true synonyms. Here are some related words to investigate in a dictionary: **casing, container, mailer, pouch, repository, sheath, wrapper**

**envious** *adjective* ✦ jealous, covetous, desirous ✧ resentful I'm *envious* of anyone who can make a good living writing poetry.

**environment** *noun* ✦ setting, surroundings, atmosphere, conditions, scene ✧ locality The university library provides a quiet *environment* for studying.

**envy** *noun* ✦ jealousy ✧ desire, greed, resentment He was filled with *envy* when his friend won the lottery. —*verb* ✦ be jealous (of), be envious (of) ✧ begrudge, covet, resent I *envy* people who have secure and high-paying jobs.

**episode** *noun* 1. ✦ event, happening, development, incident, occurrence ✧ occasion The building of the transcontinental railroad was an important *episode* in the history of the American West. 2. ✦ installment, part ✧ act, chapter, show We'll have to watch next week's *episode* to find out who committed the crime.

**equal** *adjective* ✦ identical, equivalent, even ✧ like, similar, same I dealt an *equal* number of cards to each player. —*noun* ✦ match, equivalent, peer ✧ parallel, counterpart The undefeated boxer has yet to meet his *equal* in the ring. —*verb* ✦ amount (to), constitute, make, make up ✧ correspond, match One liter *equals 33.8 ounces*.

**equip** *verb* ✦ furnish, outfit, provide, supply ✧ stock The mountaineers were *equipped* with ropes and safety harnesses.

**equipment** *noun* ✦ apparatus, gear, supplies ✧ furnishings, materials, things The local department store is having a sale on sports *equipment*.

**equivalent** *adjective* ✦ equal, identical, the same, even ✧ like, similar If you buy one sandwich at full price, you can get one of *equivalent* value for half price. —*noun* ✦ counterpart, equal, same (as) ✧ match, twin One cup is the *equivalent of* eight ounces.

**era** *noun* ✦ age, epoch, period, time ✧ day, date The Victorian *era* is named after Queen Victoria, who ruled Great Britain from 1837 to 1901.

**erase** *verb* ✦ remove, rub out, wipe out, delete ✧ blot, cancel, clear I accidentally *erased* all the files on my USB drive.

**erect** *adjective* ✦ straight, upright, vertical ✧ rigid, firm *Erect* posture is good for your back. —*verb* ✦ build, construct, put up, raise, pitch ✧ make The farmer *erected* a new barn with the help of many neighbors.

**erode** *verb* ✦ wear, wear away ✧ carve, corrode, break up, eat The wind *eroded* the rocks into interesting shapes.

**errand** *noun* ✦ task, mission, assignment, chore, commission, job My boss asked me to run an *errand* for him.

**erratic** *adjective* ✦ inconsistent, changeable, irregular, unpredictable, variable ✧ bizarre, odd The weather has been so *erratic* lately that I never know if it's going to rain or shine.

**error** *noun* ✦ inaccuracy, mistake, slip ✧ blunder,

fault, flaw, lapse, oversight The accountant carefully checked the figures to make sure there were no *errors*.

**erupt** *verb* ✦ break, burst, explode ✧ blow up, gush The audience *erupted* into laughter.

**escape** *verb* 1. ✦ break out, get away, run away ✧ flee The tiger *escaped* from its cage. 2. ✦ elude, evade, get (by) ✧ avoid, dodge, get out (of) Nothing *escapes* my manager's attention. —*noun* ✦ breakout, getaway ✧ departure, flight The convicts made their *escape* on a dark and stormy night.

**escort** *noun* ✦ entourage, retinue, attendant, companion ✧ guard, guide The statesman's *escort* included his aides, interpreter, and bodyguards. —*verb* ✦ conduct, direct, guide, lead ✧ accompany, attend The usher *escorted* us to our seats.

**especially** *adverb* ✦ mainly, chiefly, mostly, particularly, primarily ✧ very I like almost all desserts, but I am *especially* fond of chocolate cake.

**essay** *noun* ✦ article, composition, paper ✧ report, theme The magazine published a special issue of *essays* about global climate change.

**essence** *noun* ✦ basis, core, heart ✧ nature, substance, soul The *essence* of democracy is the right to choose your own government.

**essential** *adjective* ✦ necessary, vital, key, basic, critical, important Proper nutrition is *essential* to maintaining good health.

**establish** *verb* 1. ✦ set up, start, create, found, institute, build My friends and I would like to *establish* our own business. 2. ✦ prove, demonstrate, show, verify, confirm Medical research has *established* the fact that smoking is hazardous to your health.

**establishment** *noun* 1. ✦ creation, development, formation ✧ start Our city is raising funds for the *establishment* of a new community college. 2. ✦ business, company, enterprise ✧ institution, organization He works for an *establishment* that makes vacuum cleaners.

**esteem** *verb* ✦ admire, honor, respect, prize, value, appreciate Albert Einstein is *esteemed* for his contributions to science. —*noun* ✦ admiration, honor, regard, respect, account ✧ reverence Everyone holds Priya in high *esteem* because she's honest and dependable.

**estimate** *verb* ✦ approximate, calculate, figure, guess, judge, reckon ✧ evaluate The news media *estimated* that about a thousand people attended the concert. —*noun* ✦ appraisal, assessment, approximation, calculation, evaluation ✧ guess The mechanic gave me an *estimate* on the cost of repairing my motorbike.

**eternal** *adjective* ✦ everlasting, perpetual, endless, infinite ✧ constant, continual The mythical Fountain of Youth is supposed to provide *eternal* agelessness.

**Antonyms** eternal

*adjective* brief, concise, fleeting, momentary, short, temporary, transitory

**etiquette** *noun* ✦ manners ✧ convention, courtesy, custom, behavior Chewing with your mouth open is not good *etiquette*.

**evacuate** *verb* ✦ get out, leave, exit, vacate, abandon ✧ clear, empty Residents were told to *evacuate* when the forest fire drew close to town.

**evade** *verb* ✦ avoid, dodge, elude, escape, lose The criminal tried to *evade* the police officers who were pursuing him.

**evaluate** *verb* ✦ appraise, rate, assess, judge ✧ calculate, value A panel of judges *evaluated* the gymnasts' performances.

**evaporate** *verb* ✦ disappear, fade, pass, dissipate, vanish ✧ vaporize My worries *evaporated* when my friend assured me she was all right.

**even** *adjective* 1. ✦ equal, identical, the same ✧ like, similar I cut the strips of paper into *even* lengths. 2. ✦ flat, level, plane, smooth ✧ horizontal, straight It's easier to walk along an *even* path than over rocky fields. 3. ✦ constant, regular, steady, unchanging, uniform When you rest, your heart beats at an *even* rate. —*adverb* ✦ still, yet ✧ actually, indeed I was encouraged to try *even* harder when my boss said I was doing a great job. —*verb* ✦ equalize, balance, tie ✧ equal, level, match Takuya's goal *evened* the score.

**evening** *noun* ✦ dusk, twilight, nightfall ✧ sundown, sunset, night The wind died down toward *evening*.

**event** *noun* 1. ✦ happening, episode, incident, occasion, occurrence ✧ circumstance Graduating from university was an important *event* in my life. 2. ✦ competition, contest, match ✧ game, tour-

**nament** Tasha won three *events* at last week's swim meet.

**ever** *adverb* ✦ forever, eternally, always ✧ continuously, constantly In fairy tales, characters typically live happily *ever* after.

**everlasting** *adjective* ✦ ceaseless, endless, enduring, eternal, perpetual, unending ✧ immortal The diamond in an engagement ring symbolizes *everlasting* love.

**every** *adjective* ✦ each, all ✧ any Please answer *every* question to the best of your ability.

**everyday** *adjective* ✦ regular, usual, customary, familiar, frequent, ordinary Making your bed and doing the dishes are examples of *everyday* chores.

**evidence** *noun* ✦ proof, facts, grounds, information ✧ indication, sign There wasn't enough *evidence* to convict the defendant of the crime.

**evident** *adjective* ✦ apparent, obvious, clear, certain, plain, visible It's *evident* that my smartphone battery needs to be recharged.

**evil** *adjective* ✦ wicked, bad, base, immoral ✧ harmful, wrong The *evil* tyrant killed everyone who opposed him. —*noun* ✦ wickedness, immorality, sin ✧ crime, harm, wrong It is often said that the love of money is the root of all *evil*.

**evolve** *verb* ✦ derive, develop, emerge, result ✧ change, grow Darwin's theory states that present-day plants and animals *evolved* from earlier forms.

**exact** *adjective* ✦ precise, accurate, correct, definite, true ✧ right What were her *exact* words?

**exactly** *adverb* ✦ precisely, just, specifically ✧ absolutely, completely, quite Shopping won't take long because I know *exactly* what I need to purchase for the party.

**exaggerate** *verb* ✦ overstate, embellish ✧ expand, inflate, magnify Takashiro was *exaggerating* when he said that he had a million books on his e-reader.

**examination** *noun* 1. ✦ check, checkup, inspection ✧ review, study, survey You will need a medical *examination* as part of your visa application. 2. ✦ exam, test, quiz, assessment It's necessary to take a written *examination* when you apply for a driver's license.

**examine** *verb* 1. ✦ inspect, check, study ✧ analyze, investigate The jeweler *examined* the sapphire very closely. 2. ✦ interrogate, query, question, quiz ✧ ask, inquire The police *examined* the suspect to see if she had an alibi.

**example** *noun* ✦ sample, specimen, representative ✧ case, instance, model This antique vase is a classic *example* of Chinese ceramics.

**exasperate** *verb* ✦ aggravate, annoy, irk, irritate, bother ✧ disturb Passengers were *exasperated* when their flight was canceled.

**excavate** *verb* ✦ dig up, uncover, unearth ✧ hollow, mine, scoop Archaeologists *excavated* King Tutankhamen's tomb in 1922.

**exceed** *verb* ✦ beat, better, outdo, surpass, top, pass My performance on the proficiency test *exceeded* my expectations.

**excel** *verb* ✦ dominate, stand out ✧ exceed, outdo, surpass Research has shown that mental focus and intelligence are necessary to *excel* in soccer.

**excellence** *noun* ✦ distinction, superiority, merit, greatness ✧ quality Nobel Prizes are awarded annually for *excellence* in five different cultural and scientific fields.

**excellent** *adjective* ✦ fine, great, outstanding, splendid, superb, terrific, superior This is an *excellent* day for a picnic.

**except** *preposition* ✦ excluding, other than, besides, but, barring I have been to all 50 US states *except* Alaska and Hawaii.

**exceptional** *adjective* ✦ unusual, uncommon, extraordinary, remarkable ✧ rare, strange When it snowed in July, everyone commented on the *exceptional* weather.

**excess** *noun* ✦ surplus, overage, oversupply ✧ overflow We gave our neighbors the *excess* from our vegetable garden. —*adjective* ✦ excessive, extra, surplus ✧ spare Kaito trimmed the *excess* fat off the steaks before he grilled them.

**excessive** *adjective* ✦ overabundant, extreme, undue, unreasonable, extravagant ✧ lavish, profuse Taking vitamins in *excessive* amounts can do more harm than good.

**exchange** *verb* ✦ trade, swap, switch ✧ barter, change, substitute My friend and I like to *exchange* books once we've read them. —*noun* ✦ interchange, trade, barter, swap, switch ✧ substitution The global economy is based on the *exchange* of money for goods or services.

**excite** *verb* ✦ arouse, rouse, stimulate, stir, thrill ✧ energize, agitate, provoke The home run *excited* the team's fans.

**exciting** *adjective* ✦ exhilarating, rousing, stimulating, stirring, thrilling, dramatic It was an *exciting* moment when Neil Armstrong first set foot on the moon.

**Antonyms** exciting

*adjective* boring, dreary, dull, monotonous, routine, tedious

**exclaim** *verb* ✦ shout, yell, call, cry ✧ bellow, roar, scream "Stop rocking the boat!" I *exclaimed* as our rowboat almost tipped over.

**exclude** *verb* ✦ ban, bar, keep out, prohibit, forbid, disallow ✧ omit The media were *excluded* from the meeting where the president announced his controversial new policy.

**excursion** *noun* ✦ jaunt, trip, outing ✧ journey, tour Next weekend we're taking an *excursion* to the beach.

**excuse** *verb* 1. ✦ condone, disregard, forgive, overlook, pardon Please *excuse* my messy apartment. 2. ✦ release, dismiss, exempt, let off ✧ relieve, spare I was *excused* from jury duty because I am a university student. —*noun* ✦ explanation, reason, apology ✧ alibi, story My boss accepted my *excuse* for being late to work.

**execute** *verb* 1. ✦ carry out, perform, accomplish, complete ✧ achieve, do The goalie *executed* a difficult save. 2. ✦ put to death ✧ kill, murder, slay The traitor was *executed* by a firing squad.

**executive** *noun* ✦ officer, official, administrator, director, manager The company's top *executives* meet once a week. —*adjective* ✦ directorial, managerial, managing, supervisory My friend has an *executive* position at the local bank.

**exempt** *verb* ✦ excuse, free, release, relieve ✧ dismiss The government *exempts* most charities from the requirement to pay taxes.

**exercise** *noun* 1. ✦ application, employment, use, usage ✧ operation The best way to stay on a diet is through the *exercise* of self-control. 2. ✦ workout, activity ✧ drill, practice, training Bicycling and swimming are excellent forms of physical *exercise*. —*verb* 1. ✦ use, utilize, apply, employ, practice Always *exercise* caution when driving a motor vehicle. 2. ✦ work out, condition ✧ drill, practice, train Haruki *exercises* by running almost every day.

**exert** *verb* ✦ apply, employ, exercise, use, utilize My friend had to *exert* a lot of willpower in order to quit smoking.

**exertion** *noun* ✦ exercise, effort, labor, struggle, toil ✧ pain, sweat I don't like to play soccer because it requires too much physical *exertion*.

**exhaust** *verb* 1. ✦ expend, use up, consume, finish ✧ drain, spend The campers quickly *exhausted* their supply of firewood. 2. ✦ fatigue, wear out, weary, tire ✧ weaken, drain The long, hard workout *exhausted* me.

**exhaustion** *noun* ✦ fatigue, tiredness, weariness ✧ weakness The soccer players were in a state of total *exhaustion* by the end of the game.

**exhibit** *verb* ✦ display, present, show ✧ demonstrate, reveal The museum will only *exhibit* the work of local artists. —*noun* ✦ display, exhibition, show ✧ presentation Isabella's watercolors were put on *exhibit* in a small art gallery.

**exhilarate** *verb* ✦ energize, invigorate, stimulate, animate ✧ elate, excite The cold winter air *exhilarated* the skiers.

**exile** *noun* ✦ banishment, expulsion ✧ deportation, removal The rebel leader was punished by permanent *exile* from his homeland. —*verb* ✦ banish, expel, deport ✧ oust, remove From 1788 to 1868, England *exiled* criminals to Australia.

**exist** *verb* ✦ live, survive ✧ continue, dwell, last A fish cannot *exist* for long out of water.

**existence** *noun* 1. ✦ life, survival ✧ being, living Some people believe that humanity's continued *existence* is being threatened by global climate change. 2. ✦ actuality, reality, fact, occurrence ✧ presence Some people believe in the *existence* of ghosts.

**exit** *noun* 1. ✦ outlet, way out, opening, passage ✧ door, gate Some buses have a roof hatch that serves as an emergency *exit*. 2. ✦ departure, escape, retreat, evacuation ✧ withdrawal When a skunk came in the front door, everyone made a hasty *exit* out the back door. —*verb* ✦ depart, go out, leave, move out ✧ retreat, withdraw A flight attendant told the passengers to *exit* at the rear of the plane.

**expand** *noun* ✦ swell, distend, enlarge, grow, increase ✧ extend A balloon *expands* when you blow air into it.

**expanse** *noun* ✦ extent, range, reach, space ✧ area, stretch, sweep Edward loves the desert because of its seemingly endless *expanse*.

**expect** *verb* ✦ anticipate, count (on), depend (on) ✧ assume, await, presume The weather forecaster said that we could *expect* rain.

**expectation** *noun* ✦ anticipation, hope, prediction ✧ belief, expectancy, prospect The movie's success exceeded the director's *expectations*.

**expedition** *noun* 1. ✦ journey, trip, trek ✧ safari, tour, voyage Someday I'd love to go on an archaeological *expedition in* the Amazon basin. 2. ✦ company, group, party, team ✧ band, troop The members of Coronado's *expedition* were the first Europeans to see America's Grand Canyon.

**expel** *noun* ✦ eject, evict, throw out ✧ banish, discharge, dismiss The college student was *expelled* for selling illegal drugs on campus.

**expense** *noun* ✦ expenditure, cost, price ✧ amount, charge, payment Wang Min works for a company that pays all her travel *expenses*.

**expensive** *adjective* ✦ costly, high-priced, extravagant ✧ rich, valuable My friend likes *expensive* clothes, but I prefer blue jeans and T-shirts.

**experience** *noun* 1. ✦ adventure, event, incident, occasion ✧ affair, ordeal Rafting down the river was an *experience* I'll never forget. 2. ✦ background, practice, training ✧ knowledge, skill The school will only hire instructors who already have teaching *experience*. —*verb* ✦ encounter, have, meet (with), undergo ✧ know, see Did you *experience* any difficulty in finding your way here?

**experiment** *noun* ✦ test, trial, investigation ✧ demonstration, research Many scientific *experiments* have been conducted on the International Space Station. —*verb* ✦ test, try, try out ✧ analyze, examine, investigate I'm *experimenting with* different recipes to see which makes the best spaghetti sauce.

**experimental** *adjective* ✦ test, trial ✧ beginning, early, initial, new A test pilot is someone who flies *experimental* aircraft.

**expert** *noun* ✦ authority, specialist ✧ master, professional That archaeologist is an *expert* on pre-

historic stone tools. —*adjective* ✦ skilled, adept, proficient, skillful ✧ experienced, knowledgeable This fine gold watch was made by an *expert* craftsperson.

**expire** *verb* 1. ✦ end, stop, cease, finish, lapse, run out My magazine subscription will *expire* in two months. 2. ✦ die, pass away, perish, succumb ✧ depart The beached whale *expired* despite our attempts to save it.

**explain** *verb* 1. ✦ describe, clarify, define ✧ demonstrate, interpret Our ESL teacher *explained* the difference between the present perfect and past perfect tenses. 2. ✦ account (for), justify, defend ✧ excuse Would you please *explain* why you are so late?

**explanation** *noun* ✦ account, justification, rationale, reason ✧ clarification The police officer wanted an *explanation* for why the motorist was driving so fast.

**explode** *verb* ✦ blow up, burst, go off, detonate ✧ blast, discharge, erupt The firecracker *exploded* with a loud bang.

**exploit** *noun* ✦ deed, feat, act, adventure ✧ achievement, stunt Davy Crockett was an American folk hero whose *exploits* have been featured in more than twenty movies. —*verb* ✦ manipulate, take advantage (of), use, control ✧ abuse, misuse The politician *exploited* the media in order to get as much favorable press coverage as possible.

**explore** *verb* 1. ✧ scout, search, survey, discover, travel, wander Sir Henry Stanley *explored* much of central Africa in the late 1800s. 2. ✦ look into, examine, investigate, research, probe My social club is *exploring* ways to raise money.

**explosion** *noun* 1. ✦ blast, detonation, discharge ✧ bang, boom, burst When workers dynamited the old building, the *explosion* could be heard for miles. 2. ✦ outbreak, outburst, eruption ✧ boom, spurt, increase There's been an *explosion* of interest in smartphone apps in recent years.

**expose** *verb* 1. ✦ subject, lay open ✧ bare, uncover The campers were *exposed* to the rain when their tent blew down. 2. ✦ disclose, divulge, reveal, show ✧ display, exhibit A reporter *exposed* the politician's lies.

---

**Antonyms** **expose**

*verb* 2. cloak, conceal, cover, disguise, hide, mask, obscure

**express** *verb* ✦ declare, state, voice, utter, indicate ◇ reveal, show, speak Everybody *expressed* a preference for pizza. —*adjective* 1. ✦ definite, distinct, particular, special, specific, precise This repository was built for the *express* purpose of storing historical documents. 2. ✦ nonstop, high-speed, fast, quick, rapid, speedy If you want to get there quickly, take the *express* train.

**expression** *noun* 1. ✦ gesture, indication, sign, token ◇ declaration, statement On Valentine's Day, it is customary to give either flowers or candy as an *expression* of love. 2. ✦ visage, look ◇ air, appearance, aspect I knew by her *expression* that she was in a good mood. 3. ✦ saying, phrase, remark ◇ motto, proverb, term "Break a leg" is a common *expression* for wishing an actor good luck.

**exquisite** *adjective* ✦ beautiful, delicate, elegant, fine, lovely Your silver necklace is *exquisite*.

**extend** *verb* 1. ✦ expand, lengthen, open, stretch out ◇ grow, increase This ladder can be *extended* to a length of twelve feet. 2. ✦ reach, stretch ◇ carry, go, run, spread The ocean *extends* much farther than the eye can see. 3. ✦ give, present, offer ◇ grant, submit I *extended* them an invitation to my party.

**extensive** *adjective* ✦ widespread, considerable, great, wide ◇ broad, huge, vast The earthquake caused *extensive* damage.

**exterior** *adjective* ✦ external, outer, outside ◇ outdoor, outward Many castles have *exterior* walls that are separate from the central stronghold. —*noun* ✦ outside, surface, facade ◇ cover, face The *exterior* of our apartment house is brick.

**exterminate** *verb* ✦ eliminate, eradicate, destroy, kill, annihilate ◇ extinguish We had to *exterminate* the termites that were damaging our house.

**external** *adjective* ✦ exterior, outer, outside, outward, surface All insects have six legs and an *external* skeleton.

**extinct** *adjective* ✦ nonexistent, vanished ◇ dead, deceased, gone Dinosaurs became *extinct* about 65 million years ago.

**extinguish** *verb* 1. ✦ put out, snuff out ◇ douse, quench, smother We used both water and dirt to *extinguish* our campfire. 2. ✦ destroy, eliminate, wipe out, end, erase ◇ abolish, suppress Last night's defeat *extinguished* our hopes of winning the championship.

**extra** *adjective* ✦ additional, spare, surplus, reserve ◇ more, new, other Andres keeps a flashlight and *extra* batteries in his car. —*adverb* ✦ extremely, exceptionally, especially, very ◇ greatly, highly, most The chef makes his chili with *extra* lean ground beef. —*noun* ✦ accessory, attachment ◇ addition, bonus, supplement My new smartphone came with many *extras*, including a case and headset.

**extract** *verb* ✦ draw out, take out, pull, remove, withdraw ◇ pluck I used a pair of tweezers to *extract* the splinter from my hand. —*noun* ✦ concentrate, essence, solution ◇ juice, oil A few drops of vanilla *extract* can flavor a whole batch of cookie dough.

**extraordinary** *adjective* ✦ exceptional, remarkable, incredible, great, outstanding, unusual ◇ amazing, rare Hercules was a mythological hero known for his *extraordinary* strength.

**extravagant** *adjective* ✦ lavish, excessive, indulgent, wasteful ◇ costly, extreme Buying ten pairs of shoes at a time would definitely be *extravagant*.

**extreme** *adjective* 1. ✦ excessive, intense, tremendous, unusual ◇ great, extravagant California's Death Valley is known for its *extreme* heat. 2. ✦ farthest, remotest, outermost, far ◇ final, last Pluto is located at the *extreme* edge of our solar system.

**eye** *verb* ✦ observe, regard, watch ◇ stare, survey, view The mouse was being *eyed* by a cat.

**eyesight** *noun* ✦ vision, seeing, sight ◇ perception I wear contact lenses to correct my *eyesight*.

**fable** *noun* ✦ parable, legend, story, tale ✧ myth, yarn The *fable* about the boy who cried wolf teaches the importance of telling the truth.

**fabric** *noun* ✦ cloth, material ✧ textile Quilts are made by sewing together little pieces of *fabric*.

**fabulous** *adjective* ✦ amazing, astonishing, fantastic, incredible, unbelievable The explorer told a *fabulous* tale about the lost city he claimed to have discovered.

**face** *noun* 1. ✦ expression, look, countenance, visage ✧ appearance I could tell by her *face* that she was not happy. 2. ✦ front, surface ✧ exterior, facade The climbers went straight up the cliff's *face*. —*verb* 1. ✦ look, point ✧ front, overlook Traditional Navajo homes *face* east to receive blessings from the rising sun. 2. ✦ brave, confront, encounter, meet, challenge Police officers sometimes have to *face* danger in the line of duty.

**facility** *noun* 1. ✦ ease, effortlessness, easiness ✧ skill, talent, fluency Miyu ice-skates with great *facility*. 2. ✦ equipment, resource ✧ convenience, aid My apartment building has laundry *facilities* in the basement.

**fact** *noun* 1. ✦ data, information ✧ detail, particular, knowledge Amit used an online encyclopedia to look up *facts* for his term paper. 2. ✦ actuality, certainty, certitude, reality, truism, truth It is a *fact* that insects have six legs.

**factor** *noun* ✦ consideration, circumstance ✧ component, detail, ingredient, element, part Bad weather was the main *factor* in canceling the picnic.

**factory** *noun* ✦ plant, shop ✧ mill, workshop In my town there is a *factory* where cars and trucks are made.

**factual** *adjective* ✦ accurate, correct, exact, real, true, valid The book gave a *factual* account of President Kennedy's life.

**fad** *noun* ✦ craze, fashion, trend, mania ✧ rage, style The hula hoop was a popular *fad* in the 1950s when more than 100 million were sold.

**fade** *verb* 1. ✦ dim, dull, pale ✧ age, whiten, wither Sunlight caused my curtains to *fade*. 2. ✦ decline, die away, diminish, lessen, wane, weaken When the thunder began to *fade away*, we knew that the storm was almost over.

**fail** *verb* 1. ✦ fall short, miss ✧ fizzle, flop, lose The pole vaulter *failed* on his first attempt to clear the bar. 2. ✦ overlook, neglect, omit ✧ avoid, ignore My boss never *fails* to notice if I'm a few minutes late. 3. ✦ decline, diminish, dwindle, lessen, wane, weaken My dog is getting old, and his hearing is beginning to *fail*.

**failure** *noun* 1. ✧ lack of success, breakdown, defeat, miss The runner's *failure* to win the race did not discourage her. 2. ✦ fiasco, dud, flop, loss ✧ disappointment, mess, ruin My first cake was a *failure*, but my second was a success.

**faint** *adjective* 1. ✦ dim, weak, feeble, indistinct, low, soft The flashlight's *faint* beam meant that the batteries were almost dead. 2. ✦ dizzy, giddy, lightheaded, delirious I felt *faint* after climbing ten flights of stairs. —*verb* ✦ black out, pass out, swoon ✧ collapse, keel over Some people *faint* at the sight of blood.

**fair** *adjective* 1. ✦ attractive, lovely, beautiful, pretty ✧ charming Welcome to our *fair* city. 2. ✦ light, pale ✧ blonde, white, ivory She sunburns easily because she has a *fair* complexion. 3. ✦ clear, cloudless, fine, sunny, bright ✧ favorable, mild The forecast is for *fair* weather this weekend. 4. ✦just, impartial, objective, unbiased ✧ equitable, indifferent, honest Good teachers are always *fair* when they grade their students. 5. ✦ decent, moderate, reasonable, average, satisfactory, adequate There's a *fair* chance that I will be able to get off work early tonight.

**faith** *noun* 1. ✦ confidence, trust, belief ✧ dependence, reliance Our coach told the team that she has *faith* in us. 2. ✦ belief, creed, religion ✧ doctrine In the United States, people of all *faiths* are allowed to worship freely.

**faithful** *adjective* ✦ loyal, devoted, staunch, steadfast, true ✧ constant, resolute My dog is my *faithful* companion.

**fake** *verb* ✦ imitate, feign, simulate ◇ counterfeit, pretend The boy *faked* being sick in order to stay home from school. —*noun* ✦ counterfeit, imitation, phony ◇ fraudulent, forgery Only an expert can tell that this diamond is a *fake*. —*adjective* ✦imitation, artificial, phony, counterfeit, false, mock My coat is lined with *fake* fur.

**fall** *verb* 1. ✦ drop, pitch, plummet, plunge, topple, tumble I bumped into the lamp, and it *fell* to the floor. 2. ✦ surrender ◇ submit, succumb, yield Rome *fell* to barbarians in the year 476 CE. 3. ✦ decrease, diminish, lower, reduce, subside ◇ ebb, lessen My friend's voice *fell* to a whisper when he told me his secret. 4. ✦ happen, occur, take place, arrive, come My birthday *falls* on a Tuesday this year. —*noun* 1. ✦ drop, plunge, descent, dive, spill, tumble The climber's safety rope stopped her *fall*. 2. ✦ downfall, overthrow, collapse, defeat ◇ plunge Democracy was restored after the dictator's *fall* from power.

**false** *adjective* ✦ untrue, untruthful, wrong, inaccurate, incorrect ◇ mistaken The dishonest witness gave *false* testimony.

**Antonyms** false

*adjective* authentic, correct, genuine, real, right, true

**fame** *noun* ✦ renown, celebrity, recognition, distinction ◇ glory, popularity Charles Lindbergh won *fame* by being the first person to fly solo across the Atlantic Ocean.

**familiar** *adjective* 1. ✦ common, ordinary, everyday, frequent, regular, routine, well-known Swings and jungle gyms are *familiar* sights at playgrounds. 2. ✦ acquainted, aware (of), knowledgeable (about) ◇ informed, experienced Are you *familiar* with the song "Happy Birthday to You"? 3. ✦ close, cordial, friendly, sociable ◇ intimate I am on *familiar* terms with most of the people who work in my department.

**family** *noun* 1. ✦ kin, kinfolk, relations, relatives ◇ household On Rosh Hashanah, Benjamin's *family* goes to temple together. 2. ✦ class, division, group, order, set ◇ category The violin and cello are part of the *family* of stringed instruments.

**famine** *noun* ✦ food shortage, starvation, hunger ◇ scarcity, lack The United Nations sent food to the country that was experiencing a *famine*.

**famous** *adjective* ✦ renowned, well-known, celebrated, prominent, eminent ◇ popular Abraham Lincoln was one of the most *famous* presidents of the United States.

**fan** *noun* ✦ admirer, devotee, enthusiast ◇ follower, lover *Fans* mobbed the rock star in an attempt to get his autograph.

**fancy** *noun* 1. ✦ impulse, whim, urge, desire, idea, notion, thought Paulina had a sudden *fancy* to go for a walk in the rain. 2. ✦ fondness, liking, love ◇ desire, longing, want I had a *fancy* for the cute kitten from the moment I saw it. —*adjective* ✦ decorative, elaborate, elegant, extravagant ◇ intricate The socialite bought *fancy* stationery for writing personal notes.

**fantastic** *adjective* 1. ✦ bizarre, odd, strange, unbelievable, weird, wild Strong onshore winds sometimes twist coastal trees into *fantastic* shapes. 2. ✦ outstanding, marvelous, remarkable, superb, terrific, wonderful Tatsuya has more than three hundred DVDs in his *fantastic* collection of foreign films.

**fantasy** *noun* ✦ daydream, dream, reverie, vision ◇ fancy, imagination The writer's favorite *fantasy* has him winning the Nobel Prize in Literature.

**far** *adverb* ✦ considerably, much, significantly, extremely ◇ greatly The book was *far* more interesting than I expected. —*adjective* ✦ distant, faraway, far-off, remote ◇ long, removed Dinosaurs lived in the *far* past.

**fare** *noun* ✦ fee, toll, charge, price ◇ cost I paid the *fare* as soon as I boarded the bus. —*verb* ✦ do, get along, get by, manage ◇ progress, prosper, thrive Zhang Jing says that she is *faring* well at her new job.

**farm** *noun* ✦ homestead ◇ field, garden, plantation, ranch, spread My neighbor gave me some corn grown on her family's *farm*. —*verb* ✦ cultivate, grow, raise, harvest, plant, till People first began to *farm* crops more than ten thousand years ago.

**fascinate** *verb* ✦ captivate, enchant, engross, enthrall, entrance ◇ charm, intrigue The explorer *fascinated* his audience with tales of his adventures in the Amazon basin.

**fashion** *noun* 1. ✦ manner, method, style, way ◇ system Hold the chopsticks in this *fashion*. 2. ✦ trend, vogue, craze, custom, fad, style The current *fashion* in clothing is strongly influenced by what celebrities are wearing. —*verb* ✦ shape, form, build, construct, fabricate, make Pottery is made by *fashioning* clay into a desired shape and then heating it in a kiln.

**fast** *adjective* 1. ✦speedy, swift, fleet, quick, rapid The cheetah is the *fastest* animal on land. 2. ✦ firm, fixed, secure, strong, tight Whenever I go on a carnival ride, I keep a *fast* grip on the safety bar. 3. ✦ faithful, loyal, steadfast, true, constant ✧ steady Alicia and Yuki have been *fast* friends for years. —*adverb* 1. ✦ speedily, swiftly, quick, quickly, rapidly I like to walk *fast*. 2. ✦ firmly, securely, soundly, tight, tightly, hard The gum was stuck *fast* to the bottom of my shoe.

**fasten** *noun* ✦ attach, connect, fix, anchor, secure ✧ bind, tie Make sure the shelf is securely *fastened* to the wall.

**fat** *noun* ✦ grease, oil ✧ lard, tallow, suet French fries contain a lot of *fat*. —*adjective* ✦ plump, heavy, obese, overweight, stout, corpulent I started exercising because I don't want to get *fat*.

**fatal** *adjective* ✦ deadly, lethal, mortal, terminal Black widow spider bites are almost never *fatal*.

**fate** *noun* ✦ destiny, fortune, luck, providence The happily married woman says that *fate* smiled on her the day she met her husband.

**fatigue** *noun* ✦ tiredness, weariness, exhaustion, weakness His *fatigue* was caused by lack of sleep. —*verb* ✦ tire, wear out, drain, exhaust, weary The long walk across town *fatigued* me.

**fault** *noun* 1. ✦ blame, responsibility ✧ culpability, guilt, offense It's my own *fault* that I failed, because I didn't study enough. 2. ✦ defect, flaw, imperfection, shortcoming ✧ error, mistake My computer is not working right because there's a *fault* in the new software.

**favor** *noun* 1. ✦ good deed, good turn, kindness, service, courtesy My brother did me a *favor* by helping me prepare for my driver's test. 2. ✦ acceptance, approval, liking, support, admiration, respect The politician worked hard to win the voters' *favor*. —*verb* 1. ✦ gratify, indulge, oblige, reward, accommodate, please The pianist *favored* her audience with two encores. 2. ✦ like, prefer, support, endorse ✧ approve, encourage Which of the two proposals do you *favor*?

**favorable** *adjective* ✦ advantageous, good, appro-priate, helpful ✧ beneficial The weather conditions today are *favorable* for sailing.

**favorite** *noun* ✦ preference, first choice, choice, ideal, love, pick New York's Times Square is a perennial *favorite* for tourists in America. —*adjective* ✦ favored, preferred, special, well-liked, dearest My *favorite* book is Tolstoy's *War and Peace*.

**fear** *noun* ✦ fright, anxiety, dread, panic, terror, alarm I experienced a moment of *fear* when the elevator stopped suddenly and its lights went out. —*verb* ✦ be afraid (of), be scared (of), dread My daredevil boyfriend seemingly *fears* nothing.

**fearless** *adjective* ✦ bold, brave, courageous, gallant, heroic, valiant The *fearless* firefighter didn't hesitate to enter the burning house.

**feast** *noun* ✦ banquet, dinner, meal ✧ repast, spread Kwanzaa is a week-long African American celebration that ends with a special *feast* on January 1st. —*verb* ✦ banquet, dine, feed ✧ devour, eat, gorge It's an old American custom to *feast* on roast turkey every Thanksgiving.

**feat** *noun* ✦ achievement, accomplishment, exploit, act, deed ✧ stunt The firefighter was decorated for her remarkable *feat* of bravery.

**feature** *noun* ✦ attribute, characteristic, quality, trait, detail Many *features* of my new apartment building remind me of the last place I lived. —*verb* ✦ emphasize, highlight, star, spotlight ✧stress, promote The concert will *feature* folk songs from around the world.

**fee** *noun* ✦ charge, toll, payment ✧ cost, price, stipend You have to pay a *fee* to use that parking lot.

**feeble** *adjective* ✦ dim, faint, weak, inadequate ✧ fragile, frail The room was completely dark except for the *feeble* light of a single candle.

**feed** *verb* 1. ✦ nourish, serve ✧ maintain, satisfy, sustain This lasagna is big enough to *feed* ten people. 2. ✦ consume, devour, eat ✧ live, subsist Polar bears *feed on* seals and fish. —*noun* ✦ fodder, food, forage, provisions, fare ✧ chow The farmer used some of his corn crop as *feed* for his cattle.

**feel** *verb* 1. ✦ handle, touch, palpate ✧ rub, stroke The doctor *felt* my arm to see if it was broken. 2. ✦ detect, notice, perceive, sense, discern I *feel* a headache coming on. 3. ✦ believe, consider, hold, think ✧ deem, know I *feel* that your story is completely true. —*noun* ✦ texture, feeling, touch ✧ sensation I love the *feel* of rabbit fur.

**feeling** *noun* 1. ✦sensation, awareness, perception, sensitivity ✧ feel, touch I had no *feeling* in my foot when it went to sleep. 2. ✦ sense, mood, emotion ✧ sentiment, reaction The author had a *feeling* of pride when his article was published in a leading journal. 3. ✦ belief, idea, notion, impression ✧ opinion, thought I have a *feeling* that it's going to rain today.

**fell** *verb* ✦ chop down, cut down, drop, hew, level, raise On average more than forty million trees are *felled* worldwide every single day.

**fence** *noun* ✦ barrier, wall ✧ railing, barricade The family installed a *fence* to keep their dog in their yard.

**ferocious** *adjective* ✦ fierce, savage, vicious, brutal, cruel ✧ wild Judging by their teeth and claws, velociraptors must have been *ferocious* dinosaurs.

**Antonyms** **ferocious**
*adjective* docile, harmless, gentle, mild, quiet, tame

**fertile** *adjective* ✦ fruitful, fecund, productive, rich ✧ bountiful The farmland in the American Midwest is very *fertile*.

**festival** *noun* ✦ celebration, jubilee, gala, fair ✧ holiday, ritual My university sponsored a *festival* where people could sample foods from all over the world.

**fetch** *verb* ✦ go (for), go get, retrieve ✧ bring, carry When Malena plays with her dog, she throws a stick for him to *fetch*.

**feud** *noun* ✦ conflict, dispute, fight, quarrel ✧ disagreement In Scotland, Clan Campbell and Clan MacDonald clashed in a famous *feud* that lasted for hundreds of years.

**few** *adjective* ✦ not many, hardly any ✧ scant, limited, occasional, rare, scarce I *felt* a few drops, but it didn't really rain.

**fib** *noun* ✦ falsehood, lie, untruth, fabrication ✧ fiction, story, tale He told a *fib* when he said that he knew a famous rock star. —*verb* ✦ lie, falsify, misrepresent ✧ exaggerate, distort I don't think people should *fib* about their age.

**fiction** *noun* ✦ concoction, fantasy, invention, tale ✧ fable, story, fib, lie I couldn't tell if his story was fact or *fiction*.

**field** *noun* 1. ✦ lot, plot, tract, clearing ✧ ground, meadow, pasture My friends and I like to play soccer in the vacant *field* just outside town. 2. ✦ athletic field ✧ arena, court, stadium, track The football coach made his players run up and down the *field*. 3. ✦ area, realm, domain, world, subject ✧ occupation, profession Dr. Seuss was a leading author in the *field* of children's literature.

**fierce** *adjective* 1. ✦ dangerous, ferocious, savage, vicious ✧ brutal, wild Mother bears can be very *fierce* when their cubs are threatened. 2. ✦ extreme, high, intense, powerful, strong, violent Antarctica's *fierce* winds have been clocked at more than two hundred miles per hour.

**fight** *noun* 1. ✦ brawl, clash, scrap, scuffle, struggle ✧ battle, combat Two of the neighborhood cats got into a noisy *fight* last night. 2. ✦ argument, quarrel, disagreement, dispute, squabble ✧ feud Their marriage has survived despite their having had a few *fights* over money. —*verb* 1. ✦ battle, combat, contend, oppose, struggle, clash Americans *fought* against each other in the Civil War. 2. ✦ argue, bicker, quarrel, squabble, dispute Let's not *fight* over what television show we watch.

**figure** *noun* 1. ✦ digit, number, numeral, ordinal Antonio can add up a long list of *figures* in his head. 2. ✦ diagram, design, pattern, illustration ✧ drawing I could tell it was a math book because its cover was decorated with geometric *figures*. 3. ✦ form, shape, silhouette ✧ contour, outline I could see two *figures* walking in the distance. 4. ✦ dignitary, leader, notable, personality ✧ character, person The Secretary-General of the United Nations is an important world *figure*. —*verb* ✦ calculate, compute, reckon ✧ estimate, solve, assess I helped my friend *figure out* how much we should tip the waiter.

**file** *noun* 1. ✦ record, document ✧ data, information Doctors keep medical *files* on all of their patients. 2. ✦ column, line, queue, row, string, chain I saw a long *file* of ants heading toward our picnic basket. —*verb* 1. ✦ arrange, order, organize, classify, sort ✧ deposit, rank, store The secretary *filed* all the office documents alphabetically by subject. 2. ✦ enter, register, submit (to), record ✧ apply, seek After the man was in a car accident, he *filed* a claim with his insurance company. ✦ march, parade, troop, walk, move, proceed Guests *filed* past the bride and groom to wish them a happy marriage.

**fill** *verb* 1. ✦ load, pack, jam, stuff, stock, stuff, pile Alden *filled* his suitcase with clothes and shoes. 2.

♦ occupy, hold ◇ act, function, perform, serve A temporary employee will *fill* the position until a permanent replacement can be hired. **3.** ♦ plug, seal, stop up ◇ block, close The dentist *filled* my cavity. **4.** ♦ fulfill, supply, execute ◇ furnish, meet, provide The clerk said that it would take fifteen minutes to *fill* our order.

**filter** *noun* ◇ screen, strainer, purifier, sieve My roommates and I installed a *filter* to purify our drinking water. —*verb* **1.** ♦ clear, cleanse, purify, screen, strain Firefighters often wear masks to *filter* their air when fighting a wildland fire. **2.** ♦ flow, seep, trickle ◇ drain, leak, ooze Sunlight *filtered* down through the leaves and branches.

**filthy** *adjective* ♦ dirty, grimy, unclean, grubby, muddy, soiled ◇ messy, unkempt The gas station's restroom was so *filthy* I didn't want to use it.

**final** *adjective* **1.** ♦ closing, concluding, last, finishing, end, ending I missed the *final* part of the movie because I fell asleep. **2.** ♦ conclusive, decisive, definite ◇ authoritative Decisions made by referees or umpires are *final*.

**finale** *noun* ♦ climax, close, conclusion, finish ◇ end, ending The concert's grand *finale* included stirring music and lots of fireworks.

**find** *verb* **1.** ♦ come (upon), locate, spot, detect ◇ recover, retrieve I *found* a beautiful conch shell at the beach. **2.** ♦ determine, discover, learn, perceive, see, notice Have you *found* the answer to my riddle yet?

**fine** *adjective* **1.** ♦ little, minute, small, tiny, wee ◇ miniature, light, thin You need a magnifying glass to read the *fine* print in this unabridged dictionary. **2.** ♦ excellent, good, splendid, superb, superior, terrific It's a *fine* day for going to the beach. —*adverb* ♦ excellently, nicely, splendidly, well, superbly Christina is getting along *fine* at her new job.

**finish** *verb* **1.** ♦ accomplish, complete, conclude, end ◇ achieve, close I *finished* my chores in almost no time at all. **2.** ♦ consume, use up, expend, exhaust ◇ drain, empty I wanted more pie, but someone had *finished* it. —*noun* ♦ close, completion, conclusion, end, ending, finale I missed the start of the race, but I saw the *finish*.

| **Antonyms** finish |
| --- |

*verb* **1.** arise, begin, commence, launch, start
*noun* beginning, inception, opening, start

**fire** *noun* **1.** ♦ blaze, conflagration ◇ burning, combustion, flame The biggest forest *fire* in history burned 47 million acres in Siberia in 2003. **2.** ♦ gunfire, firing, shooting, shots The soldiers took cover when they were exposed to enemy *fire*. —*verb* **1.** ♦ ignite, kindle, light ◇ spark, flame I used extra-long matches to *fire* the barbecue grill. **2.** ♦ discharge, shoot ◇ trigger The race will start when the starting pistol is *fired*. **3.** ♦ discharge, dismiss, drop, let go, release, lay off The man was *fired* because he was always late to work.

**firm¹** *adjective* **1.** ♦ hard, rigid, stiff, solid ◇ compact, dense I like to sleep on a *firm* mattress. **2.** ♦ certain, definite, steadfast, steady, unwavering, resolute Carla is *firm* in her beliefs. **3.** ♦ fast, secure, steady, strong, sure, tight Keep a *firm* grip on the rope.

**firm²** *noun* ♦ business, company, corporation, enterprise, establishment, organization More than a dozen lawyers work for that *firm*.

**first** *noun* ♦ beginning, outset, start ◇ origin, inception The night was dark at *first*, but then the moon came out. —*adjective* ♦ earliest, initial, original ◇ pioneer Amelia Earhart was the *first* woman to fly across the Atlantic Ocean. —*adverb* ♦ initially, originally ◇ firstly When did the baby *first* learn to crawl?

**fit** *verb* **1.** ♦ suit, conform (to), correspond (to), match ◇ agree Your clothes *fit* the occasion perfectly. **2.** ♦ equip, furnish, outfit ◇ provide, supply I'm having my apartment *fitted* with new drapes. —*adjective* **1.** ♦ suitable, appropriate, correct, proper, right, fitting This is not a *fit* time to ask your boss for a promotion. **2.** ♦ robust, healthy, strong, well ◇ hale, sound I exercise regularly to stay *fit*.

**fix** *verb* **1.** ♦ anchor, install, secure, set ◇ attach, fasten The fence posts are *fixed* in concrete. **2.** ♦ arrange, conclude, designate, determine, establish, settle Before I left the dentist's office, I *fixed* a time for my next appointment. **3.** ♦ mend, repair, remedy ◇ correct, patch, overhaul A computer technician *fixed* my laptop. —*noun* ♦ jam, plight, predicament, mess ◇ difficulty, trouble I was in a *fix* when I couldn't find my apartment key.

**flag** *noun* ♦ banner, ensign, pennant, standard, colors A pirate's *flag* usually has a white skull and crossbones on a black background. —*verb* ♦ hail, signal, beckon ◇ gesture, motion, wave When I ran out of gas, I *flagged* a passing motorist for assistance.

**flame** *noun* ✦ fire, blaze, flare ✧ glow, light Moths are attracted to a candle's *flame*.

**flap** *verb* ✦ flutter, wave ✧ beat, fly, swing The *flag* was flapping in the wind.

**flash** *verb* 1. ✦ flare, blaze, flame, gleam ✧ glimmer, shimmer, shine Lightning *flashed* on the horizon. 2. ✦ dash, fly, race, rush, speed ✧ hasten, hurry Race cars *flashed* by the grandstand. —*noun* 1. ✦ blaze, burst, flare, gleam ✧ glimmer, shimmer, glow The fireworks exploded with colorful *flashes* and a lot of noise. 2. ✦ jiffy, instant, moment, second, wink Don't worry, I'll be back in a *flash*.

**flat** *adjective* 1. ✦ horizontal, level, even, smooth ✧ flush I sanded the tabletop until it was perfectly *flat*. 2. ✦ constant, firm, fixed, set, uniform The restaurant charges a *flat* rate for delivery, regardless of how much food is ordered. 3. ✦ bland, flavorless, tasteless, insipid ✧ dull, stale If you think that the soup seems *flat*, add a little salt.

---
**Antonyms** flat

*adjective* 1. coarse, craggy, jagged, rugged, uneven 3. delicious, flavorful, luscious, savory, tasty, toothsome

---

**flatter** *verb* ✦ compliment, praise ✧ humor, charm, gratify, please Do you really think that I look like a movie star, or are you just *flattering* me?

**flavor** *noun* ✦ tang, taste, relish, savor ✧ zest This salad dressing has a great *flavor*. —*verb* ✦ season, spice ✧ tinge, salt When Lucas makes chili, he *flavors* it with pepper and barbecue sauce.

**flaw** *noun* ✦ blemish, defect, fault, imperfection ✧ shortcoming, deformity This sweater is inexpensive because it has a *flaw*.

**flee** *noun* ✦ run away, take off, leave, scamper, scoot ✧ depart The mice *fled* when they saw a cat enter the room.

**fleet** *adjective* ✦ fast, quick, rapid, speedy, swift The cheetah is a *fleet* runner.

**flexible** *adjective* 1. ✦ bendable, pliable, elastic ✧ springy, supple My fishing pole is made of *flexible* bamboo. 2. ✦ adjustable, changeable, variable, adaptable, versatile My job has such *flexible* hours, I can take time off whenever I need.

**flicker** *verb* ✦ flash, twinkle, blink, wink ✧ flutter, glimmer Lightning bugs are easy to see because they *flicker* in the dark. —*noun* ✦ flash, flare, glimmer ✧ ray, spark, blink There was a *flicker* of lightning in the stormy sky.

**flight** *noun* 1. ✦ flying ✧ gliding, soaring, winging Ostriches, emus, and penguins are birds that are incapable of *flight*. 2. ✦ formation, squadron, wing ✧ flock, swarm, group We watched in awe as a *flight* of jets passed overhead.

**flimsy** *adjective* ✦ fragile, frail, delicate, thin, weak ✧ feeble Tissue paper is too *flimsy* for making paper airplanes.

**flinch** *verb* ✦ start, draw back, recoil, shrink back ✧ cower, cringe, wince I *flinched* as a snowball went whizzing past my head.

**fling** *verb* ✦ hurl, pitch, throw, toss, cast, heave, sling The angry toddler *flung* his toy across the room. —*noun* ✦ throw, toss, cast, heave, pitch, lob When I played darts with my friend, he got a bull's-eye on his first *fling*.

**float** *verb* ✦ drift, glide, sail, skim, wash A model boat *floated* all the way across the pond.

**flock** *noun* ✦ herd, pack ✧ crowd, group, swarm, throng A shepherd watches over a *flock* of sheep. —*verb* ✦ collect, crowd, gather, press, swarm, throng, congregate Eager fans *flocked* around the movie star.

**flood** *noun* ✦ deluge, inundation, overflow, torrent ✧ stream, tide This room has so many windows that on sunny days it is filled with a *flood* of light. —*verb* ✦ inundate, drown, submerge, cover, deluge, fill, overflow After the storm, water *flooded* all of the valley's low-lying farmland.

**floor** *noun* 1. ✦ bottom, ground, base, bed ✧ foundation Stalagmites form on cave *floors*. 2. ✦ level, story ✧ deck, tier, stage My apartment is on the building's thirteenth *floor*. —*verb* ✦ drop, fell, flatten, knock down, level The boxer *floored* his opponent with a single punch.

**flow** *verb* ✦ pour, stream, gush, run, surge, spill Water *flowed* from the drainpipe. —*noun* ✦ current, river, stream, tide, surge There was a steady *flow* of traffic on the busy highway.

**flower** *noun* ✦ bloom, blossom ✧ bud He gave his girlfriend a bouquet of *flowers* for Valentine's Day. —*verb* ✦ bloom, blossom ✧ bud, sprout Cherry trees *flower* in the springtime.

**fluid** *noun* ✦ liquid ✧ beverage, juice, drink, water I drank a lot of *fluids* when I was sick. —*adjective* ✦ liquid, runny, watery, running ✧ flowing Freshly mixed concrete is *fluid*, but it becomes hard when it sets.

**flush** *verb* 1. ✦ blush, color, redden ✧ glow Carlos *flushed* when I told him how nice he looked. 2. ✦ wash, rinse, clean, cleanse, drown, flood I like to drink lots of water to *flush* toxins out of my body. —*noun* ✦ blush, color, glow, rosiness ✧ redness Becky's face had a healthy *flush* after basketball practice.

**flutter** *verb* ✦ flap, wave ✧ fly, sail, beat, swish A flag *fluttered* in the breeze.

**fly** *verb* 1. ✦ take flight ✧ glide, sail, soar, wing Pterodactyls were reptiles that could *fly*. 2. ✦ bolt, dash, hasten, hurry, run, rush, zoom, shoot My cat *flew* to the kitchen when he heard me opening his can of food.

**focus** *noun* ✦ center, core, heart, hub, seat, spotlight I enjoyed being the *focus* of attention at my graduation party. —*verb* ✦ center, direct, fix, concentrate, address, devote, give Yuka *focused* her attention on the computer screen.

**foe** *noun* ✦ adversary, antagonist, opponent, rival, competitor, enemy The two senators were political *foes*.

**fog** *noun* ✦ haze, mist, cloud ✧ vapor, whiteout, murk The captain would not set sail until the *fog* lifted. —*verb* ✦ cloud, mist, blur ✧ blanket, obscure Steam from the kettle *fogged* my kitchen window.

**foggy** *adjective* 1. ✦ cloudy, hazy, misty, murky ✧ bleary The airport had to be closed because the day was so *foggy*. 2. ✦ confused, dim, fuzzy, indistinct, unclear, vague I have only a *foggy* recollection of my dream.

**foil** *verb* ✦ check, defeat, frustrate, hinder, thwart, prevent An alert police officer *foiled* the gang's attempt to paint graffiti on the storefront.

**fold** *verb* 1. ✦ bend, double over, crease ✧ pleat Danielle *folded* the note and put it into her pocket. 2. ✦ enfold, envelop, clasp, hug, embrace, wrap ✧ close, tuck My boyfriend *folded* me in his arms and gave me a big hug. —*noun* ✦ crease, pleat, wrinkle ✧ furrow I ironed the *folds* out of my new blouse.

**follow** *verb* 1. ✦ come (after), go (after), succeed ✧ replace, trail February *follows* January. 2. ✦ abide (by), heed, obey, observe, mind, regard Our softball game was a success because everybody *followed* the rules. 3. ✦ catch, comprehend, get, grasp, understand, perceive I wasn't able to *follow* what you were saying.

**following** *adjective* ✦ next, coming, succeeding, subsequent ✧ later The man was admitted to the hospital in the evening and released the *following* morning. —*noun* ✦ audience, public ✧ fans, followers, supporters A social media star is someone who has a large *following* on the internet.

**fond** *adjective* ✦ affectionate, loving, warm ✧ close, devoted When I came home from college, family and friends gave me a *fond* greeting.

## Word Groups

Anything that is taken in by a living organism and used for nourishment is **food**. **Food** is a general term with no true synonyms. Here are some related words to investigate in a dictionary: **cuisine, edibles, fare, provisions, rations, sustenance**

**fool** *noun* ✦ dummy, idiot, moron, simpleton, imbecile A *fool* and his money are soon parted. —*verb* 1. ✦ deceive, trick, dupe, con ✧ bluff, mislead My friend *fooled* me into thinking that today was his birthday. 2. ✦ jest, joke, kid, tease ✧ pretend, play I was only *fooling* when I said that I hate ice cream.

**foolish** *adjective* ✦ dumb, silly, stupid ✧ crazy, senseless, unwise, idiotic I felt *foolish* when I realized I had put my T-shirt on backwards.

**foot** *noun* ✦ base, bottom ✧ foundation, floor, ground There's a lake near the *foot* of the mountain.

**forbid** *verb* ✦ ban, bar, disallow, prohibit, prevent, outlaw The rules *forbid* swimming without a lifeguard.

**force** *noun* 1. ✦ energy, might, power, strength, vigor The wind blew with so much *force* that it knocked down trees and power lines. 2. ✦ crew, group, team, corps ✧ body, gang, team, unit The company has a work *force* of about fifty people. —*verb* 1. ✦ coerce, compel, make, require, obligate ✧ oblige Darkness *forced* us to stop our baseball game. 2. ✦ press, push, thrust, wrench, break, pry ✧ drive The door was stuck, and I had to *force* it open.

**forceful** *adjective* ✦ dynamic, powerful, strong, vigorous, effective, compelling The governor drew large crowds because he was such a *forceful* speaker.

**forecast** *verb* ✦ call for, foretell, predict, project ✧ anticipate, foresee The weather bureau is *forecasting* snow for tomorrow. —*noun* ✦ outlook, projection, prediction ✧ anticipation, prophecy The economic *forecast* is for lower prices and higher wages.

**foreign** *adjective* ✦ alien, exotic ✧ distant, faraway, remote, unfamiliar Liam speaks English with a *foreign* accent.

**foremost** *adjective* ✦ chief, top, leading, main, primary, principal ✧ prime Solar power is the *foremost* source of renewable energy.

**forest** *noun* ✦ woods, woodland ✧ grove, thicket, timberland *Forests* provide food and shelter for many animal species.

**foretell** *verb* ✦ forecast, foresee, predict, project, prophesy, tell Do you believe that some people can *foretell* the future?

**forever** *adverb* ✦ always, eternally, perpetually, evermore ✧ constantly, continuously Most people get married hoping their love will last *forever*.

**forfeit** *verb* ✦ give up, lose, sacrifice, surrender ✧ drop, yield The customer had to *forfeit* his deposit when he canceled his order.

**forge** *verb* 1. ✦ create, make, fashion, form, shape, mold The artist *forged* a unique chair out of horseshoes and an old tractor seat. 2. ✦ copy, counterfeit, fake, falsify, imitate, duplicate An expert discovered that the painting had been *forged*.

**forget** *verb* ✦ fail to remember ✧ disregard, neglect, overlook Don't *forget* your card when you go to the library.

**forgive** *verb* ✦ excuse, pardon ✧ condone, acquit, clear Please *forgive* me for interrupting you.

**form** *noun* 1. ✦ figure, shape, design ✧ outline, pattern Topiary is the practice of trimming foliage into animal or geometric *forms*. 2. ✦ kind, sort, type, style, variety Television is a popular *form* of entertainment. 3. ✦ document, paper, sheet, application ✧ questionnaire The catalog came with a *form* for placing orders. —*verb* 1. ✦ create, fashion, make, shape ✧ produce The city council voted to *form* a new school district. 2. ✦ devel-

op, grow, appear, materialize, emerge Mold has *formed* on this old loaf of bread.

**formal** *adjective* ✦ official, proper, conventional, regular ✧ established The businessman was successful despite not having a *formal* education.

**formation** *noun* ✦ arrangement, design, pattern ✧ layout, order, figure I saw a cloud *formation* that looked like a horse.

**former** *adjective* ✦ previous, prior, past ✧ earlier, preceding My *former* manager is now head of the entire company.

**forsake** *verb* ✦ abandon, desert, disown, renounce, leave, quit I love my country, and I will never *forsake* it.

**fort** *noun* ✦ fortification, fortress, stockade, stronghold, citadel In America's Old West, *forts* were usually made of logs.

**forth** *adverb* ✦ forward, out, outward, on, onward ✧ ahead The cavalrymen rode *forth* to meet the enemy.

**fortunate** *adjective* ✦ blessed, favored, lucky ✧ happy, well-off, good I feel *fortunate* that my best friend lives in the same apartment building.

**fortune** *noun* 1. ✦ luck, fate, destiny, chance, providence *Fortune* was with us when we won the big football game. 2. ✦ treasure, riches, wealth ✧ assets, capital The founder of the new online company has already made a *fortune*.

**forward** *adjective* ✦ front, fore ✧ advance, head, leading My seat is in the plane's *forward* cabin. —*adverb* ✦ forth, out, outward ✧ ahead, before, onward Please step *forward* when your name is called. —*verb* ✦ deliver, send, dispatch, ship, transmit I had my mail *forwarded* to a friend while I was on vacation.

**foul** *adjective* 1. ✦ disgusting, nasty, offensive, repulsive, revolting, sickening Rotten eggs have a *foul* odor. 2. ✦ bad, inclement, blustery, rainy, stormy, wet ✧ threatening We had to cancel our soccer game because of *foul* weather.

**found** *verb* ✦ create, start, begin, establish, institute ✧ originate My friends and I decided to *found* an online translating service.

**foundation** *noun* 1. ✦ basics, basis, framework, root ✧ cause, reason Reading, writing, and arithmetic are the traditional *foundations* of a good education. 2. ✦ base, bottom, footing ✧ bed, foot,

**support** The house's *foundation* is made of concrete blocks.

**fraction** *noun* ✦ part, portion, section, fragment ✧ piece, share He sold his house for only a *fraction* of what he had thought it was worth.

**fracture** *noun* ✦ break, crack ✧ rupture, separation, split Our first aid instructor showed us how to splint a *fracture*. —*verb* ✦ break, crack, shatter, splinter, split, fragment The bone *fractured* in two places.

**fragile** *adjective* ✦ breakable, brittle, delicate ✧ feeble, frail, weak If you mail something that's *fragile*, be sure to pack it very carefully.

**Antonyms** fragile
*adjective* hardy, robust, rugged, strong, sturdy, tough

**fragment** *noun* ✦ bit, chip, piece, scrap ✧ part, portion, shred The archaeologist found a *fragment* of ancient pottery.

**frail** *adjective* 1. ✦ infirm, sickly, weak, feeble ✧ crippled He's robust now, but he was *frail* as a child. 2. ✦ brittle, delicate, flimsy, fragile, crumbly Flowers that have been dried and pressed are very *frail*.

**frame** *noun* 1. ✦ framework, framing, shell ✧ mount, mounting, structure My new bicycle has a titanium *frame* that is much lighter than my old one. 2. ✦ body, build, form, physique, figure He is a good wrestler in part because he has a small, wiry *frame*. —*verb* ✦mount, border, enclose ✧ assemble, build I *framed my* college diploma and hung it on the wall of my apartment.

**frank** *adjective* ✦ candid, honest, direct, straightforward ✧ blunt, open Please be *frank* and tell me what you really think.

**frantic** *adjective* ✦ frenzied, agitated, distressed, distraught, excited ✧ wild The mother robin became *frantic* when she saw a hawk circling over her nest.

**fraud** *noun* 1. ✦ deceit, deception, trickery ✧ swindle, swindling If an advertiser makes false claims about a product, he or she is guilty of *fraud*. 2. ✦ impostor, fake, faker, phony, pretender ✧ swindler One of the characters in the book *The Adventures of Huckleberry Finn* claims to be a king, but he's actually a *fraud*.

**fray** *verb* ✦ come apart, unravel, shred, tatter, wear ✧ tear The cuffs on my shirt are beginning to *fray*.

**free** *adjective* 1. ✦ liberated, independent, self-governing, autonomous ✧ unconfined The former slave rejoiced when he became a *free* man. 2. ✦ clear, empty, void ✧ open, vacant The doctor said that my cut was *free* of infection. 3. ✦ complimentary, free of charge, gratis, gratuitous, on the house If you buy two movies, the third one is *free*. —*verb* ✦ let go, liberate, release, set free ✧ emancipate We *freed* the rabbit that was caught in our garden netting.

**freedom** *noun* ✦ independence, liberty ✧ emancipation, immunity My grandparents came to the United States in part so they would have the *freedom* to practice their religious beliefs.

**freeze** *verb* 1. ✦ ice over, ice up ✧ chill, frost, nip The river *freezes* in winter. 2. ✦ stand still, stop, halt ✧ stay The deer *froze* when it saw the car's headlights.

**frenzy** *noun* ✦ furor, turmoil ✧ agitation, commotion, excitement, fever I was in a *frenzy* trying to finish my project on time.

**frequent** *adjective* ✦ constant, numerous, repeated ✧ regular, routine, usual While on vacation in Hawaii, I made *frequent* trips to the beach.

**fresh** *adjective* 1. ✦ unspoiled, unpreserved, new ✧ current, recent The local supermarket always has *fresh* fruits and vegetables. 2. ✦ another, new, additional, further ✧ different, more These dingy walls sure could use a *fresh* coat of paint. 3. ✦ clean, pure, invigorating, refreshing ✧ healthy I opened a window to let some *fresh* air into the room.

**Antonyms** fresh
*adjective* 1. musty, old, stale 3. dirty, impure, polluted, tainted

**friction** *noun* 1. ✦ grinding, rubbing, scraping, abrasion If your foot rubs against your shoe, the *friction* can produce a blister. 2. ✦ antagonism, conflict, disagreement, discord, tension There was constant *friction* between the bossy director and the conceited star.

**friend** *noun* ✦ buddy, chum, comrade, pal, mate ✧ acquaintance, companion The two women have been good *friends* for years.

**friendship** *noun* ✦ companionship, comradeship, fellowship, attachment ✧ intimacy Your *friendship* is important to me.

**fright** *noun* ✦ fear, alarm, apprehension, dread, panic, terror The scary movie filled me with *fright*.

**frighten** *verb* ✦ scare, terrify, alarm, intimidate ✧ startle, shock Flying in an airplane *frightens* me.

**frigid** *adjective* ✦ cold, freezing, icy, chill, chilly ✧ wintry, cool A *frigid* wind blew swiftly over the Arctic tundra.

**fringe** *noun* ✦ outskirts, edge, margin, rim, border People on the *fringes* of the crowd weren't able to hear the speaker.

**frolic** *verb* ✦ play, romp, cavort ✧ prance, caper The kittens often *frolic* with each other.

**front** *noun* ✦ beginning, head, start, fore, forepart, lead Locomotives are usually at the *front* of a train. —*adjective* ✦ first, initial, foremost, beginning, fore Some people like to sit in the *front* row of a theater.

**frontier** *noun* ✦ border, borderland, borderline, boundary ✧ edge, outpost, outskirts, territory The *frontier* between the United States and Canada is not fortified.

**frosting** *noun* ✦ icing, glaze ✧ topping, meringue I think that the best part of a cupcake is the *frosting*.

**frosty** *adjective* ✦ icy, frigid, freezing, frozen ✧ wintry, arctic I was happy to stay indoors on the overcast and *frosty* day.

**frown** *verb* ✦ scowl, grimace, glower ✧ pout, glare The man *frowned* as he listened to the disturbing news. —*noun* ✦ grimace, pout, scowl, glower, glare The clown painted a *frown* on his face.

**frustrate** *verb* 1. ✦ defeat, foil, thwart, ruin, hamper ✧ cancel, prevent The falling snow *frustrated* my efforts to keep the driveway clear. 2. ✦ disappoint, discourage, upset, exasperate ✧ depress My inability to advance to a higher level in this computer game is beginning to *frustrate* me.

**fugitive** *noun* ✦ escapee, runaway ✧ outlaw, criminal, refugee Police caught the *fugitive* who had escaped from prison.

**fulfill** *verb* 1. ✦ accomplish, achieve, realize, attain, finish My friend has *fulfilled* her dream of starting her own online craft store. 2. ✦ fill, finish, meet, satisfy, answer, perform Rahul has *fulfilled* all of the requirements to get a visa to study abroad.

**full** *adjective* 1. ✦ filled, loaded, packed, stuffed, jammed, crowded I couldn't find a seat because the subway car was *full*. 2. ✦ complete, entire, whole, intact ✧ comprehensive, thorough You need a *full* deck of cards to play solitaire. —*adverb* ✦ completely, entirely, wholly, thoroughly, totally The ship turned *full* about and sailed off in the opposite direction.

**fumble** *verb* ✦ blunder, grope, feel, flounder, stumble I *fumbled* around in the dark for a flashlight.

**function** *noun* 1. ✦ job, purpose, role, task, duty ✧ operation, use One *function* of a judge is to preside over trials. 2. ✦ affair, ceremony, meeting, ritual ✧ celebration, occasion The president has to attend many political *functions*. —*verb* ✦ work, act, perform, serve, operate ✧ run, do This knife also *functions* as a screwdriver.

**fund** *noun* ✦ account, holding, reserve ✧ stock, supply, reservoir This charity has set up a *fund* to help resettle refugees.

**fundamental** *adjective* ✦ basic, essential, key, major, primary, necessary Addition is a *fundamental* part of mathematics. —*noun* ✦ basic, essential, foundation, principle, element This book discusses the *fundamentals* of existential philosophy.

**funny** *adjective* 1. ✦ amusing, comical, hilarious, humorous, witty My friend told me a *funny* story. 2. ✦ odd, peculiar, strange, unusual, weird, curious There is a *funny* smell coming from the refrigerator.

**furious** *adjective* 1. ✦ angry, enraged, irate, mad, wrathful, incensed The *furious* bear stood on its hind legs and roared. 2. ✦ fierce, strong, violent, turbulent, wild, intense The *furious* gale knocked down a lot of trees.

**furnish** *verb* 1. ✦ equip, fit, outfit ✧ appoint, decorate, stock The businessman *furnished* his office with bookshelves and a desk. 2. ✦ give, provide, supply ✧ deliver, present, grant My friend *furnished* the tools that I needed to repair my bike.

## Word Groups

**Furniture** is the movable articles in a room that make it fit for living or working. **Furniture** is a general term with no true synonyms. Here are some common types of furniture to investigate in a dictionary: **bed, bookcase, chair, chest of drawers (dresser), couch (sofa), desk, divan, nightstand, ottoman, table, wardrobe**

**further** *adverb* ✦ more, additionally, longer ✧ still, also, yet I'll have to study the problem *further* before I can give you any advice. —*adjective* ✦

added, additional, extra, more, new, other The television announcer said to stay tuned for *further* details. —*verb* ✦ advance, forward, promote, encourage, aid, assist, support The politician was more interested in *furthering* his career than helping solve problems.

**fury** *noun* 1. ✦ anger, ire, rage, wrath, furor The college student was filled with *fury* when his computer crashed. 2. ✦ ferocity, intensity, severity, violence, turbulence The storm raged with awesome *fury*.

**Antonyms** fury
*noun* 1. bliss, happiness, joy, rapture, satisfaction

**fuse** *verb* ✦ blend, combine, melt, merge, mix, unite Bronze is made by *fusing* copper and tin.

**fuss** *noun* ✦ commotion, disturbance, stir, bother, bustle The toddler made a big *fuss* when she couldn't find her favorite toy. —*verb* ✦ worry, fret, concern ✧ bustle, chafe The whole family *fussed* over the little baby when she had a cold.

**futile** *adjective* ✦ useless, pointless, hopeless, fruitless ✧ vain "Resistance is *futile*" is a phrase made famous by the *Star Trek* television series.

**future** *adjective* ✦ approaching, coming, forthcoming, prospective ✧ later, next My friends and I like to plan our *future* activities well in advance.

# G

**gadget** *noun* ✦ contraption, apparatus, appliance, device, implement, tool My roommate bought a *gadget* that automatically grinds a garlic bulb.

**gain** *verb* ✦ acquire, attain, get, pick up ✧ reach, win I *gained* a lot of experience working as an intern last summer. —*noun* ✦ advance, advancement ✧ addition, improvement, increase The quarterback carried the ball for a *gain* of fifteen yards.

**gale** *noun* ✦ wind, windstorm ✧ squall, storm, tempest The *gale* blew with so much fury that several small boats were sunk.

**gallant** *adjective* ✦ brave, courageous, heroic, valiant, daring, bold Firefighters made a *gallant* attempt to save the burning building.

**gallop** *noun* ✧ canter, trot, jog, run, lope Sayaka exercised her horse by taking it for a *gallop.* —*verb* ✦ fly, race, rush, speed, zoom, hurry Summer is *galloping* by so fast it's almost over.

**gamble** *verb* ✦ bet, wager ✧ chance, risk, put If you *gamble* your money, you risk losing it. —*noun* ✦ chance, risk ✧ bet, wager, hazard We took a *gamble* with the weather when we went picnicking on a cloudy day.

**game** *noun* 1. ✦ pastime ✧ amusement, entertainment, fun, play, recreation, sport My favorite party *game* is charades. 2. ✦ competition, contest, match ✧ meet, race, tournament The Super Bowl is the most important *game* of the American football season.

**gang** *noun* ✦ band, pack, ring, outfit ✧ crew, crowd, group, mob Jesse James led a famous *gang* of American outlaws.

**gap** *noun* ✦ opening, space ✧ break, crack, hole My rabbit has a big *gap* between its two front teeth.

**garbage** *noun* ✦ refuse, rubbish, trash, waste ✧ litter I take the *garbage* out every day so my kitchen won't smell bad.

**garment** *noun* ✦ apparel, attire, clothes, clothing, garb I buy most of my dresses at a store that specializes in women's *garments.*

**gasp** *verb* ✦ gulp, pant ✧ huff, puff, wheeze, blow Kazuki *gasped* for air after he swam a pool length under water. —*noun* ✦ gulp, pant, puff ✧ wheeze, blow Miranda was breathing in short *gasps* by the time she had run up to the top of the steep hill.

**gate** *noun* ✧ gateway, entrance, entry, door, doorway I made sure that the *gate* was closed behind me so that my dog wouldn't get out.

**gather** *verb* 1. ✦ accumulate, assemble, cluster, collect, congregate, group Pigeons *gathered* around the woman who was tossing out bread crumbs. 2. ✦ harvest, pick, pluck ✧ garner, glean, reap Let's go out to the woods and *gather* some blueberries.

**gathering** *noun* ✦ assembly, meeting, party ✧ company, crowd, group We are having a family *gathering* to celebrate the Lunar New Year.

**gauge** *noun* ✦ test, mark, measure ✧ meter, standard How we survive a month of travel together will be a *gauge* of our friendship. —*verb* ✦ calculate, compute, measure ✧ estimate, figure, judge It is difficult to *gauge* the speed of the wind unless you have the right equipment.

**gaunt** *adjective* ✦ lean, skinny, thin, bony, slim Many wild animals become *gaunt* during winter because their food is scarce.

**gaze** *verb* ✦ look, stare, peer ✧ eye, gape, gawk It was such a beautiful night that I couldn't stop *gazing* at the stars. —*noun* ✦ stare, look, eye, glance ✧ gape When the boss's *gaze* fell on me, I knew that she was going to ask me a question.

**gear** *noun* ✦ equipment, outfit, stuff, things, apparatus ✧ tackle The hikers all carried their own *gear* to the campsite.

**gem** *noun* 1. ✦ gemstone, jewel, precious stone The king's crown was covered with diamonds and other *gems.* 2. ✦ treasure, marvel, wonder, prize, masterpiece Yosemite is one of many *gems* in the American national park system.

**general** *adjective* 1. ✦ common, whole ✧ total, universal, communal The museum's library is open to the *general* public three days a week. 2. ✦ broad, overall, widespread, popular ✧comprehensive

There was *general* satisfaction with the plan, though a few people were still unhappy. **3.** ✦ normal, routine, usual, typical, ordinary, regular With computers, it's a *general* rule that you should save your work often in case the program crashes.

**generally** *adverb* **1.** ✦ normally, routinely, typically, usually, regularly ✧ often I *generally* have cereal and toast for breakfast. **2.** ✦ broadly, commonly, popularly, widely, universally It is not *generally* known that Russia is only thirty-six miles away from Alaska.

**generate** *verb* ✦ create, make, produce ✧ develop, form, cause A fire *generates* both heat and light.

**generous** *adjective* ✦ considerate, kind, thoughtful, unselfish, gracious I appreciate your *generous* offer to give me a ride.

**genius** *noun* **1.** ✦ expert, master, ace, whiz, wizard ✧ prodigy The politician proved to be a real *genius* at organizing people. **2.** ✦ brilliance, creativity, talent, inspiration, ability ✧ gift, intelligence Mozart's operas are widely thought to be works of great *genius*.

**gentle** *adjective* **1.** ✦ light, low, mild, moderate, slight, soft A *gentle* breeze made the evening cool and pleasant. **2.** ✦ tender, docile, tame ✧ easy, kind My dog is very *gentle* when she plays with me.

**genuine** *adjective* ✦ actual, authentic, real, true, original ✧ legitimate My friend's father has a *genuine* Model-T Ford antique car.

**gesture** *noun* ✦ motion, movement, sign, signal ✧ indication Police officers use hand and arm *gestures* to direct traffic. —*verb* ✦ motion, sign, signal ✧ indicate, wave My friend *gestured* for me to be silent because her baby was sleeping.

**get** *verb* **1.** ✦ become, grow, turn ✧ develop, come It's *getting* cold out. **2.** ✦ arrive, reach, show up, turn up ✧ approach, come When will the bus *get* here? **3.** ✦ go, move, travel, run ✧ proceed, progress I use my motorbike to *get* around. **4.** ✦ acquire, obtain, receive, procure ✧ earn, gain, win Camila *got* a new smartphone for her birthday. **5.** ✦ fetch, pick up, collect ✧ capture, catch, carry, go (after) Please *get* some peanut butter when you go to the store. **6.** ✦ convince, influence, persuade, coax ✧ urge I'm trying to *get* my boss to give me a day off. **7.** ✦ catch, comprehend, grasp, understand, apprehend I didn't *get* the joke at first.

**ghastly** *adjective* ✦ dreadful, gruesome, hideous, horrible, terrible, terrifying The movie was about a *ghastly* monster that was half human and half bug.

**ghost** *noun* ✦ apparition, phantom, specter, spirit, spook, wraith The house was supposed to be haunted by two *ghosts*.

**giant** *adjective* ✦ colossal, enormous, gigantic, huge, immense, mammoth, mighty That *giant* oak is taller than most houses.

**gift** *noun* **1.** ✦ contribution, donation, present, offering ✧ grant The man gave a *gift* of one thousand dollars to his favorite charity. **2.** ✦ aptitude, faculty, knack, talent, flair ✧ ability My sister has a *gift* for making people laugh.

**gifted** *adjective* ✦ talented, accomplished, expert, skilled, skillful, capable My friend Hans is a *gifted* photographer.

**gigantic** *adjective* ✦ colossal, enormous, giant, huge, immense, tremendous Redwoods are *gigantic* trees that can grow to be over 350 feet high.

**giggle** *verb* ✦ laugh, titter ✧ cackle, chuckle, guffaw, snicker The teenagers *giggled* nervously when they saw the handsome celebrity. —*noun* ✦ chuckle, laugh, laughter, snicker ✧ cackle *Giggles* filled the room when someone cracked a joke while we were having a meeting.

**give** *verb* **1.** ✦ present, bestow ✧ contribute, donate, hand out My girlfriend *gave* me her old iPod when she got a new one. **2.** ✦ hand, pass, provide, supply, deliver ✧ hand over, let have Please *give* me a glass of water. **3.** ✦ allow, grant, permit, let have ✧ accord, offer My boss *gave* me an extra day to complete my assignment. **4.** ✦ furnish, provide, supply, produce, yield, make This bulb doesn't *give* enough light to read by. **5.** ✦ have, hold, stage, conduct ✧ do, perform Let's *give* a party to surprise our roommate on her birthday.

**glad** *adjective* ✦ happy, delighted, pleased ✧ cheerful, joyful I'm always *glad* when I can spend time with my best friend.

**glamorous** *adjective* ✦ exciting, fascinating, enchanting ✧ attractive, charming, lovely Directing movies sounds like a *glamorous* career to me.

**glance** *verb* ✦ look, peek, peep, glimpse ✧ peer I *glanced* into the oven to see if the brownies were done. —*noun* ✦ glimpse, look, peek, peep A quick *glance* in the mirror told me that I needed a haircut.

**glare** *verb* 1. ✦ glower, scowl, stare ✧ frown, gaze The librarian *glared* at the students who were talking loudly. 2. ✦ blaze, flash, shine, sparkle ✧ dazzle, glisten Sunlight *glared* off the snow and ice. —*noun* 1. ✦ glower, scowl, stare ✧ frown, gaze My cat gave me a *glare* when I served him the wrong food. 2. ✦ blaze, glow, light, shine ✧ brilliance, dazzle The *glare* from the rocket's engines could be seen for miles.

**glaring** *adjective* 1. ✦ blinding, bright, brilliant, dazzling, blazing The *glaring* sunlight made my eyes water. 2. ✦ conspicuous, evident, blatant, noticeable, obvious I made a *glaring* error on my English proficiency test.

**gleam** *noun* ✦ flash, flicker, glimmer, sparkle, twinkle ✧ glow The campers saw the distant *gleam* of someone's lantern. —*verb* ✦ glisten, glow, shine, sparkle ✧ radiate, shimmer I polished the silver tea set until it *gleamed.*

**glee** *noun* ✦ delight, gladness, happiness, joy ✧ merriment, mirth The little girl cried out with *glee* when she saw the kitten her father brought her.

**glide** *verb* ✦ coast, sail, soar, drift ✧ flow, slide, slip An eagle *glided* through the sky above us.

**Antonyms** glee
*noun* anguish, grief, misery, sadness, sorrow, woe

**glimmer** *noun* ✦ flicker, flash, gleam, sparkle ✧ glow, twinkle The campfire's dying embers gave off faint *glimmers* of reddish light. —*verb* ✦ shimmer, gleam, flash, flicker, sparkle, twinkle ✧ shine Stars *glimmered* in the night sky.

**glimpse** *noun* ✦ peek (at), peep (at) ✧ glance, look Emilio caught a *glimpse* of the cardinal before it flew away. —*verb* ✦ detect, make out, spot, spy ✧ see I barely *glimpsed* my friend in the crowd.

**glitter** *noun* ✦ brilliance, radiance, sparkle ✧ light, shine The *glitter* of the sun on the water looked like diamonds. —*verb* ✦ glisten, shine, sparkle, twinkle ✧ flash, flicker Paris *glitters* at night with the lights of buildings, traffic, and the Eiffel Tower.

**gloat** *verb* ✦ exult, boast, brag, vaunt ✧ crow The modest runner didn't *gloat* over winning the race.

**globe** *noun* 1. ✦ sphere, ball, orb My kitchen light is covered by a glass *globe.* 2. ✦ earth, planet, world My grandparents' travels have taken them all over the *globe.*

**gloom** *noun* 1. ✦ dark, darkness, dimness, murk ✧ blackness, bleakness We couldn't see very far in the *gloom* of the long tunnel. 2. ✦ dejection, glumness, sadness, unhappiness ✧ depression, despair I was filled with *gloom* when I thought of my best friend moving far away.

**gloomy** *adjective* 1. ✦ bleak, dark, dismal, dreary, somber, glum The castle was cold and *gloomy.* 2. ✦ dejected, glum, sad, unhappy ✧ depressed, sullen The team has been in a *gloomy* mood ever since they lost in the playoffs.

**glorious** *adjective* ✦ gorgeous, magnificent, marvelous, splendid, stunning, superb, amazing, incredible America's Grand Canyon is one of the most *glorious* sights I've ever seen.

**glory** *noun* 1. ✦ honor, praise, fame, prestige, renown ✧ distinction The knight's heroic deeds brought him much *glory.* 2. ✦ grandeur, magnificence, splendor ✧ majesty, brilliance The sun rose in a blaze of *glory.*

**glow** *verb* ✦ shine ✧ beam, gleam, glimmer, radiate My alarm clock has a dial that *glows* in the dark. —*noun* ✦light, radiance, shine, gleam, glimmer ✧ glare, brightness The room was lit by the *glow* of a single candle.

**glue** *noun* ✦ adhesive ✧ cement, mucilage, paste, rubber cement I needed just a few drops of *glue* to reattach the cup's broken handle. —*verb* ✦ paste, stick ✧ cement, fasten, gum I *glued* pictures of my family into my scrapbook.

**gnaw** *verb* ✦ chew, nibble, bite ✧ eat, munch Dogs love to *gnaw* on bones.

**go** *verb* 1. ✦ travel, journey ✧ move, proceed, progress I'd like to *go* to Hawaii someday. 2. ✦ depart, leave, run along ✧ exit, retire, withdraw, quit I have to *go* now. 3. ✦ lead, head ✧ extend, reach, run, stretch Where does this road *go?* 4. ✦ fare, transpire ✧ happen, occur, result How did things *go* at work today? 5. ✦ pass, slip away ✧ elapse, lapse, fade The summer *went by* too fast. 6. ✦ fit, match, suit ✧ agree, belong, conform Does this tie *go with* my jacket and shirt?

**goal** *noun* ✦ aim, ambition, objective, target ✧ end, purpose My *goal* is to read five books this summer.

**gobble** *verb* ✦ bolt, gulp, wolf ✧ devour, eat, stuff It's not polite to *gobble* your food.

**good** *adjective* 1. ✦ enjoyable, fine, nice ✧ excel-

lent, great That was a *good* movie we just saw. **2.**
✦ **advantageous, beneficial** ✧ **proper, favorable,
helpful, useful** A *good* diet includes lots of fruits
and vegetables. **3.** ✦ **able, capable, competent,
skilled, skillful, talented** She is a *good* teacher. **4.**
✦ **serviceable, dependable, reliable, sound, trustworthy** My bicycle is old, but it's still *good*. **5.** ✦
**obedient, well-behaved** ✧ **nice, honorable, virtuous** When my dog is *good*, I give her a treat.
—*noun* ✦ **advantage, benefit, interest, welfare,
profit, success** Our coach urges us to play for the
*good* of the team.

**gorge** *noun* ✦ **ravine, canyon** ✧ **chasm, gulch, de-
file, valley** A river runs through the *gorge*. —*verb*
✦ **cram, fill, stuff** ✧ **devour, eat, indulge** We *gorged*
ourselves with cake and ice cream at the birthday
party.

**gorgeous** *adjective* ✦ **beautiful, glorious, magnificent, splendid** ✧ **handsome, lovely, pretty** It was
such a *gorgeous* and sunny day that we spent the
whole afternoon at the beach.

**gossip** *noun* ✦ **hearsay, rumor** ✧ **scandal, slander,
talk** I read some *gossip* about my favorite movie
star in a fan magazine. —*verb* ✦ **chatter, chitchat,
jabber, talk** ✧ **tattle, whisper** We sat around all
morning long *gossiping* about last night's party.

**govern** *verb* ✦ **direct, lead, head, manage, run** ✧
**control, rule** In a democracy, public elections determine who will *govern* the country.

**government** *noun* ✦ **state, administration, rule** ✧
**regime, regulation** Monarchies, democracies, and
republics are three different forms of national *government*.

**gown** *noun* ✦ **dress** ✧ **frock, garment, robe** The actress wore an elegant *gown* to the awards ceremony.

**grab** *verb* ✦ **seize, snatch, pluck, take, clutch, grasp**
My dog *grabbed* a sandwich right out of my hand.
—*noun* ✦ **lunge, snatch** ✧ **clutch, grasp, pass** The
bear made a *grab* for the salmon.

**grace** *noun* **1.** ✦ **elegance, gracefulness, ease, polish** ✧ **charm** The figure skater performed with
remarkable *grace*. **2.** ✦ **decency, manners, politeness** ✧ **kindness, tact** He at least had the *grace*
to apologize for his careless behavior. —*verb* ✦
**adorn, decorate** ✧ **ornament, dignify, favor, hon-
or** The bank lobby had several beautiful paintings
*gracing* its walls.

**graceful** *adjective* ✦ **refined, smooth** ✧ **agile,**
charming, elegant, lovely, easy Shiori's dive was
so *graceful* she hardly made a splash.

**Antonyms** graceful
*adjective* **awkward, clumsy, gawky, uncoordinated**

**gracious** *adjective* ✦ **cordial, courteous, hospitable,
polite, warm, kind** They are always *gracious* hosts
at their annual holiday party.

**grade** *noun* **1.** ✦ **category, degree, level, rank** ✧
**class, kind, type** Sandpaper comes in different
*grades* of coarseness. **2.** ✦ **incline, pitch, slant,
slope, rise** I had to walk my bicycle up the hill
because the *grade* was so steep. **3.** ✦ **mark, score**
✧ **evaluation, rating, assessment** Good *grades* in
high school are usually necessary to get admitted
to a top university. —*verb* **1.** ✦ **categorize, classify, order, rank, sort, group** Lumber is *graded* according to its quality. **2.** ✦ **mark, score, correct** ✧
**evaluate, rate** Teachers commonly *grade* papers in
red ink. **3.** ✦ **even out, flatten, level, smooth** ✧
**bulldoze** Before construction can begin, the land
will have to be *graded*.

**gradual** *adjective* ✦ **moderate, slow, steady** ✧ **even,
regular, gentle** The mountaineers made *gradual*
progress up the steep slope.

**graduate** *verb* **1.** ✧ **complete, finish, pass** My best
friend and I *graduated* from college together. **2.**
✦ **calibrate, mark off** ✧ **arrange, divide, measure**
This measuring cup is *graduated* in ounces.

**grand** *adjective* **1.** ✦ **excellent, great, splendid, superb, wonderful, terrific** We had a *grand* time on
our trip to Beijing. **2.** ✦ **luxurious, magnificent,
majestic, stately, grandiose** The dance will be held
in the palace's *grand* ballroom.

**grant** *verb* **1.** ✦ **allow, permit, accord, award, give**
✧ **authorize** The company's director *granted* my
request for an interview. **2.** ✦ **acknowledge, admit, agree, concede, yield** I'll *grant* that you're a
faster runner than I am. —*noun* ✦ **contribution,
donation, gift** ✧ **allotment, award, offering** The
scientist received a *grant* to help pay for her research project.

**grasp** *verb* **1.** ✦ **comprehend, perceive, see, understand, apprehend** ✧ **know** Do you *grasp* the
meaning of this poem? **2.** ✦ **clasp, clutch, grab,
grip, seize** We all *grasped* the rope tightly and
pulled to win the tug-of-war. —*noun* **1.** ✦ **clasp,
clutch, grip, hold** ✧ **possession, embrace** Sebas-
tian caught a frog, but it wriggled out of his *grasp*.

**2.** ✦ comprehension, perception, understanding, awareness ✧ knowledge I think I have a good *grasp* of the situation.

**grateful** *adjective* ✦ appreciative, thankful ✧ gratified, pleased My roommate was *grateful* when I said I'd help her cook dinner.

**gratify** *verb* ✦ cheer, delight, gladden, please, tickle The librarian said that it *gratifies* him to see me so interested in reading.

**gratitude** *noun* ✦ appreciation, gratefulness, thankfulness, thanks When the singer won the award, she expressed her *gratitude* to everyone who had been of help.

**grave** *noun* **1.** ✦ serious, severe, consequential, significant, weighty ✧ critical At my university, cheating and plagiarism are *grave* offenses. **2.** ✦ solemn, somber, sober, serious ✧ thoughtful, quiet The newscaster described the accident in a *grave* tone of voice.

**graze¹** *verb* ✦ browse ✧ crop, eat, feed, forage Sheep were *grazing* in the pasture.

**graze²** *verb* ✦ brush, scrape, swipe, touch ✧ glance off, skim The thorn just *grazed* my leg as I passed.

**grease** *noun* **1.** ✦ drippings, fat, lard ✧ tallow, suet Some people fry their eggs in bacon *grease*. **2.** ✦ oil, lubricant ✧ petroleum The mechanic was covered with *grease* after working on a car's engine. —*verb* ✦ lubricate, oil I *greased* the hinges of the squeaky door.

**great** *adjective* **1.** ✦ huge, enormous, big, large, tremendous ✧ vast Elephants are known for their *great* size. **2.** ✦ important, significant, notable, outstanding, remarkable, excellent Many people think Franklin D. Roosevelt was a *great* American president.

**greed** *noun* ✦ avarice, craving, desire, hunger, longing The dishonest politician was motivated by *greed* for power and fame.

**greet** *verb* ✦ hail, salute ✧ meet, receive, welcome I *greeted* my friend with a warm handshake.

**grief** *noun* ✦ sadness, sorrow, heartache, heartbreak ✧ despair, distress *Grief* is a natural response to the death of a loved one.

**grieve** *verb* ✦ mourn, lament, sorrow ✧ cry, weep Everyone at the funeral *grieved* for the friend they had lost.

**grim** *adjective* ✦ forbidding, hard, harsh, severe,

stern ✧ firm, stubborn The judge had a *grim* look on his face.

**grimace** *noun* ✦ scowl, frown, pout ✧ sneer, smirk, glower The patient's face twisted into a *grimace* as the doctor set his broken arm. —*verb* ✦ scowl, frown, pout ✧ sneer, smirk, glower The woman *grimaced* when she opened the door and an icy blast of air swept into the room.

**grime** *noun* ✦ dirt, filth ✧ dust, mire, mud, soil, muck The garage windows were covered with *grime*.

**grimy** *adjective* ✦ dirty, filthy, grubby, soiled, squalid ✧ messy, unclean My hands were *grimy* after I fixed my bike chain.

**grin** *verb* ✦ beam, smile My little sister *grinned* happily when I offered her a piggyback ride. —*noun* ✦ smile, beam I could tell from Leticia's *grin* that she was in a good mood.

**grind** *verb* **1.** ✦ mill, pulverize ✧ crumble, crush, powder, pound Millstones were once used to *grind* grain into flour. **2.** ✦ abrade, file, rub, scrape ✧ grate, polish, rasp, sand, sharpen, smooth Early peoples made stone axes by *grinding* the axe head against a sandstone slab.

**grip** *noun* ✦ clasp, grasp, hold ✧ clutch, clench My tennis instructor told me to keep a firm *grip* on the racket. —*verb* ✦ clasp, clutch, grasp, hold ✧ grab, seize The baseball player *gripped* his bat tightly.

**grit** *noun* ✦ dirt, dust, sand ✧ debris The wind blew a piece of *grit* into my eye. —*verb* ✦ clamp, clench ✧ gnash, grate, grind The boy *gritted* his teeth as he jumped into the icy water.

**groan** *verb* ✦ moan, sigh ✧ complain, gripe, grumble, whine I *groaned* when I saw all the dishes I had to wash. —*noun* ✦ cry, moan, sigh ✧ sob, whine The traveler gave a *groan* of relief when he set down his heavy luggage.

**groom** *verb* ✦ curry, tend ✧ brush, clean, comb Tracey *grooms* her horse after every ride.

**groove** *noun* ✦ channel, slot ✧ cut, furrow, rut, trench My desk drawer has *grooves* for holding pens and pencils.

**grope** *verb* ✦ feel, fumble ✧ poke, probe, flounder, search The theater was so dark that I had to *grope* for my seat.

**gross** *adjective* **1.** ✦ flagrant, glaring, obvious, plain, blatant ✧ extreme The tabloid article contained nothing but *gross* lies. **2.** ✦ **disgusting, offensive, repulsive, revolting, repellent** The smell from the garbage can was really *gross*.

**grotesque** *adjective* ✦ **bizarre, strange, unnatural, weird, freakish** ✧ **ugly** The mythical Cerberus was a *grotesque* dog that had three heads.

**grouchy** *adjective* ✦ **bad-tempered, cranky, cross, grumpy, irritable, surly** Some people become *grouchy* when they're tired.

**ground** *noun* **1.** ✦ **land, terra firma** ✧ **dirt, earth, soil** I was glad to be back on the *ground* after our bumpy flight. **2.** ✧ **field, lot, property, terrain, yard, area** The school's band uses the football field as a parade *ground*. **3.** ✦ **basis, cause, evidence, reason** ✧ **motive, justification** The lawyer believed that there were not sufficient *grounds* for taking the case to court. —*verb* ✦ **base, establish, found** ✧ **build, fix, rest, set** The French Revolution was *grounded* on the principles of liberty, equality, and fraternity.

**group** *noun* **1.** ✦ **bunch, cluster, crowd** ✧ **gang, party, batch, company** A *group* of students gathered on the playground. **2.** ✦ **category, class, classification, division** ✧ **branch, grade, set** Fruits and vegetables form one of the basic food *groups*. —*verb* ✦ **arrange, organize, sort, classify** ✧ **distribute, divide** The clothes were *grouped* by size.

**grove** *noun* ✦ **stand, thicket, copse** ✧ **forest, woods, orchard** There's a little *grove* of oak trees by the duck pond in the park.

**grow** *verb* **1.** ✦ **enlarge, expand, increase, swell** ✧ **develop, soar** The population in our city is *growing* rapidly. **2.** ✦ **flourish, live, thrive, exist** ✧ **arise, sprout** Weeds can *grow* almost anywhere. **3.** ✦ **cultivate, plant, produce, raise** ✧ **breed, farm, sow** Aztec farmers *grew* corn, tomatoes, and chilies. **4.** ✦ **become, come to be, get, turn** It *grows* light just before dawn.

**growl** *noun* ✦ **snarl, bark, bellow, grunt, roar** We heard a low *growl* in the dark. —*verb* ✦ **snarl, bark, bellow, grunt, roar, bay** My dog *growled* when a stranger came to the door.

**growth** *noun* **1.** ✦ **development, expansion, increase** ✧ **advance, progress, rise** The mayor was pleased by the rapid *growth* of new businesses in the town. **2.** ✦ **accumulation, buildup** ✧ **collection, mass, crop** There was a thick *growth* of weeds around the abandoned house.

**grudge** *noun* ✧ **hard feelings, ill will, resentment, malice, spite, rancor** Hugo doesn't stay mad long, and he never holds a *grudge*.

**gruesome** *adjective* ✦ **ghastly, grim, horrendous, hideous, horrible, shocking, terrible** There was a story on the news last night about a *gruesome* accident.

**gruff** *adjective* ✦ **abrupt, curt, harsh, stern** ✧ **impolite, rude, short** In a classic fairy tale, the father bear spoke to Goldilocks in a *gruff* manner.

**grumble** *verb* ✦ **complain, gripe, grouse, whine** ✧ **moan, mutter** My little brother *grumbles* when he has to go to bed early.

**grumpy** *adjective* ✦ **surly, grouchy, irritable, bad-tempered, cranky, cross** The player was *grumpy* because he had to sit out the first half of the game.

**guarantee** *noun* ✦ **assurance, promise** ✧ **pledge, warranty** There are no *guarantees* when it comes to predicting the weather. —*verb* ✦ **certify, secure** ✧ **assure, pledge, promise, warrant** The victory *guarantees* that our team will be in the finals.

**guard** *verb* ✦ **defend, protect, safeguard, shield** ✧ **preserve, watch** One of the missions of the American Secret Service is to *guard* the president. —*noun* **1.** ✦ **sentinel, sentry** ✧ **caretaker, lookout** This bank is protected by three armed *guards*. **2.** ✦ **supervision, security** ✧ **control, protection, watch** Police kept the two prisoners under *guard*. **3.** ✦ **protector** ✧ **defense, safeguard, shield, screen** Baseball catchers wear shin *guards*.

### Word Groups

A **guardian** is someone who protects or defends, often out of a legal duty. **Guardian** is a general term with no true synonyms. Here are some different kinds of guardians to investigate in a dictionary: **caretaker, conservator, custodian, guard, keeper, parent**

**guess** *verb* **1.** ✦ **estimate, speculate, judge, reckon** ✧ **calculate** Can you *guess* how many beans are in this jar? **2.** ✦ **assume, suppose, surmise, presume** ✧ **believe, think** Since the new employee is not here yet, I *guess* she's not coming to work today. —*noun* ✦ **assumption, conjecture, belief, opinion, speculation** ✧ **estimate** It's my *guess* that we'll have a mild winter this year.

**guest** *noun* **1.** ✦ **company** ✧ **visitor, caller, friend** My roommate and I have *guests* coming for dinner tonight. **2.** ✦ **patron, customer** ✧ **lodger, tenant, client** This hotel can accommodate more than 250 *guests*.

**guide** *noun* ✦ **leader, usher** ✧ **escort, scout** A park ranger was our *guide* for the nature hike. —*verb* ✦ **conduct, escort, lead, usher** ✧ **direct, steer, show** An attendant *guided* us through each wing of the museum.

**guilt** *noun* ✦ **blame, fault, offense** ✧ **responsibility** The jury ruled that the defendant was free of *guilt*.

**guilty** *adjective* **1.** ✦ **at fault, blameworthy, responsible, wrong** The suspect claimed that she was not *guilty*. **2.** ✦ **contrite, regretful, remorseful, sorry, repentant** I felt *guilty* when I forgot my friend's birthday.

**gulf** *noun* **1.** ✦ **bay** ✧ **inlet, lagoon, sound, cove** The explorers made a map of the newly discovered *gulf*. **2.** ✦ **gap, disparity, separation, split, difference, space** There's a big *gulf* between the richest and the poorest members of our society.

**gullible** *adjective* ✦ **believing, trustful, trusting, unsuspecting, naive** When I was younger, I was so *gullible* that I believed the moon was made out of cheese.

**gully** *noun* ✦ **channel** ✧ **ditch, ravine, trench, gulch** The rain created *gullies* in the hillside.

**gulp** *verb* ✦ **bolt, gobble, wolf** ✧ **guzzle, devour, swallow** When I offered my dog a taste of my ice cream, he *gulped* down the whole cone. —*noun* ✦ **mouthful, swallow, swig** ✧ **sip** I was so thirsty that I downed a glass of water in just three *gulps*.

**gush** *verb* ✦ **flow, pour, run, rush, stream, spurt, surge** Water *gushed* from the broken fire hydrant.

**gust** *noun* ✦ **blast** ✧ **blow, breeze, draft, wind** A strong *gust* of wind knocked down some power lines.

**gusto** *noun* ✦ **zest, enthusiasm, zeal, eagerness** ✧ **delight, pleasure** The hungry man ate his pizza with *gusto*.

**gutter** *noun* ✦ **ditch, drain** ✧ **channel, pipe, trough, culvert** Rainwater pools up in our yard because our street doesn't have *gutters*.

**guy** *noun* ✦ **fellow, chap, person** ✧ **boy, lad, man** Your brother is a great *guy*.

# H

**habit** *noun* ✦ custom, practice, routine, pattern ✧ mannerism, trait I make a *habit* of reading for half an hour before going to bed.

**habitual** *adjective* ✦ customary, normal, regular, routine, usual, standard Everyone in my family has a *habitual* place at the dinner table.

**hack** *verb* ✦ chop, slash, whack ✧ cut, slice, hew I *hacked* at the weeds with a garden hoe.

**hail** *verb* ✦ flag down, flag, signal ✧ call, summon, greet The man *hailed* a passing driver when his car broke down.

**hall** *noun* 1. ✦ corridor, hallway, passageway, passage My friend's office is just down the *hall* from where I work. 2. ✦ auditorium, chamber, gallery ✧ room, building, theater University classes are often taught in huge *halls*.

**halt** *noun* ✦ stop, end, close, pause, rest ✧ break, recess Chatting came to a *halt* when a supervisor entered the room. —*verb* ✦ stop ✧ cease, discontinue, pause, rest, hold School buses *halt* at railroad tracks.

**hammer** *verb* ✦ beat, pound, strike, smash, tap, thump, whack The blacksmith *hammered* the horseshoe into shape.

**hamper** *verb* ✦ hinder, impede, obstruct, thwart, restrain, restrict The rain *hampered* our efforts to light a campfire.

**hand** *noun* 1. ✦ aid, assistance, help, support, relief I gave my girlfriend *a hand* with her chores. 2. ✦ helper, assistant, employee, laborer, worker, aide The rancher hired extra *hands* to help with the roundup. 3. ✦ part, role, share ✧ piece, portion Everyone on the team had a *hand* in winning the game. —*verb* ✦ give, pass ✧ convey, deliver, transfer, turn over, present I *handed* a pencil to my friend.

**handicap** *noun* ✦ disadvantage, drawback, hindrance, impediment ✧ disability Lack of education can be a serious *handicap* when looking for a job. —*verb* ✦ burden, hamper, hinder, impede, restrain, limit The runner was *handicapped* by a sore ankle.

**handle** *noun* ✦ grip, handgrip, shaft ✧ arm, stem, haft This shovel has a wooden *handle*. —*verb* 1. ✦ hold, touch, grasp, grip ✧ feel, finger I *handled* the crystal bowl with care. 2. ✦manage, command, control, direct, supervise Dominique *handles* her horse well.

**handsome** *adjective* ✦ attractive, good-looking, beautiful, lovely ✧ fine, pleasing The little boy looks *handsome* in his new suit.

**handy** *adjective* 1. ✦ proficient, skilled, skillful, adept, expert My friend is *handy* with carpentry tools. 2. ✦ at hand, accessible, available, close, nearby, ready It is smart to keep a flashlight *handy* during a storm in case the electricity goes off. 3. ✦ convenient, helpful, practical, useful, efficient An almanac is a *handy* reference book.

**hang** *verb* 1. ✦ dangle, suspend, swing ✧ attach, fasten, droop The child's swing *hangs* from a tree limb. 2. ✦ lynch, string up ✧ execute In America's Old West, outlaws were commonly *hanged*.

**haphazard** *adjective* ✦ chance, random, disorganized, unplanned, careless The books were in *haphazard* stacks on the shelf.

**happen** *verb* ✦ arise, develop, occur, take place, pass ✧ chance What *happened* at work while I was absent?

**happiness** *noun* ✦ bliss, cheer, delight, gladness, joy, pleasure, elation Seeing my friends always fills me with *happiness*.

**happy** *adjective* 1. ✦ delighted, glad, pleased, joyful, joyous, cheerful ✧ satisfied, thrilled I'm *happy* to make your acquaintance. 2. ✦ lucky, fortunate, favorable, beneficial ✧ convenient, helpful The woman picked winning lottery numbers by *happy* chance.

**Antonyms** **happy**
*adjective* 1. dejected, despondent, gloomy, miserable, sad, sorrowful, unhappy

**harass** *verb* ✦ annoy, bother, disturb, pester, trouble, torment Ants and flies frequently *harass* picnickers.

**harbor** *noun* ✦ port ✧ bay, cove, inlet, lagoon, gulf Two tugboats guided the ocean liner into the *harbor*.

**hard** *adjective* 1. ✦ firm, stiff ✧ rigid, solid, compact That bed is much *harder* than it looks. 2. ✦ heavy, forceful, powerful, severe, strong, serious I arrived at home just before a *hard* rain began to fall. 3. ✦ difficult, laborious, rough, tough, arduous We had a *hard* time driving up the slick mountain road. —*adverb* 1. ✦ diligently, earnestly, intently, laboriously I worked *hard* to finish my work project on time. 2. ✦ forcefully, forcibly, heavily, powerfully, energetically You have to pull *hard* on that drawer because it sticks.

**hardly** *adverb* ✦ barely, just, scarcely ✧ only, somewhat I can *hardly* hear you.

**hardship** *noun* ✦ adversity, difficulty, trouble, trial ✧ danger, misfortune The Pilgrims experienced many *hardships* during their first winter in America.

**hardy** *adjective* ✦ robust, strong, sturdy, tough ✧ fit, healthy, hearty The *hardy* tree in our yard survived a hurricane that uprooted many other trees in the neighborhood.

**harm** *noun* ✦ injury, hurt ✧ damage, misfortune, loss Automobile seat belts help protect passengers from *harm*. —*verb* ✦ hurt, injure ✧ damage, mar My dog won't *harm* you.

**harmful** *adjective* ✦ damaging, injurious, unhealthy ✧ bad, dangerous Exposure to too much sunlight is *harmful*.

**harmless** *adjective* ✦ safe, nontoxic, benign ✧ innocent, good Some berries are poisonous, but many others are *harmless*.

**harmony** *noun* ✦ rapport, peace, accord, concord, agreement ✧ balance, tune, unity My cat and dog live together in peaceful *harmony*.

**harsh** *adjective* 1. ✦ grating, raspy, jarring, squawky, coarse, hoarse A blue jay has a *harsh* cry. 2. ✦ bitter, brutal, cruel, hard, rough, severe, stark We had a *harsh* winter last year.

**harvest** *noun* ✦ crop, yield ✧ produce, product, fruit Florida typically has an abundant *harvest* of oranges. —*verb* ✦ reap ✧ gather, collect, garner, glean, pick Winter wheat is planted in the fall and *harvested* in the spring or early summer.

**haste** *noun* ✦ hurry, rush, rapidity, speed ✧ hustle, quickness Because I overslept, I had to dress in great *haste*.

**hasten** *verb* ✦ hurry, race, run, rush, dash, speed I *hastened* to answer the phone.

**Antonyms** hasten

*verb* delay, hesitate, lag, loiter, slow, tarry

**hasty** *adjective* ✦ fast, hurried, quick, rapid, speedy, swift, abrupt The hikers made a *hasty* retreat when they saw a moose coming towards them.

**Word Groups**

A **hat** is a covering for the head, especially one with a shaped crown and brim. **Hat** is a general term with no true synonyms. Here are some common types of hats to investigate in a dictionary: **baseball cap, beret, bowler, derby, fedora, fez, kepi, kufi, Panama, sombrero, Stetson (cowboy hat), taqiyah**

**hatch** *verb* ✦ concoct, create, devise, invent, make up, plot, contrive My friends and I *hatched* a plan to give a surprise party for our roommate.

**hate** *verb* ✦ despise, detest, dislike, loathe, abhor, scorn I *hate* taking out the garbage.

**hatred** *noun* ✦ abhorrence, loathing, hate, aversion, disgust, dislike ✧ animosity My *hatred* of racist comments increases every time I hear one.

**haughty** *adjective* ✦ arrogant, conceited, proud, vain, egotistical In the story of Snow White, the *haughty* queen believed she was the most beautiful woman in her realm.

**haul** *verb* 1. ✦ drag, tug, lug, draw, pull, tow, cart It took four men to *haul* the piano up a flight of stairs. 2. ✦ carry, convey, move, transport, truck, take My roommates and I hired a truck to *haul* our furniture to our new house. —*noun* ✦ catch, take, yield, load, cargo ✧ booty The fishermen sailed back to port with a large *haul* of fish.

**haunt** *verb* 1. ✦ torment, trouble, worry, obsess, vex My first piano recital was so embarrassing that the memory of it still *haunts* me. 2. ✧ infest, possess, inhabit, dwell in, visit This show is about a phantom that *haunts* an opera house.

**have** *verb* 1. ✦ own, possess ✧ hold, keep, maintain I *have* a smartphone and a laptop. 2. ✦ comprise, contain, embrace, include ✧ involve A week *has* seven days. 3. ✦ accept, receive, take ✧ acquire, get, obtain, procure Will you *have* another piece of cake? 4. ✦ experience, encounter ✧ endure,

**know, meet, see, undergo** Did you *have* a good day at the beach? **5. ✦ need, must ✧ ought, should, require** I *have* to go home right after work today.

**haven** *noun* **✦ refuge, retreat, sanctuary, shelter, asylum** My room is my *haven*.

**hazard** *noun* **✦ danger, peril, risk ✧ threat, jeopardy** The beekeeper said that an occasional sting is one of the *hazards* of that occupation.

**hazardous** *adjective* **✦ dangerous, perilous, risky, unsafe ✧ treacherous** Gasoline is a *hazardous* substance.

**hazy** *adjective* **1. ✦ cloudy, foggy, misty, overcast, murky** The sky was *hazy* this morning when I left for work. **2. ✦ dim, faint, indistinct, uncertain, vague, fuzzy** I have only a *hazy* recollection of my early childhood.

**head** *noun* **1. ✦ brain, mind, intellect, intelligence ✧ aptitude, instinct, talent** My grandfather says that you have to use your *head* to solve a crossword puzzle. **2. ✦ director, leader, manager, boss, chief, supervisor** My friend is the *head* of her company's publicity department. **3. ✦ forefront, beginning, front, start ✧ top, source** A high school band marched at the *head* of the parade. —*adjective* **✦ chief, principal, leading, main, top, foremost** The *head* waiter oversees the other staff at a restaurant. —*verb* **1. ✦ aim, direct, guide, steer, turn, point** We *headed* our sailboat into the wind. **2. ✦ direct, lead, govern, manage, run, supervise** The District Attorney will *head* a special committee to investigate police misconduct.

**headstrong** *adjective* **✦ obstinate, stubborn, willful ✧ impulsive, unruly** The *headstrong* politician refused to follow the advisors' recommendations.

**heal** *verb* **✦ mend, recover, restore ✧ cure, remedy, treat** The doctor said that my broken arm will *heal* in six weeks or less.

**health** *noun* **✦ well-being, wellness, healthiness ✧ haleness, welfare** My girlfriend says that yoga helps her to maintain her *health*.

**healthy** *adjective* **1. ✦ well, hale, fit, sound, hearty ✧ all right** I was sick last week, but I'm *healthy* now. **2. ✦ healthful, nourishing, wholesome, sustaining ✧ beneficial, helpful** Vegetables and fruits are important parts of a *healthy* diet.

**heap** *noun* **✦ mass, mound, pile, stack ✧ hill, deposit** I raked the leaves into a big *heap*. —*verb* **✦** pile, stack, load, lump, mound ✧ pack** My grandmother always *heaps* lots of food onto my plate.

**hear** *verb* **✦ attend (to), heed, listen (to), regard** The captain called for the crew's attention by saying, "Now *hear* this."

**heart** *noun* **1. ✦ soul, nature ✧ emotion, feeling, sentiment, sympathy** My friend has a kind *heart* and is considerate of others. **2. ✦ courage, mettle, nerve, pluck, spirit, fortitude, enthusiasm** Our team has a lot of *heart*. **3. ✦ center, core, middle, hub ✧ essence, nucleus** We went for a long walk through the *heart* of the city.

**heat** *noun* **✦ warmth, hotness, warmness ✧ temperature** That fire is putting out a lot of *heat*. —*verb* **✦ warm, warm up, make hot ✧ cook** I'll set the table while you *heat* the soup.

**heave** *verb* **1. ✦ hoist, lift, pick up, raise, heft ✧ boost** It took two strong sailors to *heave* the ship's anchor. **2. ✦ fling, hurl, pitch, throw, toss, chuck** The child *heaved* a big rock into the pond just to see the splash.

**heaven** *noun* **✦ bliss, ecstasy, paradise ✧ joy, rapture** My aunt was in *heaven* when she got to meet her favorite author.

**heavenly** *adjective* **✦ lovely, blissful, delightful, marvelous, pleasing, wonderful** These roses have a *heavenly* scent.

**heavy** *adjective* **1. ✦ massive, weighty ✧ big, bulky, huge, large** My friend helped me lift the *heavy* trunk. **2. ✦ abundant, ample, plentiful, bountiful, substantial ✧ extreme** Last night's *heavy* snowfall left drifts several feet high. **3. ✦ demanding, difficult, hard, arduous, laborious, rigorous, tough** Digging a deep ditch is *heavy* work.

**hedge** *noun* **✦ hedgerow ✧ bushes, shrubbery, thicket** There's a tall *hedge* between our yard and our neighbor's. —*verb* **✦ edge, enclose, ring, surround ✧ fence, border** We *hedged* our garden with rose bushes.

**heed** *verb* **✦ obey, observe, follow, mind, regard ✧ listen (to), attend** Everyone is expected to *heed* traffic laws.

**height** *noun* **1. ✦ elevation, stature ✧ altitude, extent** The *height* of the Empire State Building is 1,250 feet. **2. ✦ peak, top, zenith, climax, crest, summit** At the *height* of the baseball season, there are games almost every day.

**help** *verb* 1. ✦ aid, assist ✧ support, contribute, benefit, serve I *helped* my friend plant her garden. 2. ✦ ease, relieve, improve, cure, heal I had a cup of ginger tea to *help my* upset stomach. —*noun* ✦ aid, assistance, support ✧ hand, service When it came time to move the dining table, my roommate asked for my *help.*

**helpful** *adjective* ✦ beneficial, useful, valuable, handy ✧ practical, good My friend gave me some *helpful* advice.

**helpless** *adjective* ✦ defenseless, dependent ✧ feeble, weak, vulnerable Baby kittens are *helpless* for about eight weeks after birth.

**herd** *noun* ✦ drove ✧ pack, group, horde, swarm, throng The rancher has more than 500 cattle in his *herd.* —*verb* ✦ drive, guide, lead, round up ✧ collect, gather Collies were once bred for the purpose of *herding* sheep.

**heritage** *noun* ✦ legacy, tradition, inheritance ✧ ancestry, endowment, history There are numerous museums, festivals, and exhibits that commemorate the rich *heritage* of African Americans.

**hero** *noun* ✦ champion, inspiration, role model, idol, star ✧ heroine Some of my *heroes* are real people, and some are from stories and legends.

**heroic** *adjective* ✦ bold, brave, courageous, fearless, gallant, valiant The legendary Sir Lancelot was a *heroic* knight of King Arthur's court.

**hesitant** *adjective* ✦ reluctant ✧ doubtful, indecisive, uncertain, unsure I was *hesitant* to go in the baby's room while she was sleeping.

---

**Antonyms** **hesitant**
*adjective* certain, decisive, definite, positive, secure, sure

---

**hesitate** *verb* ✦ waver, delay, pause, wait, falter ✧ balk The boys *hesitated* a moment before entering the carnival's haunted house.

**hide** *verb* ✦ conceal, cover up, mask, screen, veil, camouflage Some men wear toupees to *hide* their baldness.

**hideous** *adjective* ✦ revolting, disgusting, ghastly, gruesome, horrible, repulsive, ugly I bought a *hideous* mask to wear to the Halloween party.

**high** *adjective* 1. ✦ tall, lofty ✧ big, towering, soaring, long Mount Everest is 29,029 feet *high.* 2. ✦ heavy, strong, powerful, excessive, extreme, fierce, furious A hurricane's *high* winds can do considerable damage. 3. ✦ important, leading, prominent, lofty, eminent, significant ✧ chief The diplomat has a *high* position with the US Foreign Service. 4. ✦ piercing, sharp, shrill, treble I call my dog with a special whistle that has a *high* pitch. —*noun* ✦ maximum, peak, zenith ✧ top, summit The overall value of stocks in the American market recently reached an all-time *high.*

**highway** *noun* ✦ expressway, freeway, interstate, turnpike ✧ road, thoroughfare This *highway* goes from Chicago to Indianapolis.

**hike** *verb* ✦ trek, walk, travel ✧ march, ramble, stroll, tramp The backpackers *hiked* seventeen miles to reach the top of the mountain. —*noun* ✦ ramble, stroll, trek, walk ✧ trip, journey I enjoy taking *hikes* through the hills behind my apartment building.

**hill** *noun* ✦ knoll, rise, mound, elevation ✧ hilltop, promontory I rode my bike all the way up the steep *hill.*

**hinder** *verb* ✦ impede, obstruct, slow down, bog down, hamper, delay ✧ stall Heavy snow *hindered* the flow of traffic.

**hint** *noun* ✦ clue, cue, tip ✧ sign, suggestion, pointer I was able to guess the answer to my sister's riddle even though she refused to give me any *hints.* —*verb* ✦ imply, indicate, insinuate, suggest ✧ mention I *hinted* that I would like a new smartphone for my birthday.

**hire** *verb* 1. ✦ employ, engage, retain, take on ✧ enlist, appoint The restaurant is doing so well the manager has to *hire* more staff. 2. ✦ rent, lease, charter, let We *hired* a limousine to surprise our friend on her birthday.

**history** *noun* ✦ background, past, antiquity ✧ account, chronicle, record, story My grandparents are a great source for learning our family's *history.*

**hit** *verb* 1. ✦ hammer, pound, beat, strike, knock, smack, club, punch In order to drive a nail straight, you have to *hit* it on the head. 2. ✦ affect, move, touch, impress ✧ influence, occur (to) News of my grandfather's illness *hit* me hard. —*noun* 1. ✦ impact, strike, blow ✧ bang, crack, knock, shot, swat My arrow scored a direct *hit* on the bull's-eye. 2. ✦ sensation, smash, success, triumph, achievement The new musical was an instant Broadway *hit.*

**hitch** *verb* ✦ yoke, harness, attach, fasten, join, tie

"*Hitch* your wagon to a star" is an old saying that means you should follow your dreams. —*noun* ✦ mishap, problem, snag, difficulty ✧ delay, impediment Luckily our trip to the mountains went off without a *hitch*.

**hoard** *noun* ✦ stock, stockpile, store, supply, treasure, cache The miser kept a watchful eye on his *hoard* of gold coins. —*verb* ✦ lay away, stockpile, store ✧ accumulate, gather, save Squirrels *hoard* nuts for the winter.

**hoarse** *adjective* ✦ coarse, croaking, harsh, husky, raspy, rough, scratchy ✧ grating, jarring A *hoarse* voice is a common symptom of a sore throat.

**hoax** *noun* ✦ joke, prank, trick ✧ deception, fraud My friend always thinks of a funny *hoax* to pull on April Fools' Day.

**hobby** *noun* ✦ pastime ✧ amusement, diversion, pursuit, recreation Shannon's *hobby* is collecting stamps.

**hoist** *verb* ✦ lift, raise, pick up, haul up, run up ✧ boost, elevate A crane is used to *hoist* shipping containers on and off ships.

**hold** *verb* 1. ✦ grip, grasp, clasp, clutch, squeeze, clench You should *hold* the bat with both hands. 2. ✦ contain, accommodate, include ✧ comprise, have This carton *holds* a dozen eggs. 3. ✦ bear, support, take, carry, sustain The porch swing will *hold* the weight of two people. 4. ✦ continue, endure, last, persist, remain, stay, keep I hope that this good weather will *hold* for a few more days. 5. ✦ have, conduct, give, stage ✧ direct, run We are planning to *hold* a garage sale next Saturday. —*noun* ✦ grip, grasp, clasp, clutch, embrace I kept a firm *hold* on the ladder.

**hole** *noun* 1. ✦ gap, opening, breach, slit, slot, aperture The dog got out of the yard through a *hole* in the fence. 2. ✦ pit ✧ cavity, crater, depression, hollow, dip I helped my friend dig *holes* for her new rose bushes.

**holiday** *noun* 1. ✦ celebration, festival, fete, jubilee ✧ holy day The Fourth of July is a *holiday* that celebrates the United States' independence. 2. ✦ vacation, break, leave, recess, rest I am going to visit my grandparents during the summer *holiday*.

**hollow** *adjective* ✦ empty, unfilled ✧ vacant, void, sunken Some people say you can hear the ocean roar when you hold a *hollow* seashell to your ear. —*noun* ✦ cavity, hole, pocket ✧ crater, depres-

sion, pit Raccoons sometimes make their dens in the *hollows* of trees. —*verb* ✦ dig, scoop, shovel ✧ excavate, remove A dugout is a type of canoe that is made by *hollowing* out a large log.

**holy** *adjective* ✦ divine, sacred, religious ✧ revered, hallowed The Koran is the Muslim *holy* book.

**home** *noun* 1. ✦ house, residence, abode, dwelling, domicile ✧ lodging Several new *homes* are being built in our neighborhood. 2. ✦ institution, asylum, hospital ✧ shelter, hospice My elderly neighbor just moved to a nursing *home*.

**homely** *noun* ✦ ugly, unattractive, unlovely, repulsive, plain I think vultures are *homely*.

**honor** *noun* 1. ✦ laurels, acclaim, distinction, award ✧ praise, tribute The straight-A student graduated with *honors*. 2. ✦ honesty, integrity, virtue ✧ dignity, reputation, morality A sense of *honor* makes us want to do the right thing. —*verb* ✦ eulogize, celebrate, acclaim, commend, praise, recognize, hail This memorial *honors* the people who died in the American Civil War.

**hook** *noun* ✦ catch, clasp, fastener There is a *hook* undone on the back of your dress. —*verb* ✦ catch, fasten, latch, secure ✧ attach Please *hook* the screen door so it will stay closed.

**hop** *verb* ✦ bounce, bound, jump, leap, skip, spring A rabbit *hopped* across the corn field. —*noun* ✦ bounce, bound, jump, leap, skip, spring The robin moved across the lawn in short *hops*.

**hope** *verb* ✦ wish, look forward, want ✧ anticipate, expect, pray Mariana *hopes* to get a smartphone for her birthday. —*noun* ✦ desire, dream, longing, wish ✧ expectation, want The player's *hope* is to win the tennis tournament.

**hopeful** *adjective* 1. ✦ expectant, optimistic, anticipatory, confident My friend is *hopeful* that she will find a good job now that she has finished college. 2. ✦ encouraging, favorable, good, heartening, promising, bright The doctor said that there were many *hopeful* signs that the patient would soon make a full recovery.

**hopeless** *adjective* ✦ desperate, bad, poor, forlorn, futile ✧ despairing, pessimistic My team was in a *hopeless* situation when we were behind by fifty points at halftime.

**horde** *noun* ✦ crowd, herd, mob, pack, swarm, throng There was a *horde* of people downtown at the New Year's Eve celebration.

**horrible** *adjective* ✦ dreadful, frightful, awful, ghastly, grim, horrid, terrible Fog caused a *horrible* accident on the freeway.

**horrid** *adjective* ✦ ghastly, gruesome, hideous, horrible, revolting, grim The mythological Gorgon is a *horrid* creature with snakes for hair.

**horror** *noun* ✦ alarm, dread, fear, fright, panic, terror The movie characters screamed with *horror* when they saw the monster.

**host** *noun* ✦ hostess, receptionist, attendant ✧ entertainer The party's *hosts* greeted all their guests at the front door.

**hostile** *adjective* ✦ antagonistic, belligerent ✧ malicious, unfriendly, aggressive A *hostile* force had the soldiers surrounded.

**hot** *adjective* 1. ✦ scorching, searing, sweltering, sizzling, torrid On *hot* summer days, I like to cool off by going swimming. 2. ✦ spicy, zesty, sharp ✧ acrid, biting I like to put *hot* sauce on my hamburgers. 3. ✦ angry, fiery, intense, passionate, raging ✧ ardent Some people have *hot* tempers.

### Word Groups
A **hotel** provides a place for people to stay in return for payment. **Hotel** is a general term with no true synonyms. Here are some different kinds of hotels to investigate in a dictionary: **bed-and-breakfast, hostel, inn, lodge, motel, motor inn, resort**

**hound** *noun* ✦ dog, hunting dog ✧ pointer, retriever, setter The *hounds* began baying when they caught the fox's scent. —*verb* ✦ badger, nag, pester, prod, bother, harass The child sometimes *hounds* his mom to let him stay up late.

**house** *noun* 1. ✦ abode, dwelling, home, residence My friend lives in a small *house* that has just one bedroom. 2. ✦ place ✧ building, hall, structure, shelter A Jewish *house* of worship is called a synagogue. —*verb* ✦ lodge, put up, shelter, quarter ✧ board, dwell, reside The horses are *housed* in the barn.

**hover** *verb* 1. ✦ hang, float, drift ✧ flap, flutter, pause, poise A butterfly *hovered* over the flower. 2. ✦ hang around, linger, loiter, remain The dog *hovered* near the dining table, hoping for a snack.

**however** *conjunction* ✦ nevertheless, still, yet, but ✧ though My library book is not due until next week; *however*, I plan to return it today.

**howl** *noun* ✦ cry, scream, wail, yell, yowl, shriek I let out a *howl* of pain when I stubbed my toe. —*verb* ✦ bay, wail, yowl ✧ bawl, bellow, cry, scream Wolves *howl* at night to keep in touch with other members of their pack.

**hub** *noun* ✦ center, headquarters, seat, nub ✧ core, middle Kansas City, Missouri, is a transportation *hub* where many railroads and highways meet.

**huddle** *noun* ✦ knot, clump, cluster, mass, bunch ✧ group The football players formed a *huddle* to plan their next play. —*verb* ✦ bunch, cluster, crowd, flock, gather, press Sheep *huddle* together for warmth.

**hue** *noun* ✦ color, shade, tint, tone, tinge I would like that sweater in a darker *hue*.

**hug** *verb* ✦ clasp, embrace, squeeze, hold ✧ cuddle, nestle My grandmother always *hugs* me because she is so happy to see me. —*noun* ✦ clasp, embrace, squeeze ✧ clinch, caress My mother gave me a big *hug* when I returned from studying abroad.

**huge** *adjective* ✦ big, enormous, gigantic, immense, large, massive, colossal We usually think of dinosaurs as being *huge*, but some were as small as chickens.

**human** *noun* ✦ person, individual, human being, mortal ✧ man, woman All *humans* deserve to be treated with respect.

**humane** *adjective* ✦ compassionate, kind, merciful, tender ✧ good It is important to be *humane* to your pets.

**humble** *adjective* 1. ✦ modest, unassuming, reserved ✧ bashful, meek, shy The *humble* man never bragged about his accomplishments. 2. ✦ common, lowly, simple ✧ mean, obscure, poor My grandfather is proud of his *humble* background.

**humid** *adjective* ✦ damp, moist, muggy, steamy ✧ clammy, soggy, sultry The bathroom was *humid* after I took a hot shower.

**humiliate** *verb* ✦ disgrace, embarrass, shame ✧ dishonor, degrade The coach was *humiliated* when the team lost a game everyone thought they would win.

**humor** *noun* 1. ✦ wit, wittiness, comedy, fun ✧ amusement, funniness A good sense of *humor* makes life more enjoyable. 2. ✦ mood, disposition, temper, spirits ✧ nature The salesman has been in a good *humor* ever since he won the award for most sales. —*verb* ✦ cater (to), indulge, pamper, spoil, coddle I *humor* my parakeets by whistling to them all the time.

**humorous** *adjective* ✦ amusing, comic, comical, funny, witty Our friend told us a *humorous* story that made us laugh.

**Antonyms** humorous

*adjective* grave, grim, serious, sober, solemn, somber

**hump** *noun* ✦ bulge, bump, lump, mound ◇ swelling, knob Depending upon the species, camels have either one or two *humps* on their backs.

**hunch** *noun* ✦ feeling, idea, notion, suspicion, impression I had a *hunch* that my friends were planning a surprise party for me.

**hunger** *noun* ✦ lack of food, hungriness, starvation ◇ appetite, famine The stray kitten was weak from *hunger*. —*verb* ✦ crave, desire, long (for), want, yearn (for) Some people *hunger for* praise and recognition.

**hungry** *adjective* 1. ✦ famished, ravenous, starved, starving I was *hungry* after the bike ride. 2. ✦ avid, eager, greedy, yearning, needful, desirous I am always *hungry* for a new book by my favorite author.

**hunt** *verb* 1. ✦ chase, pursue, stalk, track, trail ◇ kill, shoot I think that people should *hunt* wild animals with cameras instead of guns. 2. ✦ look, search, seek ◇ probe, quest I helped my friend *hunt* for her missing keys. —*noun* ✦ quest, search, probe ◇ chase, pursuit The prospector spent his life in a *hunt* for gold.

**hurdle** *noun* ✦ barrier, obstacle, difficulty, impediment, obstruction, problem, bar Getting the president's signature is the last *hurdle* a bill faces before it becomes law. —*verb* ✦ jump, leap, spring over, vault, bound In a steeplechase, horses have to *hurdle* hedges, walls, and other obstacles.

**hurl** *verb* ✦ fling, launch, heave, pitch, throw, toss The little dog *hurled* himself into the air to make the catch.

**hurry** *verb* ✦ dash, hasten, fly, race, run, rush, speed, hustle I grabbed my jacket as I *hurried* out of the house. —*noun* ✦ rush, hustle ◇ dispatch, haste, quickness I was in a *hurry* to get home before the rain started.

**hurt** *verb* 1. ✦ ache, smart, pain ◇ throb, suffer My arms *hurt* from all the push-ups I did yesterday. 2. ✦ damage, harm, impair, ruin, spoil, injure, cripple All of this bad weather is *hurting* the local tourist trade.

**hustle** *verb* ✦ hasten, hurry, race, run, rush, speed The basketball players *hustled* up and down the court.

**hut** *noun* ✦ shack, shanty, shed, shelter ◇ cabin Some ski resorts have warming *huts*.

**hysterical** *adjective* ✦ frantic, frenzied, panic-stricken, upset, distraught, excited Some people become *hysterical* when they see a snake.

**icy** *adjective* ✦ frozen ✧ freezing, frosty, wintry, frigid, chilly, cold It's important to drive extra carefully on *icy* roads.

**idea** *noun* ✦ opinion, thought, notion ✧ view, belief, concept Everyone had a different *idea* about where we should go for vacation.

**ideal** *noun* ✦ dream, wish, goal ✧ aim, ambition, goal My *ideal* is to somehow make the world a better place. —*adjective* ✦ excellent, fitting, perfect ✧ satisfactory, suitable This field is *ideal* for playing softball.

**identical** *adjective* ✦ matching ✧ equal, exact, like, same, twin My best friend and I bought *identical* wristwatches.

**identify** *verb* ✦ distinguish, know, recognize ✧ describe, pinpoint Javier had no problem *identifying* his dog at the animal shelter.

**idiot** *noun* ✦ dummy, dunce, fool, moron, imbecile My grandfather said that he felt like an *idiot* the time he went golfing and forgot to bring his clubs.

**idle** *adjective* 1. ✦ inactive, unused, still ✧ inert, vacant The town's snowplow stood *idle* all summer long. 2. ✦ lazy, shiftless, slothful, listless I love *idle* days at the beach doing nothing but sunbathing. 3. ✦ empty, hollow, useless, vacant ✧ vain, worthless We passed the time in *idle* chatter during the long bus ride. —*verb* ✦ dawdle, fiddle, while ✧ loaf, lounge, waste I like to *idle* away rainy days by reading a good book.

**idol** *noun* 1. ✦ deity, god, goddess ✧ image, statue, effigy The archaeologist found a gold *idol* in the ruins of an ancient temple. 2. ✦ hero, heroine ✧ celebrity, star My *idol* is a famous writer.

**ignite** *verb* ✦ catch fire, kindle, light, burn, combust ✧ flame Dry leaves *ignite* easily.

**ignorant** *adjective* 1. ✦ uneducated, untaught ✧ illiterate *Ignorant* people sometimes make poor decisions. 2. ✦ oblivious, unaware, unconscious, uninformed ✧ unfamiliar Many pioneers were *ignorant* of the dangers that they would have to face.

**ignore** *verb* ✦ disregard, overlook, forget about ✧ neglect I tried to *ignore* the sound of the loud party.

**ill** *adjective* 1. ✦ sick, unwell ✧ ailing, unhealthy I went to bed early because I felt *ill*. 2. ✦ bad, adverse ✧ evil, harmful, unfavorable It's an old superstition that spilling salt will bring *ill* fortune. —*noun* ✦ affliction, evil, misery, misfortune, trouble Poverty is one of the *ills* that affect society today.

**illegal** *adjective* ✦ illicit, unlawful, criminal ✧ lawless, prohibited, wrongful Vandalism is *illegal*.

**illness** *noun* ✦ sickness, ailment, malady ✧ affliction, disease, disorder My *illness* caused me to miss two days of work.

**illuminate** *verb* ✦ light, light up ✧ brighten, lighten Floodlights *illuminated* the entire baseball field.

**illusion** *noun* ✦ fantasy, misbelief, misconception, mistake, falsehood ✧ delusion, mirage The notion that money can buy happiness is an *illusion*.

**illustrate** *verb* 1. ✦ clarify, demonstrate, explain ✧ show, illuminate The teacher *illustrated* her point by giving several specific examples. 2. ✧ draw, paint, sketch, adorn, decorate *Where the Wild Things Are* is a popular children's book written and *illustrated* by Maurice Sendak.

**image** *noun* ✦ likeness, picture, portrait, representation ✧ reflection, resemblance An American dollar bill bears the *image* of George Washington.

**imaginary** *adjective* ✦ fictional, nonexistent, unreal, fanciful, legendary Dragons and unicorns are *imaginary* creatures.

**imagination** *noun* 1. ✦ fancy, fantasy, whimsy, mind ✧ impression, notion, thought The child claimed there was a monster in her closet, but it existed only in her *imagination*. 2. ✦ creativity, originality ✧ inspiration, vision When my friend read my short story, she said that I have a lot of *imagination*.

**imagine** *verb* 1. ✦ picture, visualize, envision ✧ conceive, fancy, fantasize As I listened to the story, I could *imagine* the whole scene perfectly. 2. ✦ assume, guess, presume, suppose ✧ suspect,

**think** I *imagine* you'll want to know all the details about what happened at the party.

**imitate** *verb* ✦ copy, mimic, ape, reproduce ✧ duplicate, repeat Comedians often *imitate* the voices of famous people.

**imitation** *noun* ✦ copy, duplicate, likeness, replica, reproduction, simulation This statue is an *imitation* of an authentic Egyptian artifact.

**immature** *adjective* ✦ childish, juvenile ✧ babyish, foolish, infantile, young, youthful It was *immature* of me to think that I could always get my own way.

**immediate** *adjective* 1. ✦ instant, prompt, instantaneous, quick, speedy, swift ✧ sudden This medicine is guaranteed to give *immediate* relief. 2. ✦ close, near ✧ adjacent, direct, next My aunt is planning a small wedding, and only the *immediate* family will be invited.

**Antonyms immediate**

*adjective* 1. deferred, delayed, late, overdue, slow, tardy 2. distant, faraway, remote, removed

**immediately** *adverb* ✦ at once, instantly, now, promptly, right away, directly We need to leave *immediately* or we'll be late.

**immense** *adjective* ✦ colossal, enormous, gigantic, huge, large, massive, mammoth, vast The volcano erupted with enough force to hurl *immense* boulders into the air.

**immerse** *verb* 1. ✦ submerge, dunk, plunge, dip, douse ✧ soak, steep A fox will *immerse* itself in water to get rid of fleas. 2. ✦ absorb (by), engage (with), engross (by), interest, involve (with), occupy (with) The boy was so deeply *immersed in* his video game that he lost track of the time.

**immigrate** *verb* ✦ migrate, move, relocate ✧ colonize, settle Lian and her family *immigrated* to the United States from Vietnam.

**imminent** *adjective* ✦ at hand, close, near, immediate ✧ likely, looming, inevitable Defeat seemed *imminent*, but we won the game by scoring a touchdown at the last moment.

**immoral** *adjective* ✦ bad, wrong ✧ evil, sinful, unethical, wicked Most people would agree that cheating is *immoral*.

**immortal** *adjective* ✦ eternal, everlasting, undying ✧ ceaseless, endless, perpetual According to

ancient Greek religion, Zeus was the king of the *immortal* gods.

**immune** *adjective* ✦ resistant ✧ exempt, free, protected, safe Some people are *immune* to poison ivy.

**impact** *noun* 1. ✦ collision, crash, strike ✧ blow, contact, jolt This crater was formed by the *impact* of a meteor. 2. ✦ effect, influence, impression ✧ force, meaning, consequence Advances in technology have had a strong *impact* on the way we live.

**impair** *verb* ✦ hinder, reduce, decrease ✧ damage, harm, hurt, injure, cripple Clipping a bird's wing feathers *impairs* its ability to fly.

**Antonyms impair**

*verb* amend, better, correct, help, improve, refine

**impartial** *adjective* ✦unbiased, unprejudiced, neutral, objective, fair ✧ just A good referee is *impartial*.

**impatient** *adjective* 1. ✦ anxious, avid, eager, keen ✧ restless, ardent I am *impatient* to get back home to see family and friends. 2. ✦ annoyed, exasperated, irritated ✧ intolerant, irritable The *impatient* driver kept honking her horn at pedestrians in the crosswalk.

**imperative** *adjective* ✦ essential, mandatory, necessary, urgent, crucial, dire It was *imperative* for the deep-sea diver to return to the surface because she was low on air.

**imperfect** *adjective* ✦ defective, deficient, faulty, flawed ✧ incomplete *Imperfect* vision can usually be corrected with eyeglasses.

**imperial** *adjective* ✦ royal, regal ✧ sovereign, stately, majestic The emperor was protected by his *imperial* guard.

**implement** *noun* ✦ device, instrument, tool ✧ utensil, object, gadget Pencils and pens are writing *implements*.

**imply** *verb* ✦ hint, indicate, suggest ✧ mean, signify, allude My boyfriend's expression *implied* that he disagreed with what I said.

**impolite** *adjective* ✦ discourteous, disrespectful, inconsiderate, rude, crude, unmannerly It is *impolite* to chew with your mouth open.

**important** *adjective* 1. ✦ significant, consequential, critical ✧ meaningful, serious, valuable, big I have an *important* meeting at work today. 2. ✦

distinguished, eminent, influential, prominent, notable ✧ **powerful** The most *important* guests were seated at the head of the table.

**impose** *verb* 1. ✦ assess, decree, levy, place, put ✧ **dictate** The city council *imposed* a new tax on luxury items. 2. ✦ intrude (on), bother, inconvenience, trouble I'd love to stay for dinner, if you're sure I wouldn't be *imposing on* you.

**impossible** *adjective* ✦ unattainable ✧ impractical, futile, hopeless, unreal It's *impossible* to be in two places at one time.

**impostor** *noun* ✦ fake, fraud, phony, pretender, charlatan The man claimed to be a movie star, but he was an *impostor* who had never done any acting.

**impress** *verb* ✦ excite, awe, affect, move, strike ✧ influence, touch Seeing Saturn's rings through the telescope really *impressed* me.

**impression** *noun* 1. ✦ effect, impact ✧ appearance, image, influence The new teacher made a good *impression* on her first day at school. 2. ✦ feeling, hunch, idea, notion ✧ suspicion, opinion I have the *impression* that you're ready to go now. 3. ✦ imprint, indentation, outline, trace ✧ mark, stamp This rock contains the fossilized *impression* of a leaf.

**impressive** *adjective* ✦ awesome, moving, stirring, affecting, remarkable ✧ influential, touching America's Grand Canyon is an *impressive* sight.

**improper** *adjective* ✦ inappropriate, unfit, unsuitable ✧ incorrect, wrong Sweatpants are *improper* attire for a formal wedding.

**improve** *verb* ✦ better, enhance, develop, help ✧ perfect, polish, refine Rasheeda's visit to America *improved* her English.

**improvement** *noun* ✦ enhancement, advance, upgrade (from) ✧ change, progress, revision Our new car is a big *improvement* over the one we used to have.

**improvise** *verb* ✦ devise, concoct, contrive ✧ invent, originate The child *improvised* a toy airplane using a milk carton and some coat hangers.

**impulse** *noun* ✦ whim, urge, inclination ✧ fancy, motive, stimulus Stores commonly display merchandise in a way that encourages people to buy on *impulse*.

**impulsive** *adjective* ✦ impetuous, spontaneous, rash, reckless, hasty ✧ foolish I soon regretted my *impulsive* offer to babysit all day for the kids next door.

**Antonyms** **impulsive**
*adjective* careful, cautious, deliberate, intentional, planned

**in** *preposition* ✦ inside, within, into ✧ at, to Please put your jacket *in* the closet.

**inaccurate** *adjective* ✦ false, erroneous, incorrect, mistaken, wrong ✧ faulty The tabloid article was full of *inaccurate* information.

**inappropriate** *adjective* ✦ improper, unfit, unsuitable ✧ incorrect, wrong Blue jeans are considered *inappropriate* attire where I work.

**inaugurate** *verb* 1. ✦ induct, install ✧ commission The new president will be *inaugurated* next month. 2. ✦ begin, commence, initiate, start, institute ✧ introduce, open Soon after taking office, the president *inaugurated* a new immigration policy.

**incapable** *adjective* ✦ unable ✧ helpless, incompetent, powerless, unfit Whales are *incapable* of breathing underwater.

**incense** *verb* ✦ anger, enrage, infuriate, madden ✧ irritate, provoke It *incenses* me when someone cuts in front of me in a line.

**incentive** *noun* ✦ inducement, stimulus, encouragement, motivation, spur ✧ reason The store offered big discounts as an *incentive* to bring in new customers.

**incident** *noun* ✦ affair, event, experience, happening, occurrence, circumstance My friend didn't remember the funny *incident* until I reminded her.

**incline** *verb* ✦ lean, slant, slope, tilt, tip, cant ✧ list The Leaning Tower of Pisa *inclines* more than fourteen feet to one side. —*noun* ✦ grade, rise, slope, gradient ✧ hill Monique walked her bike down the steep *incline*.

**include** *verb* ✦ encompass, contain, cover, take in ✧ hold, involve The price of the meal *includes* one medium drink and a dessert.

**income** *noun* ✦ earnings, salary, pay ✧ money, revenue, wage, resources I'm looking for a better job in order to increase my *income*.

**incompetent** *adjective* ✦ incapable, unskilled, inept, inadequate, unqualified ✧ inefficient It's hard to learn from an *incompetent* teacher.

**incomplete** *adjective* ✦ deficient, unfinished, partial, lacking ✧ **fragmentary, spotty** My coin collection is *incomplete* because I'm missing a couple of rare pennies.

**inconvenience** *noun* ✦ **annoyance, bother, difficulty, trouble** ✧ **drawback, nuisance** It was a real *inconvenience* when we lost the television's remote control. —*verb* ✦ **bother, disturb, trouble** ✧ **annoy, upset** Would it *inconvenience* you to give me a ride home?

**incorrect** *adjective* ✦ **inaccurate, mistaken, erroneous, wrong, false, untrue** The *incorrect* answers are marked with red ink.

**increase** *verb* ✦ **boost, enlarge, expand, amplify, augment** ✧ **grow, multiply, swell** Regular practice will *increase* our chances of winning. —*noun* ✦ **expansion, gain, growth, rise** ✧ **advance, raise** The world is experiencing a population *increase* of about eighty million people per year.

**incredible** *adjective* 1. ✦ **unbelievable, unconvincing, inconceivable, improbable, doubtful** No one believed the woman's *incredible* account of being abducted by Martians. 2. ✦ **amazing, astonishing, astounding, extraordinary, fantastic** ✧ **fabulous** The hurricane struck land with *incredible* fury.

**indeed** *adverb* ✦ **certainly, definitely, positively, really, truly, genuinely** You are *indeed* my best friend.

**indefinite** *adjective* ✦ **open, uncertain, undecided, vague, unclear** ✧ **doubtful** My plans for the weekend are still *indefinite*.

**independence** *noun* ✦ **freedom, liberty, autonomy, self-reliance** The child had a feeling of *independence* the first time she walked to school by herself.

**independent** *adjective* 1. ✦ **free, autonomous, self-governing, sovereign** ✧ **liberated** The United States became an *independent* nation on September 3, 1783. 2. ✦ **self-reliant, self-sufficient, self-supporting, free** I feel very *independent* now that I have my own apartment.

**indicate** *verb* ✦ **designate, mark, point out, specify, reveal, show** The pirate put a big "X" on the map to *indicate* where the treasure was buried.

**indifferent** *adjective* ✦ **apathetic (toward), unconcerned (about), uninterested (in)** ✧ **detached, neutral, passive** How could anyone be *indifferent* to the suffering of others?

**indirect** *adjective* 1. ✦ **circuitous, roundabout** ✧ **long, rambling, winding** I wasn't in a hurry, so I took an *indirect* route home from work. 2. ✦ **ambiguous, evasive, vague** ✧ **unclear, indefinite** The politician gave an *indirect* answer to the embarrassing question.

**individual** *adjective* 1. ✦ **separate, single** ✧ **lone, sole, solitary** This store allows you to buy candy in bulk or by the *individual* piece. 2. ✦ **personal, private** ✧ **distinctive, particular, special** Which movies we enjoy is a matter of *individual* taste. —*noun* ✦ **person, being, human, human being** ✧ **creature, fellow, soul** My friend is a thoughtful *individual*.

**indulge** *verb* ✦ **appease, gratify, satisfy, content** ✧ **baby, pamper, spoil** I *indulged* my craving for ice cream by having a chocolate sundae.

**industrious** *adjective* ✦ **active, busy, energetic, productive, diligent** Beavers are considered to be *industrious* animals.

**industry** *noun* ✦ **business** ✧ **commerce, trade, manufacturing** The American automobile *industry* is centered in Detroit.

**inert** *adjective* ✦ **immobile, motionless, still, unmoving, stationary** ✧ **lifeless** An opossum will sometimes lie *inert* in order to trick its enemies into thinking that it is dead.

**inevitable** *adjective* ✦ **certain, inescapable, sure, unavoidable** ✧ **destined** Increasing levels of carbon dioxide in the atmosphere are making global climate change *inevitable*.

**inexpensive** *adjective* ✦ **cheap, low-cost, low-priced, economical** ✧ **reasonable, budget** An animal shelter is an *inexpensive* place to get a pet.

**inexperienced** *adjective* ✦ **green, new, raw, untried** ✧ **unskilled, untrained** Our soccer team is composed mostly of *inexperienced* players.

**infant** *noun* ✦ **baby, newborn, babe** ✧ **child, toddler, tot** The *infant* slept peacefully in the crib.

### Word Groups

To **infect** someone is to transmit an illness to them. **Infect** is a very specific term with no true synonyms. Here are some related words to investigate in a dictionary: **afflict, contaminate, poison, pollute, soil, taint**

**infectious** *adjective* ✦ **contagious, communicable** ✧ **catching, spreading** Vaccines are helpful in preventing the spread of many *infectious* diseases.

**infer** *verb* ✦ conclude, deduce, gather, presume, surmise ✧ know, understand I *infer* from your smile that you are in a good mood.

**inferior** *adjective* 1. ✦ lesser, lower, subordinate, secondary ✧ under Silver is *inferior* in value to gold. 2. ✦ mediocre, poor, substandard ✧ bad, shoddy This radio is inexpensive because it is of *inferior* quality.

**infinite** *adjective* ✦ boundless, endless, limitless, unlimited, immeasurable The number of stars in the night sky is seemingly *infinite*.

**inflate** *verb* ✦ blow up ✧ expand, swell, stretch He can *inflate* a balloon with just one breath.

**influence** *noun* ✦ effect, impact ✧ control, force, power, sway, weight My friends have had a great *influence* on the kinds of books I like to read. —*verb* ✦ effect, alter, change, shape, affect ✧ determine, sway The internet has greatly *influenced* the way people get their news.

**influential** *adjective* ✦ important, powerful, significant ✧ forceful, persuasive, effective The blogger is *influential* because so many people read her comments.

**inform** *verb* ✦ tell, advise, notify, apprise ✧ relate, report I called my friend to *inform* her that I would be a little late.

**informal** *adjective* ✦ casual, easygoing, simple, relaxed ✧ spontaneous I had an *informal* dinner at my friend's house.

**information** *noun* ✦ data, facts, knowledge, intelligence ✧ learning, news Online encyclopedias are useful sources for *information* about almost anything.

**infrequent** *adjective* ✦ rare, uncommon, unusual, irregular ✧ isolated, occasional Total solar eclipses are *infrequent* events.

**infuriate** *verb* ✦ enrage, incense, anger, madden, inflame ✧ provoke The baseball umpire's bad call *infuriated* the batter.

**Antonyms** **infuriate**
*verb* calm, comfort, compose, ease, pacify, soothe

**ingredient** *noun* ✦ component, constituent, element ✧ factor, part, piece Milk and ice cream are the main *ingredients* of a milkshake.

**inhabit** *verb* ✦ abide (in), dwell (in), live (in), occu-py, reside (in) ✧ settle I discovered that a mouse was *inhabiting* a shoebox in my closet.

**inheritance** *noun* ✦ legacy, bequest ✧ estate, heritage I received a gold ring as part of my *inheritance* from my grandmother.

**initial** *adjective* ✦ earliest, first, original ✧ beginning, introductory My *initial* opinion of my neighbor changed when I got to know her better.

**initiate** *verb* 1. ✦ begin, commence, start, launch ✧ establish, introduce The Foreign Minister *initiated* an investigation into the charges of corruption. 2. ✦ induct ✧ admit, install, receive, invest He recited the Scout Oath when he was *initiated* into the Boy Scouts.

**injure** *verb* ✦ harm, hurt, wound ✧ damage, impair According to a British study, over 60,000 people *injure* themselves every year trying to open food packages.

**injury** *noun* ✦ wound, hurt ✧ damage, harm, affliction I received only a minor *injury* when I fell off my motorbike.

**injustice** *noun* ✦ inequity, wrong, unfairness, offense, outrage ✧ crime, misdeed Sending an innocent person to prison is a terrible *injustice*.

**inner** *adjective* ✦ inside, interior ✧ central, internal, inward The *inner* bark of a willow tree is edible.

**innocent** *adjective* ✦ blameless, guiltless, not guilty ✧ faultless According to American law, a person is *innocent* until proven guilty.

**inquire** *verb* ✦ ask, query ✧ examine, question, quiz My friends and I *inquired* about the apartment that was for rent.

**inquisitive** *adjective* ✦ curious, inquiring, questioning, investigative, searching ✧ nosy, prying, snoopy Infants like to explore their surroundings because they are naturally *inquisitive*.

**insane** *adjective* ✦ absurd, foolish, idiotic, ridiculous, silly, mad Your idea for saving money by not taking baths sounds *insane* to me.

**inscribe** *verb* ✦ carve, chisel, cut, engrave, etch, impress, imprint, stamp Old tombstones sometimes have witty remarks *inscribed* on them.

**inscription** *noun* ✦ engraving, imprint, lettering, writing ✧ impression, mark Many married couples have *inscriptions* on their wedding rings.

**insecure** *adjective* ✦ shaky, unstable, unsteady,

wobbly, precarious ✧ dangerous, weak The old ladder looked too *insecure* to risk climbing it.

**insert** *verb* ✦ put in, place ✧ enter, inject, introduce To unlock the drawer, *insert* the key and turn it to the left.

**inside** *noun* ✦ interior ✧ center, core, middle, heart The *inside* of my jewelry box is lined with red velvet. —*adjective* ✦ inner, interior ✧ internal, central, inward My new suit jacket has two *inside* pockets.

**insignia** *noun* ✦ badge, crest, emblem ✧ mark, sign, symbol A three-leaf clover is the official *insignia* of the Girl Scouts of America.

**insignificant** *adjective* ✦ trivial, unimportant, meaningless, petty, trifling, slight My boss said that my mistake was too *insignificant* to worry about.

**insincere** *adjective* ✦ artificial, phony, pretended ✧ deceitful, dishonest, fake I could tell that her smile was *insincere*.

**insist** *verb* 1. ✦ demand, require ✧ command, urge, request My boss *insists* that all work assignments be finished on time. 2. ✦ affirm, assert, claim, contend, declare, state The lawyer *insisted* that his client was innocent.

**inspect** *verb* ✦ check, examine, investigate, survey ✧ observe, study, search Schools and other public buildings are *inspected* regularly by fire department officials.

**inspection** *noun* ✦ check, checkup, examination, review, survey, investigation Commercial airplanes undergo regular safety *inspections*.

**inspiration** *noun* 1. ✦ encouragement, incentive, motivation ✧ stimulation, uplift, vigor The coach's dramatic speech at halftime gave *inspiration* to his players. 2. ✦ idea, revelation, vision, concept ✧ brainstorm, creativity, thought Some inventors say that they have gotten their best *inspirations* from dreams.

**inspire** *verb* ✦ encourage, motivate, prompt, stimulate, stir, urge The crowd's cheers *inspired* the runner to try harder.

**install** *verb* ✦ put in, set up ✧ place, position, establish, locate My roommates and I had a hard time *installing* our new air conditioner.

**instance** *noun* ✦ case, occasion, time, situation ✧ example, illustration, sample I can think of only one *instance* all year long when I was late for work.

**instant** *noun* ✦ minute, moment, second ✧ flash, jiffy I saw the deer for just an *instant* before it disappeared into the forest. —*adjective* ✦ instantaneous, immediate, prompt ✧ fast, quick, swift The new movie was an *instant* success.

**instantly** *adverb* ✦ at once, immediately, right away ✧ quickly, directly, now When Wang Jing picked up the phone, she *instantly* recognized her friend's voice.

**instead** *adverb* ✦ in place (of), rather (than), in lieu (of) ✧ alternatively We decided to go bowling *instead of* seeing a movie.

**instinct** *noun* ✦ inclination, feeling, hunch, intuition ✧ impulse, tendency, urge My *instinct* is to never bother my friend when she is in a quiet mood.

**instinctive** *adjective* ✦ instinctual, inborn, innate, reflexive, automatic, intuitive Many animals have an *instinctive* fear of shadows because a predator might be approaching.

**institute** *verb* ✦ establish, set up, start, begin, introduce, organize ✧ found, originate The city government *instituted* a new recycling program. —*noun* ✦ academy, school, institution ✧ establishment, foundation My sister wants to study at an art *institute* after she graduates from high school.

**institution** *noun* ✦ academy, school, institute ✧ establishment, foundation Colleges and universities are *institutions* of higher education.

**instruct** *verb* 1. ✦ teach, train, educate, school, guide, coach ✧ inform My skydiving coach *instructed* me in the proper use of a parachute. 2. ✦ direct, order, command, bid, charge, tell A police officer *instructed* onlookers to move away from the crime scene.

**instruction** *noun* 1. ✦ teaching, training, education, schooling ✧ lesson, guidance You'll need some *instruction* before you can safely go hang-gliding on your own. 2. ✦ command, order, demand, direction, directive ✧ mandate The captain expected the crew to follow his *instructions*.

**instrument** *noun* ✦ device, implement, mechanism, tool ✧ utensil, appliance A barometer is an *instrument* for measuring atmospheric pressure.

**insult** verb ✦ affront, offend ✧ humiliate, scorn, snub, taunt I did not mean to *insult* you. —noun ✦ affront, offense ✧ slight, scorn, snub, taunt It was an *insult* to my intelligence to expect me to believe that excuse.

**Antonyms** insult

verb acclaim, applaud, commend, compliment, flatter, laud, praise

**integrity** noun ✦ honesty, honor, virtue, principle, character ✧ morality It takes *integrity* to always do the right thing.

**intellectual** adjective ✦ scholarly, cerebral, learned ✧ intelligent, thoughtful, mental My friend likes to read *intellectual* books about science and philosophy. —noun ✦ mind, thinker, brain, intellect ✧ genius, sage, scholar Albert Einstein was one of the greatest *intellectuals* of the twentieth century.

**intelligence** noun ✦ brains, brain power, intellect, mind, brightness, cleverness The cosmologist Stephen Hawking is renowned for his *intelligence*.

**intelligent** adjective ✦ bright, brilliant, smart, sharp, clever, wise ✧ alert The *intelligent* student graduated from her university with top honors.

**intend** verb ✦ aim, expect, mean, plan, propose ✧ hope, wish, design What to you *intend* to do on your vacation this year?

**intense** adjective ✦ extreme, great, strong, terrible, terrific, fierce ✧ furious, heightened, violent The continent of Antarctica is known for its *intense* cold.

**intensity** noun ✦ energy, ferocity, fury, power, strength, violence, severity The forest fire burned with great *intensity*.

**intent** adjective ✦ absorbed, attentive, preoccupied, determined, earnest ✧ deep, resolute Joshua had an *intent* look on his face as he worked on the difficult problem. —noun ✦ aim, ambition, goal, intention, objective ✧ end, purpose It is my *intent* to go to graduate school abroad.

**intentional** adjective ✦ deliberate, intended ✧ planned, premeditated, voluntary Doctors take an oath in which they promise to never do any *intentional* harm to anyone.

**intercept** verb ✦ cut off, head off ✧ block, catch, seize, stop Two fighter planes were sent to *intercept* the enemy aircraft.

**interest** noun 1. ✦ attention, curiosity, absorption ✧ care, concern, notice, regard Whenever I'm cooking, my dog looks on with *interest*. 2. ✦ activity, hobby, pastime, pursuit ✧ recreation My *interests* include reading books and playing soccer. 3. ✦ advantage, benefit, good ✧ profit, welfare, gain It is in your best *interest* to cooperate with your coworkers. —verb ✦ intrigue, engage, fascinate, absorb, attract ✧ occupy Everything about airplanes *interests* me.

**interesting** adjective ✦ absorbing, appealing, entertaining, fascinating, gripping, riveting, exciting I listened attentively as my friend told an *interesting* story about his encounter with an elephant.

**interfere** verb ✦ interrupt, intervene, meddle ✧ disturb, hinder, tamper My friends were having a private talk, and I knew that I shouldn't *interfere*.

**interior** noun ✦ inside ✧ center, core, heart, middle Our car has a leather *interior*. —adjective ✦ inner, inside, internal, inward Many ancient Roman houses had *interior* courtyards.

**intermediate** adjective ✦ halfway, middle, midway, transitional ✧ central, median, medium A cocoon is the *intermediate* stage between a caterpillar and a moth.

**intermission** noun ✦ break, pause, recess, interlude ✧ rest, stop, time-out There will be a brief *intermission* halfway through the play.

**internal** adjective ✦ inner, inside, interior, inward The *internal* workings of a clock are very complicated.

**Word Groups**

Something that is **international** relates to two or more countries. **International** is a general term with no true synonyms. Here are some related words to investigate in a dictionary: **communal, global, national, planetary, universal, worldwide**

**interpret** verb ✦ decipher, explain, understand ✧ clarify, define, solve I am reading a book about how to *interpret* dreams.

**interrupt** verb ✦ break (into), cut off, halt, stop, cease ✧ disturb, hinder, interfere The alarm clock *interrupted* my dream.

**interval** noun ✦ period, span, interlude, spell, stretch ✧ break, gap, pause, space There was an *interval* of warm weather between the two snowstorms.

**interview** *noun* ✦ consultation, conference, meeting ✧ discussion, talk The final step in getting my American visa was an *interview* at the US Embassy. —*verb* ✦ talk (to) ✧ examine, interrogate, question, consult The company *interviewed* many applicants before filling the open position.

**intolerant** *adjective* ✦ biased, close-minded, narrow-minded, prejudiced, bigoted I try not to be *intolerant* when I meet people whose beliefs are different from my own.

**intricate** *adjective* ✦ complex, complicated, detailed, elaborate ✧ fancy Leonardo da Vinci's drawings are known for their *intricate* detail.

---

**Antonyms** intricate

*adjective* clear, elementary, modest, plain, simple, straightforward

---

**intrigue** *verb* ✦ fascinate, interest, enchant ✧ attract, excite, charm Many people are *intrigued* by the possibility that there might be life on other planets.

**introduce** *verb* 1. ✦ present ✧ acquaint, announce, familiarize Amanda *introduced* herself to her new coworkers. 2. ✦ begin, launch, start, inaugurate ✧ establish, originate, put forth The city government *introduced* new measures to curb crime.

**invade** *verb* ✦ assault, attack, assail, raid, strike, overrun, penetrate ✧ occupy Germany *invaded* Russia during World War II.

**invaluable** *adjective* ✦ precious, priceless, valuable, worthy ✧ expensive, indispensable Reading and writing are *invaluable* skills.

**invasion** *noun* ✦ assault, attack, raid, incursion ✧ aggression, offensive The Great Wall of China was built to protect the country from foreign *invasion*.

**invent** *verb* ✦ devise, develop, originate, contrive, create ✧ concoct, dream up The telephone was *invented* by Alexander Graham Bell in 1876.

**invention** *noun* ✦ development, creation ✧ discovery, design, production Thomas Edison is credited with the *invention* of the first practical light bulb.

**inventory** *noun* 1. ✦ list, record ✧ catalog, file, register, summary The stockroom clerk made an *inventory* of all the company's supplies. 2. ✦ stock, stockpile, store, supply ✧ reserve, backlog The

department store had a sale to reduce its *inventory* of winter clothing.

**investigate** *verb* ✦ look (into), probe, analyze, examine, inspect, study ✧ explore, follow The police are *investigating* clues related to last week's robbery.

**invisible** *adjective* ✦ imperceptible, unnoticeable, unobservable, indistinguishable ✧ concealed, hidden, disguised The snowshoe rabbit was almost *invisible* against the white snowdrift.

**invite** *verb* ✦ ask ✧ bid, request, summon, beckon I *invited* two of my friends to come over for dinner.

**involuntary** *adjective* ✦ automatic, reflexive, spontaneous ✧ impulsive, instinctive Breathing and digestion are *involuntary* actions.

**involve** *verb* 1. ✦ call (for), entail, include, require ✧ contain, have My job *involves* a lot of traveling. 2. ✦ absorb, engage, immerse, occupy (with) We were so *involved in* our conversation that we didn't hear the phone ring.

**irregular** *adjective* ✦ uneven, variable, unsteady, unequal ✧ abnormal, unusual The patient had an *irregular* heartbeat.

**irritate** *verb* 1. ✦ annoy, bother, disturb, exasperate, provoke, vex ✧ anger That noisy car alarm is beginning to *irritate* me. 2. ✦ aggravate, inflame, exacerbate ✧ hurt, worsen You'll only *irritate* that mosquito bite if you continue to scratch it.

**island** *noun* ✦ isle, islet, cay ✧ archipelago, atoll There's a little *island* in the center of the lake.

**isolate** *verb* ✦ quarantine, segregate, separate, set apart, seclude The veterinarian *isolated* the sick puppy so that it wouldn't infect any other animals.

**issue** *noun* ✦ matter, subject, topic, question, point ✧ problem Health care is an *issue* that affects everyone. —*verb* ✦ dispense, distribute, give out, hand out, allot ✧ deliver, release The coach *issued* new uniforms to everyone on the team.

**item** *noun* 1. ✦ article, object, thing ✧ product, element, particular I made a list of the *items* that I need for my trip abroad. 2. ✦ account, article, feature, report, story, entry Did you read the *item* in the paper about tomorrow's solar eclipse?

**itemize** *verb* ✦ detail, document, list, record ✧ catalog This receipt *itemizes* our purchases.

**jab** *verb* ✦ thrust, plunge, stab, poke, push ✧ nudge, prod I *jabbed* a fork into the baked potato to see if it was done. —*noun* ✦ blow, punch ✧ strike, nudge, poke, hit The boxer threw a series of quick *jabs* at his opponent.

**jacket** *noun* 1. ✦ coat ✧ parka, windbreaker, blazer I took a warm *jacket* with me to the football game. 2. ✦ cover, wrapper, dust jacket ✧ case, container, sheath, envelope The collector keeps his rare books in protective plastic *jackets*.

**jagged** *adjective* ✦ serrated, ragged, uneven, pointed ✧ notched, rough She cut her finger on a *jagged* piece of broken glass.

**jail** *noun* ✦ jailhouse, prison ✧ pen, penitentiary, lockup The sheriff kept the outlaws in *jail*. —*verb* ✦ imprison, lock up, incarcerate ✧ confine, detain The police arrested and *jailed* two suspects.

**jam** *verb* ✦ cram, squeeze, pack, stuff, wedge, crowd, load, press My sister tried to *jam* more clothes into her suitcase. —*noun* 1. ✦ blockage, block, obstruction ✧ barrier, congestion, crush A log *jam* stopped the river's flow. 2. ✦ predicament, difficulty, plight, trouble ✧ problem, dilemma The tourists were in a real *jam* when they lost all of their money.

**jar¹** *noun* ✦ bottle ✧ jug, container, vase, vessel I keep my loose change in a *jar* on my desk.

**jar²** *verb* 1. ✦ rock, jolt, rattle, shake, vibrate, jiggle The earthquake *jarred* our house but didn't cause any damage. 2. ✦ grate (on), jangle, irritate, upset ✧ annoy, disturb The sound of chalk scraping on a blackboard *jars* my nerves. —*noun* ✦ jolt, bounce, bump, jounce ✧ crash, impact I felt repeated *jars* as we drove down the bumpy dirt road.

**jealous** *adjective* 1. ✧ insecure, possessive, threatened, angry, anxious The little girl was *jealous* when her parents paid extra attention to her baby brother. 2. ✦ resentful, covetous, envious, desirous Who wouldn't be *jealous* of your fantastic new car?

**jealousy** *noun* ✦ envy, enviousness, resentment ✧ grudge, spite The man was filled with *jealousy* when his neighbor won the lottery.

**jeer** *verb* ✦ ridicule, laugh (at), heckle, mock, taunt ✧ insult I thought the comedian was very good, but some people in the audience *jeered* him.

**jeopardy** *noun* ✦ danger, peril, risk, vulnerability ✧ threat Police officers sometimes place their lives in *jeopardy* in order to protect the public.

**jerk** *verb* ✦ pull, yank, wrench, tear, tug, wrest My dog *jerked* the leash out of my hand and ran off after a cat. —*noun* ✦ bump, jolt, lurch, snap, bounce ✧ pull, tug, yank The roller coaster started with a *jerk* and then quickly picked up speed.

**jest** *noun* ✦ joke, gag ✧ hoax, prank, trick I hope your statement that dinner would be three hours late was a *jest*. —*verb* ✦ joke, kid, tease, fool, spoof My grandfather was *jesting* when he said that mice are the best bait for catfish.

**jet** *noun* ✦ spray, spurt, spout, squirt, stream ✧ flow An erupting geyser shoots a *jet* of boiling water high into the air.

**jewel** *noun* ✦ gem, gemstone, precious stone ✧ ornament Emeralds and amethysts are my favorite *jewels*.

### Word Groups

A piece of **jewelry** is an ornament that is worn as decoration on the body. **Jewelry** is a general term with no true synonyms. Here are some different kinds of jewelry to investigate in a dictionary: **anklet, brooch, diadem, locket, pendant, ring, stickpin, tiara**

**jiffy** *noun* ✦ instant, moment, flash, minute, second Lunch will be ready in a *jiffy*.

**jingle** *verb* ✦ chime, tinkle, ring, clink ✧ jangle The bell on the shop door *jingled* as I entered. —*noun* ✦ chime, tinkle, ring, clink ✧ jangle I enjoy listening to the *jingle* of our wind chimes.

**job** *noun* 1. ✦ chore, duty, task, assignment ✧ obligation, responsibility My roommate's *job* is to cook dinner tonight, and mine is to wash the dishes. 2. ✦ position, situation ✧ employment, work,

**occupation** Andrea just got a *job* as a computer programmer.

**jog** *verb* ✦ run, trot, lope ✧ sprint, race, dash I *jogged* around the track. —*noun* ✦ run ✧ dash, race, sprint, trot, lope I went for a *jog* this morning.

**join** *verb* 1. ✦ link, attach, connect, couple, fasten, unite A special coupling mechanism is used to *join* railroad cars. 2. ✦ ally, combine, merge, unite, assemble ✧ associate Two scout troops *joined* together to paint the playground equipment. 3. ✦ enroll (in), enter, sign up (for), enlist (in) I plan to *join* a photography club.

**joint** *noun* ✦ junction, seam ✧ connection, link, union The clacking sound that a train makes is caused by the wheels rolling over *joints* in the track. —*adjective* ✦ mutual, shared, common, communal ✧ combined My parents have a *joint* bank account.

**joke** *noun* ✦ jest, gag, witticism ✧ prank, trick Everyone laughed out loud when the comedian started with a funny *joke.* —*verb* ✦ fool, jest, kid, tease, josh I was *joking* when I said that I wanted a peanut-butter pizza.

**jolly** *adjective* ✦ cheerful, happy, jovial, merry, gleeful Our *jolly* neighbor is always smiling and laughing.

**jolt** *verb* ✦ bounce, jar, jerk, shake, lurch, bump We were almost *jolted* out of our seats when our car hit a big pothole. —*noun* 1. ✦ bump, bounce, jar, jerk, lurch ✧ shake The plane landed with a small *jolt.* 2. ✦ shock, surprise, start ✧ blow I got a big *jolt* when I looked at my new haircut.

**jostle** *verb* ✦ bump, joggle, press, push, shove, crowd The pigs *jostled* each other as they tried to get to their feeding trough.

**jot** *verb* ✦ write, scribble, note, record, register I *jotted* my friend's new phone number on the back of an envelope.

**journal** *noun* 1. ✦ log, diary, chronicle, record ✧ history, notebook The American explorers Lewis and Clark kept detailed *journals* while on their expedition. 2. ✦ magazine, periodical, publication, review ✧ bulletin, newspaper, paper I read an article about ancient Greece in a history *journal.*

**journalist** *noun* ✦ reporter, correspondent, newsperson ✧ writer, columnist A *journalist* interviewed the mayor for a newspaper article.

**journey** *noun* ✦ expedition, trip, trek ✧ excursion, tour, voyage Marco Polo's famous *journey* to China lasted twenty-four years. —*verb* ✦ tour, travel, trek, ramble, roam, voyage ✧ go Zhang Min would love to *journey* through South America.

**jovial** *adjective* ✦ jolly, cheerful, gleeful, merry, mirthful A *jovial* clown with a big smile greeted everyone who entered the circus tent.

**joy** *noun* ✦ delight, happiness, ecstasy, bliss, glee ✧ enjoyment, pleasure Jeong was filled with *joy* when she was admitted to a prestigious university.

**joyful** *adjective* ✦ happy, joyous, blissful, cheerful, glad, merry, festive This year Thanksgiving was especially *joyful* because our whole family was together.

**jubilant** *adjective* ✦ ecstatic, elated, exultant, thrilled, delighted ✧ triumphant The prospector was *jubilant* when he discovered a rich vein of gold.

**judge** *noun* 1. ✦ justice, justice of the peace, magistrate The *judge* typically gives instructions to the jury before a trial begins. 2. ✦ evaluator, reviewer, critic ✧ referee, umpire A panel of three *judges* selected the winning contestant. —*verb* ✦ decide, determine, assess, settle ✧ decree, rule, try The defendant's guilt or innocence will be *judged* in a court of law.

**judgment** *noun* 1. ✦ conclusion, decision, finding, ruling, verdict, determination The *judgment* of a court is always based on the law as well as the evidence presented. 2. ✦ common sense, sense, discretion ✧ prudence, wisdom I am glad to have parents who respect my *judgment.*

**jug** *noun* ✦ bottle, jar ✧ flask, crock, pitcher, vessel We bought a *jug* of maple syrup while vacationing in Maine.

**juggle** *verb* ✦ manipulate, shuffle, alter, change, modify ✧ maneuver I had to *juggle* my schedule in order to attend a yoga class.

**jumble** *verb* ✦ muddle, scramble, snarl ✧ confuse, disorder, mess up My desk is full of papers *jumbled* together. —*noun* ✦ clutter, mess, muddle, tangle, disarray ✧ chaos, confusion, disarray, disorder My roommate left a *jumble* of dirty clothes on the floor of his room.

**Antonyms** **jumble**
*verb* assemble, classify, distribute, group, order, organize, sort

*noun* collection, pattern, plan, sequence, set, system

**jumbo** *adjective* ✦ huge, colossal, enormous, gigantic, immense, large I ordered a *jumbo* plate of French fries.

**jump** *verb* ✦ leap, spring, bound, hop, hurdle, vault The deer *jumped* out of the cyclist's way. —*noun* ✦ leap, spring, bound, hop, vault, bounce My cat made it up on the table in a single *jump*.

**junction** *noun* ✦ convergence, intersection, confluence, joining, linking, meeting, union The city of St. Louis is located at the *junction* of the Mississippi and Missouri rivers.

**jungle** *noun* ✦ rainforest, tropical forest, primeval forest ✧ bush, wilderness *Jungles* are humid because they receive a lot of rain.

**junior** *adjective* 1. ✦ adolescent, juvenile, younger ✧ youthful The boy entered the *junior* division of the surfing tournament. 2. ✦ subordinate, minor, secondary ✧ lesser, lower, under, new The *junior* partner in the law firm was always assigned the easiest cases.

**junk** *noun* ✦ debris, rubbish, garbage, litter, refuse, trash, waste To clear the lot for our community garden we had to throw away a lot of *junk*.

**just** *adjective* ✦ fair, impartial, objective, unbiased ✧ honest, right This judge is known for making *just* decisions. —*adverb* 1. ✦ exactly, precisely, completely, entirely, perfectly, thoroughly My mom says that I look *just* like my grandfather. 2. ✦ recently, now, newly ✧ lately, presently The concert had only *just* started when we arrived at the park. 3. ✦ barely, hardly, scarcely, only, merely You'll *just* have time to get to the store before it closes.

**Antonyms** just

*adjective* biased, narrow-minded, one-sided, partial, prejudiced, unfair

**justice** *noun* ✦ fairness, justness, rightness ✧ honesty, lawfulness If *justice* is to be achieved, the innocent man must be released.

**justify** *verb* ✦ confirm, verify, vindicate, validate, support, sustain, uphold Divya *justified* my trust when she returned the money that I had loaned her.

**jut** *verb* ✦ stick out, protrude, project, extend, hang ✧ bulge The Rock of Gibraltar *juts* into the Mediterranean Sea.

**juvenile** *adjective* ✦ young, youthful, immature, adolescent ✧ childish, infant *Juvenile* elephants stay with their mothers for up to ten years. —*noun* ✦ child, minor, youngster, youth ✧ boy, girl *Juveniles* under the age of eighteen may not sign a legal contract.

# K

**keen** *adjective* 1. ✦ sensitive, sharp, acute, perceptive, strong ✧ fine, quick Bears have a *keen* sense of smell. 2. ✦ eager, enthusiastic, ardent, avid ✧ excited, hot I'm not too *keen* on the idea of going to the movie by myself.

**keep** *verb* 1. ✦ retain, have, hold, maintain, own, possess My friend said that I could *keep* the pen I had borrowed from her. 2. ✦ continue, persevere (in), persist (in), carry on ✧ remain, stay I *keep* trying to improve my time for running the one-hundred yard dash. 3. ✦ store, place, put ✧ carry, stock Where do you *keep* the mayonnaise and mustard? 4. ✦ fulfill, honor, observe, adhere (to), abide (by) ✧ obey Bich *kept* her promise to send me a postcard from Vietnam. 5. ✦ prevent, stop, restrain ✧ hinder, impede A storm *kept* us from going sailing. —*noun* ✦ living, livelihood, room and board, upkeep ✧ income, support The nanny earned her *keep* by caring for three small children.

**keepsake** *noun* ✦ memento, souvenir, remembrance, reminder, token ✧ trophy This album of old family photos is one of my most treasured *keepsakes*.

**keg** *noun* ✦ barrel, cask ✧ drum, tub, tank Carpenters used to buy their nails by the *keg*.

**kettle** *noun* ✦ pot, teakettle, teapot, cauldron ✧ vat, vessel In colonial times, a *kettle* of hot water was usually kept hanging in the fireplace.

**key** *noun* 1. ✦ solution, answer, clue, explanation, guide, means The *key* to solving a riddle is to listen carefully to its exact wording. 2. ✦ means, path, route, ticket, way, secret, formula Hard work is frequently the *key* to success. —*adjective* ✦ crucial, vital, chief, leading, main, major, top ✧ essential, necessary Your contribution was a *key* factor in making our book fair such a success.

**kick** *verb* ✦ boot ✧ hit, knock, strike, tap The forward scored a goal by *kicking* the ball past the goalie. —*noun* ✦ blow, hit, poke ✧ knock, stroke, nudge The rider gave her horse a gentle *kick* in the ribs to get it moving.

**kid** *noun* ✦ child, youngster, youth ✧ boy, girl, juvenile Some of the neighborhood *kids* got together to play a game of hide-and-seek. —*verb* ✦ tease, taunt ✧ jest, joke, ridicule, fool I like to *kid* my roommate about her younger boyfriend.

**kidnap** *verb* ✦ abduct, carry off, snatch, steal ✧ capture, seize, hijack The little girl's brother *kidnapped* her favorite doll and demanded a candy bar as ransom.

**kill** *verb* 1. ✦ slay, exterminate ✧ assassinate, execute, murder, slaughter I don't like to *kill* spiders, so I catch them and take them outside. 2. ✦ destroy, demolish, eliminate, end, extinguish, ruin, wipe out My injury *killed* any chance that I might have had to win the race tomorrow. —*noun* ✦ prey, victim, quarry ✧ game The lion stood guard over its *kill*.

**kin** *noun* ✦ family, kinfolk, kindred, relations, relatives I hope that all of my *kin* can make it to the next family reunion.

**kind**[1] *adjective* ✦ kindly, compassionate, considerate, generous, good, goodhearted, helpful ✧ gentle A *kind* woman helped me pick up all the books that I had dropped.

**kind**[2] *noun* ✦ sort, type, variety, category, class, manner There are two *kinds* of pandas—the giant panda and the red panda.

**kindle** *verb* 1. ✦ ignite, light, fire ✧ burn I used a match and some crumpled newspaper to *kindle* our campfire. 2. ✦ arouse, awake, awaken, inspire, stir, stimulate, excite My friend *kindled* my interest in traveling abroad.

**kindly** *adjective* ✦ kind, kindhearted, benevolent, good, goodhearted, humane The Tin Woodman is one of many *kindly* characters in *The Wonderful Wizard of Oz* by L. Frank Baum. —*adverb* ✦ generously, thoughtfully, helpfully ✧ courteously, graciously, politely My roommate *kindly* offered to help me with my housework.

**kindness** *noun* ✦ compassion, benevolence, decency, humanity, charity, goodwill ✧ generosity I believe all animals should be treated with *kindness*.

**king** *noun* ✦ monarch, sovereign, majesty, ruler ✧ lord Henry VIII was the *king* of England from 1509 to 1547.

**Word Groups**

A **kingdom** is a country that is ruled by a king or queen. **Kingdom** is a very specific term with no true synonyms. Here are some related words to investigate in a dictionary: **colony, commonwealth, dominion, empire, nation, realm, republic**

**kink** *noun* 1. ✦ curl, twist, bend, crimp ✧ coil, knot, tangle The garden hose had a *kink* in it. 2. ✦ cramp, spasm, knot, pain, pang, crick I got a *kink* in my back when I tried to lift the heavy box.

**kit** *noun* ✦ outfit, set, gear, implements ✧ equipment, materials, tools I bought a sewing *kit* as a gift for my friend.

**knack** *noun* ✦ talent, gift, aptitude, flair, facility ✧ ability, skill My friend has a *knack* for drawing funny cartoon characters.

**kneel** *verb* ✦ stoop, crouch ✧ bend, bow, curtsy I *knelt* down to pet the kittens.

**Word Groups**

A **knife** is a sharp instrument used for cutting and piercing. **Knife** is a general term with no true synonyms. Here are some different kinds of knives to investigate in a dictionary: **cleaver, dagger, dirk, jackknife, machete, pocketknife, scalpel, stiletto, switchblade**

**knit** *verb* 1. ✧ crochet, weave, sew, stitch My grandmother is teaching me how to *knit* a scarf. 2. ✦ heal, mend ✧ repair, attach, join, unite The doctor said that my broken arm should *knit* in about six weeks.

**knob** *noun* ✦ handle, hold, handhold ✧ button, dial, grip Our kitchen cabinets have white plastic *knobs* on them.

**knock** *verb* ✦ strike, hit, smash, whack ✧ beat, pound, rap, tap I *knocked* my head against the new light fixture. —*noun* ✦ rap, tap, thump, pounding ✧ blow, hit, punch, stroke I just heard a *knock* at the door.

**knot** *noun* 1. ✦ bow, hitch ✧ braid, loop, splice, tie The child is learning how to tie a *knot* in her shoelaces. 2. ✦ snarl, tangle, snag, gnarl, kink, lump I helped my sister brush the *knots* out of her hair. 3. ✦ clump, cluster, clutch, group, swarm, band, batch, bunch A *knot* of people gathered around the street musician.

**know** *verb* 1. ✦ understand, comprehend, grasp ✧ apprehend, fathom Do you *know* how to write a computer program? 2. ✦ identify, recognize, distinguish, tell ✧ notice, perceive My cousin said that I'd *know* her by the bright green suitcase she would be carrying.

**knowledge** *noun* 1. ✦ data, facts, information, learning, wisdom, ideas An encyclopedia is a storehouse of *knowledge*. 2. ✦ awareness, comprehension, consciousness, understanding, recognition The *knowledge* that skydiving is dangerous keeps many people from trying the sport.

**label** *noun* ✦ tag, sticker, ticket, marker, sign ✧ seal At the used clothing shop, each item had a *label* showing its price. —*verb* ✦ mark, tag, ticket ✧ identify, classify, describe, name All of my storage boxes have been *labeled* with their contents.

**labor** *noun* 1. ✦ work, toil, exertion, effort ✧ drudgery, struggle It took years of *labor* to dig the canal. 2. ✦ workers, laborers, help, workmen, workwomen ✧ crew, employees The company is a success because it uses highly skilled *labor*. —*verb* ✦ work, toil ✧ strain, strive, struggle The highway crew *labored* all week to get the road repaired.

**lack** *verb* ✧ miss, need, require, want Our town *lacks* the money to build a new public swimming pool. —*noun* ✦ scarcity, shortage, absence, deficiency ✧ need, want Not many plants grow in the desert because of the *lack* of rain.

**lad** *noun* ✦ boy, young man, youngster, youth, adolescent, teenager My grandfather likes to tell stories about his adventures as a *lad*.

**laden** *adjective* ✦ burdened, loaded, weighed down ✧ full, heavy The mule train was *laden* with heavy sacks of food and other supplies.

**lag** *verb* ✦ straggle, trail, dawdle, linger, poke along ✧ delay, loiter I *lagged* behind my friends on our walk home from swimming because I was tired. —*noun* ✦ break, pause, gap, interruption ✧ delay, hesitation, interval There was a *lag* in the conversation when we all ran out of things to say.

**lair** *noun* ✦ den ✧ burrow, refuge, nest, retreat A wolf's *lair* is commonly a hole dug in the ground.

**lake** *noun* ✧ pond, pool, reservoir, sea, lagoon These *lakes* were formed when the glaciers melted at the end of the Ice Age.

**lance** *noun* ✦ spear ✧ javelin, harpoon, pike The horse soldiers were armed with swords and *lances*. —*verb* ✦ pierce, puncture, prick, cut, cut open, incise I *lanced* my blister with a needle.

**land** *noun* 1. ✦ country, nation, state ✧ region, territory, realm America is sometimes called the *land* of opportunity. 2. ✦ earth, ground, soil, dirt, loam ✧ property, real estate This is good *land* for growing soybeans. —*verb* 1. ✦ alight, set down, touch down ✧ arrive, disembark Astronauts first *landed* on the moon on July 20, 1969. 2. ✦ get, obtain, procure, gain, secure, win ✧ catch The basketball star just *landed* a big five-year contract.

**lane** *noun* ✦ avenue, road, roadway ✧ route, street, path My grandparents live on a country *lane* that is lined with oak trees.

**language** *noun* 1. ✦ tongue ✧ dialect, speech My best friend can speak three *languages*. 2. ✧ communication, expression, symbolism, signals Native Americans used sign *language* to communicate with other tribes.

**lapse** *noun* 1. ✦ failure, slip ✧ blunder, error, mistake, omission I had a momentary memory *lapse* and couldn't remember my colleague's name. 2. ✦ interval, interruption, pause, lull, break ✧ gap I started taking yoga lessons again after a *lapse* of six months. —*verb* ✦ slip, fall, slide, sink, drop ✧ decline, fade The baby squirmed for a while, but finally she *lapsed* into sleep.

**large** *adjective* ✦ big, huge, enormous, immense, great, giant, sizable ✧ considerable A *large* crowd attended the free rock concert.

**lark** *noun* ✦ escapade, adventure, affair, celebration ✧ caper, prank The boy expects that his summer vacation will be a carefree *lark*.

**lash**[1] *noun* ✦ stroke, blow, hit, rap, smack, whack It took just one *lash* of the whip to get the mule moving. —*verb* ✦ whip, switch, thrash, wave, move ✧ beat, hit, strike A violent wind *lashed* the trees back and forth.

**lash**[2] *verb* ✦ fasten, secure, bind, strap, tie, leash The driver used rope to *lash* the cargo to the truck.

**lass** *noun* ✦ girl, young lady, young woman, maid, maiden The young man married a *lass* from a neighboring village.

**last**[1] *adjective* 1. ✦ final, closing, concluding, ending ✧ terminal The *last* episode of my favorite television series airs tonight. 2. ✦ latest, most recent ✧ newest, preceding, previous I can't remember the name of the *last* movie I saw.

**last²** *verb* ✦ continue, go on, endure, persist ✧ remain, stay Does anyone know how long this rain is supposed to *last*?

**latch** *noun* ✦ catch ✧ hook, bar, bolt, clamp, lock The *latch* on the screen door needs to be replaced. —*verb* ✦ fasten, secure ✧ bar, bolt, lock, close, shut Be sure to *latch* the gate when you leave.

**late** *adjective* **1.** ✦ delayed, belated, tardy ✧ overdue, slow I got a *late* start but managed to finish all of my housework before dinner. **2.** ✦ most recent, newest, current ✧ fresh, modern Have you read that author's *latest* book? —*adverb* ✧ behind, belatedly, tardily, behindhand My friend arrived at the party two hours *late*.

**lately** *adverb* ✦ recently, of late ✧ currently, presently, now The weather has been hot *lately*.

**latter** *adjective* ✦ end, final, last, later ✧ rear, terminal, concluding Where I live, it usually gets cold by the *latter* part of October.

**Word Groups**

To **laugh** is to express amusement or scorn by making sounds in the throat. **Laugh** is a general term with no true synonyms. Here are some words describing different kinds of laughing: **cackle, chortle, chuckle, giggle, guffaw, howl, roar, snicker, snigger**

**laughable** *adjective* ✦ amusing, comical, funny, humorous ✧ ridiculous, silly I thought my mistake was *laughable* when I discovered that my socks didn't match.

**launch** *verb* **1.** ✦ send off, put in orbit, blast off ✧ fire, propel, shoot The Soviet Union *launched* the world's first satellite on October 4, 1957. **2.** ✦ begin, commence, initiate, open, start ✧ originate, introduce The mayor held a press conference to *launch* her campaign for reelection.

**launder** *verb* ✦ wash, clean, cleanse ✧ scrub, soap I *launder* my clothes once a week.

**lavish** *adjective* ✦ extravagant, fancy, abundant, generous, sumptuous ✧ luxurious The cruise ship was famous for its *lavish* meals. —*verb* ✦ bestow, heap, pour, shower ✧ squander, waste Ariana *lavishes* a lot of care and attention on her pet.

**law** *noun* ✦ ordinance, regulation, rule, statute ✧ bill, decree, order If you break a traffic *law*, you usually have to pay a fine.

**lawful** *adjective* ✦ legal, legitimate, rightful, authorized ✧ just, proper The stolen car was returned to its *lawful* owner.

**lawyer** *noun* ✦ attorney, counsel, counselor, jurist, legal advisor People in America have the legal right to be represented by a *lawyer*.

**lay** *verb* ✦ leave, place, put, set, deposit, position Please *lay* the package on the table.

**layer** *noun* ✦ coat, coating, cover, covering ✧ blanket, sheet The chocolate cake had a thick *layer* of vanilla icing.

**lazy** *adjective* ✦ idle, listless, slothful, sluggish, lethargic, inactive *Lazy* people don't get much done.

**lead** *verb* **1.** ✦ guide, conduct, direct, escort ✧ show, steer A search dog *led* rescuers to the lost hiker. **2.** ✦ go, run, reach ✧ extend, stretch, proceed This path *leads* straight to the beach. **3.** ✦ command, direct ✧ govern, manage, supervise, head General Robert E. Lee *led* the Confederate army during the American Civil War. —*noun* ✦ advantage, vantage, edge, front ✧ advance, head, fore The game isn't over yet, but our team has the *lead*.

**leader** *noun* ✦ chief, director, head ✧ ruler, supervisor, commander I'm the *leader* of the refreshment committee for next week's dance.

**league** *noun* ✦ alliance, association, union ✧ group, organization The countries formed a *league* for common defense.

**leak** *noun* ✦ hole, opening, crack ✧ break, chink, puncture They finally fixed the *leak* in the roof of my apartment building. —*verb* **1.** ✦ drip, flow, ooze, seep, trickle, dribble ✧ escape, spill Oil slowly *leaked* from the car's engine. **2.** ✦ disclose, release, reveal, divulge, tell Someone on the governor's staff has been *leaking* secrets to the press.

**lean¹** *verb* ✦ incline, slant, slope, tilt, tip, cant The telephone pole was *leaning* dangerously after the storm.

**lean²** *adjective* ✦ slender, slim, thin, skinny, spare ✧ gaunt The athlete was *lean* and muscular.

**leap** *verb* ✦ spring, hop, bound, jump ✧ bounce, skip, vault A kangaroo can *leap* over twenty-five feet with a single bound. —*noun* ✦ spring, hop, bound, jump ✧ bounce, skip, vault The deer made a graceful *leap* over the fallen tree.

**learn** *verb* **1.** ✦ study ✧ grasp, master, memorize, understand The child is *learning* how to use a computer. **2. ✦ find out, discover, determine ✧ detect, hear, realize** Doctors hoped to *learn* how to cure the mysterious disease.

**lease** *noun* **✦ agreement, contract ✧ arrangement, deal** We signed a one-year *lease* for our new apartment. —*verb* **✦ rent ✧ hire, charter, engage** My girlfriend didn't want to buy a new car, so she *leased* one instead.

**leash** *noun* **✦ tether, lead, strap ✧ cord, rein, rope, chain** The lady put a *leash* on her pet iguana and took it for a walk around her front yard. —*verb* **✦ tether ✧ hold, rein, restrain, tie up, strap, chain, rope** You will have to *leash* your dog if you want to take him to the park.

**least** *adjective* **✦ slightest, smallest, tiniest ✧ lowest, fewest, minimum** Of all my pets, my hamster requires the *least* amount of food.

**leave¹** *verb* **1. ✦ depart, go, set out, start out, take off ✧ exit** I have to *leave* by 7:00 to catch the bus to my office. **2. ✦ keep ✧ maintain, retain, sustain, hold** Please *leave* the door unlocked. **3. ✦ will, bequeath ✧ endow, entrust, give, hand down** The millionaire *left* her entire fortune to charity.

**leave²** *noun* **✦ furlough, liberty ✧ holiday, vacation, absence** The soldier was home on *leave*.

**lecture** *noun* **✦ talk, speech, address ✧ lesson, chat** The forest ranger gave a *lecture* on bird identification. —*verb* **✦ address, speak (to), talk (to) ✧ preach, teach, instruct** A police officer *lectured* the schoolchildren about the dangers of using drugs and alcohol.

**ledge** *noun* **✦ shelf, projection, overhang ✧ edge, ridge, bench** Eagles often build their nests on small, rocky *ledges*.

**legal** *adjective* **✦ lawful, legitimate ✧ allowable, permissible, authorized** The *legal* voting age in the United States is eighteen.

**legend** *noun* **✦ fable, folklore, lore ✧ myth, mythology, story, tale** According to *legend*, Robin Hood robbed from the rich in order to give to the poor.

**legendary** *adjective* **✦ fabled, storied, fabulous ✧ mythical, mythological, celebrated** El Dorado was a *legendary* city whose streets were said to be paved with gold.

**legible** *adjective* **✦ readable, clear, distinct ✧ understandable, comprehensible** I am practicing my penmanship in order to make my handwriting more *legible*.

**legion** *noun* **✦ throng, flock, horde, multitude, swarm, mob, mass, crowd** The singer has a *legion* of fans who attend every concert.

**legitimate** *adjective* **✦ valid, justifiable, sound, real, proper ✧ lawful, legal, official** My colleague had a *legitimate* excuse for being late to work.

**leisure** *noun* **✦ free time, downtime ✧ recreation, relaxation, rest, ease** The busy doctor had very little *leisure*.

**Antonyms** **leisure**
*noun* **activity, effort, exertion, labor, toil, work**

**lend** *verb* **✦ loan ✧ advance, furnish, give, provide, supply, extend** My friend *lent* me his bicycle for the afternoon.

**length** *noun* **1. ✦ extent, size ✧ distance, measure, reach, space** Tyrannosaurus rex had teeth that were up to seven inches in *length*. **2. ✦ duration, extent ✧ span, term, period, stretch** Summer vacation for most American schools is about three months in *length*.

**lengthen** *verb* **✦ elongate, stretch, extend ✧ expand, increase, prolong, protract** Pulling on a piece of taffy will *lengthen* it.

**lenient** *adjective* **✦ tolerant, merciful, compassionate, mild, easy ✧ gentle, kind** The judge was known for giving *lenient* sentences.

**less** *adjective* **✦ reduced, shortened, diminished, limited ✧ fewer, lower, smaller** I have *less* time to read now that I am working full time.

**lessen** *verb* **✦ decrease, diminish, lower, reduce ✧ shrink, lighten** This medicine should *lessen* the pain of your headache.

**lesson** *noun* **✦ instruction, education, class, schooling, teaching, session** My younger brother has his first driving *lesson* tomorrow.

**let** *verb* **✦ allow (to), permit (to) ✧ authorize, grant, approve, sanction** My boss *let* me have the day off.

**Word Groups**

A **letter** of the alphabet is a written mark used in spelling words. **Letter** in this sense is a specific term with no true synonyms. Here are some related words to investigate in a dictionary: **character, figure, mark, sign, symbol**

**level** *noun* 1. ✦ **height, elevation, point, stage, mark** ✧ **altitude, depth** The flood waters reached a *level* that was thirty feet above normal. 2. ✦ **grade, standard, degree** ✧ **step, position, rank** My younger sister reads at the same *level* as a university student. —*adjective* 1. ✦ **flat, horizontal, even** ✧ **smooth, straight, plane** We don't have any *level* ground in the yard for planting a garden. 2. ✦ **even, flush, parallel** ✧ **aligned, equal** The top of my little brother's head is *level* with my shoulder. —*verb* 1. ✦ **even out, flatten, grade, smooth** ✧ **straighten** A park employee used a rake to *level* the sand in the children's play area. 2. ✦ **demolish, destroy, knock down, tear down, raze, wreck** Construction workers *leveled* several old buildings in order to clear the site.

**liable** *adjective* 1. ✦ **accountable, answerable, responsible** ✧ **obligated** If you lose a library book, you might be held *liable* for the replacement cost. 2. ✦ **apt, likely, prone, subject** ✧ **inclined, open, probable** You're *liable* to get wet if you don't take your umbrella.

**liar** *noun* ✦ **fibber, falsifier** ✧ **storyteller** You can believe anything that she says because she's not a *liar*.

**liberal** *adjective* 1. ✦ **abundant, plentiful, generous, ample** ✧ **full, lavish** This sapling needs *liberal* amounts of water to help it grow. 2. ✦ **broad, open-minded, progressive, tolerant, unbiased** My friends have *liberal* ideas about raising their children.

**liberty** *noun* 1. ✦ **freedom, independence, sovereignty** ✧ **self-government, liberation** Mexico won its *liberty* from Spain in 1821. 2. ✦ **privilege, right, freedom** ✧ **authorization, permission** Free speech is one of the *liberties* guaranteed by the American Bill of Rights.

**license** *noun* ✦ **certificate, permit** ✧ **authorization, permission, form** My best friend and her fiancé just got their marriage *license*. —*verb* ✦ **certify, accredit** ✧ **authorize, approve, permit, qualify, allow** In America, teachers must be *licensed* by the state.

**lid** *noun* ✦ **cover, top** ✧ **cap, stopper, plug** I used a screwdriver to pry the *lid* off the can of paint.

**lie¹** *verb* 1. ✦ **lie down, recline, stretch out** ✧ **sprawl, lounge** I like to *lie* on the couch when I watch television. 2. ✦ **be located, be situated, sit, reside** ✧ **exist, rest** The local lake *lies* just beyond that grove of trees.

**lie²** *noun* ✦ **falsehood, fib, untruth, fabrication** No one has ever known Rachelle to deliberately tell a *lie*. —*verb* ✦ **fib** ✧ **falsify, deceive, distort, mislead** Sometimes I am tempted to *lie* about my age.

**life** *noun* 1. ✦ **living being, existence, being, organism** ✧ **animation, vitality** I frequently wonder if there is *life* on other planets. 2. ✦ **lifetime, existence, lifespan, time** ✧ **days, duration, term** I've only been outside the United States once in my *life*. 3. ✦ **human, human being, individual, person** ✧ **mortal, soul** Luckily, no *lives* were lost when the ship sank. 4. ✦ **liveliness, vitality, energy, high spirits, spirit, vim, vigor** My puppy is so full of *life* that he can never sit still.

**lift** *verb* 1. ✦ **pick up, hoist, heft, raise** ✧ **boost, elevate, heave** This crate is too heavy for me to *lift* by myself. 2. ✦ **ascend, climb, rise** ✧ **soar, take off** Airplanes have to gain sufficient speed before they can *lift* into the air. 3. ✦ **disappear, disperse, dissipate** ✧ **scatter, vanish, fade** The fog *lifted* at noon. —*noun* ✦ **boost, hoist** ✧ **heave, assist** My little sister couldn't reach the water fountain, so I gave her a *lift*.

**light¹** *noun* 1. ✦ **illumination, radiance, glow** ✧ **brightness, brilliance, shine** The river looked silver in the *light* of the moon. 2. ✦ **aspect, perspective, regard, attitude** ✧ **angle, facet** I saw things in a different *light* after hearing my friend's side of the story. —*adjective* 1. ✦ **bright** ✧ **brilliant, sunny, radiant, illuminated** My bedroom is very *light* when I open the curtains. 2. ✦ **pale, pallid** ✧ **whitish, fair** I painted the water *light* blue and the fish bright yellow. —*verb* 1. ✦ **ignite, kindle, fire, set fire (to)** ✧ **burn** My friend *lit* the campfire while I got the marshmallows. 2. ✦ **light up, illuminate, brighten** ✧ **lighten, shine** Do you think one lamp will be enough to *light* the entire room?

**light²** *adjective* 1. ✦ **lightweight** ✧ **scant, slight, sparse, underweight** My dog is *light* enough that I can easily pick her up. 2. ✦ **slight, moderate, gentle, soft** ✧ **faint, mild, weak** Yesterday's *light* rain barely got the ground wet. 3. ✦ **easy, simple** ✧ **effortless, moderate, undemanding** I should be able to quickly finish this *light* housework.

**lighten¹** *verb* ✦ **brighten, light up** ✧ **illuminate, shine, gleam** The sky began to *lighten* just before the sun appeared.

**lighten²** *verb* ✦ **make lighter** ✧ **empty, lessen, re-**

duce, unload The box was too heavy for me to lift, so I *lightened* it by removing some of the contents.

**like¹** *verb* ✦ enjoy, love, relish, savor ✧ admire, adore, fancy I *like* playing computer games after work.

**like²** *preposition* ✦ identical (to), the same (as), similar (to), equivalent (to) Your car is *like* mine except for the color. —*adjective* ✦ similar, equivalent, comparable, equal, identical, matching We got five inches of snow yesterday and a *like* amount today.

**likely** *adjective* 1. ✦ apt, expected, liable, probable ✧ destined, inclined The weather report said that a storm is *likely* to hit tomorrow morning. 2. ✦ suitable, acceptable, appropriate, fit, proper, reasonable The pregnant cat began looking for a *likely* spot in which to have her kittens. —*adverb* ✦ probably, presumably, doubtless, no doubt ✧ seemingly I'll *likely* be late, so don't wait for me.

**limit** *noun* 1. ✦ limitation, restriction, maximum, quota ✧ ceiling, end There is a *limit* on how many fish you are allowed to catch in this lake. 2. ✦ boundary, bounds ✧ border, edge, extent, extreme Before the children play hide-and-seek, they agree on the *limits* beyond which no one is allowed to go. —*verb* ✦ restrict, confine ✧ set, fix, check, restrain The coach decided to *limit* the basketball team to ten players.

**limp** *verb* ✦ hobble ✧ shuffle, stagger, stumble, totter, waddle I *limped* around for two weeks after I sprained my ankle. —*noun* ✦ hobble ✧ shuffle, stagger, waddle Our old dog walks with a *limp*. —*adjective* ✦ droopy, floppy ✧ loose, slack, soft, weak Flowers get *limp* if you don't water them.

**line** *noun* 1. ✦ stripe, strip, streak, band ✧ bar, mark White *lines* were painted on the pavement to indicate parking places. 2. ✦ border, boundary, edge, limit ✧ margin This fence sits right on our property *line*. 3. ✦ file, column, row ✧ rank, string There was a long *line* of people waiting to get into the government office. 4. ✦ wire, cable ✧ cord, rope, strand, string My telephone doesn't work because the *line* is down. 5. ✦ note, card, letter, message, postcard Please drop me a *line* while you're on vacation. 6. ✦ assortment, range, variety ✧ kind, make, type This store carries a full *line* of smartphones.

**linger** *verb* ✦ stay, remain, endure, go on, last, persist, continue ✧ delay The thunderstorms should be over today, but a few light showers may *linger* through tomorrow morning.

**link** *noun* ✦ association, connection, relationship, relation ✧ bond, tie Detectives found no apparent *links* between the two robberies. —*verb* ✦ connect, join, unite ✧ couple, attach, combine, fasten The Brooklyn Bridge *links* Brooklyn with Manhattan Island.

**lip** *noun* ✦ brim, rim ✧ edge, border, margin The *lip* of a cup or mug is usually smooth and rounded.

**liquid** *noun* ✦ fluid ✧ solution Water, oil, and milk are all *liquids*. —*adjective* ✦ fluid, flowing, liquefied ✧ runny, watery, wet, molten Some rockets use *liquid* oxygen as part of their fuel.

**list** *noun* ✦ listing, record ✧ catalog, file, inventory, register Before I went to the grocery store, I made a *list* of everything I needed. —*verb* ✦ itemize, record, write down ✧ catalog, file, register Our boss asked us to *list* all of our ideas for making the company more efficient.

**listen** *verb* ✦ pay attention ✧ hear, heed, mind, attend When the teacher gave the assignment, she told everyone to *listen* carefully to the directions.

**literacy** *noun* ✦ knowledge, education, learning, proficiency ✧ background, skill Computer *literacy* is an important skill for anyone desiring a good job.

**litter** *noun* ✦ debris, refuse, rubbish, trash ✧ garbage, junk, mess Volunteers picked up the *litter* along the lakeshore. —*verb* ✦ clutter, mess up, strew ✧ cover, scatter Our living room was *littered* with wrapping paper after my birthday party.

**little** *adjective* 1. ✦ small, tiny, wee ✧ miniature, minute, petite A Chihuahua is a very *little* dog. 2. ✦ brief, limited, short ✧ scant, slight, meager I only have a *little* time left before my report is due. —*adverb* ✦ slightly, somewhat ✧ barely, hardly, scarcely I'm getting a *little* tired of eating leftovers. —*noun* ✦ bit, portion ✧ fragment, particle, speck, touch, trace I read a *little* of this book every night.

**live¹** *verb* 1. ✦ exist, survive, endure ✧ be, continue, last, thrive Humans need food, water, and air to *live*. 2. ✦ reside (in), dwell (in), inhabit, occupy ✧ stay, abide My friends and I *live in* a three bedroom apartment.

**live²** *adjective* ✦ alive, living, animate ✧ existing,

breathing, **conscious** Yogurt is made by adding *live* bacteria to milk.

**lively** *adjective* ✦ **spirited, vigorous, dynamic, energetic** ✧ **active, brisk** The *lively* music made me want to dance.

**living** *adjective* ✦ **alive, live, animate** ✧ **existing, breathing, conscious** I believe that all *living* creatures should be treated with respect. —*noun* 1. ✦ **existence, life** ✧ **being, existing, lifestyle** I love city *living*. 2. ✦ **livelihood, income, keep, subsistence** ✧ **career, occupation, support** My aunt makes her *living* as a writer.

**Word Groups**

A **lizard** is a reptile that has a scaly body, tapering tail, and four legs. **Lizard** is a specific term with no true synonyms. Here are some common types of lizards: **chameleon, chuckwalla, gecko, Gila monster, iguana, Komodo dragon**

**load** *noun* ✦ **burden, weight** ✧ **cargo, freight, shipment** Camels can carry heavy *loads* on their backs for long distances without needing water. —*verb* ✦ **fill, pack** ✧ **heap, pile, stuff, cram** We'll be ready to leave on vacation as soon as we finish *loading* the car.

**loaf** *verb* ✦ **lounge, relax, laze, rest, idle** ✧ **loiter** I plan on *loafing* around the house for the first few days of my vacation.

**loan** *noun* ✧ **advance, allowance, credit** I asked my roommate for a *loan* to help cover my share of the rent.

**loathe** *verb* ✦ **despise, detest, hate, dislike, abhor** I *loathe* being exposed to cigarette and cigar smoke.

**loathsome** *adjective* ✦ **abhorrent, disgusting, hideous, revolting, hateful** ✧ **nasty** The movie was about some *loathsome* creatures that came out of the swamp at night.

**local** *adjective* ✦ **community, neighborhood** ✧ **close, near, nearby, neighboring** I get most of my reading material from the *local* library.

**locate** *verb* 1. ✦ **find, detect, discover, come (upon)** ✧ **spot** Moles rely mainly on smell and touch to *locate* food. 2. ✦ **place, situate, position, put, set, install** The shipping company will *locate* its new office near the airport.

**location** *noun* ✦ **site, place, address, locale, spot** ✧ **locality, point, position** My company will be moving to a new *location* next year.

**lock** *noun* ✧ **fastening, bolt, catch, clasp, hook, latch, padlock** We need to replace the broken *lock* on our garage door. —*verb* 1. ✦ **secure** ✧ **fasten, latch, bar, bolt, clamp** Did you *lock* the car doors? 2. ✦ **join, link, interlock, connect, couple, fasten** ✧ **grasp, hold, entwine** These plastic blocks are designed to *lock* together.

**Antonyms** lock

*verb* 1. **open, open up, unclose, unfasten, unlock** 2. **free, liberate, loose, release, uncouple**

**lodge** *noun* ✦ **inn, hotel, chalet** ✧ **cabin, cottage, shelter** The ski resort has a *lodge* for people who want to stay overnight. —*verb* 1. ✦ **reside, stay, live, dwell** ✧ **accommodate, house** I plan to *lodge* in hostels on my bike trip through Europe. 2. ✦ **catch, snag, stick, wedge** ✧ **fix, snare** My kite is *lodged* in the branches of that tree.

**lofty** *adjective* ✦ **towering, high, tall** ✧ **sky-high, soaring** The mountain's *lofty* summit was hidden by clouds.

**logical** *adjective* ✦ **intelligent, rational, reasonable, sensible, sound, wise** If you are hungry, the *logical* thing to do would be to eat something.

**loiter** *verb* ✦ **dawdle, dally, dilly-dally, linger, idle, lag** ✧ **delay, pause** I could not *loiter* over breakfast because I was late for work.

**lone** *adjective* ✦ **single, sole, solitary** ✧ **individual, alone, lonely, only** A *lone* pear tree grew in the middle of the open field.

**lonely** *adjective* 1. ✦ **companionless, lonesome, friendless, solitary** ✧ **alone, lone, single** The old hermit leads a *lonely* life. 2. ✦ **desolate, forlorn, deserted** ✧ **isolated, remote, secluded** This desert is a *lonely* place.

**long**[1] *adjective* ✦ **extended, extensive, lengthy, prolonged** ✧ **big, great, large** I spent a *long* time preparing for my English proficiency test.

**long**[2] *verb* ✦ **ache, yearn, desire, want, wish, pine** ✧ **crave** My grandmother *longs* to visit her childhood home in Japan.

**look** *verb* 1. ✦ **search, hunt, seek** ✧ **explore, scout** I'll help you *look* for your missing book. 2. ✦ **gaze (at), stare (at), observe, watch, see, view** ✧ **glance** Everyone was *looking at* the man who was making a disturbance. 3. ✦ **appear, seem** ✧ **resemble, show** Do you think this shirt *looks* nice enough to wear to the party? —*noun* 1. ✦ **glance, glimpse,**

**peek, peep** ✧ **gaze, inspection, view** I took a *look* out the window to see if my ride had come. **2.** ✦ **appearance, expression, countenance** ✧ **bearing, manner** The parents of the sick boy had a worried *look*.

**loom** *verb* ✦ **appear, arise, materialize, take shape** ✧ **emerge, show** Storm clouds *loomed* on the horizon.

**loop** *noun* ✦ **coil, noose, ring, circle** ✧ **spiral** The cowboy slipped a *loop* of rope over the bull's horns. —*verb* ✦ **coil, turn, twist, wind, circle** ✧ **bend** The climber anchored her rope by *looping* it around a tree.

**loose** *adjective* **1.** ✦ **free, untied, unattached, unbound, unfastened** The boat came *loose* and floated down the stream. **2.** ✦ **at liberty, at large, free, unconfined, unrestrained** I called the police about a big dog that was *loose* in our neighborhood. **3.** ✦ **baggy, roomy, slack** ✧ **big, comfortable, oversize** Hyun likes to wear *loose* clothing when he plays tennis.

**loosen** *verb* ✦ **slacken, untighten, unloosen** ✧ **ease, relax, untie** My necktie was too tight, so I *loosened* it.

**loot** *noun* ✦ **booty, plunder, spoils** ✧ **haul, treasure, pillage** The robbers hid their *loot* in the hollow of an old tree. —*verb* ✦ **plunder, sack, pillage** ✧ **raid, rob, steal** Pirates *looted* the town and took the valuables back to their ships.

**lose** *verb* **1.** ✦ **mislay, misplace** ✧ **forget, miss** I'm always *losing* my car keys. **2.** ✦ **be defeated** ✧ **succumb, fail, forfeit, surrender, yield** Our team won the first two games but *lost* in the semifinals.

**loss** *noun* **1.** ✦ **reduction** ✧ **removal, shrinkage, depletion** My friend is on a diet, and he is pleased with his weight *loss*. **2.** ✦ **misfortune, setback** ✧ **damage, injury, suffering, trouble** It was a great *loss* for the company when two of its best employees moved away.

**lost** *adjective* **1.** ✦ **missing, mislaid, misplaced** ✧ **absent, gone, vanished** I found my *lost* sweater under the bed. **2.** ✦ **absorbed, deep, occupied, preoccupied** ✧ **distracted** I didn't hear you come in because I was *lost* in thought.

**lot** *noun* **1.** ✦ **an abundance (of), lots (of), many, numerous, plenty (of)** ✧ **much** I received *a lot of* presents for my birthday this year. **2.** ✦ **batch, set, assortment** ✧ **bunch, collection, group** The store

will be receiving a new *lot* of furniture tomorrow. **3.** ✦ **plot, parcel, tract** ✧ **land, property, real estate** Neighborhood children use the vacant *lot* as a playground.

**loud** *adjective* **1.** ✦ **noisy, deafening** ✧ **blaring, ear-splitting, roaring, shrill** The band was so *loud* that my friends and I could hardly hear each other speak. **2.** ✦ **bright, gaudy, flashy, showy, colorful** The *loud* T-shirt has orange lettering on a purple background.

**love** *noun* ✦ **affection, fondness, liking, tenderness, warmth, attachment** I have much *love* for my family. —*verb* **1.** ✦ **adore, cherish, hold dear** ✧ **treasure, worship** My cat is grumpy sometimes, but I *love* him anyway. **2.** ✦ **enjoy, like, relish, delight (in)** ✧ **fancy** I *love* going to the movies with my friends.

**lovely** *adjective* ✦ **attractive, beautiful, enchanting, adorable, pretty, good-looking** That is a *lovely* dress you're wearing.

**loving** *adjective* ✦ **affectionate, caring, devoted, tender, adoring** We have a warm and *loving* family.

**low** *adjective* **1.** ✦ **short, squat** ✧ **little, small, shallow** The horse easily jumped over the *low* fence. **2.** ✦ **inadequate, inferior, unsatisfactory, bad, poor** This job has excellent benefits, but the pay is *low*. **3.** ✦ **hushed, quiet, soft, subdued, muted** The two friends spoke to each other in *low* voices in the museum. **4.** ✦ **sad, dejected, depressed, downcast, gloomy, unhappy** I've been feeling a little *low* ever since my best friend moved away.

**lower** *verb* **1.** ✦ **let down, move down, drop** ✧ **descend, sink** The stage crew *lowered* the curtain after the final act. **2.** ✦ **decrease, diminish, lessen, reduce, drop** My friend *lowered* her voice when she told me her secret.

**loyal** *adjective* ✦ **dependable, devoted, faithful, steadfast, true, trustworthy, staunch** A *loyal* friend will stand by you even when you have troubles.

**loyalty** *noun* ✦ **allegiance, devotion, faithfulness, fidelity** ✧ **dependability** The king knew that he could count on the *loyalty* of his knights.

**luck** *noun* **1.** ✦ **chance, fortune** ✧ **destiny, fate, providence** I prefer games of skill over games of *luck*. **2.** ✦ **good fortune, good luck, luckiness** ✧ **favor, success** Finding a four-leaf clover is said to bring *luck*.

**lucky** *adjective* ✦ fortunate, successful, good ✧ favorable, happy I made a *lucky* guess on the proficiency test and chose the right answer.

**lug** *verb* ✦ carry, haul, tote, bear ✧ drag, tow, tug I *lugged* the heavy suitcases up the stairs.

**luggage** *noun* ✦ baggage, bags, suitcases, trunks ✧ belongings, gear A porter helped us carry our *luggage* to the train.

**lull** *verb* ✦ calm, soothe, quiet, settle ✧ pacify, still The soft music *lulled* me to sleep. —*noun* ✦ break, lapse, pause, interlude ✧ calm, hush, quiet The rain started up again after a brief *lull*.

**lump** *noun* 1. ✦ clump, chunk, clod, hunk, mass, piece ✧ wad My friend uses a hoe to break up the *lumps* of dirt in her garden. 2. ✦ bump, swelling, bulge ✧ knot, hump The bee sting raised a big *lump* on my arm.

**lunge** *noun* ✦ charge, dive, pounce, rush, spring, jump When I dangled a toy mouse in front of my kitten, she made a *lunge* for it. —*verb* ✦ charge, dive, jump, leap, spring ✧ pounce, thrust I *lunged* forward to catch the lamp as it started to fall to the floor.

**lurch** *verb* 1. ✦ stagger, stumble, reel, weave, wobble ✧ teeter, totter The exhausted runner *lurched* across the finish line. 2. ✦ roll, pitch, yaw, sway, toss, swing ✧ tilt, list The ship *lurched* from side to side in heavy seas.

**lure** *noun* ✦ attraction, draw, invitation, temptation, enticement ✧ bait The *lure* of adventure makes me want to travel and see new places. —*verb* ✦ attract, draw, pull, tempt, entice ✧ hook, invite We were *lured* into the bakery by the wonderful smells coming from within.

**lush** *adjective* ✦ abundant, dense, luxuriant, rich, sumptuous, thick We saw deer browsing on the *lush* grass of a mountain meadow.

**luster** *noun* ✦ sheen, shine, brilliance, glow, radiance I admired the *luster* of the polished marble statues in the museum.

**luxurious** *adjective* ✦ sumptuous, elegant, magnificent, splendid ✧ expensive, rich The princess wore a *luxurious* gown to the grand ball.

**Antonyms** **luxurious**
*adjective* cheap, poor, ragged, shabby, threadbare, worn

**luxury** *noun* 1. ✦ extravagance, pleasure, treat ✧ delight, enjoyment Dining at an expensive restaurant is a rare *luxury* for me. 2. ✦ affluence, comfort, extravagance, splendor ✧ riches, wealth The wealthy movie star lived in *luxury*.

**machine** *noun* ✦ appliance, device, mechanism, instrument ✧ engine, motor I love my new sewing *machine.*

**mad** *adjective* 1. ✦ angry, furious, incensed, indignant, wrathful ✧ upset I was *mad* when my roommate borrowed my smartphone without asking. 2. ✦ crazy, demented, lunatic ✧ delirious, foolish, idiotic This movie is about a *mad* scientist who travels through time. 3. ✦ ardent, enthusiastic, excited, fanatic, wild, zealous The audience erupted into *mad* cheering when the rock star came onto stage.

**magazine** *noun* ✦ journal, periodical, publication, digest ✧ newsletter Kari subscribes to a *magazine* for horse lovers.

**magic** *noun* ✦ witchcraft, wizardry, sorcery ✧ enchantment, charm The genie used *magic* to grant people their three wishes. —*adjective* ✦ magical, enchanting, entrancing ✧ charming, fascinating It was a *magic* moment when I first saw the man I will marry.

**magician** *noun* ✦ entertainer ✧ enchanter, witch, wizard, sorcerer The *magician* pulled a rabbit out of his hat.

**magnetic** *adjective* ✦ appealing, captivating, charismatic, charming, fascinating The actor was known for his *magnetic* personality as well as his acting ability.

**magnificent** *adjective* ✦ beautiful, fantastic, glorious, grand, splendid, wonderful A peacock looks *magnificent* when it spreads its tail feathers.

**magnify** *verb* ✦ enlarge, expand, amplify ✧ increase, inflate, boost, grow Whenever my grandfather reads, he wears glasses that *magnify* the print.

**mail** *noun* ✧ cards, letters, messages, packages, parcels More *mail* is delivered during the Christmas season than at any other time of the year. —*verb* ✦ post, send ✧ dispatch, forward, ship, transmit Please *mail* this letter for me.

**main** *adjective* ✦ chief, principal, primary ✧ head, leading, major This is the *main* road leading into town.

**mainly** *adverb* ✦ chiefly, generally, mostly, primarily, usually, predominantly I like all types of books, but I *mainly* read science fiction novels.

**maintain** *verb* 1. ✦ preserve, keep, retain, sustain ✧ continue, extend I exercise regularly to help *maintain* my health. 2. ✦ care (for), look (after), manage ✧ service, fix, repair My roommate helps me *maintain* our yard. 3. ✦ affirm, assert, declare, insist, state, profess, claim Throughout his trial, the defendant *maintained* that he was innocent.

**majestic** *adjective* ✦ grand, impressive, magnificent, splendid ✧ stately, noble, dignified Redwoods are *majestic* trees that can grow to be more than three hundred feet tall.

**major** *adjective* ✦ chief, leading, main, primary, first, foremost My *major* focus this year has been improving my English vocabulary.

**Antonyms** major
*adjective* insignificant, minor, slight, trivial, unimportant

**make** *verb* 1. ✦ create, fashion, produce ✧ build, form, manufacture My grandmother *made* me a quilt for my birthday. 2. ✦ cause (to), compel (to), force (to) ✧ bring, bring about, induce Peeling onions always *makes* my eyes water. 3. ✦ earn, acquire, get, obtain ✧ gain, receive I *make* enough money to save a little every week. 4. ✦ add up (to), amount (to), come (to), equal, total Four quarts *make* one gallon. —*noun* ✦ brand, kind, model, style, type, variety, name My friend liked his old car so much that he got a new one of the same *make.*

**makeshift** *adjective* ✦ improvised, make-do, substitute, stopgap, temporary ✧ emergency I fashioned some *makeshift* bookshelves out of bricks and boards.

**malicious** *adjective* ✦ spiteful, hateful, mean, nasty, wicked, evil I would never dream of spreading *malicious* gossip.

## Word Groups

A **mammal** is a warm-blooded animal that has a backbone, hair or fur, and glands that produce milk in the female. **Mammal** is a general term with no true synonyms. Here are some unusual mammals to investigate in a dictionary: **aye-aye, bat, cavy, dugong, echidna, gerenuk, jerboa, loris, manatee, pangolin, platypus**

**mammoth** *adjective* ✦ colossal, enormous, gigantic, huge, immense, large Sending astronauts to the moon is a *mammoth* undertaking.

**man** *noun* ✦ fellow, gentleman, guy, gent ✧ male A kind *man* helped me fix my flat tire.

**manage** *verb* 1. ✦ supervise, direct, run, head, control, administer My aunt *manages* a flower shop. 2. ✦ fare, get by, succeed ✧ accomplish, achieve, do, function Although it won't be easy to carry all my luggage, I'll *manage* somehow.

**management** *noun* ✦ supervision, control, direction, leadership ✧ administration The restaurant reopened under new *management*.

**manager** *noun* ✦ supervisor, head, boss, director, leader, administrator When I applied for a job, I had to speak to the store's *manager*.

**maneuver** *noun* ✦ move, movement, turn, operation ✧ action, play, stunt The marching band executed a series of complicated *maneuvers*. —*verb* ✦ guide, navigate, pilot, steer, direct, move The pilot carefully *maneuvered* his riverboat past a sandbar.

**manner** *noun* ✦ way, style, fashion, mode ✧ method, system My parents taught me to speak in a polite *manner* to everyone.

## Word Groups

A **mansion** is a large stately house. **Mansion** is a general term with no true synonyms. Here are some related words to investigate in a dictionary: **chateau, estate, hacienda, hall, manor, plantation, villa**

**manual** *adjective* ✦ physical, done by hand ✧ hand-operated, human Gardening is a *manual* activity. —*noun* ✦ guide, guidebook, handbook ✧ text, textbook I read the instruction *manual* before assembling my new bicycle.

**manufacture** *verb* ✦ assemble, fabricate, build, construct, make, produce ✧ create That factory *manufactures* air conditioners.

**many** *adjective* ✦ numerous, countless, abundant ✧ endless, several There are *many* interesting books in our local library.

**map** *noun* ✦ chart, plan ✧ diagram, drawing, graph, sketch We used a *map* of the city to find our hotel. —*verb* ✦ chart ✧ diagram, draw, plot, sketch, portray Astronomers use images received from spacecraft to *map* the planet Mars.

**mar** *verb* ✦ deface, damage, flaw, spoil, blemish ✧ injure, impair The surface of the antique writing table was *marred* by a long scratch.

**march** *verb* ✦ parade ✧ stride, hike, trek, walk, stroll The soldiers *marched* past the reviewing stand. —*noun* ✦ parade, procession, demonstration ✧ walk, trek, hike Environmentalists are planning a *march* to protest the proposed oil pipeline.

**margin** *noun* 1. ✦ border, edge, fringe ✧ boundary, rim I have my word processor set to leave a one-inch *margin* around each page. 2. ✦ room, range, leeway, space ✧ freedom, surplus Space flight is so complicated there's very little or no *margin* for error.

**mark** *noun* 1. ✦ spot, stain, blemish ✧ impression, imprint The wet glass left a *mark* on the table. 2. ✦ token, sign, symbol, indication, measure ✧ emblem Everyone stood up as a *mark* of respect when the senator entered the room. 3. ✦ target, goal, objective ✧ aim, end, destination I tried to hit the tree with a snowball, but I missed my *mark*. 4. ✦ grade, rating, score ✧ evaluation, standing I earned a better *mark* on this proficiency test than I did on the last one. —*verb* 1. ✦ mar, spot, stain, blemish ✧ scar Be careful not to *mark* the freshly waxed floor. 2. ✦ designate, identify, indicate, point out, show, reveal Flags were used to *mark* the corners of the playing field. 3. ✦ correct, grade, rate, score ✧ evaluate, assess An aide helped the teacher *mark* the spelling tests.

**market** *noun* 1. ✦ grocery, store, supermarket ✧ marketplace, shop, shopping center Could you get me a candy bar when you go to the *market*? 2. ✦ call, demand, need ✧ business, commerce, trade There is a very large *market* for health foods in this city. —*verb* ✦ sell ✧ offer, peddle, trade, barter These television sets are *marketed* worldwide.

**marriage** *noun* ✦ matrimony, wedlock ✧ match, union, wedding The man and woman were joined in *marriage*.

**marry** *verb* ✦ wed ✧ mate, couple, join, unite My friend is planning to *marry* her fiancé next June.

**marshal** *noun* ✦ law officer, peace officer, officer ✧ sheriff, constable Wyatt Earp was a famous American *marshal* back in the 1880s. —*verb* ✦ arrange, array, order, organize, assemble The colonel *marshaled* his troops for inspection.

**marvel** *noun* ✦ wonder ✧ spectacle, astonishment, curiosity, miracle, sensation Egypt's ancient *marvels* include the Sphinx and the Great Pyramid of Cheops. —*verb* ✦ wonder, gape, gaze, stare ✧ admire Visitors to America's Grand Canyon usually pause to *marvel at* its great length and depth.

**marvelous** *adjective* ✦ amazing, fantastic, incredible, outstanding, wonderful, extraordinary My girlfriend is a *marvelous* singer.

**mash** *verb* ✦ crush, squash, smash, pound ✧ pulverize, press *Mash* the garlic before you add it to the pasta sauce.

**mask** *noun* ✦ disguise ✧ camouflage, cloak, cover, veil The little boy wore a gorilla *mask* to the costume party. —*verb* ✦ conceal, cover up, disguise, hide, camouflage, veil Whenever I eat fish, I *mask* its flavor by adding lots of lemon and butter.

**Antonyms** mask
*verb* display, exhibit, expose, reveal, uncover

**mass** *noun* 1. ✦ pile, heap, mound, batch, bunch ✧ clump, lump The plow left a *mass* of snow in front of our house. 2. ✦ bulk, size, volume ✧ extent, magnitude, weight The *mass* of a blue whale is much greater than that of a goldfish. —*verb* ✦ accumulate, assemble, cluster, collect, gather, amass I knew that a storm was coming when I saw dark clouds *massing* on the horizon.

**massacre** *noun* ✦ killing, slaughter, slaying ✧ mass murder, butchery Many people are outraged by the *massacre* of baby seals. —*verb* ✦ kill, slaughter, slay ✧ murder, exterminate African elephants are being *massacred* for their ivory tusks.

**massage** *noun* ✦ rubdown ✧ back rub, rub, stroking The doctor prescribed *massages* as part of the athlete's physical therapy. —*verb* ✦ knead, rub ✧ stroke, manipulate I *massaged* my neck to ease the stiffness.

**massive** *adjective* ✦ enormous, gigantic, huge, immense, mammoth, large ✧ bulky, heavy Mount Rushmore is famous for its *massive* portraits of four US presidents.

**master** *noun* 1. ✦ owner, keeper ✧ leader, lord, ruler, superior A well-trained dog will always obey its *master*. 2. ✦ expert, genius, professional, wizard, ace ✧ authority The chef was a *master* at creating new dishes. —*adjective* 1. ✦ masterful, expert, professional, skilled, accomplished, competent This antique dresser was made by a *master* craftsman. 2. ✦ chief, main, primary, principal ✧ major The *master* bedroom in most homes is much larger than the other bedrooms. —*verb* ✦ learn, acquire, pick up, grasp ✧ command, conquer, control My friend has yet to *master* the art of driving a motorcycle.

**match** *noun* 1. ✦ complement, companion, counterpart, mate, supplement My striped tie is a good *match* for my white shirt. 2. ✦ double, duplicate, equal, equivalent, twin We need a *match* for the bedroom wallpaper so we can fix a tear. 3. ✦ competition, contest, game ✧ meet, tournament, bout I played well, but my girlfriend won our tennis *match*. —*verb* 1. ✦ agree (with), correspond (to), duplicate, resemble, fit This paint *matches* the color of my curtains. 2. ✦ compare (with), equal, rival, compete (with) ✧ challenge No one on their team can *match* our quarterback.

**material** *noun* 1. ✦ substance, component, element, ingredient ✧ matter, stuff Wood is a common building *material*. 2. ✦ cloth, fabric, textile, dry goods I picked out *material* for a new dress. —*adjective* ✦ concrete, physical, real, solid, tangible ✧ bodily Anything that you can see or touch is a part of the *material* world.

**matter** *noun* 1. ✦ material, substance ✧ components, elements, stuff, constituents A space that has no *matter* is known as a vacuum. 2. ✦ affair, business, concern, issue, point, subject, transaction I went to the bank to take care of some financial *matters*. 3. ✦ difficulty, problem, trouble ✧ predicament, bother What's the *matter* with the car? —*verb* ✦ be important ✧ concern, count, influence, affect It *matters* to me that you remembered my birthday.

**mature** *adjective* 1. ✦ adult, full-grown, grown, developed ✧ ready, ripe A *mature* elephant can weigh as much as five tons. 2. ✦ experienced, grown-up, responsible, sensible ✧ wise The girl's parents feel that she is *mature* enough to stay at home without a babysitter. —*verb* ✦ develop, evolve, grow ◇ age, ripen Most trees *mature* very slowly.

**maximum** *noun* ✦ limit, ceiling ◇ peak, top, zenith, most This elevator is designed to carry a *maximum* of twenty people. —*adjective* ✦ greatest, supreme, top, ultimate, best ◇ biggest, largest A Boeing 747 jetliner can reach a *maximum* speed of more than six hundred miles per hour.

**maybe** *adverb* ✦ conceivably, perhaps, possibly, perchance *Maybe* my work will be done in time for me to join you.

**maze** *noun* ✦ network, labyrinth, web ◇ knot, snarl, tangle America's Carlsbad Caverns is a complex *maze* of interconnecting tunnels and chambers.

**meager** *adjective* ✦ inadequate, poor, scant, scanty, small, sparse, deficient The coyote is thin because his winter food supply was *meager*.

**meal** *noun* ✦ banquet, feast, repast ◇ breakfast, dinner, lunch, supper My family celebrates Thanksgiving by having a special *meal* of turkey and all the trimmings.

**mean**[1] *verb* 1. ✦ denote, indicate, signify ◇ designate, imply, convey A red traffic light *means* that drivers are supposed to stop. 2. ✦ aim, expect, intend, plan, propose ◇ want, contemplate What do you *mean* to do with all this leftover food?

**mean**[2] *adjective* ✦ nasty, rotten, rude, cruel, malicious, unkind, spiteful The *mean* man screamed at us to get out of his way.

**mean**[3] *noun* ✦ average, medium, middle, balance, center ◇ norm The best speed for driving is a *mean* between too fast and too slow. —*adjective* ✦ average, median, central, intermediate, middle The annual *mean* temperature of the continental United States is 55 degrees Fahrenheit.

**meaning** *noun* ✦ message, idea, intent, purpose, significance ◇ sense I have read the story two times, but I still don't understand its *meaning*.

**measure** *verb* ✦ calculate, compute, figure ◇ count, gauge, rule We *measured* the size of our garage to see if a pickup truck would fit. —*noun* 1. ✦ amount, portion, share, ration ◇ dimension, extent, size This brownie recipe calls for equal *measures* of flour and sugar. 2. ✦ gauge, test ◇ scale, standard, unit, yardstick, rule An IQ test is not always a true *measure* of a person's intelligence. 3. ✦ step, action, procedure ◇ course, move,

**means** We took *measures* to keep our dog out of the neighbor's yard.

**mechanism** *noun* ✦ apparatus, device ◇ instrument, machine, tool The coffeemaker has a *mechanism* that automatically shuts it off after an hour.

**medal** *noun* ✦ medallion ◇ award, badge, ribbon, decoration American swimmer Michael Phelps has won twenty-three Olympic gold *medals*.

**meddle** *verb* ✦ interfere, intervene, intrude ◇ fool, mess, tamper It's not polite to *meddle* in other people's affairs.

**medicine** *noun* ✦ medication, drug, prescription ◇ cure, remedy The doctor gave me *medicine* that helped bring my temperature back to normal.

**meditate** *verb* ✦ contemplate, deliberate, ponder, reflect, think, consider I *meditated* for a long time before deciding on which university to attend.

**medium** *noun* 1. ✦ environment, setting, substance, surroundings Moist soil in a dark room is the perfect *medium* for growing mushrooms. 2. ✦ agency, agent, instrument, means ◇ tool, vehicle Gold was commonly used as a *medium* of exchange before paper money was introduced. —*adjective* ✦ average, intermediate, middle, median ◇ moderate, normal These shirts come in small, *medium*, and large sizes.

**meet** *verb* 1. ✦ come together, cross, intersect, converge ◇ connect, join, link A new truck stop was built at the spot where the two highways *meet*. 2. ✦ get together (with), see ◇ contact, encounter, rendezvous, greet I plan to *meet* my friends at a coffee shop after work. 3. ✦ assemble, congregate, convene ◇ collect, gather, muster My yoga class *meets* once a week. 4. ✦ fill, fulfill, satisfy ◇ equal, reach, comply (with) I received a letter saying that I *meet* all the university's admission requirements. —*noun* ✦ competition, contest, match, tournament ◇ event My friend Li Wei will be competing in next week's swim *meet*.

**meeting** *noun* ✦ conference, assembly, gathering ◇ affair, session The *meeting* will begin as soon as everyone gets here.

**melancholy** *noun* ✦ dejection, depression, gloom, sadness, unhappiness A feeling of *melancholy* came over me as I listened to the sad song. —*adjective* ✦ sad, saddening, depressing, dreary, gloomy, sorrowful The *melancholy* movie made me cry.

**mellow** *adjective* ✦ soothing, soft, gentle, mild, smooth, sweet The woman sang a *mellow* tune to lull her baby to sleep.

**melody** *noun* ✦ music, tune, harmony ✧ refrain, song I was awakened by the *melody* of a robin chirping outside my window.

**melt** *verb* ✦ thaw, liquefy ✧ disappear, dissolve, fade, soften The snowman began to *melt* as soon as the sun came out.

**member** *noun* ✦ participant, associate, enrollee ✧ constituent, part, piece I am a *member* of several different environmental organizations

**memorable** *adjective* ✦ important, noteworthy, remarkable, significant, unforgettable My college graduation was the most *memorable* event of my life.

**memorial** *noun* ✦ monument, shrine ✧ remembrance, tribute This *memorial* honors the Americans who died in the Vietnam War. —*adjective* ✦ commemorative ✧ dedicatory, testimonial The city will hold a *memorial* service for the police officer who died in the line of duty.

**memory** *noun* ✦ recollection, remembrance ✧ recall, thought The earliest *memory* I have is of my father reading me a story.

**menace** *noun* ✦ threat, hazard, peril, danger ✧ risk, jeopardy Our cat is a *menace* to any bird that enters our yard. —*verb* ✦ endanger, imperil, threaten ✧ jeopardize, frighten, scare The shepherd protected his sheep from the wolf that *menaced* them.

**mend** *verb* 1. ✦ fix, patch, repair ✧ correct, restore, renovate The crew *mended* the ship's torn sails. 2. ✦ heal, recover, cure, recuperate ✧ improve The doctor said that my broken arm would *mend* in about six weeks.

**mental** *adjective* ✦ intellectual, cerebral, thinking ✧ rational, reasoning I enjoy solving crossword puzzles because I like the *mental* challenge.

**mention** *verb* ✦ remark, say, divulge, disclose ✧ declare, state, tell My friend *mentioned* that she would be away next weekend. —*noun* ✦ comment, note, notice, reference, remark, statement, acknowledgement Last night's thunderstorm received only a brief *mention* on the morning news.

**menu** *noun* ✦ index, list, register, file ✧ inventory, table A computer's *menu* lists the available programs.

**merchandise** *noun* ✦ goods, products, stock, wares ✧ articles, things All the sale *merchandise* is marked with a red tag.

**merchant** *noun* ✦ retailer, shopkeeper, storekeeper ✧ dealer, trader, vendor Several *merchants* have shops on the corner strip mall.

**mercy** *noun* ✦ clemency, compassion, charity, kindness ✧ pity, sympathy I showed *mercy* to the spider by putting it outside.

**mere** *adjective* ✦ insignificant, minor, negligible, plain, simple ✧ only, scant I had a bike accident, but a *mere* scratch was my only injury.

**merge** *verb* ✦ combine, come together, join, meet ✧ link, unite I know of a good fishing spot where two creeks *merge*.

**merit** *noun* ✦ value, worth, virtue ✧ benefit, quality, excellence My editor said that my story idea has real *merit*. —*verb* ✦ deserve, justify, rate, warrant ✧ earn, gain, get My boss thinks that my proposal *merits* further consideration.

**Antonyms** merge
*verb* break, divide, part, separate, split

**merry** *adjective* ✦ cheerful, happy, jolly, jovial, mirthful Everyone at the party was in a *merry* mood.

**mess** *noun* ✦ clutter, litter, shambles ✧ disorganization, eyesore I am cleaning up the *mess* I left in the kitchen. —*verb* ✦ disarrange, disorder, muss, tangle ✧ clutter, dirty, litter The wind *messed up* my hair.

**message** *noun* ✦ note, communication, statement ✧ notice, notification, report, word The easiest way to reach my friends is to text them a *message*.

**messenger** *noun* ✦ courier ✧ carrier, delivery person, emissary The queen gave the letter to her most trusted *messenger*.

**messy** *adjective* ✦ cluttered, disorderly, disorganized, untidy, dirty ✧ sloppy I cleaned up my *messy* room.

**method** *noun* ✦ manner, mode, style ✧ fashion, system, technique, way Traveling by bus is just one of the many *methods* of transportation available to us.

**middle** *noun* ✦ center, core, inside, heart ✧ midpoint These candies have soft *middles*. —*adjective* ✦ center, central, inner, inside ✧ intermediate My friend held up three straws, and I picked the *middle* one.

**mighty** *adjective* ✦ powerful, strong, potent, sturdy ✧ colossal, gigantic, huge Crocodiles have *mighty* jaws for crushing their prey.

**migrate** *verb* ✦ immigrate, journey, move, travel ✧ emigrate, wander, trek The American West was settled by pioneers who *migrated* from the East.

**mild** *adjective* ✦ gentle, delicate ✧ calm, easy, moderate, pleasant, smooth, soft I use a *mild* detergent that doesn't fade my clothes.

**mimic** *verb* ✦ copy, echo, imitate, repeat ✧ mock, ape My parrot *mimics* a lot of what he hears.

**mind** *noun* ✦ brain, intellect ✧ head, intelligence, thinking, reasoning A good education helps to develop a person's *mind*. —*verb* 1. ✦ care, object ✧ disapprove, dislike, resent Do you *mind* if I borrow your sweater? 2. ✦ attend (to), care (for), look (after), tend, watch, protect Who is going to *mind* the cat while we're away? 3. ✦ heed, obey, listen (to) ✧ follow, observe The parents told their child to *mind* the babysitter.

**mine** *noun* ✦ mineshaft, shaft ✧ excavation, pit, quarry, tunnel, hole The world's deepest gold *mine* is in South Africa. —*verb* ✦ excavate, dig up, quarry ✧ extract, remove More gold is *mined* in China than anywhere else in the world.

**mingle** *verb* ✦ blend, combine, compound, join, mix ✧ merge, unite When I saw the bear I felt fear *mingled* with awe.

**miniature** *adjective* ✦ little, minute, small, tiny, wee, miniscule The *miniature* painting was no bigger than a postage stamp.

**minimum** *adjective* ✦ lowest, slowest, least ✧ slightest, smallest, littlest The *minimum* speed at which a jumbo jet can be flown is 160 miles per hour.

**minor** *adjective* ✦ insignificant, petty, slight, small, trivial, unimportant ✧ lesser The accident victim felt fortunate to have only *minor* injuries. —*noun* ✦ adolescent, child, juvenile, youngster, youth, teenager *Minors* cannot vote in state or federal elections.

**minuscule** *adjective* ✦ tiny, small, little, minute, microscopic, wee ✧ miniature The *minuscule* amount of rain did nothing to help alleviate the drought.

**minute**[1] *noun* ✦ instant, jiffy, moment, second, trice, twinkling, flash I'll be with you in just a *minute*.

**minute**[2] *adjective* ✦ little, small, tiny, wee, minuscule ✧ microscopic, miniature The bug was so *minute* that I almost couldn't see it.

**miracle** *noun* ✦ marvel, wonder ✧ sensation, surprise, rarity It was a *miracle* that no one was injured in the car wreck.

**miraculous** *adjective* ✦ amazing, astonishing, extraordinary, incredible, marvelous, remarkable The gravely ill man made a *miraculous* recovery.

**miscellaneous** *adjective* ✦ assorted, diverse, mixed, varied, various, different The top drawer contains *miscellaneous* art supplies.

**mischief** *noun* ✦ mischievousness, misbehavior, misconduct, trouble ✧ damage, harm, injury I wonder what kind of *mischief* my dog is up to now.

**mischievous** *adjective* ✦ misbehaving, naughty, bad, troublesome, annoying The *mischievous* puppy chewed up two pairs of shoes.

**miserable** *adjective* 1. ✦ unhappy, sad, dejected, desolate, gloomy, wretched We all felt *miserable* until our missing cat was found. 2. ✦ awful, bad, lousy, poor, rotten ✧ inferior, unsatisfactory I had *miserable* luck the last time we played poker.

**misery** *noun* ✦ distress, hardship, misfortune, sorrow, suffering, torment The flood victims endured much *misery* before the rescue team arrived.

**misfortune** *noun* 1. ✦ bad luck, ill fortune, ill luck, adversity We had the *misfortune* to get a flat tire just as we were leaving for our trip. 2. ✦ blow, setback, catastrophe, disaster, tragedy ✧ trouble The loss of our best player was a great *misfortune* for our volleyball team.

**misgiving** *noun* ✦ qualm, reservation, concern, doubt, anxiety, fear, worry ✧ suspicion I have some *misgivings* about doing a back dive off the high board.

**mislead** *verb* ✦ deceive, fool, trick, dupe ✧ misinform The advertisement *misled* people into thinking that the exercise machine would be easy to use.

**misplace** *verb* ✦ lose, mislay ✧ forget, miss I occasionally *misplace my* eyeglasses.

*verb* detect, discover, find, locate, pinpoint, spot

**miss** *verb* 1. ✦ fail to notice, overlook, forget, neglect, skip ✧ drop, let go I fell asleep on the subway and *missed* my stop. 2. ✦ long (for), yearn (for), pine (for) ✧ crave, desire, want I *missed* my family while I was studying abroad. 3. ✦ avoid, dodge, evade, bypass, escape ✧ lose We'll *miss* the lunch-hour rush if we go to the restaurant early.

**mission** *noun* 1. ✦ assignment, job, objective, task ✧ obligation, responsibility, goal The spy's *mission* was to gather information about the enemy. 2. ✦ commission, delegation, task force ✧ embassy, legation The United Nations sent a peacekeeping *mission* to help stop the war.

**mist** *noun* ✦ fog, haze, cloud ✧ vapor, steam, drizzle A heavy *mist* hung in the air just before sunrise. —*verb* ✦ fog, steam, cloud, blur ✧ drizzle, sprinkle The bathroom mirror *mists* up whenever anyone takes a hot shower.

**mistake** *noun* ✦ error, inaccuracy ✧ blunder, fault, lapse, slip I made only one *mistake* on my driver's license test. —*verb* ✦ confuse (with), mix up (with) ✧ misinterpret, blunder, err I *mistook* Natalia for her twin sister.

**mistaken** *adjective* ✦ false, inaccurate, incorrect, wrong, erroneous, faulty People once had the *mistaken* belief that the Earth was flat.

**mistreat** *verb* ✦ abuse, harm, hurt, injure ✧ mishandle, damage People should never *mistreat* their pets.

**misty** *adjective* ✦ foggy, hazy, cloudy ✧ dim, murky, vague We were not able to see the lunar eclipse because the evening was *misty*.

**misunderstand** *verb* ✦ misinterpret, confuse ✧ misjudge, mistake, misread I had trouble finding my friend's house because I *misunderstood* her directions.

**misunderstanding** *noun* ✦ misconception, mix-up ✧ confusion, error, mistake There was a *misunderstanding* about the time of our meeting.

**mix** *verb* ✦ blend, combine, merge, scramble, stir ✧ mingle Concrete is made by *mixing* cement with gravel and water. —*noun* ✦ assortment, combination, mixture, variety ✧ jumble There was an interesting *mix* of food at our potluck supper.

**mixture** *noun* ✦ blend, combination, compound, mix ✧ assortment My favorite drink is a *mixture* of iced tea and lemonade.

**moan** *noun* ✦ wail, howl, yowl, groan ✧ sob, whimper, murmur I heard an eerie *moan* that turned out to be the wind. —*verb* ✦ wail, howl, yowl, groan, keen ✧ cry, sigh Every Halloween my little brother walks around the house *moaning* like a ghost.

**mob** *noun* ✦ crowd, horde, mass, pack, swarm, throng ✧ group There was a *mob* of people at the shopping mall on the day before Christmas. —*verb* ✦ crowd (around), press (toward), surround, swarm (around), throng (around) Dozens of shouting reporters *mobbed* the politician.

**mobile** *adjective* ✦ movable, moving, portable, transportable, traveling Volunteers set up a *mobile* kitchen to help feed the homeless.

**mock** *verb* ✦ laugh (at), ridicule, taunt, tease, insult, jeer, scorn Many people *mocked* early aviators by saying that if humans were meant to fly, they would have wings. —*adjective* ✦ artificial, imitation, simulated ✧ fake, false, phony The film crew built a *mock* spaceship for the science-fiction movie.

**mode** *noun* ✦ manner, means, method, style, system, way ✧ fashion, procedure, form Steamboats and stagecoaches are two old-fashioned *modes* of transportation.

**model** *noun* 1. ✦ miniature, replica ✧ copy, duplicate, imitation, facsimile The boy likes to build *models* of military airplanes. 2. ✦ make, design, kind, style, type, variety, version We traded in our old car for a newer *model*. 3. ✦ example, ideal, pattern, standard, paragon, prototype ✧ subject Many people expect the president to be a *model* of moral integrity. —*verb* ✦ design, fashion, make, shape, form ✧ copy, imitate The courthouse building was *modeled* after an ancient Greek temple. —*adjective* ✦ ideal, perfect, good ✧ representative, standard, typical I believe that being active in community affairs is part of being a *model* citizen.

**moderate** *adjective* ✦ modest, reasonable, conservative ✧ average, medium, temperate This store sells quality merchandise at *moderate* prices. —*verb* ✦ restrain, tame, tone down, control ✧ lessen, reduce My uncle has to *moderate* his eating habits for health reasons.

**modern** *adjective* ✦ contemporary, current, new, present, recent ✧ fresh High-rise office buildings are a *modern* form of architecture.

**modest** *adjective* 1. ✦ humble, quiet, reserved ✧ shy, demure, silent The research scientist was *modest* about her many discoveries. 2. ✦ limited, moderate, small ✧ average, reasonable My grandparents live on a *modest* income now that they have retired.

**modify** *verb* ✦ adjust, alter, change, revise, vary ✧ reorganize, transform The weather forced us to *modify* our vacation plans.

**moist** *adjective* ✦ damp, dank, wet ✧ soggy, humid I used a *moist* rag to clean the dirt off my bicycle.

**moisten** *verb* ✦ dampen, wet, soak ✧ drench, rinse, wash, water *Moisten* the sponge before you wipe the counter.

**moisture** *noun* ✦ dampness, wetness, water ✧ fluid, liquid Try to keep your books dry because *moisture* will harm them.

**mold**[1] *noun* ✦ form, cast, die ✧ shape, pattern Candles are made by pouring hot wax into a *mold*. —*verb* ✦ fashion, form, shape, model ✧ build, forge, make Alexa took a lump of clay and *molded* it into a cup.

**mold**[2] *noun* ✦ fungus, blight ✧ rot, mildew There's *mold* on this loaf of bread.

**moment** *noun* ✦instant, jiffy, minute, second, trice, twinkling, flash The doctor will be with you in a *moment*.

**momentary** *adjective* ✦ short, brief, fleeting, fleet, temporary, passing I felt only *momentary* pain when I got the injection.

**momentous** *adjective* ✦ historic, important, major, significant ✧ serious, memorable The lunar landing on July 20, 1969, was a *momentous* occasion.

**momentum** *noun* ✦ speed, velocity, impetus ✧ energy, force, power The bicyclist gained *momentum* as he coasted down the hill.

**monarch** *noun* ✦ queen, ruler, sovereign, majesty ✧ king Queen Elizabeth I was England's *monarch* from 1558 to 1603.

**money** *noun* ✦ cash, currency ✧ funds, revenue, riches, wealth, capital I use credit cards because I don't like to carry a lot of *money*.

**monitor** *noun* ✦ overseer, guardian ✧ director, guide, supervisor The school selects older students to be hallway *monitors*. —*verb* ✦ check, observe, watch, supervise, follow ✧ control Doctors closely *monitored* the seriously ill patient.

**monotonous** *adjective* ✦ boring, dull, tedious, tiresome, dreary, uninteresting ✧ routine The long plane trip was *monotonous*.

**monster** *noun* ✦ beast, creature ✧ brute, demon, fiend, giant, ogre My favorite movie *monster* is a giant lizard that destroys Tokyo.

**monstrous** *adjective* 1. ✦ colossal, enormous, gigantic, huge, immense, mammoth, massive The sailboat was almost capsized by a *monstrous* wave. 2. ✦ frightening, gruesome, hideous, horrible, terrifying, dreadful ✧ ugly According to folklore, ogres are *monstrous* creatures that eat human beings.

**monument** *noun* ✦ memorial, shrine, remembrance ✧ testament, tribute This statue is a *monument* to the pioneers who founded our town.

**mood** *noun* ✦ frame of mind, attitude, disposition ✧ spirit, temper, temperament When my *mood* is cheerful in the morning, I am usually happy all day long.

**moody** *adjective* ✦ gloomy, sulky, melancholy, sullen ✧ unstable, temperamental I prefer to be by myself when I feel *moody*.

**moor** *verb* ✦ fasten, fix, lash, secure, tie, tether ✧ anchor The crew *moored* their ship to the dock.

**mop** *verb* ✦ swab, sponge, wipe, clean ✧ scrub, wash Please *mop* up the spilled milk.

**moral** *adjective* ✦ honorable, upright, virtuous, good, honest, ethical A *moral* person does not lie or cheat. —*noun* ✦ lesson, meaning, message, teaching ✧ proverb A fable is a story that has a *moral*.

**morale** *noun* ✦ spirit, mood, attitude, confidence ✧ self-esteem *Morale* at my office has really improved since we got a new manager.

**more** *adjective* ✦ additional, extra, added, further ✧ new, other, another Do you need *more* time to finish? —*noun* ✧ extra, addition, another, increase, supplement, refill When we ran out of bagels, I went to the bakery to get some *more*.

—*adverb* ✦ additionally, further, longer ✧ better, beyond, still, too, yet Our coach said that we will have to practice *more*.

**morsel** *noun* ✦ bit, bite, crumb, piece, mouthful ✧ fragment, scrap When we were finished eating the cake, there wasn't a *morsel* left.

**mortal** *adjective* ✦ fatal, lethal, terminal, deadly, killing A lion delivers a *mortal* wound by biting its prey in the back of the neck. —*noun* ✦ human, human being, person ✧ man, woman, individual In Roman mythology, Hercules was a *mortal* who possessed godlike strength.

**most** *adjective* ✦ greater, greatest, larger, largest, maximum ✧ better, best, top The person with the *most* strength will probably win the weightlifting contest. —*noun* ✦ almost all, nearly all, best part ✧ majority, maximum, peak I spend *most* of my paycheck on food and rent. —*adverb* ✦ exceedingly, extremely, exceptionally, quite, very ✧ extra, notably Everyone in the audience thought that the magician's performance was *most* impressive.

**mostly** *adverb* ✦ chiefly, largely, mainly, primarily, principally My yoga class is *mostly* women, but a couple of men also attend.

**motion** *noun* ✦ movement, flux ✧ action, activity, move, stir Because sharks are very heavy, they have to remain in constant *motion* or they will sink. —*verb* ✦ beckon, gesture, indicate, signal, wave ✧ direct My grandmother *motioned* for me to sit down beside her.

**motive** *noun* ✦ motivation, incentive, objective, aim, purpose, reason, cause My *motive* for taking an exercise class is to lose some weight.

**motor** *noun* ✦ engine, power plant, power source ✧ machine, mechanism The model airplane has a miniature battery-powered *motor*. —*adjective* ✦ mobile, moving, traveling ✧ mechanized, motorized My grandparents are driving through Alaska in their *motor* home.

**motto** *noun* ✦ maxim, saying, slogan, expression ✧ principle, rule The Boy Scout *motto* is "Be Prepared."

**mound** *noun* ✦ hill, pile, stack, heap, mass ✧ mountain Some species of ants form huge *mounds* of soil when they dig their nests.

**mount** *verb* 1. ✦ build, grow, increase, rise, lift ✧ ascend, climb, scale Excitement *mounted* as the swimmers neared the finish line. 2. ✦ install, place, position, set, fix ✧ exhibit, frame, show The bank has surveillance cameras *mounted* above the doors.

**mountain** *noun* 1. ✦ peak, summit, mount ✧ crag, hill, mound We camped at the base of a majestic snowcapped *mountain*. 2. ✦ heap, mass, pile, stack, mound ✧ abundance, accumulation We have a *mountain* of trash that we need to take to the dump.

**mourn** *verb* ✦ grieve, sorrow, lament ✧ cry, despair, suffer It is natural to *mourn* when someone we care about dies.

**move** *verb* 1. ✦ shift, carry, convey ✧ change, go, transport I *moved* my chair closer to the television. 2. ✦ relocate, migrate, transfer ✧ depart, leave, travel My uncle recently *moved* from New York to Iowa. 3. ✦ affect, disturb, touch, stir, impress I was deeply *moved* by the tragic love story that I just finished reading. 4. ✦ cause, influence, inspire, motivate, persuade, stimulate, prompt What *moved* you to join the karate club? —*noun* ✦ motion, movement ✧ action, maneuver, step The police officer ordered the suspect to stand still and not make a *move*.

**movement** *noun* 1. ✦ motion, stirring, move ✧ action, activity, shift A sudden *movement* in the bushes caught my attention. 2. ✦ campaign, crusade, drive, push ✧ group, organization There is a *movement* in my neighborhood to start a community garden.

**movie** *noun* ✦ film, motion picture, feature, picture, show, cinema My favorite *movie* will soon be available through online streaming.

**mow** *verb* ✦ clip, cut, trim, crop, shear ✧ hack The grass is too wet to *mow* right now.

**mud** *noun* ✦ mire, muck, slime ✧ dirt, ooze I always wear my boots when I have to walk through *mud*.

**muffle** *verb* ✦ dampen, silence, soften, stifle, suppress, gag I put my hand over my mouth to *muffle* my laughter.

**muggy** *adjective* ✦ clammy, humid, sticky, sultry ✧ damp, moist I never feel like doing much on hot, *muggy* days.

**multiply** *verb* ✦ build up, grow, increase, mount, swell, expand, mushroom The difficulties of the climb *multiplied* as the mountaineers got close to the summit.

**multitude** *noun* ✦ crowd, horde, pack, swarm, throng, mass, mob A *multitude* of tourists boarded the ferryboat.

**mumble** *verb* ✦ murmur, mutter, whisper It's hard for me to understand you when you *mumble*.

**munch** *verb* ✦ snack, eat ✧ bite, chew, gnaw, chomp I love to *munch on* popcorn while I watch television.

**murder** *noun* ✦ homicide, killing, slaying, manslaughter ✧ assassination, massacre The suspect has been charged with attempted *murder*. —*verb* ✦ assassinate, kill, slay ✧ massacre, slaughter American President Abraham Lincoln was *murdered* by John Wilkes Booth on April 14, 1865.

### Word Groups

**Music** is a pleasing or meaningful combination of sounds. **Music** is a general term with no true synonyms. Here are some different forms of music to investigate in a dictionary: **air, harmony, lyrics, melody, singing, song, strain, tune**

**must** *verb* ✦ have to, need to ✧ ought to, should My work assignment *must* be turned in no later than next Wednesday.

**mutiny** *noun* ✦ rebellion, revolt, uprising, insurrection ✧ revolution, riot The *mutiny* on HMS Bounty in 1789 is one of the most famous in history. —*verb* ✦ rebel, revolt, rise up ✧ resist, riot The sailors *mutinied* and took over the ship.

**mutual** *adjective* ✦ common, joint, shared, similar ✧ general, related My best friend and I have a *mutual* love of dancing.

**mystery** *noun* ✦ enigma, puzzle, question, riddle ✧ problem, secret The reason why so many ships have been lost in the Devil's Triangle is an unsolved *mystery*.

**mystify** *verb* ✦ baffle, bewilder, perplex, puzzle, confuse, stump Easter Island's huge statues *mystify* archaeologists because no one knows why the statues were made.

**myth** *noun* ✦ folk tale, legend, story ✧ fable, lore, saga There are *myths* from many cultures describing how the world was made.

**mythical** *adjective* ✦ fictitious, imaginary, legendary, fabled, fanciful, fantastic ✧ unreal Shangri-La is a *mythical* paradise where people never grow old.

**mythology** *noun* ✦ myth, folklore, legend, lore ✧ tradition, tales In Greek *mythology*, Poseidon was the god of the sea.

**nab** *verb* ✦ arrest, apprehend, capture, catch, seize, snatch, grab Police *nabbed* the robber as he was leaving the bank.

**nag** *verb* ✦ carp (at), harass, badger, bother, hound, pester ✧ annoy, complain, scold My parents constantly *nag* me about getting a better job.

**Word Groups**

A **nail** is a pointed piece of metal that is hammered into pieces of wood to fasten them. **Nail** is a very specific term with no true synonyms. Here are some related words to investigate in a dictionary: **brad, peg, pin, spike, tack**

**naked** *adjective* **1.** ✦ nude, bare, unclad, unclothed ✧ exposed, uncovered The little boy ran *naked* through the house after his bath. **2.** ✦ unaided, unassisted ✧ natural, plain, simple, direct Bacteria are too small to be seen by the *naked* eye.

**name** *noun* **1.** ✦ appellation, designation ✧ label, term, title The *name* of the tallest mountain in the world is Mount Everest. **2.** ✦ reputation, repute ✧ character, distinction, fame I want to go to a college that has a good *name*. —*verb* **1.** ✦ call, designate ✧ label, term, title, dub I *named* my pet rabbit Blackie. **2.** ✦ identify, itemize, list, specify, cite ✧ mention Can you *name* all the countries in Asia? **3.** ✦ appoint, designate, choose, select, nominate ✧ elect The president *named* a new ambassador to the United Nations.

**nap** *noun* ✦ catnap, doze, rest, snooze, siesta ✧ sleep I like to take an afternoon *nap* whenever my schedule permits. —*verb* ✦ catnap, doze, drowse, snooze, sleep My cat enjoys *napping* in the sun.

**narcotic** *noun* ✦ opiate, sedative ✧ painkiller, drug, medicine Doctors sometimes prescribe *narcotics* for patients who are in great pain.

**narrate** *verb* ✦ describe, recount, relate, tell ✧ recite, report, detail In the book I just read, an old sailor *narrates* his adventures on the high seas.

**narrow** *adjective* **1.** ✦ confined, cramped, snug, tight, constricted ✧ slender, thin The cavers inched their way along the *narrow* passage. **2.** ✦ close, small, little, slim, meager ✧ limited The

horse won the race by a *narrow* margin. —*verb* ✦ taper, contract, constrict ✧ reduce, tighten The road *narrows* as it goes through the tunnel.

**nasty** *adjective* **1.** ✦ mean, vicious, wicked, cruel, evil, hateful The movie audience cheered when the *nasty* villain was defeated. **2.** ✦ awful, bad, disgusting, foul, offensive, unpleasant, vile There's a *nasty* smell coming from the garbage can. **3.** ✦ serious, severe ✧ dangerous, harmful, injurious, painful The skier took a *nasty* fall.

**nation** *noun* ✦ country, state ✧ domain, land, realm, republic Canada and Mexico are the two *nations* that border on the United States.

**native** *adjective* **1.** ✦ innate, natural, hereditary, inherited, inborn My friend has so much *native* intelligence she can succeed at almost anything. **2.** ✦ indigenous, domestic, aboriginal, original ✧ internal, national Pandas are *native* to China. —*noun* ✦ citizen, inhabitant, resident, local, national ✧ dweller My friend Chihiro is a *native* of Japan.

**natural** *adjective* **1.** ✦ inborn, instinctive, innate ✧ hereditary, inherited Dogs have a *natural* tendency to chase anything that runs away from them. **2.** ✦ native, lifelike, realistic, wild ✧ normal, regular, typical The San Diego Zoo is famous for displaying animals in their *natural* surroundings.

**naturally** *adverb* **1.** ✦ normally, regularly ✧ genuinely, routinely, typically I felt nervous having a solo part in the play, but I tried to just speak *naturally*. **2.** ✦ obviously, of course, clearly, certainly, logically, surely *Naturally*, we'll be having turkey for Thanksgiving dinner.

**nature** *noun* **1.** ✦ the outdoors, the environment ✧ wilderness, world, creation, universe I enjoy hiking in the woods because I love being out in *nature*. **2.** ✦ character, disposition, personality, makeup ✧ essence, quality, temper I like people who have a gentle *nature*.

**naughty** *adjective* ✦ bad, disobedient, ill-behaved, mischievous ✧ impish, unruly My dog was being *naughty* when she chewed up my shoes.

**nausea** *noun* ✦ upset stomach ◇ indigestion, sickness, queasiness My *nausea* was probably caused by eating too much just before I got on the roller coaster.

**nautical** *adjective* ✦ marine, maritime, naval, boating, sailing "Forecastle" is a *nautical* term that refers to the forward part of a ship's deck.

**navigate** *verb* ✦ pilot, steer, guide ◇ direct, maneuver Early sailors *navigated* by using the stars as a guide.

**navy** *noun* ✦ naval forces, armada, fleet, flotilla, ships England's *navy* gained control of the seas by defeating the Spanish in 1588.

**near** *adjective* 1. ✦ approaching, at hand, coming, imminent Winter is *near* when the days begin to be shorter and colder. 2. ✦ close ◇ adjacent, adjoining, nearby, immediate We live in the country, and our *nearest* neighbor is two miles away.

**nearly** *adverb* ✦ almost, about, approximately, roughly, virtually I was *nearly* asleep when the phone rang.

**neat** *adjective* 1. ✦ orderly, organized, tidy, precise ◇ clean, trim The old magazines were stacked in *neat* piles. 2. ✦ clever, deft, skillful ◇ fine, great, wonderful My grandfather showed me a really *neat* magic trick.

**necessary** *adjective* ✦ essential, needed, required, requisite ◇ imperative, important, urgent The art teacher said that she would furnish all *necessary* supplies for making ceramic bowls.

**necessity** *noun* ✦ essential, requirement, need, must ◇ condition, fundamental Water is a *necessity* for all life on Earth.

**need** *noun* 1. ✦ essential, necessity, requirement, want ◇ resource Pioneer families had to provide for most of their own *needs*. 2. ✦ call, necessity ◇ demand, obligation, imperative There is no *need* for further discussion of this matter. —*verb* ✦ require, want, desire ◇ demand, lack We *need* two more players for our team.

**needless** *adjective* ✦ pointless, useless ◇ unnecessary, superfluous It is *needless* to ask me again because I have made up my mind.

**needy** *adjective* ✦ destitute, impoverished, penniless, poor, poverty-stricken, broke A local charity collects food and clothing for *needy* families throughout the country.

**negative** *adjective* ✦ adverse, bad, unfavorable, pessimistic, unsatisfactory The movie received many *negative* reviews.

**neglect** *verb* ✦ fail, omit, overlook, forget ◇ disregard, ignore, skip The man's phone was disconnected because he *neglected* to pay the bill. —*noun* ✦ disregard, inattention, indifference, oversight, negligence The dilapidated old barn has suffered from years of *neglect*.

**negligent** *adjective* ✦ careless, inattentive, irresponsible ◇ forgetful, indifferent, neglectful The *negligent* driver got a ticket for running a red light.

**negotiate** *verb* ✦ arrange, determine, conclude, set, settle ◇ confer, discuss, bargain The details of the agreement still have to be *negotiated*.

**neighborhood** *noun* ✦ area, community, district, locality, quarter ◇ block, street I have lived in the same *neighborhood* for ten years.

**nerve** *noun* ✦ boldness, daring, bravery, courage, pluck ◇ mettle, spirit It took a lot of *nerve* to ski down the steep mountainside.

**nervous** *adjective* ✦ anxious, distressed, fearful, tense, uneasy, upset, edgy Loud noises make my cat very *nervous*.

**Antonyms** nervous
*adjective* calm, collected, cool, relaxed, serene

**nestle** *verb* ✦ cuddle, snuggle, clasp, embrace ◇ hug, squeeze The toddler always goes to sleep with his teddy bear *nestled* in his arms.

**neutral** *adjective* 1. ✦ impartial, unbiased, detached, indifferent, uninvolved A referee is supposed to be *neutral* so that each team has an equal chance of winning. 2. ✦ bland, drab, flat, toneless, indistinct, ordinary, plain My dentist's office is painted a *neutral* color.

**nevertheless** *adverb* ✦ anyway, anyhow, nonetheless, regardless, even so ◇ however, still, yet I didn't feel very well this morning, but I went to work *nevertheless*.

**new** *adjective* 1. ✦ brand-new, up-to-date ◇ current, latest, modern, recent Everyone in the family wants to use our *new* digital camcorder. 2. ✦ fresh, unfamiliar, unknown, different, strange There are several *new* employees at my office this year. 3. ✦ novel, original, unique, unusual, different, creative The company is promoting a *new* way to recycle old soda bottles.

**newly** *adverb* ✦ just, freshly, lately, recently I love my *newly* redecorated bedroom.

**news** *noun* ✦ information, report, story, word, tidings ✧ intelligence, knowledge Have you heard the *news* about the movie that is going to be made in our town?

**next** *adjective* 1. ✦ coming, following, subsequent, ensuing, succeeding ✧ adjacent, close I ordered a book by express delivery, and it arrived the *next* day. —*adverb* ✦ hereafter ✧ after, afterward, later, subsequently I've seen this movie before, but I don't remember what happens *next*.

**nibble** *verb* ✦ chew, gnaw, munch ✧ bite, eat My rabbit *nibbled* on the carrot that I gave him. —*noun* ✦ bite, taste, bit, morsel ✧ snack The mouse took one *nibble* of the cheese and decided that he liked it.

**nice** *adjective* 1. ✦ agreeable, delightful, enjoyable, good, pleasant, pleasing The roses that grow in our garden have a *nice* smell. 2. ✦ decent, kind, thoughtful, considerate ✧ courteous, polite, proper It was *nice* of you to share your umbrella with me.

**nick** *noun* ✦ scratch, chip, cut, dent, notch, scar The antique table was in perfect condition except for a few *nicks* on its legs. —*verb* ✦ cut, scratch, scrape ✧ chip, dent, mar, notch, scar I *nicked* myself while shaving this morning.

**night** *noun* ✦ nighttime, evening, nightfall, sundown, twilight ✧ dark I enjoy seeing fireflies when they come out at *night*.

**nimble** *adjective* ✦ agile, deft, adroit, spry, swift, lively, quick ✧ clever You have to have *nimble* fingers to play a guitar.

**noble** *adjective* 1. ✦ aristocratic, highborn, royal, titled ✧ upper-class The prince was required to marry a woman who was of *noble* birth. 2. ✦ honorable, virtuous, moral, selfless ✧ courageous, excellent, generous Helping the homeless is a *noble* cause. 3. ✦ grand, grandiose, imposing, magnificent, majestic, stately California's Sierra Nevada is a chain of *noble* mountains. —*noun* ✦ aristocrat ✧ lord, lady, nobleman, noblewoman, royalty *Nobles* came from all over the land to attend the queen's coronation.

**noise** *noun* ✦ clamor, din, racket, sound ✧ tumult, uproar The garbage collectors made so much *noise* they woke me up.

**noisy** *adjective* ✦ loud ✧ blaring, booming, clamorous, deafening, earsplitting This old lawnmower is really *noisy*.

**nominate** *verb* ✦ choose, designate, name, propose, select ✧ appoint In 1872, Victoria Woodhull was the first woman ever *nominated* as a candidate for president of the United States.

**nonsense** *noun* ✦ absurdity, craziness, foolishness, silliness ✧ stupidity, drivel As we sat around the campfire, we made up a funny story that was pure *nonsense*.

**normal** *adjective* ✦ average, ordinary, regular, standard, typical, usual, general The river returned to its *normal* level one week after the flood.

**notable** *adjective* ✦ eminent, famous, great, important, memorable, noteworthy The signing of the Declaration of Independence was a *notable* event in American history.

**notch** *noun* ✦ groove, indentation, nick ✧ chip, cut, dent An arrow has a *notch* on its end in order to get a better grip on the bowstring. —*verb* ✦ slot, cut, chip, nick ✧ chop, scratch When making a log cabin, the logs usually are *notched* so that they fit together snugly.

**note** *noun* 1. ✦ card, letter, message, memo ✧ communication I sent my friend a *note* thanking her for my birthday present. 2. ✦ notation, comment, observation, remark ✧ memorandum, record This book has explanatory *notes* at the end of each chapter. 3. ✦ hint, indication, suggestion, trace, bit ✧ evidence, sign There was a *note* of sadness in my friend's voice when she told us that she was moving away. —*verb* ✦ notice, observe, mark, mind ✧ perceive, regard, see Please *note* that your appointment is for three o'clock.

**nothing** *noun* ✦ naught, nought, zero, nil, zilch ✧ not anything The final score was ten to *nothing*.

**notice** *verb* ✦ note, observe, see, spot ✧ perceive, recognize Did you *notice* the flock of chickadees in the yard? —*noun* 1. ✦ attention, consideration, heed, regard ✧ observation I was happy that my work received such favorable *notice*. 2. ✦ directive, announcement, declaration, statement ✧ bulletin, pronouncement I received a *notice* that said I had to report for jury duty. 3. ✦ notification, warning, forewarning ✧ information, instruction We gave the landlord a month's *notice* before we moved out of our apartment.

**notify** *verb* ✦ advise, alert, inform, tell, apprise ✧ instruct, mention We *notified* the post office that we were going on vacation.

**notion** *noun* ✦ belief, idea, thought, conviction ✧ concept, opinion The little boy has somehow gotten the *notion* that there's a monster in his closet.

**notorious** *adjective* ✦ infamous, scandalous ✧ famous, leading, well-known Edward Teach, known also as Blackbeard, was a *notorious* pirate.

**nourish** *verb* ✦ feed, nurture, maintain, supply, sustain ✧ provide, support Your blood *nourishes* your body by carrying oxygen and nutrients to every living cell.

**nourishment** *noun* ✦ feed, food, sustenance ✧ nutrition, provision, support All baby animals need *nourishment* to grow.

**novel** *adjective* ✦ fresh, new, original, unusual, different ✧ odd, uncommon, unique Someone came up with a *novel* idea for turning old automobile tires into pavement.

**Antonyms** novel

*adjective* common, familiar, ordinary, usual, well-known

**novelty** *noun* ✦ freshness, newness ✧ originality, strangeness, uniqueness Some people lose interest in new undertakings once the *novelty* wears off.

**now** *adverb* ✦ at once, right away, directly, immediately, instantly, presently If I don't leave *now*, I'll be late for work.

**nucleus** *noun* ✦ center, core ✧ focus, heart, kernel, seed This year's team will be formed around a *nucleus* of returning players.

**nudge** *verb* ✦ push, shove, prod, propel ✧ jab, poke, touch A tugboat *nudged* the ocean liner away from the pier. —*noun* ✦ poke, jab, prod, push ✧ shove, touch My friend gave me a *nudge* with her elbow.

**nuisance** *noun* ✦ aggravation, annoyance, bother, irritation, pest, pain That barking dog is a real *nuisance*.

**numb** *adjective* ✦ unfeeling, insensitive ✧ asleep, dead, deadened, frozen My ears were *numb* from walking in a cold wind. —*verb* ✦ blunt, deaden, dull ✧ desensitize, chill, freeze The dentist gave me a shot to help *numb* the pain.

**number** *noun* 1. ✦ numeral, digit ✧ character, figure, sign, symbol My clock is easy to read because it has big *numbers* on it. 2. ✦ amount, quantity ✧ sum, total, whole Five is the maximum *number* of players that a basketball team can have on the court at one time. 3. ✦ company, crowd, group, bunch, collection ✧ multitude A large *number* of guests attended my sister's wedding.

**numeral** *noun* ✦ digit, number ✧ character, figure, sign, symbol My car's license plate is a combination of letters and *numerals*.

**numerous** *adjective* ✦ abundant, many, plentiful, profuse ✧ infinite On a clear night, the stars are too *numerous* to be counted.

**nurse** *verb* ✦ care (for), take care (of), tend, treat, minister (to) ✧ aid, nourish The kind woman found an injured owl and *nursed* it till it was able to fly again.

**Word Groups**

A **nut** is a fruit having a hard shell and one seed. Nut is a general term with no true synonyms. Here are some common types of nuts to investigate in a dictionary: **almond, Brazil, cashew, filbert, macadamia, peanut, pecan, pistachio, walnut**

**nutrition** *noun* ✦ diet, food, nourishment ✧ nutriment, sustenance Good *nutrition* is essential to a healthy and active life.

**nutritious** *adjective* ✦ healthful, healthy, nourishing, wholesome, nutritional Fresh fruits and vegetables are *nutritious* foods.

**nuzzle** *verb* ✦ cuddle, nestle, snuggle, rub ✧ press, touch My kitten likes to *nuzzle* against me when she's in an affectionate mood.

**oath** *noun* ✦ pledge, vow ✧ affirmation, assertion, declaration, promise, statement The Knights of the Round Table took an *oath* of loyalty to King Arthur.

**obedient** *adjective* ✦ compliant, docile, submissive ✧ dutiful, loyal, conscientious The *obedient* dog always came when his master called.

**obese** *adjective* ✦ fat, heavy, overweight, plump, stout, portly The vet told me to put my cat on a diet because he's getting *obese*.

**obey** *verb* ✦ abide (by), carry out, follow, heed ✧ fulfill, observe, respect Soldiers are expected to *obey* the orders given by an officer.

**object** *noun* 1. ✦ article, item, thing, commodity ✧ device This antique store has many unusual *objects* for sale. 2. ✦ focus, subject, target, recipient ✧ mark The author was the *object* of much attention when her book won a prestigious prize. 3. ✦ aim, goal, objective ✧ end, purpose, idea The *object* of chess is to checkmate your opponent's king. —*verb* ✦ dispute, protest, complain (about) ✧ argue, challenge, oppose The ball player *objected to* the umpire's decision.

**objection** *noun* ✦ protest, complaint, challenge, opposition ✧ argument, dispute No one had any *objections* to the proposal to lower taxes.

**objective** *adjective* ✦ fair, impartial, just, unbiased, unprejudiced ✧ honest, sincere The referee was careful to be *objective* when making her calls. —*noun* ✦ aim, goal, object, point ✧ end, purpose The *objective* of a popular outdoor game is to capture the other team's flag.

**obligation** *noun* ✦ commitment, duty, requirement, responsibility, burden ✧ promise Police officers have an *obligation* to uphold the law.

**oblige** *verb* ✦ obligate, require, compel, bind ✧ force, make, pressure Employers are legally *obliged* to pay workers the minimum wage.

**obscure** *adjective* 1. ✦ unclear, vague, ambiguous ✧ hidden, indistinct The meaning of this poem is *obscure*. 2. ✦ little known, unknown, unheard-of, minor ✧ insignificant, unimportant The actress isn't a big star because all of her roles have been in *obscure* movies. —*verb* ✦ block, conceal, cover, hide, screen, obstruct ✧ veil In a solar eclipse, the moon *obscures* the sun.

**observation** *noun* 1. ✦ examination, inspection, observance, study ✧ view, watch Scientists have made careful *observations* of the Earth's weather patterns. 2. ✦ comment, remark, statement ✧ opinion, view, idea My boyfriend made an interesting *observation* about the movie we were watching.

**observe** *verb* 1. ✦ notice, see, spot, witness ✧ watch, glimpse I called the fire department when I *observed* smoke coming from the neighbor's garage. 2. ✦ abide (by), comply (with), follow, heed, keep, obey ✧ respect The referee warned both boxers to *observe* the rules at all times.

**obstacle** *noun* ✦ impediment, difficulty, hurdle, barrier, obstruction ✧ barricade, block, check A steep cliff was the last *obstacle* standing between the climbers and the mountain's summit.

**obstinate** *adjective* ✦ stubborn, headstrong, contrary ✧ uncontrollable, unruly The *obstinate* mule refused to budge.

**obstruct** *verb* ✦ block, close up, stop up, choke ✧ bar, delay, prevent Our rain gutter overflowed because leaves were *obstructing* it.

**obstruction** *noun* ✦ barrier, obstacle, block, hindrance, impediment ✧ bar, blockage, check, clog, hurdle The fallen tree was an *obstruction* to traffic.

**obtain** *verb* ✦ acquire, attain, gain, get ✧ earn, secure You have to be sixteen years old before you can *obtain* a driver's license.

**obvious** *adjective* ✦ clear, distinct, evident, unmistakable ✧ apparent, plain Our volleyball team has an *obvious* advantage because we have taller players.

**Antonyms obvious**

*adjective* ambiguous, hidden, obscure, unclear, vague

**occasion** *noun* 1. ✦ event, happening, incident, occurrence, time ✧ circumstance My grandparents' fiftieth anniversary was an important *occasion* for the entire family. **2.** ✦ **chance, opportunity, opening** ✧ **possibility, excuse** I haven't had many *occasions* to play tennis this summer.

**occasional** *adjective* ✦ **infrequent, odd, random, periodic, intermittent** ✧ **irregular, rare, uncommon** The weather has been fine except for an *occasional* afternoon shower.

**occupant** *noun* ✦ **inhabitant, resident** ✧ **renter, tenant, lodger** The former *occupants* left the apartment very clean.

**occupation** *noun* **1.** ✦ **career, profession, business, vocation, job, work** My father's *occupation* is teaching school. **2.** ✦ **control, possession, rule, subjugation** ✧ **capture, conquest** China was under Japanese *occupation* during World War II.

**occupy** *verb* **1.** ✦ **dwell (in), inhabit, live (in), reside (in), lodge (in)** My parents have *occupied* the same house for more than twenty years. **2.** ✦ **take up, engage, fill, use up** ✧ **busy, employ** Santiago's job *occupies* most of his time. **3.** ✦ **take control (of), take possession (of), hold** ✧ **capture, command, conquer, seize** During the War of 1812, British troops briefly *occupied* Washington, D.C.

**occur** *verb* ✦ **happen, come about, take place, result** ✧ **appear, develop** Thunder *occurs* when the heat from a flash of lightning expands the surrounding air.

**occurrence** *noun* ✦ **development, circumstance, event, experience, incident** ✧ **affair, occasion** The local airport is very busy, and flight delays are a common *occurrence*.

**odd** *adjective* **1.** ✦ **curious, peculiar, strange, unusual** ✧ **weird, bizarre, outlandish** My friend has the *odd* habit of scratching his ear whenever he's thinking. **2.** ✦ **lone, single, unmatched** ✧ **extra, leftover, surplus** I have several *odd* socks that are missing their mates. **3.** ✦ **miscellaneous, various, random** ✧ **chance, irregular, occasional** A handyman earns money by doing *odd* jobs such as minor carpentry, plumbing and yardwork.

**odor** *noun* ✦ **scent, smell, aroma** ✧ **fragrance, stench, stink, reek** Onions and garlic have a strong *odor*.

**offend** *verb* ✦ **anger, annoy, displease, irritate, upset, vex, insult** ✧ **disgust, outrage** My friend was *offended* when I forgot to meet her at the movies as planned.

**offense** *noun* **1.** ✦ **crime, misdeed, violation** ✧ **misdemeanor, error, sin, wrong** Jaywalking is only a minor *offense*. **2.** ✦ **disrespect, insult** ✧ **indignation, outrage, resentment** I meant no *offense* when I said that you look different today.

**offensive** *adjective* **1.** ✦ **disgusting, foul, nasty, revolting, unpleasant, atrocious** Sulfur hot springs have an *offensive* odor similar to that of rotten eggs. **2.** ✦ **discourteous, disrespectful, insulting, rude, unmannerly** My friend is so tactful that she can point out a person's faults without being *offensive*. —*noun* ✦ **assault, attack, offense** ✧ **aggression, charge, strike** The generals hoped that their big *offensive* would end the war.

**offer** *verb* **1.** ✦ **volunteer, proffer** ✧ **propose, submit** My roommate *offered* to help clean up after the party. **2.** ✦ **furnish, present, provide, supply, afford** ✧ **give** Our city *offers* a wide variety of cultural activities. —*noun* ✦ **proposal, proposition, bid** ✧ **suggestion, invitation** A friend accepted my *offer* to buy his old motorbike.

**office** *noun* **1.** ✦ **workroom, workplace** ✧ **headquarters, room, shop, department** The accountant will be back in her *office* this afternoon. **2.** ✦ **position, post** ✧ **job, role, situation, task** Five candidates are running for the *office* of mayor.

**official** *adjective* ✦ **authorized, formal, legitimate, proper, approved** ✧ **real, true** An ambassador is an *official* representative from one country to another. —*noun* ✦ **executive, officer, authority** ✧ **administrator, director, leader** The president is the highest elected *official* in the United States.

**often** *adverb* ✦ **commonly, frequently, regularly** ✧ **generally, usually** The zipper on my backpack *often* gets stuck.

**old** *adjective* **1.** ✦ **aged, elderly, senior** ✧ **mature, ancient, antique** The United States Social Security Administration was created primarily to benefit *old* people after they retire. **2.** ✦ **rundown, used, worn, worn-out, shabby** These shoes are so *old* that they're starting to fall apart. **3.** ✦ **former, past, previous** ✧ **late, onetime** It's been six years since we moved from our *old* house to the one we live in now.

**omen** *noun* ✦ **indication, sign, token** ✧ **prediction, portent, prophecy** Some people think that finding a four-leaf clover is an *omen* of good luck.

**omit** *verb* ✦ **exclude, neglect, skip, forget, drop, elim-**

inate, **ignore** I want to hear everything that happened at the party, so please don't *omit* any details.

**once** *adverb* ✦ **at one time, formerly, previously** ✧ **already, before, earlier, heretofore** Dinosaurs were *once* the largest creatures living on the Earth.

**only** *adjective* ✦ **lone, one, single, sole, solitary** ✧ **individual, unique** My friend was the *only* student who earned a perfect score on the vocabulary quiz. —*adverb* ✦ **just, merely, solely, simply, exclusively** I have two brothers, but *only* one sister.

**ooze** *verb* ✦ **seep, trickle, dribble, drip, leak, drain, discharge** Sap *oozed* from the tree's broken branch.

**open** *adjective* 1. ✦ **ajar, unclosed** ✧ **unfastened, unlocked** Somebody left the window *open*, and our parakeet got out. 2. ✦ **uncapped, uncovered, unsealed** ✧ **exposed, unprotected** Don't leave the soda bottle *open* or all the fizz will go out. 3. ✦ **empty, vacant** ✧ **bare, clear, deserted, wide** The children like to play in the *open* field behind their apartment building. 4. ✦ **accessible, available, allowable** ✧ **free, public** This contest is only *open* to writers under the age of thirty. —*verb* 1. ✦ **unwrap, unfasten, untie** ✧ **free, release, undo** The little girl eagerly *opened* her birthday presents. 2. ✦ **begin, commence, start** ✧ **initiate, launch, institute** Many schools *open* on the day after Labor Day.

**operate** *verb* 1. ✦ **function, perform, run, work** ✧ **go, behave** The toaster isn't *operating* properly. 2. ✦ **drive, handle, manage, use** ✧ **manipulate, work** The farmer taught his daughter how to *operate* a tractor.

**operation** *noun* ✦ **action, functioning, performance, working, running** ✧ **effect, use** This new factory has computers that control the *operation* of its machinery.

**opinion** *noun* ✦ **belief, conviction, judgment, view** ✧ **idea, evaluation** In my *opinion*, Tolstoy's *War and Peace* is one of the best books ever written.

**opponent** *noun* ✦ **adversary, challenger, competitor, rival** ✧ **enemy, foe** The winning candidate defeated two *opponents* in the primary election.

**opportunity** *noun* ✦ **chance, occasion** ✧ **moment, situation, time, opening** I haven't had an *opportunity* to fly my new kite yet.

**oppose** *verb* ✦ **disagree (with), disapprove (of), object (to), protest, resist** ✧ **contest, deny, fight** I wonder if my parents will *oppose* my plan to study abroad.

**opposite** *adjective* 1. ✦ **facing, opposing, reverse** ✧ **other** The football teams lined up on *opposite* sides of the field. 2. ✦ **conflicting, contradictory, contrary, counter** ✧ **different** "Up" and "down" have *opposite* meanings.

**opposition** *noun* ✦ **disagreement (with), disapproval (of), objection** ✧ **defiance, resistance** Local residents have expressed *opposition* to the proposal to build a new freeway exit.

**opt** *verb* ✦ **choose, decide, elect, pick, select** ✧ **go for, prefer** Which movie did you finally *opt* to see?

**optimistic** *adjective* ✦ **confident, hopeful, positive, trusting** ✧ **upbeat, cheerful** The drama teacher was *optimistic* that the school play would be a great success.

**optional** *adjective* ✦ **not required, elective, voluntary** ✧ **free, possible** The test included an *optional* question that could be answered for extra credit.

**Antonyms optional**
*adjective* **compulsory, mandatory, necessary, obligatory, required**

**oral** *adjective* ✦ **spoken, verbal** ✧ **vocal, voiced, verbalized** Vietnam has a rich heritage of *oral* poetry that has been passed down through the generations.

**orbit** *noun* ✦ **revolution, rotation** ✧ **circuit, course, path, trajectory** Russia's *Sputnik I* was the first artificial satellite to be placed in *orbit* around the Earth. —*verb* ✦ **circle, revolve around, circumnavigate** ✧ **rotate, spin, turn** The Earth *orbits* the sun once every year.

**ordeal** *noun* ✦ **trial, trouble, difficulty, hardship, distress** ✧ **experience** The shipwrecked sailors said that the worst part of their *ordeal* was going without water.

**order** *noun* 1. ✦ **condition, form, shape, state, trim, repair** The pilot checked her plane to ensure that all the equipment was in working *order*. 2. ✦ **sequence, arrangement, classification, organization** ✧ **pattern, system** I shelve my books in alphabetical *order* by author. 3. ✦ **calm, control, discipline, peace, quiet, silence** The teacher had trouble restoring *order* after a bird flew in the classroom window. 4. ✦ **command, directive, direction, instruction** ✧ **demand, rule** The soldier received an *order* to report to his commanding officer. —*verb* 1. ✦ **command, direct, instruct, tell, bid** ✧ **force,**

require Firefighters *ordered* everyone to leave the building immediately. **2.** ✦ **ask (for), request** ✧ **buy, purchase, reserve, hire** We *ordered* a large pizza with extra cheese.

**orderly** *adjective* **1.** ✦ **methodical, neat, organized, regular, trim** ✧ **clean, tidy** The band marched in *orderly* lines. **2.** ✦ **calm, disciplined, peaceful, quiet, well-behaved, civil** The fans remained *orderly* even though the concert did not start on time.

**ordinarily** *adverb* ✦ **generally, normally, typically, usually** ✧ **customarily, regularly, routinely** My friend is on vacation this week, but *ordinarily* he would be at work now.

**ordinary** *adjective* **1.** ✦ **average, normal, regular, standard, typical, usual** On an *ordinary* day, my work begins at 8 o'clock in the morning. **2.** ✦ **common, commonplace, everyday, modest, plain, simple** We were surprised to see the famous actress dressed in *ordinary* clothes.

**organic** *adjective* ✦ **natural, unadulterated** ✧ **additive-free, pesticide-free** I believe that *organic* fruits and vegetables are healthier.

**organization** *noun* **1.** ✦ **planning, organizing, arrangement** ✧ **design, form, order, structure** The entire staff helped with the *organization* of this year's company picnic. **2.** ✦ **association, group, society** ✧ **club, league, party** Priyana joined an *organization* that works to protect endangered species.

**organize** *verb* **1.** ✦ **arrange, categorize, classify, group, order, sort** I need to *organize* the stamps in my collection. **2.** ✦ **establish, form, set up, start** ✧ **create, develop, found, institute** My town *organized* a tree-planting campaign to celebrate Arbor Day.

**origin** *noun* ✦ **beginning, source, start** ✧ **root, basis, cause, foundation** Explorers traveled up the river to find its *origin*.

**original** *adjective* **1.** ✦ **first, initial** ✧ **beginning, early, primary** My old car still has its *original* coat of paint. **2.** ✦ **fresh, imaginative, new, novel, unique, unusual, creative** The idea for your story should be *original*, not copied from something you've read.

**originate** *verb* ✦ **begin, commence, start, arise** ✧ **create, introduce, invent** The use of paper money *originated* in China more than one thousand years ago.

**ornament** *noun* ✦ **decoration, trimming** ✧ **accessory, adornment** My mother bought a box of new *ornaments* for our Christmas tree. —*verb* ✦ **adorn, decorate** ✧ **beautify, enhance, trim, embellish** The castle was *ornamented* with bright flags and banners.

**other** *adjective* ✦ **alternate, different, additional, more** ✧ **extra, new** Does this shirt come in any *other* colors?

**ought** *auxiliary verb* ✦ **had best, should** ✧ **have, must, need** As long as I'm at the pet store, I *ought to* buy some rabbit food.

**oust** *verb* ✦ **remove, banish, expel, dismiss** ✧ **eject, evict** The city council voted to *oust* the corrupt mayor.

**out** *adverb* ✦ **outdoors, outside, out-of-doors** The children went *out* to play. —*adjective* ✦ **dead, gone** ✧ **absent, done, finished, over, expired** I can't use my computer because the power is *out*.

**outbreak** *noun* ✦ **epidemic, outburst, surge** ✧ **eruption, uprising** Measles vaccinations can help prevent *outbreaks* of the disease.

**outburst** *noun* ✦ **burst, eruption, outbreak** ✧ **flood, gush, torrent, fit** I apologized to my friend for my *outburst* of anger.

**outcome** *noun* ✦ **conclusion, end, result** ✧ **aftermath, consequence, issue** I couldn't wait to hear about the *outcome* of the game.

**outdo** *verb* ✦ **beat, better, exceed, surpass, top** ✧ **excel, eclipse** Shantay is determined to *outdo* her previous personal record for the long jump.

**outdoor** *adjective* ✦ **out-of-doors, outside, open-air** ✧ **external** The local park is sponsoring a series of *outdoor* concerts.

**outer** *adjective* ✦ **exterior, external, outside** ✧ **outward** Crabs, lobsters, and clams all have hard *outer* shells for protection.

**outfit** *noun* ✦ **clothing, dress, garb** ✧ **equipment, gear, costume** A hunter's *outfit* usually includes a brightly colored vest and cap. —*verb* ✦ **equip, provision, supply** ✧ **furnish, provide, stock, rig** We went shopping to *outfit* ourselves for the week-long canoe trip.

**outing** *noun* ✦ **excursion, jaunt, tour, trip** ✧ **expedition, vacation** We're planning a family *outing* to Catalina Island.

**outlaw** *noun* ✦ **bandit, criminal, crook, robber** ✧ **gangster, felon** Billy the Kid was a notorious *outlaw* of America's Old West. —*verb* ✦ **abolish,**

ban, forbid, prohibit, bar ✧ banish, prevent The Eighteenth Amendment to the US Constitution *outlawed* the sale of alcoholic beverages.

*verb* allow, authorize, legalize, license, permit

**outlet** *noun* ✦ release, vent, channel ✧ exit, opening, passage, escape My friend has taken up painting as an *outlet* for her creative energy.

**outline** *noun* 1. ✦ silhouette, profile, contour ✧ form, shape I could just see the mountain's *outline* against the evening sky. 2. ✦ draft, plan, summary, sketch, synopsis Writing an essay is easier if you have an *outline* to follow. —*verb* ✦ plan out, summarize, sketch ✧ draft, draw up The author *outlined* the plot of his new novel.

**outlook** *noun* 1. ✦ attitude (toward), perspective, view (of), point of view, viewpoint A positive *outlook* on life can help you get through a bad day. 2. ✦ forecast, prediction, prospect, projection ✧ chance, future The weatherman said that the *outlook* for the next few days is quite good.

**output** *noun* ✦ production, productivity ✧ volume, harvest, yield The companies that make exercise equipment have recently been increasing their *output.*

**outrage** *noun* ✦ anger, fury, indignation ✧ resentment, wrath, vexation The principal expressed her *outrage* when she learned that the school budget was to be cut. —*verb* ✦ anger, incense, offend ✧ affront, insult, shock, vex We were *outraged* when we saw the polluted beach.

**outrageous** *adjective* ✦ despicable, disgraceful, offensive, shameful, shocking, awful The movie star said that the scandal was based on an *outrageous* lie.

**outside** *noun* ✦ exterior ✧ surface, face, front, facade We painted the *outside* of the old shed. —*adjective* ✦ exterior, external, outer, outward These caramels have an *outside* layer of chocolate.

**outstanding** *adjective* ✦ excellent, exceptional, remarkable, superior, superb, great My boss said I am doing *outstanding* work.

**over** *preposition* ✦ higher (than), above, beyond, past ✧ across Manuel hit the ball *over* the outfield fence. —*adjective* ✦ finished ✧ complete, done, through, past The television show was *over* in time for supper.

**overcast** *adjective* ✦ cloudy, gray ✧ dark, hazy, misty, murky The sky was *overcast* all day long, but it never rained.

**overcome** *verb* ✦ beat, conquer, defeat, master, subdue, surmount ✧ win I have been trying to *overcome* my shyness.

**overdue** *adjective* ✦ past due ✧ behind, late, tardy I have three *overdue* books that I must get back to the library by tonight.

**overflow** *verb* ✦ cascade, pour, spill, gush, flood When I accidentally left the bathtub faucet on, water *overflowed* onto the floor.

**overhaul** *verb* ✦ rebuild, repair, service, fix, mend ✧ examine, inspect Mechanics *overhauled* the plane's jet engines.

**overlook** *verb* ✦ miss, neglect, pass over, skip ✧ disregard, forget, omit I *overlooked* two misspelled words when I proofread my report.

**overrule** *verb* ✦ disallow, reject ✧ repeal, revoke, veto, nullify The judge *overruled* most of the lawyer's objections.

**oversight** *noun* ✦ lapse, slip, omission, blunder, error, mistake ✧ fault, neglect It was an unfortunate *oversight* to forget to take a stove on our camping trip.

**overtake** *verb* ✦ catch, catch up (with), pass, overhaul ✧ beat, reach, surpass The motorboat easily *overtook* our rowboat.

**overthrow** *verb* ✦ bring down, oust, remove, topple, depose ✧ conquer, defeat, destroy The people rose up to *overthrow* their oppressive dictator. —*noun* ✦ downfall, ouster, removal ✧ collapse, defeat, undoing The king's aides plotted his *overthrow.*

**overturn** *verb* ✦ capsize, roll over, turn over, upset ✧ spill, topple A kayak is a type of canoe that can be easily righted if it *overturns.*

**overweight** *adjective* ✦ fat, heavy, obese, plump, stout, pudgy The doctor told the *overweight* patient to exercise more and eat fewer snacks.

**overwhelm** *verb* ✦ crush, defeat, overpower, overrun ✧ destroy, wipe out The attacking army quickly *overwhelmed* the small band of defenders.

**own** *verb* ✦ have, possess ✧ hold, keep, retain I *own* more than five hundred books.

# P

**pace** *noun* **1.** ✦ stride, step, footstep ◆ gait In ancient Rome, a mile was exactly 1,000 *paces* long. **2.** ✦ rate, speed, velocity, clip ◆ motion, movement My friend can run at a faster *pace* than I can. —*verb* ✦ step, stride, tread, walk ◆ march The lion *paced* back and forth in its cage.

**pack** *noun* **1.** ✦ packet, package ◆ bag, bundle, carton, container, parcel Please get me a *pack* of gum when you go to the store. **2.** ✦ band, bunch, group ◆ gang, herd, mob We could hear a *pack* of coyotes howling in the distance. —*verb* ✦ cram, crowd, squeeze, stuff, load ◆ fill Kwame had so many items *packed* in his duffel bag that he could barely get it to close.

**package** *noun* ✦ box, carton, parcel ◆ bundle, container, pack The mail carrier left a *package* on our front porch.

**pact** *noun* ✦ accord, concord, agreement, alliance, treaty ◆ bargain, deal The two nations signed a *pact* to help defend each other.

**pad** *noun* **1.** ✦ cushion, mat ◆ mattress, pillow I used a blanket and a foam *pad* to make a bed for my dog. **2.** ✦ notepad, tablet, writing tablet ◆ notebook Each student received two pencils and a *pad* of paper.

**pageant** *noun* ✦ play, show, performance, spectacle ◆ celebration, parade, procession I'll be playing a Pilgrim in this year's Thanksgiving *pageant*.

**pail** *noun* ✦ bucket ◆ can, container, vessel, receptacle The woman uses a plastic *pail* to carry water to her flower garden.

**pain** *noun* **1.** ✦ ache, hurt, pang, soreness, stitch ◆ twinge, discomfort I felt a sudden *pain* in my side from running. **2.** ✦ agony, anguish, distress, misery, suffering, woe Losing a good friend can cause a lot of *pain*. —*verb* ✦ distress, trouble, hurt, sadden ◆ injure, wound It *pains* me to see you so unhappy.

**paint** *noun* ◆ pigment, color, coloring, dye, stain, tint I put two coats of green *paint* on the old picnic table. —*verb* ✦ color, tint ◆ decorate, dye, shade, cover The clown *painted* his face red and white.

**painting** *noun* ✦ picture, portrait, artwork ◆ canvas, drawing, oil, sketch One of the world's most famous *paintings* is the *Mona Lisa* by Leonardo da Vinci.

**pair** *noun* ✦ couple, duo, twosome, team ◆ combination, match, unit I think you and I would make a good *pair*. —*verb* ✦ match, match up, team, couple, join ◆ combine, mate The coach *paired* the wrestlers according to their weight.

**pal** *noun* ✦ buddy, chum, companion, comrade, friend, mate Wang Wei and I have been *pals* for years.

**pale** *adjective* ✦ faint, light, dim, pallid ◆ colorless, whitish The sky turned *pale* blue as the sun came up.

**pamper** *verb* ✦ baby, cater (to), coddle, indulge, spoil ◆ humor My aunt *pampers* her cat by feeding it fresh tuna and chicken.

**pamphlet** *noun* ✦ booklet, brochure ◆ book, text, manual My new bicycle came with a *pamphlet* on safety tips.

## Word Groups

A **pan** is an open container used for cooking. **Pan** is a general term with no true synonyms. Here are some different kinds of pans to investigate in a dictionary: **broiler, casserole, frying pan, griddle, roaster, saucepan, skillet**

**pandemonium** *noun* ✦ chaos, uproar, tumult, bedlam, racket ◆ clamor, turbulence There was *pandemonium* at the zoo when the elephants broke out of their enclosure.

**panel** *noun* ✦ group, board, team ◆ assembly, commission, committee The talk show featured a *panel* of teachers who discussed ways to improve educational quality.

**pang** *noun* ✦ ache, pain, twinge ◆ discomfort, smart, throe I get hunger *pangs* if I go too long without eating.

**panic** *noun* ✦ alarm, dread, fear, fright, terror ◆ dis-

**tress, horror** I felt a sudden *panic* when I thought the bus was going to go off the road. *—verb* ✦ **alarm, frighten, scare, terrify** ✧ **terrorize, startle** The horse galloped away after a rattlesnake *panicked* it.

**pant** *verb* ✦ **gasp, huff, puff, wheeze** ✧ **blow, heave** We were all *panting* hard after taking the stairs up to the 12th floor.

**pants** *noun* ✦ **slacks, trousers** ✧ **blue jeans, dungarees, jeans** Some of the women wore *pants* while others wore dresses.

**paper** *noun* 1. ✦ **writing paper, notepaper, stationery** ✧ **page, parchment, sheet** I need a piece of *paper* to jot down my shopping list. 2. ✦ **document, legal paper, form** ✧ **certificate, contract, deed** I had to sign a bunch of *papers* when I applied for my American visa. 3. ✦ **newspaper, tabloid** ✧ **gazette, journal, periodical, publication** Our local *paper* is called *The Daily Enterprise*. 4. ✦ **article, essay, composition, treatise** ✧ **report, theme** The scientist's *paper* was published in a prestigious journal.

**parade** *noun* ✧ **march, procession, cavalcade** Many cities around the world have annual *parades* to celebrate New Year's Day. *—verb* ✦ **file, march, stride** ✧ **step, stroll, walk** The graduating students *paraded* across the stage to pick up their diplomas.

**paradise** *noun* ✦ **heaven, utopia** ✧ **bliss, delight, ecstasy, glory** Many people think that Hawaii is a tropical *paradise*.

**parallel** *adjective* 1. ✦ **side by side** ✧ **aligned, alongside, even** The rails of a railroad track are *parallel* to each other. 2. ✦ **alike, corresponding, equivalent, like, similar, duplicate** The two scientists are conducting *parallel* experiments to see if they can get the same results. *—noun* ✦ **similarity, likeness, resemblance** ✧ **comparison, analogy** There are some obvious *parallels* between the two bank robberies. *—verb* ✦ **correspond (to), equal, match, duplicate** ✧ **resemble** The subjects covered in home schooling *parallel* those taught in public schools.

**paralyze** *verb* ✦ **cripple, disable, immobilize** ✧ **numb, stun, knock out** A massive power failure *paralyzed* America's entire West Coast.

**parcel** *noun* ✦ **package, box, carton** ✧ **bundle, container, pack** The post office delivers millions of *parcels* every year.

**parch** *verb* ✦ **dehydrate, dry out** ✧ **burn, roast, scorch, wither, bake** The long drought has *parched* all the cornfields.

**pardon** *verb* ✦ **excuse, forgive, condone** ✧ **absolve, overlook, tolerate, acquit** Please *pardon* my barging in like this. *—noun* ✦ **forgiveness** ✧ **excuse, mercy, acquittal** I beg your *pardon*, but I didn't mean to bump into you.

**pare** *verb* ✦ **peel** ✧ **skin, strip, trim, cut, shave** I helped my roommate *pare* apples for the pie she was baking.

**part** *noun* 1. ✦ **passage, section, segment, portion, element** ✧ **piece** Some *parts* of the book were better than others. 2. ✦ **share, piece** ✧ **role, duty, responsibility, task, function** Everyone did their *part* to help clean up the office. *—verb* ✦ **divide, separate, split, cleave** ✧ **break up, open** The axe *parted* the wood right down the middle.

**partial** *adjective* 1. ✦ **incomplete, limited, part** ✧ **fragmentary, fractional, unfinished** Police have only a *partial* description of the suspect. 2. ✦ **biased, one-sided, prejudiced, unfair** ✧ **unjust, slanted** A good referee is never *partial*.

**participate** *verb* ✦ **join, take part** ✧ **contribute, cooperate, share, engage** Everybody *participated* in the sing-along.

**particle** *noun* ✦ **bit, fragment, scrap, grain, piece, speck, trace** The dog ate every last *particle* of food in his dish.

**particular** *adjective* 1. ✦ **special, specific, detailed, close** ✧ **thorough, unusual** Whenever I get ready to go out, I pay *particular* attention to my hair. 2. ✦ **choosy, fussy, picky, finicky** ✧ **careful, demanding** Because my sister is a vegetarian, she's very *particular* about what she eats. *—noun* ✦ **detail, fact, factor, point, specific** ✧ **circumstance, item** Please tell me all the *particulars* about your trip to Mexico.

**partition** *noun* ✦ **barrier, divider, screen** ✧ **wall, panel** Some libraries have *partitions* between desks so that patrons can study in privacy. *—verb* ✦ **divide, section, separate** ✧ **break up, cut, split** We *partitioned* off part of the garage to make a workshop.

**partly** *adverb* ✦ **partially, partway, slightly, somewhat, incompletely** Please leave the window *partly* open until the room cools off.

**partner** *noun* ✦ **associate, colleague, affiliate** ✧

ally, companion, mate My best friend and I are business *partners*.

**partnership** *noun* ✦ alliance, association, affiliation ✧ business, company Two of my friends have formed a business *partnership*.

**party** *noun* 1. ✦ celebration, festivity ✧ get-together, social, affair We're going to give our parents a surprise *party* for their anniversary. 2. ✦ group, company ✧ band, bunch, crowd, gang, crew Ask the server if he can seat our entire *party* at one table.

**pass** *verb* 1. ✦ go, proceed, travel, journey, move, progress The parade will *pass* along Forest Street and turn onto Monument Avenue. 2. ✦ go away, cease, disappear, end, lapse ✧ depart, die, expire If you take these aspirin, your pain should soon *pass*. 3. ✦ give, hand ✧ convey, deliver, transmit, send Please *pass* me the butter. 4. ✦ complete, fulfill, satisfy, finish ✧ accomplish, achieve I just *passed* all the requirements to get my driver's license. 5. ✦ adopt, approve, enact, ratify, sanction ✧ confirm The state legislature *passed* a bill requiring all bicyclists to wear helmets.

**passage** *noun* 1. ✦ passing, course, flow, movement, progression ✧ journey, travel My parents say I will grow wiser with the *passage* of time. 2. ✦ corridor, passageway, walkway, way, route ✧ channel, path There is an underground *passage* that connects these two buildings. 3. ✦ excerpt, selection, section, segment, part, portion Sophia read me a *passage* from her favorite book.

**passenger** *noun* ✦ rider, traveler, voyager ✧ commuter, tourist The Airbus A380 jet airliner can carry more than eight hundred *passengers*.

**passion** *noun* ✦ emotion, enthusiasm, ardor, fervor, feeling, fire, intensity The author spoke with *passion* about the book she is writing.

**passionate** *adjective* ✦ emotional, forceful, impassioned, heated, intense, moving The charity's spokesperson made a *passionate* plea for donations.

**past** *adjective* ✦ just over, preceding, previous, prior ✧ finished, former, gone I've been pretty busy for the *past* few days. —*noun* ✦ former times, previous times ✧ yesterday, yesteryear, antiquity In the *past*, people had shorter lifespans than they do today. —*preposition* ✦ after, beyond ✧ behind, over, through To get to the municipal swimming pool, turn left just *past* the library.

**Word Groups**

**Pasta** refers to dough that is molded into a variety of shapes and boiled. **Pasta** is a general term with no true synonyms. Here are some different kinds of pasta to investigate in a dictionary: **cannelloni, fettuccine, lasagna, linguine, macaroni, manicotti, ravioli, rigatoni, spaghetti, tortellini, vermicelli, ziti**

**paste** *noun* ✦ adhesive, glue, mucilage, cement The children made scrapbook *paste* by mixing flour with cold water. —*verb* ✦ glue, stick, cement ✧ attach, fasten, bind I *pasted* a photograph into my album.

**pastime** *noun* ✦ diversion, entertainment, amusement ✧ hobby, recreation, sport Baseball is one of America's most popular *pastimes*.

**pasture** *noun* ✦ field, meadow, pastureland ✧ clearing, grassland The farm boy's morning chore was to put the cows out to graze in the *pasture*.

**pat** *verb* ✦ pet, stroke, tap ✧ caress, cuddle, fondle, rub My dog likes being *patted* on the head.

**patch** *noun* ✦ area, space, spot ✧ stretch, section, tract, lot There were some *patches* of ice on the road this morning. —*verb* ✦ cover, mend ✧ fix, repair, restore I used colorful fabric to *patch* the hole in my blue jeans.

**path** *noun* ✦ pathway, trail, walk, walkway, way ✧ course, route This *path* goes all the way around the lake.

**pathetic** *adjective* ✦ forlorn, sad, woeful, heartbreaking, moving, pitiful, touching ✧ miserable, unfortunate The lost puppy looked so *pathetic* that I decided to take it home.

**patience** *noun* ✦ calmness, restraint, self-control, composure, serenity, tolerance When the concert didn't start on time, the audience waited with admirable *patience*.

**patient** *adjective* ✦ calm, tolerant, understanding, forbearing, serene ✧ gentle The teenager is a popular babysitter because she is very *patient* with young children.

**Antonyms** patient

*adjective* anxious, hasty, impatient, restless, uneasy

**patrol** *verb* ✦ police, cruise, guard, watch ✧ defend, protect, supervise The sheriff said that more deputies would be made available to *patrol* the streets after dark.

**patron** *noun* ✦ client, customer, regular ◈ backer, sponsor, supporter The barber shop has dozens of regular *patrons* who have been coming there for many years.

**pattern** *noun* 1. ✦ arrangement, design ◈ figure, form, shape The shadows of the trees made interesting *patterns* on the snow. 2. ✦ plan, guide, model, standard ◈ example, ideal, sample Making a dress is easier if you have a *pattern* to follow. —*verb* ✦ fashion, form, model (on) ◈ copy, follow, imitate This museum building is *patterned* after a medieval castle.

**pause** *noun* ✦ break, interruption, lull ◈ delay, halt, rest, stop There was a brief *pause* in our conversation. —*verb* ✦ discontinue, hesitate, stop, cease, halt ◈ delay, rest, wait The speaker *paused* for a moment to glance at his notes.

**pave** *verb* ✦ surface, coat, cover, top, layer ◈ tar We had our driveway *paved* with asphalt.

**pay** *verb* ✦ compensate, remunerate ◈ give, render, reward (with), earn, gain, get I don't have any cash; could you *pay* the taxi driver? —*noun* ✦ compensation, salary, wages, earnings, money, remuneration ◈ fee An experienced restaurant cook can get very good *pay*.

**peace** *noun* 1. ✦ amity ◈ accord, armistice, harmony, neutrality, truce There has always been *peace* between the United States and Canada. 2. ✦ calm, peacefulness, quiet, serenity, tranquility I love the sense of *peace* that I find while walking in the forest.

**peaceful** *noun* 1. ✦ nonviolent, peaceable, pacific ◈ friendly, neutral Switzerland is a *peaceful* country that hasn't been at war since 1848. 2. ✦ calm, quiet, restful, serene, tranquil, placid I found a *peaceful* spot in the park in which to read my book.

**peak** *noun* 1. ✦ summit, crest, crown, top, tip ◈ roof, pinnacle The mountain's *peak* was covered with snow. 2. ✦ climax, height, top, zenith ◈ limit, maximum The actress is now at the *peak* of her career.

**peculiar** *adjective* ✦ curious, odd, strange, weird, unusual ◈ distinctive, unique The duck-billed platypus has a *peculiar* mouth that looks like a bird's beak.

**peddle** *verb* ✦ hawk, vend, sell, market ◈ barter, trade Vendors were *peddling* caps, pennants, and other souvenirs at the baseball stadium.

**pedestrian** *noun* ✦ walker ◈ hiker, stroller, rambler The sidewalk was crowded with *pedestrians* enjoying the warm weather.

**peek** *verb* ✦ glance, glimpse, look, peep ◈ peer, spy I *peeked* into the closet to see if that's where my brother was hiding. —*noun* ✦ glance, glimpse, look, peep ◈ view I was tempted to take a *peek* at my girlfriend's diary, but I knew that I shouldn't.

**peer¹** *verb* ✦ gaze, look, stare ◈ examine, search, inspect, scan I *peered* into the stream to see if I could spot any fish.

**peer²** *noun* ✦ associate, colleague, fellow, equal ◈ counterpart, teammate The young doctor gained the respect of her *peers*.

**pelt¹** *noun* ✦ coat, hide, skin ◈ fur, hair, fleece Fur coats are made from the *pelts* of animals such as mink and fox.

**pelt²** *verb* ✦ batter, beat, hammer, hit, pummel, strike ◈ knock, tap We listened to the hail *pelting* the roof.

**pen** *noun* ✦ enclosure ◈ sty, cage, coop, corral, stockade Close the gate to the *pen* or the pigs will get out. —*verb* ✦ cage, confine, coop, enclose, shut away, shut up ◈ corral We *penned* the geese for the night.

**penalize** *verb* ✦ punish, discipline ◈ correct, fine, sentence In ice hockey, players who break the rules are *penalized* by being removed from the game for a few minutes.

**penalty** *noun* ✦ punishment ◈ fine, correction, discipline A late charge is often the *penalty* for not paying a bill on time.

**penetrate** *verb* ✦ pierce, pass (through), enter ◈ perforate, puncture, impale An arrow can *penetrate* several inches of wood.

**pennant** *noun* ✦ banner, flag ◈ colors, standard, streamer, ensign Taka collects the *pennants* of his favorite baseball and football teams.

**people** *noun* 1. ✦ human beings, humans, persons, individuals ◈ folks, souls There are approximately eight billion *people* living on the planet Earth. 2. ✦ citizens, citizenry, populace, public ◈ community, nation, society The *people* voted in favor of the new recycling law.

**perceive** *verb* 1. ✦ discover, note, notice, observe, see, spot, tell Can you *perceive* any difference between the two twins? 2. ✦ apprehend, comprehend, grasp, realize, understand ◇ know The teacher quickly *perceived* that some students had not understood her directions.

**percentage** *noun* ✦ fraction, part, percent, proportion, share ◇ ratio A large *percentage* of voters are opposed to the new tax.

**perfect** *adjective* 1. ✦ accurate, exact, precise, true, complete ◇ correct, right This model steam locomotive is *perfect* in every detail. 2. ✦ faultless, flawless, unflawed ◇ sound, whole My friend can speak *perfect* Russian. 3. ✦ excellent, ideal, superb, superlative ◇ fine, good This is a *perfect* day for a picnic. —*verb* ✦ develop, polish, refine, hone ◇ accomplish, achieve, complete The gymnast *perfected* her technique by practicing several hours every day.

**perform** *verb* 1. ✦ accomplish, complete, do, carry out, conclude ◇ achieve, fulfill The surgeon *performed* five operations in one day. 2. ✦ enact, give, present, put on, produce ◇ act, play, portray The local theater company will *perform* Shakespeare's *Romeo and Juliet*.

**perhaps** *adverb* ✦ conceivably, maybe, possibly, perchance *Perhaps* we'll be able to get together tomorrow night.

**peril** *noun* ✦ danger, hazard, risk, threat ◇ jeopardy, menace The explorers faced many *perils* on their journey across Antarctica.

**period** *noun* ✦ interval, phase, span, spell, stretch, time ◇ era, season We've been having a *period* of rainy weather.

**perish** *verb* ✦ die, expire, pass away, succumb, decease ◇ cease, end, vanish Many animals *perished* in the forest fire.

**Antonyms** **perish**
*verb* endure, flourish, last, survive, thrive

**permanent** *adjective* ✦ durable, enduring, lasting, long-lasting ◇ old, constant, stable I have a *permanent* scar on my arm where I cut it in a biking accident.

**permit** *verb* 1. ✦ allow, authorize, sanction, let ◇ approve, consent, tolerate In soccer, only the goalkeeper is *permitted* to touch the ball with his or her hands. 2. ✦ allow, be favorable, oblige,

**enable** If the weather *permits*, we can go swimming. —*noun* ✦ authorization, license, permission, sanction ◇ pass My younger brother has a learner's *permit* that allows him to drive a car if an adult is present.

**perplex** *verb* ✦ baffle, bewilder, confuse, mystify, puzzle, stump, dumbfound The car's strange noises *perplexed* its owner.

**persecute** *verb* ✦ harass, oppress, punish, torment ◇ abuse, wrong Throughout history, many religious groups have been *persecuted* for their beliefs.

**persist** *verb* ✦ continue, endure, go on, last, remain, linger ◇ persevere The hailstorm *persisted* long enough to damage most of the crops.

**persistent** *adjective* 1. ✦ insistent, persevering, stubborn, determined, firm, steadfast The *persistent* salesman would not take "no" for an answer. 2. ✦ chronic, continuing, lasting, lingering, long-lived ◇ constant I went to the doctor because I had a *persistent* cough.

**person** *noun* ✦ human, human being, individual ◇ man, woman On July 20, 1969, astronaut Neil Armstrong became the first *person* to set foot on the moon.

**personal** *adjective* ✦ intimate, private ◇ individual, own, particular, peculiar I keep my *personal* thoughts in my diary, which I don't let anyone read.

**Antonyms** **personal**
*adjective* common, communal, mutual, public, shared

**personality** *noun* ✦ character, disposition, temperament, nature, makeup, identity ◇ qualities, traits The twin brothers look alike, but they have very different *personalities*.

**perspective** *noun* ✦ context, proportion, relation, reference ◇ outlook, viewpoint To put the size of a blue whale into *perspective*, a fully-grown one can weigh as much as two thousand men.

**perspire** *verb* ✦ sweat ◇ lather, drip, pour, flush, secrete I was *perspiring* heavily after I finished the long run.

**persuade** *verb* ✦ coax, convince, get, influence, sway, talk (into) ◇ urge, entice I'm trying to *persuade* my parents to let me study abroad.

**pertain** *verb* ✦ apply (to), bear (on), concern, refer

**(to), regard, relate (to), touch** The judge would only allow testimony that *pertained to* the case that was being tried.

**pessimistic** *adjective* ✦ **dark, dismal, dim, gloomy, glum, discouraging** ✧ **doubtful, hopeless** The movie we saw takes a *pessimistic* view of human nature.

**pest** *noun* ✦ **annoyance, bother, irritation, nuisance, pain** ✧ **trouble** My little brother can be a big *pest* when he won't leave me alone.

**pester** *verb* ✦ **annoy, bother, disturb, harass, irritate, torment, trouble, vex** The mosquitoes *pestered* me while I was on a camping trip.

**pet** *noun* ✦ **darling, dear, favorite** ✧ **love, beloved** The adorable little girl was her grandmother's *pet.* —*adjective* ✦ **cherished, favored, favorite, preferred, special** ✧ **precious** My friend's *pet* project is the model railroad that he's been working on for years. —*verb* ✦ **caress, fondle, stroke** ✧ **cuddle, pat, rub** My cat purrs when I *pet* her.

**petition** *noun* ✦ **appeal, plea, proposal, request** ✧ **application, suit** Hundreds of parents signed a *petition* asking the city to hire more teachers. —*verb* ✦ **appeal (to), apply (to), ask, call (upon), entreat** ✧ **request** The scientists *petitioned* the government for more money to support their research.

**petrify** *verb* **1.** ✧ **dry, harden, set, solidify, congeal** Under the right conditions, wood will *petrify* into stone. **2.** ✦ **frighten, horrify, scare, terrify** ✧ **alarm, shock, stun** The monster movie *petrified* my little sister.

**petty** *adjective* **1.** ✦ **insignificant, minor, small, little, trifling, trivial, unimportant** I don't let *petty* problems bother me. **2.** ✦ **mean, narrow-minded, small-minded, spiteful, intolerant** ✧ **stingy** Gossip is spread by *petty* people.

**phantom** *noun* ✦ **ghost, spirit, wraith, specter** ✧ **spook, vision** In a famous story by French writer Gaston Leroux, a *phantom* haunts an opera house.

**phase** *noun* ✦ **period, stage, step, level, state** ✧ **condition, development** A tadpole is one *phase* in the life cycle of a frog.

**phenomenal** *adjective* ✦ **exceptional, extraordinary, remarkable, outstanding, amazing, marvelous, stupendous, wonderful** The winner of the lottery couldn't believe her *phenomenal* luck.

**phony** *adjective* ✦ **artificial, pretended, counterfeit,**

**fake, false** ✧ **unreal** The actor's *phony* accent didn't fool anyone. —*noun* ✦ **fake, fraud, impostor, pretender** ✧ **forgery, hoax, imitation** The woman claimed to be a fortuneteller, but she turned out to be just another *phony.*

**photograph** *noun* ✦ **photo, picture, snapshot** ✧ **image, portrait, print** My grandmother has dozens of family *photographs* on display in her home.

**phrase** *noun* ✦ **expression, saying** ✧ **motto, slogan, idiom, clause** The word "good-bye" is derived from the *phrase* "God be with you." —*verb* ✦ **express, formulate, present, put, state, word, term** Perhaps your question will be easier to answer if you *phrase* it differently.

**physical** *adjective* **1.** ✦ **bodily, corporal, corporeal** ✧ **living, personal** Athletes exercise regularly to maintain their *physical* fitness. **2.** ✦ **concrete, material, solid, substantial, tangible** ✧ **actual, real** Anything that you can touch is a *physical* object.

**physician** *noun* ✦ **doctor, medical doctor** ✧ **healer, intern** If your cold doesn't go away soon, you should see a *physician.*

**pick** *verb* **1.** ✦ **choose, decide (on), elect, select, name** We *picked* Jiwon to be the captain of our soccer team. **2.** ✦ **collect, gather, harvest, pluck** ✧ **garner, reap, get** I helped our next-door neighbor *pick* tomatoes. —*noun* ✦ **choice, preference, selection, option** ✧ **best, prize** You can take your *pick* of any piece of candy in the box.

**picture** *noun* **1.** ✦ **image, portrait** ✧ **drawing, illustration, sketch, painting, photograph** Do you want me to draw your *picture?* **2.** ✦ **film, motion picture, movie** ✧ **cinema, feature, show** My favorite movie won an award for Best *Picture.* —*verb* ✦ **conceive, envision, imagine, visualize** ✧ **see, think, vision** I'm trying to *picture* what my room will look like with new curtains and wallpaper.

**piece** *noun* ✦ **part, portion, section, segment** ✧ **share, unit, division** I cut the cake into six *pieces.*

**pier** *noun* ✦ **dock, wharf, jetty** ✧ **quay, breakwater** Several gift shops and a seafood restaurant are located out on the *pier.*

**pierce** *verb* ✦ **prick, puncture, stick, penetrate** ✧ **stab, cut, gash** I hardly felt it when the nurse *pierced* my skin with a needle.

**pile** *noun* ✦ **heap, lump, mass, mound, stack** ✧ **accumulation, collection** I changed in a hurry and left my old clothes in a *pile* on the floor. —*verb*

✦ heap, lump, mass, mound, stack ✧ accumulate, collect The children *piled* all the cushions on the floor and jumped on them.

**pill** *noun* ✦ capsule, tablet ✧ lozenge, medication, medicine I take a vitamin *pill* every morning.

**pillar** *noun* ✦ column, post ✧ support, prop, shaft The local courthouse has two big *pillars* on either side of the door.

**Word Groups**

A **pillow** is a case filled with something soft and used to support or cushion. **Pillow** is a general term with no true synonyms. Here are some different kinds of pillows to investigate in a dictionary: **bolster, cushion, headrest, pad, sham**

**pilot** *noun* 1. ✧ aviator, airman, captain, flyer, flier Small aircraft usually require only one *pilot*. 2. ✦ helmsman, steersman ✧ conductor, guide, navigator As the ship neared land, a licensed *pilot* came on board to guide it into port. —*verb* ✦ fly, operate ✧ guide, navigate, steer, maneuver I'd love to learn how to *pilot* an airplane.

**pin** *noun* ✦ brooch ✧ clasp, clip, ornament, stickpin, tiepin The woman wore a silver and turquoise *pin* that was shaped like a little dolphin. —*verb* 1. ✦ attach, fasten, fix, secure, stick ✧ staple I have lots of souvenir buttons *pinned* to my backpack. 2. ✦ hold, press ✧ restrain, immobilize, clasp The wrestler won the match by *pinning* his opponent to the mat.

**pinch** *verb* ✦ squeeze ✧ crush, compress, cramp, nip, tweak I accidentally *pinched* my hand in the front door. —*noun* 1. ✦ squeeze, nip ✧ tweak My friend gave me a playful *pinch* on the arm. 2. ✦ bit, dash, speck, trace, dab ✧ little, taste I added a *pinch* of salt to my bowl of chili. 3. ✦ crisis, emergency, predicament ✧ difficulty, trouble, plight This umbrella isn't very good, but it will do in a *pinch*.

**pioneer** *noun* 1. ✦ settler ✧ homesteader, colonist, explorer, frontiersman, pathfinder, scout During the 1800s, many *pioneers* made the difficult journey westward across North America. 2. ✦ creator, developer, forerunner, founder, originator, innovator The Wright brothers were among the *pioneers* of aviation.

**pious** *noun* ✦ devout, religious, reverent ✧ holy, saintly, godly The *pious* man went to church every day.

**pirate** *noun* ✦ buccaneer, privateer, corsair ✧ marauder, plunderer, outlaw, robber *Pirates* sometimes attacked coastal cities as well as ships at sea.

**pistol** *noun* ✦ handgun, side arm, automatic ✧ revolver, firearm, gun Police officers in America are usually armed with *pistols*.

**pit**[1] *noun* ✦ hole, excavation, cavity, basin, hollow ✧ crater, shaft, well The city turned the old gravel *pit* into a fishing pond. —*verb* ✦ match, oppose, set ✧ counter, play off In wrestling matches, people of about the same weight are *pitted* against each other.

**pit**[2] *noun* ✦ kernel, seed ✧ nut, stone, pip We put the avocado *pit* in a glass of water to see if it would grow.

**pitch** *verb* 1. ✦ throw, toss, cast, fling, heave, hurl, lob I *pitched* the stone far out into the lake. 2. ✦ erect, put up, raise, set up ✧ establish, place This looks like a good spot to *pitch* our tent. 3. ✦ heave, rock, roll, toss ✧ lurch, plunge Waves *pitched* our rowboat back and forth. —*noun* 1. ✦ throw, toss ✧ cast, delivery, fling, heave, lob The batter hit a home run on the first *pitch*. 2. ✦ degree, level, point ✧ height, peak, intensity The crowd reached a high *pitch* of excitement as the band began to play. 3. ✦ angle, grade, incline, slant, slope, tilt, cant The roof of a Swiss chalet has a steep *pitch* so that snow will slide off easily.

**pitiful** *adjective* ✦ pathetic, forlorn, heartbreaking, moving, sad, sorrowful The injured bird looked *pitiful*, but we were able to nurse it back to health.

**pity** *noun* ✦ compassion, mercy, sympathy ✧ charity, empathy, kindness Many people donated clothes and money out of *pity* for the hurricane victims. —*verb* ✦ feel sorry (for) ✧ sympathize, empathize I *pity* the people left homeless by the earthquake.

**pivot** *verb* ✦ swing, swivel, turn ✧ revolve, rotate, swerve, veer The telescope is mounted in a way that allows it to *pivot* sideways as well as up and down.

**place** *noun* 1. ✦ site, space, spot, area, location, point, position This is a good *place* to plant the rosebush. 2. ✦ district, locale, locality, region ✧ vicinity My uncle thinks that Cape Cod is a great *place* to live. 3. ✦ home, house, residence ✧ abode, dwelling, quarters I invited some friends to my *place* for dinner. 4. ✦ position, post, rank, station ✧ **situation, status** George Washington occupies a *place* of honor in America's history. —*verb* **1. ✦ put, set, position, situate, locate** ✧ **arrange, deposit** Please *place* the silverware on the table. **2. ✦ identify, recognize, remember** ✧ **connect, know** I know I've seen that man before, but I just can't *place* him.

**placid** *adjective* **✦ still, calm, peaceful, quiet, serene, tranquil, undisturbed** The lake is *placid* and smooth whenever the wind dies down.

**plague** *noun* **1. ✦ epidemic, disease** ✧ **illness, infection, outbreak, sickness** A deadly *plague* hit Europe in the mid-fourteenth century. **2. ✦ affliction, burden, curse, hardship, ill, problem, trouble, scourge** Poverty and crime are two *plagues* that society is trying to overcome. —*verb* **✦ afflict, burden, curse, torment, trouble** ✧ **annoy, bother** The patient was *plagued* by a cough that lasted all winter long.

**plain** *adjective* **1. ✦ apparent, clear, distinct, evident, obvious, unmistakable** You have made your meaning perfectly *plain*. **2. ✦ common, everyday, ordinary, standard** ✧ **average, routine** Many police detectives wear *plain* clothes instead of a uniform. **3. ✦ candid, frank, honest, simple, sincere, straightforward** ✧ **absolute, total** Please tell me the *plain* truth. —*noun* **✦ grassland, prairie** ✧ **steppe, field, plateau** Enormous herds of buffalo once roamed the North American *plains*.

**plan** *noun* **✦ aim, goal, intent, intention, idea** ✧ **design, scheme, strategy** Guadalupe's *plan* is to go to law school after she graduates from college. —*verb* **✦ 1. organize, arrange, design, devise, formulate** ✧**invent** I helped *plan* the annual office picnic. **2. aim, intend, propose, mean, foresee, contemplate** I *plan* to travel through Europe next summer.

**plane** *noun* **1. ✦ level, degree, grade, stage** ✧ **condition, rank, standard** Ancient Chinese civilization reached a very high *plane* of development. **2. ✦ aircraft, airplane** ✧ **airliner, jet** Hundreds of *planes* land at Los Angeles International Airport every day.

**plant** *noun* **1. ✧ herb, vegetable, flower, bush, grass, shrub, tree** We have lots of different *plants* in our garden. **2. ✦ factory** ✧ **facility, mill, shop, works, foundry** My uncle works at an automobile *plant*. —*verb* **✦ seed, sow** ✧ **farm, grow, raise** Winter wheat is *planted* in the fall.

**play** *verb* **1. ✦ recreate, sport, frolic, romp** ✧ **amuse (oneself), entertain (oneself)** The neighborhood children like to *play* together after school. **2. ✦ compete, participate, take part** ✧ **join in, contend** Everyone on our soccer team got a chance to *play* in yesterday's game. **3. ✦ act, perform, portray, represent, depict** ✧ **impersonate** My niece is going to *play* Snow White in the school show. —*noun* **1. ✦ drama, performance, show, production, theatrical** Every student will have a role in the class *play*. **2. ✦ amusement, diversion, entertainment, fun, game, sport, recreation, pleasure** I think it's sad that many adults work so much they never have time for *play*.

**playful** *adjective* **✦ energetic, frisky, frolicsome, lively, sprightly** ✧ **amusing, joking** My kitten is always in a *playful* mood.

**plea** *noun* **✦ appeal, request, petition, entreaty** ✧ **cry, prayer** The Red Cross made a *plea* for donations of warm clothing.

**plead** *verb* **✦ appeal, beg, entreat, implore, press** ✧ **ask, request** The little girl *pleaded* for a puppy of her very own.

**pleasant** *adjective* **✦ agreeable, delightful, enjoyable, nice, pleasing, pleasurable, satisfying** I like springtime because the days are warm and *pleasant*.

**please** *verb* **1. ✦ delight, gladden, gratify, overjoy** ✧ **cheer, satisfy** My parents were *pleased* when I was admitted to a top university. **2. ✦ choose, desire, like, prefer, want, will, wish, elect** My grandparents gave me fifty dollars to buy whatever I *please* for my birthday.

**pleasure** *noun* **✦ enjoyment, delight, gladness, happiness, joy** ✧ **cheer, satisfaction** My little brother laughs with *pleasure* when I give him a piggyback ride.

**pledge** *noun* **✦ agreement, commitment, promise** ✧ **contract, oath, vow** I made a *pledge* to contribute money to the homeless shelter. —*verb* **✦ promise, swear, vow, guarantee, declare** ✧ **agree, affirm** The president *pledged* to never raise taxes.

**plenty** *noun* **✦ an abundance, a great deal, lots, a quantity** ✧ **enough, much, sufficient** We have *plenty* of food for tomorrow's picnic.

**plod** *verb* **✦ trudge, tramp, drag, toil, slog** ✧ **tread, walk** We *plodded* wearily up the steep hill.

**plot** *noun* **1. ✦ patch, lot, parcel, tract** ✧ **area, ground, land, space** My grandfather has a small *plot* of land that he uses for a vegetable garden. **2.** ✦ **story, story line** ✧ **narrative, theme, scenario** This novel has an exciting *plot* about traveling in a time machine. **3.** ✦ **conspiracy, intrigue, plan, scheme** ✧ **design** There was a *plot* to overthrow the cruel dictator. —*verb* ✦ **conspire, intrigue, plan, scheme** ✧ **contrive** The bandits were *plotting* to rob a bank.

**plug** *noun* ✦ **stopper** ✧ **cork, block, cap, filling** Pull the *plug* to let water drain out of the sink. —*verb* ✦ **block, close, cover, fill, seal, stop, stuff, stopper** I tried to *plug* the leak in the pipe with a piece of bubble gum.

**Antonyms** plug

*verb* **clear, free, open, unblock**

**plump** *adjective* ✦ **fat, stout, well-fed, chubby** ✧ **beefy, bulky, fleshy, full, obese** My grandmother bought a nice *plump* turkey for our Thanksgiving dinner.

**plunder** *verb* ✦ **loot, pillage, raid, sack, ransack** ✧ **rob, steal** About 1,000 years ago, Vikings *plundered* Europe's coastal villages. —*noun* ✦ **booty, loot, pillage, spoils** ✧ **treasure, winnings, prize** The Vikings divided their *plunder* into equal shares.

**plunge** *verb* **1.** ✦ **dive, jump, leap** ✧ **dip, dunk, immerse, submerge** I ran down the path and *plunged* into the pond. **2.** ✦ **drop, fall, tumble, plummet** ✧ **descend, topple, pitch** The climber would have *plunged* fifty feet if his rope hadn't caught him. —*noun* ✦ **dip, dive, swim, dunk** ✧ **jump, leap, drop, fall** The man enjoys taking a *plunge* in his pool after work.

**pocket** *noun* ✦ **cavity, hole, hollow, chamber** ✧ **compartment, receptacle, pit** The miner found a *pocket* of gold deep in the mine. —*adjective* ✦ **compact, little, portable, small, concise** ✧ **miniature** My *pocket* dictionary has a lot of useful information in it.

**Word Groups**

A **poem** is a verbal composition designed to convey experiences, ideas, or emotions in a vivid and imaginative way. **Poem** is a general term with no true synonyms. Here are some different kinds of poems to investigate in a dictionary: **ballad, couplet, epic, free verse, haiku, limerick, lyric poem, prose poem, sonnet**

**point** *noun* **1.** ✦ **end, tip** ✧ **head, peak, prong, spike, top** Your pencil will write better if you sharpen its *point.* **2.** ✦ **cape, headland, promontory** ✧ **peninsula** A lighthouse sits out on the end of this *point.* **3.** ✦ **locality, location, place, area, site, spot, position** There are many *points* of interest in Yellowstone National Park. **4.** ✦ **time, instant, moment, juncture, stage** ✧ **period, phase** At this *point* in the voting, it's impossible to know yet who will win. **5.** ✦ **item, matter, particular, subject, topic, detail** The mayor's speech covered many important *points.* **6.** ✦ **purpose, reason, idea, value** ✧ **aim, end, objective** There isn't much *point* in watering the lawn on a rainy day. —*verb* **1.** ✦ **aim, direct** ✧ **turn, level, head** You have to *point* the remote control straight at the television or it won't work. **2.** ✦ **indicate, show, designate** ✧ **mention, name** The tour guide *pointed* out many interesting sights.

**poise** *verb* ✦ **balance, perch** ✧ **hang, hover, suspend** The girl *poised* for a moment on the edge of the diving board before she jumped. —*noun* ✦ **assurance, composure, confidence, self-control** ✧ **balance** It's not easy to maintain your *poise* while speaking in front of a large group.

**poisonous** *adjective* ✦ **toxic, dangerous** ✧ **deadly, fatal, lethal, venomous** Most insecticides are *poisonous* to humans.

**poke** *verb* **1.** ✦ **jab, nudge, prod, stab, stick** ✧ **dig, hit** My friend *poked* me in the ribs to get my attention. **2.** ✦ **stick, thrust** ✧ **push, shove, raise** The gopher *poked* its head cautiously out of its hole.

**police** *noun* ✦ **police officers, peace officers, officers** ✧ **patrolmen, patrolwomen, policemen, policewomen** The *police* are looking for the hit-and-run driver who caused last night's accident. —*verb* ✦ **patrol, defend, guard, protect, watch, control** The mayor promised to add extra officers to *police* the crime-ridden streets.

**policy** *noun* ✦ **guidelines, procedure, rules** ✧ **code, custom, practice** According to school *policy,* students may not smoke on campus.

**polish** *verb* **1.** ✦ **buff, shine, burnish** ✧ **brighten, clean, rub, wax** My grandmother always *polishes* her silverware before she hosts big family dinners. **2.** ✦ **improve, perfect, refine, touch up** ✧ **enhance, smooth, finish** The president's aides spent several weeks *polishing* his State of the Union address. —*noun* **1.** ✦ **shine, gloss, glow, luster,**

**sheen** ◇ **glaze, sparkle** I buffed my shoes until they had a beautiful *polish*. **2.** ✦ **elegance, grace, refinement, style, class** The actor worked hard to give *polish* to his performance.

**polite** *adjective* ✦ **civil, considerate, courteous, respectful, well-mannered, gracious** A *polite* person treats everyone with respect.

**poll** *noun* ✦ **survey, sampling, census** ◇ **tally, vote** The latest *poll* shows that the senator is likely to be reelected. —*verb* ✦ **interview, question, survey, interrogate** ◇ **sample, examine** One hundred students were *polled* about their summer vacation plans.

**pollute** *verb* ✦ **contaminate, foul** ◇ **dirty, poison, soil, stain, tarnish** The exhaust from cars and trucks *pollutes* the air.

**ponder** *verb* ✦ **consider, contemplate, think about, deliberate, reflect** ◇ **study** Let's *ponder* the situation a while longer before we decide what to do.

**poor** *adjective* **1.** ✦ **destitute, impoverished, needy, penniless, poverty-stricken** ◇ **bankrupt** This shelter provides free meals for people who are too *poor* to buy their own food. **2.** ✦ **bad, deficient, inadequate, inferior, unsatisfactory** ◇ **worthless** You can't get a good crop out of *poor* soil. **3.** ✦ **pathetic, pitiful, unfortunate, unlucky, wretched, sad** That *poor* cat was abandoned by its owners.

**popular** *adjective* **1.** ✦ **widespread, general, public** ◇ **democratic, universal** Due to *popular* demand, the circus will stay in town for another week. **2.** ✦ **favored, favorite, preferred, well-liked** ◇ **leading** Soccer is a *popular* sport in most parts of the world.

**popularity** *noun* ✦ **celebrity, fame, renown, acceptance, acclaim, favor, support** That singer is currently enjoying great *popularity*.

**population** *noun* ✦ **citizenry, populace** ◇ **inhabitants, natives, people, residents** The little village where my father grew up has a *population* of only two hundred people.

**portable** *adjective* ✦ **movable, transportable, mobile** ◇ **compact, light, lightweight** Laptop computers are small enough to be easily *portable*.

**Antonyms portable**
*adjective* **firm, fixed, immovable, permanent, stationary, steadfast**

**portion** *noun* ✦ **part, percentage, fraction, share** ◇ **piece, section, segment** Andrea saves a *portion* of her weekly paycheck. —*verb* ✦ **deal out, dispense, distribute, divide, parcel out** ◇ **disperse** We *portioned out* the snacks so that everyone got an equal share.

**portray** *verb* **1.** ✦ **characterize, depict, describe, represent, show, render** ◇ **picture** History books often *portray* Thomas Jefferson as an effective and honest president. **2.** ✦ **act, perform, play** ◇ **impersonate** A young girl is going to *portray* an elderly woman in the school play.

**pose** *verb* **1.** ✦ **sit, model** ◇ **posture, stand** Once a year, we get dressed up and *pose* for a family portrait. **2.** ✦ **impersonate, masquerade (as), pass (for), pretend to be** ◇ **act, feign** The man was able to get into the sold-out concert by *posing as* a reporter. **3.** ✦ **propose, advance, present, raise, state, suggest** My friend *posed* a philosophical question that none of us could answer. —*noun* ✦ **position, posture, stance** ◇ **attitude, bearing** As the ballet ended, all of the dancers held their *poses* until the curtain came down.

**position** *noun* **1.** ✦ **place, spot, station, location, site** ◇ **area, orientation** The parade will start as soon as all of the floats are in their proper *positions*. **2.** ✦ **condition, situation, state** ◇ **circumstances, status** I'm not in a good *position* to ask my friend for a favor because she's still mad at me. **3.** ✦ **stand, view, stance, belief, conviction, feeling, opinion** The senator stated her *position* on the new tax bill. **4.** ✦ **post, appointment, office, job** ◇ **employment, duty** In 1933, Frances Perkins became the first woman to hold a cabinet *position* in the United States government.

**positive** *adjective* **1.** ✦ **favorable, good, optimistic** ◇ **constructive, helpful, useful** Our boss always has something *positive* to say about our work. **2.** ✦ **certain, confident, convinced, definite, sure** I'm *positive* that I have seen this movie before.

**possess** *verb* ✦ **have, hold, own, retain** ◇ **command, control** Our local library *possesses* more books than I can ever hope to read.

**possession** *noun* **1.** ✦ **ownership, custody, title** ◇ **control, hold, occupancy** We will be able to take *possession* of our new condominium any day now. **2.** ✦ **belonging** ◇ **asset, effect, property, resource** My most valuable *possession* is a quilt that my great-grandmother made.

**possibility** *noun* ✦ **chance, likelihood, probability, prospect** ◇ **odds** There's a good *possibility* that we'll get out of work early because tomorrow is a holiday.

**possible** *adjective* ✦ **conceivable, potential, workable, feasible** ◇ **likely, probable** There is more than one *possible* solution to this riddle.

**possibly** *adverb* ✦ **perhaps, conceivably, maybe, feasibly** ◇ **likely, probably** The doctor said the problem was *possibly* just a bad cold.

**post¹** *noun* ✦ **pole** ◇ **picket, pillar, prop, stake, column, rail** The fence *posts* were spaced ten feet apart. —*verb* ✦ **display, fasten, place, put, attach** ◇ **install, set** Next week's work schedule will be *posted* on the bulletin board.

**post²** *noun* 1. ✦ **base, camp, garrison, station** ◇ **fort, headquarters** The soldiers returned to their *post* after the maneuvers. 2. ✦ **appointment, assignment, office, position** ◇ **duty, job** My uncle just received an important *post* in the state government. —*verb* ✦ **station, place, position, situate** ◇ **assign, locate** Two guards were *posted* near the bank's entrance.

**post³** *verb* ✦ **inform, apprise, advise, brief, notify** ◇ **report, tell** I'm interested in hearing about how you're doing, so please keep me *posted*.

**postpone** *verb* ✦ **defer, delay, put off** ◇ **hold, stay, suspend** The weather forced us to *postpone* our picnic.

**potential** *adjective* ✦ **possible, likely, probable, promising** ◇ **conceivable** I had a *potential* buyer for my motorbike, but she changed her mind.

**pounce** *verb* ✦ **jump, leap, spring** ◇ **strike, ambush, attack** The cat *pounced* on the toy mouse.

**pound** *verb* ✦ **beat, hammer, hit, pummel, strike, batter** ◇ **punch, thrash, wallop** The impatient man *pounded* on the door with his fists.

**pour** *verb* ✦ **cascade, spill, flow, stream, run, rush** ◇ **gush, surge** After a heavy rain, water *poured* over the top of the dam.

**poverty** *noun* ✦ **destitution, neediness, pennilessness** ◇ **lack, need, want** The actor had to endure years of *poverty* before he started to get good roles.

**power** *noun* 1. ✦ **ability, capability, capacity, might, strength** ◇ **energy, force** The fictional Superman has the *power* to leap tall buildings and stop speeding bullets. 2. ✦ **authority, command, control** ◇ **dominion, mastery, rule** The election will decide which party will be in *power*. —*verb* ✦ **activate, operate, run, supply** ◇ **energize** The toy car is *powered* by batteries.

**powerful** *adjective* ✦ **effective, forceful, influential, compelling, strong, vigorous** ◇ **mighty, heavy** The speaker presented a *powerful* argument in favor of ending the war.

**Antonyms** **powerful**
*adjective* **feeble, frail, helpless, ineffectual, weak**

**practical** *adjective* ✦ **helpful, realistic, sensible, sound, useful, worthwhile** ◇ **efficient** Your suggestion to fix my glasses with a paperclip was quite *practical*.

**practice** *verb* 1. ✦ **drill, rehearse, train, prepare** ◇ **exercise, study, discipline** The marching band is *practicing* for next Saturday's performance. 2. ✦ **apply, employ, perform, use** ◇ **do, follow, observe** *Practicing* good oral hygiene helps to prevent tooth decay. —*noun* 1. ✦ **rehearsal, training, preparation, drill** ◇ **exercise, study, discipline** It takes a lot of *practice* to become a good violinist. 2. ✦ **custom, habit, routine** ◇ **way, tradition, rule, policy** It is my *practice* to have dinner at 6 p.m. every day. 3. ✦ **action, application, operation, use, execution** ◇ **performance** The company will soon put its new hiring procedures into *practice*.

**praise** *noun* ✦ **acclaim, commendation, compliments, recognition** ◇ **approval, kudos** The student received a lot of *praise* for her outstanding science project. —*verb* ✦ **commend, compliment, congratulate, acclaim** ◇ **honor, approve** The conductor *praised* the orchestra for having played so well.

**pray** *verb* ✦ **appeal, beg, implore, plead** ◇ **desire, hope, long, want, wish, yearn** The farmer *prayed* for rain.

**precaution** *noun* ✦ **safeguard, safety measure, care, caution, prevention** If you take a few simple *precautions*, rock climbing can be quite safe.

**precede** *verb* ✦ **come before, go before, usher in** ◇ **lead, introduce, preface** High winds and dark clouds *preceded* the thunderstorm.

**precious** *adjective* ✦ **costly, expensive, valuable** ◇ **invaluable, priceless, rare, dear** Diamonds and emeralds are *precious* stones.

**precise** *adjective* ✦ **exact, specific, literal** ◇ **accurate, correct, definite, true** What were her *precise* words?

**precision** *noun* ✦ accuracy, correctness, exactness, preciseness ◇ attention, care, carefulness Computers perform calculations with great speed and *precision.*

**predicament** *noun* ✦ fix, jam, mess, crisis ◇ difficulty, trouble, problem, mess The man was in a *predicament* when he locked his keys in his car.

**predict** *verb* ✦ forecast, foresee, foretell, prophesy, divine, see, tell ◇ project The fortuneteller at the carnival claimed to be able to *predict* the future in a crystal ball.

**preface** *noun* ✦ foreword, introduction, prologue ◇ beginning, overture, prelude The book's *preface* included a discussion of the author's background.

**prefer** *verb* ✦ like, favor, fancy, choose, elect, pick, select Which would you *prefer*, frozen yogurt or ice cream?

**preference** *noun* ✦ choice, desire, pick, option, selection ◇ fancy, liking, favorite My *preference* is to go to a movie rather than stay home and watch television.

**prejudice** *noun* ✦ bias, one-sidedness, partiality ◇ intolerance, unfairness, bigotry Judges must be without *prejudice* if they are to render fair verdicts. —*verb* ✦ bias, predispose ◇ influence, sway, turn against Don't be *prejudiced* against the movie just because you don't like one of the actors.

**preliminary** *adjective* ✦ beginning, introductory, opening, preparatory, starting, initial The speaker made a few *preliminary* remarks before addressing his main topic.

**premature** *adjective* ✦ early, untimely, beforehand, hasty ◇ impulsive, rash The swimmer was disqualified for making a *premature* start.

**prepare** *verb* ✦ fix, make, get ready ◇ arrange, form, organize My roommate often helps me *prepare* dinner.

**presence** *noun* 1. ✦ appearance, existence, occurrence ◇ attendance, being, development The *presence* of smoke usually means that there is a fire. 2. ✦ company, vicinity, proximity ◇ midst, nearness, neighborhood There are some things that the girl's parents wouldn't discuss in her *presence.*

**present¹** *adjective* 1. ✦ current, existing, present-day, contemporary ◇ immediate, latest, recent My friend wants to quit her *present* job and try to find a better one. 2. ✦ at hand, attending, here ◇ near, nearby, there The meeting will start as soon as everyone is *present.*

**present²** *verb* 1. ✦ award, confer, give, bestow ◇ donate, grant, offer The football coach will *present* the trophy for Best Athlete. 2. ✦ introduce, make known ◇ acquaint A visiting nobleman was *presented* to the queen. 3. ✦ furnish, produce, show, display, exhibit, provide ◇ perform The lawyer *presented* evidence that proved the innocence of his client. —*noun* ✦ gift ◇ donation, favor, grant, offering, presentation I got this shirt as a birthday *present.*

**preserve** *verb* ✦ save, conserve, maintain, protect, defend, guard, safeguard Everyone should help to *preserve* our natural resources. —*noun* 1. ◇ spread, jam, jelly, marmalade I like to put strawberry *preserves* on my toast. 2. ✦ refuge, reservation, reserve, sanctuary ◇ park, haven I'm taking a field trip to a wildlife *preserve.*

**press** *verb* 1. ✦ depress, push ◇ shove, compress, crush, squeeze *Press* this button to start the elevator. 2. ✦ iron ◇ smooth, steam, flatten Now that I live on my own, I have to *press* my own shirts and pants. 3. ✦ entreat, urge, implore, beg ◇ plead, demand, insist My friend *pressed* me to stay for dinner.

**pressure** *noun* 1. ✦ weight, burden, strain ◇ compression, force, power, strength The shelf sagged under the *pressure* of the heavy books. 2. ✦ strain, stress, duress ◇ anxiety, distress, tension The author is under a lot of *pressure* to get her book finished on time.

**prestige** *noun* ✦ distinction, importance, influence, status ◇ honor, reputation The president occupies a position of great *prestige* in the United States government.

**presume** *verb* ✦ assume, suppose, surmise, think, believe ◇ guess, imagine I stopped by my friend's house because I *presumed* that he would be home.

**pretend** *verb* 1. ✦ fake, feign, simulate, pose ◇ act, claim I *pretended* to be asleep so that my little brother wouldn't bother me. 2. ✦ make believe, play-act, fantasize, imagine ◇ act, masquerade The children sometimes *pretend* that they are grown-ups.

**pretty** *adjective* ✦ attractive, beautiful, lovely ◇ cute, good-looking, handsome, fair, sweet The little girl looks *pretty* in her new holiday dress.

—*adverb* ✦ fairly, quite, rather, somewhat, very ✧ reasonably It's *pretty* cold out for a spring day.

**prevent** *verb* ✦ avert, forestall, head off, halt, stop ✧ avoid, hinder, obstruct Making sure your campfire is completely out is a good way to help *prevent* forest fires.

**previous** *adjective* ✦ prior, past, earlier, former, preceding ✧ advance Only people with *previous* experience should apply for this job.

**prey** *noun* ✦ quarry, catch, game, kill ✧ target, victim The tiger pounced on its *prey*. —*verb* ✦ eat, feed (on), live (on), hunt, pursue ✧ attack, seize Spiders *prey on* flies and other small insects.

**price** *noun* ✦ cost, charge (for), expense ✧ amount, value, worth The *price* of admission at the local movie theater just went up. —*verb* ✦ appraise, assess, estimate, evaluate, value, rate The merchant *priced* the diamond necklace at three thousand dollars.

**priceless** *adjective* ✦ invaluable, precious, valuable ✧ costly, expensive, dear The museum has several works of art that are rare and *priceless*.

**pride** *noun* 1. ✦ self-esteem, self-respect, ego ✧ dignity, honor The author's *pride* was hurt after failing to win the writing contest. 2. ✦ fulfillment, satisfaction, gratification ✧ delight, enjoyment, pleasure My roommate takes great *pride* in his ability to fix things around the house. 3. ✦ arrogance, conceit, self-importance, vanity, egotism ✧ insolence The man didn't apologize for making a mistake because he had too much *pride*.

**primary** *adjective* 1. ✦ beginning, first, initial, earliest, original, elementary The project is still in its *primary* stage of development. 2. ✦ chief, foremost, leading, main, prime, principal, top My *primary* interests are reading books, listening to music, and playing soccer.

**primitive** *adjective* ✦ crude, rough, simple ✧ ancient, early, prehistoric, basic, raw Archaeologists have found *primitive* stone tools in Kenya that are 3.3 million years old.

**principal** *adjective* ✦ foremost, leading, main, major, primary, top, key, dominant The state of Idaho's *principal* crop is potatoes. —*noun* ✧ administrator, director, head, leader, chief, ruler The *principal* of the local high school was once a teacher herself.

**principle** *noun* 1. ✦ assumption, doctrine, fundamental, rule, standard, axiom ✧ law The United States is founded on the *principle* that all people are created equal. 2. ✦ character, honesty, integrity, morality, virtue ✧ honor A person of high *principle* is not likely to lie, steal, or cheat.

**print** *verb* 1. ✦ imprint ✧ stamp, impress, engrave, letter, mark My friend had her name and address *printed* on her new stationery. 2. ✦ issue, publish, release, bring out ✧ reissue, reprint The publisher *printed* ten thousand copies of the new cookbook. —*noun* 1. ✦ impression, imprint, mark ✧ indentation, stamp My dog left a paw *print* in the wet cement. 2. ✦ printing, letters, type, text ✧ typeface, writing My grandfather prefers to read books that have large *print*. 3. ✦ reproduction, illustration ✧ engraving, etching, photograph These *prints* have been signed and numbered by the artist.

**prior** *adjective* ✦ past, previous, earlier, former, preceding, beforehand The beginner's class is for people who have no *prior* experience doing yoga.

**prison** *noun* ✦ penitentiary, jail ✧ pen, brig, cell, dungeon, stockade The thief was caught and sent to *prison*.

**private** *adjective* 1. ✦ individual, personal ✧ exclusive, reserved, restricted I like to have *private* time to write in my journal every day. 2. ✦ secret, clandestine, confidential ✧ hidden, concealed, classified The two children have a *private* meeting place that no one else knows about.

**privilege** *noun* ✦ benefit, right, advantage ✧ freedom, liberty, allowance The company's top executives enjoy certain *privileges* that are not available to other employees.

**prize** *noun* ✦ award, premium, reward, winnings ✧ recognition, trophy The *prize* for first place was a scholarship for five thousand dollars. —*adjective* ✦ champion, winning, acclaimed ✧ cherished, top, valued The rancher's *prize* bull won a blue ribbon at the county fair. —*verb* ✦ cherish, treasure, value, esteem ✧ admire, appreciate, like The man has one coin in his collection that he *prizes* more than all the others.

**probable** *adjective* ✦ likely, presumed, presumable

✧ **apparent, possible, reasonable** Investigators are trying to determine the fire's *probable* cause.

**probe** *noun* ✦ **inquiry, investigation** ✧ **examination, exploration, research** The police *probe* revealed that several people were involved in the crime. —*verb* ✦ **examine, inspect, investigate, search** ✧ **explore, study** The dentist *probed* inside my mouth to see if I had any problems with my teeth.

**problem** *noun* 1. ✦ **question** ✧ **mystery, puzzle, riddle, topic** I helped my little brother solve the difficult math *problem*. 2. ✦ **complication, difficulty, trouble, fault, flaw** ✧ **issue, predicament** It took the company a few days to work all of the *problems* out of its new computer system.

**procedure** *noun* ✦ **method, process, technique, way** ✧ **course, policy, system** Luckily we have a booklet that explains the *procedure* for programming our GPS.

**proceed** *verb* ✦ **advance, continue, go on, move on, progress** ✧ **start** When drivers encounter a flashing red light, they must come to a full stop before *proceeding*.

**process** *noun* ✦ **method, procedure, system, technique, way** ✧ **operation, routine, formula** In 1856, Henry Bessemer developed a new *process* for making steel from cast iron. —*verb* ✦ **deal (with), handle, treat** ✧ **prepare, ready, alter** The college admissions office *processes* thousands of applications every year.

**proclaim** *verb* ✦ **announce, declare, state** ✧ **call, claim, profess, reveal** The governor *proclaimed* a state of emergency in response to the hurricane.

**procure** *verb* ✦ **acquire, gain, get, obtain, secure** ✧ **buy, win** The coin collector finally managed to *procure* the rare silver dollar that he had long desired.

**Antonyms** procure
*verb* drop, forfeit, give up, lose, sell

**prod** *verb* 1. ✦ **jab, nudge, poke, shove, push** ✧ **dig, thrust** When the mule refused to budge, its owner *prodded* it with a stick. 2. ✦ **prompt, urge, encourage, motivate, stimulate, spur, inspire, goad, incite** ✧ **nag** Environmentalists are *prodding* energy companies to be more efficient.

**produce** *verb* 1. ✦ **furnish, give, provide, supply, yield, generate** ✧ **bear** This well *produces* more than one hundred barrels of oil every day. 2. ✦ **assemble, make, manufacture** ✧ **build, construct,**

**create** My friend works at a factory that *produces* microwave ovens. 3. ✦ **bring forward, bring out** ✧ **display, exhibit, present, show** The magician reached into his hat and *produced* a rabbit.

**product** *noun* 1. ✦ **commodity, goods, merchandise, ware, article, item** This store carries televisions, stereos, and other electronic *products*. 2. ✦ **outcome, result, effect, consequence, issue** The businessman's success is a *product* of his hard work.

**production** *noun* 1. ✦ **manufacture, making, construction, fabrication, building, assembly** Henry Ford introduced mass *production* of automobiles with the development of the assembly line in 1908. 2. ✦ **drama, play, show, performance, presentation** ✧ **film, motion picture, movie** The playwright's latest *production* will open on Broadway next year.

**profess** *verb* ✦ **affirm, announce, declare, proclaim, state, assert** ✧ **confirm** The engaged couple *professed* their love for each other.

**profession** *noun* 1. ✦ **career, field, occupation, vocation, calling** ✧ **business, job, work** Medicine and law are *professions* that require years of specialized education. 2. ✦ **assertion, affirmation, declaration, statement, announcement, pledge** The jury did not believe the defendant's *profession* of innocence.

**profile** *noun* ✦ **side view** ✧ **portrait, likeness, silhouette, contour, outline** A *profile* of Abraham Lincoln appears on US pennies.

**profit** *noun* 1. ✦ **advantage, benefit, use, value** ✧ **good, improvement, blessing** The time non-native speakers spend studying English will be of *profit* to them in the future. 2. ✦ **earnings, gains, returns** ✧ **income, revenue, money, pay** *Profits* for smartphone makers are expected to grow this year. —*verb* ✦ **benefit, gain, capitalize** ✧ **advance, earn, help, improve** A lot of companies will *profit* from the plan to lower corporate taxes.

**profound** *adjective* 1. ✦ **thoughtful, wise, deep** ✧ **intellectual, intelligent, knowledgeable** The historian's book presented some *profound* insights into the effects of war. 2. ✦ **deep, intense, extreme, great, strong, thorough, total** I have *profound* admiration for people who risk their lives to rescue others from danger.

**program** *noun* 1. ✦ **show, broadcast, performance, production, series, presentation** My favorite television *program* airs at 7:00 tonight. **2.** ✦ project, procedure, plan, policy ✧ arrangement, list, schedule The company has a *program* to help employees with their child-care needs.

**progress** *noun* ✦ improvement, headway, advancement ✧ development, growth Learning to play a French horn is difficult, but I'm making good *progress*. —*verb* ✦ advance, go forward, proceed, move ✧ develop, grow, improve Work on the new gymnasium is *progressing* at a steady pace.

**prohibit** *verb* ✦ ban, disallow, forbid, outlaw ✧ restrict, stop, prevent Parking is *prohibited* on this street.

**project** *noun* ✦ enterprise, task, undertaking, venture ✧ plan, scheme, design My latest *project* is to build an outdoor barbecue. —*verb* ✦ extend, jut, protrude, stick out ✧ bulge, overhang The rocky promontory *projected* several hundred feet into the water.

**prolong** *verb* ✦ draw out, extend, lengthen, protract, stretch out, continue We decided to *prolong* our visit for two more days.

**Antonyms** **prolong**
*verb* abbreviate, abridge, crop, cut, lop, shorten

**prominent** *adjective* **1.** ✦ conspicuous, noticeable, obvious, visible, evident The two skyscrapers are the most *prominent* buildings in the whole city. **2.** ✦ distinguished, eminent, important, notable, outstanding ✧ famous, great The mayor invited several *prominent* citizens to lunch to discuss the city's future.

**promise** *noun* **1.** ✦ pledge, vow, word, oath ✧ assurance, commitment People trust Vani because she always keeps her *promises*. **2.** ✦ possibility, prospect, potential, hope ✧ ability, capacity, talent The rookie baseball player showed a lot of *promise*. —*verb* ✦ pledge, swear, vow ✧ agree, assure, guarantee, vouch You may borrow my laptop if you *promise* to return it tomorrow.

**promote** *verb* **1.** ✦ encourage, foster, further, support, aid, assist, boost Proper eating habits *promote* good health. **2.** ✦ advance, elevate, move up, raise, upgrade ✧ graduate The store *promoted* two sales clerks to management positions.

**prompt** *adjective* ✦ quick, rapid, swift, timely ✧ immediate, instant, punctual Fast food restaurants always try to give *prompt* service to their customers. —*verb* ✦ cause, inspire, motivate, prod, stimulate, spur ✧ arouse My curiosity *prompted* me to skip to the last page of the book.

**prone** *adjective* **1.** ✦ face down, flat, horizontal ✧ prostrate, reclining Everyone lay in a *prone* position, waiting for the coach's command to start doing pushups. **2.** ✦ apt, given, inclined, liable, likely, disposed ✧ subject People sometimes tell me that I'm *prone* to talk too much.

**pronounce** *verb* **1.** ✦ articulate, enunciate, utter, vocalize, say ✧ express, speak Vietnamese is a tonal language that has many words foreigners find difficult to *pronounce*. **2.** ✦ announce, declare, decree, proclaim, state, rule The jury's foreperson *pronounced* a verdict of "not guilty."

**pronounced** *adjective* ✦ distinct, evident, noticeable, obvious, strong ✧ clear, plain The tourist spoke English with a *pronounced* accent.

**proof** *noun* ✦ evidence, verification, authentication, certification, documentation I had to show *proof* of my citizenship to get a passport.

**propel** *verb* ✦ drive, move, run, operate ✧ launch, push, start, thrust This toy airplane is *propelled* by a rubber band.

**proper** *adjective* ✦ appropriate, correct, right, suitable, fitting ✧ apt, useful If you wear the *proper* clothing, you can stay warm and dry on stormy days.

**property** *noun* **1.** ✦ assets, belongings, effects, goods, possessions, things, stuff My personal *property* includes all of my clothes, books, sports equipment, and smartphone. **2.** ✦ land, real estate ✧ acreage, estate, plot, tract My grandparents bought *property* out in the country. **3.** ✦ attribute, characteristic, feature, quality, trait, ingredient ✧ element, part Heat and light are *properties* of fire.

**prophecy** *noun* ✦ prediction, foretelling, divination ✧ forecast, vision, warning The wizard made a *prophecy* that the king's reign would be long and prosperous.

**prophesy** *verb* ✦ foresee, foretell, predict ✧ forecast, warn A fortuneteller *prophesied* that I will someday be a famous writer.

**proportion** *noun* **1.** ✦ ratio, measure, distribution ✧ amount, degree, extent, size The *proportion* of milk to ice cream in a milk shake is usually about two to one. **2.** ✦ balance, perspective, symmetry, relation ✧ harmony, agreement In the funhouse mirror, my features appeared to be out of *proportion*.

**proposal** *noun* 1. ✦ offer, proposition, invitation, suggestion, request ◇ appeal I'm thinking about my friend's *proposal* to travel through Europe together. 2. ✦ idea, plan, recommendation, scheme ◇ program, project The city council is studying the mayor's *proposal* to hire more police officers.

**propose** *verb* 1. ✦ present, offer, submit, suggest, introduce, recommend I *proposed* the idea that we save time and effort by just ordering pizzas for our office party. 2. ✦ aim, expect, intend, mean, plan ◇ contemplate My brother *proposes* to go to college after he graduates from high school.

**prospect** *noun* ✦ chance, expectation, hope, possibility, likelihood ◇ anticipation, outlook Sumin is excited by the *prospect* of studying abroad. —*verb* ✦ explore, look, probe, search, seek, survey In 1849, thousands of people journeyed to California to *prospect* for gold.

**prosper** *verb* ✦ boom, flourish, thrive ◇ gain, increase, succeed The town *prospered* when an automobile factory was built nearby.

**Antonyms** prosper
*verb* decline, dwindle, fade, fail, weaken

**prosperity** *noun* ✦ affluence, comfort, ease, wealth ◇ fortune, riches, success The author lived in *prosperity* after her book became an international bestseller.

**protect** *verb* ✦ defend, guard, safeguard, shield ◇ preserve, save A mother bear can be very dangerous when *protecting* its cubs.

**protection** *noun* ✦ safety, security, safekeeping, defense, refuge, shelter, cover When the little girl gets scared, she runs to her mother for *protection*.

**protest** *noun* ✦ challenge, objection, complaint, resistance ◇ demonstration, disagreement, opposition *Protests* have been made by people who are opposed to the new nuclear power plant. —*verb* ✦ argue (against), challenge, object (to), oppose ◇ complain, demonstrate The coach loudly *protested* the umpire's decision.

**proud** *adjective* 1. ✦ pleased (with), satisfied (with) ◇ delighted, glad, happy I'm *proud* of my mother for returning to college after I left home. 2. ✦ arrogant, conceited, haughty, self-important, vain,

smug The *proud* nobleman refused to socialize with common people.

**prove** *verb* ✦ certify, confirm, establish, show, verify, validate, demonstrate My birth certificate *proves* that I'm an American citizen.

**proverb** *noun* ✦ adage, saying, motto ◇ maxim, moral, rule "The early bird gets the worm" is a *proverb* that late sleepers may not appreciate.

**provide** *verb* ✦ furnish, supply, contribute ◇ bring, deliver, give, produce I am *providing* the dessert for my church's potluck dinner.

**provoke** *verb* 1. ✦ instigate, cause, incite, set off, start, produce ◇ arouse, prompt That bully is always trying to *provoke* a fight. 2. ✦ aggravate, anger, annoy, bother, disturb, irritate, vex Our dog is usually gentle, but he growls at people who *provoke* him.

**prowl** *verb* ✦ slink, creep, sneak, stalk, lurk, steal ◇ roam We saw a raccoon *prowling* around our garbage can.

**prudent** *adjective* ✦ careful, cautious, sensible, thoughtful, wary, wise *Prudent* pilots always check their airplanes before takeoff.

**Antonyms** prudent
*adjective* foolhardy, hasty, impulsive, madcap, rash

**pry¹** *verb* ✦ lever, lift, raise, force ◇ break, move, work I used a screwdriver to *pry* the lid off the paint can.

**pry²** *verb* ✦ meddle, intrude, nose, snoop, interfere ◇ investigate, poke My friend said she didn't want to talk about why she was upset, so I decided not to *pry*.

**public** *adjective* ✦ civic, civil, communal, community ◇ common, general I believe that we have a *public* duty not to litter. —*noun* ✦ citizens, citizenry, community, populace, people ◇ everyone The university museum is open to the *public* on weekends only.

**publish** *verb* ✦ bring out, issue, put out, release ◇ print I can't wait for my favorite author to *publish* another book.

**pull** *verb* 1. ✦ tow, haul, drag, draw ◇ lug, tug My friend's pickup truck can *pull* a horse trailer. 2. ✦ draw out, extract, remove, take out ◇ pluck, yank The dentist said that she would have to *pull* my bad tooth. **3.** ✦ **rip, shred, tear, rend** ✧ **break, divide, separate** The puppy *pulled* my old sock to pieces. —*noun* ✦ **jerk, tug, wrench, yank** ✧ **drag, draw** The fisherman hooked a fish by giving the line a quick *pull*.

**pulse** *noun* ✦ **beat, throb** ✧ **rhythm, stroke, vibration, drumbeat** Many people in the audience were tapping their feet in sync with the music's *pulse*.

**punch** *verb* ✦ **hit, jab, knock, strike, box** ✧ **poke, smack, wallop** The boxer tried to *punch* his opponent in the jaw. —*noun* ✦ **blow, hit, jab** ✧ **poke, smack, wallop, thrust** The *punch* missed because the other boxer ducked.

**punctual** *adjective* ✦ **on time, prompt, timely** ✧ **early, dependable, reliable** The nurse urged me to be *punctual* for my appointment with the doctor.

**puncture** *verb* ✦ **penetrate, perforate, pierce, prick** ✧ **cut, stick** A piece of glass *punctured* my bicycle tire. —*noun* ✦ **hole, perforation, prick** ✧ **break, cut, opening, leak** Fortunately I had a repair kit, and I was able to patch the *puncture* in my bike tire.

**punish** *verb* ✦ **discipline, penalize, admonish** ✧ **correct, sentence** The little boy avoids doing anything that his parents will *punish* him for.

**punishment** *noun* ✦ **discipline, penalty, correction** ✧ **consequence, payment, sentence** The usual *punishment* for misbehaving in class is detention after school.

**pupil** *noun* ✦ **student** ✧ **learner, schoolchild, schoolboy, schoolgirl, scholar** In the United States, the average elementary class size is 21 *pupils*.

### Word Groups

A **puppet** is a toy that looks like a person or animal and is designed to be moved around. **Puppet** is a general term with no true synonyms. Here are some different kinds of puppets to investigate in a dictionary: **doll, dummy, figurine, mannequin, marionette**

**purchase** *verb* ✦ **buy, pay for** ✧ **acquire, get, obtain, procure** Binh is saving his money until he has enough to *purchase* a new motorbike. —*noun* ✦ **acquisition, buy** ✧ **asset, possession, property** Though I could have afforded more, I made only one *purchase* at the music store.

**pure** *adjective* **1.** ✦ **genuine, real, undiluted, un-** mixed ✧ **plain, simple, straight** Choi's new necklace is made of *pure* gold. **2.** ✦ **absolute, complete, sheer, thorough, total, utter, perfect** My grandfather thinks that the whole idea of UFO abductions is *pure* nonsense.

**purify** *verb* ✦ **clean, cleanse, decontaminate, filter** ✧ **sterilize** The city has a filtration plant to *purify* the water supply.

**purpose** *noun* ✦ **aim, intent, intention, objective, point, goal** ✧ **design, end** The *purpose* of my visit is to ask you a favor.

**pursue** *verb* **1.** ✦ **chase, go (after), run (after), follow** ✧ **hunt, track, trail** A police officer *pursued* the thief on foot. **2.** ✦ **strive (for), work (for)** ✧ **undertake, lead, live** My sister is *pursuing* her dream of becoming a veterinarian.

**pursuit** *noun* **1.** ✦ **chase** ✧ **following, hunt, quest, search** A rabbit dashed across the yard with two dogs in *pursuit*. **2.** ✦ **activity, hobby, pastime, recreation** ✧ **job, occupation, vocation** Reading is my favorite leisure *pursuit*.

**push** *verb* **1.** ✦ **depress, press** ✧ **move, nudge, shove, thrust, force** *Push* this button to turn on the camcorder. **2.** ✦ **encourage, pressure, prod, prompt, urge** ✧ **coerce, motivate** The mayor is *pushing* the city council to adopt new parking regulations. —*noun* **1.** ✦ **shove** ✧ **jolt, nudge, poke, pressure, thrust** The door won't open unless you give it a hard *push*. **2.** ✦ **endeavor, effort, attempt, drive** ✧ **ambition, energy, enterprise** The candidate who was behind made a last-minute *push* to attract support.

**put** *verb* **1.** ✦ **place, set** ✧ **deposit, lay, position, situate, settle** Please *put* the dishes back in the cupboard as soon as I have dried them. **2.** ✦ **set, assign** ✧ **cause, commit, make, require** My roommate *put* me to work cleaning up the mess I made in the kitchen. **3.** ✦ **express, formulate, phrase** ✧ **say, state, word, articulate** Sometimes I have trouble *putting* my thoughts into words.

**puzzle** *noun* ✦ **mystery, riddle** ✧ **problem, question, enigma** It's still a *puzzle* why the dinosaurs died out so suddenly. —*verb* ✦ **baffle, bewilder, confuse, mystify, perplex** The man's unusual symptoms *puzzled* his doctor.

**quaint** *adjective* ✦ old-fashioned, picturesque ✧ charming, cute, enchanting The *quaint* cottage had stone walls and a slate roof.

**quake** *verb* ✦ shiver, tremble, quiver, shake, shudder, convulse ✧ quaver, vibrate The rabbit was so terrified that its whole body began to *quake*.

**qualification** *noun* 1. ✦ requirement, prerequisite, condition, provision ✧ skill, talent One of the main *qualifications* for this job is that applicants must have a driver's license. 2. ✦ exception, limitation, reservation, restriction, doubt I can say without *qualification* that Ariel is the funniest person I've ever met.

**qualify** *verb* 1. ✦ authorize, entitle ✧ permit, enable, fit, prepare, suit A teaching certificate *qualifies* a person to be a teacher. 2. ✦ limit, restrict, moderate, soften ✧ change, modify My friend *qualified* her criticism by saying my idea did have some good points.

**quality** *noun* 1. ✦ attribute, characteristic, feature, property, trait The candidate has many of the *qualities* necessary to make a good mayor. 2. ✦ merit, value, worth, caliber ✧ excellence, status This advertisement claims that the new discount store offers goods of high *quality* for low prices.

**quantity** *noun* ✦ amount, measure, volume ✧ portion, mass, number, total My family consumes a large *quantity* of milk every week.

**quarrel** *noun* ✦ argument, dispute, fight, squabble ✧ disagreement, altercation The roommates got into a *quarrel* over whose turn it was to wash the dishes. —*verb* ✦ argue, bicker, fight, squabble, dispute, clash The married couple sometimes *quarrels* about money.

**quarter** *noun* ✦ area, district, neighborhood, zone, locale ✧ region, part New Orleans is known for its picturesque French *Quarter*.

**quaver** *verb* ✦ quake, quiver, shake, tremble ✧ shudder, vibrate, waver My voice *quavered* with nervousness as I read my story to the writer's group.

**queen** *noun* ✦ monarch, sovereign, ruler ✧ majes-ty, empress Victoria was the *queen* of Great Britain from 1837 to 1901.

**quench** *verb* ✦ douse, extinguish, put out, smother ✧ kill, suppress The campers *quenched* their fire with a bucketful of water.

**query** *noun* ✦ inquiry, question ✧ concern, doubt, problem, reservation The bank manager will help all customers who have *queries* about their accounts. —*verb* ✦ ask, question, quiz ✧ examine, inquire, interrogate When two students were late getting to class, the teacher *queried* them about where they had been.

**question** *noun* 1. ✦ query ✧ inquiry The teacher asked if anybody had *questions* about the assignment. 2. ✦ issue, matter, subject, topic, point ✧ motion, problem The meeting dealt with the *question* of whether a new wing for the library was needed. 3. ✦ doubt, uncertainty, reservation ✧ confusion, controversy, suspicion Without any *question*, you are my best friend. —*verb* 1. ✦ examine, interrogate, query, quiz, interview ✧ ask, inquire The police *questioned* two witnesses to the robbery. 2. ✦ challenge, distrust, doubt, dispute, refute, suspect ✧ disbelieve I never *question* my coach's judgment.

**quick** *adjective* ✦ fast, hasty, rapid, speedy, swift ✧ prompt, brief, short I have to make a *quick* stop at the bakery on my way home tonight.

**quicken** *verb* ✦ accelerate, speed up, step up ✧ hasten, hurry, rush My pulse *quickened* when our team scored the run that tied the game.

**quiet** *adjective* 1. ✦ noiseless, silent, soundless ✧ hushed, still, mute Our new air conditioner is very *quiet*. 2. ✦ calm, peaceful, restful, serene, tranquil, undisturbed, still I'm looking forward to a *quiet* evening at home after my hectic day at work. —*noun* ✦ quietness, silence, stillness, hush ✧ calm, tranquility, serenity The hikers enjoyed the *quiet* that they found in the forest. —*verb* ✦ calm, settle ✧ shut up, silence, still, hush If we don't *quiet* down, we might wake the baby.

**quit** *verb* 1. ✦ cease, discontinue, give up, stop, finish ✧ end, halt, terminate I *quit* smoking one year ago today. **2. ✦ abandon, depart, leave, forsake ✧ desert, resign** Our neighbors decided to *quit* the city and move to the country.

**Antonyms** quit

*verb* **1. begin, commence, initiate, start 2. bide, remain, stay**

**quite** *adverb* **1. ✦ completely, entirely, fully, totally, wholly, perfectly ✧ thoroughly** These two puzzle pieces don't *quite* fit together. **2. ✦ extremely, really, very, considerably ✧ rather, somewhat** It's *quite* warm for a winter day.

**quiver** *verb* **✦ shiver, tremble, shake ✧ quake, quaver, vibrate, shudder** My dog *quivers* with excitement whenever she hears the word "walk."

**quiz** *noun* **✦ exam, examination, test ✧ inquiry** The teacher announced there would be a spelling *quiz* the next day. *—verb* **✦ ask, question, query, interrogate, examine ✧ check, test** My roommate spent the evening *quizzing* me about my new boyfriend.

**quota** *noun* **✦ limit, maximum, ration, allotment ✧ allowance, portion, share, part** There is a *quota* on the number of immigrants allowed into the country every year.

**quotation** *noun* **✦ quote, excerpt, passage, selection ✧ extract, reference** The online article about the author included numerous *quotations* from her novels and short stories.

**quote** *verb* **✦ cite ✧ refer (to), extract, mention, reference** The candidate *quoted* the Declaration of Independence in his campaign speech. *—noun* **✦ quotation, excerpt, passage, selection ✧ extract, reference** The newspaper article included a *quote* from the president's speech.

**race** *noun* ✦ competition, contest ✧ match, meet, relay, tournament A triathlon is an endurance *race* that typically includes swimming, running, and cycling. —*verb* ✦ dash, hurry, run, rush, scramble, scurry, speed, sprint, fly, bolt, dart Because my plane was late, I had to *race* to catch my connecting flight.

**rack** *noun* ✦ stand, frame, hanger ✧ holder, counter, shelf We have a *rack* near the front door for holding coats and jackets.

**racket** *noun* ✦ din, clamor, commotion, noise, uproar ✧ clatter The *racket* from the party could be heard a block away.

**radiant** *adjective* 1. ✦ bright, brilliant, gleaming, shining, sparkling, dazzling It was a *radiant* morning without a cloud in the sky. 2. ✦ beaming, blissful, happy, joyful, merry, glowing, ecstatic My parents look *radiant* in their wedding picture.

**radical** *adjective* ✦ extreme, fanatic, fanatical, zealous ✧ revolutionary, thorough, total The *radical* environmentalist chained himself to a tree to save it from being cut down. —*noun* ✦ extremist, fanatic, revolutionary, zealot ✧ rebel Early American patriots were considered *radicals* by those who supported the British monarchy.

**rag** *noun* ✦ piece of cloth, scrap of cloth, shred, tatter ✧ piece, remnant I used a flannel *rag* to clean my bicycle.

**rage** *noun* 1. ✦ frenzy, fury, tantrum, furor ✧ anger, wrath The toddler flew into a *rage* when she couldn't find her favorite toy. 2. ✦ craze, fad, fashion, style, trend ✧ passion Hula hoops were all the *rage* in the late 1950s. —*verb* ✦ rant, fume, rave, scream, yell, seethe, blow up An angry customer *raged* at the store manager about the bad service he'd gotten.

**ragged** *adjective* ✦ frayed, raggedy, tattered, worn, shabby ✧ ripped, torn The old blanket was *ragged* from much use.

**raid** *noun* ✦ assault, attack ✧ invasion, offensive, foray, strike The police prepared for the *raid* by putting on bulletproof vests. —*verb* ✦ assault, attack, invade, storm ✧ loot, pillage, plunder, ransack Viking warriors *raided* many European coastal towns in the Middle Ages.

**rain** *verb* ✦ pour, shower, sprinkle, drop ✧ heap, lavish The guests *rained* rose petals on the bride and groom.

**raise** *verb* 1. ✦ lift, lift up, elevate, hoist ✧ haul up, pull up, pick up If you have a question, *raise* your hand. ✦ improve, increase, boost, heighten ✧ advance, upgrade The student studied hard to *raise* her test scores. 3. ✦ bring up, rear, nurture ✧ breed, cultivate, grow My girlfriend was born and *raised* in China. 4. ✦ accumulate, collect, gather, get, obtain, acquire ✧ mass The local Girl Scout troop *raises* money by selling cookies.

### Word Groups

A **rake** is a tool with a long handle and teeth that is used for gardening or yardwork. **Rake** is a very specific term with no true synonyms. Here are some related words to investigate in a dictionary: **cultivator, hoe, scraper, shovel, spade, trowel**

**rally** *verb* 1. ✦ assemble, collect, gather, marshal, muster, convene The commander *rallied* his troops around him. 2. ✦ get better, improve, recover, revive, rebound ✧ perk up The patient *rallied* quickly after his fever broke. —*noun* ✦ assembly, gathering, get-together, meeting ✧ convention, muster There will be a pep *rally* before the big game.

**ramble** *verb* 1. ✦ amble, roam, saunter, stroll, wander ✧ trek, rove My friends and I like to *ramble* around the shopping mall. 2. ✦ babble, chatter, rattle ✧ speak, talk The old man *rambled* on about his days as a gold prospector. —*noun* ✦ saunter, stroll, walk ✧ hike, trek, jaunt I went for a *ramble* in the woods with my dog.

**random** *adjective* ✦ chance, arbitrary, haphazard, unorganized, unplanned ✧ accidental The books were in *random* order on the shelf.

**range** *noun* 1. ✦ array, assortment, selection, variety ✧ choice, field, collection Commercial pastels come in a wide *range* of colors. 2. ✦ scope, sphere, reach, stretch, limit, bounds, domain My friend feels that her new job is well within her *range* of ability. 3. ✦ grassland ✧ pasture, pastureland, plains, territory The cattle ranch contains over 1,100 acres of open *range*. 4. ✦ band, chain, line, row, series ✧ ridge, tier I can see a *range* of hills from my bedroom window.

**rank¹** *noun* ✦ grade, level, position, status, station ✧ class, degree During the American Civil War, George Armstrong Custer attained the *rank* of general when he was only twenty-three years old. —*verb* 1. ✦ come first, stand, place, rate, count ✧ judge A new smartphone *ranks* high on my wish list. 2. ✦ arrange, array, categorize, organize, classify ✧ align, marshal The teams were *ranked* according to their win-loss records.

**rank²** *adjective* ✦ bad, foul, offensive, pungent, rotten, putrid Skunks have a *rank* smell.

**rap** *verb* ✦ tap, knock, bang, hit, strike, thump, whack We were interrupted by someone *rapping* on the window.

**rapid** *adjective* ✦ fast, quick, speedy, swift ✧ brisk, fleet, hasty, prompt The jet made a *rapid* climb at takeoff.

**rapture** *noun* ✦ bliss, delight, happiness, joy, elation, enchantment The little girl was filled with *rapture* when she finally got to ride a pony.

**rare** *adjective* ✦ scarce, uncommon, unusual ✧ exceptional, infrequent, unique Diego's hobby is collecting *rare* coins.

**rarely** *adverb* ✦ infrequently, not often, seldom ✧ hardly, little, occasionally It *rarely* rains in the desert.

**rascal** *noun* ✦ mischief-maker, prankster, trickster, rogue ✧ scoundrel, villain In Native American myth, the coyote is usually an impish *rascal*.

**rash** *adjective* ✦ reckless, brash, hasty, impetuous, impulsive ✧ foolhardy, foolish, thoughtless It was *rash* of the student to raise his hand when he didn't know the answer.

**rate** *noun* 1. ✦ pace, speed, velocity, clip ✧ tempo, time The roller coaster was going at a breakneck *rate* when it went into the last turn. 2. ✦ charge, cost, price, fee ✧ amount What is the *rate* for a double room at this motel? —*verb* ✦ appraise, evaluate, grade, judge, rank ✧ gauge, assess The students were asked to *rate* their favorite TV shows for a class assignment.

**ratify** *verb* ✦ affirm, approve, authorize, sanction, adopt ✧ confirm, pass The ambassadors met to *ratify* the trade agreement.

**ratio** *noun* ✦ proportion, distribution, relation, share ✧ percentage The *ratio* of men to women on our office softball team is two to one.

**ration** *noun* ✦ allotment, allowance, quota, measure, provision ✧ portion, share The refugees were provided with a daily food *ration*. —*verb* ✦ allot, deal out, distribute, dispense, issue ✧ disperse The local utility company *rationed* water during the long drought.

**rational** *adjective* ✦ logical, prudent, reasonable, sensible, sound ✧ sane, wise When you have had a sore throat for many days, the *rational* thing to do is to see a doctor.

**rattle** *verb* 1. ✦ shake, jangle, jingle, clink ✧ clang, clank, clatter The earthquake *rattled* our windows. 2. ✦ chatter, jabber, babble, run on, gush My friend apologized for *rattling* on about his new job. 3. ✦ confuse, disturb, fluster, muddle, upset The near accident *rattled* the driver so much he missed his exit. —*noun* ✦ clatter, banging, clang, clanging, clank, racket When I heard the *rattle* of pots and pans, I knew my roommate must be fixing dinner.

**ravine** *noun* ✦ gorge, canyon, gulch, chasm ✧ gap, gully, valley I stood on the edge of the *ravine* to look at the stream below.

**raw** *adjective* 1. ✦ uncooked, unprepared ✧ fresh, natural Broccoli is more nutritious if eaten *raw*. 2. ✦ inexperienced, unskilled, untrained, green, unschooled, new The coach took the *raw* players and made them into a good team. 3. ✦ harsh, biting, bitter, chilly, cold, bleak, numbing, severe, wet The cold, *raw* weather made me glad to be inside by the fire.

**reach** *verb* 1. ✦ achieve, attain, accomplish, arrive (at), make, realize I *reached* my goal of reading ten books over the summer. 2. ✦ extend, stretch, go, run, span, continue ✧ spread Interstate 40 *reaches* across the entire United States. 3. ✦ contact, get hold (of), get (to), communicate (with), find Your friend tried to *reach* you to say that she would be late. —*noun* ✦ grasp, range, touch ✧ expanse, length, span, stretch The goat poked his head through the fence and ate all the grass within *reach*.

**react** *verb* ✦ respond ✧ act, answer, reply, count-

**er** Tanya *reacted* with a smile when she heard the good news.

**reaction** *noun* ✦ reflex, response, result ✧ answer, effect, reply The doctor tapped my knee to check for a *reaction*.

**ready** *adjective* ✦ prepared, set ✧ arranged, fixed, organized It's time to get *ready* for work. —*verb* ✦ prepare, equip, fix ✧ arrange, fit, outfit, organize We waited while the ground crew *readied* the plane for takeoff.

**real** *adjective* ✦ genuine, authentic, true, actual ✧ legitimate This necklace is made of *real* gold.

**reality** *noun* ✦ actuality, fact ✧ certainty, event, existence, truth My friend's dream of owning a house is about to become a *reality*.

**realize** *verb* 1. ✦ comprehend, grasp, perceive, recognize, understand I suddenly *realized* that the surprise party was for me. 2. ✦ fulfill, accomplish, achieve, attain, complete, gain, reach By taking a class, Joaquin *realized* his goal of learning to write computer programs.

**realm** *noun* ✦ kingdom, empire, country, domain, dominion ✧ territory, area The king traveled to all parts of his *realm*.

**reap** *verb* ✦ cut, mow, garner, glean, harvest ✧ gather, obtain, pick Before the invention of modern farm machinery, scythes were used to *reap* grain.

**rear**[1] *noun* ✦ back, end, rear end, tail, tail end ✧ stern My friend and I like to sit in the *rear* of a roller coaster car. —*adjective* ✦ back, rearmost ✧ last, hind, hindmost, aft My car's *rear* window sometimes gets fogged up.

**rear**[2] *verb* 1. ✦ bring up, care (for), raise, nurture ✧ foster, develop My grandmother *reared* three children on her own after my grandfather died. 2. ✦ raise, rise, lift ✧ elevate, loom, soar, tower The bear *reared* up on his hind legs when he smelled something strange.

**reason** *noun* 1. ✦ excuse, explanation, justification, basis, cause, motive I hope my boyfriend has a good *reason* for being late. 2. ✦ logic, rationality, reasoning ✧ comprehension, sense, wisdom, judgment Scientists are conducting experiments to see whether animals possess powers of *reason*. —*verb* 1. ✦ solve, figure out, calculate, deduce ✧ reckon, understand Juanita *reasoned out* the math problem without assistance. 2. ✦ debate, discuss,

get through (to), talk (to) ✧ argue, convince, persuade It is difficult to *reason with* someone who is angry.

**reasonable** *adjective* 1. ✦ logical, rational, sensible, practical ✧ intelligent, sane, wise The negotiator proposed a *reasonable* compromise. 2. ✦ moderate, acceptable, fair, just ✧ honest, suitable This store has good quality clothing at *reasonable* prices.

**rebel** *verb* ✦ revolt, rise up, strike ✧ challenge, defy, mutiny, resist The workers *rebelled* against the low pay and unsafe working conditions. —*noun* ✦ revolutionary, insurgent ✧ freedom fighter, mutineer, striker Guy Fawkes was an English *rebel* who tried to blow up Parliament in 1605.

**rebellion** *noun* ✦ revolt, revolution, insurgency ✧ mutiny, uprising The American Revolution was a *rebellion* against British control.

**recall** *verb* ✦ remember, think (of), recollect, summon ✧ retain, place I can't *recall* the name of that restaurant that I liked so much. —*noun* ✦ memory, recollection, remembrance, retention The elderly man improves his *recall* of names by writing them down.

**recede** *verb* ✦ ebb, go out, retreat, subside, withdraw ✧ diminish, dwindle, leave You can find lots of interesting creatures in the pools that are left behind when the tide *recedes*.

**receive** *verb* ✦ get, acquire, gain, obtain ✧ attain, accept, gather, procure My sister *received* her college diploma last spring.

**recent** *adjective* ✦ new, brand-new, current ✧ contemporary, fresh, modern I went to the bookstore to find a *recent* book by my favorite author.

**reception** *noun* 1. ✦ greeting, welcome ✧ acceptance, response, treatment, reaction I received a warm *reception* from everyone at the family reunion. 2. ✦ function, gathering, party ✧ affair, social, celebration A *reception* for the new club members will be held next Friday night.

**recess** *noun* ✦ break, intermission, interlude, rest ✧ halt, pause, stop The students have fifteen minutes for *recess* in the morning and again in the afternoon.

**recite** *verb* ✦ quote, narrate, repeat, speak ✧ deliver, report, tell My friend can *recite* her favorite poems from memory.

**reckless** ✦ careless, heedless, irresponsible, rash,

thoughtless, foolhardy *Reckless* driving is the cause of many accidents.

---

**Antonyms** reckless

*adjective* careful, cautious, deliberate, prudent, thoughtful

---

**recline** *verb* ✦ lie down, lounge, rest, stretch out, repose My grandfather fell asleep while *reclining* in his favorite lounge chair.

**recognize** *verb* 1. ✦ distinguish, identify, place, tell ✧ know, make out Yuri can *recognize* many species of birds by just their songs. 2. ✦ acknowledge, admit, accept ✧ endorse, support, sanction The scientist is *recognized* as a leading authority in her field.

**recollect** *verb* ✦ recall, remember, think (of), summon ✧ place, retain I know my friend gave me her phone number, but I can't *recollect* it right now.

**recommend** *verb* ✦ advise, advocate, counsel, endorse, promote, suggest ✧ back, urge My doctor *recommends* regular exercise.

**recommendation** *noun* ✦ advice, counsel, guidance, endorsement, suggestion ✧ proposal I am following all of my doctor's *recommendations*.

**record** *noun* 1. ✦ account, chronicle, log, register, journal ✧ diary, report The businessman keeps a daily *record* of all his expenses. 2. ✦ mark, performance, time ✧ achievement, deed The swimmer is hoping to beat his own *record* for this event. —*verb* ✦ chronicle, document, note, write down, post, list ✧ register The secretary *records* everything that happens at our club meetings.

**recover** *verb* 1. ✦ find, get back, reclaim, regain, retrieve ✧ salvage I was happy to *recover* the book that I thought was lost. 2. ✦ get better, improve, rally, revive ✧ heal, mend You certainly *recovered* quickly from your cold.

**recovery** *noun* ✦ recuperation ✧ convalescence, healing, improvement We were pleased to hear that my uncle made a full *recovery* from his illness.

**recreation** *noun* ✦ leisure pursuit, sport, pastime, amusement, entertainment, fun, play ✧ hobby Mountain biking is my favorite form of *recreation*.

**recruit** *verb* ✦ draft, enlist, round up, enroll, muster ✧ induct, obtain Our church is *recruiting* people to help with the craft fair.

**reduce** *verb* ✦ decrease, diminish, lessen, restrict, cut, curtail The doctor advises her overweight patients to *reduce* the amount of calories they consume.

**reel** *verb* ✦ lurch, roll, spin, stagger, sway, weave, wobble, totter I was *reeling* when I got off the carnival ride.

**refer** *verb* 1. ✦ direct, send, recommend, transfer, turn over ✧ introduce, pass The doctor *referred* her patient to a specialist. 2. ✦ consult, look (at), turn (to), use ✧ go, resort Students are not allowed to *refer to* the glossary in the back of the book while they take the test. 3. ✦ allude (to), speak (of), bring up, cite, mention, point out, touch (on) My art teacher *referred to* an artist whose work is the subject of a special exhibit at the museum.

**refine** *verb* ✦ process, purify ✧ clean, filter, strain, treat Sugar was first *refined* about 2,500 years ago.

**reflect** *verb* 1. ✦ cast back, give back, return, send back ✧ mirror The windowpane *reflected* the light from my candle. 2. ✦ consider, contemplate, deliberate, ponder, think, meditate My parents encourage me to stop and *reflect* before I make an important decision.

**reform** *verb* ✦ change, revise, correct, improve, alter, amend, modify, remedy Both presidential candidates claimed that the federal tax system needed to be *reformed*. —*noun* ✦ change, revision, reformation, correction, improvement, progress The 1960s were a decade of significant social *reform* in the United States.

**refresh** *verb* ✦ freshen, renew, revive, perk up ✧ restore, invigorate, stimulate The bicyclists took a break to *refresh* themselves.

---

**Antonyms** refresh

*verb* drain, exhaust, sap, tire, weary

---

**refreshments** *noun* ✦ snacks, treats ✧ drink, food, nourishment We bought *refreshments* before the movie.

**refrigerate** *verb* ✦ keep cold, chill, cool, ice ✧ freeze Mayonnaise needs to be *refrigerated* after opening to keep it from spoiling.

**refuge** *noun* ✦ preserve, sanctuary ✧ haven, retreat, shelter, asylum My friends and I took a tour of a wildlife *refuge*.

**refund** *verb* ✦ return, repay, reimburse, give back, pay back ✧ restore The store will *refund* your money if you are not satisfied.

**refuse¹** *verb* ✦ decline, reject, turn down, spurn ✧ balk, resist Rashid *refused* any help in finishing the crossword puzzle.

**refuse²** *noun* ✦ garbage, rubbish, trash, waste ✧ litter, debris The *refuse* from cleaning up our yard filled several trash cans.

**regard** *verb* ✦ observe, scrutinize, view, eye, consider ✧ scan, watch The art dealer *regarded* the painting for several minutes before making any comments. —*noun* **1.** ✦ admiration, esteem, respect, appreciation ✧ honor, homage We have great *regard* for the firefighters who saved our home from burning down. **2.** ✦ attention, consideration, heed, contemplation, notice, care Please give more *regard* to the advice that I give you.

**region** *noun* ✦ locale, area, zone, territory, district, tract ✧ section Tropical *regions* receive a lot of rainfall.

**register** *noun* ✦ log, logbook, list, record, roll, journal The school has a *register* that contains the names and addresses of all its students. —*verb* ✦ enroll, sign up, check in ✧ enlist, schedule, enter My brother has *registered* to take classes next fall at the community college.

**regret** *verb* ✦ be sorry, feel sorry, lament ✧ grieve, mourn I *regret* that I will not be able to attend this year's New Year's Eve celebration. —*noun* ✦ remorse, qualms, misgivings, sorrow, disappointment, discontent, dissatisfaction I have no *regrets* about my decision to major in English literature.

**regular** *adjective* ✦ usual, customary, normal, routine, standard, common My *regular* route to work goes past my favorite coffee shop.

**regulate** *verb* ✦ control, manage, direct, govern, supervise ✧ adjust, modify, tune The veterinarian told me to *regulate* my cat's diet more strictly.

**regulation** *noun* ✦ rule, law, statute, requirement, decree, order, guideline The factory had to make a few changes to meet the new safety *regulations*.

**rehearse** *verb* ✦ practice, drill, study, review, prepare ✧ learn The cast of the school play got together to *rehearse* their lines.

**reign** *noun* ✦ regime, rule, dominion, monarchy, sovereignty ✧ administration The British Empire reached its peak during the *reign* of Queen Victoria. —*verb* ✦ govern, rule ✧ command, lead, administer Queen Victoria *reigned* from 1837 to 1901.

**reinforce** *verb* ✦ bolster, fortify, brace, support, strengthen ✧ tighten, toughen The beavers added twigs and branches to *reinforce* their dam.

**reject** *verb* ✦ dismiss, veto, deny, refuse, turn down, spurn The city council *rejected* the proposal to build a new courthouse.

**rejoice** *verb* ✦ be happy, celebrate, exult, glory ✧ delight, revel The whole family *rejoiced* when my cousin recovered from her serious illness.

**relate** *verb* **1.** ✦ describe, recount, narrate, tell ✧ communicate, recite The author's latest book *relates* his experiences in Africa. **2.** ✦ apply, bear (on), concern, pertain, refer, connect The teacher showed a video that *related* to the subject the class was studying.

**relation** *noun* **1.** ✦ relationship, similarity, connection, link, association ✧ tie, bond Many movies about America's Old West have almost no *relation* to the way things really were. **2.** ✦ family member, relative ✧ kin, kinfolk, in-law I met many distant *relations* for the first time at my grandmother's birthday party.

**relative** *adjective* **1.** ✦ relevant, connected, related, pertinent ✧ comparative Your remarks are interesting, but they are not *relative* to our discussion. —*noun* ✦ family member, relation ✧ kin, kinfolk, in-law My sister invited only close friends and *relatives* to her wedding.

**relax** *verb* ✦ rest, unwind, calm down ✧ ease, loosen, slacken I like to *relax* after work by taking a walk in the park.

**release** *verb* **1.** ✦ free, let go, liberate, set loose, loose ✧ discharge The fish hatchery will *release* the baby salmon as soon as they are big enough. **2.** ✦ issue, publish, put out, distribute ✧ offer, present The publisher plans to *release* several new books this spring.

**relent** *verb* ✦ give in, acquiesce, submit, yield ✧ soften, weaken The parents finally *relented* and allowed their daughter to spend the night at her friend's house.

**relevant** *adjective* ✦ applicable, pertinent, related, connected, fitting ✧ significant The student referred to an online encyclopedia for information *relevant* to her report.

**reliable** *adjective* ✦ dependable, responsible, trustworthy, committed, faithful ✧ honest I need a *reliable* person to help organize the talent show.

**relic** *noun* ✦ keepsake, souvenir, memento, remembrance ✧ heirloom My grandfather collects medals and other *relics* from World War II.

**relief** *noun* 1. ✦ ease, comfort, release ✧ cure, remedy This medicine provides immediate *relief* for an upset stomach. 2. ✦ aid, assistance, help, support ✧ rescue, charity The Red Cross sent *relief* to the hurricane victims.

**relieve** *verb* 1. ✦ alleviate, soothe, ease, help, lighten, aid, comfort ✧ lessen, reduce These lozenges should *relieve* your sore throat. 2. ✦ replace, take over (for) ✧ discharge, free, release The sentry had to stay on duty until someone could *relieve* him.

**religion** *noun* ✦ creed, faith, belief ✧ devotion, worship Christianity, Islam, Hinduism, and Buddhism are the four *religions* that have the most followers.

**religious** *adjective* ✦ devout, pious, reverent, spiritual ✧ divine, holy The *religious* woman prays several times every day.

**reluctant** *adjective* ✦ hesitant, resistant, unwilling ✧ averse, opposed, wary The horse was *reluctant* to jump the wide ditch.

**rely** *verb* ✦ count (on), depend (on), trust, expect ✧ believe I'm *relying on* you to bring the buns and potato chips to our cookout.

**remain** *verb* ✦ stay, endure, continue, last, linger, persist ✧ wait A beautiful pink glow *remained* in the sky long after sunset.

**remark** *noun* ✦ comment, observation, statement ✧ expression, mention, utterance Everyone listened attentively to the president's *remarks* about his new tax proposal. —*verb* ✦ comment (on), mention, note, observe ✧ express, say My friend *remarked on* how nice the weather has been lately.

**remarkable** *adjective* ✦ impressive, astonishing, exceptional, extraordinary, outstanding Modern computers can process information at *remarkable* speeds.

**remedy** *noun* ✦ therapy, treatment, cure ✧ antidote, medicine, medication The traditional *remedy* for a cold is to drink lots of fluids and get plenty of rest.

**remember** *verb* ✦ recall, recollect, call to mind ✧ think (of), retain Do you *remember* who played the villain in that movie?

**remind** *verb* ✦ notify, prompt, inform ✧ admonish, caution, suggest, warn Please *remind* me when it's time to leave for my music lesson.

**remote** *adjective* 1. ✦ distant, faraway, far-off, isolated, removed, secluded The explorers were shipwrecked on a *remote* island. 2. ✦ faint, slight, slim, small, unlikely, poor There is only a *remote* possibility that we will get another dog.

**Antonyms** remote
*adjective* 1. adjacent, close, nearby, neighboring

**removal** *noun* ✦ elimination, riddance, withdrawal, extraction ✧ evacuation, relocation, transfer The city made arrangements for the *removal* of debris from the empty lot.

**remove** *verb* 1. ✦ take away, withdraw, clear ✧ move, shift, transfer The landscapers *removed* the old shrubs and replaced them with rose bushes. 2. ✦ eliminate, eradicate, extract, get rid (of), take away ✧ clean, erase You can *remove* some stains by soaking them with vinegar or soda water.

**renew** *verb* 1. ✦ refresh, recondition, renovate, restore The finish on our wood floors needs to be *renewed*. 2. ✦ continue, extend, update ✧ begin again, restart, resume, revive I need to *renew* my magazine subscription.

**rent** *noun* ✦ rental, payment, fee ✧ cost, price, dues I'm pleased with my new apartment because the monthly *rent* is quite reasonable. —*verb* ✦ charter, hire, lease ✧ contract, borrow, let My family *rented* a sailboat for the weekend.

**repair** *verb* ✦ fix, mend, rebuild, restore, patch ✧ overhaul, renovate I used glue to *repair* my model airplane's broken wing. —*noun* ✦ fixing, servicing, mending ✧ overhaul, renovation, restoration Our washing machine is in need of *repair*.

**repeal** *verb* ✦ revoke, rescind, cancel ✧ abolish, reverse, withdraw The state legislature voted to *repeal* the unpopular law.

**repeat** *verb* ✦ restate, retell, reiterate, say again ✧ recite, recount The teacher *repeated* her instructions to make sure that everyone understood them.

**repel** *verb* 1. ✦ repulse, chase away, drive away, hold off, keep off ✧ resist, scatter A porcupine's quills help it to *repel* attackers. 2. ✦ disgust, appall, irritate, offend, revolt, sicken The last scene in that movie really *repelled* me.

**replace** *verb* ✦ change, exchange, substitute ✧ alter, restore, return I need to *replace* the batteries in my flashlight.

**reply** *verb* ✦ respond (to), answer, return ✧ acknowledge, react Everyone who *replies to* the survey will receive a free gift. —*noun* ✦ response, answer ✧ acknowledgment, reaction, return I emailed my friend a party invitation yesterday, and I received her *reply* today.

**report** *noun* ✦ account, article, story, statement, description ✧ narrative, summary The journalist used a smartphone to file her *report*. —*verb* 1. ✦ describe, relate, state, tell, narrate, disclose The army scout returned to headquarters to *report* what he had seen. 2. ✦ check in (at), go, proceed ✧ appear (at), arrive, reach New students have to *report to* the principal's office for their classroom assignment.

**represent** *verb* 1. ✦ symbolize, signify, stand (for), indicate ✧ characterize, illustrate, portray The stars on the American flag *represent* the fifty states. 2. ✦ act (for), speak (for), stand (for), serve Many writers have a literary agent who *represents* them when conducting business with a publisher.

**representative** *noun* ✦ delegate ✧ ambassador, deputy, emissary, agent In 1917, Jeannette Rankin became the first woman to be elected as a *representative* to the US Congress. —*adjective* 1. ✦ democratic, elected, republican ✧ chosen The United States has a *representative* form of government. 2. ✦ characteristic, typical, illustrative, indicative, descriptive This portrait is *representative* of the artist's early style.

## Word Groups

A **reptile** is a cold-blooded animal that has a backbone, is covered with scales or horny plates, and breathes with lungs. **Reptile** is a very specific scientific term with no true synonyms. Here are some kinds of reptiles to investigate in a dictionary: **alligator, crocodile, dinosaur, lizard, snake, tortoise, turtle**

**reputation** *noun* ✦ name, standing, status ✧ position, respect, stature This restaurant has a good *reputation* because the food is always excellent.

**request** *verb* ✦ ask (for), seek, apply (for), appeal (for) ✧ call (for), entreat, petition I *requested* permission to leave work early because I had a doctor's appointment. —*noun* ✦ appeal, call, plea ✧ demand, petition, summons The relief agency issued an urgent *request* for food and warm clothing to give to victims of the flood.

**require** *verb* ✦ direct, command, order, compel, oblige ✧ demand, expect A California law *requires* bicyclists under the age of eighteen to wear a helmet.

**rescue** *verb* ✦ save, help, deliver, recover ✧ free, release, extricate The Coast Guard *rescued* the crew of a sinking ship. —*noun* ✦ aid, assistance, help, relief, deliverance ✧ recovery, salvation After the earthquake, many people helped in the *rescue* of victims trapped in collapsed buildings.

**research** *noun* ✦ investigation, study, inquiry, probe ✧ analysis, experimentation The author traveled abroad to do the *research* for her new book. —*verb* ✦ investigate, study, explore, examine ✧ analyze, test The internet has countless websites that are useful for *researching* almost any topic.

**resemblance** *noun* ✦ likeness, similarity, correspondence ✧ closeness, comparison, sameness Do you see any physical *resemblance* between my sister and me?

**resentful** *adjective* ✦ bitter, indignant, offended ✧ hurt, angry, upset I felt *resentful* when my friend forgot my birthday.

**resentment** *noun* ✦ anger, bitterness, animosity, annoyance, indignation, rancor There was much *resentment* when taxes were raised.

**reservation** *noun* 1. ✦ booking, engagement ✧ appointment, arrangement, accommodation We have a *reservation* for two nights at the Grand Hotel. 2. ✦ doubt, qualm, hesitancy, misgiving, reluctance, uncertainty The cyclist had some *reservations* about riding his mountain bike down the steep hill.

**reserve** *verb* 1. ✦ conserve, save, hold back, keep, preserve, retain The runner *reserved* some of her strength for the final lap. 2. ✦ book, engage, schedule ✧ register, retain, secure We *reserved* a train compartment for our trip. —*noun* 1. ✦ stock, stockpile, store, supply, cache ✧ hoard, inventory The explorers kept an emergency *reserve* of food and water at their base camp. 2. ✦ aloofness, coolness, restraint, detachment, self-control The man's apparent *reserve* was really shyness.

**reside** *verb* ✦ abide, dwell, live, lodge ✧ inhabit,

**stay** My uncle's family *resides* in a small town in Nebraska.

**residence** *noun* ✦ **abode, dwelling, habitation, home, house, domicile** ◇ **household** The American president's official *residence* is the White House in Washington, D.C.

**resident** *noun* ✦ **citizen, dweller, inhabitant, native, householder, local** My grandmother is a longtime *resident* of Milwaukee.

**resign** *verb* ✦ **leave office, quit, step down** ◇ **abdicate, forsake, give up** The mayor had to *resign* for reasons of health.

**resist** *verb* ✦ **refuse, reject, forgo, turn down** ◇ **oppose, withstand** I can't *resist* my friend's offer of half-price tickets to the championship basketball game.

**resistance** *noun* ✦ **opposition, protest, struggle, defiance, fight** ◇ **rebellion** My dog puts up a lot of *resistance* when I try to bathe him.

**resolve** *verb* 1. ✦ **decide, determine, plan, mean, propose** ◇ **desire** The student *resolved* to study harder for his next test. 2. ✦ **clear up, fix, settle, solve, work out** ◇ **answer** The company's staff holds regular meetings to *resolve* any problems that might have developed.

**resort** *verb* ✦ **refer (to), turn (to), use, utilize, employ** ◇ **apply, go** I had to *resort to* the instruction manual to figure out how to use my new smartphone. —*noun* 1. ✦ **tourist spot, vacation place** ◇ **hideaway, retreat, destination** Cancún, Mexico, is a popular *resort*. 2. ✦ **alternative, choice, option, possibility, recourse** ◇ **hope, resource** If we can't get plane or train tickets, we can take the bus as a last *resort*.

**resource** *noun* 1. ✦ **aid, help, source, support** ◇ **reserve, storehouse** A thesaurus is an excellent *resource* for people who want to expand their vocabulary. 2. ✦ **asset, capital, cash, funds, money, wealth, revenue** My friend said that he doesn't have the *resources* to buy a new house at this time.

**respect** *noun* ✦ **admiration, esteem, regard, praise** ◇ **approval, honor, reverence** I have great *respect* for people who spend their lives helping others. —*verb* ✦ **esteem, honor, regard, value, revere** ◇ **admire, praise** My parents taught me to *respect* my elders.

**respectful** *adjective* ✦ **civil, considerate, courteous, mannerly, polite** ◇ **attentive, gallant, thoughtful**

Our team maintained a *respectful* silence during the singing of the national anthem before the game.

**respond** *verb* ✦ **answer, reply** ◇ **acknowledge, return, act, react** I sent an email to my friend last week, but she hasn't *responded* yet.

**Antonyms** **respond**
*verb* **disregard, ignore, neglect, scorn, slight, snub**

**response** *noun* ✦ **acknowledgment, answer, reaction** ◇ **reply, return, action** I knocked on the door, but got no *response*.

**responsibility** *noun* ✦ **chore, duty, function, job, obligation, task, charge** It is my roommate's *responsibility* to cook dinner this week.

**responsible** *adjective* ✦ **dependable, reliable, trustworthy** ◇ **accountable, honest, capable, solid** Children my go on the rafting trip only if they are accompanied by a *responsible* adult.

**rest¹** *noun* 1. ✦ **break, halt, pause, recess, time-out, intermission** ◇ **holiday** I sat down for a while to take a *rest* from my chores. 2. ✦ **relaxation, sleep, slumber** ◇ **calm, peace, quiet** You should get plenty of *rest* before the game tomorrow. —*verb* 1. ✦ **lie down, relax, take a break, lounge** ◇ **doze, nap, sleep** After lunch, I always *rest* for a little while before I go swimming. 2. ✦ **lay, lean, place, position, prop, set, stand** The worker *rested* his shovel against a tree.

**rest²** *noun* ✦ **balance, excess, remainder, surplus, leftovers** ◇ **remains** We ate half the pizza and took the *rest* home for tomorrow's lunch.

**restless** *adjective* ✦ **agitated, fidgety, jumpy, nervous, uneasy, fretful** The *restless* tiger paced back and forth in its cage.

**restore** *verb* ✦ **recondition, renew, revive, reestablish, renovate** ◇ **return, patch** This wax should help to *restore* the table's original finish.

**restrain** *verb* ✦ **stop, check, control, curb, hold, hold back, hamper** I have to use a leash to *restrain* my dog from jumping up on people.

**restrict** *verb* ✦ **limit, contain, confine** ◇ **check, moderate, bound** The new government plans to *restrict* the number of immigrants allowed into the country.

**restriction** *noun* ✦ **check, condition, limit, limitation, bound, constraint** ◇ **regulation** The city has *restrictions* on where it's permissible to open a business.

**result** *noun* ✦ consequence, effect, outcome, product ✧ end, outgrowth One *result* of the election is that our city now has a new mayor. —*verb* ✦ arise, develop, emerge, stem, follow, issue, flow ✧ happen The student's good grades *resulted* from his improved study habits.

**resume** *verb* ✦ begin again, continue, proceed, reopen, restart, go on The meeting will *resume* after a one-hour lunch break.

**retain** *verb* ✦ hold, keep, maintain, preserve, save, contain A thick layer of blubber helps whales *retain* heat even in arctic waters.

**retire** *verb* ✦ depart, step down, leave ✧ resign, withdraw, exit, give up Next month, my grandfather is going to *retire from* his job as a civil engineer.

**retreat** *verb* ✦ draw back, fall back, withdraw ✧ depart, escape, flee, retire The army was forced to *retreat* when the enemy attacked. —*noun* 1. ✦ fallback, withdrawal ✧ departure, escape, flight, getaway The soldiers made an orderly *retreat*. 2. ✦ asylum, haven, refuge, sanctuary, shelter The doctor's private office is a *retreat* from the pressures of the job.

**retrieve** *verb* ✦ fetch, get back, reclaim, recover, regain, repossess I *retrieved* my hat after the wind blew it away.

**return** *verb* 1. ✦ come back, go back ✧ reappear, revisit The Scouts *returned* to camp after their hike. 2. ✦ give back, hand back ✧ replace, restore, repay I will *return* your book as soon as I finish reading it. —*noun* 1. ✦ homecoming, reappearance ✧ arrival, entrance My cat's sudden *return* delighted me because I had thought that he was lost. 2. ✦ earnings, gain, income, profit, yield ✧ revenue The businessman was pleased with the *return* on his investment.

**reveal** *verb* ✦ disclose, expose, give away, tell ✧ uncover, show Please don't *reveal* how the movie ends.

**reverse** *adjective* ✦ back, opposite, obverse ✧ counter, contrasting, other Instructions for playing the game are on the *reverse* side of the box. —*noun* ✦ opposite, counter, contrary ✧ contrast I thought that you were older than I am, but it turns out that the *reverse* is true. —*verb* ✦ over-

ride, overturn, counter, turn around ✧ alter, repeal In the United States, a higher court has the power to *reverse* a lower court's ruling.

**review** *verb* 1. ✦ go over, look over, reconsider, reexamine ✧ examine, study In my ESL class, we start each lesson by *reviewing* what we learned the day before. 2. ✦ criticize, evaluate, judge ✧ assess, analyze, discuss Our writing assignment is to *review* a book and write about it in English. —*noun* 1. ✦ drill, study ✧ examination, investigation, survey The students had an oral *review* the day before they took the test. 2. ✦ criticism, evaluation, judgment, notice ✧ assessment, analysis The movie received favorable *reviews* from most critics.

**revise** *verb* ✦ alter, amend, change, modify, reconsider, vary The weather forced us to *revise* our vacation plans.

**revive** *verb* ✦ refresh, renew, restore, revitalize ✧ bring around I was very tired, but a short nap *revived* me.

**revoke** *verb* ✦ cancel, annul, nullify, recall, repeal, withdraw ✧ abolish If a driver has too many traffic tickets, his or her license can be *revoked*.

**revolt** *verb* 1. ✦ rebel, rise up ✧ mutiny, protest, riot, strike In 1789, the people of France *revolted* against the rich noblemen who ruled the country. 2. ✦ disgust, repel, horrify, offend, sicken, nauseate ✧ shock Gory movies *revolt* me. —*noun* ✦ rebellion, revolution, uprising, insurrection ✧ mutiny, protest, riot Patrick Henry was one of the leaders of the American *revolt* against Great Britain.

**revolution** *noun* 1. ✦ rebellion, revolt, uprising, insurrection ✧ overthrow, upheaval, coup The *revolution* in Russia in 1917 created the world's first communist state. 2. ✦ circle, circuit, rotation, cycle, turn ✧ spin The Earth makes one full *revolution* around the sun every 365¼ days.

**revolve** *verb* ✦ circle, orbit, spin, turn ✧ reel, rotate, wheel Earth *revolves* around the sun at a rate of 18.5 miles per second.

**reward** *noun* ✦ award, bounty, compensation, payment ✧ prize We offered a *reward* for the return of our lost cat. —*verb* ✦ award, compensate, pay back, repay ✧ acknowledge, honor The coach *rewarded* me for my hard work by making me captain of the team.

**rhythm** *noun* ✦ beat, pulse, throb ✧ measure, cadence, meter, tempo The doctor listened to the *rhythm* of my heartbeat.

**rich** *adjective* 1. ✦ prosperous, wealthy, affluent, well-off, well-to-do Whoever owns that yacht must be very *rich*. 2. ✦ bountiful, fertile, fruitful, productive, plentiful, prolific ✧ lush The Midwest region of the United States is known for its *rich* farmland. 3. ✦ heavy, creamy, fattening ✧ sweet, buttery Cheesecake is a *rich* dessert.

**rid** *verb* ✦ purge, free, clear, relieve ✧ eliminate, remove Our neighbor hired an exterminator to *rid* his house of termites.

**riddle** *noun* ✦ brainteaser, puzzle, enigma, problem ✧ question, mystery In many myths, the hero has to solve a *riddle* before continuing on a journey.

**ride** *verb* ✦ drive, handle, control, manage ✧ steer, take, travel (in) My friend is teaching me how to *ride* a dirt bike. —*noun* ✦ drive, jaunt, spin ✧ excursion, journey, trip, tour My roommate suggested that we go for a *ride* in the country.

**ridicule** *noun* ✦ mockery, scorn, disdain, sarcasm, sneering, teasing The inventor's idea was met with *ridicule* until he proved that it actually worked. —*verb* ✦ insult, jeer, laugh (at), mock, sneer, taunt ✧ tease, belittle The politician *ridiculed* his opponent at a press conference.

**ridiculous** *adjective* ✦ absurd, silly, comical, foolish, funny, laughable, crazy My father has a *ridiculous* tie that lights up like a Christmas tree.

**right** *noun* 1. ✦ morality, virtue, goodness, justice ✧ honor, integrity, propriety Parents are responsible for teaching their children the difference between *right* and wrong. 2. ✦ freedom, liberty, privilege ✧ license, permission When a suspect is arrested in the United States, that person has the *right* to remain silent. —*adjective* 1. ✦ accurate, correct ✧ exact, perfect, true, valid All of the answers on my driver's test were *right*. 2. ✦ honorable, ethical, virtuous, just, noble, proper, fair You did the *right* thing in returning the wallet that you found on the subway.

**rigid** *adjective* ✦ hard, immovable, inflexible, solid, stiff, firm The frozen fish were very *rigid*.

---

**Antonyms** **rigid**

*adjective* elastic, flexible, malleable, pliable, supple

---

**rim** *noun* ✦ brim, brink, edge, lip ✧ border, ledge, margin Hikers stood on the *rim* of Bryce Canyon and admired the magnificent view.

**ring¹** *noun* ✦ circle ✧ coil, hoop, loop, band, wheel The Scouts sat in a *ring* around their campfire. —*verb* ✦ circle, encompass, wreathe, enclose, surround ✧ hem, loop We *ringed* the fish pond with stones.

**ring²** *verb* ✦ jingle, jangle, sound ✧ chime, peal, toll, trill Did you hear the phone *ring*? —*noun* ✦ chime, peal, toll, knell, ringing, sound, clang ✧ tinkle, trill Every Sunday morning I hear the *ring* of church bells.

**riot** *noun* ✦ disorder, disturbance, unrest, uprising, upheaval ✧ protest, turmoil Many windows were broken and cars burned during the *riot*.

**rip** *verb* ✦ tear, cut, slash, slit, split ✧ run, shred I *ripped* my jeans on a barbed wire fence. —*noun* ✦ tear, slit, split, hole ✧ cut, gash, run The *rip* in my shirt is too big to mend.

**ripe** *adjective* ✦ mature, ready, developed, full-grown ✧ plump Pick only the *ripe* strawberries.

**rise** *verb* 1. ✦ arise, ascend, climb, go up ✧ lift, soar The sun *rises* in the east and sets in the west. 2. ✦ expand, grow, increase, swell ✧ strengthen, wax It rained so heavily that the river *rose* and overflowed its banks. —*noun* ✦ increase, jump, surge, boost, expansion, gain ✧ ascent, climb There was a *rise* in donations to the charity after their appeal on TV.

**risk** *noun* ✦ chance, gamble ✧ danger, hazard, jeopardy, peril The photographer took a *risk* by standing in an open field during the lightning storm. —*verb* ✦ endanger, imperil, jeopardize, hazard ✧ bet, chance, gamble The doctors *risked* their own health trying to discover the cause of the new disease.

**rival** *noun* ✦ competitor, adversary, challenger, opponent ✧ enemy, foe, contestant The two friends are *rivals* for the lead in the new Broadway play. —*verb* ✦ equal, match, approach ✧ challenge, compete (with), meet, oppose The amateur chef's cooking *rivals* the food at the best restaurants in both taste and aroma.

**road** *noun* ✦ route, street, avenue, boulevard, drive, roadway ✧ freeway, highway, lane, thoroughfare, way Our town is building a *road* that will lead from the shopping mall to the highway.

**roam** *verb* ✦ wander, rove, meander, ramble, drift, range, stray The sheep *roamed* over a wide area of the mountainside.

**roar** *noun* ✧ cry, growl, bawl, bay, bellow, howl The gazelles stampeded when they heard the lion's *roar*. —*verb* ✦ bellow, shout, howl, scream, shriek, bawl ✧ call, cry The drill instructor *roared* commands at the new recruits.

**rob** *verb* ✦ burglarize, hold up, stick up ✧ pilfer, steal The police caught the people who *robbed* a convenience store last week.

**robust** *adjective* ✦ healthy, hearty, hale, strong, sturdy, vigorous, lusty I feel much more *robust* in the summer than I do in wintertime.

**rock**[1] *noun* ✦ stone ✧ boulder, cobblestone, pebble The cabin's fireplace is made out of big, flat *rocks*.

**rock**[2] *verb* ✦ heave, pitch, roll, toss, sway ✧ jar, shake I almost fell in the lake when a wave *rocked* our canoe.

### Word Groups

A **rodent** is a mammal with large front teeth for gnawing or nibbling. **Rodent** is a very specific scientific term with no true synonyms. Here are some kinds of rodents to investigate in a dictionary: **beaver, gerbil, hamster, lemming, mouse, muskrat, porcupine, prairie dog, rat, squirrel**

**role** *noun* ✦ character, part ✧ function, place, portrayal Many actors auditioned for the lead *role* in the new play.

**roll** *verb* 1. ✦ throw, toss, pitch ✧ revolve, rotate, tumble, flip Yoon *rolled* the dice and took her turn in the game. 2. ✦ wind, wrap, twist ✧ coil, curl, turn, loop I *rolled* the leftover wrapping paper back onto the tube. —*noun* 1. ✦ attendance ✧ lineup, list, register, schedule, roster The coach calls *roll* at the beginning of every practice. 2. ✧ biscuit, bun, croissant, pastry, bread We got fresh *rolls* at the bakery. 3. ✦ rumble ✧ boom, clap, peal, thunder There was a drum *roll* before the announcement of the winner.

**romance** *noun* 1. ✦ love affair, affair, love, courtship, passion, relationship My parents' *romance* began when a friend introduced them. 2. ✦ adventure, excitement, glamor, mystery ✧ passion Some people think that jumbo jets and superhighways have taken the *romance* out of travel.

**room** *noun* 1. ✦ chamber ✧ compartment, den, cell, apartment, lodging The palace has over one hundred *rooms*. 2. ✦ area, space, expanse ✧ extent, territory There's no *room* to put anything more on my shelves.

**root** *noun* ✦ beginning, origin, source ✧ base, bottom, foundation We're trying to get to the *root* of the problem.

**rot** *verb* ✦ spoil, decay, decompose, go bad, break down The overripe bananas are beginning to *rot*. —*noun* ✦ decay, decomposition, rottenness ✧ blight, fungus, mildew, mold The old barn is beginning to show signs of *rot*.

**rotate** *verb* ✦ revolve, spin, turn, twirl, whirl ✧ swivel, wind *Rotate* this knob to focus the binoculars.

**rough** *adjective* 1. ✦ coarse, grainy, gritty, scratchy ✧ jagged, uneven Nail files have a *rough* surface. 2. ✦ crude, preliminary, incomplete, unfinished ✧ basic The artist made a *rough* sketch before she started painting. 3. ✦ approximate, general, inexact, vague ✧ quick, hasty We made a *rough* estimate of the amount of lumber we would need to build a fence around the entire yard. 4. ✦ taxing, demanding, difficult, hard, tough, unpleasant I was tired after a *rough* day at work.

**round** *adjective* 1. ✦ circular, spherical ✧ elliptical, oval The full moon looks perfectly *round* in the sky. 2. ✦ curved, rounded ✧ arched, bowed The restaurant has a *round* booth in the corner. —*noun* 1. ✦ circuit, beat, route, tour, course ✧ watch The museum guard makes an hourly *round* of the building. 2. ✦ series, string, succession, sequence ✧ chain, cycle There was a *round* of parties for the newly engaged couple. —*verb* ✦ go (around), turn ✧ circle, travel The cyclists were going at top speed when they *rounded* the bend.

**rout** *noun* ✦ defeat, drubbing, thrashing ✧ disaster, overthrow, upset The game ended in a complete *rout* with the home team winning by seven touchdowns. —*verb* ✦ beat, conquer, defeat, overcome, overwhelm, triumph (over), crush Guerrilla forces *routed* the government troops.

**route** *noun* ✦ course, way ✧ lane, path, road, avenue, track We planned the *route* for our trip. —*verb* ✦ send, ship, direct, dispatch, forward, transfer ✧ convey My overseas package was *routed* through San Francisco.

**routine** *noun* ✦ custom, habit, pattern, procedure ✧ practice, program Having a cup of coffee is the first step of my morning *routine.* —*adjective* ✦ standard, regular, customary, familiar, normal, usual The school children followed *routine* procedure during the fire drill.

**row** *noun* ✦ line, string, file, sequence, series, chain ✧ column The homeowner planted a *row* of lilac bushes along the back of her property.

**royal** *adjective* 1. ✦ regal, imperial ✧ aristocratic, highborn, noble The *royal* family appeared on the palace balcony. 2. ✦ grand, magnificent, majestic, splendid, superb, stately The troops received a *royal* sendoff.

**rub** *verb* ✦ knead, massage, stroke, manipulate ✧ scour, scrub *Rubbing* my temples helps me to relax. —*noun* ✦ massage, rubdown, kneading, manipulation ✧ scouring, scrubbing Will you give me a back *rub*, please?

**rubbish** *noun* ✦ garbage, junk, refuse, trash, waste ✧ litter, debris We threw away a lot of *rubbish* when we cleaned out the garage.

**rude** *adjective* 1. ✦ discourteous, disrespectful, impolite, inconsiderate Please forgive me, I didn't mean to be *rude.* 2. ✦ coarse, crude, makeshift, primitive, rough, simple, rustic The sheepherder built a *rude* shelter out of stones and brush.

**ruffle** *verb* ✦ mess up, disorder, disturb, jumble, tangle, upset If you put on this scarf, the wind won't *ruffle* your hair.

**rugged** *adjective* ✦ solid, sturdy, tough, durable ✧ hardy, rough I have a pair of *rugged* boots to wear when I go hiking.

**ruin** *noun* 1. ✦ collapse, destruction, downfall, catastrophe ✧ havoc, wreck The company is facing financial *ruin.* 2. ✦ rubble, wreckage, debris, remains, remnant ✧ relics We explored the *ruins* of an old silver mine. —*verb* ✦ demolish, destroy, wreck, mangle ✧ smash, spoil The puppy *ruined* my leather belt by chewing on it.

**rule** *noun* 1. ✦ guideline, regulation ✧ law, order, principle, edict The swimming pool's lifeguard enforces the safety *rules.* 2. ✦ dominion, reign ✧ administration, government, sovereignty The legendary Robin Hood is said to have lived during the *rule* of King Richard the Lion-Hearted. —*verb* 1. ✦ govern, reign ✧ administer, head, lead, command, control Empress Catherine the Great *ruled* Russia from 1762 until 1796. ✦ decide, determine, judge, decree, conclude, resolve The referee *ruled* that the player had committed a foul.

**rumble** *verb* ✦ growl, grumble ✧ boom, resound, roar, roll, thunder My stomach *rumbled* because I was hungry. —*noun* ✦ boom, roar, roll, thunder ✧ growl, crash We knew a storm was coming because we could hear the *rumble* of distant thunder.

**rumor** *noun* ✦ gossip, hearsay, talk, news ✧ report, story, tale The *rumor* is that you will get the lead in the musical. —*verb* ✦ suggest, say, report, gossip ✧ talk, tattle, whisper It is *rumored* that we will get Friday off work.

**run** *verb* 1. ✦ dash, hasten, hurry, hustle, race, rush, scurry I must *run* to the post office before it closes. 2. ✦ campaign ✧ compete, contend, contest, stand The senator is going to *run* for office again. 3. ✦ function, go, operate, perform, work, drive A car *runs* better after a tune-up. 4. ✦ manage, supervise, direct ✧ administer, control, maintain My parents *run* a donut shop. —*noun* 1. ✦ jog, race, sprint, trot, dash We went for a *run* around the block. 2. ✦ streak, stretch, string, sequence, spell ✧ series I've been having a *run* of good luck.

**rupture** *noun* ✦ break, crack, fracture, gap, hole, split, breach The basement was flooded because of a *rupture* in the hot water tank. —*verb* ✦ break, burst, split ✧ breach, crack, fracture, explode The water balloon *ruptured* when the child filled it too full.

**rural** *adjective* ✦ country, provincial ✧ agricultural, farm, pastoral, rustic My family comes from a *rural* village in southern China.

**rush** *verb* ✦ dash, hasten, hurry, hustle, race, run, sprint I *rushed* over to my friend's house as soon as she got home from vacation. —*noun* ✦ hurry, scramble, haste ✧ dash, race, run We were in a *rush* to finish our holiday shopping.

**ruthless** *adjective* ✦ brutal, cruel, harsh, heartless, merciless ✧ severe, callous The *ruthless* queen treated her enemies harshly.

**sack¹** *noun* ✦ **bag** ✧ **pack, pouch, receptacle** I bought a *sack* of potatoes at the grocery store. —*verb* ✦ **bag, pack, package** ✧ **load, fill** The clerk *sacked* my groceries for me.

**sack²** *verb* ✦ **pillage, plunder, ransack, loot** ✧ **attack, raid** The Vikings *sacked* many villages over a period of about three hundred years. —*noun* ✦ **pillage, plundering, looting** ✧ **burning, destruction, robbing** The *sack* of Rome by the Vandals occurred in 455 CE.

**sacred** *adjective* ✦ **holy, religious, divine, blessed, hallowed** ✧ **saintly, spiritual** Jerusalem is a *sacred* city to Christians, Jews, and Muslims alike.

**sacrifice** *noun* 1. ✦ **offering, gift, homage** ✧ **victim** The ancient Greeks made *sacrifices* to their gods by killing sheep and other animals. 2. ✦ **concession, forfeit** ✧ **loss, surrender, cost** My parents had to make *sacrifices* in order to put me through college. —*verb* ✦ **give up, lose, offer up, surrender, yield, let go** In chess, it is often necessary to *sacrifice* pieces in order to win the game.

**sad** *adjective* ✦ **dejected, depressed, gloomy, melancholy, unhappy, blue** ✧ **joyless** I was *sad* that I could not go skiing with my friends.

**saddle** *noun* ✦ **riding saddle** ✧ **packsaddle, seat, pad, perch** The cowboy put a *saddle* on his horse. —*verb* ✦ **burden, load, tax, weigh down, weight** ✧ **impose, inflict** I was *saddled* with extra responsibilities while my coworker was on vacation.

**safe** *adjective* ✦ **protected, secure** ✧ **defended, guarded, unhurt, snug** The rabbit felt *safe* and comfortable in its burrow. —*noun* ✦ **vault** ✧ **safe-deposit box, strongbox, chest** Access to the bank's *safe* is controlled by a time lock.

**sag** *verb* ✦ **dip, droop, drop, sink, slump, bow** ✧ **flop, wilt** The clothesline *sagged* when we hung up wet towels.

**sail** *noun* ✦ **boat trip, cruise, voyage** ✧ **excursion, passage** We decided to go on a *sail* across the bay. —*verb* 1. ✦ **cruise, voyage, float** ✧ **cross, set sail** It took us two hours to *sail* across the bay. 2. ✦ **navigate, pilot, helm, captain, guide, steer** ✧ **control, manage** My boyfriend is teaching me how to *sail* a boat. 3. ✦ **fly, drift, float, glide, soar, wing** ✧ **flutter, skim** A little bird *sailed* through my open window.

**salary** *noun* ✦ **compensation, earnings, pay, wage** ✧ **fee, income** The store owner raised her employee's *salary*.

**sale** *noun* 1. ✦ **selling, exchange, transfer** ✧ **marketing, purchase** Our neighbor hopes that the *sale* of his house will go smoothly. 2. ✦ **bargain, deal, discount, markdown** ✧ **closeout** We plan to take advantage of the big holiday *sales*.

**same** *adjective* ✦ **identical, matching, alike** ✧ **equal, exact, similar, duplicate** My sister and I have eyes of the *same* color.

**sample** *noun* ✦ **example, specimen** ✧ **model, representative, cross section** This is just a *sample* of the kind of drawing I can make. —*verb* ✦ **experience, taste, test, try, judge** ✧ **sip** The clerk asked if we would like to *sample* the new ice cream flavor.

**sanctuary** *noun* ✦ **asylum, haven, protection, refuge, safety** ✧ **shelter** The refugees found *sanctuary* at the embassy.

**sane** *adjective* ✦ **prudent, rational, reasonable, sensible, sound, wise** I need some *sane* advice about the problems I'm having with my best friend.

**sanity** *noun* ✦ **mental health, reason, common sense, judgment, mind** My friends questioned my *sanity* when I told them that I wanted to go bungee jumping.

**sarcastic** *adjective* ✦ **derisive, insulting, jeering, mocking, scornful, sneering, taunting** The politician made a *sarcastic* remark about her opponent's campaign promises.

**satisfaction** *noun* ✦ **contentment, fulfillment, happiness, pleasure, pride** ✧ **comfort, relief** Renata felt immense *satisfaction* when she completed her science project.

**satisfactory** *adjective* ✦ **acceptable, adequate, all right, sufficient, decent** ✧ **suitable, enough** I have agreed to sell my motorbike because the buyer made a *satisfactory* offer.

**satisfy** *verb* 1. ✦ appease, content, gratify, fulfill, satiate, please, pacify I was so hungry that I knew a bowl of soup would not be enough to *satisfy* me. 2. ✦ assure, convince, persuade, reassure, sway ✧ answer The suspect's alibi *satisfied* the police that he was not guilty of committing the crime.

**saturate** *verb* ✦ soak, drench, douse ✧ fill, sop, wet Camila *saturated* her houseplants with water before she left for the week.

**savage** *adjective* ✦ brutal, cruel, ferocious, fierce, ruthless, vicious The hungry shark made a *savage* attack on its prey.

**save** *verb* 1. ✦ rescue, help, deliver, aid ✧ free, protect, recover, safeguard Many volunteers joined in to *save* the birds that had been caught in an oil spill. 2. ✦ lay away, put aside, reserve, store, maintain Jonah is *saving* a little money each week until he has enough for a new laptop.

**Antonyms save**

*verb* 1. endanger, imperil, risk, threaten 2. consume, spend, squander, waste

**say** *verb* ✦ articulate, enunciate, pronounce, recite, utter, state Can you *say* "the frog flopped" ten times in a row? —*noun* ✦ voice, vote ✧ chance, opinion, view, turn All the club members had a *say* in the decision.

**saying** *noun* ✦ adage, expression, motto, proverb, maxim ✧ statement "There's no use crying over spilt milk" is a common *saying*.

**scan** *verb* ✦ search, survey, examine, inspect, study ✧ explore, look The lookout used binoculars to *scan* the horizon.

**scandal** *noun* ✦ disgrace, dishonor, embarrassment, outrage, shame ✧ offense The mayor's dishonesty created a public *scandal*.

**scant** *adjective* ✦ little, meager, scanty, skimpy, sparse, poor ✧ insufficient I paid *scant* attention to the boring television show.

**scar** *noun* ✦ blemish, mark ✧ cut, injury, wound My mother has a *scar* from when she had her appendix removed. —*verb* ✦ disfigure, blemish, damage, deface, injure, mark The man's legs were permanently *scarred* after his mountain bike accident.

**scarce** *adjective* ✦ rare, sparse, uncommon, unusual ✧ infrequent, scant, scanty Water is *scarce* in the desert.

**scarcely** *adverb* ✦ barely, hardly, just, only ✧ slightly, merely I had *scarcely* hung up the phone when it rang again.

**scare** *verb* ✦ frighten, alarm, terrify, shock, startle ✧ terrorize, panic I had a bad nightmare that really *scared* me. —*noun* ✦ alarm, fright, shock, start, startle ✧ surprise, terror You gave me quite a *scare* when you came in without knocking.

**scatter** *verb* ✦ strew, spread, disperse, distribute, sprinkle, sow ✧ separate We *scatter* rock salt on our front steps when they get icy.

**scene** *noun* 1. ✦ setting, site, locale, location ✧ area, place, spot The police are investigating the *scene* of the crime. 2. ✦ act, episode, segment ✧ chapter, part, section The murderer was revealed in the last *scene* of the play.

**scenic** *adjective* ✦ picturesque, beautiful, panoramic, pretty, spectacular Instead of the shorter road, we took a *scenic* route through the mountains.

**scent** *noun* ✦ aroma, fragrance, odor, smell, bouquet ✧ whiff These roses have a lovely *scent*. —*verb* ✦ smell, sniff, nose out ✧ detect, perceive, sense The hounds started baying when they *scented* the fox.

**schedule** *noun* ✦ calendar, lineup, timetable ✧ list, program, register The coach gave each player a copy of this year's game *schedule*. —*verb* ✦ arrange, book, slate, reserve ✧ plan, prepare, program I *scheduled* a doctor's appointment for my annual checkup.

**scheme** *noun* ✦ plan, program, system, procedure, strategy ✧ plot, design Diet *schemes* that promise quick results usually don't work. —*verb* ✦ conspire, contrive, intrigue, plan, plot, maneuver The con artist *schemed* to cheat people out of their life's savings.

**scholar** *noun* ✦ academic, intellectual ✧ sage, specialist, authority, pupil, student Many *scholars* use university libraries to do their research.

**Word Groups**

A **school** is a place for teaching and learning. **School** is a general term with no true synonyms. Here are some different kinds of schools to investigate in a dictionary: **academy, college, grammar school, high school, middle school, institute, kindergarten, seminary, university**

**scold** *verb* ✦ admonish, criticize, chastise, lecture ✧ blame, denounce The mother gently *scolded* her unruly toddler.

**scope** *noun* ✦ extent, range, reach, spread ✧ realm, sphere, space The *scope* of my professor's knowledge is impressive.

**scorch** *verb* ✦ char, singe, sear, blacken ✧ bake, burn, roast, toast The flames *scorched* the wall, but the house didn't catch on fire.

**score** *noun* ✦ mark, grade, total, result ✧ count, points, record People who take this English proficiency test will receive a *score* of from 1 to 9. —*verb* ✦ achieve, attain, earn, gain, make ✧ win, count The team *scored* three goals during the last quarter.

**scoundrel** *noun* ✦ rogue, rascal, villain ✧ crook, thief, swindler Many people thought the dishonest politician was a *scoundrel*.

**scour** *verb* ✦ scrub, polish, rub, buff ✧ cleanse, wash I *scoured* my dirty pots and pans until they gleamed.

**scout** *noun* ✦ advance guard, guide, lookout ✧ explorer, spy Kit Carson was a famous American frontier *scout*. —*verb* ✦ reconnoiter, explore, search, inspect, observe, examine, survey My friend went ahead to *scout* the next block for a place we could eat.

**scramble** *verb* 1. ✦ hasten, hurry, hustle, race, rush, scurry, run All the students *scrambled* to put their books and papers away when the bell rang. 2. ✦ disorder, jumble, mess up, mix, shuffle, disorganize I like to solve word puzzles in which all the letters are *scrambled*. —*noun* ✦ free-for-all, tussle, struggle, tumult, confusion ✧ race, rush There was a *scramble* in the end zone when one of the players dropped the ball.

**scrap** *noun* ✦ bit, fragment, part, piece, portion, shred, segment Natasha is saving *scraps* of cloth to make a quilt. —*verb* ✦ abandon, discard, dispose (of), dump, junk ✧ throw away The Navy plans to *scrap* this old battleship.

**scrape** *verb* 1. ✦ clean off, remove, rub off, scour ✧ peel, skin The man *scraped* the ice from the windshield of his car. 2. ✦ scratch, scuff, skin, abrade, bruise ✧ hurt, injure I wear pads when I go roller-skating so that I won't *scrape* my knees. —*noun* ✦ mark, scratch, scuff, abrasion ✧ bruise, damage, injury My car has a *scrape* on the right front fender.

**scratch** *verb* ✦ rub, scrape, abrade ✧ scuff, mar, mark Bears like to *scratch* their backs against trees. —*noun* ✦ gash, mark, scrape, scuff, score ✧ damage, injury This wax should cover the *scratch* on the table.

**scream** *verb* ✦ cry out, howl, screech, shout, shriek, yell, bellow ✧ wail Everybody *screamed* as the roller coaster looped the loop. —*noun* ✦ cry, howl, screech, shout, shriek, yell ✧ wail We heard lots of *screams* coming from the carnival's haunted house.

**screech** *noun* ✦ cry, scream, shriek, squawk ✧ squeal, wail The *screech* of a blue jay woke me up. —*verb* ✦ cry out, scream, shriek ✧ squawk, squeal, wail The child *screeched* when a mouse scurried across the floor.

**screen** *noun* 1. ✦ cover, protection, shade, shield ✧ shelter, veil This elm tree acts as a *screen* to keep the sun off our porch. 2. ✦ mesh, netting, net, screening Our tent has a small *screen* that serves as a window. —*verb* ✦ cloak, conceal, hide, obscure, veil, shroud ✧ protect, shelter The dark night *screened* the attacking army.

**screw** *noun* ✧ fastener, pin, bolt, nail My bookshelves are held together with metal *screws*. —*verb* ✦ turn, twist, rotate, wind, twirl ✧ attach, fasten, tighten I had a hard time *screwing* the childproof cap off the aspirin bottle.

**scribble** *verb* ✦ draw, scrawl, write, doodle ✧ jot The toddler *scribbled* on the bedroom wall with crayons.

**scrub** *verb* ✦ scour, cleanse, clean, wash ✧ buff, polish, rub I *scrubbed* the kitchen sink after doing the dishes. —*noun* ✦ scrubbing, cleaning, cleansing, scouring, washing ✧ polish, rub This tub needs a good *scrub*.

**sculpture** *noun* ✦ statue, figure ✧ bust, figurine, model, carving America's Statue of Liberty is an enormous *sculpture* made of copper.

**seal** *noun* ✦ emblem, insignia, mark, sign, stamp ✧ badge Legal documents often have an official *seal* on them. —*verb* ✦ bind, close, fasten, secure, shut ✧ bar, lock I *sealed* the carton with packing tape.

**search** *verb* ✦ explore, hunt, look, seek, probe ✧ investigate The prospector spent his life *searching* for gold. —*noun* ✦ hunt, exploration, probe ✧ investigation, pursuit, inquiry The rescue team began a *search* for the missing boy.

**season** *noun* ✦ period, time ✧ occasion, spell, term, era A lot of people decorate their homes during the holiday *season*. —*verb* ✦ flavor, spice ✧ enhance, pep up, salt My roommate uses curry powder to *season* her baked chicken.

**secret** *adjective* ✦ confidential, private ✧ concealed, hidden, personal, classified, unknown Manuel has a *secret* password to access his email account. —*noun* ✦ confidential information, private information ✧ intrigue, mystery Don't you dare tell anyone my *secret*!

---

**Antonyms** secret

*adjective* explicit, obvious, open, plain, public

---

**section** *noun* ✦ part, portion, segment, piece, unit ✧ area, division, slice Hiro likes to read the sports *section* of the newspaper. —*verb* ✦ cut, divide, separate, slice, split, partition I *sectioned* the pie into six pieces.

**secure** *adjective* 1. ✦ safe, defended, protected, sheltered, guarded ✧ immune Having my dog with me when I take a walk makes me feel *secure*. 2. ✦ assured, certain, guaranteed, stable, steady, sure My father has a *secure* position with his company. —*verb* 1. ✦ defend, guard, protect, safeguard ✧ shelter, shield, preserve The new alarm system will help *secure* the office against burglars. 2. ✦ anchor, attach, bind, chain, fasten, tie, moor We *secured* the boat to the dock so it would not drift away. 3. ✦ acquire, gain, get, obtain, procure, attain ✧ win We were able to *secure* good seats for the baseball game.

**see** *verb* 1. ✦ view, observe, behold, glimpse, spot, watch ✧ notice You can *see* the ocean from here. 2. ✦ comprehend, perceive, understand, grasp ✧ detect, realize I can *see* why you're upset. 3. ✦ ascertain, determine, find out, learn, discover, detect I answered the phone just to *see* who was calling so late.

**seed** *noun* ✦ nut, kernel, pip, pit ✧ germ, grain, nucleus, source The giant redwood tree grows from a tiny *seed* that is only an eighth of an inch long.

**seek** *verb* ✦ hunt (for), look (for), search (for) ✧ go (after), pursue, want Birds *seek* safe places to build their nests.

**seem** *verb* ✦ appear, look ✧ resemble, sound, suggest That person over there *seems* to be waving at you.

**seep** *verb* ✦ dribble, drip, leak, ooze, trickle, drain Oil *seeped* from the car's engine onto the driveway.

**segment** *noun* ✦ part, piece, portion, section, slice ✧ division, bit I gave my friend several *segments* of my orange.

**seize** *verb* ✦ clutch, grab, grasp, grip, snatch ✧ capture, catch, take I *seized* my little sister to keep her from running into the street.

**seldom** *adverb* ✦ hardly ever, infrequently, not often, rarely I *seldom* forget to brush my teeth before bed.

**select** *verb* ✦ choose, decide (on), pick, settle (on), elect, name The ice cream shop offered so many flavors, I took a long time to *select* the one I wanted. —*adjective* ✦ chosen, elect, choice, exclusive ✧ first-class, special, superior Only a few *select* employees will be allowed to attend the conference.

**selection** *noun* ✦ assortment, choice, pick, range, variety ✧ preference, option The stationery store has a large *selection* of birthday cards.

**self-conscious** *adjective* ✦ bashful, modest, shy ✧ embarrassed, nervous The student felt a little *self-conscious* while giving an oral report in front of the class.

**selfish** *adjective* ✦ greedy, self-centered, stingy, ungenerous ✧ inconsiderate I was *selfish* and took the last piece of pie.

---

**Antonyms** selfish

*adjective* bighearted, charitable, generous, giving, unselfish

---

**sell** *verb* ✦ deal (in), market, peddle, retail ✧ offer, stock, trade This bookstore *sells* both new and used books.

**send** *verb* ✦ mail, ship, forward ✧ dispatch, transfer, transmit I *sent* the package by priority mail.

**senior** *adjective* 1. ✦ older, old, elderly, elder ✧ aged, advanced Many restaurants give discounts to *senior* citizens. 2. ✦ chief, higher, leading, major, superior, top, ranking My uncle is a *senior* official in the governor's office. —*noun* ✦ superior, chief, better, boss ✧ elder, oldster The army officer was constantly trying to impress his *seniors*.

**sensational** *adjective* ✦ fantastic, spectacular, superb, terrific, thrilling, wonderful, exciting The special effects in that movie were absolutely *sensational.*

**sense** *noun* 1. ✦ faculty, capability, capacity, power, sensation ✧ function An Alsatian dog has a *sense* of smell that is about one million times stronger than a human's. 2. ✦ feeling, sentiment ✧ appreciation, understanding, impression I have a strong *sense* of loyalty to my friends. —*verb* ✦ detect, feel, perceive, recognize, see, notice ✧ think I *sense* that you are anxious to leave.

**sensible** *adjective* ✦ logical, prudent, rational, reasonable, wise, intelligent ✧ thoughtful It is *sensible* to warm up before you exercise.

**sensitive** *adjective* ✦ perceptive (about), aware (of), receptive, sympathetic, understanding (about) ✧ feeling A teacher needs to be *sensitive* to the needs of each student.

**sentiment** *noun* ✦ opinion, belief, attitude, position, view, leaning ✧ emotion, feeling The city conducted a survey to determine people's *sentiments* about a new sales tax.

**separate** *verb* ✦ divide, part, split, detach ✧ break up, sever To make vanilla pudding, you should *separate* the egg whites from the yolks. —*adjective* ✦ different, distinct, independent, individual ✧ solitary, unique Put the light and dark laundry into *separate* piles.

**sequence** *noun* ✦ order, arrangement, succession, placement ✧ course, series A combination lock will not open if the numbers are dialed out of *sequence.*

**serene** *adjective* ✦ tranquil, placid, calm, peaceful, quiet, restful The lake looked *serene* in the evening twilight.

**series** *noun* ✦ course, cycle, run, sequence, set, succession ✧ assortment, collection, group The science channel is airing a *series* of shows on African wildlife.

**serious** *adjective* 1. ✦ grave, grim, sober, solemn, somber ✧ sad You look very *serious* today—is there something wrong? 2. ✦ in earnest, sincere, resolved, resolute, decided, definite Are you *serious* about not going to the party? 3. ✦ important, momentous, significant, urgent, vital ✧ heavy Drug abuse is a *serious* problem. 4. ✦ alarming, bad, critical, dangerous, difficult, tough The sailors were in a *serious* situation when their ship started to sink.

**sermon** *noun* ✦ address, lecture, speech, talk ✧ lesson The principal gave a *sermon* on the value of a good education.

**serve** *verb* 1. ✦ act, function, work, perform, labor ✧ behave My friend and I *serve* as volunteer firefighters. 2. ✦ aid, assist, attend, help, wait (on) ✧ support The salesclerk was very polite when she *served* us. 3. ✦ give, provide, supply, deliver, pass, offer Please *serve* each guest a piece of your birthday cake.

**service** *noun* 1. ✦ aid, assistance, attendance, help, support, attention The sick man needed the *services* of a doctor. 2. ✦ armed forces, military ✧ Air Force, Army, Coast Guard, Marine Corps, Navy My boyfriend is home on leave from the *service.* 3. ✦ agency, bureau, department, office ✧ facility, utility Some college students work for the Forest *Service* during the summer. 4. ✦ ceremony ✧ celebration, function, ritual, observance The wedding *service* was lovely. —*verb* ✦ fix, repair, overhaul ✧ adjust, maintain, restore We had our broken washing machine *serviced* by a repairman.

**set**[1] *verb* 1. ✦ lay, place, put ✧ locate, install, rest, stick Please *set* the groceries on the counter. 2. ✦ congeal, dry, harden, solidify, stiffen, thicken This glue will *set* in fifteen minutes. 3. ✦ adjust, arrange, fix, order, prepare, regulate I *set* my alarm clock to ring at 7 a.m. 4. ✦ depart, embark, start, start out, begin, commence ✧ undertake The cruise ship weighed anchor and *set off* on its voyage. —*adjective* ✦ established, fixed, customary, definite, habitual, regular, specific It's necessary to follow the *set* procedure in order to file a claim.

**set**[2] *noun* ✦ assortment, batch, collection, group, array ✧ bunch My friend bought a *set* of metric wrenches to fix his foreign car.

**settle** *verb* 1. ✦ agree (on), arrange, choose, decide, fix, set Let's *settle* the date for the party so I can send out invitations. 2. ✦ locate, move (to) ✧ dwell, live, reside, inhabit Many European immigrants *settled in* New York City in the 1880s. 3. ✦ alight, land, set down ✧ descend, drop, sink The flock of crows *settled* on the top branches of the tree. 4. ✦ calm, relieve, pacify, quiet, soothe ✧ relax This herbal tea should *settle* your upset stomach.

**several** *adjective* ✦ a few, some, numerous, various ✧ a number That actor has been in *several* of my favorite movies.

**severe** *adjective* 1. ✦ heavy, serious, strict, tough, grave, stern At my university there is a *severe* penalty for cheating. 2. ✦ bitter, brutal, difficult, hard, harsh, rough, grim I hope that this winter won't be as *severe* as the last one.

**shack** *noun* ✦ hut, shanty, shed, lean-to, hovel ✧ cabin, shelter We found an abandoned *shack* in the woods.

**shade** *noun* 1. ✦ shadow, shadiness ✧ cover, darkness, gloom, murk My dog likes to lie in the *shade* of our big oak tree. 2. ✦ hue, tint, tone, tinge, color ✧ gradation The sunset turned the clouds different *shades* of pink and orange.

**shadow** *noun* 1. ✧ reflection, silhouette, trace, image, outline Your *shadow* is always shortest at noon. 2. ✦ darkness, dimness, gloom, murk, shade I can see my little brother hiding in the *shadows*.

**shady** *adjective* ✦ shaded, shadowy ✧ dark, dim, covered, sheltered Let's find a *shady* spot for our picnic.

**shake** *verb* 1. ✦ jiggle, rattle, joggle, vibrate ✧ agitate, wag Audra *shook* her tambourine in time to the music. 2. ✦ tremble, quake, quiver, shiver, convulse, shudder The rabbit *shook* with fear when it saw a fox. 3. ✦ diminish, discourage, weaken, undermine, disturb ✧ move, shift No one can *shake* my determination to study abroad. —*noun* ✦ shaking ✧ jar, jiggle, jolt, vibration, bounce I gave my sweater a good *shake* to get the dog hair off.

**shame** *noun* 1. ✦ humiliation, disgrace, embarrassment ✧ regret, sorrow, remorse The student was filled with *shame* when she was caught cheating. 2. ✦ pity, misfortune, disappointment, sorrow ✧ crime, scandal It is a *shame* that your injury kept you from playing in the last game of the season. —*verb* ✦ disgrace, dishonor, humiliate ✧ discredit, embarrass The spy *shamed* his country by selling secrets to the enemy.

**shape** *noun* 1. ✦ configuration, figure, form, outline, pattern, contour, profile We made Christmas cookies in the *shape* of snowmen, wreaths, and candy canes. 2. ✦ condition, health, state, trim, fitness ✧ order My cat is still in good *shape* even though he's seventeen years old. —*verb* ✦ fashion, form, mold, model ✧ design, make, sculpt I *shaped* the bread dough into a loaf.

**share** *verb* ✦ divide, split ✧ deal out, distribute, partition, ration The three friends *shared* their lunches. —*noun* ✦ division, part, percentage, portion ✧ piece, segment, fraction Each employee got a *share* of the profits.

**sharp** *adjective* 1. ✦ keen, sharp-edged, honed ✧ acute, pointed, pointy Piranhas have teeth that are as *sharp* as a razor. 2. ✦ abrupt, rapid, sudden, steep ✧ clear, distinct The temperature took a *sharp* drop last night. 3. ✦ bitter, harsh, severe, stinging, cutting ✧ nasty The actor was upset over the director's *sharp* criticism. 4. ✦ alert, bright, clever, intelligent, quick, smart, shrewd It takes a *sharp* mind to solve this riddle . —*adverb* ✦ exactly, precisely, promptly, punctually, on time, right The train will leave at 8 p.m. *sharp*.

**sharpen** *verb* ✦ hone, whet ✧ file, grind, edge This carving knife needs to be *sharpened*.

**shatter** *verb* 1. ✦ burst, break, smash, splinter, fragment ✧ disintegrate, crumble The jar slipped out of my hand and *shattered* on the floor. 2. ✦ demolish, destroy, finish, ruin, spoil, undo, devastate Last night's loss *shattered* our dream of winning the championship.

**shed** *verb* 1. ✦ cast off, molt ✧ discard, drop, remove, eliminate Snakes *shed* their skin to make room for continued growth. 2. ✦ cast, emit, give, project, spread, radiate ✧ release, throw The sun *sheds* little warmth on cold winter days.

**sheer** *adjective* 1. ✦ see-through, thin, translucent ✧ clear, transparent The *sheer* lace curtains let a lot of sunlight into the room. 2. ✦ absolute, complete, pure, thorough, total, utter The little boy made up a story that was *sheer* nonsense. 3. ✦ perpendicular, steep, vertical, abrupt The climbers scaled the cliff's *sheer* face.

**shelter** *noun* 1. ✦ cover, protection, refuge ✧ safety, security We sought *shelter* when it began to rain. 2. ✦ asylum, haven, home, refuge, sanctuary ✧ hospital, retreat Our veterinarian runs a *shelter* for homeless cats and dogs.

**shield** *noun* ✦ cover, guard, safeguard, screen, protection ✧ defense A power saw has a *shield* that is designed to protect the user from injury. —*verb* ✦ cover, screen, protect, guard, shelter ✧ defend I used a newspaper to *shield* my head from the hot sun.

**shift** *verb* 1. ✦ move, maneuver, relocate, transfer ✧ **carry, transport** The boy *shifted* his book-bag from one shoulder to the other. **2.** ✦ **alter, change, switch, vary** ✧ **adjust, swerve, veer** The wind *shifted* direction. —*noun* **1.** ✦ **alteration, change, changeover, switch, move** ✧ **transfer** I haven't gotten used to the *shift* from regular to daylight savings time. **2.** ✦ **duty, tour, watch, assignment, period** ✧ **crew, staff** The night *shift* begins at midnight.

**shimmer** *verb* ✦ **glimmer, glisten, glitter, sparkle, twinkle, flash, shine** The lights from the cruise ship *shimmered* on the dark water.

**shine** *verb* **1.** ✦ **beam, flash** ✧ **glare, gleam, glow, radiate** Please *shine* the flashlight over here. **2.** ✦ **buff, polish, wax, gloss** ✧ **brush, rub** I need to *shine* my shoes for the party. —*noun* ✦ **luster, sheen, gleam, gloss, glow, polish, sparkle** The man buffed his car until it had a bright *shine*.

**ship** *noun* ✦ **boat, vessel, watercraft** ✧ **freighter, ocean liner, steamer, tanker** There were more than a dozen large *ships* in the harbor. —*verb* ✦ **send, dispatch, convey, deliver, forward, transport** ✧ **move** How much will it cost to *ship* this package to Japan?

**shiver** *verb* ✦ **tremble, shake, shudder** ✧ **quake, quiver, vibrate** The skiers *shivered* from the cold as they waited for the chair lift. —*noun* ✦ **shudder, tremble, tremor, shake, jitter** ✧ **quake, quiver** The eerie story sent a *shiver* down my spine.

**shock** *noun* ✦ **blow, jar, jolt** ✧ **start, surprise, upset, trauma** It was a *shock* to the family when my father lost his job. —*verb* ✦ **appall, outrage, dismay, stagger, startle, stun, surprise, shake** The terrorist attack *shocked* the world.

### Word Groups

A **shoe** is an outer covering for the human foot. **Shoe** is a general term with no true synonyms. Here are some different kinds of shoes to investigate in a dictionary: **boot, clog, loafer, moccasin, pump, sandal, slipper, sneaker**

**shoot** *verb* **1.** ✦ **launch, let fly, propel** ✧ **discharge, fire, hurl** I *shot* an arrow into the air. **2.** ✦ **bolt, dart, dash, flash, rocket, run, rush, hurry** A rabbit *shot* out of the sagebrush when we rode by on our dirt bikes. —*noun* ✦ **bud, sprout** ✧ **runner, stem, sucker, tendril** The crocuses sent up new *shoots* through the spring snow.

**shop** *noun* ✦ **store** ✧ **boutique, department store,** outlet, market This mall has over a hundred different *shops*. —*verb* ✦ **go shopping, browse, look** ✧ **buy, purchase** My friend and I like to *shop* for clothes together.

**shore** *noun* ✦ **beach, coast, seacoast, seashore, seaside, waterfront** The children built a sandcastle at the *shore*.

**short** *adjective* **1.** ✦ **little, small, diminutive** ✧ **low, slight, tiny, wee** The little child was too *short* to ride the roller coaster. **2.** ✦ **brief, concise, terse, succinct** ✧ **fast, speedy, swift** Our boss gave us a *short* talk about the importance of being on time. —*adverb* ✦ **abruptly, instantly, quickly, suddenly, unexpectedly, immediately** The hikers stopped *short* when they came to the edge of a cliff.

**shortage** *noun* ✦ **deficit, lack, scarcity, shortfall** ✧ **deficiency, insufficiency** There are so many players on my soccer team that we have a *shortage* of uniforms.

**shortcoming** *noun* ✦ **drawback, fault, flaw, imperfection** ✧ **defect, weakness** My friend's impatience is her only *shortcoming*.

**shorten** *verb* ✦ **decrease, reduce, lessen, cut, trim** ✧ **abridge, condense** Research shows that every cigarette *shortens* the smoker's life by eleven minutes.

**shout** *verb* ✦ **yell, scream, cry out, bellow** ✧ **howl, roar** I had to *shout* in order to be heard over the loud music. —*noun* ✦ **yell, cry, call, scream** ✧ **bellow, howl, roar** When I heard my neighbor's *shout*, I went outside to see what he wanted.

**shove** *verb* ✦ **move, push, nudge** ✧ **press, thrust, propel** The students *shoved* their desks into a circle. —*noun* ✦ **nudge, push, thrust** ✧ **boost, prod** I gave my model boat a *shove*, and it floated across the pool.

**show** *verb* **1.** ✦ **display, exhibit, present** ✧ **demonstrate, reveal** The museum guide *showed us* a fossil and described how it was formed. **2.** ✦ **conduct, escort, guide, lead, direct, steer** The usher *showed* us to our seats. —*noun* **1.** ✦ **display, exhibition, pageant, presentation** ✧ **demonstration, exhibit** I entered my border collie in the local dog *show*. **2.** ✦ **performance, production, program** ✧ **entertainment, spectacle, drama** The school *show* was a big success.

**shred** *noun* ✦ **piece, scrap, strip, tatter, bit** ✧ **fragment, particle** The children tore the newspapers into *shreds* for their papier-mâché project. —*verb* ✦ cut up, rip up, tear up ✧ grate, slice, dice I *shredded* some lettuce for a salad.

**shrewd** *adjective* ✦ clever, intelligent, smart, keen, sharp, wise ✧ practical Li Qiang made a *shrewd* guess and got the answer right.

**shriek** *noun* ✦ cry, scream, screech, shout, squeal, yell, holler I let out a *shriek* when I saw the snake. —*verb* ✦ cry out, scream, screech, shout, squeal, yell, holler Lots of people began *shrieking* when the rock band came onstage.

**shrink** *verb* 1. ✦ contract, decrease, reduce, shorten, dwindle ✧ constrict, shrivel Shadows *shrink* as the sun rises higher. 2. ✦ back away, draw back, retreat, withdraw ✧ cower, cringe, flinch The frightened cat *shrank back* from the dog that was barking.

**shrivel** *verb* ✦ dry up, wilt, wither ✧ fade, droop, shrink, wrinkle The rose petals *shriveled* after they fell to the ground.

**shudder** *verb* ✦ shiver, tremble, quake, quiver, shake ✧ convulse, twitch The children *shuddered* as they listened to the scary ghost story. —*noun* ✦ quiver, shiver, tremble, tremor ✧ convulsion, twitch I gave a *shudder* of relief when I got safely back to shore.

**shuffle** *verb* 1. ✦ hobble, limp, straggle, stumble ✧ drag, scuff, scuffle The injured player *shuffled* off the field. 2. ✦ jumble, mix up, scramble, rearrange, reorder ✧ shift The teacher *shuffled* the papers on her desk. —*noun* ✦ hobble, limp ✧ scuffle, stumble I walked with a *shuffle* when I sprained my ankle.

**shut** *verb* 1. ✦ close ✧ fasten, latch, lock, seal, secure Please *shut* the window. 2. ✦ cage, confine, coop up, enclose, pen ✧ imprison Tamara *shut* her parrot in its cage for the night.

**shy** *adjective* 1. ✦ bashful, meek, reserved, timid, modest, sheepish ✧ coy I felt a little *shy* on the first day at my new job. 2. ✦ lacking, missing, short, under ✧ deficient, wanting Our soccer team is *shy* one player. —*verb* ✦ cringe, flinch, jerk away, recoil, shrink back The horse *shied away* when I reached out to pet it.

**Antonyms shy**

*adjective* 1. bold, brash, brave, confident, fearless 2. enough, over

**sick** *adjective* ✦ ill, sickly, unwell, queasy ✧ ailing, unhealthy The greasy dinner made me feel *sick*.

**sickly** *adjective* ✦ in poor health, unhealthy, infirm, ailing ✧ feeble, weak The homeless kitten was frail and *sickly*.

**side** *noun* 1. ✦ end, edge, border, boundary, margin ✧ rim The teams lined up on opposite *sides* of the field. 2. ✦ face, surface ✧ part, half I turned the letter over and read what was on the other *side*. 3. ✦ version, view, viewpoint, opinion, position ✧ aspect The judge listened to both *sides* before she made up her mind. 4. ✦ squad, team, faction ✧ group, party, sect Which *side* do you think will win the game?

**sift** *verb* ✦ filter, strain, winnow, screen ✧ separate, sort The cook *sifted* flour into the cake batter.

**sight** *noun* 1. ✦ eyesight, seeing, vision, eye ✧ perception A hawk's *sight* is very keen. 2. ✦ view, scrutiny ✧ appearance, glance, glimpse, look The hot-air balloon came into *sight* over the ridge. 3. ✦ spectacle, scene, picture, show ✧ marvel, wonder A magnolia tree is a beautiful *sight* when it is in full bloom. —*verb* ✦ glimpse, observe, perceive, see, spot, view, behold The soldiers *sighted* an enemy plane approaching.

**sign** *noun* 1. ✦ gesture, mark, signal ✧ expression, symbol, token The teacher raised her hand as a *sign* for the class to be quiet. 2. ✦ announcement, bulletin, notice, poster ✧ billboard We put *signs* all around the neighborhood advertising our yard sale. 3. ✦ evidence, indication, hint, suggestion, trace, clue The space probe will look for *signs* of life on Mars. —*verb* ✦ endorse, inscribe, autograph ✧ initial All the students *signed* their teacher's birthday card.

**significance** *noun* ✦ consequence, importance, meaning, relevance ✧ value, weight This language proficiency test is of great *significance* to my job prospects.

**significant** *adjective* ✦ big, consequential, historic, important, notable, meaningful My family's move to the United States was a *significant* event in my life.

**silence** *noun* ✦ hush, quiet, quietness, stillness ✧ calm, peace A *silence* came over the room when the teacher walked in. —*verb* ✦ hush, shush, quiet, quieten, calm ✧ muffle, shut up My mother *silenced* my crying brother by rocking him gently.

**silent** *adjective* 1. ✦ quiet, hushed, soundless, still, noiseless ✧ mute The congregation was *silent* during the minister's sermon. 2. ✦ implied, undeclared, unexpressed, unsaid, unspoken, understood The two children have a *silent* agreement not to tell on each other.

*adjective* 1. clamorous, loud, noisy 2. declared, spoken

**silly** *adjective* ✦ absurd, comical, foolish, crazy, ridiculous, stupid, dumb ✧ frivolous The little boy looked *silly* in his father's business suit.

**similar** *adjective* ✦ close, comparable, equivalent, like, corresponding ✧ identical My best friend and I have *similar* tastes when it comes to books and movies.

**similarity** *noun* ✦ resemblance, closeness, relation, likeness, sameness ✧ agreement The movie had a disclaimer saying that any *similarity* to a real person or event was strictly a coincidence.

**simple** *adjective* 1. ✦ easy, effortless, uncomplicated ✧ basic, elementary I finished the *simple* work assignment in twenty minutes. 2. ✦ plain, modest, basic ✧ natural, unadorned I enjoy a *simple* meal of bread, fruit, and cheese.

**sin** *noun* ✦ evil, misdeed, offense, trespass, violation, wrong, vice Many religions consider lying and stealing to be *sins*.

**sincere** *adjective* ✦ earnest, genuine, heartfelt, honest, real, true My friend's apology seemed to be *sincere*.

**Word Groups**

To **sing** is to utter words or sounds in musical tones. **Sing** is a general term with no true synonyms. Here are some different ways of singing to investigate in a dictionary: **carol, chant, croon, hum, serenade, vocalize, warble**

**single** *adjective* ✦ lone, solitary, one, only, sole ✧ individual, alone The contest's rules said to submit a *single* poem.

**sink** *verb* 1. ✦ go down, go under, submerge, submerse ✧ descend, dip, plunge The RMS Titanic *sank* in less than three hours after hitting an iceberg on April 10, 1912. 2. ✦ bore, drill, dig, penetrate ✧ excavate The farmer *sank* the well to a depth of two hundred feet.

**sit** *verb* 1. ✦ be seated, sit down ✧ perch, rest, settle You may *sit* wherever you like. 2. ✦ be located, be situated, lie ✧ occupy, reside, stand The farm *sits* on one hundred acres of rich farmland.

**site** *noun* ✦ area, location, place, position, spot, locale We picked a level *site* on which to set up the tent.

**situation** *noun* ✦ circumstance, condition, state, status ✧ place, predicament The heavy rains have created a dangerous *situation* for people living near the river.

**size** *noun* ✦ dimension, extent, measurement, proportion, volume ✧ area, mass The stegosaurus was a large dinosaur, but it had a brain that was only about the *size* of a walnut.

**sketch** *noun* ✦ drawing, picture, illustration ✧ diagram, draft, portrait Alejandra made a pencil *sketch* of the blooming cherry tree. —*verb* ✦ draw, depict, portray ✧ diagram, outline, illustrate The art teacher asked her students to *sketch* a horse from memory.

**skill** *noun* ✦ talent, ability, capability, aptitude, technique ✧ art, craft I can ski reasonably well, but I don't have the *skill* to do a jump.

**skillful** *adjective* ✦ adept, capable, competent, expert, good, masterful, skilled The cellist's *skillful* performance was a pleasure to experience.

**skinny** *adjective* ✦ gaunt, lean, slender, slim, thin, scrawny, spare My grandmother is always feeding me because she thinks I'm too *skinny*.

**skip** *verb* 1. ✧ bounce, bound, gambol, hop, jump, leap, spring The girl was so happy that she *skipped* all the way home from school. 2. ✦ miss, omit, leave out, cut ✧ avoid, dodge, neglect I had to *skip* breakfast because I woke up late. —*noun* ✦ bounce, spring, hop, bound, jump, leap The happy child walked down the street with a *skip* in his step.

**skirt** *noun* ✧ dress, frock, gown, garment The school's uniform for girls is a blue sweater and a plaid *skirt*. —*verb* ✦ bypass, go around, circle ✧ avoid, dodge, evade This freeway *skirts* the city to avoid the downtown traffic.

**slack** *adjective* 1. ✦ limp, loose, relaxed ✧ flexible, soft, pliant My muscles felt *slack* after a few minutes in the hot tub. 2. ✦ down, off, slow, sluggish ✧ idle, quiet, weak During the winter, business is *slack* at the beach resort.

*adjective* 1. rigid, stiff, taut, tense, tight 2. active, busy, employed, engaged

**slam** *verb* ✦ bang, dash, smack ✧ crash, hit, smash, strike A gust of wind *slammed* the door shut. —*noun* ✦ bang, crash, smack, smash, wham ✧ blow The car door made a loud *slam* when I flung it shut.

**slant** *verb* ✦ lean, incline, slope, tilt, tip, cant, pitch ✧ list The telephone pole *slants* to one side ever since someone backed into it. —*noun* ✦ incline, slope, tilt, cant, pitch ✧ list I position my keyboard at a *slant* in order to make typing easier on my wrists.

**slap** *verb* ✦ hit, smack, strike, swat, wallop ✧ pat, spank The little baby likes to *slap* the water when taking a bath. —*noun* ✦ blow, hit, smack, swat, wallop, clap ✧ pat, rap, spank The prospector gave his mule a *slap* on the rump to get it to move.

**slash** *verb* 1. ✦ hack, chop, cut, slice ✧ carve, gash The explorers *slashed* at the thick undergrowth with their machetes. 2. ✦ decrease, drop, lower, mark down, pare, reduce, diminish After the holidays, stores usually *slash* prices on leftover Christmas decorations. —*noun* ✦ cut, gash, laceration, slice, slit ✧ rip, split, tear The doctor stitched up the *slash* on my hand.

**slavery** *noun* ✦ enslavement, bondage, servitude ✧ captivity, serfdom The 13th Amendment abolished *slavery* in the United States.

**slay** *verb* ✦ kill, slaughter, exterminate ✧ assassinate, execute, murder This book is about a knight who *slays* dragons.

**sleek** *adjective* ✦ glossy, lustrous, shiny, silky, glistening, gleaming ✧ polished The seal's fur was *sleek* and smooth when it came out of the water.

**sleep** *noun* ✦ slumber ✧ nap, rest, snooze, repose We spend about one third of our lives in *sleep*. —*verb* ✦ doze, drowse, snooze, slumber ✧ nap, rest I like to *sleep* late on Saturday mornings.

**slender** *adjective* ✦ lean, skinny, slim, thin, spare ✧ bony, gaunt, scrawny Deer have long, *slender* legs.

**slice** *noun* ✦ wedge, slab, chunk, piece ✧ portion, section, segment I had a *slice* of melon and some grapes for my snack. —*verb* ✦ carve, cut, divide, split ✧ section, segment, separate Renee *sliced* her birthday cake and served it to her guests.

**slick** *adjective* ✦ slippery, glassy ✧ smooth, glossy, shiny, sleek Be careful, the ice on the sidewalk is very *slick*.

**slide** *verb* ✦ coast, glide, skid, skim, slip ✧ shoot The hockey puck *slid* across the ice. —*noun* ✦ avalanche ✧ landslide, mudslide, rockslide The road was closed because it was blocked by a *slide*.

**slight** *adjective* 1. ✦ faint, insignificant, minor, small, trivial, unimportant, negligible There is only a *slight* difference between these two colors. 2. ✦ slender, slim, thin, skinny ✧ petite, delicate, frail The man is so *slight* that he can wear boy's clothing. —*verb* ✦ snub, spurn, affront, insult, offend ✧ disregard, ignore I didn't mean to *slight* you, but I haven't had a chance to return your call. —*noun* ✦ affront, insult, snub ✧ disrespect, offense I meant my remark as a joke, not a *slight*.

**slim** *adjective* ✦ lean, slender, slight, thin, spare ✧ gaunt, skinny You're looking *slim* since you began exercising.

**sling** *verb* ✦ cast, fling, heave, hurl, pitch, throw, toss The boys were *slinging* stones at tin cans.

**slip** *verb* 1. ✦ glide, slide, steal, slink ✧ move, pass, slither The wolf *slipped* silently through the woods. 2. ✦ slide, fall, stumble ✧ trip, tumble, skid I *slipped* on the icy sidewalk. 3. ✦ decline, decrease, drop off, fall off, lapse ✧ sink, vanish, sag My attention began to *slip* as I grew tired. —*noun* 1. ✦ fall, trip, stumble, tumble, misstep ✧ skid, slide I've been careful walking on ice ever since I had a nasty *slip*. 2. ✦ error, mistake, blunder ✧ lapse, oversight I could tell my friend was distracted when he made a *slip* and called me by his sister's name.

**slit** *noun* ✦ slot, aperture, hole, opening ✧ cut, slash Castle walls commonly had *slits* through which archers could shoot at enemy soldiers. —*verb* ✦ cut, slash, slice, split ✧ carve, rip, sever The clerk *slit* the cardboard box open.

**slogan** *noun* ✦ motto, saying ✧ expression, phrase, jingle The company printed its *slogan* on all of its packaging.

**slope** *verb* ✦ angle, incline, slant ✧ lean, pitch, tip, list The parkland *slopes* down to the river. —*noun* ✦ slant, pitch, angle, grade, incline ✧ tilt, cant The *slope* of this roof is very steep.

**sloppy** *adjective* ✦ disorderly, messy, slovenly, untidy ✧ **careless, poor** Whenever I write too fast, my handwriting looks *sloppy*.

**slow** *verb* ✦ **decrease, reduce, moderate, slacken** ✧ **brake, delay** The truck *slowed* its speed as it approached the icy bridge. —*adjective* ✦ **gradual, moderate, plodding, sluggish, unhurried, leisurely** The turtle made *slow* progress across the sand.

**sluggish** *adjective* ✦ **lethargic, listless, slow, torpid** ✧ **idle, inactive, lazy** Reptiles are *sluggish* in cold weather.

**slumber** *verb* ✦ **sleep, snooze, doze, drowse, nap** ✧ **rest** My cat likes to *slumber* on the windowsill. —*noun* ✦ **sleep** ✧ **snooze, doze, nap, rest** I fell into a deep *slumber* that lasted all night long.

**sly** *adjective* ✦ **clever, crafty, sneaky, veiled** ✧ **cunning, shrewd, tricky** Chau gave us a *sly* hint that her birthday was coming up.

**smack** *verb* ✦ **hit, slap, strike, swat, slam** ✧ **punch, smash, squash** I *smacked* at the mosquito that was on my arm. —*noun* ✦ **blow, hit, slam, strike, swat, thump** ✧ **pat, slap, tap** The carpenter gave the nail a hard *smack* with his hammer.

**small** *adjective* 1. ✦ **little, miniature, minute, tiny, wee** ✧ **puny, petite** Compsognathus was a *small* dinosaur no bigger than a chicken. 2. ✦ **limited, meager, scant, scanty, slight, paltry** There is only a *small* amount of seed left in the bird feeder. 3. ✦ **insignificant, minor, petty, trifling, trivial, unimportant** There's only a *small* difference between these two brands of blue jeans.

**smart** *adjective* ✦ **bright, brilliant, intelligent, quick, sharp, clever** My friend is so *smart* that she can do long division in her head. —*verb* ✦ **ache, hurt, sting, throb** ✧ **burn, itch** Does that bee sting still *smart*?

**smash** *verb* ✦ **crumble, crush, pound, pulverize, break, disintegrate** ✧ **demolish, splinter** I *smashed* the graham crackers to make a crust for my cheesecake.

**smear** *verb* 1. ✦ **apply, dab, daub, layer, spread** ✧ **coat, cover** Ji-young *smeared* sunscreen on her arms and shoulders. 2. ✦ **smudge, streak, blur** ✧ **blot, rub, soil** Juan was careful not to *smear* the paint before it dried. —*noun* ✦ **smudge, blot, blotch, spot, stain, streak, dab** There was a *smear* of jam on the little boy's cheek.

**smell** *verb* 1. ✦ **scent, sniff, whiff** ✧ **detect, nose, perceive, sense** We could *smell* bread baking in the oven. 2. ✦ **reek, stink** Rotten eggs really *smell*. —*noun* ✦ **aroma, fragrance, scent, odor** ✧ **whiff, stink** I love the *smell* of lilacs in the springtime.

**smile** *noun* ✦ **grin, beam** ✧ **smirk, simper** The photographer asked us for a big *smile*. —*verb* ✦ **beam, grin** ✧ **smirk** The boy *smiled* at his parents when his name was called for the science award.

**smooth** *adjective* 1. ✦ **calm, tranquil, undisturbed** ✧ **even, flat, level** The surface of the lake turns *smooth* when the wind dies down. 2. ✦ **easy, effortless, orderly, uneventful, untroubled, simple** The plane made a *smooth* landing. —*verb* ✦ **even, flatten, make level, straighten** ✧ **press, iron** Please *smooth* the tablecloth before you set out the dishes.

**smother** *verb* ✦ **extinguish, snuff, stifle, suffocate** ✧ **choke, strangle** We threw sand on our campfire to *smother* the flames.

**smudge** *verb* ✦ **blur, rub, smear, mess up** ✧ **soil, spot, stain** I *smudged* the lines of my pencil drawing to give it a soft look. —*noun* ✦ **smear, blot, blotch, spot, stain, streak** I wiped the *smudge* of dirt off my face.

**snake** *noun* ✦ **serpent** ✧ **reptile** A *snake* wriggled through the grass. —*verb* ✦ **meander, twist, weave, wind** ✧ **coil, spiral** A little stream *snakes* through the valley.

**snap** *verb* 1. ✦ **break, crack, fracture, splinter, split** ✧ **crackle, pop** The twig *snapped* when I stepped on it. 2. ✦ **bite, nip, snatch, strike, lunge** ✧ **grasp, seize** Don't put your finger in the cage or the parrot might *snap* at it. —*noun* 1. ✦ **crack, crackle, pop** ✧ **click, bang** We could hear the *snap* of the logs as they started to burn. 2. ✦ **clasp, fastener** ✧ **catch** Western shirts commonly have mother-of-pearl *snaps*.

**snare** *noun* ✦ **trap** ✧ **bait, lure, net, noose** The Scouts learned how to make a *snare* in their outdoor survival class.

**snatch** *verb* ✦ **grab, pluck, seize, snap up, take** ✧ **catch, clutch** Jung *snatched* an apple from the bowl as he ran out the door. —*noun* ✦ **bit, fragment, part, portion, segment** ✧ **piece** I caught brief *snatches* of the TV news while making dinner.

**sneak** *verb* 1. ✦ **crawl, creep, slink, steal** ✧ **slither, prowl** I could just see the skunk *sneaking* along the fence. 2. ✦ **smuggle, spirit, slip** ✧ **hide** Occasionally someone will *sneak* a camera into a movie theater.

**snip** *verb* ✦ clip, cut ✧ nip, slice, trim, shear The student *snipped* some pictures out of a magazine for her report.

---

**Word Groups**

Snow is water that falls to the earth as frozen crystals. Snow is a very specific term with no true synonyms. Here are some related words to investigate in a dictionary: **frost, hail, ice, powder, sleet, slush, snowflake**

---

**snub** *verb* ✦ avoid, ignore, shun, spurn ✧ insult, offend, slight My cat *snubbed* me after I left him alone for the weekend. —*noun* ✦ insult, offense, slight, rebuff, discourtesy ✧ oversight It was an unintentional *snub* when I forgot to respond to my friend's invitation.

**snug** *adjective* 1. ✦ cozy, comfortable ✧ homey, safe, secure, sheltered The cabin was warm and *snug* during the storm. 2. ✦ confining, small, tight, cramped ✧ close, compact, narrow The jacket was too *snug* on me, so I gave it to my younger sister.

**snuggle** *verb* ✦ cuddle, curl up, nestle, nuzzle ✧ embrace, hug Kana likes to *snuggle* with her kitten.

**soak** *verb* 1. ✦ immerse, steep, marinate ✧ drench, saturate, wet These beans should be *soaked* in water overnight. 2. ✦ absorb, sop up, take up ✧ dry, mop I used a paper towel to *soak up* the spilled milk.

**soar** *verb* 1. ✦ float, fly, glide, hover, sail, coast ✧ lift The hot-air balloon *soared* high above us. 2. ✦ increase, climb, lift, mount, multiply, rise, grow, ascend The company's profits *soared* as their product became popular.

**sob** *verb* ✦ weep, bawl, cry, wail, whimper ✧ yowl, keen The baby *sobbed* because it was tired and hungry. —*noun* ✦ cry, wail, whimper, weeping, sobbing ✧ yowl There were *sobs* from the audience at the end of the sad movie.

**sober** *adjective* ✦ grave, grim, sad, serious, solemn, somber, mournful We were all in a *sober* mood after we heard the bad news.

**sociable** *adjective* ✦ cordial, friendly, genial, neighborly, social ✧ hospitable Our *sociable* neighbor is always coming over for a visit.

**social** *adjective* 1. ✦ civic, communal, community, public ✧ common, popular The quality of public education is an important *social* issue. 2. ✦ amiable, cordial, friendly, outgoing, sociable, neighborly Everyone says that I am a *social* person because I have lots of friends.

**society** *noun* 1. ✦ the community, the people, the public ✧ civilization, humanity The criminal was sent to prison because he was a threat to *society*. 2. ✦ association, club, group, organization ✧ union, league Trisha and Marianna joined a birdwatching *society*.

**soft** *adjective* 1. ✦ mushy, pulpy, spongy, squishy ✧ fleshy, yielding These apples have gotten too *soft* to eat. 2. ✦ satiny, silky, downy, delicate, fine, fluffy, smooth Guinea pigs and rabbits have *soft* fur. 3. ✦ low, mellow, quiet, subdued, hushed ✧ gentle, mild The father uses a *soft* voice when he reads his little daughter to sleep.

**soggy** *adjective* ✦ sodden, sopping, saturated, soaked, soaking, wet ✧ damp The cardboard box was *soggy* after being left outside in the rain.

**soil**¹ *noun* ✦ dirt, earth, humus, loam ✧ ground, topsoil We mixed fertilizer with the *soil* when we planted our garden.

**soil**² *verb* ✦ dirty, muddy, smear, smudge, stain ✧ foul, spot We *soiled* our football uniforms playing on the muddy field.

**soldier** *noun* ✦ combatant, fighter, serviceman, servicewoman ✧ warrior, trooper There were hundreds of *soldiers* involved in the battle.

**sole** *adjective* ✦ one, only, lone, single, solitary ✧ particular My *sole* reason for going to the mall was to look for my friend.

**solemn** *adjective* ✦ grave, grim, serious, sober, somber, earnest Everybody at the funeral had *solemn* expressions on their faces.

**solid** *adjective* 1. ✦ substantial, firm, sound, sturdy, stable ✧ concrete, dense, hard The building may be old, but it has good, *solid* walls. 2. ✦ continual, continuous, unbroken, uninterrupted, steady, constant There was a *solid* line of traffic all the way to the airport. 3. ✦ dependable, secure, steady, strong, steadfast My best friend and I have a *solid* friendship.

**solitary** *adjective* ✦ lone, solo, individual, isolated, single ✧ alone, lonely The cyclists passed a *solitary* runner on the bike path.

**solution** *noun* 1. ✦ mixture, compound, blend, infusion ✧ fluid, liquid I cleaned the carpet with a special *solution* designed to remove stains. 2. ✦

answer, explanation, key ✧ interpretation, result Li Jie guessed the *solution* to my riddle.

**solve** *verb* ✦ answer, figure out, resolve, work out ✧ explain, analyze It took the student a long time to *solve* the tough math problem.

**somber** *adjective* ✦ dismal, grim, melancholy, sad, serious, sober, solemn, gloomy We were in a *somber* mood after hearing about the accident.

**sometimes** *adverb* ✦ at times, now and then, occasionally, periodically, irregularly I usually walk to work, but *sometimes* I take the bus.

**song** *noun* ✦ melody, tune, ballad, hymn ✧ air, anthem, carol We sang folk *songs* around the campfire.

**soon** *adverb* ✦ before long, promptly, quickly, rapidly, shortly ✧ directly If we don't get there *soon*, we might miss the start of the movie.

**soothe** *verb* ✦ ease, relax, relieve ✧ calm, quiet, settle I took a hot bath to *soothe* my stiff muscles.

**Antonyms** soothe

*verb* agitate, fluster, irritate, unsettle, upset

**sore** *adjective* ✦ aching, hurting, painful, sensitive, tender My sprained wrist is still *sore*. —*noun* ✦ hurt, injury, wound ✧ bruise, infection, inflammation I need a bandage for the *sore* on my knee.

**sorrow** *noun* ✦ anguish, distress, grief, heartache, sadness, unhappiness It is believed that elephants feel great *sorrow* when one of their herd dies or is injured.

**sorry** *adjective* 1. ✦ regretful, apologetic, contrite ✧ sad, sorrowful, remorseful I am *sorry* that I forgot your birthday. 2. ✦ inferior, pitiful, poor, miserable, ridiculous, wretched No one believed the boy's *sorry* excuse for being late.

**sort** *noun* ✦ kind, manner, type, variety, style ✧ brand, category Bianca and I tried all *sorts* of different foods at the international fair. —*verb* ✦ arrange, categorize, classify, group, organize, order, separate Volunteers *sorted* the items that would be sold at the fundraiser.

**sound**¹ *noun* ✦ noise ✧ clamor, din, racket, tone, roar Do you hear that strange *sound*? —*verb* 1. ✦ ring, peal, toll, chime ✧ resound The cook *sounded* the dinner bell. 2. ✦ appear, look, look like, seem It *sounds* as if you had a good day at work.

**sound**² *adjective* 1. ✦ solid, strong, sturdy, firm, in-

tact, undamaged The old barn is still *sound*. 2. ✦ good, logical, prudent, reasonable, sensible, wise, intelligent My older friend gave me some *sound* advice about relationships.

**sour** *adjective* 1. ✦ acidic, tart, bitter, tangy, sharp, lemony The *sour* candy made my mouth water. 2. ✦ spoiled, rancid, bad, curdled ✧ fermented *Sour* milk has a disgusting smell. —*verb* ✦ curdle, go bad, spoil ✧ ferment, turn Milk will *sour* if it is left unrefrigerated.

**source** *noun* 1. ✦ resource, reference ✧ authority, basis, fountain, reservoir An online encyclopedia is a good *source* for facts. 2. ✦ beginning, head, origin, start, outset The Colorado River has its *source* in the Rocky Mountains.

**souvenir** *noun* ✦ memento, keepsake ✧ gift, reminder, token My boyfriend brought me a *souvenir* from his trip to Hawaii.

**sovereign** *noun* ✦ monarch, ruler ✧ emperor, king, queen The United States has never had a *sovereign*. —*adjective* 1. ✦ regal, royal ✧ absolute, imperial, supreme The queen exercised her *sovereign* power when she declared a national holiday. 2. ✦ free, independent, autonomous, self-governing, self-ruling Mozambique became a *sovereign* nation in 1975.

**space** *noun* 1. ✦ gap, opening, separation ✧ break, crack, hole My little sister is wearing braces to close up the *spaces* between her teeth. 2. ✦ area, expanse, room, volume ✧ distance, spread Our new piano takes up a lot of *space* in the living room. —*verb* ✦ arrange, array, place, separate ✧ order, organize The trees were *spaced* far enough apart to give them room to grow.

**span** *noun* ✦ duration, interval, length, period, range, term A sequoia tree's life *span* can be several thousand years. —*verb* ✦ bridge, cover, cross, stretch (over) ✧ reach, traverse The fallen telephone pole *spanned* the width of the road.

**spare** *verb* 1. ✦ save, not harm, protect, exempt, pardon, rescue We *spared* the mouse's life by using a no-kill trap. 2. ✦ part (with), let go ✧ donate, give, lend, provide Can you *spare* a few sheets of paper? —*adjective* 1. ✦ additional, extra, reserve, unused ✧ surplus, substitute We have a *spare* bedroom for overnight guests. 2. ✦ lean, skinny, slender, slim, thin ✧ gaunt, scrawny Greyhound dogs have a *spare* build.

**sparkle** *verb* ✦ gleam, glimmer, glitter, shimmer, twinkle ✧ flash The snow *sparkled* in the moonlight. —*noun* ✦ flash, flicker, gleam, glimmer, glitter, twinkle The diamond earrings gave off *sparkles* of light.

**spasm** *noun* ✦ contraction, cramp, twitch, convulsion ✧ seizure A muscle *spasm* can be painful.

**speak** *verb* 1. ✦ talk, chat, converse ✧ chatter, communicate We were just *speaking* about you, and here you are. 2. ✦ declare, say, state, tell, express, utter The witness swore that he *spoke* the truth.

**spear** *noun* ✦ javelin, lance ✧ harpoon, pike Roman soldiers usually carried a short sword and two *spears* into battle. —*verb* ✦ jab, stab, stick, impale, lance, pierce ✧ thrust I *speared* a piece of chicken with my fork.

**special** *adjective* ✦ particular, specific, distinctive ✧ individual, unique My grandfather is on a *special* diet to lower his cholesterol.

**specialty** *noun* ✦ specialization, strong point, strength ✧ accomplishment, skill, talent As a cook, my roommate's *specialties* are grilled cheese sandwiches and tuna melts.

**species** *noun* ✧ category, classification, kind, sort, type, variety It has been estimated that there are more than two million *species* of insects.

**specific** *adjective* ✦ clear, definite, exact, explicit, particular, precise The teacher gave the students *specific* directions for their science project.

*adjective* ambiguous, general, open, unclear, vague

**specimen** *noun* ✦ example, sample ✧ item, piece, sort, type Yuki showed me some different *specimens* of quartz from his rock collection.

**speck** *noun* ✦ bit, grain, particle, mote ✧ fleck, drop, spot The wind blew a *speck* of dirt into my eye.

**spectacle** *noun* ✦ display, exhibition, performance, presentation, show, sight The laser light show was a fascinating *spectacle*.

**spectacular** *adjective* ✦ impressive, magnificent, remarkable, sensational, dramatic On New Year's Eve we watched a *spectacular* display of fireworks.

**speculate** *verb* ✦ ponder, contemplate, deliberate (about), reflect (on), think (about) The philosopher *speculated on* the meaning of life.

**speech** *noun* 1. ✦ speaking, talk, talking, utterance ✧ dialect, language Parrots can be trained to imitate human *speech*. 2. ✦ address, lecture, talk ✧ oration, discussion, sermon The mayor gave a *speech* at the annual Fourth of July picnic.

**speed** *noun* ✦ pace, rate, velocity ✧ haste, quickness, swiftness The cheetah can run at a *speed* of about sixty miles per hour. —*verb* ✦ race, rush, bolt, dart, fly, shoot ✧ whiz, zoom The black horse *sped* past the others to win the race.

**spell**[1] *noun* ✦ charm, enchantment, magic spell, fascination ✧ formula, incantation We fell under the *spell* of the beautiful tropical beach.

**spell**[2] *noun* ✦ interval, period, span, stretch, time, stint ✧ bout The sunshine was welcome after the long *spell* of rainy weather.

**spend** *verb* 1. ✦ expend, lay out, pay out, dispense ✧ exchange, trade How much money did you *spend* at the book fair? 2. ✦ consume, fill, occupy, pass, put in, use up Cho *spends* a lot of time surfing the internet.

**sphere** *noun* 1. ✦ ball, globe, spheroid ✧ bulb, oval The Earth is a *sphere* that is slightly flattened at its poles. 2. ✦ area, domain, realm, range, reach, scope ✧ field, territory England's *sphere* of influence formerly included India and parts of Africa.

**Word Groups**

A **spider** is a small animal that has eight legs and a body divided into two parts. **Spider** is a specific term with no true synonyms. Here are some common American spiders: **black widow, brown recluse, daddy longlegs, garden, house, huntsman, orb weaver, tarantula, trapdoor, wolf**

**spice** *noun* ✦ flavoring, seasoning ✧ condiment, herb, relish, zest Ginger is a *spice* that is commonly used in Chinese cooking. —*verb* ✦ flavor, season ✧ enhance, enliven, improve I *spiced* the hot apple cider with cinnamon, nutmeg, and cloves.

**spill** *verb* ✦ flow, pour, run, slop, splash, splatter ✧ overflow Root beer *spilled* all over when I dropped my glass. —*noun* ✦ fall, tumble, dive, plunge ✧ accident Shannon took a *spill* when she went skateboarding yesterday.

**spin** *verb* 1. ✦ narrate, recount, relate, tell, recite ✧ report I like to hear my grandmother *spin* tales about her childhood. 2. ✦ revolve, rotate, turn, twirl, whirl, swirl How long can you make this top *spin*? —*noun* 1. ✦ revolution, rotation, turn, twirl,

**whirl** I gave the bicycle wheel a *spin* to see if it was in balance. **2.** ✦ drive, jaunt, ride ✧ excursion, run I took my new car for a *spin* around the neighborhood.

**spirit** *noun* **1.** ✦ soul ✧ consciousness, essence, heart, mind Many religions teach that the *spirit* lives on after the body dies. **2.** ✦ apparition, ghost, phantom, specter People say that this house is haunted by *spirits*. **3.** ✦ energy, enthusiasm, pep, vigor, vim ✧ bravery, courage, pluck The cheerleaders shouted with lots of *spirit*. —*verb* ✦ carry, smuggle, sneak ✧ abduct, make off (with) The documents couldn't be found because someone *spirited* them away.

**spite** *noun* ✦ animosity, ill will, malice, nastiness, resentment He said that nasty remark out of *spite*. —*verb* ✦ annoy, irritate, needle, nettle, provoke, upset, aggravate She withheld the information just to *spite* him.

**splendid** *adjective* ✦ beautiful, glorious, impressive, magnificent, remarkable, wonderful The peacock's tail looked *splendid* in the sun.

**splendor** *noun* ✦ beauty, brilliance, glory, magnificence, majesty, grandeur We were impressed by the *splendor* of the Great Smoky Mountains.

**split** *verb* **1.** ✦ cut, slice, carve, sever ✧ break, burst, crack Phoung *split* the watermelon in two with a big knife. **2.** ✦ distribute, divide, separate, share ✧ allot We agreed to *split* the work so that we could get it done faster. —*noun* ✦ rip, slash, tear, slit ✧ break, crack, separation There is a *split* in the seam of my blue jeans.

**spoil** *verb* **1.** ✦ foul up, mess up, ruin, upset, wreck, mar ✧ destroy The sudden rainstorm *spoiled* our day at the beach. **2.** ✦ decay, decompose, go bad, rot, putrefy ✧ curdle, sour I threw the fruit away because it had *spoiled*. **3.** ✦ baby, cater (to), coddle, indulge, pamper The woman *spoiled* her cats by feeding them fresh fish.

**sponsor** *noun* ✦ backer, contributor (to), promoter, supporter, benefactor ✧ patron My friend's company is one of the *sponsors* of our roller hockey team. —*verb* ✦ back, finance, promote, support, fund That bakery *sponsors* an annual pie-eating contest.

**spontaneous** *adjective* ✦ ad-lib, improvised, impromptu, unplanned, impulsive, informal The

teacher set aside her lesson plan and gave her class a *spontaneous* talk.

**sport** *noun* ✦ athletics ✧ competition, contest, game, recreation My father played *sports* in high school and college.

**spot** *noun* **1.** ✦ patch, blotch, dot, mark, speck, fleck ✧ blot, stain Dalmatians have black *spots* on white fur. **2.** ✦ location, place, site, area, point, position, locale This looks like a good *spot* to set up our tent. —*verb* **1.** ✦ dot, fleck, mark, spatter, splatter, sprinkle ✧ stain The floor in the artist's studio was *spotted* with paint. **2.** ✦ glimpse, observe, see, spy, perceive ✧ detect, find, locate The boaters were thrilled when they *spotted* the migrating whales.

**spray** *noun* ✦ mist, shower, sprinkle ✧ drizzle, squirt, spout There are birds bathing in the *spray* from the fountain. —*verb* ✦ shower, spurt, squirt, shoot ✧ splash, spout, sprinkle Firefighters *sprayed* water on the burning building.

**spread** *verb* **1.** ✦ extend, open up, stretch out, unfold, unfurl, expand The pigeon *spread* its wings and flew away. **2.** ✦ layer, put, smear, smooth ✧ coat, cover Maria *spread* cream cheese on her bagel. **3.** ✦ circulate, distribute, repeat, report ✧ broadcast, transmit I believe that it's not nice to *spread* gossip. —*noun* **1.** ✦ advance, development, expansion, growth ✧ increase, extension This ointment can stop the *spread* of your rash. **2.** ✦ breadth, extent, span, stretch, reach, width ✧ expanse, range, size, sweep The wandering albatross has wings with a *spread* of twelve feet. **3.** ✦ bedspread, cover ✧ blanket, quilt My aunt made me a quilted *spread* for my bed.

**spring** *verb* **1.** ✦ bounce, bound, jump, leap ✧ hop, skip My dog *sprang* up and ran to the door when he heard the mail carrier. **2.** ✦ appear, arise, emerge, grow, rise, sprout, issue Flowers *sprang up* in the desert after the heavy rainfall.

**sprinkle** *verb* **1.** ✦ shake, pour, scatter, spread ✧ dribble, dust, trickle Rachel *sprinkled* salt on her popcorn. **2.** ✦ drizzle ✧ rain, shower, precipitate, mist It *sprinkled* lightly at first, but a heavy rain soon started. —*noun* **1.** ✦ bit, dash, touch, trace, pinch ✧ dribble, trickle I put a *sprinkle* of sugar on top of the cookies. **2.** ✦ drizzle ✧ rain, shower, precipitation, mist This afternoon's *sprinkle* barely wet the pavement.

**sprout** *verb* ✦ come up, arise, bud, grow, germinate ✧ bloom, flower Everything that we planted in our garden is now beginning to *sprout.* —*noun* ✦ seedling, shoot ✧ bud, runner, stem, tendril I grow alfalfa *sprouts* in a jar.

**spur** *verb* ✦ stimulate, motivate, inspire, egg (on), goad, move ✧ prompt, urge The coach's pep talk *spurred* the team to victory over their rivals.

**spurt** *noun* 1. ✦ jet, spout, spray, squirt, stream ✧ gush, eruption Steamboat Geyser in Yellowstone National Park can send a *spurt* of water 300 feet into the air. 2. ✦ burst, rush ✧ blast, gust, outbreak The marathoner won the race with a final *spurt* of energy. —*verb* ✦ gush, splash, spray, squirt, erupt ✧ spout Water *spurted* all over the floor from the broken faucet.

**spy** *noun* ✦ secret agent, undercover agent, agent, operative ✧ informer The *spy* stole some secret government documents. —*verb* 1. ✦ scout out, snoop around, watch ✧ eavesdrop, peep, pry The scout was sent to *spy* on the enemy camp. 2. ✦ detect, glimpse, notice, see, spot, observe, perceive I *spied* my friend in the crowd.

**squabble** *verb* ✦ bicker, quarrel, argue, dispute, fight ✧ feud My roommate and I *squabbled* over whose turn it was to clean the bathroom. —*noun* ✦ argument, disagreement, dispute, fight, quarrel ✧ feud The two friends quickly resolved their *squabble.*

**squad** *noun* ✦ detail, group, unit, outfit ✧ company, platoon, team A *squad* of soldiers was sent to guard the embassy.

**squall** *noun* ✦ gale, storm, windstorm ✧ flurry, tempest We got caught in a *squall* on our fishing trip.

**square** *noun* ✦ box ✧ block, cube, rectangle Graph paper is marked into many small *squares.*

**squash** *verb* ✦ mash, smash, crush ✧ compress, press, squeeze Nhan *squashed* the bananas to make banana bread.

**squat** *verb* ✦ crouch, hunker ✧ bend, hunch, kneel, stoop The father *squatted* down to help his little daughter tie her shoe.

**squeal** *noun* ✦ scream, screech, shriek, yell, yowl ✧ wail, cry The toddler let out a *squeal* when she stubbed her toe. —*verb* ✦ scream, screech, shriek, yell, yowl ✧ wail, cry The girls *squealed* with laughter during their pillow fight at the slumber party.

**squeeze** *verb* 1. ✦ cram, crowd, jam, pack, stuff,

wedge ✧ compress We were barely able to *squeeze* the Thanksgiving leftovers into the refrigerator. 2. ✦ force, wring, press, twist, express ✧ crush, extract You pull this lever to *squeeze* the water from the mop. —*noun* ✦ embrace, hug ✧ clasp, clutch, grasp, press My father put his arm around my shoulder and gave me a *squeeze.*

**squirm** *verb* ✦ twist, wiggle, wriggle, writhe ✧ jerk, shift, turn The garter snake *squirmed* out of my grasp.

**squirt** *verb* ✦ spray, spurt, discharge, eject, expel, jet ✧ gush, splash An octopus *squirts* a cloud of ink when it is frightened. —*noun* ✦ jet, spray, spurt, stream ✧ gush, splash, spout A *squirt* of juice from the grapefruit hit me in the eye.

**stab** *verb* ✦ jab, plunge, thrust, ram, prick, stick ✧ puncture The zoo's veterinarian *stabbed* a big needle through the elephant's thick, wrinkled skin. —*noun* ✦ jab, poke, thrust ✧ lunge, plunge, swipe I made a *stab* at the meatball with a toothpick.

**stable** *adjective* ✦ firm, steady, solid, fixed, secure, immovable ✧ sound Before Miki climbed up the ladder, she made sure that it was *stable.*

**Antonyms** stable
*adjective* precarious, shaky, unstable, unsteady, wobbly

**stack** *noun* ✦ pile, mound, heap, mass ✧ batch, bundle We have *stacks* of old magazines in the basement. —*verb* ✦ pile, mound, heap ✧ assemble, group, load I *stacked* all my books in one corner of my room.

**staff** *noun* 1. ✦ crook, stave, walking stick ✧ cane, pole, rod, wand The shepherd used a *staff* to herd the sheep. 2. ✦ assistants, employees, help, personnel, retinue ✧ crew, team The senator's *staff* did the research for the proposed bill.

**stage** *noun* ✦ phase, period, step ✧ degree, level, point The new housing project is in its final *stage* of development. —*verb* ✦ act out, dramatize, perform, present, put on, produce ✧ direct The neighborhood children like to *stage* plays for their parents.

**stagger** *verb* 1. ✦ lurch, reel, stumble, sway, weave, wobble, totter The boy whirled around and around until he *staggered* from dizziness. 2. ✦ amaze, astonish, astound, overwhelm, startle, dumbfound ✧ **surprise** The man was *staggered* by the news that he had won the lottery.

**stagnant** *adjective* ✦ **stale, dirty, foul** ✧ **contaminated, polluted** I changed the *stagnant* water in my vase of flowers.

**stain** *verb* ✦ **discolor, smear, smudge, soil, dirty** ✧ **blemish, blot** The leaky ballpoint pen *stained* my fingers. —*noun* ✦ **blot, blotch, mark, smear, smudge, spot, blemish** I hope this paint *stain* on my shirt will come out.

**stake** *noun* ✦ **picket, pole, post, stick** ✧ **peg, pin, spike** We supported the tomato plant by tying it to a *stake*. —*verb* ✦ **mark, mark off, outline** ✧ **define, limit** We *staked* out the borders for our new flower garden.

**stale** *adjective* ✦ **dry, hard, old** ✧ **moldy, rotten, spoiled, rancid** Let's feed this *stale* bread to the ducks at the park.

**stalk** *verb* 1. ✦ **stamp, stomp, stride, tramp, march** ✧ **swagger** The angry customer *stalked* out of the store. 2. ✦ **pursue, follow, hunt, shadow, track, trail** ✧ **chase** The lion *stalked* its prey with great patience.

**stall** *noun* 1. ✦ **enclosure, compartment, cubicle, pen** ✧ **corral, stable, coop, sty** The barn has a separate *stall* for each horse. 2. ✦ **booth, stand** ✧ **counter, shop, store, table** We set up a *stall* at the swap meet to sell our homemade jams and jellies. —*verb* ✦ **die, quit, stop, halt** ✧ **cease, delay, interrupt** I took my car to the mechanic because the engine is always *stalling*.

**stammer** *verb* ✦ **stutter, sputter** ✧ **falter, mumble, stumble** I *stammer* sometimes when I get excited.

**stamp** *verb* 1. ✦ **tramp, trample, crush, mash, squash, step, tread** I *stamped* the aluminum can flat before putting it in the recycling bin. 2. ✦ **imprint, print** ✧ **label, mark, inscribe, seal** I *stamped* the package with my return address. —*noun* ✦ **seal, emblem, label, mark** ✧ **symbol, sign** The clerk put the bank's *stamp* on the important document.

**stampede** *noun* ✦ **charge, dash, flight, race, rush** ✧ **panic** There was a *stampede* to the creek when the thirsty cattle smelled the water. —*verb* ✦ **bolt, flee, take flight, scatter** ✧ **panic** The buffalo *stampeded* when they sensed danger.

**stand** *verb* 1. ✦ **arise, get up, rise** We all *stood up*

when the national anthem began to play. 2. ✦ **be located, be situated** ✧ **rest, sit, perch** The Eiffel Tower *stands* in Paris, France. 3. ✦ **apply, hold, persist, remain, stay, last** ✧ **exist** I tried to change my friend's mind, but she said that her decision still *stands*. 4. ✦ **abide, bear, endure, take, tolerate, withstand** ✧ **deal (with), handle** I moved away because I could no longer *stand* all the noise in my apartment building. —*noun* 1. ✦ **booth, stall** ✧ **counter, shop, store, pushcart** We bought oranges at the fruit *stand*. 2. ✦ **rack, pedestal, support** ✧ **counter, platform, table** I need a *stand* to hold my music book while I practice. 3. ✦ **attitude, position, viewpoint, stance** ✧ **opinion, policy** My grandfather tends to take a conservative *stand* on political issues.

**standard** *noun* 1. ✦ **ideal, principle, guideline, requirement** ✧ **example, model, pattern** The teacher set high *standards* for the students. 2. ✦ **banner, ensign, flag, pennant, colors** An honor student carried the school *standard* in the parade. —*adjective* ✦ **customary, normal, ordinary, regular, typical, usual** ✧ **average, routine** A *standard* baseball team has nine players.

**stanza** *noun* ✦ **verse** ✧ **paragraph, part, section, segment** Thalia recited all three *stanzas* of her favorite poem.

**star** *noun* ✦ **lead, principal** ✧ **leading lady, leading man, hero, heroine** My little sister was the *star* of her school play. —*verb* ✦ **feature, showcase** ✧ **introduce, present, promote** This opera *stars* my favorite singer.

**stare** *verb* ✦ **gape, gawk, gaze, look, peer** ✧ **glare, observe, ogle, watch** My dog *stares* at me whenever I am eating something. —*noun* ✦ **glare, glower, look, glance** ✧ **gape, gaze** The librarian gave the children a disapproving *stare* when they talked too loudly.

**start** *verb* 1. ✦ **depart, embark, get going, leave, set out, go** We'll need to *start* early if we want to get back before dark. 2. ✦ **begin, commence, initiate, open** ✧ **activate, undertake** I *start* my day with a cup of coffee. 3. ✦ **create, establish, found, institute, launch, originate, pioneer** Automobiles *started* a new age of transportation. —*noun* ✦ **beginning, commencement, onset, opening** ✧ **initiation, outset** I am looking forward to the *start* of the holiday season.

**startle** *verb* ✦ **surprise, frighten, scare, shock,**

alarm, jolt You *startled* me because I hadn't heard you come home.

**state** *noun* 1. ✦ condition, situation, status, circumstance ✧ position, shape Our house was in a *state* of confusion while we were having the kitchen remodeled. 2. ✦ country, nation ✧ dominion, land, republic The *state* of Israel was founded in 1948. —*verb* ✦ announce, declare, express, proclaim, say, speak The witness *stated* her name for the record.

**stately** *adjective* ✦ august, dignified, grand, majestic, noble, regal, royal, solemn The presidential inauguration is a *stately* occasion.

**statement** *noun* ✦ announcement, bulletin, declaration, proclamation ✧ commentary, comment The senator's aide read a *statement* to the press.

**station** *noun* 1. ✦ position, post ✧ location, place, stand The guard was instructed not to leave her *station* beside the entrance. 2. ✦ headquarters, station house, office ✧ base, center I went to the police *station* to turn in the purse that I had found. 3. ✦ depot, terminal ✧ stop, terminus The bus *station* is on Main Street. —*verb* ✦ assign to, place at, position at, post at ✧ locate, situate Soldiers were *stationed at* the outside of the embassy building.

**stationary** *adjective* ✦ fixed, immobile, motionless, unmoving ✧ steady, still I like to exercise inside on a *stationary* bike.

**stationery** *noun* ✦ notepaper, paper, writing paper ✧ parchment I wrote my grandmother a letter on a piece of my favorite *stationery*.

**statue** *noun* ✦ sculpture, image, figure ✧ bust, likeness The *statue* of Abraham Lincoln at his memorial in Washington, D.C., was sculpted by Daniel Chester French in 1922.

**status** *noun* ✦ position, rank, standing, station ✧ grade, place, situation The president of a bank holds a position of high *status*.

**stay** *verb* 1. ✦ linger, remain, wait, tarry ✧ loiter, pause We *stayed* in the movie theater until everyone else had left. 2. ✦ abide, dwell, live, lodge, reside, room ✧ visit I have a friend in Japan I can *stay* with whenever I go there. —*noun* ✦ visit, stopover ✧ holiday, vacation, stop I am looking forward to having a nice *stay* at my cousin's.

**steady** *adjective* 1. ✦ stable, firm, solid, secure ✧ sound, strong Is that old ladder *steady* enough to hold my weight? 2. ✦ constant, continuous, even, regular, uniform The ferry made *steady* progress toward the island. —*verb* ✦ stabilize, brace, hold fast, secure, support ✧ balance Please help *steady* the canoe while I get in.

**steal** *verb* 1. ✦ pilfer, snatch, rob, thieve, loot, plunder, swipe Magpies often *steal* shiny objects and take them back to their nests. 2. ✦ creep, slip, sneak, slide, glide, slink, tiptoe ✧ prowl I didn't hear my little brother *steal* into the room.

**steam** *noun* ✦ mist, condensation, vapor ✧ fog, moisture *Steam* from the shower fogged up the bathroom mirror. —*verb* ✦ cruise, navigate, ply ✧ run, sail, travel, voyage During the 1800s, riverboats *steamed* up and down the Mississippi River.

**steep**[1] *adjective* ✦ perpendicular, sheer, vertical, abrupt, upright ✧ high The walls of the Grand Canyon are *steep* cliffs.

**steep**[2] *verb* ✦ immerse, soak, submerge, brew ✧ saturate, drench *Steep* the tea leaves in water that is hot but not boiling.

**steer** *verb* ✦ direct, guide, maneuver, operate, control ✧ navigate, pilot I can *steer* my bicycle with no hands.

**stem**[1] 1 *noun* ✦ trunk, stalk, shoot ✧ branch, cane, stock, twig The *stem* of the giant bamboo can grow up to three feet in 24 hours. —*verb* ✦ originate, spring, rise, issue, derive, arise, result The town's financial difficulties *stem* from a lack of tax revenue.

**stem**[2] *verb* ✦ stop, check, arrest, halt, stanch, control, restrain The medic used a pressure bandage to *stem* the bleeding.

**step** *noun* 1. ✦ footstep, pace, stride ✧ move, tread, walk The soldier took a *step* forward when his name was called. 2. ✦ measure, procedure, tactic, act, action ✧ level, stage Installing a smoke alarm is an important *step* in fire safety. —*verb* ✦ walk, tread, tramp ✧ pace, shuffle, stride Devout Buddhists try not to *step* on any insects or other living creatures.

**sterilize** *verb* ✦ disinfect, sanitize, clean, cleanse,

**purify** ✧ **pasteurize** Dentists *sterilize* their tools after each use.

**stern¹** *adjective* ✦ **hard, harsh, severe, sharp, strict** ✧ **grave, grim** My roommate gave me a *stern* look when I slammed the door.

**stern²** *noun* ✦ **back, end, rear, tail, poop** ✧ **heel** We stood at the *stern* of the boat to watch the dolphins.

**stick** *noun* ✦ **branch, twig, stem, switch** ✧ **limb, pole, rod, shaft** I used a *stick* to write my name in the sand. —*verb* **1.** ✦ **jab, stab, pierce, poke, puncture, prick, spear** Katlyn *stuck* holes in the potato so that it wouldn't explode in the microwave. **2.** ✦ **attach, fasten, put up** ✧ **glue, nail, paste, pin, tape** The boy *stuck up* basketball posters all over his bedroom walls. **3.** ✦ **adhere, cling, hold** ✧ **bond, catch, fix, stay** Static electricity made the balloon *stick* to my hair. **4.** ✦ **extend, poke, protrude, push, put, thrust** ✧ **place, position** My dog loves to *stick* his head out the car window when I take him for a ride.

**sticky** *adjective* **1.** ✦ **gluey, gummy, tacky** ✧ **adhesive, syrupy** The sap of a pine tree is very *sticky*. **2.** ✦ **clammy, humid, muggy, sultry** ✧ **damp, moist, wet** The rain was a relief after the hot and *sticky* weather.

**stiff** *adjective* **1.** ✦ **inflexible, rigid, hard, inelastic, unbending, unyielding** ✧ **taut** Coat hangers are made from *stiff* wire. **2.** ✦ **intense, tough, keen, powerful, strong** ✧ **forceful** Competition was *stiff* at the football playoffs.

**stifle** *verb* ✦ **control, hold back, restrain, muffle, smother, stop, suppress** I tried to *stifle* my laughter as I read the funny book in the library.

**still** *adjective* **1.** ✦ **quiet, silent, hushed, noiseless, soundless** The students were *still* as their teacher read them a story. **2.** ✦ **calm, motionless, placid, unmoving, tranquil, serene** ✧ **stationary** The lake was perfectly *still* after the wind died down. —*noun* ✦ **quiet, quietness, silence, hush, stillness, tranquility** The *still* of the night was broken by an owl's screech. —*adverb* ✦ **nevertheless, nonetheless** ✧ **however, yet, too, but** The concert tickets are expensive, but I *still* plan on going.

**stimulate** *verb* ✦ **arouse, awaken, encourage, excite, quicken, spur, spark** Going to the air show *stimulated* my desire to become a pilot.

**sting** *verb* ✦ **bite, burn, chafe** ✧ **smart, hurt, injure, wound** The cold wind *stung* my cheeks.

**stingy** *adjective* ✦ **miserly, tight, ungenerous, cheap** ✧ **greedy, selfish** The *stingy* boy wouldn't share his Halloween candy with anyone.

---

**Antonyms** **stingy**
*adjective* **free, generous, lavish, liberal, unselfish**

---

**stink** *verb* ✦ **smell bad, reek, smell** That rotting fish on the beach is beginning to *stink*. —*noun* ✦ **bad smell, foul odor, stench, reek, smell** There is quite a *stink* coming from the garbage can.

**stir** *verb* ✦ **blend, churn, mix, whip, agitate, beat, whisk** I *stirred* the cake batter until it was smooth. —*noun* ✦ **commotion, disturbance, tumult, turmoil, uproar, fury** The woman's long-lost brother caused quite a *stir* when he showed up at her front door.

**stock** *noun* **1.** ✦ **hoard, reserve, store, supply, cache** ✧ **inventory** We keep a *stock* of canned foods for emergency use. **2.** ✦ **livestock, farm animals, herd** ✧ **cattle, pigs, sheep** The rancher branded the *stock* before turning them loose on the range. **3.** ✦ **ancestry, blood, descent, line, lineage, origin, parentage** ✧ **clan, kindred** My father likes to say that he comes from sturdy farming *stock*. —*verb* ✦ **fill, furnish, provide, supply, provision** ✧ **equip, store** We *stocked* our refrigerator with fresh fruits and vegetables.

**stocky** *adjective* ✦ **heavyset, stout, sturdy, thick, thickset, solid** I'm just like my uncle—short and *stocky*.

**stomach** *noun* ✦ **belly, tummy, gut** ✧ **abdomen, midsection** My *stomach* is growling because I am hungry.

**stone** *noun* **1.** ✦ **pebble, rock** ✧ **boulder, cobble, cobblestone** Carlos skipped a *stone* across the pond. **2.** ✦ **gem, gemstone, jewel, precious stone** The *stone* in my ring is an opal.

**stoop** *verb* **1.** ✦ **bend down, lean over, crouch** ✧ **bow, duck, kneel, squat** I *stooped down* to pick up the pencil I dropped. **2.** ✦ **resort, sink, submit, succumb** ✧ **descend, fall, lower** I would never *stoop* to cheating. —*noun* ✦ **slouch, droop** ✧ **bend, bow, sag** The elderly man walks with a slight *stoop*.

**stop** *verb* **1.** ✦ **cease, discontinue, halt, quit** ✧ **pause, suspend** I had to *stop* running because I got a cramp in my leg. **2.** ✦ **bar, block, check, pre-**

vent, restrain ✧ intercept The manager *stopped* the children from entering the pool hall because they weren't eighteen. —*noun* ✦ **halt, standstill** ✧ **pause, delay, end, finish** Drivers have to come to a full *stop* at a flashing red light.

**store** *noun* 1. ✦ **shop, business, retailer** ✧ **boutique, department store, market** I bought my friend's present at a stationery *store*. 2. ✦ **hoard, reserve, stock, supply, cache, accumulation** ✧ **inventory** We keep a *store* of candles for use when the power goes out. —*verb* ✦ **hoard, stockpile, put away, save, stash, stock, keep** ✧ **collect** Squirrels *store* nuts in the fall so they'll have food in the winter.

**storm** *noun* 1. ✦ **tempest** ✧ **blizzard, downpour, gale, hurricane, rainstorm, snowstorm, tornado** The *storm* was accompanied by lots of thunder and lightning. 2. ✦ **outbreak, outburst, eruption, deluge, flood** ✧ **shower** There was a *storm* of protest against the unjust law. —*verb* 1. ✦ **bluster, blow** ✧ **hail, pour, rain, snow** It *stormed* all night, but in the morning the sky was bright and clear. 2. ✦ **assail, assault, attack, charge, raid, rush, beset** Enemy soldiers *stormed* the castle.

**story**[1] *noun* 1. ✦ **account, anecdote, narrative, report, description** ✧ **version** My grandmother told me the *story* about how she met my grandfather. 2. ✦ **tale, yarn** ✧ **fable, fiction, legend, narrative** The little girl likes to read ghost *stories* by flashlight under the covers.

**story**[2] *noun* ✦ **floor, level** ✧ **layer, tier** The Empire State Building has 102 *stories*.

**stout** *adjective* ✦ **brawny, burly, heavyset, husky, stocky, thickset, sturdy** Saint Bernards are big, *stout* dogs.

> **Antonyms** stout
> *adjective* **gaunt, lean, skinny, spare, thin, weedy**

**straggle** *verb* ✦ **trail, lag, linger, dawdle** ✧ **ramble, stray, wander** I *straggled* so far behind my friends when we went shopping that I almost lost track of them.

**straight** *adjective* 1. ✦ **upright, erect, in line, perpendicular, vertical** ✧ **even** My dance instructor often reminds me to keep my back *straight*. 2. ✦ **direct, frank, candid, honest, true, truthful, reliable** I gave my girlfriend a *straight* answer when she asked where I had been. —*adverb* ✦ **at once, directly, immediately, instantly, right** When I got

home from work, I went *straight* to the refrigerator for a snack.

**strain** *verb* 1. ✦ **labor, strive, struggle, try, work, toil** ✧ **exert** I couldn't get the top off the jar no matter how hard I *strained*. 2. ✦ **pull, sprain, wrench** ✧ **hurt, injure, twist** I *strained* my calf muscles by carrying such a heavy load on the hike.

**strange** *adjective* ✦ **odd, peculiar, unusual, weird, bizarre, eccentric** Taking baths and fetching sticks is *strange* behavior for a cat.

**stranger** *noun* ✦ **unknown person, newcomer** ✧ **alien, foreigner, immigrant** Parents commonly teach their children to not talk to *strangers*.

**strangle** *verb* ✦ **choke, suffocate, throttle, gag** ✧ **smother** I loosened my tie because it was almost *strangling* me.

**strap** *noun* ✦ **band, strip, thong** ✧ **cord, lash, string** My sandals have two *straps* in front and one in back. —*verb* ✦ **lash, tie, tether, bind** ✧ **attach, fasten, secure** We *strapped* our luggage to the roof of the car.

**strategy** *noun* ✦ **method, plan, procedure, scheme, system, tactic, program** The new company has a marketing *strategy* that seems to be working.

**stray** *verb* ✦ **drift, wander, ramble, range, roam** ✧ **digress, meander** My mind *strayed* during the boring movie. —*adjective* ✦ **abandoned, homeless, lost, wandering, vagrant** We adopted the *stray* dog because it was so friendly.

**streak** *noun* 1. ✦ **stripe, strip, band, line** ✧ **bar, vein** The golden-crowned sparrow has a yellow *streak* on its head. 2. ✦ **interval, period, run, spell, stretch, string** ✧ **bout** I've had a *streak* of good luck lately. —*verb* 1. ✦ **band, stripe, bar** ✧ **mark, smear, smudge, stain** The sky was *streaked* with red at dawn. 2. ✦ **dash, flash, race, rush, sprint, fly** ✧ **zoom** The runner *streaked* across the finish line.

**stream** *noun* 1. ✦ **brook, creek, rill** ✧ **channel, river** This little *stream* dries up in the summer. 2. ✦ **gush, jet, spurt, flow** ✧ **current, torrent** Choi sprayed a *stream* of water on her vegetable garden. —*verb* ✦ **course, flow, gush, pour, run, rush, spill** I was laughing so hard that tears *streamed* down my face.

**street** *noun* ✦ **avenue, boulevard** ✧ **drive, lane, road, alley** My best friend and I live on the same *street*.

**strength** *noun* ✦ power, brawn, might ✧ force, muscle, vigor My boyfriend has been working out with weights to improve his *strength*.

**strengthen** *verb* ✦ brace, buttress, fortify, reinforce ✧ support, toughen Workers added new beams to *strengthen* the old bridge.

**strenuous** *adjective* ✦ active, brisk, dynamic, energetic, vigorous ✧ hard, tough Our soccer coach put us through a *strenuous* practice this afternoon.

**stress** *noun* 1. ✦ emphasis, importance, significance, value, weight ✧ concern My family puts a lot of *stress* on getting a college education. 2. ✦ anxiety, distress, strain, tension, worry, nervousness Some people experience *stress* when they go to a dentist. —*verb* ✦ emphasize, highlight, underscore, assert ✧ feature, insist, affirm My boss *stresses* the importance of creativity.

**stretch** *verb* ✦ draw out, pull out, extend ✧ expand, lengthen, spread, widen It's a good idea to *stretch* your muscles after exercising. —*noun* ✦ expanse, extent, length, span, reach, space ✧ distance We drove down a *stretch* of dirt road to get to our campsite.

**strict** *adjective* ✦ rigorous, firm, inflexible, rigid, stern, unyielding ✧ meticulous The school has a *strict* policy against the use of illegal drugs.

**Antonyms** strict

*adjective* flexible, indulgent, lax, lenient, relaxed

**strike** *verb* 1. ✦ hit, knock, slam, smack, whack ✧ pound, punch, tap The tennis ball *struck* me on the shoulder. 2. ✦ impress ✧ affect, touch, appear, occur, seem My cousin's joke didn't *strike* me as being very funny. 3. ✦ walk out, go on strike ✧ boycott, picket, protest The coal miners are planning to *strike* for better working conditions. —*noun* ✦ stroke, blow, hit ✧ knock, punch, smack The old oak tree was destroyed by a lightning *strike*.

**strip**[1] *verb* ✦ remove, take away, take off ✧ peel, skin, uncover The first step in refinishing furniture is to *strip* the old paint or varnish.

**strip**[2] *noun* ✦ band, ribbon ✧ piece, section, segment, shred The children wove place mats out of *strips* of construction paper.

**stripe** *noun* ✦ band, bar, line, streak ✧ strip, vein A zebra has black and white *stripes*.

**stroke**[1] *noun* 1. ✦ blow, hit, strike, impact, tap ✧ knock, swing I split the piece of firewood with a single *stroke* of my axe. 2. ✦ event, feat, occurrence, act ✧ accomplishment, achievement Getting home before the snow started was a *stroke* of good luck.

**stroke**[2] *verb* ✦ pet, rub, caress, pat ✧ brush, smooth, touch The girl likes to *stroke* her pet rabbit's fur.

**stroll** *verb* ✦ hike, walk, amble, ramble, roam, saunter, wander I like to *stroll* through the woods behind my house. —*noun* ✦ walk, hike, ramble, saunter ✧ excursion, promenade My friend and I took a *stroll* around the neighborhood.

**strong** *adjective* 1. ✦ brawny, mighty, muscular, powerful ✧ forceful, hale Elephants are *strong* enough to carry big logs with their trunks. 2. ✦ firm, secure, solid, stout, sturdy, substantial, sound This tree limb is *strong* enough to bear my weight.

**structure** *noun* 1. ✦ building ✧ construction, establishment, shed The ranch has a house, a barn, and several smaller *structures*. 2. ✦ arrangement, form, organization, pattern, design ✧ shape The human brain has a complex *structure*.

**struggle** *verb* ✦ battle, contend (with), fight, wrestle, combat ✧ compete, labor, toil The tired swimmer *struggled against* the current. —*noun* ✦ effort, endeavor, strain, trouble ✧ battle, fight It was a *struggle* to get the big chair into my small car.

**stubborn** *adjective* ✦ determined, headstrong, obstinate, uncooperative, unyielding, willful The *stubborn* camel refused to budge.

**student** *noun* ✦ pupil, learner ✧ schoolchild, schoolboy, schoolgirl, scholar The *students* bought a birthday present for their teacher.

**study** *noun* 1. ✦ analysis, examination, investigation ✧ learning, research The *study* of insects is called entomology. 2. ✦ office, den ✧ library, studio, workroom My parents turned their spare bedroom into a *study*. —*verb* ✦ review, go over, learn, read over, examine ✧ cram, meditate, research The student has to *study* her notes for tomorrow's history quiz.

**stuff** *noun* ✦ articles, goods, items, things, gear ✧ belongings, possessions Here's a list of the *stuff* that we need for the camping trip. —*verb* ✦ cram, crowd, fill, jam, load, pack ✧ squeeze, heap The piñata was *stuffed* with candy.

**stuffy** *adjective* 1. ✦ airless, close, stifling, suffocating ✧ muggy, sweltering I opened the windows to air out my *stuffy* room. 2. ✦ blocked, clogged, congested, filled My sinuses are *stuffy* because I have allergies.

**stumble** *verb* ✦ trip, slip, tumble, stagger ✧ blunder, fall The hiker *stumbled* and almost fell when her foot caught on a tree root.

**stump** *verb* ✦ baffle, bewilder, mystify, puzzle, thwart, stymie ✧ frustrate The crossword clue *stumped* me, so I asked my roommate for help.

**stun** *verb* ✦ shock, amaze, astonish, overwhelm, startle ✧ surprise I was *stunned* to hear that I had won the dance contest.

**stunning** *adjective* ✦ remarkable, sensational, spectacular, astonishing, dazzling, marvelous The ballerina thrilled the audience with her *stunning* performance.

**stunt**[1] *verb* ✦ check, curb, curtail, impede, limit, restrict ✧ retard, slow Doctors warn that poor nutrition can *stunt* a child's growth.

**stunt**[2] *noun* ✦ feat, trick ✧ act, exploit, performance, achievement My dog's best *stunt* is to roll over and play dead.

**stupid** *adjective* ✦ dumb, foolish, silly, unintelligent ✧ simple-minded, idiotic The student hesitated to ask a question because he worried that he might sound *stupid*.

**sturdy** *adjective* ✦ strong, solid, stout, substantial, firm ✧ rugged, tough I thought that the lawn chair was *sturdy*, but it broke under my weight.

**stutter** *verb* ✦ stammer ✧ falter, mumble, sputter, stumble My friend *stutters* when she feels shy. —*noun* ✦ stammer, stammering, stuttering, speech impediment He is going to a speech therapist to help correct his *stutter*.

**style** *noun* ✦ arrangement, design, fashion ✧ mode, pattern, shape That haircut is a great *style* for you.

**subdue** *verb* ✦ check, control, reduce, suppress, quiet ✧ pacify The medicine *subdued* my coughing.

**subject** *noun* 1. ✦ subject matter, theme, topic ✧ issue, point, question The professor told us to pick a report *subject* by the end of the week. 2. ✦ class, course, topic ✧ field, discipline My favorite *subject* in college was English literature.

**submerge** *verb* 1. ✦ immerse, submerse, soak, dip, douse, plunge, duck ✧ sink The tired hiker *submerged* her feet in the cold mountain stream. 2. ✦ flood, deluge, engulf, inundate, swamp ✧ drench, drown, overflow It rained so heavily that the river overflowed its banks and *submerged* the downtown streets.

**submit** *verb* 1. ✦ defer, give in, surrender, yield ✧ accept, comply, obey The dictator expected everyone to *submit* to his demands. 2. ✦ present, hand in, turn in, offer ✧ propose, advance Marissa *submitted* her short story to a prestigious literary magazine.

**subordinate** *adjective* ✦ junior, lower ✧ auxiliary, inferior, lesser, minor, secondary The company's president accepts suggestions from *subordinate* employees. —*noun* ✦ aide, assistant, employee, servant ✧ slave, attendant A good manager treats his or her *subordinates* with respect.

**subsequent** *adjective* ✦ following, ensuing, later, succeeding, successive ✧ future The misunderstanding and *subsequent* bad feelings were quickly resolved.

**subside** *verb* ✦ abate, decrease, diminish, dwindle, ebb, lessen, wane When the storm *subsided*, I went outside to shovel the walks.

**substance** *noun* 1. ✦ element, material, matter, stuff, item ✧ ingredient Water is the only *substance* that occurs naturally in three forms—gas, liquid, and solid. 2. ✦ essence, meaning, significance, depth ✧ reality, truth, worth The movie was enjoyable, but it didn't have much *substance*.

**substantial** *adjective* ✦ ample, considerable, generous, great, large, significant, sizable The new employee got a *substantial* raise after completing her internship.

**substitute** *noun* ✦ replacement, alternate, alternative, stand-in, equivalent I use honey as a *substitute* for sugar when making oatmeal cookies. —*verb* ✦ change, exchange, replace, swap, switch, trade, alternate The coach *substituted* the players every ten minutes to let everyone get some experience.

**subtract** *verb* ✦ deduct, remove, take off ✧ discount, withdraw The clerk *subtracted* the value of our coupons from our grocery bill.

**succeed** *verb* ✦ be successful, flourish, prosper, thrive ✧ triumph, work Retail stores need a good location in order to *succeed*.

**success** *noun* ✦ triumph, victory ✧ achievement, accomplishment, attainment, sensation The school's fundraising drive was a big *success*.

**successful** *adjective* 1. ✦ effective, efficient, favorable, productive, winning ✧ perfect My parents helped me to develop *successful* study habits. 2. ✦ accomplished, famous, notable, popular, prominent, well-known My dream is to be a *successful* poet.

**sudden** *adjective* ✦ abrupt, quick, rapid, hasty, unexpected, unforeseen ✧ instant The driver had to make a *sudden* stop in order to avoid hitting a dog.

**suffer** *verb* ✦ accept, bear, endure, experience, sustain, undergo, tolerate The coach told her players they'd have to *suffer* the consequences if they don't train hard.

**sufficient** *adjective* ✦ adequate, enough, ample ✧ abundant, satisfactory Do we have *sufficient* time to stop at the drugstore?

**suffocate** *verb* ✦ asphyxiate, choke, smother ✧ gag, stifle, strangle Dense smoke can *suffocate* a person.

**suggest** *verb* ✦ propose, put forward, recommend, offer, submit ✧ advise, counsel My boss *suggested* a work assignment that she thought I might like.

**suggestion** *noun* ✦ proposal, proposition, recommendation, idea ✧ advice, counsel I like your *suggestion* that we go to a movie after dinner.

**suit** *verb* ✦ agree (with), fit, please, satisfy, serve ✧ content, delight, gratify My new office *suits* me better than my old one did.

**suitable** *adjective* ✦ appropriate, apt, fit, good, proper, right ✧ acceptable I bought a new dress because I didn't have anything *suitable* for my friend's wedding.

**sullen** *adjective* ✦ surly, moody, resentful, sulky ✧ angry, cross, bitter, hostile My friend gets *sullen* whenever she thinks nothing is going her way.

**Antonyms** **sullen**

*adjective* cheerful, chipper, happy, pleasant, sunny

**sum** *noun* ✦ amount, grand total, sum total, total, gross ✧ aggregate, entirety, number Ticket sales for the raffle came to a larger *sum* than we had expected. —*verb* ✦ add up, calculate, compute, figure, total The businessman *summed up* the expenses from his trip.

**summary** *noun* ✦ digest, outline, review, synopsis ✧ abridgment, condensation The students had to read a book over the summer and turn in a *summary* of its contents in the fall.

**summit** *noun* ✦ peak, pinnacle, tip, top, crest ✧ crown There is snow all summer long on the mountain's *summit*.

**sunrise** *noun* ✦ dawn, daybreak, sunup ✧ daylight, morning Why is it that roosters always crow right around *sunrise*?

**sunset** *noun* ✦ nightfall, sundown, twilight, dusk ✧ evening The planet Venus will be visible just after *sunset*.

**superb** *adjective* ✦ excellent, fine, magnificent, splendid, superior, terrific The actress received an award for her *superb* performance.

**superior** *adjective* ✦ better, preferable, exceptional, first-rate, premium, excellent ✧ admirable, fine, high This store carries furniture of *superior* quality.

**supervise** *verb* ✦ administer, direct, manage, oversee, run ✧ govern, head The third-grade teacher is going to *supervise* the afterschool program.

**supervisor** *noun* ✦ overseer, director, head, manager, boss, chief ✧ administrator The factory has a *supervisor* in charge of each shift.

**supplement** *noun* ✦ addition, complement, extra, companion ✧ appendix, insert The professor gave us a reading packet as a *supplement* to our textbook. —*verb* ✦ add (to), augment, boost, extend ✧ complete, increase Lev *supplements* his regular income with the money that he makes as a part-time tutor.

**supply** *verb* ✦ equip, furnish, provide, outfit ✧ contribute, give, present Our team sponsor *supplied* us with new basketball uniforms. —*noun* ✦ stock, store, quantity ✧ hoard, inventory, reserve The corner store gets a fresh *supply* of milk every morning.

**support** *verb* 1. ✦ hold up, prop up, bear, brace, buttress ✧ reinforce The cabin has a big beam that *supports* the roof. 2. ✦ back, endorse, encourage, foster, promote, uphold ✧ aid, assist, help My parents have always *supported* my interest in studying abroad. —*noun* 1. ✦ backing, encouragement, help ✧ aid, assistance My friends have given me lots of *support*. 2. ✦ brace, buttress, pillar, post, prop ✧ **frame** The boy used toothpicks as *supports* for his miniature bridge.

**suppose** *verb* ✦ **believe, expect, guess, imagine, think** ✧ **assume, presume** Do you *suppose* it will snow tonight?

**supreme** *adjective* ✦ **top, highest, foremost, head, primary, principal, chief** The US president is the *supreme* commander of the nation's military forces.

**sure** *adjective* 1. ✦ **certain, confident, definite, positive, convinced** I am *sure* that I can finish my chores before noon. 2. ✦ **secure, steady, firm, reliable, stable, solid** Mountain goats are known for their *sure* footing.

**surface** *noun* ✦ **exterior, outside** ✧ **cover, face, top, skin** The Earth's *surface* is 80% water. —*verb* ✦ **cover, pave, top** ✧ **coat, overlay, spread** Ancient Roman roads were *surfaced* with stone.

**surpass** *verb* ✦ **better, eclipse, exceed, outdo, pass, top, beat** Robyn *surpasses* all of her teammates in speed and endurance.

**surprise** *verb* ✦ **amaze, astonish, astound, awe** ✧ **shock, startle, stun** I was *surprised* by how big the redwoods really are when I saw them up close. —*noun* ✦ **amazement, astonishment, wonder** ✧ **awe, shock, bewilderment** The boy's mother was filled with *surprise* when he cleaned his room without being told.

**surrender** *verb* ✦ **give up, capitulate, submit, yield** ✧ **quit, succumb** The army *surrendered* after being surrounded by enemy troops. —*noun* ✦ **capitulation, submission, yielding, concession** ✧ **resignation** Displaying a white flag to the enemy is the traditional sign of *surrender*.

**surround** *verb* ✦ **circle, encircle, envelop, ring, mob** ✧ **crowd, enclose, skirt** The actor was *surrounded* by reporters after he announced his retirement.

**survey** *verb* ✦ **inspect, observe, scan, view, check** ✧ **watch, regard** The general *surveyed* the battlefield as he planned his attack.

**survive** *verb* ✦ **exist, live, persist, thrive, endure, last** ✧ **withstand** Polar bears can *survive* in extremely cold climates.

**suspect** *verb* ✦ **distrust, doubt, mistrust, question, query** ✧ **challenge** We *suspected* our neighbors' motives when they showed up for a visit right at dinnertime.

**suspend** *verb* 1. ✦ **hang, dangle, sling, swing** ✧

**attach, fasten** I *suspended* my hammock between two trees. 2. ✦ **break off, discontinue, interrupt, postpone, delay, defer** The baseball game had to be *suspended* because of rain.

**suspense** *noun* ✦ **anxiety, apprehension, tension, uncertainty** ✧ **doubt, anticipation** The *suspense* was almost unbearable as we waited for the judges to announce the winner.

**suspension** *noun* ✦ **interruption, pause (in), halt (in), stoppage** ✧ **break, discontinuity** The cable company announced a brief *suspension* of service while they replaced their old equipment.

**suspicion** *noun* 1. ✦ **feeling, guess, hunch, idea, inkling, notion** ✧ **belief** I have a *suspicion* that my cubicle mate is the one who left a rubber chicken in my desk drawer. 2. ✦ **distrust, mistrust, doubt** ✧ **question, skepticism** When we discovered that the hamburger meat was missing, our *suspicions* fell on the dog.

**sustain** *verb* 1. ✦ **bear, carry, hold up, support** ✧ **brace, prop** This tripod doesn't look strong enough to *sustain* the weight of my telescope. 2. ✦ **hold, keep up, maintain** ✧ **preserve, retain, uphold** I turned off the TV program because it didn't *sustain* my interest.

**swallow** *verb* ✦ **take, ingest** ✧ **bolt, consume, gulp, guzzle** Some people can *swallow* a pill without taking any water. —*noun* ✦ **drink, gulp, mouthful, sip** ✧ **bite, taste, bit** I tried a *swallow* of beer once, but I didn't like it very much.

**swamp** *noun* ✦ **bog, marsh, marshland, swampland, wetland** ✧ **mire, morass** There are alligators living in Florida's *swamps*. —*verb* ✦ **deluge, engulf, flood, inundate, overwhelm** ✧ **immerse, submerge** The post office gets *swamped* with letters during the holidays.

**swarm** *noun* ✦ **crowd, horde, host, mass, multitude, throng, mob** A *swarm* of fans ran onto the field as the game ended. —*verb* ✦ **congregate, crowd, flock, mass, throng, cluster** ✧ **teem** At the school dance, most of the students *swarmed* around the refreshment table.

**sway** *verb* ✦ **move, ripple, wave, swing** ✧ **beat, flap, weave** The flowers *swayed* in the evening breeze.

**swear** *verb* ✦ **pledge, promise, vow** ✧ **affirm, assert, state, testify** All of the witnesses *swore* to tell the whole truth and nothing but the truth.

**sweep** *verb* ✦ **brush, whisk** ✧ **clean, dust, tidy,**

**wipe** I *swept* the leaves off the sidewalk. —*noun* ✦ pass, stroke, swoop, thrust, swing ✧ motion, movement I cleaned off the cookie crumbs with one *sweep* of my hand.

**sweet** *adjective* 1. ✦ sugary, sweetened ✧ rich This cereal is too *sweet* for my tastes. 2. ✦ considerate, nice, gracious, courteous, friendly, kind It was *sweet* of my friend to send me a get-well card.

**swell** *verb* ✦ bulge, expand, grow, puff, rise ✧ increase, enlarge That bee sting is beginning to *swell*. —*noun* ✦ wave, roller, billow ✧ breaker, comber, ripple The ocean *swells* gently rocked our boat.

**swerve** *verb* ✦ turn aside, dodge, veer ✧ move, shift, swing, twist The driver *swerved* in order to avoid hitting a pothole.

**swift** *adjective* ✦ fast, fleet, quick, rapid, speedy ✧ brisk, hasty Jamar is the *swiftest* runner on our track team.

**Antonyms** swift

*adjective* gradual, leisurely, poky, slow, sluggish, tardy

**swindle** *verb* ✦ defraud, cheat, deceive, exploit, fool, trick ✧ steal The dishonest jeweler tried to *swindle* people by selling them fake diamonds. —*noun* ✦ deception, fraud, hoax, racket, trick After the *swindle* was discovered, the responsible people were sent to jail.

**swing** *verb* 1. ✦ dangle, hang, suspend, sway ✧ move, shift, rock Monkeys seem to love *swinging* by their arms. 2. ✦ circle, curve, swerve, turn, veer ✧ twist The boomerang *swung* around and came back to me. —*noun* ✦ stroke, swat ✧ blow, hit, strike, thrust, poke The golfer took a *swing* at the ball.

**swirl** *verb* ✦ spin, twirl, twist, whirl ✧ reel, swish The dancer's skirt *swirled* around her as she moved.

**switch** *noun* 1. ✦ stick, branch, rod, twig, stalk ✧ cane, whip The child improvised a fishing pole from a long *switch* and a piece of string. 2. ✦ alteration, change, shift, modification ✧ exchange, swap, trade We had to make a last-minute *switch* in our vacation plans. —*verb* ✦ change, exchange, swap, trade, shift, substitute The sisters sometimes *switch* bedrooms for the night.

**Word Groups**

A **sword** is a weapon that has a long blade set in a handle, or hilt. **Sword** is a general term with no true synonyms. Here are some common types of swords: **broadsword, claymore, cutlass, épée, foil, gladius, rapier, saber, scimitar**

**symbol** *noun* ✦ emblem, mark, sign, token ✧ badge, indication The dove and the olive branch are both *symbols* of peace.

**sympathize** *verb* ✦ feel bad (for), feel sorry (for), empathize ✧ pity, relate, understand I *sympathized with* my friend when she told me about her accident.

**sympathy** *noun* ✦ empathy, comfort, support, understanding, compassion ✧ concern, pity My friends gave me lots of *sympathy* when I lost my job.

**symptom** *noun* ✦ indication, sign, evidence, feature, trait ✧ warning, note A runny nose is often a *symptom* of a cold.

**synthetic** *adjective* ✦ artificial, manmade, manufactured ✧ unnatural, imitation Plastic is a *synthetic* material made from petroleum.

**system** *noun* 1. ✦ set, unit ✧ arrangement, combination, complex, network My roommate just bought a new stereo *system*. 2. ✦ method, order, pattern, plan, procedure, scheme In 1876, Melvil Dewey developed a *system* for organizing library books that is still in use today.

**tab¹** *noun* ✦ flap, pull, tag, tongue, strip ✧ lip, projection A popular type of children's book has *tabs* that can be pulled or slid to reveal something new.

**tab²** *noun* ✦ bill, check, invoice, statement ✧ account, cost, price The waiter brought our *tab* when we had finished eating.

**table** *noun* 1. ✦ dining table ✧ bar, bench, board, counter, stand, surface Please set the *table* for dinner. 2. ✦ list, index, chart ✧ appendix, graph, record, register Most nonfiction books start with a *table* that shows the book's contents.

**tablet** *noun* ✦ capsule, pill, lozenge ✧ medication, medicine, dosage, dose When I have a headache, I usually take two aspirin *tablets*.

**tack** *verb* ✦ pin, stick ✧ attach, fasten, fix, secure, nail The girl *tacked* a poster of her favorite singer to her closet door.

**tackle** *verb* ✦ begin, deal (with), take on, undertake ✧ attempt, confront, try I'll *tackle* the new assignment as soon as I finish this project.

**tact** *noun* ✦ tactfulness, consideration, diplomacy, thoughtfulness ✧ courtesy, politeness It takes *tact* to tell people about their faults without offending them.

**tag** *noun* ✦ label, sticker, ticket ✧ marker, slip, tab All items with red *tags* are on sale. —*verb* 1. ✦ label, mark, ticket ✧ designate, identify The baggage handler *tagged* each piece of luggage to show its destination. 2. ✦ follow, tail, trail ✧ accompany, attend, dog, heel The little boy likes to *tag* along wherever his father goes.

**tail** *noun* ✦ back, end, rear, tail end ✧ stern, extremity, stern, tip The airplane's identification number was painted on its *tail*. —*verb* ✦ follow, trail ✧ pursue, stalk, track, shadow A police detective *tailed* the suspect from the airport to her apartment.

**take** *verb* 1. ✦ capture, seize, gain, secure ✧ acquire, get, obtain, win The invading army was unable to *take* the enemy fort. 2. ✦ bring, carry, bear, convey, haul ✧ move, transport I *take* my lunch to work every day. 3. ✦ swallow, ingest, consume ✧ chew, drink, eat *Take* this medicine twice a day. 4. ✦ make, execute, give, perform ✧ act, do The actors each *took* a bow at the end of the play. 5. ✦ need, require, call (for) ✧ demand, involve, want, use This assignment *takes* about one hour to complete. 6. ✦ abide, endure, suffer, tolerate, withstand ✧ accept, brave I'm not sure if I can *take* another day of this rainy weather. 7. ✦ interpret, understand, comprehend, perceive ✧ assume, grasp Did you *take* her comment the same way I did? 8. ✦ deduct, remove, subtract, withdraw ✧ eliminate If you have eighteen quarters and *take away* two, how many dollars would you have?

**tale** *noun* ✦ anecdote, story, yarn, narrative, narration ✧ fable, tall tale The old sailor had many *tales* to tell about his days at sea.

**talent** *noun* ✦ aptitude, flair, gift, knack ✧ skill, ability, capability, power Mariana has a *talent* for expressing her thoughts in an original manner.

**talk** *verb* ✦ chat, speak, converse ✧ chatter, communicate, discuss, confer My friends and I often *talk* on the phone for hours. —*noun* 1. ✦ conference, consultation, conversation, discussion ✧ chat, dialogue I had a *talk* with my boss about how to improve my work performance. 2. ✦ address, speech, presentation, lecture ✧ commentary, sermon A firefighter gave the students a *talk* about fire safety.

**tall** *adjective* ✦ high, lofty ✧ big, lengthy, long, towering, soaring The rebuilt World Trade Center is the *tallest* building in the United States.

**Antonyms** **tall**
*adjective* diminutive, low, short, small, squat

**tame** *adjective* ✦ docile, gentle, mild ✧ broken, domesticated, meek, obedient My parakeet is so *tame* that he will sit on my finger. —*verb* ✦ break, domesticate ✧ discipline, master, subdue, train It's not easy to catch and *tame* a wild horse.

**tamper** *verb* ✦ fool around, meddle, mess, play, tinker ✧ alter, interfere Someone *tampered* with the bank's ATM machine, but no money was stolen.

**tang** *noun* ✦ sharpness, zest, bite ✧ flavor, relish, savor, taste Some cheeses are aged for many months to give them more *tang*.

**tangle** *verb* ✦ kink, knot, snarl, twist ✧ disorder, scramble, mess The wind *tangled* Priya's long hair. —*noun* ✦ kink, knot, snarl, twist ✧ maze, mess, muddle, web Priya combed the *tangles* out of her hair.

**tantalize** *verb* ✦ taunt, tease, tempt, torment ✧ captivate, entice, provoke My boyfriend likes to *tantalize* me by giving clues about my birthday presents.

**tantrum** *noun* ✦ blowup, fit, temper tantrum ✧ outburst, rage, scene When I was little I had big *tantrums* when I didn't get what I wanted.

**tap**[1] *verb* ✦ drum, rap, knock, thump, beat ✧ hit, pat, slap, strike The professor always *taps* his pencil on his desk when he's thinking. —*noun* ✦ knock, rap, thump ✧ hit, pat, slap, strike Did you hear a *tap* on the window?

**tap**[2] *noun* ✦ faucet, spigot ✧ spout, valve, nozzle We need to fix that dripping *tap*.

**tape** *noun* ✦ band, ribbon, strap, strip, cord ✧ reel, roll, spool The lead runner broke the *tape* that was stretched across the finish line. —*verb* ✧ attach, fasten, secure, stick, clip, seal The boy *taped* basketball posters all over his wall.

**tardy** *adjective* ✦ late, delayed, detained ✧ belated, slow Students who are frequently *tardy* will likely be disciplined.

**target** *noun* ✦ goal, mark, objective ✧ aim, end, object, purpose We have set a *target* of $1,000 for our fund-raising drive.

**tarnish** *verb* ✦ corrode, oxidize, darken, dim, discolor, dull ✧ rust, stain Some metals *tarnish* after they've been exposed to air for a while. —*noun* ✦ corrosion, oxidation, discoloration ✧ rust, stain The antique silver pitcher had a lot of *tarnish* on it.

**tart** *adjective* ✦ sour, acid, bitter, tangy ✧ sharp, dry, vinegary Lemons are so *tart* that they make my mouth pucker up.

**task** *noun* ✦ assignment, chore, duty, job, obligation, responsibility, mission One of the manager's *tasks* is to train new employees.

**taste** *noun* 1. ✦ flavor, savor ✧ relish, tang, zest, essence Hoa loves foods that have a sweet *taste*. 2. ✦ bit, bite, morsel, nibble, piece, sample ✧ sip,

swallow May I have a little *taste* of your burrito? 3. ✦ liking, preference, leaning, judgment ✧ fashion, style You and I have the same *taste* in music. —*verb* ✦ sample, test, try, experience ✧ eat, relish, savor Please *taste* this soup and tell me if it needs a little more salt.

**tasteless** *adjective* 1. ✦ bland, flavorless, flat, plain ✧ unsavory, mild The spaghetti sauce was rather *tasteless*, so I added more herbs and spices. 2. ✦ vulgar, crude, offensive, rude, tactless ✧ improper No one laughed at the *tasteless* joke.

**taut** *adjective* ✦ stretched, tight ✧ drawn, firm, rigid, stiff, tense Please hold the measuring tape *taut*.

**tax** *noun* ✦ assessment, levy ✧ charge, duty, tariff, toll The main way the government raises money is by *taxes*. —*verb* 1. ✦ assess ✧ charge, levy Our county government *taxes* property owners to pay for services like schools and sewers. 2. ✦ drain, exhaust, sap, weaken ✧ burden, strain Playing the whole game with no substitutes *taxed* my strength.

**taxi** *noun* ✦ cab, taxicab ✧ hired car, limousine I called a *taxi* to take me to the airport.

**teach** *verb* ✦ educate, instruct, train, inform ✧ lecture, tutor, coach I'm helping my parents *teach* my little sister how to read.

**teacher** *noun* ✦ schoolteacher, educator, instructor ✧ professor, trainer, tutor It takes skill and hard work to be a really good *teacher*.

**team** *noun* ✦ group, squad, unit, crew ✧ band, company, force A *team* of investigators thoroughly examined the accident site. —*verb* ✦ combine, join up, pair up, couple up, unite ✧ associate, connect, link The two authors *teamed up* to write a book together.

**tear**[1] *verb* 1. ✦ pull apart, rip up, shred ✧ cut, slice, split, tatter My gerbils *tore up* a piece of cardboard to build a nest. 2. ✦ charge, fly, race, rush, speed ✧ bolt, dash, hurry, run A group of kids came *tearing* down the street on their bicycles. —*noun* ✦ rip, split, slit ✧ break, cut, gap, hole I sewed up the *tear* in my jeans.

**tear**[2] *noun* ✦ teardrop ✧ drop, moisture I laughed so hard that I had *tears* running down my cheeks.

**tease** *verb* ✦ annoy, bother, harass, irritate, pester, torment, vex The dog growled at the boys who were *teasing* him.

**technique** *noun* ✦ form, style, skill, art, craft ✧

method, procedure, system The guitarist practiced hard in order to improve her *technique.*

**tedious** *adjective* ✦ boring, dull, tiresome, dreary, uninteresting, wearisome, weary Pulling up weeds in the garden can be a *tedious* task.

**televise** *verb* ✦ air, broadcast, telecast, show ✧ transmit The baseball game will be *televised* live.

**tell** *verb* 1. ✦ say, speak, state, utter ✧ communicate, talk, voice I always *tell* the truth. 2. ✦ narrate, recite, relate, recount ✧ describe, report When I was young, my father would *tell* me a story every night. 3. ✦ disclose, divulge, expose, give away, reveal ✧ betray I promised my friend that I wouldn't *tell* her secret to anyone. 4. ✦ differentiate, distinguish, know, separate ✧ determine, discover Do you know how to *tell* a ripe watermelon from an unripe one? 5. ✦ bid, direct, instruct, command, order, demand, require My boss *told* me to get the assignment done today.

**temper** *noun* 1. ✦ nature, disposition, mood ✧ attitude, spirit Our dog has a very sweet *temper.* 2. ✦ anger, fury, rage, wrath ✧ irritation, agitation When I am upset, I count to ten to control my *temper.*

**temporary** *adjective* ✦ brief, short-lived, short-term ✧ fleeting, momentary, passing The storm caused a *temporary* loss of power.

**Antonyms** temporary

*adjective* enduring, lasting, long-lived, permanent, perpetual

**tempt** *verb* ✦ entice, lure, attract, invite, persuade ✧ coax, inspire, urge The bakery put a gingerbread house in the window to *tempt* people to come inside.

**temptation** *noun* ✦ enticement, attraction, lure ✧ draw, pull, bait Chocolate is a *temptation* that many people find difficult to resist.

**tenant** *noun* ✦ lodger, renter ✧ inhabitant, occupant, resident My parents have found a *tenant* for their rental house.

**tend¹** *verb* ✦ be apt, be likely, be inclined ✧ lean, slant, trend New Mexico's climate *tends* to be hot and dry.

**tend²** *verb* ✦ attend, care (for), look (after), watch, see (to) ✧ guard, protect My neighbor asked me to *tend* his yard and garden while he's away on vacation.

**tendency** *noun* ✦ habit, inclination, disposition ✧ bias, leaning, trend I have a *tendency* to stay up late on weekends.

**tender** *adjective* 1. ✦ soft, supple, delicate ✧ fragile, frail, weak Carrots become *tender* when they are steamed. 2. ✦ painful, sensitive, sore, uncomfortable ✧ aching, throbbing I sprained my ankle last week, and it's still *tender.* 3. ✦ caring, gentle, loving ✧ compassionate, kindhearted, warm The mother cat was very *tender* with her newborn kittens.

**tense** *adjective* 1. ✦ rigid, stiff, strained ✧ stretched, taut, tight When I'm frightened, my whole body gets *tense.* 2. ✦ anxious, apprehensive, nervous, uneasy, restless, jittery The actor was *tense* on the opening night of his first play.

**term** *noun* 1. ✦ interval, period, time, duration ✧ span, stretch The president of the United States is elected for a *term* of four years. 2. ✦ expression, word ✧ name, designation, phrase, terminology This dictionary defines more than 1,500 science and computer *terms.* 3. ✦ condition, provision, qualification, requirement, specification ✧ clause One of the *terms* of the loan was that it had to be paid off in two years.

**terminal** *noun* ✦ depot, station, terminus ✧ destination, stopping place We arrived at the *terminal* just in time to catch our bus.

**terrible** *adjective* 1. ✦ severe, violent, fierce, intense ✧ alarming, frightful The *terrible* fire destroyed more than 5,000 homes. 2. ✦ awful, bad, dreadful, horrible ✧ poor, rotten I'm usually pretty good at tennis, but my game was *terrible* today.

**terrific** *adjective* 1. ✦ intense, powerful, severe, fierce ✧ horrible, terrible The hurricane had *terrific* winds of more than 110 miles per hour. 2. ✦ great, magnificent, marvelous, splendid, superb, wonderful, awesome I had a *terrific* time at your party last night.

**terrify** *verb* ✦ alarm, frighten, panic, petrify, scare, terrorize Thunder and lightning *terrify* my new puppy.

**territory** *noun* ✦ area, region, domain, realm ✧ district, locality, terrain A grizzly bear roams over a *territory* of about one hundred square miles.

**terror** *noun* ✦ alarm, fear, fright ✧ dread, horror, panic The rabbit froze in *terror* when it saw a hawk circling overhead.

**test** *noun* ✦ exam, examination, quiz ✧ check, investigation, study, probe The students are having a spelling *test* tomorrow. —*verb* ✦ analyze, check, examine, investigate, assess ✧ question, quiz Cities routinely *test* their water to make sure that it is safe to drink.

**testify** *verb* ✦ affirm, assert, avow, claim, confirm, declare, swear Two witnesses *testified* that they saw the defendant commit the crime.

**testimony** *noun* ✦ declaration, statement, assertion, claim ✧ evidence, proof The jury listened carefully as the witness gave her *testimony*.

**text** *noun* 1. ✦ contents, subject matter, words, writing ✧ theme, topic My *American Heritage Dictionary* contains 2,112 pages of *text*. 2. ✦ book, schoolbook, textbook, reference ✧ manual, primer, reader The student has to read a chapter in her history *text* by tomorrow.

**textile** *noun* ✦ fabric, cloth, material ✧ fiber, thread, yarn Rayon was the first synthetic *textile* to be developed.

**texture** *noun* ✦ feel, consistency, composition, grain ✧ character, quality Sandpaper has a rough *texture*.

**thankful** *adjective* ✦ appreciative, grateful ✧ content, glad, pleased, happy We were *thankful* to be inside all warm and snug while the blizzard raged outside.

**thankless** *adjective* ✦ unappreciated, unacknowledged, unrecognized, unrewarded ✧ boring, dreary, dull Garbage collectors do important work, but their job often seems *thankless*.

### Word Groups

A **theater** is a building where plays or movies are presented. **Theater** is a general term with no true synonyms. Here are some related words to investigate in a dictionary: **auditorium, cinema, movie theater, playhouse, stage**

**theft** *noun* ✦ larceny, stealing ✧ burglary, robbery, pilfering The man reported the *theft* of his car to the police.

**theme** *noun* 1. ✦ point, premise, subject, subject matter, topic, argument The *theme* of the mayor's speech was that more money is needed for law enforcement. 2. ✦ composition, essay, paper, report, article ✧ commentary, piece The students

had to write a *theme* about what they did during summer vacation.

**theory** *noun* ✦ idea, hypothesis ✧ assumption, guess, speculation, explanation I have a couple of different *theories* about how my lamp was broken.

**thick** *adjective* 1. ✦ broad, thickset, wide, deep ✧ big, bulky, fat, large A castle's walls are typically quite *thick*. 2. ✦ stiff, firm ✧ solid, heavy Honey gets *thick* when it is cold. 3. ✦ crowded, dense, packed, tight, abundant, plentiful The branches were so *thick* that we couldn't see very far into the woods.

**thief** *noun* ✦ burglar, robber ✧ bandit, criminal, crook, stealer The police are looking for the *thief* who broke into our neighbor's house.

**thin** *adjective* 1. ✦ lean, slender, slim, spare, slight, lanky ✧ gaunt, skinny Plenty of exercise helps keep our dog *thin*. 2. ✦ scarce, sparse, meager, scant, scanty ✧ rare My father's hair is getting *thin* on top. 3. ✦ dilute, runny, watered-down, watery ✧ weak *Thin* paint is easier to apply than thick paint. —*verb* ✦ decrease, diminish, reduce ✧ dilute, water down, weaken The crowd began to *thin* before the game was over.

**thing** *noun* 1. ✦ article, item, object ✧ device, gadget, stuff I saw some really unusual *things* at the museum. 2. ✦ act, action, deed ✧ accomplishment, feat, task I know that I did the right *thing* when I returned the wallet to its rightful owner. 3. ✦ belongings, goods, personal effects, possessions, property My roommate asked me to pick up my *things* and take them to my room. 4. ✦ affairs, circumstances, conditions, matters ✧ business, concern How are *things* at work?

**think** *verb* 1. ✦ consider, contemplate, deliberate, ponder, reflect, meditate I had to *think* a few moments before I could solve the riddle. 2. ✦ assume, presume, believe, conclude, guess, suppose, deem People sometimes *think* that my friend and I are related because we look so much alike.

**thorough** *adjective* ✦ complete, exhaustive, extensive, full, total ✧ careful, entire Tanya gave her horse a *thorough* brushing.

**thought** *noun* 1. ✦ consideration, contemplation, deliberation, reflection, study I have given your suggestion a lot of *thought*. 2. ✦ idea, notion, opinion, view ✧ belief, concept What are your *thoughts* on this subject?

**thoughtful** *adjective* 1. ✦ contemplative, meditative, reflective ✧ thinking, pensive My friend gets very quiet when she is in a *thoughtful* mood. 2. ✦ caring, considerate, kind, kindly ✧ courteous, polite It was *thoughtful* of you to send me a get-well card.

**thrash** *verb* ✦ beat, crush, defeat, overwhelm, trounce, whip ✧ conquer Our softball team *thrashed* our opponents by a score of 7 to 0.

**threat** *noun* 1. ✦ warning ✧ caution, notice, notification, promise The teacher carried out her *threat* to send the noisy students to the principal's office. 2. ✦ danger, hazard, menace, peril, risk ✧ trouble A spokesperson said that the forest fire does not pose a *threat* to any homes.

**threaten** *verb* 1. ✦ intimidate, menace, bully ✧ caution, warn, terrorize The belligerent country *threatened* its neighbor by moving troops to the border. 2. ✦ endanger, jeopardize, put at risk, put in jeopardy, imperil This year's harvest is being *threatened* by drought.

**thrifty** *adjective* ✦ economical, frugal ✧ careful, prudent, saving A *thrifty* shopper buys things on sale whenever possible.

**thrill** *verb* ✦ delight, excite, please, tickle ✧ stir, move, stimulate, inspire The student was *thrilled* when she got a perfect score on the math test. —*noun* ✦ excitement, joy, pleasure, sensation ✧ adventure, fun I can still recall the *thrill* of my first roller coaster ride.

**thrive** *verb* ✦ flourish, prosper, succeed ✧ advance, grow, progress, bloom My uncle is pleased that his new business is *thriving*.

**throb** *verb* ✦ pulsate, pulse, beat, pound, thump ✧ flutter, tremble, vibrate After running the race, I could feel my pulse *throbbing*. —*noun* ✦ beat, pulse, tremor, vibration, reverberation ✧ spasm The crew could feel the *throb* of the engines as the tugboat began to move.

**throng** *noun* ✦ crowd, flock, horde, mass, mob, multitude, swarm A *throng* of eager visitors waited outside the gates of the amusement park. —*verb* ✦ crowd, flock, mob, press, swarm, jam ✧ assemble, gather After the game, fans *thronged* around the players.

**through** *preposition* ✦ around, in, throughout ✧ among, between, into, past We took a drive *through* the countryside. —*adjective* ✦ done, finished ✧ completed, ended, over Are you *through* with your chores yet?

**throw** *verb* ✦ pitch, toss ✧ cast, fling, heave, hurl, sling, lob Will you please *throw* that pillow over here? —*noun* ✦ pitch, toss ✧ cast, fling, hurl, delivery The pitcher's first *throw* was high and wide.

**thrust** *verb* ✦ shove, push, plunge, force, jam, ram ✧ drive Choi *thrust* his hands into his pockets to keep them warm. —*noun* ✦ lunge, stab, plunge, advance ✧ drive, push, shove In fencing, competitors use their swords to block their opponents' *thrusts*.

**thus** *adverb* ✦ accordingly, as a result, consequently, hence, therefore, so I overslept, and *thus* I was late for work.

**thwart** *verb* ✦ defeat, foil, frustrate, hinder, obstruct, prevent, stop, check I *thwarted* my dog's attempt to eat the cat's food.

**ticket** *noun* 1. ✦ admission, pass ✧ coupon, permit, authorization My friend has two free *tickets* for tonight's concert. 2. ✦ label, tag, marker, slip, sticker ✧ tab The price on the *ticket* says this shirt costs thirty dollars.

**tickle** *verb* 1. ✧ stroke, touch, brush, caress, pet, scratch My little sister always squirms and giggles when I *tickle* her feet. 2. ✦ amuse, delight, entertain, gladden, please, cheer The children's performance *tickled* the entire audience.

### Word Groups

The regular rising and falling of the surface level of oceans is the **tide**. **Tide** is a very specific term with no true synonyms. Here are some related words to investigate in a dictionary: **current, drift, flow, stream, surf, undertow, wave**

**tidy** *adjective* ✦ neat, orderly, organized ✧ clean, trim, spruce Michele likes to keep her desk *tidy*. —*verb* ✦ neaten, organize, straighten up ✧ arrange, clean, spruce We *tidied* the kitchen when we were done making cookies.

**tie** *verb* 1. ✦ attach, bind, fasten, secure ✧ connect, join, knot We used a strong rope to *tie* the mattress to the top of the car. 2. ✦ balance, equal, even, match, deadlock ✧ draw, meet That last touchdown *tied* the score. —*noun* 1. ✦ fastener, fastening ✧ cord, line, ribbon, rope, string Do you have a *tie* for this garbage bag? **2.** ✦ **attachment, bond, connection, link, relationship, kinship** There is a strong *tie* between my brother and me. **3.** ✦ **deadlock, draw, standoff, stalemate** The hockey game ended in a *tie*.

**tier** *noun* ✦ **layer, level** ✧ **step, story, rank, row** The wedding cake had three *tiers*.

**tight** *adjective* **1.** ✦ **fixed, set, fast, secure** ✧ **sealed, strong** The knot was so *tight* that I could hardly undo it. **2.** ✦ **snug, little, small** ✧ **constricted, narrow** My favorite jeans are getting too *tight* for me. **3.** ✦ **taut, tense, stretched** ✧ **firm, rigid, stiff** The lines holding up our tent weren't very *tight*, and it collapsed in the night. **4.** ✦ **close, compact, packed, compressed** ✧ **crowded, full, thick** The military jets were flying in a *tight* formation.

**tighten** *verb* ✦ **contract, shorten, stiffen, tense** ✧ **fortify, strengthen** Your muscles *tighten* when you pick up something heavy.

**till¹** *verb* ✦ **plow, cultivate, furrow, harrow** ✧ **hoe, turn** American farmers once *tilled* their fields with horse-drawn plows.

**till²** *conjunction* ✦ **until, before** ✧ **prior (to), sooner than, up (to)** We can't leave *till* the meeting is over.

**till³** *noun* ✦ **register, cash register, cash box, cash drawer** ✧ **safe, vault** The money in the *till* has to be counted every night.

**tilt** *verb* ✦ **lean, tip, incline, slant, angle** ✧ **pitch, slope** I *tilted* my head toward my friend so I could hear what she was whispering to me. —*noun* ✦ **lean, slant, slope, incline** ✧ **list, pitch, angle** This table has a noticeable *tilt* because one of the legs is shorter than the others.

**time** *noun* **1.** ✦ **interval, space, span, spell, stretch, term, while** It seems like a long *time* until my next vacation. **2.** ✦ **age, day, epoch, era, period** ✧ **season** I like to read stories set in the *time* of King Arthur. **3.** ✦ **chance, moment, occasion, opening, opportunity, point** Now seems like a good *time* to ask my boss for a raise. —*verb* ✦ **schedule, set, adjust, regulate** ✧ **measure, pace, plan** Our sprinklers are *timed* to go on at regular intervals.

**timid** *adjective* ✦ **shy, bashful, apprehensive** ✧ **afraid, cautious, hesitant** When the little boy is feeling *timid*, he hides behind his father's legs.

**tint** *noun* ✦ **hue, shade, tinge, tone** ✧ **color, dye** "Emerald" and "jade" are two different *tints* of

green. —*verb* ✦ **color, dye** ✧ **shade, stain, tinge** I *tinted* my hair a lighter brown.

**tiny** *adjective* ✦ **diminutive, little, small, miniature, minute, wee** A Chihuahua is a very *tiny* dog.

**tip¹** *noun* ✦ **peak, point, top, tiptop, head** ✧ **end, extremity** Only the *tip* of an iceberg shows above water.

**tip²** *verb* ✦ **knock over, overturn, upset, topple** ✧ **overthrow, tilt** I accidentally *tipped over* my cup of tea.

**tip³** *noun* **1.** ✦ **gratuity** ✧ **bonus, reward, gift, present** We left a generous *tip* for the waiter. **2.** ✦ **pointer, suggestion** ✧ **advice, clue, hint, information** A police officer gave the students several *tips* on bicycle safety.

**tire** *verb* **1.** ✦ **exhaust, fatigue, wear out, weary, drain, weaken** The long bike ride *tired* me. **2.** ✦ **grow weary, lose interest (in), become bored (with)** ✧ **annoy, bother** Micah never seems to *tire* of playing computer games.

**tired** *adjective* **1.** ✦ **exhausted, fatigued, weary, worn-out, drained, spent** The *tired* wolf lay panting on the ground. **2.** ✦ **fed up (with), sick, bored (with), exasperated (by)** ✧ **impatient** I am *tired of* your constant complaining.

**title** *noun* **1.** ✦ **name** ✧ **designation, heading** What is the *title* of the book you are reading? **2.** ✦ **claim, ownership (of), possession (of)** ✧ **deed, interest, right** There is some question as to who really has legal *title* to the mansion. **3.** ✦ **championship, crown** ✧ **trophy, honors, laurels** The boxer that wins this bout will win the world *title*. —*verb* ✦ **entitle, name, call, designate** ✧ **label, term** The author has decided to *title* her new book *How I Survived College*.

**toil** *verb* ✦ **labor, slave, work** ✧ **strain, strive, struggle** The farm workers *toiled* in the fields from dawn to dusk. —*noun* ✦ **drudgery, exertion, labor, work** ✧ **effort, struggle, sweat** The coal miner was finally able to retire after years of hard *toil*.

**toast** *verb* ✦ **heat, warm, warm up, bake** ✧ **roast, burn, char, scorch** It felt good to *toast* our cold feet in front of the campfire.

**token** *noun* ✦ **expression, mark, sign, symbol, indication** ✧ **keepsake, souvenir** The couple exchanged rings as a *token* of their love for each other.

**tolerant** *adjective* ✦ open-minded (about), patient (with), understanding (toward) ✧ charitable, forgiving, sympathetic I try to be *tolerant* of people who think differently from me.

**tolerate** *verb* 1. ✦ allow, permit, stand (for), condone, have ✧ approve, authorize The teacher said she will not *tolerate* any boisterous behavior in her classroom. 2. ✦ endure, bear, take, suffer, withstand, abide I can *tolerate* hot weather better than cold weather.

**toll¹** *noun* ✦ charge, fee, price ✧ expense, cost, tariff, tax Drivers have to pay a *toll* to use this expressway.

**toll²** *verb* ✦ peal, ring, chime, knell, sound ✧ strike Church bells *toll* when it's time for the faithful to attend a service.

**tomb** *noun* ✦ burial chamber, mausoleum ✧ crypt, grave, sepulcher, vault The Taj Mahal in India is a luxurious *tomb* built for an emperor's wife.

**tone** *noun* 1. ✦ note, pitch, sound, intonation ✧ noise This whistle has a high *tone*. 2. ✦ shade, hue, tinge, tint ✧ color Our new drapes have three *tones* of blue in them. 3. ✦ feel, mood, spirit, attitude, quality ✧ manner, mode The brightly colored paper lanterns gave the patio a festive *tone*. 4. ✦ firmness, fitness, strength ✧ health, vigor My grandmother does yoga to maintain her muscle *tone*.

**tongue** *noun* ✦ language ✧ dialect, speech, talk, voice My friend Tuyen's native *tongue* is Vietnamese.

**too** *adverb* 1. ✦ also, as well, likewise ✧ additionally, besides, furthermore I told Mira that if she tried out for the play, I would *too*. 2. ✦ excessively, overly, unduly ✧ extremely, greatly, very This shirt is *too* small for me.

**tool** *noun* ✦ implement ✧ apparatus, device, instrument, utensil, machine A hammer is one *tool* that every carpenter is likely to have.

**top** *noun* 1. ✦ summit, tip, crest, peak ✧ crown, head, zenith The *top* of Mount Everest is 29,029 feet above sea level. 2. ✦ cap, stopper, cover, lid ✧ cork I can't find the *top* to my tube of toothpaste. —*adjective* ✦ best, greatest, highest, topmost ✧ chief, leading, main This car's *top* speed is one hundred miles per hour. —*verb* ✦ beat, better, exceed, outdo, surpass ✧ excel That joke *tops* the one you told yesterday.

**topic** *noun* ✦ subject, theme, point, matter, issue, business, question The weather is a common *topic* of conversation.

**topple** *verb* ✦ knock over, knock down, overturn, upset ✧ drop, fall, overthrow Last night's strong wind *toppled* the old oak tree in our yard.

**torch** *noun* ✧ flare, fire, flame, lamp, light At the start of the Olympic Games, a *torch* is used to light the Olympic Flame.

**torment** *noun* ✦ agony, anguish, distress, misery, suffering, pain A bad toothache can be a source of great *torment*. —*verb* ✦ annoy, bother, pester, plague, trouble ✧ distress, pain, torture A thick cloud of mosquitoes *tormented* the campers all night long.

**torrent** *noun* ✦ deluge, flood, river ✧ downpour, flow, overflow, stream Heavy rain turned the gentle creek into a rushing *torrent*.

**torture** *noun* ✦ abuse, persecution, punishment ✧ agony, anguish, misery, suffering, torment The Geneva Conventions outlaw the *torture* of prisoners of war. —*verb* ✦ torment, distress, pain, punish ✧ maim, mutilate These new boots are *torturing* my feet.

**Antonyms** **torture**
*noun* comfort, contentment, ease, pleasure
*verb* ease, relieve, soothe

**toss** *verb* 1. ✦ fling, throw, cast, sling ✧ heave, hurl, pitch Ashley *tossed* her coat on the bed. 2. ✦ heave, pitch, rock, roll, thrash ✧ stir, sway, writhe Our little rowboat *tossed* this way and that in the choppy water. —*noun* ✦ throw, cast, fling, roll, shake ✧ heave, pitch Many board games start with a *toss* of the dice.

**total** *noun* ✦ sum, sum total ✧ aggregate, amount, tally, whole We collected a *total* of 241 cans during our food drive. —*adjective* ✦ complete, entire, full, whole ✧ absolute, thorough The *total* cost of the party was less than we expected. —*verb* ✦ add, calculate, compute, figure, sum up, reckon When we *totaled* the score for our game, I had won by ten points.

**touch** *verb* 1. ✦ feel, finger, handle ✧ manipulate, stroke, rub Please don't *touch* my model airplane before the paint dries. 2. ✦ contact, meet, come (to), reach (to), abut ✧ border, press Let's move the couch out a little so that it doesn't *touch* the wall. **3. ✦ affect, move, stir ✧ impress, influence, strike** Your thoughtfulness *touched* me deeply. —*noun* **1. ✦ contact, feel, pressure, sensation ✧ feeling, handling, touching** I looked up when I felt the *touch* of someone's hand on my shoulder. **2. ✦ bit, dash, pinch, trace ✧ crumb, dab, hint, shade, tinge** I added a *touch* of oregano to the spaghetti sauce.

**touchy** *adjective* **✦ oversensitive, sensitive, testy, irritable ✧ crabby, nervous, resentful** My brother is so *touchy* that he takes every remark as a criticism.

**tough** *adjective* **1. ✦ strong, sturdy, durable, rugged ✧ hardy, stout** Leather is a *tough* material. **2. ✦ difficult, hard, demanding ✧ rough, strenuous** The boy spent a long time trying to solve the *tough* math problem.

---

**Antonyms tough**

*adjective* **1.** brittle, delicate, flimsy, fragile **2.** easy, facile, simple

---

**tour** *noun* **✦ excursion, outing, trip ✧ expedition, journey, visit** If we take this *tour*, we'll be able to see the Tower of London. —*verb* **✦ journey (through), travel (through), visit ✧ explore, see, rove** My whole family *toured* Japan and Korea last summer.

**tourist** *noun* **✦ sightseer, traveler, visitor, voyager** *Tourists* from all over the world come to Egypt to see the pyramids.

**tournament** *noun* **✦ competition, contest, match, meet, tourney ✧ challenge, games, series** This chess *tournament* is open to players of all ages.

**tow** *verb* **✦ pull, tug, drag, draw ✧ haul, lug** Powerful tugboats *towed* the ocean liner out of the harbor.

**tower** *noun* **✧ belfry, minaret, spire, steeple, turret** The Italian city of Pisa has a famous bell *tower* that leans at an angle of almost four degrees. —*verb* **✦ soar, rise, loom, rear up ✧ dominate, overlook** The new high-rise *towers* over all the nearby buildings.

**town** *noun* **✦ community, municipality, settlement ✧ city, village** My father grew up in a small *town* in Japan.

**toxic** *adjective* **✦ harmful, injurious, poisonous ✧ deadly, venomous** *Toxic* chemicals have to be handled very carefully.

**toy** *noun* **✦ plaything ✧ trifle, trinket, model** When I was young, my favorite *toy* was a yellow dump

truck. —*verb* **✦ play, trifle ✧ putter, fiddle, tinker, tease** I *toyed* with my dinner because I wasn't all that hungry.

**trace** *noun* **1. ✦ remains, remnants, indications, signs, evidence ✧ mark, proof** The hikers found *traces* of an old mining camp. **2. ✦ bit, dash, pinch, touch ✧ hint, inkling, suggestion, tinge** There's just a *trace* too much salt in this soup. —*verb* **1. ✦ hunt down, track down, trail ✧ follow, pursue, search, seek** The FBI helped *trace* the missing person. **2. ✦ copy, outline, reproduce ✧ diagram, draw, sketch, portray** The little girl spends hours *tracing* pictures from her coloring book.

**track** *noun* **1. ✦ footprint, print ✧ mark, sign, trace, impression** Who left these dirty *tracks* all over the kitchen floor? **2. ✦ footpath, path, pathway, trail, way ✧ course** A dirt *track* winds through the forest. —*verb* **1. ✦ follow, hunt, pursue, trail, stalk ✧ search, seek, trace** The wildlife photographer *tracked* a bear and her cubs through the forest. **2. ✦ bring, carry, drag, trail ✧ bear, transport** I took off my sandals so that I wouldn't *track* sand into the house.

**tract** *noun* **✦ lot, parcel, plot, piece, section ✧ area, district, region, site** This *tract* of land is going to be used for a housing development.

**trade** *noun* **1. ✦ business, commerce ✧ exchange, traffic, marketing** The United States engages in *trade* with most of the countries in the world. **2. ✦ exchange, swap, switch, barter ✧ substitution, deal** Do you think that my baseball glove would be a fair *trade* for your tennis racket? **3. ✦ occupation, profession, vocation, business, craft ✧ career, work** People in the plumbing *trade* usually have to serve an apprenticeship. —*verb* **✦ exchange, swap, switch, change, substitute ✧ barter** My roommate and I sometimes *trade* chores.

**tradition** *noun* **✦ custom, habit, practice, ritual ✧ convention, standard** It is our family *tradition* to celebrate Passover at my grandparents' house.

**traditional** *adjective* **✦ conventional, customary, regular ✧ habitual, normal, routine, usual** My friend and her fiancé decided to have a *traditional* wedding.

**traffic** *noun* **1. ✦ travel ✧ movement, transit, transport** *Traffic* is heavy on this freeway during rush hour. **2. ✦ commerce, market, trade ✧ business, exchange, sale** The government is trying to stop the *traffic* in illegal drugs. —*verb* **✦ deal, trade**

✧ **barter, buy, market, sell** It is against the law to *traffic in* stolen goods.

**tragedy** *noun* ✦ **catastrophe, disaster, calamity, misfortune** ✧ **accident, mishap** The sinking of the *Titanic* was one of the worst maritime *tragedies* of the twentieth century.

**tragic** *adjective* ✦ **sad, sorrowful, unfortunate, unhappy, doomed** ✧ **dreadful, mournful** The tale of Romeo and Juliet is a *tragic* love story.

**trail** *verb* 1. ✦ **drag, draw, pull, tow** ✧ **haul, lug** My dog ran off, *trailing* his leash behind. 2. ✦ **trace, track** ✧ **hunt, pursue, search, seek** The shepherd and his dog *trailed* the lost sheep. 3. ✦ **follow, lag, straggle, tag along** ✧ **linger, tail** The ducklings *trailed* behind their mother. —*noun* 1. ✦ **trace, track** ✧ **mark, scent, sign, spoor** The fox followed a rabbit's *trail* through the snow. 2. ✦ **footpath, path, route, track** ✧ **course, way** This *trail* leads to the pond.

**train** *noun* ✦ **caravan, convoy, procession** ✧ **column, line, string** In America's Old West, mule *trains* were used to transport military supplies. —*verb* ✦ **teach, coach, drill, instruct** ✧ **educate, tutor** I'm trying to *train* my dog to roll over and to shake hands.

**trait** *noun* ✦ **attribute, characteristic, feature, quality** ✧ **property** Honesty and kindness are two of my friend's best *traits*.

**traitor** *noun* ✦ **betrayer, double-crosser** ✧ **informer, spy, turncoat** A *traitor* sold secret plans to the enemy.

**tramp** *verb* ✦ **plod, stamp, trek, trudge, hike, march, walk** ✧ **trample** We got wet feet *tramping* through the snow. —*noun* ✦ **hike, march, trek, ramble, stroll, walk, excursion** We went for a *tramp* through the woods.

**trample** *verb* ✦ **crush, flatten, squash** ✧ **stamp, tramp, tread** Our dog *trampled* our newly planted petunias.

**tranquil** *adjective* ✦ **peaceful, quiet, restful, serene, soothing, calm** We enjoyed a *tranquil* weekend at the lake.

**transfer** *verb* ✦ **convey, move, shift** ✧ **carry, send, ship, transport** Anusha used a flash drive to *transfer* a file between computers. —*noun* ✦ **reassignment, relocation, transferal** ✧ **change, move, shift** My uncle got a *transfer* from Pennsylvania to Oregon.

**transform** *verb* ✦ **alter, change, convert, modify, turn** ✧ **renew** In the classic folk tale, Cinderella's fairy godmother *transformed* a pumpkin into a carriage.

**transition** *noun* ✦ **shift, transformation, alteration, change, modification** The country made a peaceful *transition* from monarchy to democracy.

**translate** *verb* ✦ **render** ✧ **alter, change, convert, modify, transform, interpret** Do you know Chinese well enough to *translate* this letter into English?

**transmission** *noun* 1. ✦ **transfer, transference, conveyance** ✧ **passage, sending** Regular washing of the hands helps prevent the *transmission* of germs. 2. ✦ **broadcast, signal, communication** ✧ **message, report** We can receive *transmissions* from a radio station that is more than 220 miles away.

**transmit** *verb* ✦ **send, convey, pass, relay, transfer** ✧ **deliver** Fax machines *transmit* images and written messages over telephone lines.

**transparent** *adjective* 1. ✦ **clear, see-through, translucent, lucid** Most jellyfish have delicate, *transparent* bodies. 2. ✦ **apparent, evident, obvious, plain, unmistakable, visible, blatant** My sister's joke was a *transparent* attempt to change the subject.

**Antonyms** **transparent**
*adjective* 1. opaque 2. concealed, hidden, obscured

**transport** *verb* ✦ **carry, convey, haul, move, take, transfer** ✧ **bear, cart, ferry, shift** There is no way that we can *transport* all this luggage in our little car. —*noun* ✦ **conveyance, shipment, shipping, transfer, transportation** ✧ **delivery** Trucks, trains, and airplanes are used for the *transport* of freight.

**transportation** *noun* ✦ **conveyance, transit, transport, movement** Leonardo's favorite form of *transportation* is a motorcycle.

**trap** *noun* ✦ **ambush, lure, snare** ✧ **deception, hoax, trick** The police set a *trap* to catch the robbers. —*verb* ✦ **capture, catch** ✧ **net, seize, snare** Many people prefer to *trap* mice alive rather than poison them.

**trash** *noun* ✦ **garbage, refuse, rubbish, waste** ✧ **debris, junk** It's your turn to take out the *trash*.

**travel** *verb* 1. ✦ **journey, roam, tour, trek, wander** ✧ **sightsee, visit** It would be fun to *travel* through Europe by bicycle. 2. ✦ **go, move, pass, proceed** ✧ **advance, progress** Light *travels* at a speed of approximately 186,000 miles per second. —*noun* ✦ **excursion, journey, tour, trek, trip** ✧ **voyage, passage** We enjoyed our *travels* through Italy and Greece.

**treacherous** *adjective* 1. ✦ **deceitful, disloyal, traitorous, treasonous, unfaithful** A *treacherous* guard assassinated Indira Gandhi, prime minister of India, in 1984. 2. ✦ **dangerous, hazardous, perilous, risky, unsafe, precarious** Sailing can be *treacherous* if the wind is too strong.

**treason** *noun* ✦ **disloyalty, treachery** ✧ **betrayal, conspiracy, deceit** Benedict Arnold committed an act of *treason* during the American Revolutionary War.

**treasure** *noun* ✦ **fortune, riches, wealth, valuables** ✧ **gems, gold, jewels** The divers found a sunken ship that was full of *treasure*. —*verb* ✦ **cherish, prize, value** ✧ **adore, esteem, love, revere** My mother *treasures* the rocking chair that she received from her grandmother.

**treat** *verb* 1. ✦ **deal (with), consider, look (upon), regard** ✧ **handle, manage** My parents taught me to *treat* everyone with respect. 2. ✦ **care (for), medicate, relieve, nurse** ✧ **cure, heal** One way to *treat* a sore throat is with lemon juice and honey in hot water. —*noun* ✦ **enjoyment, pleasure, delight, joy** ✧ **bonus, comfort** Our Friday night *treat* is pizza and a movie.

**treatment** *noun* ✦ **care, handling, attention, reception** ✧ **approach, management** I appreciated the friendly *treatment* I received from the store manager.

**treaty** *noun* ✦ **compact, pact, accord, agreement** ✧ **alliance, arrangement** Representatives from six nations were present at the signing of the peace *treaty*.

**Word Groups**

A **tree** is a woody plant having a main trunk and usually a distinct crown. **Tree** is a specific term with no true synonyms. Here are some common types of trees found in America: **alder, beech, cedar, eucalyptus, fir, juniper, maple, oak, pine, redwood, spruce, willow, yew**

**tremble** *verb* ✦ **shiver, shake, shudder** ✧ **quake, quiver, quaver** The campers *trembled* with cold until they got their fire started.

**tremendous** *adjective* ✦ **enormous, gigantic, huge, immense, large, giant, great** ✧ **intense** A *tremendous* wave capsized the boat.

**tremor** *noun* ✦ **quake, shake, shock** ✧ **earthquake, tremble, vibration** We felt little *tremors* for several days following the earthquake.

**trench** *noun* ✦ **ditch, furrow, trough** ✧ **channel, gully, depression, excavation** Workers dug a *trench* to bury the water pipe.

**trend** *noun* ✦ **direction, movement, tendency, inclination** ✧ **course, fashion, style** There has been an upward *trend* in the price of concert tickets recently.

**trial** *noun* 1. ✦ **court case** ✧ **case, hearing, inquiry, lawsuit, suit** The *trial* will start as soon as a jury is selected. 2. ✦ **check, test, tryout** ✧ **analysis, examination, experiment** The new plane will be put through a series of *trials* to see how it performs. 3. ✦ **adversity, affliction, hardship, ordeal, trouble, misfortune** For America's early pioneers, the westward trek was a time of both *trial* and adventure.

**tribute** *noun* 1. ✦ **acknowledgment (of), homage, honor (of), praise (of), recognition (of)** This statue was erected in *tribute* to the man who founded our town. 2. ✦ **payment, tax, money, levy** ✧ **bribe, offering** Ancient Rome received great amounts of *tribute* from the nations it conquered in battle.

**trick** *noun* 1. ✦ **feat, stunt, technique, skill** ✧ **accomplishment, art** I taught my dog the *trick* of rolling over to get a treat. 2. ✦ **deception, ruse, device, tactic, deceit** ✧ **fraud, scheme** An opossum will lie motionless as a *trick* to make enemies think that it is dead. 3. ✦ **prank, gag, jest, joke, antic** ✧ **mischief** The children play *tricks* on each other on April Fool's Day. —*verb* ✦ **deceive, fool, mislead, trap** ✧ **cheat, double-cross, swindle** Fake news stories on social media often *trick* people into believing things that aren't true.

**trickle** *verb* ✦ **dribble, drip, flow, run, ooze** ✧ **leak, seep** Sweat *trickled* down my back after playing tennis in the hot sun. —*noun* ✦ **dribble, drip, thin stream** ✧ **crawl, creep, drop** A *trickle* of water is coming out of the leaking faucet.

**trifle** *noun* ✦ **novelty, trinket, knickknack, bauble** ✧ **plaything, toy** We bought balloons and other *trifles* to hand out as party favors. —*verb* ✦ **fidget, fool, play, putter, toy, fiddle** Lynell *trifled* with the papers on her desk while waiting for the computer to boot up.

**trim** *verb* 1. ✦ **clip, crop, cut, snip, shear, prune** ✧ **nip, shape** My girlfriend *trims* my hair with scissors and a comb. **2.** ✦ **adorn, decorate, edge** ✧ **embroider, embellish, ornament** The little girl's dress is *trimmed* with lace. —*noun* **1.** ✦ **clip, crop, cut, shearing** ✧ **pruning, shortening** I asked the barber to give my hair a *trim*. **3.** ✦ **condition, order, repair, shape, state, form** ✧ **fitness** My uncle's sailboat is always in good *trim*. —*adjective* ✦ **fit, lean, slender, slim** ✧ **neat, sleek, tidy** My friend looked *trim* after her vacation at a health spa.

**trip** *noun* ✦ **excursion, journey, tour** ✧ **jaunt, outing, voyage, vacation** We went on a *trip* to Mexico to visit the Mayan ruins. —*verb* ✦ **stumble, fall, tumble** ✧ **flounder, slip, stagger** Our new puppy sometimes *trips* over its own feet.

**triumph** *verb* ✦ **prevail (over), beat, defeat, overpower** ✧ **conquer, outdo, succeed** We went wild when our team finally *triumphed over* our greatest rival. —*noun* ✦ **accomplishment, achievement, success, attainment** ✧ **conquest, victory, win** Paula had a feeling of *triumph* when she finally finished the quilt.

**triumphant** *adjective* ✦ **exultant, joyful, jubilant, victorious** ✧ **conquering, winning** The runner gave a *triumphant* smile as she crossed the finish line ahead of the others.

**trivial** *adjective* ✦ **insignificant, petty, slight, trifling, unimportant, small** The music students played their recital pieces with only a few *trivial* mistakes.

**troop** *noun* **1.** ✦ **group, unit** ✧ **band, company, corps, squad, bunch** The local Boy Scout *troop* will be going to next summer's jamboree. **2.** ✦ **soldiers, servicemen, servicewomen, troopers** ✧ **armed forces, military** The commanding general requested that more *troops* be committed to the war. —*verb* ✦ **file, march, parade, step, stride** ✧ **advance, proceed** The school children *trooped* off the bus and headed into the museum.

**trophy** *noun* ✧ **award, prize, medal, citation, crown, honor, laurels** The school gives *trophies* to the best students at the end of each year.

**trouble** *noun* **1.** ✦ **fix, jam, predicament, difficulty** ✧ **problem, mess** We'll be in *trouble* if we're late for work. **2.** ✦ **bother, inconvenience, annoyance** ✧ **care, effort, work** It won't be any *trouble* for me to get your tickets for you. —*verb* ✦ **distress, disturb, upset, worry, annoy, bother** Is something *troubling* you today?

**truce** *noun* ✦ **armistice, cease-fire, peace** ✧ **halt,** lull, stop The fighting will end when the *truce* takes effect at midnight.

**trudge** *verb* ✦ **plod, slog, toil, tramp** ✧ **shuffle, limp, hike, trek** The tired hikers *trudged* back to their camp.

**true** *adjective* **1.** ✦ **accurate, correct, factual, right, valid** ✧ **exact** The witness swore that everything she said was *true*. **2.** ✦ **dependable, faithful, loyal, reliable, steadfast, trustworthy, devoted** My dog is a *true* companion who always wants to be with me. **3.** ✦ **lawful, legal, legitimate, rightful** ✧ **just, official** The documents will prove who is the *true* owner of this priceless painting. **4.** ✦ **authentic, genuine, real, actual, bona fide** ✧ **undoubted** This book is a *true* first edition.

**truly** *adverb* ✦ **definitely, genuinely, positively, really** ✧ **actually** The editor said that my short story was *truly* original.

**trust** *verb* **1.** ✦ **believe (in), depend (on), rely (on), swear (by), accept** Self-confident people *trust* their instincts. **2.** ✦ **assume, believe, presume, suppose** ✧ **anticipate, expect** I *trust* that you will keep my secret. —*noun* **1.** ✦ **confidence, conviction, faith, reliance** ✧ **belief** I value the *trust* that my friends have in me. **2.** ✦ **care, custody, charge, protection, guardianship, keeping** Li Min left her cat in my *trust* while she was away on vacation.

**trustworthy** *adjective* ✦ **dependable, reliable, responsible** ✧ **faithful, loyal, honorable** I know that my friend will pay back the money I loaned him because he is very *trustworthy*.

**truth** *noun* ✦ **fact, reality, actuality** ✧ **authenticity, honesty, truthfulness** The *truth* is that I did eat the last doughnut.

**try** *verb* **1.** ✦ **sample, taste, test, experience** ✧ **check, examine, inspect** Would you like to *try* one of the cookies I made? **2.** ✦ **consider, deliberate, hear, judge, decide** The Supreme Court of the United States *tries* important cases that are referred to it by lower courts. **3.** ✦ **aim, attempt, endeavor, seek, strive** ✧ **struggle, work** The boy always *tries* to get his homework done before dinner. —*noun* ✦ **attempt, effort, endeavor, trial, turn** ✧ **experiment, test** Our old lawnmower usually doesn't start on the first *try*.

**trying** *adjective* ✦ **demanding, difficult, hard, rough, tough, troublesome** The parents had a *trying* time when their baby was sick.

**tug** *verb* ✦ pull, draw, drag, jerk ✧ haul, heave, wrench My dog *tugs* so hard on his leash that I can barely hold him. —*noun* ✦ jerk, pull, yank ✧ heave, tow, wrench Give this rope a *tug* to ring the bell.

**tumble** *verb* 1. ✦ roll, somersault, stumble, trip ✧ pitch, reel, toss The children *tumbled* over one another to get to the candy from the piñata. 2. ✦ drop, fall, plunge, topple, plummet ✧ slip, spill The lamp *tumbled* to the floor when I bumped the table. —*noun* ✦ fall, spill, slip ✧ dive, drop, plunge The toddler took a lot of *tumbles* while learning to walk.

**tune** *noun* 1. ✦ air, melody, refrain, song, ditty, theme I can't think of the name of the *tune* that keeps running through my head. 2. ✦ agreement, conformity, harmony, accord ✧ pitch The successful politician is in *tune* with the voters' wishes. —*verb* ✦ harmonize ✧ adjust, regulate, set, calibrate, adapt I haven't learned how to *tune* my new guitar yet.

**tunnel** *noun* ✦ underground passage ✧ corridor, passageway, shaft, tube, mine The longest railway *tunnel* in the world is in Switzerland. —*verb* ✦ burrow, dig ✧ excavate, mine, furrow, scoop, shovel Gophers are *tunneling* through our back yard again.

**turmoil** *noun* ✦ chaos, commotion, confusion, uproar, tumult, dither, flurry, flutter ✧ ferment The ants ran around in *turmoil* when their nest was disturbed.

**Antonyms** turmoil

*noun* calm, order, peace, serenity, tranquility

**turn** *verb* 1. ✦ rotate, swivel, revolve, pivot ✧ spin, twirl, whirl *Turn* the faucet to the left to get hot water. 2. ✦ go, move, shift, swerve ✧ detour, divert, wheel *Turn* right at the next corner to get to my friend's house. 3. ✦ become, change (into), transform (into) ✧ alter, convert, modify In a fairy tale by Hans Christian Andersen, an ugly duckling *turns into* a beautiful swan. 4. ✦ sprain, twist, wrench ✧ hurt, strain, tear, pull I *turned* my ankle playing soccer. —*noun* 1. ✦ bend, curve, angle ✧ arc, corner, rotation, twist, zigzag The path makes a *turn* to the left just before the pond. 2. ✦ change, shift, switch, alteration ✧ modification The weather has taken a *turn* for the better. 3. ✦

chance, opportunity, spell, time, stint ✧ attempt, go Whose *turn* is it to bat after Yuki?

**tutor** *noun* ✦ instructor, teacher, educator ✧ coach, trainer I'm looking for a *tutor* to help me learn English. —*verb* ✦ instruct, teach, educate, drill ✧ coach, inform, train An increasing number of students are *tutored* at home by their parents.

**twilight** *noun* ✦ dusk, nightfall, sundown, sunset ✧ evening Deer come out to feed just after dawn and just before *twilight*.

**twinkle** *verb* ✦ flash, flicker, gleam, glimmer, glitter, sparkle ✧ shine The sequins on the singer's dress *twinkled* under the spotlight.

**twirl** *verb* ✦ whirl, spin, revolve, rotate, turn ✧ swirl, wheel The drum majorette *twirled* her baton and then threw it into the air.

**twist** *verb* 1. ✦ coil, roll, wind, wrap ✧ curl, twine, weave The cowboy *twisted* his rope around the post. 2. ✦ sprain, strain, turn, wrench ✧ hurt, injure How did you *twist* your ankle? 3. ✦ alter, change, distort, contort ✧ deform, warp Some people *twist* the facts in order to make their story more interesting. —*noun* 1. ✦ bend, curve, turn, angle ✧ zigzag, dogleg This road is full of dangerous *twists*. 2. ✦ slant, interpretation, alteration, variation ✧ change, development, treatment A pun gets its humor from putting an unexpected *twist* on a word's meaning.

**twitch** *verb* ✦ jerk, quiver ✧ quaver, shake, shiver, wiggle, wriggle The cat's whiskers *twitched* when he saw the mouse.

**type** *noun* 1. ✦ category, class, kind, sort, variety ✧ group, genre Our library has all *types* of books. 2. ✦ print, printing ✧ character, letter, text My grandfather likes books with large *type* because they're easier to read.

**typical** *adjective* ✦ average, normal, ordinary, standard, usual, regular, common The *typical* American household has two or more television sets.

**tyranny** *noun* ✦ oppression, repression, suppression ✧ domination, subjugation The government's *tyranny* ended when a democratic leader was finally elected.

**tyrant** *noun* ✦ absolute ruler, dictator, despot, autocrat ✧ oppressor The *tyrant* was overthrown by the people he had been oppressing.

**ugly** *adjective* 1. ✦ bad-looking, homely, unattractive, unsightly ✧ plain In a fairy tale by Hans Christian Andersen, the *ugly* duckling is actually a beautiful swan. 2. ✦ disgusting, foul, nasty, repulsive, unpleasant, vile ✧ mean, rude There was an *ugly* smell coming from the town's garbage dump.

**ultimate** *adjective* 1. ✦ concluding, end, final, last, terminal ✧ eventual The plane will make two stops before reaching its *ultimate* destination. 2. ✦ greatest, highest, supreme, top, topmost ✧ maximum The Nobel Prize for Literature is the *ultimate* literary award.

**umpire** *noun* ✧ arbitrator, judge, ref, referee, mediator We need an *umpire* for next week's baseball game.

**unable** *adjective* ✦ incapable (of), not able ✧ powerless, unfit, unqualified Baby birds are *unable* to fly until they grow feathers.

**unanimous** *adjective* ✦ united, undivided, unified ✧ common, solid, universal The office staff voiced their *unanimous* support for the new hiring policy.

**unaware** *adjective* ✦ ignorant, unconscious, uninformed ✧ blind, heedless, oblivious I was *unaware* of how much time I was actually spending on the internet until you pointed it out to me.

**unbelievable** *adjective* ✦ dubious, flimsy, incredible, questionable, unconvincing, weak, absurd The boy's story about seeing a flying monkey was a bit *unbelievable*.

**uncanny** *adjective* ✦ eerie, mysterious, strange, weird ✧ curious, unusual There was an *uncanny* silence in the old house.

**uncertain** *adjective* 1. ✦ undecided, unsure, indecisive, unclear ✧ doubtful, dubious I am *uncertain* as to whether or not I want to go to my friend's party. 2. ✦ erratic, unpredictable, unsettled, variable, changeable ✧ fickle, freakish The *uncertain* weather forced us to cancel our fishing trip.

**uncomfortable** *adjective* 1. ✦ ill-at-ease, nervous, self-conscious, uneasy, embarrassed ✧ awkward, upset I'm usually *uncomfortable* when I have to speak in front of a large group. 2. ✦ comfortless ✧

cramped, hard, ill-fitting, painful This old couch is lumpy and *uncomfortable*.

**uncommon** *adjective* ✦ rare, scarce, unusual ✧ exceptional, remarkable, strange, unique I was excited to see an eagle because they are *uncommon* in this part of the country.

**unconcerned** *adjective* ✦ indifferent (to), uninterested (in), unmindful ✧ apathetic, careless, heedless My uncle wears whatever clothes he happens to find because he is *unconcerned* about his appearance.

**unconscious** *adjective* 1. ✦ knocked out, out cold ✧ senseless, stunned, comatose The man was *unconscious* for several minutes after falling and hitting his head. 2. ✦ heedless, ignorant, innocent, oblivious, unaware, unknowing, unmindful The speaker was *unconscious* of the fact that his mannerisms were distracting the audience.

**uncover** *verb* ✦ discover, expose, find, turn up, dig up, unearth ✧ disclose, reveal Historians are always *uncovering* new facts about events of the past.

**undecided** *adjective* ✦ unsure, indecisive, uncertain, undetermined, unresolved, indefinite My friend is still *undecided* about which college she wants to attend.

**under** *preposition* 1. ✦ below, beneath, underneath I finally found my calculator *under* a stack of papers on my desk. 2. ✦ less (than), lower (than), smaller (than) ✧ short (of), shy (of) Anyone *under* four feet in height may not ride this roller coaster. 3. ✦ according (to) ✧ controlled (by), following, subject (to), dependent (upon) *Under* the rules of basketball, each team can have only five players on the court at one time.

**undergo** *verb* ✦ experience, go (through), have, meet (with) ✧ encounter, face Babies *undergo* many significant physical changes during the first year of life.

**underground** *adjective* ✦ belowground, subterranean ✧ buried, covered, sunken Foxes, wolves, and coyotes typically live in *underground* dens.

**underneath** *preposition* ✦ beneath, under ✧ be-

**low** Saki wore a heavy wool sweater *underneath* her jacket. —*adverb* ✦ **below, beneath, under** ✧ **down, downward, lower** The leaf was green above and silver *underneath*.

**understand** *verb* 1. ✦ **comprehend, get, grasp, follow, know** ✧ **realize, recognize** The teacher took great care to ensure that every student *understood* the lesson. 2. ✦ **infer, believe, conclude, gather, presume** ✧ **hear, perceive** I *understand* that the rehearsal might be postponed.

**understanding** *noun* 1. ✦ **comprehension, concept, grasp, idea, knowledge, appreciation** My dog likes to ride in the car, but he has no *understanding* of how it operates. 2. ✦ **agreement, arrangement** ✧ **bargain, compromise, deal, pact, accord** My roommate and I have an *understanding* about the need for each of us to respect the other's privacy. —*adjective* ✦ **sympathetic** ✧ **compassionate, kind, sensitive, tender, tolerant** Whenever I feel unhappy, I tell my troubles to an *understanding* friend.

**undertake** *verb* ✦ **assume, attempt, tackle, take on** ✧ **begin, start** Cleaning out the basement was a chore that no one wanted to *undertake*.

**undo** *verb* 1. ✦ **erase, neutralize, reverse, wipe out, cancel** ✧ **defeat, spoil** I can't *undo* my mistakes, but at least I can apologize for them. 2. ✦ **loosen, unfasten, unravel, untie, free, open** ✧ **unclose** My shoelaces were tied so tight I had trouble *undoing* the knot.

**uneasy** *adjective* 1. ✦ **anxious, apprehensive, nervous, worried** ✧ **tense, troubled** I felt a little *uneasy* about diving off the high board. 2. ✦ **awkward, uncomfortable, unpleasant, embarrassed** ✧ **shy** There was an *uneasy* pause in our conversation.

**unemployed** *adjective* ✦ **jobless, out-of-work, not working** ✧ **idle, inactive** The state government has a bureau that helps *unemployed* people find jobs.

**unequal** *adjective* 1. ✦ **different, dissimilar, uneven** ✧ **irregular, unlike** The chair wobbles because the legs are of *unequal* length. 2. ✦ **lopsided, mismatched, unbalanced, uneven** ✧ **unfair, unjust** An important social issue is that women and men often receive *unequal* pay for similar work.

**uneven** *adjective* 1. ✦ **bumpy, irregular, rough, rugged** ✧ **coarse** We had difficulty walking across the *uneven* ground. 2. ✦ **lopsided, mismatched,**

one-sided, unbalanced, unequal ✧ **different, unlike** The basketball game was *uneven* because one team had much taller players than the other.

---

*adjective* 1. **level, smooth, straight, uniform** 2. **equal, equitable, fair, just**

---

**unexpected** *adjective* ✦ **unanticipated, unforeseen** ✧ **abrupt, sudden, surprising, chance** I was delighted when I received an *unexpected* present a week after my birthday.

**unfair** *adjective* ✦ **one-sided, unjust, uneven, unreasonable** ✧ **biased, prejudiced** Wrestlers are matched up according to their weight so that no one has an *unfair* advantage.

**unfamiliar** *adjective* 1. ✦ **strange, unknown, new** ✧ **different, fresh, novel, original, uncommon** The explorers moved cautiously through the *unfamiliar* territory. 2. ✦ **unacquainted, inexperienced** ✧ **ignorant, unaware, uninformed** I was *unfamiliar* with many of the foods we ate on our trip to India.

**unfortunate** *adjective* ✦ **regrettable, unlucky, unhappy** ✧ **bad, inappropriate, poor** An *unfortunate* misunderstanding caused bad feelings between the two friends.

**unfriendly** *adjective* ✦ **aloof, cold, cool, distant, unsociable** ✧ **haughty, hostile** Our cat is usually *unfriendly* to strangers.

**unhappy** *adjective* ✦ **dejected, depressed, down, downcast, gloomy, low, sad, blue** ✧ **sorrowful** Listening to my favorite song cheers me up when I'm feeling *unhappy*.

**unhealthy** *adjective* 1. ✦ **ill, sick, sickly, unwell** ✧ **infirm, frail, weak** My plant looks *unhealthy* because it hasn't been getting enough sunlight. 2. ✦ **unhealthful, dangerous, harmful, risky, unwholesome, unsafe** The smoggy air in some big cities is *unhealthy* for the people who live there.

**uniform** *adjective* 1. ✦ **constant, consistent, even, regular, steady, unchanging** ✧ **same** A good refrigerator keeps everything at a *uniform* temperature. 2. ✦ **comparable, equal, identical, like, alike, similar** ✧ **standard** Most bricks are of *uniform* size.

**Word Groups**

Clothing that someone wears to identify herself or himself as a member of a specific group is a **uniform**. **Uniform** is a very specific term with no true synonyms. Here are some related words to investigate in a dictionary: **costume, habit, livery, suit, vestment, wardrobe**

**unify** *verb* ✦ **unite, merge, combine, consolidate, join** ✧ **connect, link** In 1990, East and West Germany *unified* to form one nation.

**union** *noun* 1. ✦ **unification, merger, combination, consolidation, joining** The United Arab Emirates is a country that was formed in 1971 by the *union* of seven sheikdoms. 2. ✦ **guild, alliance, association, federation, league, organization** ✧ **society** My father is a member of a labor *union*.

**unique** *adjective* ✦ **different, distinctive, individual, separate** ✧ **remarkable, sole, unusual** Every snowflake has a *unique* shape.

**unit** *noun* 1. ✦ **quantity** ✧ **category, classification, measure, interval** Seconds, minutes, hours, and days are *units* used to measure time. 2. ✦ **system, component, device, element** ✧ **item, part, piece** I'd like to buy a new stereo *unit* for my car.

**unite** *verb* ✦ **unify, merge, combine, consolidate, join, link** ✧ **connect** Chief Tecumseh's dream was to *unite* all North American tribes into one Indian nation.

**universal** *adjective* ✦ **broad, general, wide, widespread, all-around** ✧ **boundless, total, unlimited** Some books become classics because they have *universal* appeal.

**unkempt** *adjective* ✦ **disheveled, sloppy, slovenly, messy, uncombed, untidy** ✧ **neglected, slipshod** The camper had an *unkempt* appearance after spending a week in the woods.

**Antonyms** unkempt
*adjective* **groomed, neat, orderly, shipshape, spic-and-span, spruce, tidy, trim**

**unkind** *adjective* ✦ **cruel, harsh, inconsiderate, mean, thoughtless, insensitive** I apologize for my *unkind* remark about your new boyfriend.

**unknown** *adjective* ✦ **anonymous, nameless, unidentified, unrecognized** ✧ **obscure** The uncredited donation was made by a person who wished to remain *unknown*.

**unlike** *adjective* ✦ **different, dissimilar, disparate, distinct, diverse** ✧ **opposite, unrelated** Though a whale and a mouse are both mammals, they are quite *unlike* in size and appearance.

**unlikely** *adjective* ✦ **doubtful, dubious, improb-**
able, questionable ✧ **unexpected, rare, slight** We're so far behind schedule that it's *unlikely* the project will be finished on time.

**unlucky** *adjective* ✦ **luckless, unfortunate, ill-fated** ✧ **cursed, doomed, unhappy** The *unlucky* gambler lost all of his money.

**unnatural** *adjective* ✦ **eerie, abnormal, bizarre, curious, peculiar, strange, unusual, weird** We decided to investigate when we saw an *unnatural* light coming from the abandoned house.

**unnecessary** *adjective* ✦ **needless, unrequired, nonessential, unneeded, uncalled-for** ✧ **excessive** Police officers are trained to avoid using *unnecessary* force.

**unpack** *verb* ✦ **empty, unload** ✧ **clear, discharge, dump** I had to *unpack* my whole suitcase just to find my pajamas.

**unpopular** *adjective* ✦ **disliked, friendless, unwanted, unwelcome** ✧ **unacceptable, undesirable** The *unpopular* politician was voted out of office.

**unreasonable** *adjective* 1. ✦ **absurd, foolish, illogical, irrational, senseless, ridiculous** It's *unreasonable* to expect your parents to support you forever. 2. ✦ **excessive, extreme, exaggerated, extravagant, immoderate** ✧ **needless, undue** My brother spends an *unreasonable* amount of time combing his hair.

**unreliable** *adjective* ✦ **questionable, uncertain, undependable, untrustworthy, dubious** The newspaper didn't publish the story because the information came from an *unreliable* source.

**unrest** *noun* ✦ **agitation, disorder, disturbance, trouble, turmoil, disquiet** Periods of political *unrest* can occur when people are unhappy with their leaders.

**unruly** *adjective* ✦ **disorderly, uncontrollable, unmanageable, wild, rowdy** ✧ **disobedient** More police were called in to help control the *unruly* mob.

**unsatisfactory** *adjective* ✦ **inadequate, insufficient, unacceptable** ✧ **bad, poor, inferior** The new employee almost lost his job because he was making *unsatisfactory* progress.

**unscrupulous** *adjective* ✦ **deceitful, immoral, unethical, unprincipled, corrupt** ✧ **bad, evil** The *unscrupulous* politician made promises he had no intention of keeping.

**unskilled** *adjective* ✦ inexperienced, untrained ✧ unqualified, untalented, amateur *Unskilled* workers usually make less money than professionals.

**unsteady** *adjective* ✦ shaky, unstable, wobbly, rickety ✧ insecure, unsafe, precarious The table was too *unsteady* to hold anything heavy.

**untie** *verb* ✦ loosen, unbind, undo, unfasten, unwrap ✧ detach, disconnect The knot was pulled so tight it was difficult to *untie*.

**unused** *adjective* 1. ✦ new, pristine, untouched, untried ✧ fresh, original Jeon found some ice skates at a yard sale that looked like they were *unused*. 2. ✦ unaccustomed, unfamiliar (with) ✧ inexperienced I am *unused* to getting up this early in the morning.

**unusual** *adjective* ✦ exceptional, extraordinary, rare, strange, uncommon, freakish, odd, peculiar ✧ unique Back in 1816, an *unusual* blizzard hit Nebraska in the middle of July.

**up** *adverb* ✦ overhead, upward, skyward ✧ above, aloft, higher I looked *up* just in time to see an eagle taking off from its nest.

**uphold** *verb* ✦ maintain, support, sustain ✧ defend, preserve, protect Police officers take an oath in which they promise to *uphold* the law.

**upkeep** *noun* ✦ maintenance, repair ✧ preservation, operation, support I've been spending a lot of money on the *upkeep* of my old car.

**upper** *adjective* ✦ higher, top, topmost, uppermost ✧ greater, superior There's a good view from the *upper* floors of our apartment building.

**upright** *adjective* 1. ✦ vertical, erect, raised ✧ perpendicular, standing Please place your seatback in an *upright* position before takeoff. 2. ✦ good, honest, honorable, moral, ethical, trustworthy, virtuous The *upright* politician was admired and trusted by everyone.

**uproar** *noun* ✦ clamor, commotion, disturbance, noise ✧ tumult, turmoil There was such an *uproar* from the audience that I almost couldn't hear the band.

**upset** *verb* 1. ✦ capsize, overturn, turn over, tip over ✧ knock over, topple We all got soaked when we accidentally *upset* our canoe. 2. ✦ disrupt, mess up, unsettle, disorganize ✧ jumble, muddle, change The cancellation of the flight *upset* all our travel plans. 3. ✦ agitate, distress, disturb, perturb, trouble ✧ annoy, bother The news that our favorite manager was leaving *upset* everyone in the office. —*adjective* 1. ✦ overturned, upside-down, upturned ✧ capsized, toppled, inverted The road was blocked by an *upset* garbage truck. 2. ✦ distressed, disturbed, troubled ✧ annoyed, bothered, perturbed I was *upset* when I lost my favorite necklace.

**urban** *adjective* ✦ city, metropolitan, municipal ✧ civic, cosmopolitan When the Industrial Revolution began in the eighteenth century, many people moved to *urban* areas to find work.

**Antonyms** **urban**
*adjective* agrarian, country, pastoral, rural, rustic

**urge** *verb* 1. ✦ drive, goad, press, prod, spur ✧ force, push When the cattle refused to cross the river, a cowboy *urged* them on. 2. ✦ entreat, encourage, persuade, prompt, advise ✧ beg, plead The sick man's friends *urged* him to see a doctor. —*noun* ✦ impulse, desire, longing, wish, yearning ✧ hunger, thirst I had a sudden *urge* to run outside and sing in the rain.

**urgent** *adjective* ✦ critical, crucial, dire, immediate, pressing ✧ essential, important The charity spokesperson said that there was an *urgent* need for donations.

**usage** *noun* ✦ handling, operation, treatment, use ✧ application, employment My bicycle is still in good shape despite years of hard *usage*.

**use** *verb* 1. ✦ employ, make use (of), utilize ✧ apply, exercise, practice My knife has a special blade to *use* for punching holes. 2. ✦ consume, expend, take ✧ eat up, exhaust, finish, spend Our old refrigerator *uses* too much electricity so we are getting a new one. —*noun* 1. ✦ operation, service, action, employment ✧ duty, work We will have to wait because the elevator is in *use* right now. 2. ✦ application, function, utilization, usage ✧ advantage, purpose A smartphone has many practical *uses*.

**useful** *adjective* ✦ good, handy, helpful, practical, valuable ✧ beneficial A hammer is a *useful* tool for a carpenter.

**usher** *noun* ✦ attendant, escort, guide ✧ guard, leader, pilot An *usher* showed us to our seats in the upper balcony. —*verb* ✦ conduct, escort, guide, lead ✧ direct, show, steer The waiter *ushered* us to our table.

**usual** *adjective* ✦ accustomed, customary, habitual, normal, regular, routine I took my *usual* seat near the front of the conference room before the start of the meeting.

**usually** *adverb* ✦ generally, normally, typically, commonly, customarily, routinely I *usually* get home from work at 5 pm.

**utensil** *noun* ✦ implement, instrument, tool ✧ apparatus, device, gadget, appliance Knives, forks, and spoons are *utensils* for eating.

**utter¹** *verb* ✦ pronounce, say, speak, state ✧ articulate, vocalize, talk The witch *uttered* a spell, and the prince was turned into a frog.

**utter²** *adjective* ✦ absolute, complete, total, entire, thorough, perfect When the electricity went out, the house was plunged into *utter* darkness.

**vacant** *adjective* ✦ empty, uninhabited, unoccupied ✧ abandoned, deserted Someone finally moved into the house that has been *vacant* for a year.

**vacation** *noun* ✦ break, holiday, leave, furlough, recess ✧ rest New employees get a two-week *vacation* their first year.

**vacuum** *noun* ✦ empty space, void ✧ emptiness, nothingness, vacancy Sound waves cannot travel through a *vacuum*. —*verb* ✦ clean ✧ brush, dust, sweep, mop One of my weekly chores is to *vacuum* the carpet in my apartment.

**vague** *adjective* ✦ dim, faint, fuzzy, hazy, indistinct ✧ indefinite, uncertain The lookout saw the *vague* outline of a ship approaching through the fog.

**vain** *adjective* 1. ✦ futile, ineffective, unsuccessful, useless ✧ worthless, fruitless I made a *vain* attempt to get to the post office before it closed. 2. ✦ arrogant, conceited, haughty, proud, smug, egotistic The *vain* actor assumed that everyone adored him.

**valiant** *adjective* ✦ brave, courageous, fearless, gallant, heroic, valorous A *valiant* woman helped her fellow passengers to safety after the train wreck.

**valid** *adjective* 1. ✦ good, sound, acceptable, convincing, logical, suitable, true Tomas had a *valid* excuse for being late to work. 2. ✦ lawful, legal, legitimate ✧ authentic, genuine, real, official You need to have a *valid* driver's license in order to legally operate a motor vehicle.

**valley** *noun* ✦ vale, dale, dell, glen ✧ basin, hollow The peaceful *valley* was nestled between two mountain ranges.

**valuable** *adjective* 1. ✦ costly, expensive, high-priced ✧ invaluable, precious, priceless This antique chair is very *valuable*. 2. ✦ beneficial, helpful, important, useful, worthwhile, worthy The student's summer job gave him *valuable* experience.

**value** *noun* 1. ✦ merit, worth, use, usefulness, benefit ✧ importance, significance My friend's advice usually has a great deal of practical *value*. 2. ✦ cost, price ✧ appraisal, amount, charge, expense The *value* of my parents' house has gone up since they bought it. —*verb* 1. ✦ appreciate, cherish, esteem, prize, respect, treasure, love I really *value* your friendship. 2. ✦ appraise, assess, price, estimate, evaluate, judge A jeweler *valued* the emerald ring at five hundred dollars.

**vanish** *verb* ✦ disappear, go away ✧ dissolve, evaporate, fade, perish Many ships are said to have *vanished* in the Bermuda Triangle.

**Antonyms** vanish

*verb* appear, arise, emerge, materialize

**vanity** *noun* ✦ arrogance, conceit, pride, smugness, self-admiration Anjali's friends describe her as a humble person who has little or no *vanity*.

**vapor** *noun* ✦ fog, mist ✧ haze, smog, smoke, steam Our view of the bay was obscured by *vapor* rising from the water.

**variable** *adjective* ✦ changeable, erratic, shifting, unstable, unsteady This is not a good day for sailing because the winds are so *variable*. —*noun* ✦ factor, circumstance, unknown, possibility ✧ chance There are many *variables* that could alter the outcome of this experiment.

**variety** *noun* 1. ✦ change, diversity, variation ✧ difference For the sake of *variety*, let's have something other than pepperoni on our pizza tonight. 2. ✦ array, assortment, collection, mixture, selection People usually carry a *variety* of hooks and lures when they go fishing. 3. ✦ kind, sort, type ✧ brand, category, species There are more than 7,000 different *varieties* of apples grown around the world.

**various** *adjective* ✦ assorted, different, diverse, varied ✧ numerous, several This shirt is available in *various* colors.

**vary** *verb* ✦ change, shift, alter, differ, fluctuate ✧ adjust, modify, switch Fashions *vary* from season to season.

**vast** *adjective* ✦ huge, enormous, gigantic, immense, colossal, extensive ✧ endless The Sahara Desert occupies a *vast* region in North Africa.

**vault¹** *noun* ✦ strong room ✧ safe, storeroom, treasury Bank *vaults* usually have massive steel doors.

**vault²** *verb* ✦ jump, hurdle, leap, spring ✧ bound, hop In a race known as a steeplechase, horses have to *vault* over fences, ditches, and other such barriers.

## Word Groups

A **vegetable** is a plant cultivated for its edible parts. Vegetable is a general term with no true synonyms. Here are some common types of vegetables to investigate in a dictionary: **asparagus, beet, broccoli, cabbage, carrot, cauliflower, green bean, onion, lettuce, radish, spinach, turnip**

**vegetation** *noun* ✦ flora, plant life, plants ✧ greenery, shrubbery, foliage Hawaii is famous for its lush *vegetation*.

**vehicle** *noun* ✦ conveyance, motor vehicle ✧ transport, transportation The traffic accident was caused by two *vehicles* colliding.

**veil** *noun* ✦ curtain, cloak, cover, mask, screen, shroud, mantle The mountaintop was hidden behind a *veil* of clouds. —*verb* ✦ cloak, conceal, cover, hide, mask, screen, shroud In some African cultures, men traditionally *veil* their faces.

**vein** *noun* ✦ line, seam, streak, layer ✧ stripe, deposit The prospector found a rich *vein* of gold.

**velocity** *noun* ✦ rate, speed, pace ✧ quickness, rapidity, tempo Sound waves travel at a *velocity* of more than 740 miles per hour.

**vendor** *noun* ✦ peddler, seller, dealer ✧ merchant, salesperson, supplier, trader We bought some fruit from a *vendor* on the corner.

**vengeance** *noun* ✦ revenge, retaliation, retribution, punishment ✧ fury, wrath The dictator swore *vengeance* against the people who had tried to overthrow him.

**venom** *noun* ✦ poison, toxin Black widow spiders produce a *venom* that is harmful to humans.

**vent** *noun* ✦ opening, outlet ✧ aperture, hole, passage, flue Our clothes dryer is connected to a *vent* so that heat can be released outside the house.

**venture** *noun* ✦ endeavor, enterprise, undertaking, adventure ✧ chance, gamble, risk Columbus's expeditions were risky *ventures*.

**verbal** *adjective* ✦ oral, spoken, unwritten, voiced, declared, stated The two women had a *verbal* agreement to go into business together.

**verdict** *noun* ✦ conclusion, decision, finding, judgment, ruling, decree The jury's *verdict* was that the defendant was not guilty.

**versatile** *adjective* ✦ adaptable, all-around, all-purpose, flexible ✧ handy The *versatile* hockey player was good at both defense and offense.

**version** *noun* ✦ account, description, report, statement, story, tale Each boy gave his own *version* of how the window got broken.

**vertical** *adjective* ✦ straight up, upright ✧ perpendicular, standing, erect A referee's shirt has *vertical* black and white stripes.

**very** *adverb* ✦ exceedingly, exceptionally, extremely, especially, greatly, immensely, highly My friend was *very* upset when I lost his smartphone. —*adjective* ✦ exact, precise, specific ✧ identical, same The book you gave me is the *very* one that I've been wanting.

**vessel** *noun* 1. ✦ ship, boat, craft ✧ freighter, liner, tanker, yacht Oceangoing *vessels* are usually quite large. 2. ✦ container, receptacle ✧ bottle, bowl, cup, jar, pitcher This old earthenware *vessel* appears to have been used for storing wine.

**veteran** *noun* ✦ professional, authority, expert, master, old hand Our new police chief is a *veteran* with twenty years of previous experience.

**veto** *noun* ✦ denial, disapproval, rejection ✧ ban, cancellation, prohibition The president's *veto* kept the bill from becoming law. —*verb* ✦ reject, turn down, void, disapprove ✧ block, stop, ban State governors can *veto* bills passed by their legislatures.

**vibrate** *verb* ✦ quake, quaver, quiver ✧ shake, tremble, shudder When you strike a tuning fork, it *vibrates* for several moments.

**vibration** *noun* ✦ quivering, shaking, throbbing, tremor ✧ trembling, pulse I can feel *vibrations* inside the car whenever the engine is started.

**vicinity** *noun* ✦ area, locality, neighborhood, region, surroundings, environs There are many stores and restaurants in the *vicinity* of my apartment.

**vicious** *adjective* 1. ✦ cruel, hateful, hurtful, malicious, mean, spiteful A *vicious* lie is one that is told with the intention of hurting somebody. 2. ✦

atrocious, bad, evil, immoral, terrible, wicked, vile The dictator committed many *vicious* crimes. **3.** ✦ dangerous, ferocious, fierce, savage, violent, wild Our neighbor's dog is not as *vicious* as he sounds.

**victim** *noun* ✦ casualty ✧ injured, fatality, sufferer, wounded Paramedics rushed the accident *victim* to a hospital.

**victorious** *adjective* ✦ successful, triumphant, winning ✧ champion, conquering The *victorious* candidate thanked everyone who had helped get him elected.

**victory** *noun* ✦ success, triumph ✧ conquest, win Joan of Arc was only seventeen when she led the French army to *victory* at the Battle of Orléans.

---

**Antonyms victory**
*noun* defeat, loss, overthrow, rout, upset

---

**view** *noun* **1.** ✦ look (at), glimpse, gaze ✧ glance, peek, sight The father lifted his daughter up so that she could get a better *view* of the parade. **2.** ✦ vista, outlook, panorama, scene, scenery ✧ spectacle, vision The hikers paused to admire the *view*. **3.** ✦ belief, conviction, feeling, opinion, position, thought, judgment My friend's political *views* are much stronger than my own. —*verb* ✦ look at, see, watch ✧ observe, behold, witness Special glasses are required to *view* 3-D movies.

**vigor** *noun* ✦ energy, liveliness, power, strength, zest, intensity ✧ endurance The politician spoke with great *vigor*.

**vigorous** *adjective* ✦ active, brisk, dynamic, energetic, lively, strenuous *Vigorous* exercise makes me hungry.

**village** *noun* ✦ hamlet, small town ✧ community, settlement The *village* had just one store, two churches, and fewer than one hundred houses.

**villain** *noun* ✦ bad guy, criminal, rascal, rogue, scoundrel, cad In old western movies, the good guys wore white and the *villains* wore black.

**violate** *verb* ✦ break, disobey, disregard, ignore ✧ defy, resist Police officers give tickets to drivers who *violate* traffic laws.

**violence** *noun* **1.** ✦ brutality, savagery ✧ assault, attack, cruelty The movie depicted fistfights, gunfights, and other forms of *violence*. **2.** ✦ ferocity, force, fury, intensity, power, severity, strength The wind blew with such *violence* that it snapped trees in two as if they were toothpicks.

**violent** *adjective* **1.** ✦ brutal, savage, vicious ✧ cruel, bloodthirsty, harsh, mad A *violent* act of terrorism shocked the whole nation. **2.** ✦ forceful, intense, powerful, strong, wild, rough In 2017, Hurricane Irma's *violent* winds were clocked at 185 miles per hour. **3.** ✦ fierce, fiery, furious, terrible ✧ excited, impetuous The man was able to control his *violent* temper by counting to ten when he began to feel angry.

**virgin** *adjective* ✦ pristine, unspoiled, unused, untouched ✧ fresh, pure, new, brand-new Alaska has vast tracts of *virgin* wilderness that very few people have ever seen.

**virtual** *adjective* ✧ effective, essential, practical, implied, assumed My mother's best friend has been a *virtual* aunt to me all my life.

**virtue** *noun* ✦ decency, goodness, honor, integrity, morality ✧ honesty People respect our fire chief because he is a man of great *virtue*.

**visible** *adjective* **1.** ✦ noticeable, observable, discernible, perceptible, viewable ✧ visual There are billions of stars, but fewer than six thousand are *visible* to the naked eye. **2.** ✦ apparent, clear, distinct, evident, obvious, plain The doctor said that her patient was making *visible* improvement.

**vision** *noun* **1.** ✦ eyesight, sight ✧ seeing, perception Hawks have extremely keen *vision*. **2.** ✦ farsightedness, foresight, imagination, perception, wisdom, sense Benjamin Franklin was a man of great *vision*. **3.** ✦ dream, idea, notion ✧ fancy, fantasy, plan, ideal Martin Luther King, Jr. is famous for his *vision* of all races living together in harmony.

**visit** *verb* ✦ see, call (on), go (to), stay (with) ✧ drop (by), look up Next year I will fly to Vietnam to *visit* my grandparents. —*noun* ✦ stay, visitation ✧ call, stopover, vacation, meeting My friend who moved away will be coming back for a *visit* sometime this summer.

**visitor** *noun* ✦ caller, company, guest, houseguest ✧ tourist, traveler We're expecting *visitors* from out of state for the holidays.

**visual** *adjective* ✦ visible, manifest, discernible, observable, perceivable, plain The footprints in the snow were *visual* proof that a fox had been checking out the chicken coop.

**vital** *adjective* ✦ essential, critical, crucial, important, necessary, required The drama teacher said that everyone's cooperation was *vital* if the play was to be a success.

*adjective* insignificant, irrelevant, paltry, trifling, trivial

**vivid** *adjective* 1. ✦ bright, brilliant, colorful, rich, loud The paintings of Vincent Van Gogh are famous for their *vivid* colors. 2. ✦ acute, clear, intense, keen, sharp, strong, powerful The famous pianist still has *vivid* memories of his first recital.

**vocal** *adjective* ✦ oral, voiced, uttered, phonetic ◇ spoken Parrots and parakeets don't really speak—they just make *vocal* imitations of sounds that they have heard.

**voice** *noun* 1. ◇ speech, tone, utterance, verbalization, delivery, expression When I answered the telephone, I immediately recognized my friend's *voice*. 2. ✦ part, role, say, share ◇ choice, opinion, vote In a true democracy, all citizens have a *voice* in running their government.

**volume** *noun* 1. ✦ book ◇ edition, publication, title, work I have read all three *volumes* of J. R. R. Tolkien's *The Lord of the Rings*. 2. ✦ capacity ◇ amount, extent, measure, quantity, size This plastic milk jug has a *volume* of one gallon. 3. ✦ loud-ness, sound ◇ intensity, power, strength Could you please turn down the *volume* on the TV?

**voluntary** *adjective* ✦ optional, unforced, willing, volunteer, free ◇ spontaneous The *voluntary* donations that visitors make help the museum pay for new exhibits.

**volunteer** *noun* ◇ unpaid person, voluntary person The coaches for our soccer league are all *volunteers*. —*adjective* ✦ voluntary ◇ unpaid, nonprofessional My father is a *volunteer* firefighter. —*verb* ✦ contribute, donate, give, offer, provide, present We *volunteered* our time to help with the community cleanup campaign.

**vote** *noun* ✦ ballot, election ◇ choice, preference, ticket The *vote* for president was close this year. —*verb* ✦ cast a ballot, ballot ◇ choose, elect, select American citizens are eligible to *vote* at the age of eighteen.

**vow** *noun* ✦ oath, pledge, promise ◇ assurance, guarantee, affirmation The knight took a *vow* of loyalty to his king. —*verb* ✦ pledge, promise, swear ◇ affirm, declare, resolve The husband and wife *vowed* to always love each other.

**voyage** *noun* ✦ expedition, journey, trip ◇ cruise, sail, passage Captain James Cook went to Tahiti on his first *voyage* to the South Pacific.

**wad** *verb* ✦ crush, mash, compress, press, roll, squeeze I *wadded up* the paper and threw it into the recycling bin.

**wage** *noun* ✦ salary, pay, payment, compensation, earnings, fee I will receive a higher *wage* at my new job. —*verb* ✦ carry on, carry out, conduct ◇ make, pursue, undertake The senator *waged* a successful reelection campaign.

**wail** *verb* ✦ bawl, cry, sob, weep ◇ howl, moan, whine, shriek In many cultures, it is traditional to *wail* aloud when mourning. —*noun* ✦ cry, howl, moan ◇ sob, whine, shriek The strange *wails* we heard last night were probably from a cat fight.

**wait** *verb* ✦ linger, remain ◇ stand by, stall, stay, delay I *waited* outside the movie theater for my friends to arrive. —*noun* ✦ delay, pause, postponement, interval ◇ break, lull, rest There was a long *wait* before the doctor was able to see me.

**wake¹** *verb* ✦ awake, awaken, rouse, arouse, waken ◇ stir My alarm clock *wakes* me at seven o'clock every morning.

**wake²** *noun* ✦ aftermath, path, track, trail, course The tornado left many ruined buildings in its *wake*.

**walk** *verb* ✦ go on foot, stroll ◇ amble, hike, march, stride, trek, pace If the weather is nice, I like to *walk* to work. —*noun* 1. ✦ stroll ◇ hike, jaunt, march, ramble, trek Shin took his dog for a *walk* in the park. 2. ✦ walkway, sidewalk, footpath, path ◇ lane, track There is a great view of the city from the *walk* that runs along the harbor.

### Word Groups

A solid structure that divides two areas is a **wall**. **Wall** is a general term with no true synonyms. Here are some related words to investigate in a dictionary: **divider, fence, parapet, partition, rampart, screen**

**wander** *verb* 1. ✦ roam, stroll, amble, ramble, saunter, rove My friends and I spent the afternoon *wandering* around the new shopping mall. 2. ✦ stray, drift, shift, swerve, deviate ◇ become lost The audience became restless when the speaker *wandered* from his subject.

**want** *verb* ✦ desire, crave, long, wish, yearn ◇ like, need, require The baby cried because she *wanted* to be fed. —*noun* ✦ desire, craving, need, requirement ◇ demand, necessity The old hermit had very few material *wants*.

**war** *noun* ✦ battle, fight, struggle, conflict ◇ combat, warfare, crusade The government is waging a *war* against illegal drugs.

**wares** *noun* ✦ commodities, goods, merchandise, products ◇ stock, supplies Peddlers used to roam the countryside to sell their *wares* at farms and villages.

**warm** *adjective* 1. ✦ lukewarm, tepid, heated ◇ hot, sizzling The recipe said to mix the ingredients with half a cup of *warm* water. 2. ✦ loving, tender, affectionate, friendly, hearty ◇ enthusiastic My mother gave me a *warm* hug when I got home from studying abroad. —*verb* ✦ heat, warm up, simmer ◇ cook, thaw Jazmin *warmed* some leftover soup on the stove.

**warn** *verb* ✦ alert, inform, make aware, notify, signal, forewarn, caution Beavers slap their tails on the water to *warn* others when danger is present.

**warning** *noun* ✦ notice, notification, admonition, caution ◇ alarm, precaution, signal Hazardous products contain safety *warnings* on their labels.

**warrior** *noun* ✦ fighter, soldier, combatant, brave ◇ brave, trooper Chief Sitting Bull led his *warriors* against Custer's Seventh Cavalry.

**wary** *adjective* ✦ careful, cautious, suspicious ◇ alert, watchful, vigilant My parents taught me to be *wary* of strangers.

**wash** *verb* 1. ✦ clean, cleanse, scour, scrub ◇ bathe, launder Please *wash* your hands before dinner. 2. ✦ carry, move, convey, sweep ◇ flush, remove The heavy rain *washed* sand and dirt over our patio. —*noun* 1. ✦ cleaning, cleansing, washing ◇ bath, shower My car could really use a good *wash*. 2. ✦ clothes washing, laundry I do my *wash* at the Fluff and Fold Laundromat.

**waste** *verb* 1. ✦ lose, squander, throw away ◇ consume, dissipate, eat up, misspend The hikers *wast-*

*ed* two hours trying to find a shortcut. **2. ✦ wither ✧ fade, weaken, decline, decrease, diminish** Certain diseases cause the body to *waste* away. *—noun* **1. ✦ misuse, squandering, mishandling ✧ abuse, extravagance, loss** Trying to fix that outdated computer is a *waste* of both time and money. **2. ✦ garbage, refuse, rubbish, trash ✧ debris, litter, junk** We take our household *waste* to the landfill once a week.

**wasteful** *adjective* **✦ extravagant, lavish, excessive ✧ uneconomical** Don't be *wasteful* at an all-you-can-eat buffet by taking more than you can actually eat.

**watch** *verb* **1. ✦ gaze (at), look (at), observe, see, view ✧ notice, regard** While waiting at the airport, I *watched* airplanes taking off and landing. **2. ✦ attend, tend, look (after), mind, guard ✧ care (for), protect** Would you mind *watching* my jacket while I'm in the restroom? *—noun* **1. ✦ timepiece, wristwatch ✧ clock, pocket watch** I need a new band for my *watch*. **2. ✦ guard, lookout, vigil, vigilance ✧ attention, observation** The mare kept a close *watch* over her newborn foal.

**watchful** *adjective* **✦ alert, attentive, observant, vigilant, wary ✧ aware, careful** The sheepdog kept a *watchful* eye on the entire flock.

**water** *verb* **✦ irrigate, saturate, soak ✧ dampen, moisten, spray, sprinkle, wet** In dry weather we have to *water* the vegetable garden every other day.

**wave** *verb* **1. ✦ flutter, ripple, flap ✧ sway, beat, shake, waver** The flags *waved* in the breeze. **2. ✦ gesture, motion, signal, flag, beckon** I *waved* to Krista to get her attention. *—noun* **1. ✦ swell ✧ breaker, comber, ripple, roller, surf** A huge *wave* almost capsized the rowboat. **2. ✦ gesture, motion, movement ✧ sign, signal, wag** The police officer gave us a *wave* of his hand when it was safe to cross the street.

**way** *noun* **1. ✦ manner, method, system, technique, procedure ✧ fashion, style** My friend taught me a new *way* to braid my hair. **2. ✦ direction, route ✧ course, path, road, trail** Do you know the *way* to the main library? **3. ✦ distance ✧ length, space, span, stretch** My friend's house is a long *way* from here. **4. ✦ choice, desire, preference, wish ✧ will, fancy** The spoiled child almost always gets her *way*.

**weak** *adjective* **✦ faint, feeble ✧ fragile, frail, help-** less, powerless** I felt *weak* because I hadn't eaten anything all day.

**wealth** *noun* **1. ✦ assets, capital, money, riches ✧ fortune, treasure** The man accumulated a great deal of *wealth* by investing in the stock market. **2. ✦ abundance, lot, profusion, world, store ✧ much, plenty** This online encyclopedia has a *wealth* of information on a large variety of subjects.

**wealthy** *adjective* **✦ affluent, prosperous, rich, well-off, moneyed** The *wealthy* woman gave money to our city to build a new stadium.

**wear** *verb* **1. ✦ don, dress (in), have on, put on ✧ deck, wrap** Kenisha *wore* traditional African clothing when she went to her cousin's wedding. **2. ✦ abrade, rub, wear away ✧ erode, exhaust, fray, use up** I *wore* a hole in the elbow of my favorite sweater. *—noun* **1. ✦ apparel, attire, clothes, clothing, garments** This store specializes in children's *wear*. **2. ✦ service, use, utilization ✧ application, employment, function** You certainly have gotten a lot of *wear* out of those hiking boots.

**weary** *adjective* **1. ✦ drained, exhausted, fatigued, tired, worn-out, spent, beat** The boy usually feels *weary* when he gets home from basketball practice. **2. ✦ dreary, tedious, tiresome, wearisome ✧ boring, dull** It's been a long, *weary* winter. *—verb* **✦ tire, drain, exhaust, fatigue, wear out** The long hike *wearied* all of us.

**weather** *noun* **✦ climate, temperature ✧ elements** Arizona is known for its warm *weather*. *—verb* **1. ✦ season, toughen, wrinkle, age ✧ bleach, dry** The old sailor's face has been *weathered* by long exposure to sun and wind. **2. ✦ come (through), endure, survive, withstand ✧ deal (with), brave** The president thinks that his administration can *weather* the current crisis.

**weave** *verb* **1. ✧ braid, knit, lace, plait, spin, twist** Navajo women *weave* colorful rugs and blankets from homespun wool. **2. ✦ wind, zigzag ✧ meander, twist, wander** We had to *weave* our way through the parking lot to find an exit.

**web** *noun* **✦ cobweb, webbing ✧ maze, net, snare, trap** Spiders spin *webs* in order to catch flies and other small insects.

**wed** *verb* **✦ marry ✧ couple, combine, join, link, unite** My friend will *wed* her fiancé next August.

**weep** *verb* **✦ cry, shed tears, sob ✧ bawl, blubber,**

**snivel, wail** I began to *weep* as I read the tragic story.

**weight** *noun* ✦ **heaviness** ✧ **mass, poundage, tonnage, heft** A person's *weight* on the moon would be only one-sixth of what it is here on Earth.

**weird** *adjective* ✦ **abnormal, bizarre, odd, peculiar, strange** ✧ **eerie, unnatural** I took my car to a mechanic because it was making *weird* noises.

**welcome** *verb* ✦ **greet, meet, receive** ✧ **accept, hail** The woman went to the front door to *welcome* her guests. —*noun* ✦ **greeting, reception** ✧ **acceptance, hello** I always receive a warm *welcome* at my best friend's house. —*adjective* ✦ **agreeable, favorable, nice, pleasant, pleasing, satisfying** Sunny weather will be a *welcome* change after all of this rain.

### Word Groups

A **well** is a deep hole that is dug into the ground in order to gain access to a natural deposit such as water. The noun **well** is a very specific term with no true synonyms. Here are some related words to investigate in a dictionary: **fountain, geyser, mine, pit, shaft, spring, water hole**

**well** *adverb* 1. ✦ **agreeably, favorably, nicely, satisfactorily, excellently** ✧ **adequately, all right** The girl is getting along *well* at her new school. 2. ✦ **considerably, far, much, quite** ✧ **fully, thoroughly** I got up *well* before dawn this morning. —*adjective* ✦ **fit, hale, healthy, sound** ✧ **all right, satisfactory, strong** I was sick last week, but I'm feeling *well* now.

**wet** *adjective* 1. ✦ **drenched, soaked** ✧ **damp, moist, soggy, soppy, sopping** You might get *wet* if you don't take an umbrella. 2. ✦ **rainy, stormy** ✧ **drizzly, showery** The forecast is for another *week* of wet weather. —*verb* ✦ **dampen, moisten** ✧ **drench, saturate, soak, water, douse** I have to *wet* my hair before I can comb it properly.

**wharf** *noun* ✦ **pier** ✧ **dock, jetty, quay, landing** I like to go down to the *wharf* and watch while the ships are loaded and unloaded.

**whim** *noun* ✦ **impulse, urge, inclination, notion, desire, fancy, idea, wish** I don't need any more clothes, but I had a sudden *whim* to buy a new sweater.

**whine** *verb* ✦ **fuss, whimper, snivel** ✧ **complain, cry, moan, sob** Little children often *whine* when they get tired.

**whip** *noun* ✦ **lash** ✧ **crop, strap, switch, thong** The cowboy snapped the *whip* in the air to get the cattle moving. —*verb* 1. ✦ **lash, flog, thrash** ✧ **beat, strike, switch** The pirate captain threatened to *whip* anyone who disobeyed him. 2. ✦ **crush, defeat, overcome, rout, trounce, vanquish** The Tigers *whipped* their opponents with a score of nine to nothing.

**whirl** *verb* ✦ **spin, turn, twirl, twist** ✧ **reel, rotate, swirl** I *whirled* around when I heard a strange noise behind me. —*noun* ✦ **spin, swirl, turn, twirl** ✧ **revolution, rotation** The ballet dancers executed a series of graceful leaps and *whirls*.

**whisk** *verb* 1. ✦ **brush, sweep, flick, dust** ✧ **wipe** I used a small brush to *whisk* the dirt out of my car. 2. ✦ **bustle, hurry, hustle, rush, speed** ✧ **dash, hasten, race, scoot** When the student began to feel faint, a teacher immediately *whisked* him off to the nurse's office.

**whisper** *verb* ✦ **speak softly** ✧ **mumble, murmur, mutter** Other students could hear someone *whispering* in the back of the classroom. —*noun* ✦ **undertone** ✧ **mumble, murmur, mutter** My friend lowered her voice to a *whisper* before telling me her secret.

**whole** *adjective* ✦ **entire, complete, full, total** ✧ **all** My dog ate the *whole* bag of potato chips I had left on the table. —*noun* ✦ **entirety, totality, total** ✧ **all, aggregate, bulk, lot, sum, total** We spent the *whole* of our vacation at the beach.

**wholesome** *adjective* ✦ **healthful, healthy, nourishing, nutritious, beneficial** A *wholesome* diet includes plenty of fresh fruits and vegetables.

**wicked** *adjective* ✦ **bad, evil, fiendish, mean, nasty, vicious** ✧ **immoral, sinful** In *The Wonderful Wizard of Oz*, a *wicked* witch tries to steal Dorothy's magic slippers.

**wide** *adjective* ✦ **broad, extensive, large, vast** ✧ **ample, full** I tossed some confetti into the air, and the wind scattered it over a *wide* area.

**width** *noun* ✦ **breadth, wideness, span** ✧ **measure, size, distance** Standard-size typing paper has a *width* of eight and one-half inches.

**wild** *adjective* 1. ✦ **native, natural, uncultivated** ✧ **undomesticated, untamed** Every summer, my friends and I go out to the woods to pick *wild* blueberries. 2. ✦ **disorderly, unruly, uncontrolled, undisciplined, reckless** ✧ **crazy, frantic** The camp counselor made it clear that he would not tolerate any *wild* behavior.

**will** *noun* 1. ✦ desire, determination, drive, resolve, wish ✧ conviction, resolution Roberto is a good soccer player because he has a strong *will* to win. 2. ✦ testament ✧ last wishes, legacy According to the terms of the man's *will*, his wife is to inherit all of his money. —*verb* 1. ✦ persuade ✧ choose, desire, determine, resolve, want, wish The marathon runner *willed* herself to keep going even though she was very tired. 2. ✦ bequeath, leave ✧ confer, endow, give, pass on, transfer The wealthy man *willed* most of his money to charity.

**willing** *adjective* ✦ prepared, ready, agreeable ✧ happy, delighted My friend said that she is *willing* to care for my cat while I'm on vacation.

**wilt** *verb* ✦ wither, become limp, droop, sag ✧ die, shrivel Plants will *wilt* if they don't get enough water.

**win** *verb* 1. ✦ prevail, triumph ✧ beat, conquer, defeat, vanquish My friend usually *wins* when we play Scrabble. 2. ✦ earn, gain, get, receive ✧ achieve, acquire, attain, obtain Rina *won* a trophy for being our softball team's best player. —*noun* ✦ triumph, victory ✧ conquest, success, gain Our football team has had five consecutive *wins* so far this season.

**wind**[1] *noun* 1. ✦ breeze ✧ blow, draft, gale, gust This *wind* would be perfect for flying a kite. 2. ✦ breath ✧ air, respiration The hard tackle knocked the *wind* out of me.

**wind**[2] *verb* 1. ✦ coil, loop, wrap, turn ✧ reel, roll, twist I *wound* the rope tightly around the post to make sure that it wouldn't slip. 2. ✦ meander, snake, wander, weave ✧ bend, turn This road *winds* through the village and out into the country.

**wing** *noun* ✦ addition, annex, extension, arm ✧ branch, section The new library *wing* was built to house the children's collection.

**winner** *noun* ✦ champion, victor, prizewinner ✧ conqueror, master The *winner* in the school's spelling contest will advance to the citywide competition.

**wipe** *verb* ✦ clean, wash, rub ✧ dry, dust, mop, polish, scrub I used a damp sponge to *wipe* off the kitchen table.

**wire** *noun* 1. ✧ cable, cord, filament, line, strand,

thread The rancher had to use several coils of *wire* to repair his fences. 2. ✦ cable, cablegram, telegram, telegraph The urgent message arrived by *wire*. —*verb* 1. ✦ lash ✧ bind, fasten, join, secure, tie When my kite broke, I *wired* the pieces back together. 2. ✦ cable, telegraph ✧ transmit, send When my brother was traveling through Europe, my parents had to *wire* him some money.

**wisdom** *noun* ✦ knowledge, understanding, common sense ✧ intelligence, judgment We gain *wisdom* by learning from our experiences.

**wise** *adjective* ✦ intelligent, prudent, rational, sensible, smart, sound ✧ bright, sage Angela made a *wise* decision not to go swimming alone.

**wish** *noun* ✦ desire, hope, longing, yearning ✧ need, want The schoolboy's fondest *wish* is to become an astronaut. —*verb* ✦ desire, like, want, choose ✧ crave, long (for), yearn If you *wish*, you may go first.

**wishful** *adjective* ✦ desirous, hopeful, longing, yearning ✧ daydreaming, greedy Believing you might actually win the lottery is just *wishful* thinking.

**wit** *noun* 1. ✦ wittiness, cleverness, comedy, humor, satire ✧ fun, joke Mark Twain's books successfully mix *wit* and realism. 2. ✦ mind, senses ✧ sanity, intelligence, judgment, understanding My little brother scared me out of my *wits* when he crept up behind me and yelled.

**witch** *noun* ✦ enchantress, sorceress ✧ conjurer, magician A *witch* turned the prince into a frog.

**withdraw** *verb* 1. ✦ remove, take away, take back, retract ✧ cancel, eliminate I *withdrew* my suggestion when I realized that it wasn't practical. 2. ✦ depart, leave, exit, go away, retire ✧ retreat The butler served dinner, and then he quietly *withdrew* from the room.

**wither** *verb* ✦ dry up, shrivel, wilt ✧ droop, sag, parch, die, fail Our grass *withered* during last summer's drought.

**Antonyms** **wither**
*verb* bloom, burgeon, flourish, grow, succeed, thrive

**withstand** *verb* ✦ bear, endure, stand up (to), take, tolerate ✧ oppose, resist My new tent can *withstand* winds of up to ninety miles per hour.

**witness** *noun* ✦ eyewitness, observer, onlooker,

**spectator, viewer** There have to be *witnesses* present in order for a wedding to be legal. —*verb* ✦ **observe, see, view, watch** ✧ **notice, spot** The police are hoping to find someone who *witnessed* the accident.

**witty** *adjective* ✦ **amusing, funny, humorous, clever** ✧ **smart** I laughed out loud when I heard the *witty* comment.

**wizard** *noun* 1. ✦ **magician, sorcerer** ✧ **conjurer, enchanter** The *wizard* cast a spell that made the dragon fall asleep. 2. ✦ **ace, expert, genius, prodigy, master, professional** One of my colleagues is a computer *wizard*.

**wobble** *verb* ✦ **rock, totter, teeter, shake, sway** ✧ **quake, waver** This chair *wobbles* because one of the legs is loose.

**wonder** *noun* 1. ✦ **marvel, sensation, spectacle** ✧ **curiosity, miracle** One of the Seven *Wonders* of the Ancient World was the Hanging Gardens of Babylon. 2. ✦ **awe, fascination** ✧ **amazement, astonishment, surprise** The children watched in *wonder* as their cat gave birth to kittens. —*verb* ✦ **ponder, reflect (on), speculate (about), question** ✧ **meditate, think** I sometimes *wonder* what my life will be like when I get married.

**wonderful** *adjective* 1. ✦ **amazing, astonishing, fantastic, incredible, marvelous, fascinating** The splendors of Yosemite Valley are *wonderful* to behold. 2. ✦ **terrific, splendid, excellent, great, superb** I had a *wonderful* time at your holiday party.

**wood** *noun* 1. ✦ **boards, planks, lumber** ✧ **logs, timber** I need some *wood* to make more bookshelves. 2. ✦ **forest, woodland** ✧ **grove, timber, timberland** My friends and I like to go hiking in the *woods* near my house.

**word** *noun* 1. ✦ **term** ✧ **designation, expression, name** "Gigantic" is a *word* that means "very large." 2. ✦ **conversation, discussion, talk, chat, consultation** My manager wants to have a *word* with me. 3. ✦ **word of honor, pledge, promise, vow, assurance, guarantee** My friend gave me her *word* that she would return the money I loaned her. 4. ✦ **message, news, notice** ✧ **communication, report** Our relatives sent *word* that they would be arriving a day late. —*verb* ✦ **express, phrase, put, state, formulate** ✧ **term** I *worded* my suggestion carefully so that my friend would not be offended.

**work** *noun* 1. ✦ **labor, effort, drudgery, toil** ✧ **exertion** Mowing a large yard is a lot of *work*. 2. ✦ **employment, job, occupation, career, profession** ✧ **business, trade** My friend says that he really enjoys his *work* as a salesman. 3. ✦ **task, assignment, project, duty, chore, obligation, responsibility** My boss said I can take the rest of the day off if I finish my *work* early. 4. ✦ **creation, piece, product** ✧ **accomplishment, achievement, composition** This gallery specializes in displaying the *works* of local artists. —*verb* 1. ✦ **labor, toil, strive** ✧ **endeavor, strain** We *worked* hard to get the important project finished on time. 2. ✦ **function, operate, perform, run** ✧ **go** Do you know how a computer *works*?

**worker** *noun* ✦ **employee, hand, laborer** ✧ **workingman, workingwoman, workman, workwoman** The successful company plans to hire more *workers*.

**world** *noun* 1. ✦ **Earth, globe** ✧ **planet** Ferdinand Magellan commanded the first expedition to sail around the *world*. 2. ✦ **humanity, humankind, the human race, mankind** ✧ **everyone, everybody** The *world* watched on live television as a human walked on the moon for the first time. 3. ✦ **abundance, profusion, wealth, great deal, large amount, lot** A good library contains a *world* of information on all types of subjects.

**worry** *verb* ✦ **concern, trouble, distress, disturb, upset** ✧ **fret** I'm *worried* that I might not get into the university of my choice. —*noun* ✦ **care, concern** ✧ **anxiety, apprehension, trouble, burden** My kid brother doesn't have a *worry* in the world.

**worship** *noun* ✦ **devotion, reverence, veneration** ✧ **adoration, glorification, honor** A mosque is a building that Muslims use for religious *worship*. —*verb* ✦ **revere, venerate, glorify, adore** ✧ **idolize, honor** The ancient Greeks *worshiped* many different gods and goddesses.

**worth** *noun* ✦ **importance, value, merit, usefulness, use** ✧ **significance** Miho proved her *worth* when she hit two home runs in one game.

**worthless** *adjective* ✦ **good-for-nothing, insignificant, unimportant, useless, valueless** This is just a *worthless* piece of junk mail.

**worthwhile** *adjective* ✦ **valuable, good, important, useful, worthy** ✧ **helpful, beneficial** Volunteering at the hospital is a *worthwhile* use of your time.

**worthy** *adjective* ✦ **deserving, commendable, ex-**

cellent, good, worthwhile, fitting Helping to feed the homeless is a *worthy* cause.

**wound** *noun* ✦ injury ✧ cut, abrasion, sore, harm, hurt Our first-aid instructor showed us how to clean and bandage an open *wound*. —*verb* ✦ injure, hurt ✧ harm, damage, pain A police officer was *wounded* in the shootout.

**wrap** *verb* ✦ gift-wrap, cover, enclose, package ✧ bind, bundle I *wrapped* my mother's present in bright paper.

**wrath** *noun* ✦ anger, rage, furor, fury, ire ✧ gall, indignation, rancor, resentment The dictator was filled with *wrath* when he discovered a plot to overthrow him.

**wreck** *verb* ✦ ruin, demolish, destroy, shatter, smash, damage The inexperienced driver *wrecked* his fence when he backed into it. —*noun* ✦ accident, crash, smashup, pileup ✧ destruction, devastation, disaster Fortunately no one was hurt in yesterday's train *wreck*.

**Antonyms** wreck

*verb* fix, mend, preserve, rebuild, renovate, repair

**wrench** *verb* 1. ✦ jerk, pull, snatch, tug, twist ✧ wring, rip My dog *wrenched* the stick out of my hand. 2. ✦ sprain, strain, pull ✧ turn, twist My grandfather *wrenched* his back when he tried to pick up a heavy box without help.

**wrestle** *verb* ✦ grapple, scuffle, tussle ✧ fight, jostle, struggle Sometimes the children *wrestle* with each other just for the fun of it.

**wretched** *adjective* ✦ dreadful, horrid, lousy, miserable, rotten, terrible, awful We've had *wretched* weather all winter long.

**wring** *verb* ✦ squeeze, twist ✧ compress, press, force, wrench After a shower, I *wring* the water out of my washcloth.

**wrinkle** *noun* ✦ crease, fold, crinkle ✧ furrow, groove, line, pleat Minh ironed the *wrinkles* out of her new skirt. —*verb* ✦ crease, crinkle, pucker, furrow ✧ crumple, fold My skin starts to *wrinkle* when I've been in the water a long time.

**write** *verb* 1. ✦ inscribe, jot down, record, scrawl, scribble, note Please *write* your phone number on this card. 2. ✦ compose, create, author, pen ✧ draft, produce I have to *write* a marketing report for my boss.

**wrong** *adjective* 1. ✦ inaccurate, incorrect, mistaken, erroneous ✧ false, untrue I got only one *wrong* answer when I took my driver's license test. 2. ✦ bad, immoral ✧ evil, nasty, sinful, vile, wicked It is *wrong* to tell lies about other people. 3. ✦ improper, inappropriate, unfit, unsuitable High-heeled shoes are the *wrong* thing to wear when going on a strenuous hike. 4. ✦ amiss, defective, faulty, out of order, broken There's something *wrong* with my motorbike. —*adverb* ✦ incorrectly, improperly, erroneously, inaccurately, badly Most people pronounce my name *wrong*. —*noun* ✦ misdeed, offense ✧ injustice, crime, evil, sin "Two *wrongs* don't make a right" means that it isn't proper to seek revenge. —*verb* ✦ betray, mistreat ✧ dishonor, harm, hurt, injure, offend I *wronged* my friend when I revealed her secret.

**Antonyms** wrong

*adjective* 1. accurate, correct, right 2. decent, ethical, good, moral 3. apt, fitting, proper, respectable

# XYZ

**x-ray** *noun* ✧ **diagnostic picture, medical photograph, scan** When the doctor examined the *x-rays* of my injured ankle, he discovered a hairline fracture. —*verb* ✧ **film, photograph, scan** The dentist *x-rays* my teeth once a year to make sure that I don't have any hidden cavities.

**yacht** *noun* ✦ **boat, ship** ✧ **cabin cruiser, craft, sailboat, sloop, watercraft** The crew of the *yacht* met to discuss the upcoming race.

**yank** *verb* ✦ **jerk, pull, tug, wrench** ✧ **draw, snatch, pluck** The fisherman *yanked* on his line to set the hook in the fish's mouth. —*noun* ✦ **jerk, pull, tug, wrench** ✧ **grab, jolt** Because the door was stuck, I had to give it a hard *yank* to get it to open.

**yard** *noun* ✦ **backyard, lawn** ✧ **courtyard, grounds, lot** We set up a badminton net in our *yard*.

**yarn** *noun* 1. ✦ **spun wool** ✧ **fiber, strand, thread, filament** My grandmother is knitting mittens with red and blue *yarn* as a gift for me. 2. ✦ **anecdote, story, tale, narrative** ✧ **fable, tall tale** The old sailor enjoys telling *yarns* about his years at sea.

**yawn** *verb* ✦ **gape, gap** ✧ **expand, extend, open, spread, divide** The cave explorers carefully studied the deep pit that *yawned* open in front of them.

**yearn** *verb* ✦ **ache, desire, long, want, wish, crave** ✧ **covet** My elderly neighbor *yearns* to visit her grandchildren again.

**yell** *verb* ✦ **bellow, call, cry, holler, scream, shout** ✧ **roar, bawl** The boy *yelled* from his window that he would be down in a minute. —*noun* ✦ **call, cry, scream, shout, holler** Firefighters rescued the trapped woman after they heard her *yells* for help.

**yet** *adverb* 1. ✦ **as yet, so far, thus far** ✧ **before, earlier, previously** My roommate hasn't gotten home *yet*. 2. ✦ **eventually, finally, someday, sometime, still, even** If the rain ever stops, we may *yet* go to the park. —*conjunction* ✦ **but, however, nevertheless, nonetheless, still** ✧ **although, though** I was already full, *yet* the pizza was so good I had another slice.

**yield** *verb* 1. ✦ **bear, give, produce, provide** ✧ **generate, furnish** The tree in our backyard *yielded* more than one hundred oranges last year. 2. ✦ **give in, submit, succumb, surrender** ✧ **buckle, relent** I *yielded* to temptation and had a second piece of pie. —*noun* ✦ **crop, harvest** ✧ **output, produce, production** We had a good *yield* from our garden this summer.

**yoke** *verb* ✦ **harness, hitch** ✧ **attach, connect, couple, join, link** A team of oxen were *yoked* to the covered wagon.

**young** *adjective* ✦ **immature, juvenile, youthful, underage** ✧ **new, undeveloped** My little brother is too *young* to see R-rated movies. —*noun* ✦ **babies, offspring** ✧ **brood, litter, family** Mother bears are known for keeping a close watch over their *young*.

**youngster** *noun* ✦ **child, kid, juvenile, youth** ✧ **boy, girl, lad, lass** My grandfather says that he didn't have television to watch when he was a *youngster*.

**youth** *noun* 1. ✦ **adolescence, childhood** ✧ **boyhood, girlhood** Our elderly neighbor has lived in the same house since his *youth*. 2. ✦ **adolescent, juvenile, teen, teenager, youngster** ✧ **child** My father said he started working when he was a *youth* of seventeen.

**youthful** *adjective* ✦ **adolescent, juvenile, young** ✧ **boyish, childish, girlish** This television series was made to appeal to a *youthful* audience.

**yowl** *noun* ✦ **cry, howl, moan, scream, screech, shout, wail, yell** The boy let out a *yowl* of pain when he smashed his thumb with a hammer. —*verb* ✦ **howl, screech, wail** ✧ **cry, scream, shout, yell, moan** I was awakened by two cats *yowling* in the alley.

**zenith** *noun* ✦ **height, highest point, peak, top** ✧ **apex, crest, pinnacle, summit** At the *zenith* of his career, the actor starred in three major movies in just one year.

**Antonyms** **zenith**
*noun* **abyss, base, bottom, depths, foot**

**zero** *noun* ✦ **nothing, nil, naught, none, zilch** Five subtracted from five equals *zero*.

**zest** *noun* ✦ pungency, spice, tang, taste, flavor, savor I put red pepper flakes and Parmesan cheese on my pizza to give it extra *zest*.

**zip** *verb* 1. ✦ close, fasten ◇ button, snap I *zipped* up my jacket. 2. ✦ zoom, whiz, flash, rush, fly, race, dart, dash Cars *zipped* by the slow driver on the freeway.

**zone** *noun* ✦ area, district, locality, neighborhood, quarter, region ◇ territory Our town has a business *zone* and several residential *zones*.

**zoom** *verb* ✦ zip, whiz, dart, dash, race, speed, streak, bolt ◇ fly, hurry, rush, sail The motorcycle *zoomed* past us so quickly that we barely caught a glimpse of it.

# Appendix I:
# Test Vocabulary

*The American Heritage Word Finder* is an excellent resource when preparing for an English language proficiency test or an American college admissions test. Its A–Z text includes thousands of basic words that test takers should know. But if you just want to focus on test vocabulary, this appendix lists basic words that are considered essential regardless of which test you're preparing to take.

## Tests You Might Need To Take

The SAT (formerly known as the Scholastic Aptitude Test) and the ACT (formerly known as American College Testing) are college admission aptitude tests, typically taken in the United States by high school juniors or seniors. They contain language and reading sections that test for knowledge of the vocabulary students will need in college.

Many nonnative speakers study for and take an English Language proficiency test. The three major ones are the International English Language Testing System (IELTS), the Test of English as a Foreign Language (TOEFL), and the Test of English for International Communication (TOEIC).

IELTS is a British test; however, American English is acceptable. The TOEFL, SAT, and ACT are North American tests, but British English is acceptable. The key to all tests is consistency — you shouldn't switch back and forth from one style of English to the other.

The TOEIC is a North American test, but it does not emphasize American English. The TOEIC tests for knowledge of "international English"; that is, the language used by nonnative speakers communicating in English with both native speakers and other nonnative speakers. In the listening portion of the TOEIC, it's possible to hear English spoken with a variety of different accents—American, British, Scottish, and so on. Also, even though it's a North American test, some British terms could appear. (Appendix II covers basic British terms that might be encountered on the TOEIC.)

One thing these tests have in common is the emphasis they place on vocabulary. They all expect the test taker to have knowledge of basic vocabulary and synonyms, and that's exactly what this book provides. In addition, each test requires specialized knowledge of more advanced vocabulary, including academic, business, political, and science terminology. You can find all types of vocabulary lists—either online or in printed texts—that present the vocabulary for a specific test. We recommend you use *The American Heritage Word Finder* to master the basic vocabulary all these tests expect you to know. As your English proficiency improves, you will be ready to proceed to vocabulary lists for the specific test you are preparing to take.

# Part One: Adjectives, Adverbs, Nouns, and Verbs

This is where to start your test preparations. Part One lists basic vocabulary words that commonly appear on the English language proficiency tests and American college admissions tests. All are included as main entries in *The American Heritage Word Finder*—just look them up in the A–Z text to see how they're used and to learn their synonyms. You will not be ready to proceed to more advanced vocabulary until you know these words.

## Adjectives

An *adjective* is a word that describes a noun. *The American Heritage Word Finder* contains more than 1,100 adjectives. Here are the ones that are the most common on language proficiency and college admissions tests:

| | | | | |
|---|---|---|---|---|
| abnormal | confident | extinct | obese | spectacular |
| adverse | conscious | fabulous | optimistic | spontaneous |
| amiable | convenient | fantastic | outdoor | suitable |
| ample | cool | flexible | permanent | taut |
| ancient | courteous | flimsy | pessimistic | temporary |
| anxious | critical | ghastly | practical | tranquil |
| arid | dangerous | haughty | prone | treacherous |
| beneficial | diligent | hot | prudent | typical |
| brittle | diverse | humid | quaint | unique |
| characteristic | docile | immense | rapid | valid |
| cheap | dry | immune | rash | various |
| chilly | dull | improper | reasonable | vast |
| cold | efficient | inevitable | relevant | voluntary |
| comfortable | energetic | jubilant | safe | warm |
| compact | excess | logical | satisfactory | wary |
| complex | exciting | manual | sociable | wet |
| compulsory | expensive | necessary | social | |

## Adverbs

An *adverb* is a word that describes a verb or an adjective. *The American Heritage Word Finder* has more than 100 adverbs. Here are the ones that are the most common on language proficiency and college admissions tests:

| | | | | |
|---|---|---|---|---|
| abroad | barely | exactly | nearly | perhaps |
| alike | before | immediately | nevertheless | straight |
| almost | clearly | indeed | now | thus |
| also | down | instead | often | too |
| always | especially | just | once | very |
| approximately | even | lately | only | |

## Nouns

A *noun* is a word that is used to name a person, place, or thing. Nouns can also name an idea, a feeling, or an action, such as *pride, happiness,* or *mistake. The American Heritage Word Finder* contains more than 2,100 nouns. Here are the ones that are the most common on language proficiency and college admissions tests:

| | | | |
|---|---|---|---|
| abyss | compassion | impact | opponent |
| agreement | compromise | incentive | perspective |
| ailment | conference | influence | plunge |
| annex | contract | ingredient | prejudice |
| appliance | culprit | integrity | prosperity |
| aroma | demand | inventory | reception |
| asset | depression | jeopardy | reservation |
| attendant | destination | lease | ruin |
| benefit | discipline | leash | squabble |
| bias | effort | luggage | supervisor |
| boost | endeavor | manual | tremor |
| cafeteria | excess | measure | uproar |
| candidate | expectation | merchandise | vacation |
| catastrophe | exploit | misunderstanding | vanity |
| characteristic | famine | moisture | weather |
| client | fare | nausea | zenith |
| clue | flood | neglect | |
| cold | fraud | obstacle | |
| compact | gain | occupation | |

## Verbs

A *verb* is a word that describes an action or a state of being. *The American Heritage Word Finder* contains more than 1,900 verbs. Here are the ones that are the most common on language proficiency and college admissions tests:

| | | | |
|---|---|---|---|
| abandon | anticipate | contradict | discuss |
| abbreviate | arrange | cool | donate |
| abdicate | bias | dangle | edit |
| absorb | boost | degrade | emerge |
| abstain | borrow | demand | enclose |
| accompany | collect | depart | endeavor |
| acquire | collide | deprive | endorse |
| agitate | compact | determine | engage |
| alter | compose | develop | enhance |
| analyze | compromise | dine | evolve |
| annex | concentrate | discipline | exhibit |

| | | | |
|---|---|---|---|
| exploit | learn | postpone | squabble |
| fare | lease | precede | stimulate |
| flood | lease | prejudice | strain |
| forsake | mark | proceed | suggest |
| gain | measure | publish | supervise |
| gather | meddle | reflect | support |
| grumble | mend | refund | surpass |
| harass | neglect | register | touch |
| hunt | notify | release | train |
| immigrate | nourish | resign | warm |
| impair | obtain | review | wet |
| infer | omit | revise | |
| influence | persuade | ruin | |
| interrupt | plunge | shatter | |

# Part Two: Nouns by Category

*The American Heritage Word Finder* places more emphasis on nouns than the other parts of speech. This section lists hundreds more that appear commonly on tests. Most of these nouns do not have synonyms and thus are not included as main entries in the A–Z text. We have organized them in thematic categories in order to make them more accessible and understandable. When you've mastered the basic nouns presented here and you are ready to study advanced vocabulary lists, you'll find most of them organized by subject—just like we have done here.

Nouns make up more than half of all the words in the English language. They are also the easiest words to learn because many of them refer to items that can be visualized. As a result, most beginners learn nouns first, and this is especially true for anyone studying for a test.

All of the English language proficiency tests and the American college admissions tests have sections on reading and writing. Considering that more than half of all English words are nouns, obviously they are important. In addition, the proficiency tests have sections for lis-

tening and speaking, and you simply can't say much without a good knowledge of nouns.

**Animals**: An *animal* is a living organism that ingests food rather than manufacturing it. Here are common types of animals: alligator, bear, bee, bird, butterfly, camel, cat, cow, crocodile, dog, elephant, fish, goat, horse, llama, lion, lizard, penguin, rabbit, seal, sheep, snake, tiger, tortoise, turtle, whale.

**Buildings**: A *building* is a structure that has a roof and walls. Here are some common types of buildings: apartment, auditorium, bookstore, church, factory, hall, hospital, hotel, house, library, museum, office, post office, restaurant, skyscraper, theater, warehouse.

**Business**: *Business* is the activity of buying and selling commodities, products, or services. Here are the people who engage in business: businessman, businesswoman, competitor, consultant, director, entrepreneur, executive, expert, manager, manufacturer, merchant, salesman, salesperson, saleswoman, secretary, specialist.

**Colors**: *Color* is the way things are perceived

due to differing qualities of the light they reflect or emit. Here are the basic colors you should know: black, blue, brown, gray, green, orange, pink, purple, red, white, yellow.

**Conference**: A *conference* is a meeting for consultation or discussion. Here are related terms to learn: attendance, brochure, catalog, committee, coordinator, event, member, organization, project, registration, schedule, seminar, session, workshop.

**Contracts**: A *contract* is an agreement between two or more parties, especially one that is written and enforceable by law. Here are the related terms you should know: agency, agent, agreement, client, contractor, customer, lease, party, property, provision, rent, rental.

**Crops**: A *crop* is a plant that is cultivated for food. Here are some of the most important crops in the world: cassava, corn, plantains, potatoes, rice, sorghum, soybeans, sweet potatoes, wheat, yams.

**Education**: *Education* is the act or process of receiving or giving instruction. Here are words related to education that test takers need to know: classroom, college, curriculum, diploma, faculty, graduate, graduate student, instructor, lecture, lecturer, professor, pupil, student, teacher, textbook, tuition, tutor, undergraduate, university.

**Family**: A *family* is a group of people related by blood or marriage. Here are the most common terms for members of a family: aunt, brother, cousin, daughter, father, granddaughter, grandfather, grandmother, grandson, husband, mother, nephew, niece, sister, son, uncle, wife.

**Finance**: *Finance* refers to the management of money. Here are the important financial words to know: account, accountant, asset, balance, bank, banking, budget, cash, charge, check, credit, debt, deductible, deduction, deficit, deposit, fee, income, interest, investment, loan, money, payment, profit, rate, revenue, saving account, statement, tax, transaction, withdrawal.

**Food**: *Food* is any substance that animals, people, and plants consume to maintain life and growth. Here are common food items you should know: beans, bread, cereals, cheese, eggs, fruit, meat, milk, nuts, pasta, pizza, potatoes, rice, seafood, vegetables, yogurt.

**Geographic Features**: *Geographic features* are the physical land and water aspects of the Earth. Here are the common terms you should know: basin, canyon, channel, continent, equator, gulf, hill, island, jungle, lake, mountain, ocean, peninsula, plateau, pond, reef, river, sea, valley, volcano.

**Goods and Services**: *Goods* are products that are bought and sold. A *service* is work performed by others as their occupation or business. Here are the related terms: bill, claim, cost, coupon, discount, feedback, invoice, material, packaging, price, product, receipt, refund, warranty, workmanship.

**Hobbies**: A *hobby* is an activity or interest pursued for pleasure. Here are examples of popular hobbies: birdwatching, collecting (coins, stamps, etc.), cooking, embroidery, fishing, gardening, hiking, knitting, painting, photography, pottery, reading, sculpture, woodcarving, writing.

**Identification**: *Identification* is the act of identifying or the state of being identified. Here are the related words you should learn: birth certificate, driver's license, fingerprint, ID card, photo, passport, signature, visa.

**Job**: A *job* is an activity performed in exchange for payment. Here are the related terms you should know: applicant, application, benefit, bonus, boss, candidate, compensation, employee, interview, interviewee, interviewer, offer, pay, paycheck, position, raise, salary, union, wage.

**Materials**: *Materials* are the substances out of which a thing is or can be made. Here are common types of materials: aluminum, brick, cement, concrete, fabric, glass, leather, lumber, metal, plastic, rubber, steel, stone, wood.

**Measurement**: *Measurement* refers to something's dimension, quantity, or capacity. Here are the common terms of measurement: area, breadth, depth, extent, height, length, number, size, volume, width.

**Plants**: *Plants* are living organisms that either use chlorophyll to synthesize nutrients or live as parasites stealing their nutrients from other plants. Here are the most common types of plants: algae, ferns, grasses, herbs, mosses, mushrooms, shrubs, trees.

**Shapes**: A thing's *shape* is its external form, contour, or outline. Here are the basic shapes you should know. If there is an adjective form, that form is listed too: circle/circular, cube/cubic, oval, pyramid/pyramidal, rectangle/rectangular, sphere/spherical, square, triangle/triangular.

**Sports**: A *sport* is a physical activity governed by a set of rules and commonly played competitively. There are many types of both individual and team sports. Here are some popular team sports: baseball, basketball, cricket, football, hockey, lacrosse, polo, rugby, soccer, softball, volleyball, water polo.

**Time**: *Time* is the succession of events from the past through the present to the future. Common units to measure or describe time include: century, day, decade, fortnight, hour, millennium, minute, month, second, week, year.

**Vehicles**: A *vehicle* is a device for transporting people or things. Here are some common types:

*Land vehicles:* automobile, bicycle, bus, cab, camper, car, coach, jeep, motorcycle, pickup, scooter, subway, tanker, taxi, tow truck, tractor, train, tram, truck, van, wagon.

*Water vehicles:* boat, cabin cruiser, canoe, container ship, dinghy, ferry, gondola, hovercraft, hydrofoil, kayak, lifeboat, ocean liner, punt, rowboat, sailboat, steamer.

*Air vehicles:* aircraft, airplane, airship, helicopter, hot-air balloon, jet, jumbo jet, seaplane.

# Part Three: Proper Nouns

A *proper noun* is the name of a unique individual, event, organization or place. All proper nouns are spelled with an initial capital letter. Here are the basic ones you need to know when taking a proficiency test.

**Continents**: Africa, Antarctica, Asia, Australia, Europe, North America, South America.

**Geographic Features**: Arctic, Arctic Circle, Eastern Hemisphere, Northern Hemisphere, North Pole, Southern Hemisphere, South Pole, Western Hemisphere

**Days of the Week**: Monday, Tuesday, Wednesday, Thursday, Friday, Saturday, Sunday.

**Months of the Year**: January, February, March, April, May, June, July, August, September, October, November, December.

**Religions**: Buddhism, Christianity, Confucianism, Hinduism, Islam, Judaism, Shintoism, Sikhism, Taoism

# Appendix II:
# Differences between British and American English

It's a good idea to know and use the style of English in use where you are living and working. Using the proper spelling and vocabulary for your location helps to avoid confusion, and it makes you appear more competent and experienced.

*The American Heritage Word Finder* is based on American English. If you have been studying the English language somewhere other than in the United States, you may have been learning British English. The two versions of English are sufficiently similar to be mutually understandable. However, many words are spelled differently in British vs. American English, and a few words are so different in meaning that they are likely to be unknown to someone unfamiliar with both styles of English.

Appendix II contains spelling rules for converting British English to American. There is also a listing of the most common British words that have different meanings in American English.

## Part I: Spelling Differences

This section contains spelling rules for converting British English to American English. Some spelling differences are rarely encountered, and there are too many minor ones to be able to include them all here. We have, however, included the most common spelling differences you will encounter. Do keep in mind, however, that these are only general rules, and exceptions do exist. When in doubt, consult a reliable dictionary.

Here are six rules for converting from British to American English, with examples for each:

1. Words ending in *–our* change to *–or*.

| British Spelling | American Spelling |
| --- | --- |
| colour | color |
| endeavour | endeavor |
| honour | honor |
| humour | humor |
| labour | labor |
| neighbour | neighbor |
| odour | odor |
| vigour | vigor |

2. Words ending in *–re* change to *–er*.

| British Spelling | American Spelling |
| --- | --- |
| centre | center |
| fibre | fiber |
| litre | liter |
| metre | meter |
| sombre | somber |
| theatre | theater |

3. Words ending in *–ise* change to *–ize*.

| British Spelling | American Spelling |
| --- | --- |
| apologise | apologize |
| authorise | authorize |
| itemise | itemize |
| organise | organize |
| realise | realize |
| recognise | recognize |

4. Words ending in *–nce* change to *–nse*.

| British Spelling | American Spelling |
| --- | --- |
| defence | defense |
| licence | license |
| offence | offense |
| pretence | pretense |

5. British words containing the double vowels *ae* and *oe* change to just *e* in American English.

| British Spelling | American Spelling |
| --- | --- |
| a*e*on | eon |
| arch*ae*ology | archeology |
| encyclop*ae*dia | encyclopedia |
| f*oe*tus | fetus |
| man*oe*uvre | maneuver |
| medi*ae*val | medieval |

6. When adding suffixes to verbs ending with an *l*, British English typically doubles the *l*, but American English does not.

| British Spelling | American Spelling |
| --- | --- |
| cancelled | canceled |
| fuelling | fueling |
| marvelled | marveled |
| pedalling | pedaling |
| quarrelled | quarreled |
| travelled | traveled |

# Part II: Words with Different Meanings

This section lists the most common British words that have different meanings in American English.

| British Word | American Word |
| --- | --- |
| *Baby Terms* | |
| cot | crib |
| dummy | pacifier |
| nappy | diaper |
| pram | stroller/baby carriage |

| British Word | American Word |
| --- | --- |
| *Building/Household* | |
| bench (kitchen) | countertop |
| bin/dustbin | garbage can/trashcan |
| block of flats | apartment building |
| chemist's | drugstore/pharmacy |
| first floor | second floor |
| flat | apartment |
| ground floor | first floor |
| jumble sale | yard sale |
| lift | elevator |

| British Word | American Word |
| --- | --- |
| *Clothing* | |
| boiler suit | coveralls |
| braces | suspenders |
| jumper | sweater |
| mackintosh | raincoat |
| pants | underpants |
| polo neck | turtleneck |
| pyjamas | pajamas |
| trainers | sneakers |
| vest | undershirt |
| waistcoat | vest |
| windcheater | windbreaker |

| British Word | American Word |
| --- | --- |
| *Food* | |
| aubergine | eggplant |
| banger | sausage |
| biscuit | cookie |
| candy floss | cotton candy |
| chips | French fries |
| cob | bread roll |
| courgette | zucchini |
| crisps | potato chips |
| entrée | appetizer |
| ice lolly | Popsicle |
| icing sugar | powdered sugar |
| jacket potato | baked potato |
| jelly babies | jelly beans |
| lolly | sucker |
| mangetout | snow peas |
| sultana | raisin |
| treacle | molasses |

| British Word | American Word |
| --- | --- |
| *Sports/Games/Recreation* | |
| catapult | slingshot |
| draughts | checkers |
| football | soccer |
| noughts and crosses | tic-tac-toe |
| patience | solitaire |

| British Word | American Word |
| --- | --- |
| *Things* | |
| drawing pin | thumbtack |
| full stop (punctuation) | period |
| queue | line |
| rubber | eraser |
| spanner | wrench |
| torch | flashlight |

| British Word | American Word |
| --- | --- |
| *Transportation/Vehicles* | |
| blinker (turn signal) | indicator |
| bonnet (car) | hood |
| boot (car) | trunk |
| breakdown van | tow truck |
| estate wagon | station wagon |
| flyover | overpass |
| high street | main street |
| lorry | truck |
| low loader | flatbed truck |
| metalled road | paved road |
| milometer | odometer |
| motorway | highway |
| pavement | sidewalk |
| petrol | gasoline |
| silencer (car) | muffler |
| transport café | truck stop |
| tyre | tire |
| underground/tube | subway |
| windscreen | windshield |
| zebra crossing | crosswalk |